AF477388

# Learning with Computers™ II

EDITION 2


**H. Albert Napier, Ph.D.**
*Professor of Management*
*Rice University, Jones Graduate School*
*Houston, Texas*

•

**Ollie N. Rivers**
*San Antonio, Texas*

•

**Jack P. Hoggatt, Ed.D.**
*Professor of Business Communication*
*University of Wisconsin – Eau Claire*
*Eau Claire, Wisconsin*

Australia • Brazil • Japan • Korea • Mexico • Singapore • Spain • United Kingdom • United States

**Learning with Computers™ II, Second Edition**

**H. Albert Napier, Ollie Rivers, Jack Hoggatt**

Vice President of Editorial, Business: Jack W. Calhoun

Vice President/Editor-in-Chief: Karen Schmohe

Sr. Developmental Editor: Dave Lafferty

Vice President, Marketing: Cheryl Costantini

Marketing Manager: Alla Reese

Marketing Coordinator: Julia Tucker

Sr. Marketing Communications Manager: Sarah Greber

Sr. Content Project Manager: Martha Conway

Sr. Media Editor: Sally Nieman

Sr. Print Buyer: Charlene Taylor

Production Service: Bill Smith Group

Consulting Editor: Jean Findley, Custom Editorial Productions, Inc.

Copyeditor: Marianne Miller

Sr. Art Director: Tippy McIntosh

Cover and Internal Design: Grannan Graphic Design, Ltd.

Cover Illustration: Grannan Graphic Design, Ltd.

Sr. Rights Specialist, Photography: Deanna Ettinger

Photo Research: Bill Smith Group

© 2012, 2006 South-Western, Cengage Learning

ALL RIGHTS RESERVED. No part of this work covered by the copyright herein may be reproduced, transmitted, stored, or used in any form or by any means graphic, electronic, or mechanical, including but not limited to photocopying, recording, scanning, digitizing, taping, Web distribution, information networks, or information storage and retrieval systems, except as permitted under Section 107 or 108 of the 1976 United States Copyright Act, without the prior written permission of the publisher.

For product information and technology assistance, contact us at **Cengage Learning Customer & Sales Support, 1-800-354-9706**.

For permission to use material from this text or product, submit all requests online at **www.cengage.com/permissions**. Further permissions questions can be emailed to **permissionrequest@cengage.com**.

Microsoft is a registered trademark of Microsoft Corporation in the U.S. and/or other countries.

The names of all products mentioned herein are used for identification purposes only and may be trademarks or registered trademarks of their respective owners. South-Western disclaims any affiliation, association, connection with, sponsorship, or endorsement by such owners.

ISBN-13: 978-0-538-45071-3
ISBN-10: 0-538-45071-1

**South-Western Cengage Learning**
5191 Natorp Boulevard
Mason, OH 45040
USA

Cengage Learning products are represented in Canada by Nelson Education, Ltd.

For your course and learning solutions, visit **www.cengage.com/school**
Visit our company website at **www.cengage.com**

Printed by RR Donnelley, Willard, OH,
1st Ptg., 12/2010

Printed in the United States of America
1 2 3 4 5 6 7 14 13 12 11 10

# LEARNING WITH COMPUTERS I AND II, 2E

Students learn grade-level appropriate computer skills based on the National Educational Technology Standards (NETS). Lessons are presented in the form of fun, cross-curricular projects, so students apply computer skills to relevant academic subjects. The books emphasize research, reading, and writing activities relevant to social studies, science, math, and language arts curricula.

Texts in this series consist of the level I and II books. Each text is a series of projects which introduce students to the Explorers Club. Four young members of the club — Luis, Ray, Julie, and Lin — guide students on Microsoft Office explorations.

### *Learning with Computers I* (Green), 2e

ISBN: 978-0-538-45070-6

The projects in this text cover word processing, spreadsheet, presentation, database, graphics, keyboarding, and Internet skills. Projects range from using word processing to explore the great wall of China, to using worksheets to identify biosphere reserves, to using presentations about volcanoes, to using databases for cataloging native arts of the Americas. Capstone projects are included.

### *Learning with Computers II* (Orange), 2e

ISBN: 978-0-538-45071-3

The projects in this text cover more advanced word processing, spreadsheet, presentation, database, graphics, keyboarding, and Internet skills. Projects range from using word processing to raft the Mississippi with Mark Twain, to using worksheets to explore elements from the periodic table, to using presentations about the California gold rush, to using databases for cataloging the fifty states. Capstone projects are included.

# LEARNING WITH COMPUTERS

## A Features Safari—the Instructional Plan

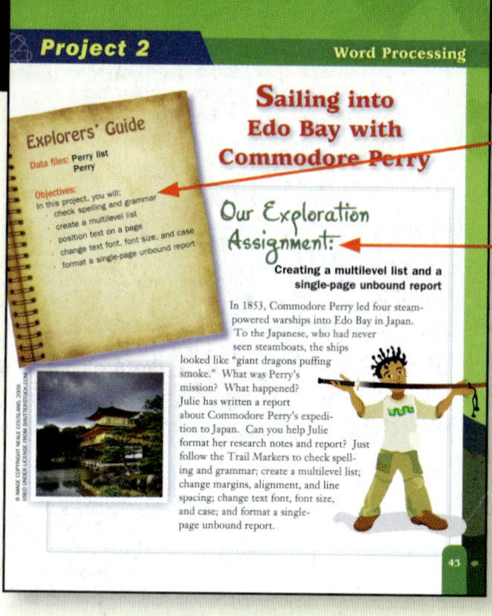


**Explorers' Guide** lists project files and provides a clear outline of learning objectives for the project.

**Our Exploration Assignment** states exactly what students will do for each project.

**Starting Out!** Gets students moving as they open and rename the data file to make the project their own.

***NEW!* Explorer Character**
Lin joins the team! Explorers introduce projects and guide students through each step.

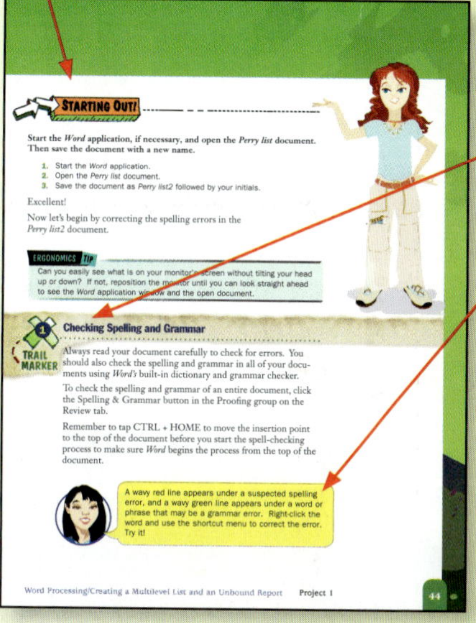


**Trail Markers** provide clear division for project tasks and explain how to perform computer functions.

**Margin Notes and Ergonomics Tips**—introduced by the explorers—support students with tips, additional information, and encouragement.

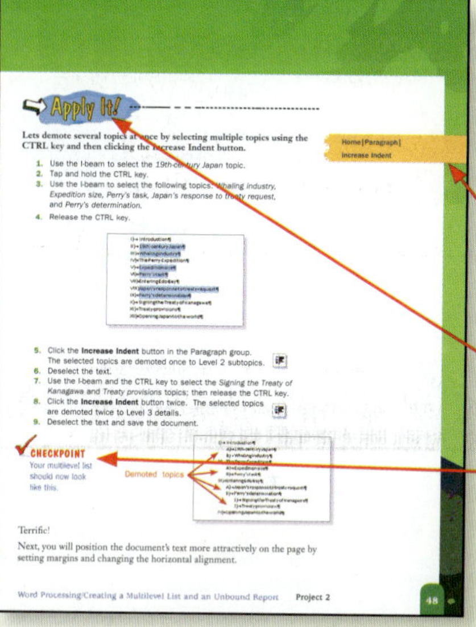


***NEW!* Ribbon Path (Tab/Group/Command)** in the margin provides a shortcut of the steps for the project.

**Apply It!** extends instruction by providing hands-on practice with the skill students learn in the Trail Marker section.

**Checkpoints** reinforce learning by providing visual examples of how the work should appear.

# WHAT'S NEW

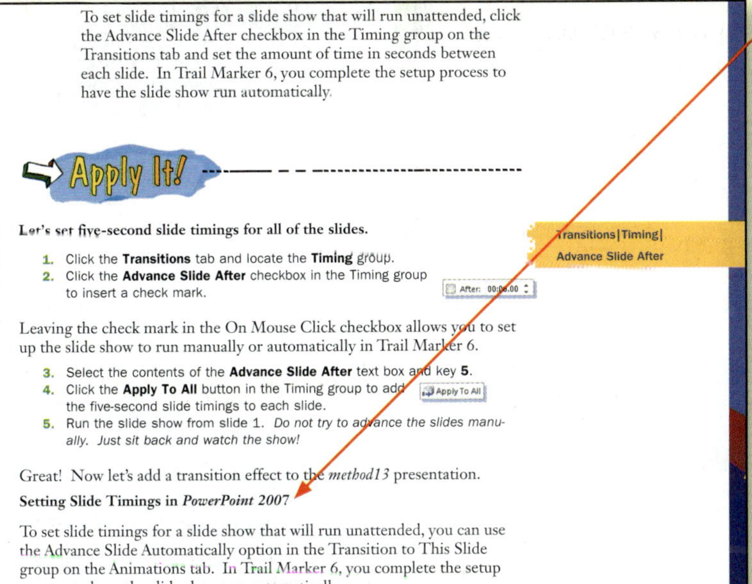

To set slide timings for a slide show that will run unattended, click the Advance Slide After checkbox in the Timing group on the Transitions tab and set the amount of time in seconds between each slide. In Trail Marker 6, you complete the setup process to have the slide show run automatically.

Apply It!

Let's set five-second slide timings for all of the slides.

1. Click the **Transitions** tab and locate the **Timing** group.
2. Click the **Advance Slide After** checkbox in the Timing group to insert a check mark.

Transitions | Timing | Advance Slide After

Leaving the check mark in the On Mouse Click checkbox allows you to set up the slide show to run manually or automatically in Trail Marker 6.

3. Select the contents of the **Advance Slide After** text box and key **5**.
4. Click the **Apply To All** button in the Timing group to add the five-second slide timings to each slide.
5. Run the slide show from slide 1. *Do not try to advance the slides manually. Just sit back and watch the show!*

Great! Now let's add a transition effect to the *method13* presentation.

**Setting Slide Timings in *PowerPoint 2007***

To set slide timings for a slide show that will run unattended, you can use the Advance Slide Automatically option in the Transition to This Slide group on the Animations tab. In Trail Marker 6, you complete the setup process to have the slide show run automatically.

***NEW!*** Instructions now cover both **Microsoft Office 2010 and Office 2007**, when needed.

***NEW!*** **Century 21 document formats** are used for reports and letters to maximize the features of Word.

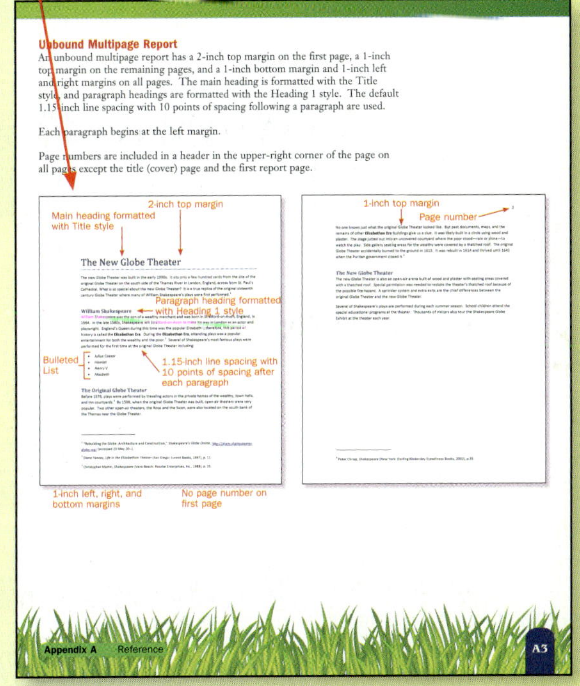

**Unbound Multipage Report**

An unbound multipage report has a 2-inch top margin on the first page, a 1-inch top margin on the remaining pages, and a 1-inch bottom margin and 1-inch left and right margins on all pages. The main heading is formatted with the Title style, and paragraph headings are formatted with the Heading 1 style. The default 1.15-inch line spacing with 10 points of spacing following a paragraph are used.

Each paragraph begins at the left margin.

Page numbers are included in a header in the upper-right corner of the page on all pages except the title (cover) page and the first report page.



Appendix A Reference A3

***NEW!*** **Unit Capstone Projects** help students apply what they have learned by integrating computer applications with a theme of "Summer Internship."

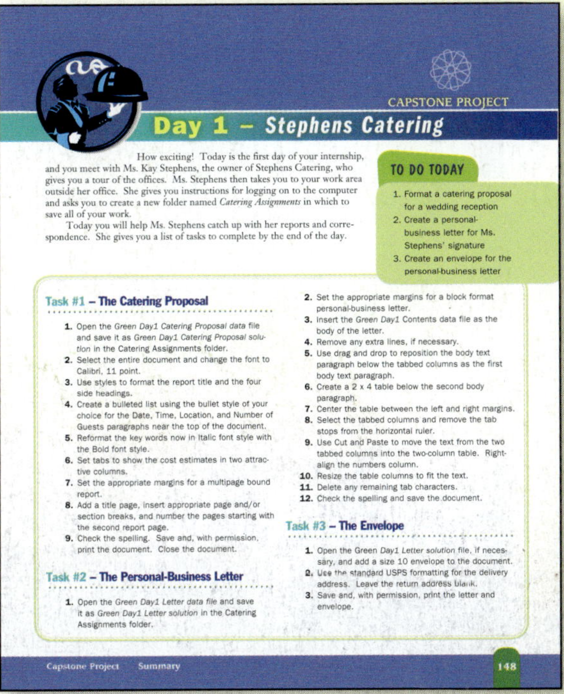

CAPSTONE PROJECT

**Day 1 – Stephens Catering**

How exciting! Today is the first day of your internship, and you meet with Ms. Kay Stephens, the owner of Stephens Catering, who gives you a tour of the offices. Ms. Stephens then takes you to your work area outside her office. She gives you instructions for logging on to the computer and asks you to create a new folder named *Catering Assignments* in which to save all of your work.

Today you will help Ms. Stephens catch up with her reports and correspondence. She gives you a list of tasks to complete by the end of the day.

TO DO TODAY

1. Format a catering proposal for a wedding reception
2. Create a personal-business letter for Ms. Stephens' signature
3. Create an envelope for the personal-business letter

**Task #1 – The Catering Proposal**

1. Open the *Green Day1 Catering Proposal* data file and save it as *Green Day1 Catering Proposal solution* in the Catering Assignments folder.
2. Select the entire document and change the font to Calibri, 11 point.
3. Use styles to format the report title and the four side headings.
4. Create a bulleted list using the bullet style of your choice for the Date, Time, Location, and Number of Guests paragraphs near the top of the document.
5. Reformat the key words now in Italic font style with the Bold font style.
6. Set tabs to show the cost estimates in two attractive columns.
7. Set the appropriate margins for a multipage bound report.
8. Add a title page, insert appropriate page and/or section breaks, and number the pages starting with the second report page.
9. Check the spelling. Save and, with permission, print the document. Close the document.

**Task #2 – The Personal-Business Letter**

1. Open the *Green Day1 Letter* data file and save it as *Green Day1 Letter solution* in the Catering Assignments folder.
2. Set the appropriate margins for a block format personal-business letter.
3. Insert the *Green Day1* Contents data file as the body of the letter.
4. Remove any extra lines, if necessary.
5. Use drag and drop to reposition the body text paragraph below the tabbed columns as the first body text paragraph.
6. Create a 2 x 4 table below the second body paragraph.
7. Center the table between the left and right margins.
8. Select the tabbed columns and remove the tab stops from the horizontal ruler.
9. Use Cut and Paste to move the text from the two tabbed columns into the two-column table. Right-align the numbers column.
10. Resize the table columns to fit the text.
11. Delete any remaining tab characters.
12. Check the spelling and save the document.

**Task #3 – The Envelope**

1. Open the *Green Day1 Letter* solution file, if necessary, and add a size 10 envelope to the document.
2. Use the standard USPS formatting for the delivery address. Leave the return address blank.
3. Save and, with permission, print the letter and envelope.

Capstone Project Summary 148

***NEW!*** **Appendices** on technology and digital citizenship add even more topics for discussion.

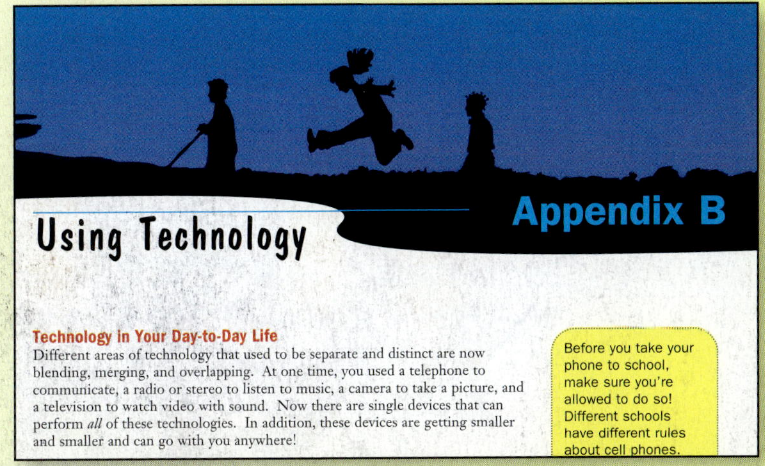

**Appendix B**

**Using Technology**

**Technology in Your Day-to-Day Life**

Different areas of technology that used to be separate and distinct are now blending, merging, and overlapping. At one time, you used a telephone to communicate, a radio or stereo to listen to music, a camera to take a picture, and a television to watch video with sound. Now there are single devices that can perform *all* of these technologies. In addition, these devices are getting smaller and smaller and can go with you anywhere!

Before you take your phone to school, make sure you're allowed to do so! Different schools have different rules about cell phones.

# Extended Learning

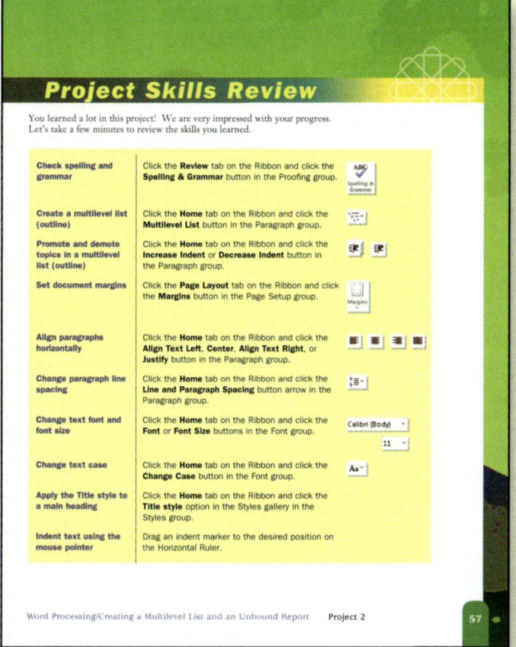

## Project Skills Review

You learned a lot in this project! We are very impressed with your progress. Let's take a few minutes to review the skills you learned.

| | |
|---|---|
| **Check spelling and grammar** | Click the **Review** tab on the Ribbon and click the **Spelling & Grammar** button in the Proofing group. |
| **Create a multilevel list (outline)** | Click the **Home** tab on the Ribbon and click the **Multilevel List** button in the Paragraph group. |
| **Promote and demote topics in a multilevel list (outline)** | Click the **Home** tab on the Ribbon and click the **Increase Indent** or **Decrease Indent** button in the Paragraph group. |
| **Set document margins** | Click the **Page Layout** tab on the Ribbon and click the **Margins** button in the Page Setup group. |
| **Align paragraphs horizontally** | Click the **Home** tab on the Ribbon and click the **Align Text Left**, **Center**, **Align Text Right**, or **Justify** button in the Paragraph group. |
| **Change paragraph line spacing** | Click the **Home** tab on the Ribbon and click the **Line and Paragraph Spacing** button arrow in the Paragraph group. |
| **Change text font and font size** | Click the **Home** tab on the Ribbon and click the **Font** or **Font Size** buttons in the Font group. |
| **Change text case** | Click the **Home** tab on the Ribbon and click the **Change Case** button in the Font group. |
| **Apply the Title style to a main heading** | Click the **Home** tab on the Ribbon and click the **Title style** option in the Styles gallery in the Styles group. |
| **Indent text using the mouse pointer** | Drag an indent marker to the desired position on the Horizontal Ruler. |

Word Processing/Creating a Multilevel List and an Unbound Report Project 2 57

**Skills Review** summarizes the skills learned in the project in a clear, easy-to-read table format.

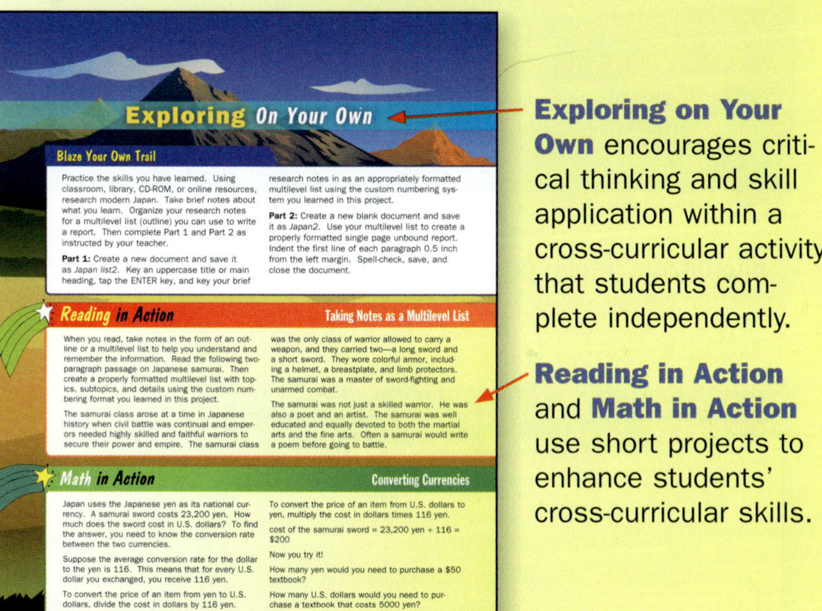

## Exploring On Your Own

### Blaze Your Own Trail

Practice the skills you have learned. Using classroom, library, CD-ROM, or online resources, research modern Japan. Take brief notes about what you learn. Organize your research notes for a multilevel list (outline) you can use to write a report. Then complete Part 1 and Part 2 as instructed by your teacher.

**Part 1:** Create a new document and save it as *Japan list2*. Key an uppercase title or main heading, tap the ENTER key, and key your brief research notes in as an appropriately formatted multilevel list using the custom numbering system you learned in this project.

**Part 2:** Create a new blank document and save it as *Japan2*. Use your multilevel list to create a properly formatted single page unbound report. Indent the first line of each paragraph 0.5 inch from the left margin. Spell-check, save, and close the document.

### Reading in Action — Taking Notes as a Multilevel List

When you read, take notes in the form of an outline or a multilevel list to help you understand and remember the information. Read the following two-paragraph passage on Japanese samurai. Then create a properly formatted multilevel list with topics, subtopics, and details using the custom numbering format you learned in this project.

The samurai class arose at a time in Japanese history when civil battle was continual and emperors needed highly skilled and faithful warriors to secure their power and empire. The samurai class was the only class of warrior allowed to carry a weapon, and they carried two—a long sword and a short sword. They wore colorful armor, including a helmet, a breastplate, and limb protectors. The samurai was a master of sword-fighting and unarmed combat.

The samurai was not just a skilled warrior. He was also a poet and an artist. The samurai was well educated and equally devoted to both the martial arts and the fine arts. Often a samurai would write a poem before going to battle.

### Math in Action — Converting Currencies

Japan uses the Japanese yen as its national currency. A samurai sword costs 23,200 yen. How much does the sword cost in U.S. dollars? To find the answer, you need to know the conversion rate between the two currencies.

Suppose the average conversion rate for the dollar to the yen is 116. This means that for every U.S. dollar you exchanged, you receive 116 yen.

To convert the price of an item from yen to U.S. dollars, divide the cost in dollars by 116 yen.

To convert the price of an item from U.S. dollars to yen, multiply the cost in dollars times 116 yen.

cost of the samurai sword = 23,200 yen ÷ 116 = \$200

Now you try it!

How many yen would you need to purchase a \$50 textbook?

How many U.S. dollars would you need to purchase a textbook that costs 5000 yen?

Exploring on Your Own/Creating a Multilevel List and an Unbound Report Project 2 58

**Exploring on Your Own** encourages critical thinking and skill application within a cross-curricular activity that students complete independently.

**Reading in Action** and **Math in Action** use short projects to enhance students' cross-curricular skills.

**Exploring Across the Curriculum** provides more academic connections by integrating computer skills practice with language arts, social studies, science, math, art, and online research skills.

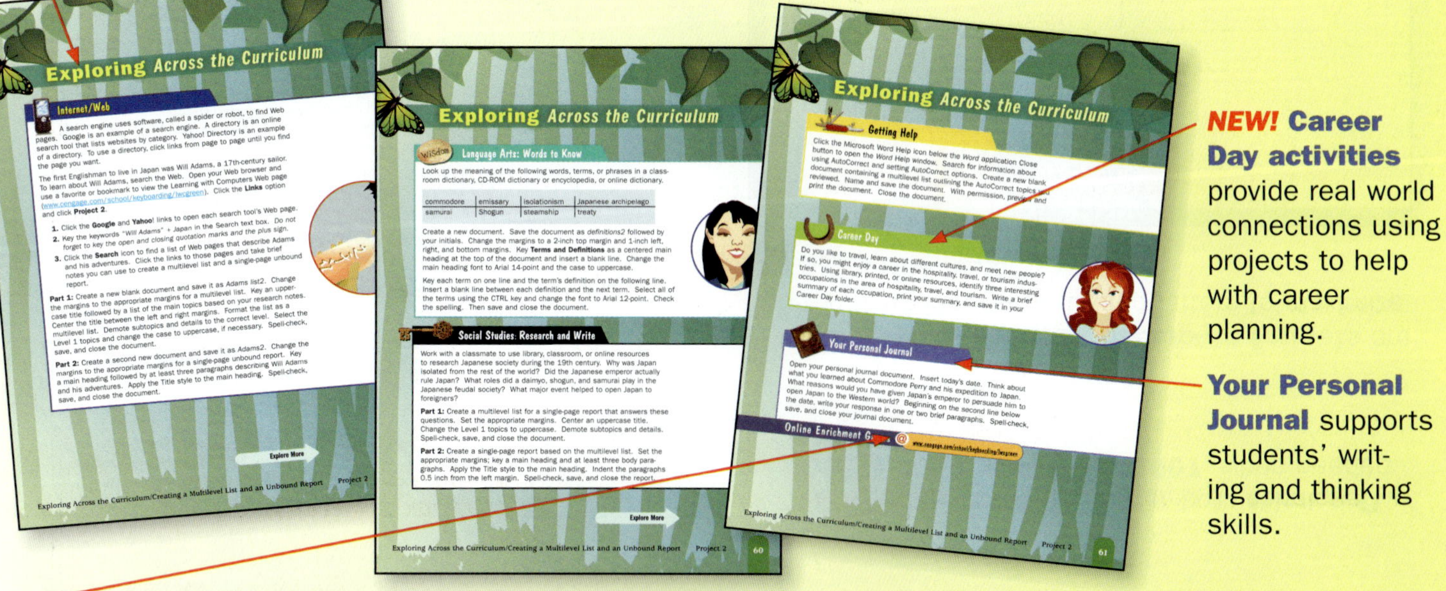


**NEW! Career Day activities** provide real world connections using projects to help with career planning.

**Your Personal Journal** supports students' writing and thinking skills.

**Online Enrichment** supports and extends students' computer skills using the Learning with Computers website.

# KEYBOARDING FOR REINFORCEMENT

**Project 2** Keyboarding

**2a Review h, e, i, r**

Key each line twice. Double-space between 2-line groups.

**TECHNIQUE TIP**

Keep your fingers curved and upright.

h
1 jh jh|hjh hjh|ha ha|hs hs|hd hd|hf hf|hj hj|hk hk;
2 has has|had had|half half|hall; halls;|dash; dash;

e
3 de de|ede ede|el el|ea ea|es es|ek ek|ef ef|ej ej;
4 seek seek|fell fell|ease ease|feed feed|jell jell;

i
5 ki ki|iki iki|i; i;|il il|ik ik|ij ij|ia ia|id id;
6 is is|his his|ill ill|kid kid|hike hike|side side;

r
7 fr fr|rfr rfr|rd rd|rj rj|rs rs|rk rk|ra ra|rl rl;
8 jar jar|hair hair|ride ride|hear hear|cards cards;

**2b Technique: ENTER**

Key each line twice single-spaced; double-space between 2-line groups.

For additional practice: **MicroType 5** New Key Review, Alphabetic Lessons 3–4

1 if;
2 if he;
3 if he did
4 if he did see
5 if he did see her

6 ask
7 ask her
8 ask her if
9 ask her if he
10 ask her if he has

Keyboarding Project 2 62

**Keyboarding** page at the end of every project offers practice and reinforcement of keyboarding skills and features a Technique Tip.

### *Enhance Keyboarding instruction with MicroType Keyboarding software!*

This engaging, easy-to-use program teaches new-key learning and skill building. MicroType features 3-D animations, videos, and fun, interactive games.

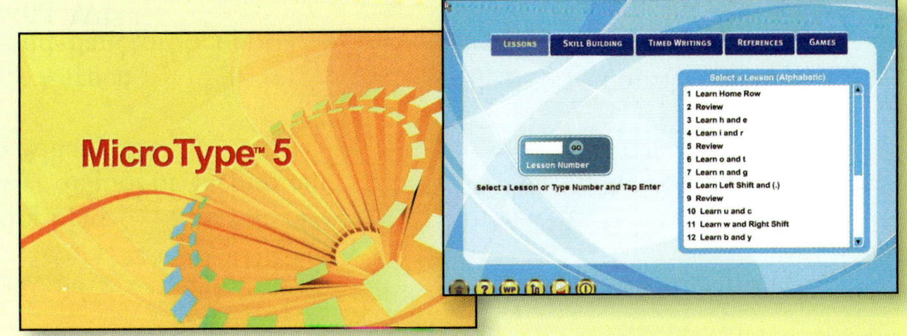


# PROGRAM SUPPLEMENTS MAKE IT EASY

### *Instructor's Resource CD-ROM*

ISBN Level I (green): 978-0-538-45073-7

ISBN Level II (orange): 978-0-538-45081-2

Now all instructor materials are available on one convenient and easy-to-use CD. Designed to help facilitate instruction, motivate students, and enhance students' knowledge and course appreciation, this Windows CD has instructor files unique to the textbook. The CD contains project data files, project solutions, PowerPoint® presentations, quizzes, quiz solutions, rubrics, character clip art, program scope & sequence, and links to the program website.

### *Teacher's Wraparound Edition*

ISBN Level I (green): 978-0-538-45072-0

ISBN Level II (orange): 978-0-538-45080-5

The teacher's edition contains annotations for the student edition pages, as well as information and features to facilitate instruction and extend student learning, such as Prepare to Teach, Resources, Focus/Prepare, Teaching Tips, Language Skills Tips, Internet Activities, Let's Discuss, and more.

### **NEW!** *ExamView® CD-ROM*

ISBN Level I (green): 978-0-538-45095-9

ISBN Level II (orange): 978-0-538-45094-2

Also available separately, this CD-ROM includes the ExamView test generator software along with test banks for most units from the student text. Exams can be customized and final exams can be created.

### *eBooks*

ISBN Level I (green): 978-0-8400-6968-9
eBook Instant Access Code (IAC)

ISBN Level II (orange): 978-1-111-30026-5
eBook Instant Access Code (IAC)

ISBN Level I (green): 978-1-111-66710-8
eBook Printed Access Code (PAC)

ISBN Level II (orange): 978-1-111-66709-2
eBook Printed Access Code (PAC)

Now teachers and students can access this dynamic, interactive program and take learning to a new level. eBooks enhance traditional instructional materials by providing them digitally. eBooks are viewed on a computer and look exactly like the printed version—including photos, graphics, and rich fonts. Additionally, they allow teachers and students the ability to customize content by Annotating text, Highlighting key passages, Inserting "sticky notes," and Bookmarking pages.

## About the Authors

**H. Albert Napier, Ph.D.** is a Professor of Management at the Jesse H. Jones Graduate School of Management, Rice University. The author and co-author of several books about using desktop applications, Al has been involved in computer education for more than 20 years.

**Ollie N. Rivers** has more than 20 years' business experience in financial and administrative management and more than 10 years' experience as a corporate trainer. She is co-author or contributing author on several Office software, Internet, Web design, and Web authoring software textbooks. She holds an M.B.A. and a B.S. in Accounting and Management from Houston Baptist University.

**Dr. Jack P. Hoggatt** is Department Chair for the Department of Business Communications and Assistant Dean at the University of Wisconsin-Eau Claire. He has taught courses in Business Writing, Advanced Business Communications, and the communication component of the university's Masters in Business Administration (MBA) program. Dr. Hoggatt has held offices in several professional organizations, including the Wisconsin Business Education Association. He has served as an advisor to local and state business organizations. He has received the Wisconsin Outstanding Business Educator Award for Post Secondary and is a member of the Wisconsin Phi Beta Lambda Hall of Fame.

## Dedications

**Al Napier:** To my family.

**Ollie Rivers:** To my darlings: Taylor, Keller, and Davis.

**Jack P. Hoggatt:** This book is dedicated to Glenda (my wife), Ashley, Logan, Erika, Cody (my children), and to Maxine Vermillion Hoggatt (my mother), who was a master teacher at providing the informal portion of my early education.


## Acknowledgements to Reviewers

Barbara Miller-Beasley
Taylor Middle-High School
Pierson, FL

Bonnie W. Brown
Clinton Junior High School
Clinton, MS

Anne Carson
The Ellison School
Vineland, NJ

Elfrieda Christensen
Spring Creek Middle School
Providence, UT

Debra Dumas
DeLand Middle School
DeLand, FL

Sandra Flatt
Prosser School of Technology
New Albany, IN

Sandy Karpen
Almond-Bancroft School
Almond, WI

Pat Kennedy
New Oxford Middle School
New Oxford, PA

Barbara T. Mathis
Lyons Creek Middle School
Coconut Creek, FL

Donald Perry
Neptune Middle School
Kissimmee, FL

Amber Reed
Bremen High School
Bremen, IN

Heather Jackson-Reed
Bridgewater Middle School
Winter Garden, FL

Elaine Reinitzer
Hudson Memorial School
Hudson, NH

Cheryl Beazley Wolfred
Independence Middle School
Virginia Beach, VA

# To the Student

## The Explorers Club Preview

Hi! Welcome to *Learning with Computers Level II.* My name is Julie, and this is Lin, Luis, and Ray. At the **Explorers Club** meetings, we learn how to use the computer while learning interesting and exciting things about our world. Come with us as we:

- **Create** and format *Word* documents
- **Solve** problems using *Excel* worksheets
- **Present** ideas and facts in *PowerPoint* slide shows
- **Organize** information in *Access* databases

Lin, Ray, Luis, and I will be your guides through the 18 projects in this book. Together we will follow the Trail Markers in each project to learn new skills. At the end of each project are several fun activities to let you practice your new skills. You will explore the World Wide Web and share your research using documents, workbooks, presentations, and databases, then record your thoughts about what you've learned in your own personal journal.

Here is the starting point on our Explorers Club trail—let's go!

GUIDEPOST 1

### Getting Started

Do you know the difference between computer hardware and software? Can you point out the different parts of your computer? Are you using good posture while working at your computer?

In the Getting Started project, you will find the answers to these and other basic computer questions, learn how to use the *Windows* desktop and create files and folders, and visit the *Learning with Computers* Web pages.

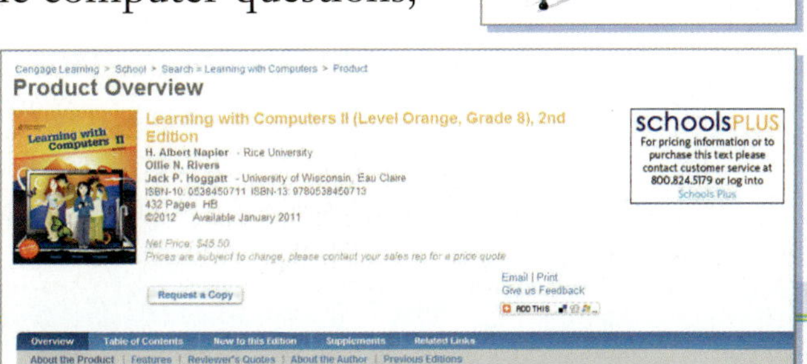

© GREG VAUGHN / ALAMY

GUIDEPOST 2

## Word Processing – Projects 1–6

Just look at the fun you will have in Projects 1–6! You will learn about the 13 original colonies; the Lewis and Clark Expedition; the nineteenth-century writers and philosophers of Concord, Massachusetts; our country's founding fathers and mothers; and the founding of our country's National Park system as you use *Word* to create multilevel lists, bound and unbound reports, letters, envelopes, and infographics.

You will learn how to create multilevel lists to organize information and then learn how to create multipage reports, which are based on the multilevel lists, that have the correct margins, fonts and font sizes, line spacing, and source citations. You will also learn how to use tables, tabbed columns, newsletter columns, and bulleted lists to present information attractively and how to create correctly formatted letters and envelopes.

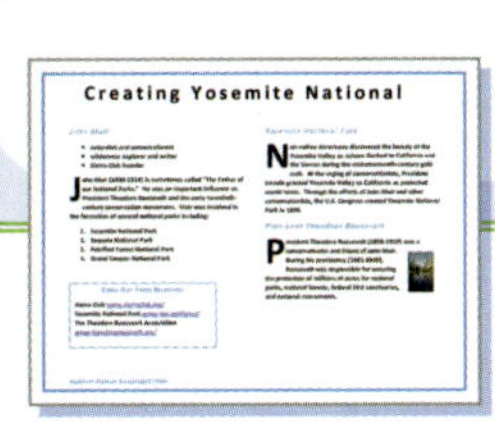

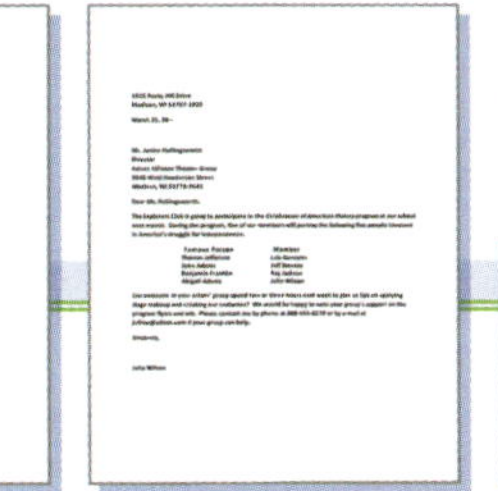

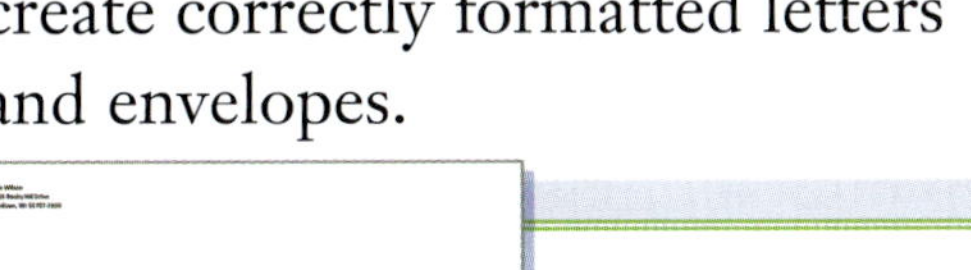

## Worksheets – Projects 7–10

I enjoy solving interesting problems and working with numbers. How about you? In Projects 7–10, you will solve problems by entering the data and formulas in *Excel* worksheets to explore elements from the Periodic Table, analyze early U.S. population data, create a budget for a fund-raising project, and chart data about the universe.

© IMAGE SOURCE/JUPITER IMAGES

GUIDEPOST 3

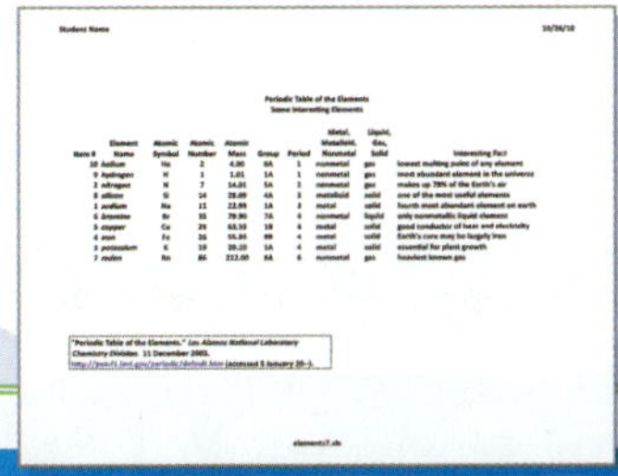

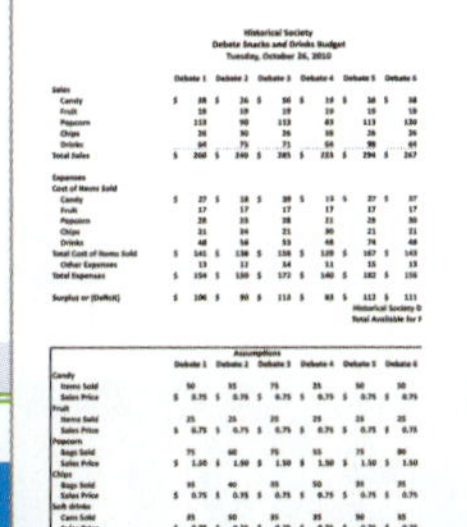

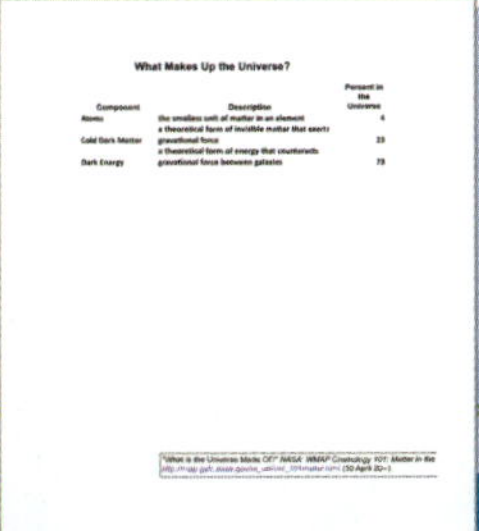

KIRK GEISLER/SHUTTERSTOCK.COM

## Presentations and Multimedia – Projects 11–15

Presenting ideas and facts to an audience is really fun! In Projects 11–15, you will create *PowerPoint* slide show presentations using different slide layouts and themes. To make your presentations more interesting and fun, you will add transitions, animations, audio, video, and hyperlinks. You will even learn how to work in two applications at once by adding worksheet data to slides!

GUIDEPOST 4

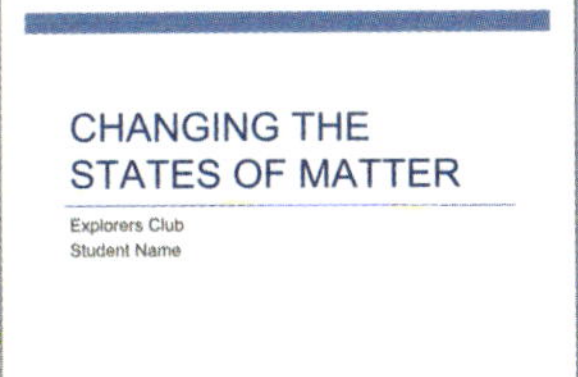


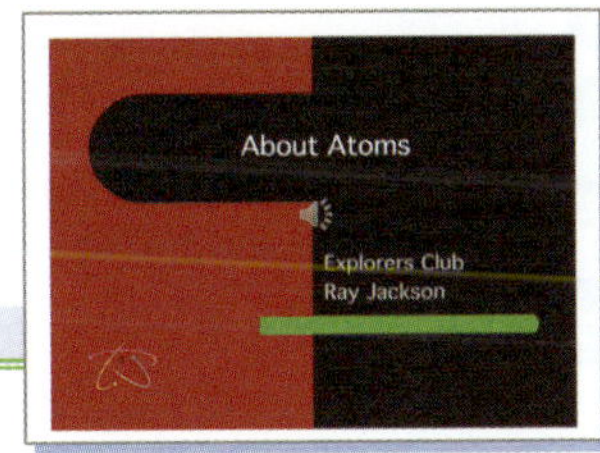

NORTH WIND PICTURE ARCHIVES VIA AP IMAGES

## Database – Projects 16–18

Did you know that databases are great tools for organizing your research data? In Projects 16–18, you will use *Access* databases to organize research data about the 50 states, nineteenth-century social reformers, and U.S. inventors and their inventions. You will learn to open and create database files, create tables, enter data in your tables, sort and filter your data, ask questions and get answers from the data, and print your data in from the datasheet or in a report.

GUIDEPOST 5

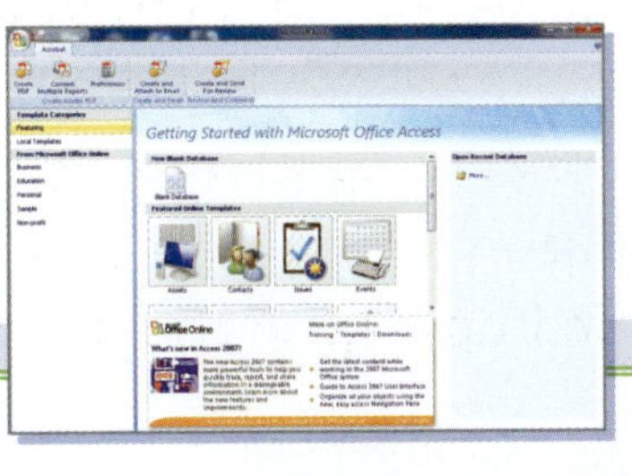


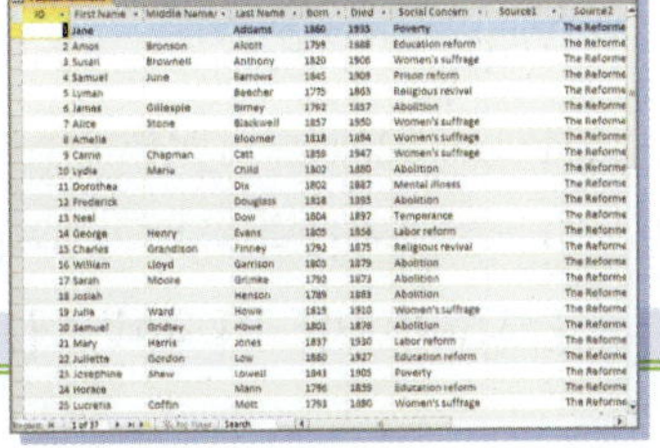

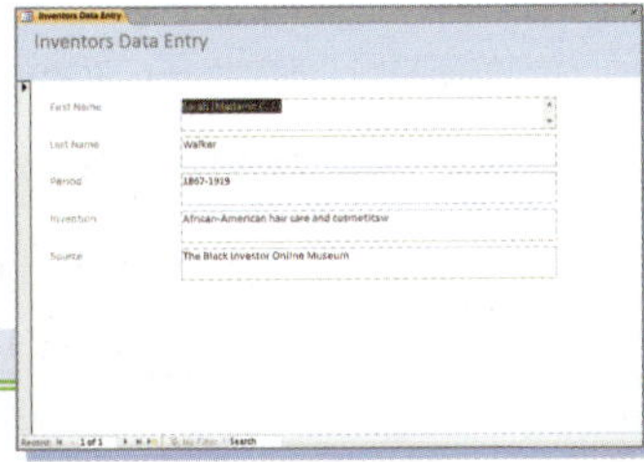


We hope you are excited about joining our Explorers Club and are looking forward to learning many new skills. Next, go to the Getting Started project to begin blazing your own trail!

# Contents

# PRESENTATIONS AND MULTIMEDIA

## Project 12 Changing the States of Matter



## Project 13 Observing the Atom



## Project 14 Rushing to California



## Project 15 Racing the Iditarod Trail

# DATABASE

# Getting Started

## Explorers' Guide

**Data file:** none

**Objectives:**
In this project, you will:
- practice computer ergonomics
- define computer hardware and software
- review the *Windows* desktop
- use the mouse
- work with windows and folders
- access the Internet and the Web

## Our Exploration Assignment:

### Learning about computer basics

Welcome to the Explorers Club! Follow the Trail Markers as we explain the right way to sit at the computer and describe computer hardware and software. Next, you will review the *Windows* desktop, learn several ways to use the mouse, and learn how to work with windows and folders. Finally, you will use the Internet to send and receive e-mail and explore a Web page.

# Day 4 – Total Care Veterinary Clinic

## Task #2 – Sort and Query a Table and Create a Report Using the Report Wizard

1. Open the *Addresses* table in Datasheet view and verify your data entry. Resize the columns as necessary.
2. Sort the table in ascending order by last name, save the changes to the table, and close it.
3. Use the Simple Query Wizard to create a select query (based on the *Addresses* table) that shows only the FirstName, LastName, and WorkPhone fields for all of the records. Save the query as **Phone List**.
4. Sort the query datasheet in ascending alphabetical order by Last Name, if necessary; then save the changes to the query and close it.
5. Use the Report Wizard to create a report based on the *Phone List* query. Sort the report in ascending order by last name; use the Tabular and Portrait layout and a style of your choice. Save the report as **Phone List**.
6. Preview and, with permission, print the report.
7. Close the report object and close *Access*.

## Task #3 – Create a New Database and Define Table Fields in Design View

1. Start *Access* and create a new database using the Blank database template. Name, save, and create the database as *Orge Day 4 Clients sol*.
2. Save the table as **Clients** and switch to Design view.
3. Name the following fields and set the field properties:

| Field Name | Data Type | Field Size | Caption |
|---|---|---|---|
| ClientName | Text | 50 | Client |
| Street | Text | 50 | None |
| City | Text | 50 | None |
| State | Text | 5 | None |
| Zip | Text | 10 | None |
| PetName | Text | 50 | Pet Names |

4. Save the table and switch to Datasheet view; then review the table datasheet and close the table.

## Task #4 – Create a Form Using the Form Wizard

1. Use the Form Wizard to create a data entry form for the *Clients* table that includes all fields except the ID field. Use the Columnar layout and the style of your choice.
2. Switch to Form view and save the form as **Clients Data Entry**.
3. Close the form and close *Access*.

## Practicing Computer Ergonomics

The rules for using a computer correctly to avoid personal injury are called computer ergonomics. Computer ergonomics rules include appropriate posture in addition to ways to correctly position and use the computer components such as the keyboard, mouse, and monitor.

Check out the way Ray is sitting at his computer. This is the way you should sit at your computer to avoid injury to your back, wrists, or fingers.

# Day 4 – Total Care Veterinary Clinic

Today is the last day of your internship! Working with Ms. Davis and others at Total Care Veterinary Clinic has been interesting and fun and allowed you to practice your new skills. Ms. Davis and Dr. Wilson encourage you to continue to develop your computer skills. To celebrate the successful completion of your internship, Dr Wilson is treating you and the entire clinic staff to lunch.

Before lunch, Ms. Davis asks you to update Dr. Wilson's electronic address book, which she maintains for him in a table in an *Access* database. She gives you a handwritten list of the new entries. She would like the table to be sorted in ascending order by last name each time Dr. Wilson or she opens it. Ms. Davis also wants you to create a report that shows only names and phone numbers.

Then after lunch, Ms. Davis wants you to create a new database containing a table of client information. She also wants you to add a data entry form to the database so that she can have Beverly, the receptionist, update the table at a later date.

## TO DO TODAY

1. Add data to a table using a form
2. Sort and query the table and create a report using the Report Wizard
3. Create a new database and define table fields and field properties in Design view
4. Create a form using the Form Wizard

## Task #1 – Data Entry Using a Form

1. Start *Access* and open the *Orange Day 4 Add Bk data* file.
2. Save the database as *Orge Day 4 Add Bk sol*.
3. Open the *Addresses Data Entry* form in Form view and enter the following new records in the *Addresses* table. Close the form when finished with your data entry.

| Name | Company | Address | Work Phone | Email Address |
|---|---|---|---|---|
| Jeff Saenz | Saenz Construction | 1234 S. Dayton, St. Paul, MN 55113-1234 | 651-555-9824 | jsaenz@ttxm.com |
| Laura Wang | Wang and Sons | 2258 Lawton Street, Chicago, IL 60609-2258 | 312-555-6789 | llwang@opzu.net |

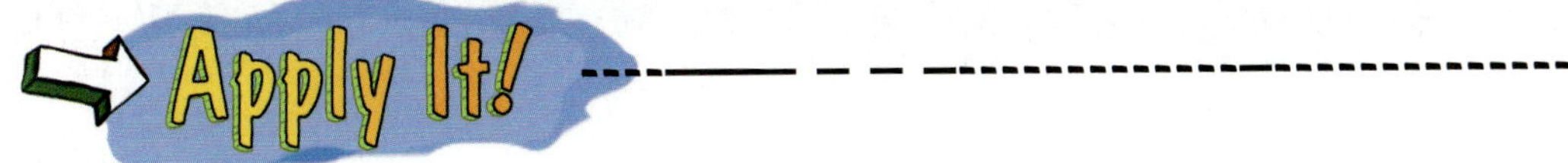


**Follow this checklist to make certain you are using correct posture each time you begin working at your computer.**

1. Are you sitting straight with your back against the chair? ☑
2. Are your forearms, wrists, and hands straight and in line on the keyboard? ☑
3. Are your feet resting flat on the floor or on a footrest? ☑
4. Are your neck, head, and shoulders in line with your body? ☑
5. Are you facing your computer's monitor and screen straight ahead? ☑
6. Are your upper arms and elbows relaxed next to your body? ☑
7. Is your computer monitor's screen at eye level? ☑
8. Is your mouse to the left or right of your keyboard for easy reach? ☑

Fantastic! After checking each item on the list, you are ready to start working at your computer.

## Defining Computer Hardware and Software

Computer hardware includes the computer parts that you can see and touch. Computer software provides instructions the computer needs to operate.

### Computer Hardware

Computer hardware components include the monitor, the keyboard, the mouse, internal and external storage devices, and the CPU. All are connected by insulated wires called cables. The CPU, or central processing unit, acts like the computer's "brain" by sending and receiving electronic instructions to and from the other hardware components, such as the storage devices and the keyboard, across these cables.

Some small computers, called notebook or laptop computers, combine the computer monitor, keyboard, storage devices, and CPU hardware elements together in one easy-to-transport case. You can use a mouse with a laptop computer, or you can use the Touch Pad that is included below the keyboard.

The documents you key on your computer's keyboard may be stored electronically on your computer's internal hard drive storage device. Your computer may be part of a local computer network. If so, you may be able to save your documents to a network storage device called a file server that is shared by everyone on the network. You may also be able to store your documents on external storage devices such as a USB flash drive, a CD, or a DVD. Check with your teacher to learn where to store the documents you create in this text.

# Project 18 — Keyboarding

## 18a Build Skill

Key each line twice. Double-space between 2-line groups.

**Balanced-hand sentences**

1 Hal and I may go to the social held on the island.
2 Alan and Glen did half of the problems on the bus.
3 The goal of the tutor is to do the problems right.
4 The six men may work down by the lake on the dock.
5 Pamela may go visit with the neighbor by the lake.

gwam 20" | 3 | 6 | 9 | 12 | 15 | 18 | 21 | 24 | 27 | 30 |

## 18b Speed Check

1. Key a 1' timing on paragraph 1.
2. Determine the number of words you keyed.
3. Key another 1' timing on paragraph 1. Try to go two words a minute faster.
4. Repeat steps 1–3 for paragraph 2.
5. Key a 2' timing on paragraphs 1–2 combined.
6. Determine the number of words you keyed.

For additional practice:
**MicroType 5**
Skill Building, Lesson F

**A** **all letters used** gwam 2'

Extraordinary would be the appropriate expression to use to 6
describe Michelangelo. It would be an outstanding word choice to 13
express how an individual may feel about the statue of David. It 19
would also be an excellent choice to describe the exquisite works of 26
art located in the Sistine Chapel. It would be just as fine a word to 33
use to tell about the beautiful dome of the St. Peter's Basilica. 40

The paintings, sculptures, and architecture of this individual 46
are recognized throughout the world. Michelangelo was born in 53
Caprese, Italy, but spent much of his early life in the city of Florence. 59
Here he spent a great deal of time in the workshops of artists. His 66
father considered artists to be beneath the dignity of his family 72
members. This did not stop the young artist who would become one 79
of the greatest of all time. 83

gwam 2' | 1 | 2 | 3 | 4 | 5 | 6 |

You view your documents on your monitor's screen and print them using a printer. If your computer has a camera, microphone, and speakers, you can record and listen to video and sounds.

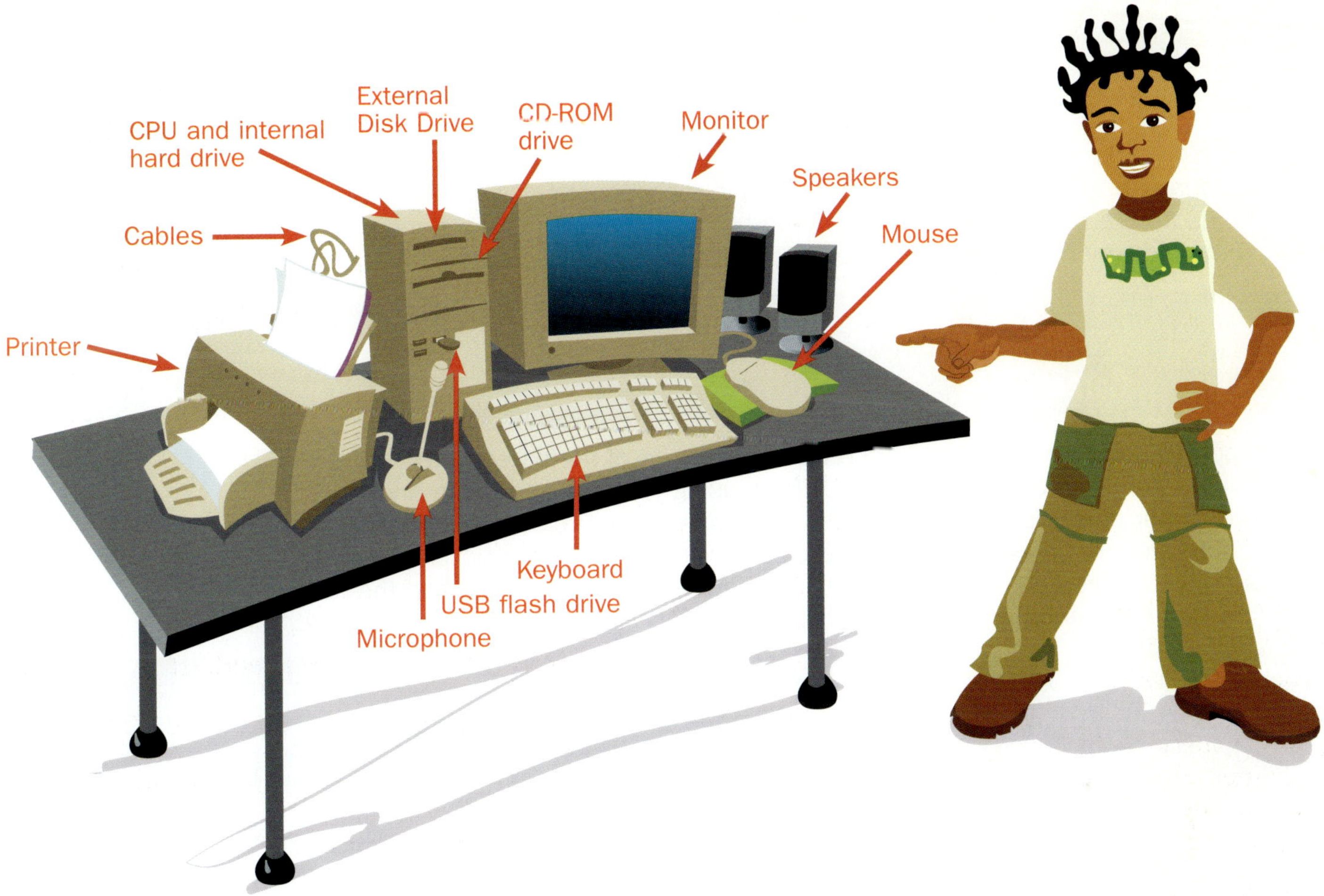

**Let's check out the hardware components on your computer.**

1. Find these hardware components on your computer: the CPU, monitor, storage devices (internal and external disk drive, CD-ROM drive, flash drive), cables, keyboard, and mouse.
2. Look to see if your computer also has the following hardware components: a printer, a microphone, or speakers.

To use your computer's hardware components, you also need computer software.

# Exploring Across the Curriculum

## Getting Help

Start *Access*, if necessary, and click the Microsoft Access Help icon to open the Help window. Key **Blank Report tool** in the search box and tap the ENTER key to research how to create a report from scratch. Open the database of your choice and create a simple report containing two or three fields from a table using the Blank Report tool. Preview the report and, with permission, print it. Save the new report and close the database.

## Career Day

Open your Career Day folder and review the results of the career interest survey you completed in Project 17. Then using your survey results and the career or occupation summaries you completed in Projects 1–16, create and print a list of the top five careers or occupations in which you are most interested. With your teacher's approval, share your list and the reasons for your choices with your classmates.

## Your Personal Journal

Open your personal journal document. Insert today's date and two blank lines. Think about what you have learned about U.S. inventors and how their inventions have changed the way people in the United States live and work. Which invention do you think made the biggest change? Why? Write two or three paragraphs explaining your choice. Spell-check, save, and close your journal.

## Online Enrichment Games

www.cengage.com/school/keyboarding/lwcorange

### Computer Software

Computer software is grouped into two categories: system software and application software. System software includes the operating system that runs your computer. *Microsoft Windows®* 7 and *Microsoft Windows® Vista*, often called *Windows*, are two versions of the most commonly used operating system software. Check with your teacher to verify which operating system your classroom or lab computers use.

Application software is used for a specific purpose. For the projects in this text, you will learn to use the *Microsoft Office®* application software suite: *Word*, *Excel*, *PowerPoint*, and *Access*. You will use *Word* to create text documents; *Excel* to create worksheets, sometimes called spreadsheets; *PowerPoint* to create multimedia slide shows; and *Access* to organize data in databases. You will also learn to use another application, *Internet Explorer*, to access Web pages.

Application software

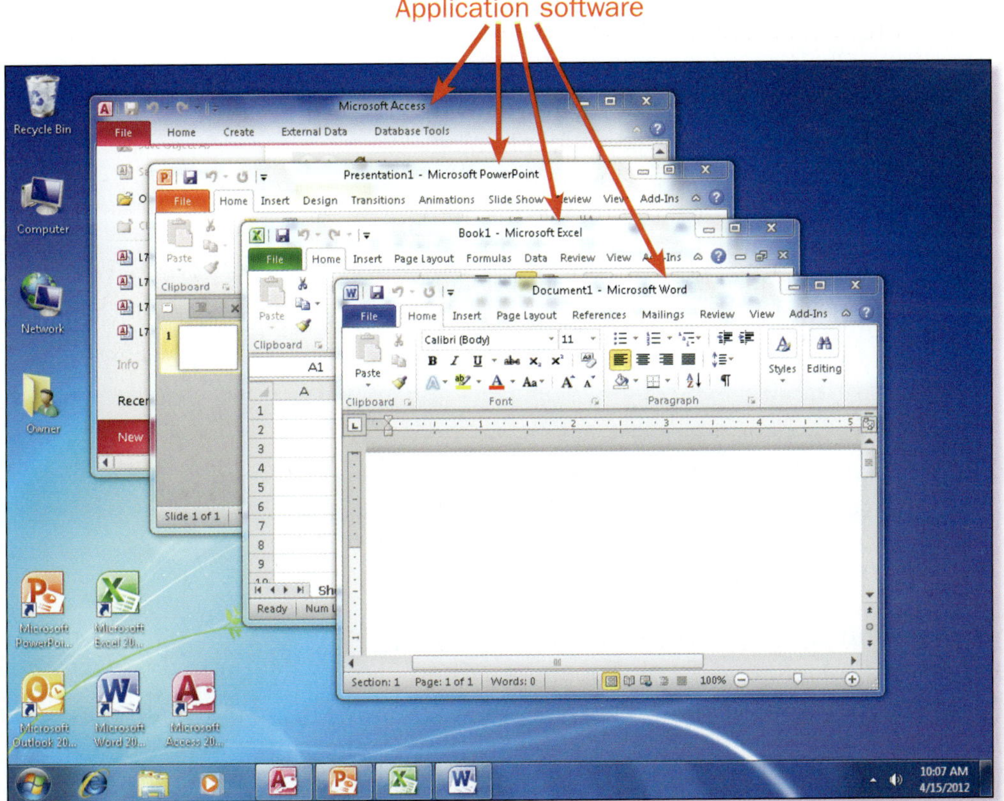


Let's start your computer and look at the *Windows* desktop. Begin by turning on your computer. Remember! Follow all classroom or lab rules when you are working at your school computer and respect other students' work that may be stored on the same computer.

Your teacher may modify the following Apply It! steps, if necessary.

## Language Arts: Words to Know

Look up the meaning of the following terms in a classroom dictionary, CD-ROM dictionary or encyclopedia, or online dictionary.

| compact disc | cotton gin | mechanical reaper | microwave oven |
|---|---|---|---|
| nylon | penicillin | Popsicle® | vinyl |

Create a new database with an empty table and save it as *definitions18*. Add the ***Term*** and ***Definition*** fields to the table in Datasheet view. Enter the term and definition for *compact disc* as the first record. Save the table as **Definitions** and let *Access* set the Data Type and other default properties. Use the Form Wizard to create a data entry form containing only the *Term* and *Definition* fields.

Use the layout and style of your choice. Save the form as **Terms Data Entry**. Use the form to enter the remaining seven records containing the terms and their definitions; then close the form. Open the table in Datasheet view, resize the columns to fit, and save and close the table. Use the Report Wizard to create a report that lists all of the terms and their definitions. Use the layout, orientation, and style of your choice. Save the report as **Terms List**. With permission, print the report; then close the database.

## Science: Research and Organize

Work with a classmate to use library or online resources to research the inventors and inventions of popular items we eat and drink: Luther Burbank, Clarence Birdseye, Rose Totino, Peter Cooper, John Pemberton, Gail Borden, Ruth Wakefield, Edwin Perkins, and Frank Epperson. Then create a new database with an empty table. Add fields to the table in Datasheet view, add the first record, and rename the fields in Datasheet view; then rename and save the table. Use the Form, Query, and Report Wizards to enter and store, query, and publish your research data. Include at least one source for each record.

Explore More

**Let's turn on your computer**

1. Turn on your computer.
2. If the Welcome screen appears, click your user name or icon and, if necessary, enter your password to log on to *Windows* and to view the *Windows* desktop.

**CHECKPOINT**
Your monitor's screen should look similar to this.

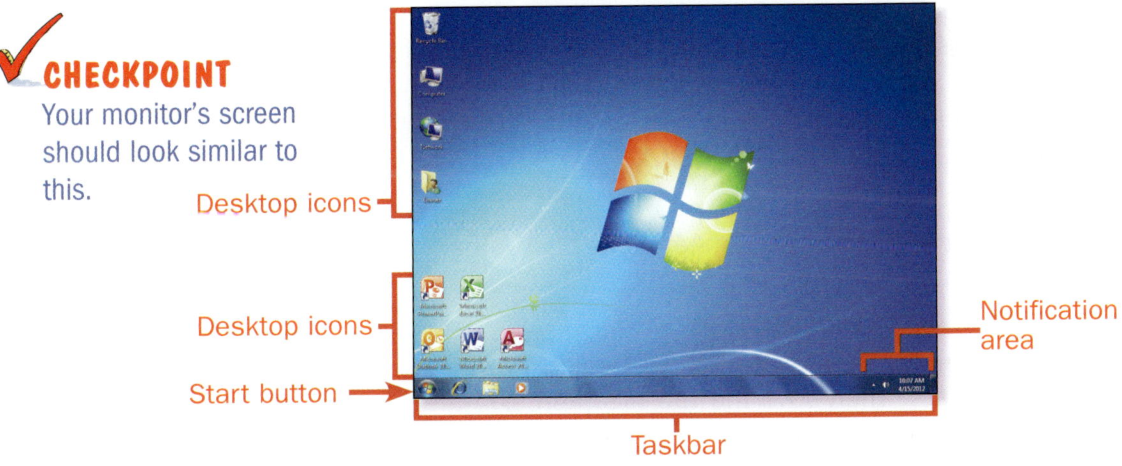

## Reviewing the *Windows* Desktop

The *Windows* desktop is the work area that covers your monitor's screen after you start your computer. The five main elements of the *Windows* desktop are:

1. a background picture or color that covers the work area
2. the taskbar that displays a button for each open application and document
3. the Start button, which opens the Start menu
4. small graphic symbols called icons, which can represent an electronic file or folder or application software
5. the notification area or *tray*, which displays small icons for system software or applications that are running in the computer's background memory, in addition to the current time.

Always take good care of your diskettes, flash drives, CDs, and DVDs to make sure you do not damage your stored documents. Check with your teacher for care instructions, if necessary.

# Exploring *Across the Curriculum*

## Internet/Web

You can learn more about inventors and their inventions on the Web. Open your Web browser and use a favorite or bookmark to view the Learning with Computers Web page (www.cengage.com/school/keyboarding/lwcorange). Click the **Links** option and click **Project 18**. Click the link to research inventors and their inventions in the field of computer science and telecommunications. List at least five inventors including their first, middle, and last names; the invention; a significant date; and the URL source of your information.

1. Create a new database containing an empty table and save it as *computers18*.
2. Add the following fields to the table in Datasheet view: *FirstName*, *MiddleName*, *LastName*, *Date*, *Invention*, and *Source*.
3. Enter the data for your first record in Datasheet view.
4. Save the table as **Computer Technology**, switch to Design view, and add appropriate captions. Then save the table, switch to Datasheet view, review the changes, and close the table.
5. Use the Form Wizard to create a data entry form containing all of the fields except the *ID* field. Use the layout and style of your choice. Save the form as **Computers Data Entry**.
6. Use the Computers Data Entry form to enter the remaining data for the table.
7. Close the data entry form and open the *Computer Technology* table in Datasheet view. Widen the columns, if necessary. Save the layout changes to the table and close it.
8. Use the Simple Query Wizard to create a query that lists each inventor's last name and invention. Save the query as **Invention**.
9. Use the Report Wizard to create a list of the inventors and their inventions based on the *Invention* query. Use the layout, orientation, and style of your choice. With permission, preview and print the report. Then close Print Preview and close the database.

Explore More

The *Windows* desktop can display many different icons, such as the Computer, Recycle Bin, or Network icons that allow you to access *Windows* features. You may also see shortcut icons for application software such as *Word*, *Excel*, *PowerPoint*, and *Access*.

The Start menu contains commands you can use to open folders and to start applications.

## Using the Mouse

The mouse is a very useful and important tool for working with desktop icons, opening files and folders, and creating and editing documents. For example, you will use the mouse and a desktop icon to open a folder, start an application, and perform tasks inside the application.

Moving the mouse on the mouse pad also moves a pointer, called the mouse pointer, across the screen. You use the mouse pointer to *point* to items on the screen.

The following table describes the common mouse actions you will use as you work in these projects.

| Mouse Action | Description |
|---|---|
| **Point** | Place the mouse pointer on a specific area of the screen. |
| **Click** | Point to a specific area on the screen and tap the left mouse button once. |
| **Double-click** | Point to a specific area on the screen and tap the left mouse button twice very quickly. |
| **Triple-click** | Point to a specific area on the screen and tap the left mouse button three times very quickly. |
| **Right-click** | Point to a specific area on the screen and tap the right mouse button once. |
| **Drag** | Tap and hold down the left mouse button and move the mouse pointer across the screen. |

Now use the mouse pointer and the *Windows* desktop to work with windows and folders.

# Exploring On Your Own

## Reading in Action

### Determining Cause and Effect

The inventions listed in the *inventors18* database had a great impact on American life. Read the paragraph below. Think about how each action or event (cause) resulted in another event (effect). Then place details from the paragraph in a cause and effect graphic organizer.

After the invention of cotton mills, which could spin cotton into thread and thread into cloth faster and more efficiently than could be done by hand, there was a need to pick and clean cotton seeds from cotton more efficiently. To address this need, Eli Whitney invented the cotton gin. By using the cotton gin, a worker could clean 1,000 pounds of cotton per day instead of just 1 pound per day by hand. Because the profit on cotton skyrocketed, more cotton was planted. Cotton growers expanded their crops, settling large areas in Alabama. To keep up with the increased crops, owners brought more enslaved workers from Africa to pick the crops. Because of the cotton gin, the growth of slavery and agriculture increased in the South.

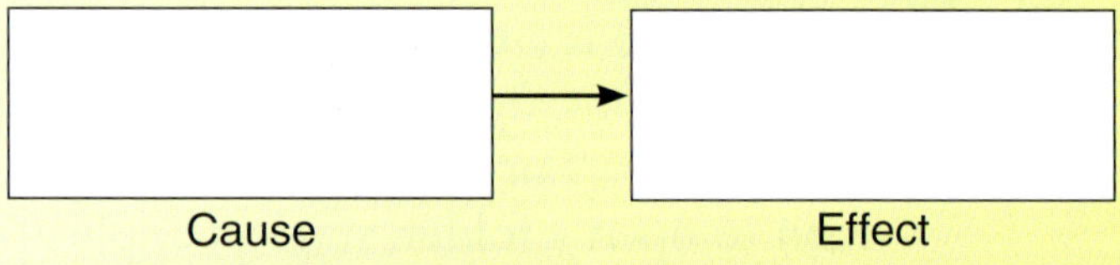


## Math in Action

### Calculating Profit

Profit is the amount of income a person earns in excess of the expenses in a transaction. A cotton grower has to spend \$100 to clean 1,000 pounds of cotton. A grower has 80,000 pounds of cotton to sell. How much should the grower charge per pound to make a profit of \$12,000?

Profit = Income – Expenses

$x$ = price of cotton per pound

Income = (80,000 pounds) ($x$)

$$\text{Expenses} = \left(\frac{\$100}{1{,}000 \text{ pounds}}\right)(80{,}000 \text{ pounds}) = \left(\frac{\$8{,}000{,}000}{1{,}000}\right) = \$8{,}000$$

$\$12{,}000 = 80{,}000x - \$8{,}000$

$80{,}000x = \$20{,}000$

$x = \$0.25$ charged per pound of cotton

Now you try it!

How much would a grower have to charge per pound to make a profit of \$4,000? to make a profit of \$8,000?

## Working with Windows and Folders

Everything that you create using the *Microsoft Office*® applications will be saved as electronic files. Electronic files are saved on diskettes, a computer's hard drive, a flash drive, a CD or DVD, or a network server.

Because you will create many electronic files, it is important to keep them organized so that you can easily find any specific file. To organize your electronic files, store them in electronic folders. An electronic folder is similar to a paper folder you might place inside a file cabinet drawer.

The *Windows* 7 operating system organizes the electronic folders and files on your computer's hard drive in virtual folders called libraries. The four default libraries are Documents, Music, Pictures, and Videos. You can open these libraries by clicking the *Windows Explorer* icon on the taskbar to open the Libraries window.

**Let's open the *Windows Explorer* window to view shortcuts to the libraries.**

1. Click the **Windows Explorer** button on the taskbar to open the Libraries window.

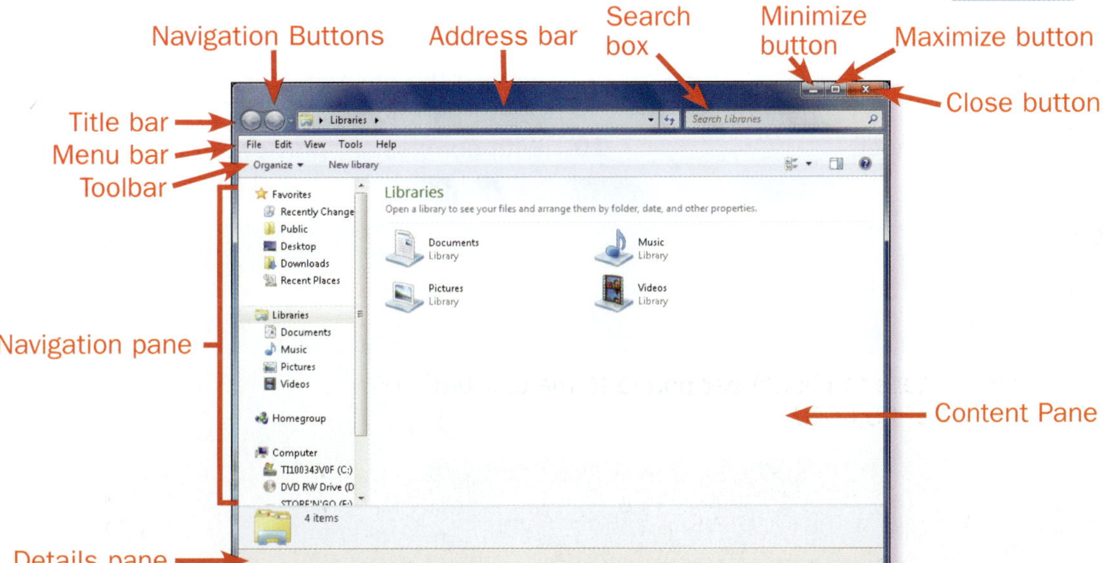

# Exploring *On Your Own*

## Blaze Your Own Trail

You have learned several new skills in this project. Now blaze your own trail by practicing these skills on your own!

**1.** Create a new database containing an empty table and save it as *contacts18 solution*.

**2.** Enter the first record in the table using the following data:

| Luis | Gonzales | lgonzales@navx.net | 608-555-8841 | Fishing and hiking |
|---|---|---|---|---|

**3.** Rename the fields as **FirstName**, **LastName**, **Email Address**, **CellPhone**, and **Hobbies**.

**4.** Save the table as **My Contacts**; then switch to Design view and add the following captions:
FirstName caption=First Name
LastName caption=Last Name
CellPhone caption=Cell Phone

**5.** Save the table; then switch back to Datasheet view, review the changes, and close the table.

**6.** Create a data entry form using the Form Wizard and include all of the fields in the *My Contacts* table except the *ID* field. Save the form as **Contacts Data Entry**. Use the new form to add the following records to the table.

| First Name | Last Name | Email Address | Cell Phone | Hobbies |
|---|---|---|---|---|
| Ray | Jackson | rayjackson@xeon.net | 608-555-2608 | Building computers |
| Tamika | Minton | tminton@nztk.com | 608-555-1579 | Designing clothes |
| Julie | Wilson | juliew@odzok.com | 608-555-6578 | Taking photos |
| Lin | Yang | lyang@xeon.net | 608-555-6654 | Cooking |

**7.** Close the form and open the table in Datasheet view. Resize the datasheet columns as necessary; then save and close the table.

**8.** Use the Simple Query Wizard to query the *My Contacts* table to view only the last name and cell phone number for each contact. Save the query as **Phone Numbers**; then run the query and close the query datasheet.

**9.** Use the Report Wizard to create a report based on the *Phone Numbers* query. Sort the report data in ascending order by last name and use the Tabular layout and the Portrait orientation. If you are using *Access 2007*, choose the style of your choice. Save the report as **Phone List**.

**10.** With permission, preview and print the report. Close Print Preview and close the database.

A window is a special area on the desktop in which files, folders, and applications are opened. All windows contain similar features you can use to manage them and view their contents. The *Windows Explorer* Libraries window features include the following:

- title bar—contains the Minimize, Maximize, Restore Down, and Close buttons, Navigation buttons; the Address Bar; and the Search box
    - o Minimize button—hides the window to a button on the taskbar
    - o Maximize button—sizes the window so that it covers the entire desktop
    - o Restore Down button—sizes the window smaller
    - o Close button—closes the window
    - o Navigation buttons—Back and Forward buttons you can click to revisit previously viewed window contents
    - o Address bar—displays the path to folders and subfolders
    - o Search box—used to search for files and folders
- menu bar—contains expandable menus of commands
- toolbar—contains clickable buttons to manage folder contents; the type of buttons that appear on the toolbar depends on the contents of the window
- Navigation pane—displays shortcuts to frequently used folders, libraries, and computers on your network and to your computer's storage devices
- Content pane—displays the contents of the open folder
- Details pane—displays information about the open folder or selected file

When you select a file in the Content pane, you see a Preview pane on the right side of the *Windows Explorer* window. The Preview pane displays a preview of the file you select in the Content pane.

**Minimizing, Maximizing, and Restoring a Window**

Windows can be minimized to a button on the taskbar, maximized to cover the entire screen, restored to its previously smaller size, and manually resized using the mouse pointer.

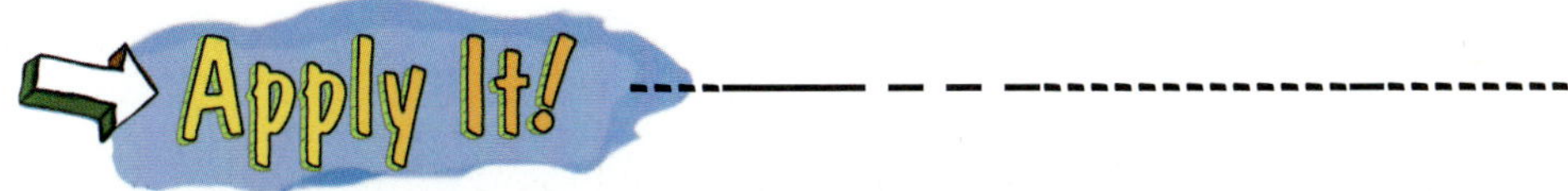


**Let's minimize, maximize, and restore the *Windows Explorer* window.**

1. Click the **Minimize** button on the window title bar to minimize the window. The window is still open, but it is hidden, or minimized, as a button on the taskbar.
2. Click the **Windows Explorer** button on the taskbar to unhide the open the window. The window is again visible on the desktop.

# Project Skills Review

You learned a lot in this project! We are very impressed with your progress. Let's take a few minutes to review the skills that you learned.

| Skill | How To | |
|---|---|---|
| **Add fields to an empty table in Datasheet view** | Enter data in the field to allow *Access* to set the Data Type property and other default properties. | |
| **Rename a field in Datasheet view** | Double-click the field name (column header) to select the field name and key another name. | |
| **Create a form using the Form Wizard** | *Access 2010*: click the **Form Wizard** button in the Forms group on the **Create** tab. | 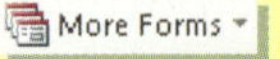  |
| | *Access 2007*: click the **More Forms** button in the Forms group on the **Create** tab and click **Form Wizard**. | More Forms |
| **Create a query using the Simple Query Wizard** | *Access 2010*: click the **Query Wizard** button in the Queries group on the **Create** tab. |   |
| | *Access 2007*: click the **Query Wizard** button in the Other group on the **Create** tab. |   |
| **Create a report using the Report Wizard** | Click the **Report Wizard** button in the Reports group on the **Create** tab. |   |

3. Click the **Maximize** button on the window's title bar to size the window larger so that it covers the entire desktop. 
4. Click the **Restore Down** button on the window's title bar to size the window back to its previously smaller size. 

If a window is not maximized, you can resize and reposition it using the mouse pointer. To resize a window, drag the top, bottom, left, or right edge of the window with the white double-headed arrow mouse pointer. To reposition a window, drag the window's title bar with the mouse pointer.

Great! Now let's practice creating and deleting a folder inside the My Documents private folder located in the Documents library folder.

### Creating and Deleting Folders

Suppose you use your computer to create and save all of your school reports during the year. Where should you put your school reports so that you can find them easily? It is easy! Just save all of your school reports together in their own private folder inside the My Documents folder! A private folder is a folder you do not share with others on a computer network.

You can create a new folder inside another folder, such as My Documents, by clicking the New Folder button on the window's toolbar. You can also create a new folder using a shortcut menu.

To create a folder inside the My Documents folder, navigate to the My Documents folder and click the New folder button on the window's toolbar. You can quickly navigate to the My Documents folder using the Navigation pane.

**Let's navigate to the My Documents folder and create a new folder named Reports.**

1. Point to the Documents icon in the Libraries group in the Navigation pane to view the folder expand icon.
2. Click the **expand** icon to the left of the Documents icon in the Navigation pane to display the My Documents folder icon.
3. Click the **My Documents** icon in the Navigation pane to view the folders and files in the My Documents folder in the Content pane.

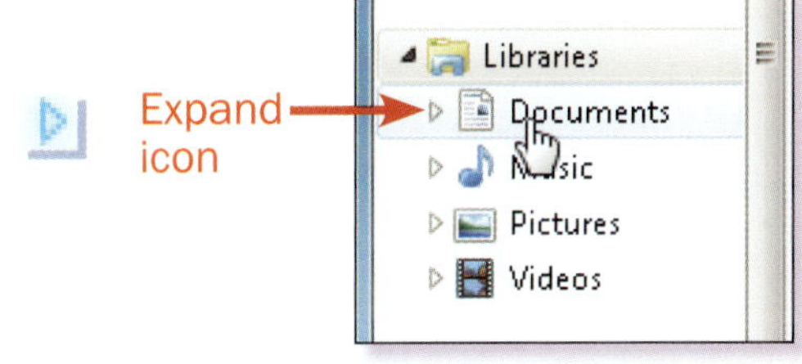


Now you are ready to create your new folder.

4. Click the **New folder** button on the window's toolbar. A New folder icon and folder name text box appears in the list of folders.
5. Key **Reports** in the folder name text box and tap the ENTER key.

Your report in Print Preview should look like this.

Custom report in Print Preview

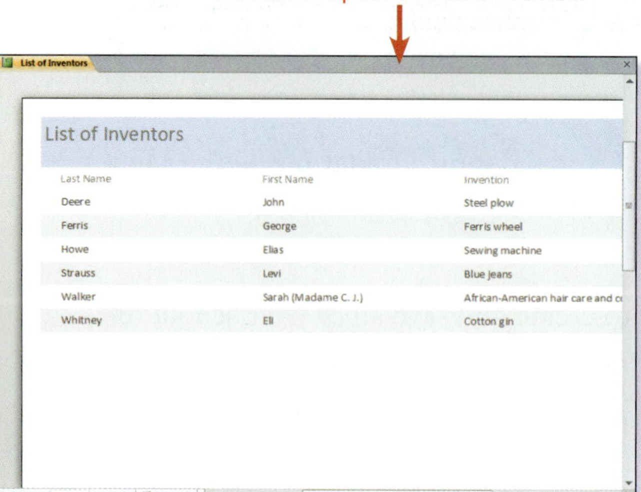


12. Close Print Preview and close the database.

Nicely done! Luis's data is organized and ready for the field trip.

**CHECKPOINT**

Your new *Reports* folder icon and name should look similar to this.

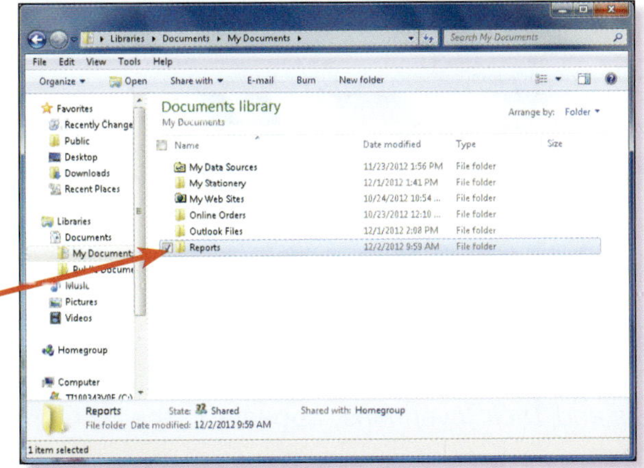


How can you tell the difference between a window and a dialog box? Unlike a window, a dialog box *does not* have Minimize, Maximize, or Restore Down buttons on its title bar!

When you no longer need the *Reports* folder, you can delete it. A quick way to delete a folder is with a shortcut menu.

A shortcut menu is a brief list of commands. You can view a shortcut menu by right-clicking a folder or file icon.

To delete the *Reports* folder, right-click the folder icon and click Delete on the shortcut menu. When you click Delete, a dialog box opens. A dialog box generally asks you a question or provides options you can click to continue your task. The dialog box that opens when you delete a file or folder asks you to confirm your deletion.

*Warning! Be careful when deleting folders.* When you delete a folder, you also delete any files stored in the folder!

**Let's delete the new *Reports* folder using a shortcut menu.**

1. Right-click the **Reports** folder icon in the Content pane to view the shortcut menu.
2. Click **Delete** to open the Delete Folder dialog box.
3. Click **Yes** to confirm your deletion.
4. Click the **Close** button on the window's title bar to close the My Documents folder and window.

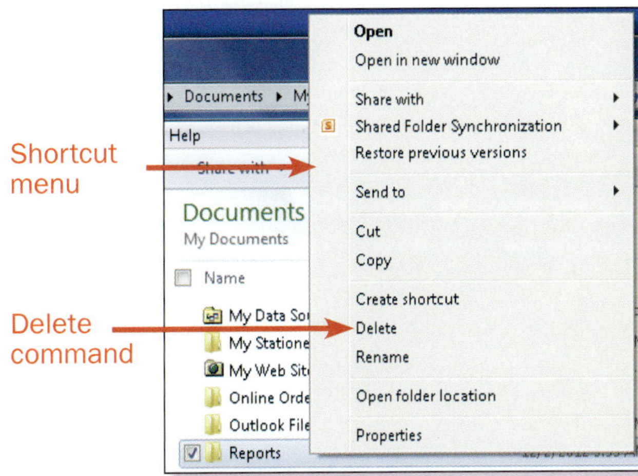

**Let's use the *Inventors and Their Inventions* query to create a report with the Report Wizard.**

**Create | Reports | Report Wizard**

1. Click the ***Inventors and Their Inventions*** query name in the Navigation Pane, if necessary.
2. Click the **Create** tab, if necessary, and locate the **Reports** group.
3. Click the **Report Wizard** button in the Reports group to start the wizard. The preselected query, *Inventors and Their Inventions*, appears in the Tables/Queries list.

Report Wizard

4. Click the double right arrows (>>) to add all three fields from the Available Fields list to the Selected Fields list.
5. Click the **Next** button to organize or group the records by the contents of a field. You do not need to group these records, so go to the next step.
6. Click the **Next** button to select a sorting order for the records.
7. Click the first arrow and click **LastName** to sort the records in ascending order by last name.
8. Click the **Next** button to select the layout of the report.
9. Click the **Tabular** and **Portrait** option buttons, if necessary, and click the **Next** button.
10. If you are using *Access 2007*, select the **Access 2007** style for your report and then click the **Next** button. Skip this step if you are using *Access 2010*.
11. In the last step, key **List of Inventors** as the report name and click the **Finish** button to save the report and view it in Print Preview.

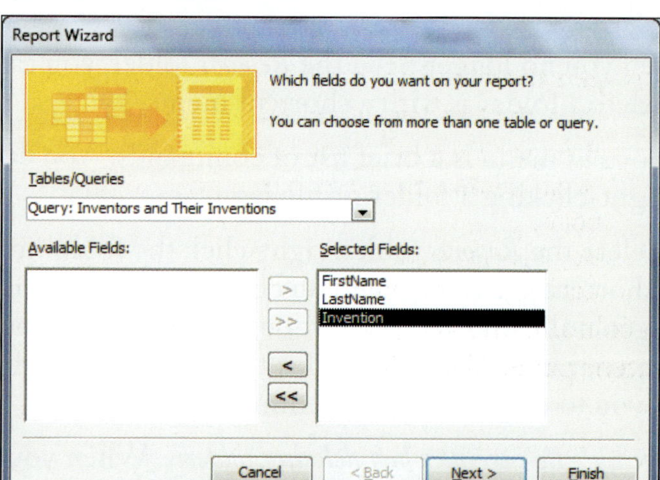


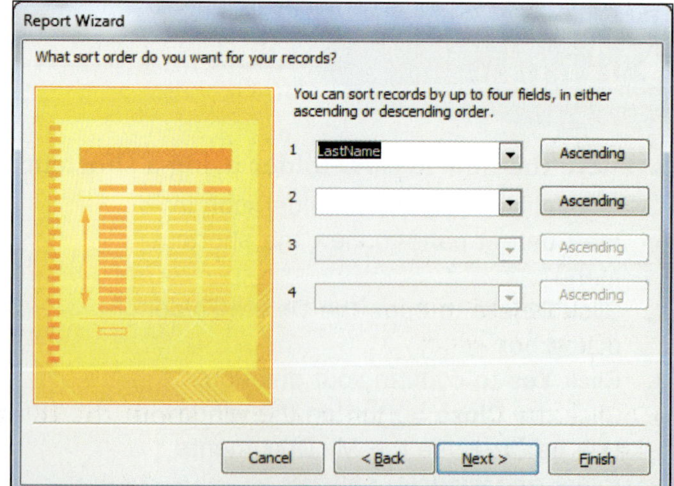

Because you will likely create many files and folders on your computer, you may occasionally need help in finding a specific file or folder.

**Finding Files and Folders**

In the projects in this text, you will create and save an electronic file or you will open and work on an existing electronic file called a data file. Your teacher will place your data files in a folder on your computer's hard drive or network drive.

Do not worry if you accidentally delete an item from your hard drive! Items deleted from the *hard drive* are temporarily stored in the Recycle Bin folder. You can double click the Recycle Bin folder to open it. Then right-click the deleted item and click Restore.

**Let's open the *Windows Explorer* window and search for your data files.**

1. Click the **Windows Explorer** button on the taskbar to open the *Windows Explorer* Libraries window.
2. Click the **Search box** on the window's title bar to position the insertion point.
3. Key the name of your data files folder in the Search box. (Your teacher will tell you the name of the folder.)

The folder name and path to your data files folder should appear in the Content pane. You can double-click the folder name to open the folder.

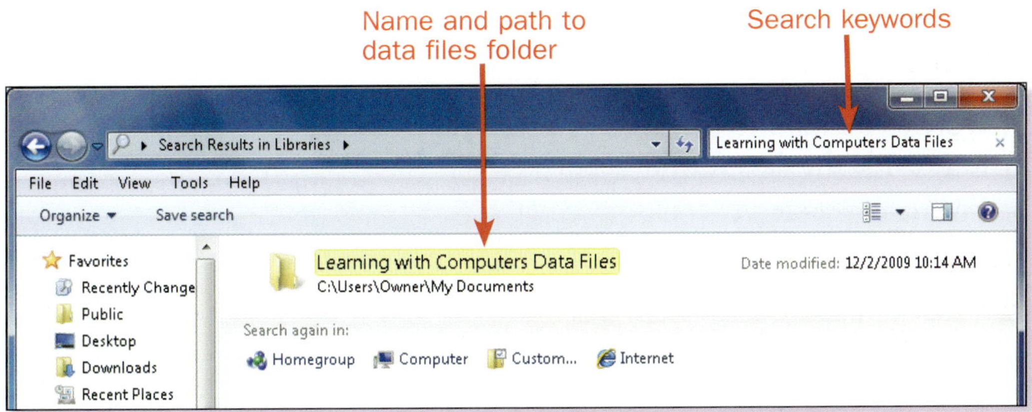

4. Double-click the folder name to open your data files folder.
5. Close the window.

Terrific! Now you are ready to learn about the Internet, e-mail, and the World Wide Web.

**CHECKPOINT**

Your query datasheet should look like this.

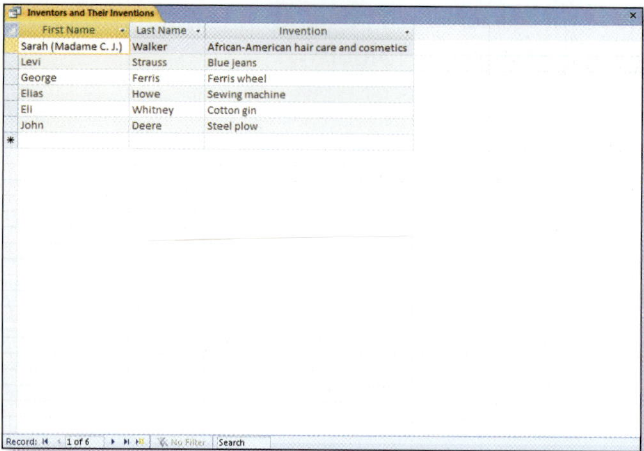

Inventors and Their Inventions

| First Name | Last Name | Invention |
|---|---|---|
| Sarah (Madame C. J.) | Walker | African-American hair care and cosmetics |
| Levi | Strauss | Blue jeans |
| George | Ferris | Ferris wheel |
| Elias | Howe | Sewing machine |
| Eli | Whitney | Cotton gin |
| John | Deere | Steel plow |



You can modify a query created with the Simple Query Wizard by switching to query Design view and adding or removing fields and setting query criteria.

8. Close the query datasheet.

Good job! Now let's create a report based on the *Inventors and Their Inventions* query.

## Creating a Report Using the Report Wizard

The Report Wizard is similar to the other wizards you have used. When you create a report using the Report Wizard, you can specify what fields you want to see in the report, how you want the data grouped, how you want the data sorted, what type of report layout you want, and what style you want to use. You can specify either a table or a query to provide the data for the report.

You can modify a report created with the Report Wizard or the Report tool in report Design view. For more information about working in report Design view, see *Access* online Help.

To start the Report Wizard, click the Create tab and then click the Report Wizard button in the Reports group.

## Accessing the Internet and the Web

The Internet is a worldwide network that links personal and business computers together. Most people connect to the Internet from their personal or business computer using a telephone line or cable connection, or they connect via satellite.

Connecting your computer to the Internet allows you to send and receive e-mail and instant messages, download or upload electronic files, and locate information stored on the World Wide Web.

### Sending and Receiving E-mail

Electronic mail, or e-mail, is one of the most popular Internet activities. Why? Because it is easy to correspond quickly with a friend, coworker, family member, or teacher by sending an e-mail to an electronic mailbox using an e-mail address. An electronic mailbox is a folder on a computer called a mail server. An e-mail address has three parts:

- the name of the person using the mail box, called the user name
- the @ symbol, which stands for *at*
- the name of the mail server where the user's electronic mail box is stored, called the host name

Here is an example of an e-mail address.

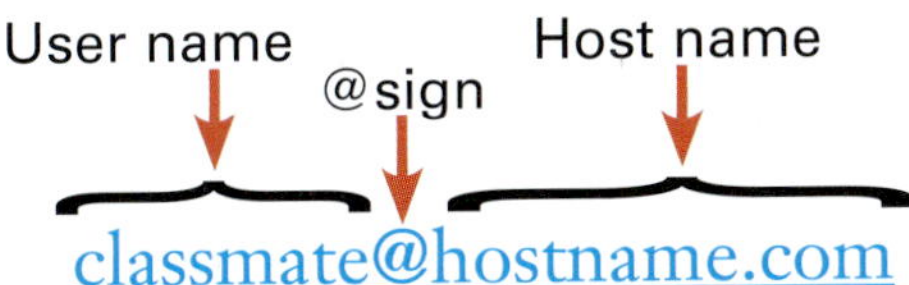


Whether you are sending or receiving an e-mail, you should remember a few simple rules of good behavior, called e-mail etiquette. Let's share some e-mail etiquette rules with a friend or classmate! With your teacher's permission, send a classmate or friend an e-mail listing a few e-mail etiquette rules.

If you are not using *Windows Live Mail* as your e-mail application, your teacher may modify the following Apply It! steps.

Your query datasheet should look like this.

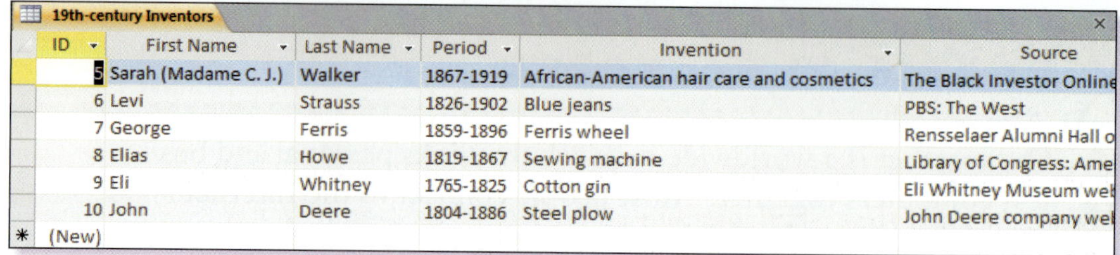

19th-century Inventors

| ID | First Name | Last Name | Period | Invention | Source |
|---|---|---|---|---|---|
| 5 | Sarah (Madame C. J.) | Walker | 1867-1919 | African-American hair care and cosmetics | The Black Investor Online |
| 6 | Levi | Strauss | 1826-1902 | Blue jeans | PBS: The West |
| 7 | George | Ferris | 1859-1896 | Ferris wheel | Rensselaer Alumni Hall o |
| 8 | Elias | Howe | 1819-1867 | Sewing machine | Library of Congress: Ame |
| 9 | Eli | Whitney | 1765-1825 | Cotton gin | Eli Whitney Museum wel |
| 10 | John | Deere | 1804-1886 | Steel plow | John Deere company wel |
| (New) | | | | | |

8. Close the query datasheet.

### Using the Simple Query Wizard in *Access 2007*

You can start the Simple Query Wizard by selecting the underlying table in the Navigation Pane and then clicking the Create tab and clicking the Query Wizard button in the Other group.

**Let's use the Simple Query Wizard to quickly create a query that lists only the FirstName, LastName, and Invention fields.**

Create | Other | Query Wizard

1. Click the ***19th-century Inventors*** table name in the Navigation Pane, if necessary.
2. Click the **Create** tab, if necessary, and locate the **Other** group.
3. Click the **Query Wizard** button in the Other group.
4. Click **Simple Query Wizard** in the list of query wizards and click **OK** to start the wizard.

Query Wizard

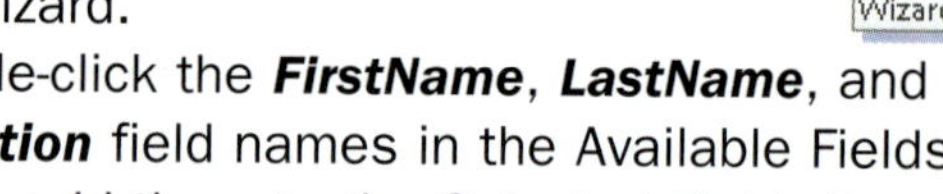

5. Double-click the ***FirstName***, ***LastName***, and ***Invention*** field names in the Available Fields list to add them to the Selected Fields list.
6. Click the **Next** button.
7. Key **Inventors and Their Inventions** as the query name and click the **Finish** button to run the query and view the query datasheet.

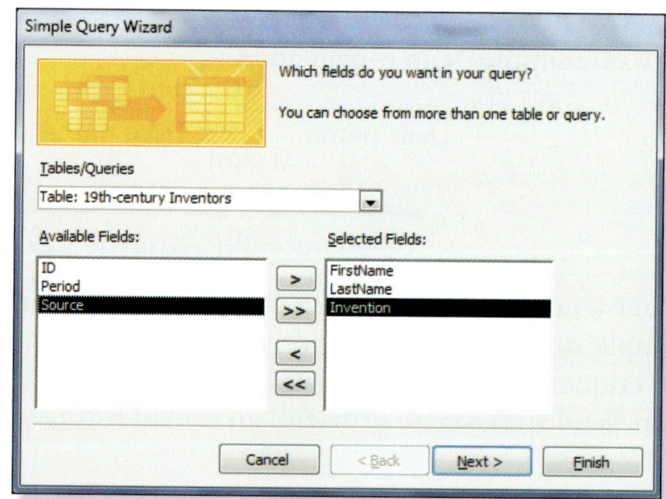

**Let's share some e-mail etiquette rules with a friend or classmate! With your teacher's permission, send a classmate or friend an e-mail listing a few e-mail etiquette rules. If you are not using *Windows Live Mail*, your teacher will tell you the name of your e-mail application and modify the following Apply It steps.**

1. Open **Windows Live Mail** or another e-mail application indicated by your teacher, using the Start menu or a desktop icon.
2. Click the **New** button on the toolbar to open the New Message window.
3. Key the e-mail address of a classmate or friend in the To text box. (Your teacher may tell you the e-mail address to use.)
4. Tap the TAB key to move to the Subject text box.
5. Key **E-mail Etiquette** and tap the TAB key to move to the message area.
6. Key the message just as you see it in the following figure and key your name instead of *Student Name* at the end of the message.

Your e-mail window should look similar to this.

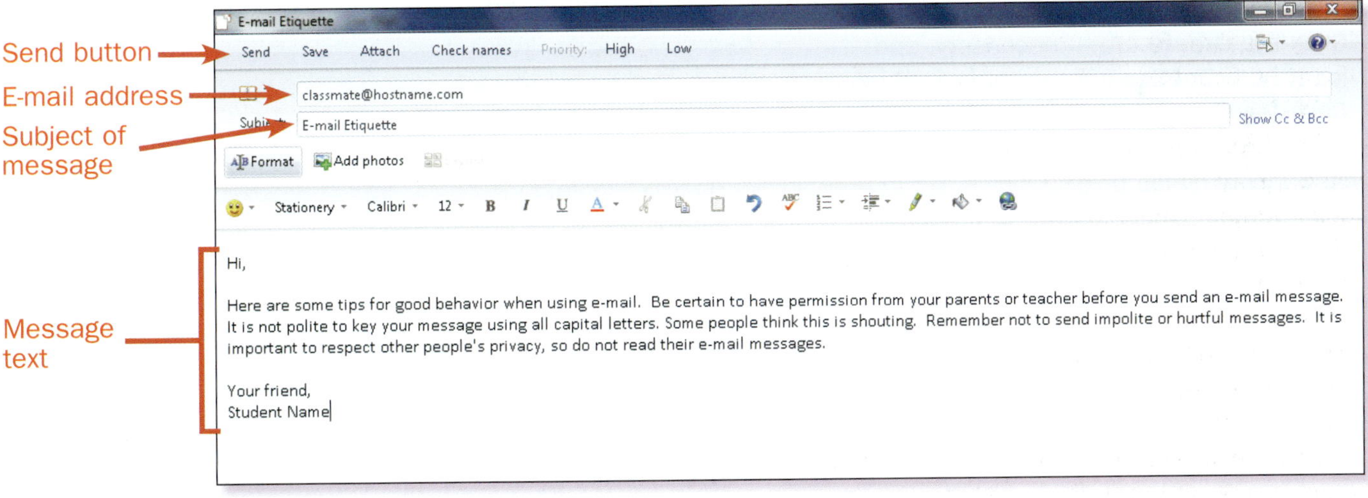


7. Click the **Send** button on the toolbar.

You can check for new e-mail at any time. Messages you receive from others are stored in the Inbox folder. You can see the Inbox folder and its contents when you open your e-mail application.

## Creating a Query Using the Simple Query Wizard

Just as you can create a form using a wizard, you can use a wizard to create a query. The Simple Query Wizard is a step-by-step process that allows you to identify a table and then specify individual fields in that table to be shown in a query datasheet when you run the query.

**Using the Simple Query Wizard in *Access 2010***

You can start the Simple Query Wizard by selecting the underlying table in the Navigation Pane and then clicking the Create tab and clicking the Query Wizard button in the Queries group.

**Let's use the Simple Query Wizard to quickly create a query that lists only the FirstName, LastName, and Invention fields.**

Create | Queries | Query Wizard

1. Click the ***19th-century Inventors*** table name in the **Navigation Pane**, if necessary.
2. Click the **Create** tab, if necessary, and locate the **Queries** group.
3. Click the **Query Wizard** button in the Queries group to open the New Query dialog box.
4. Click **Simple Query Wizard** in the list of wizards and click **OK** to start the wizard. The name of the preselected table appears in the Table/Queries list.
5. Double-click the ***FirstName***, ***LastName***, and ***Invention*** field names in the Available Fields list to add them to the Selected Fields list.
6. Click the **Next** button.
7. Key **Inventors and Their Inventions** in the What title do you want for your query? text box and click the **Finish** button to run the query and view the query datasheet.

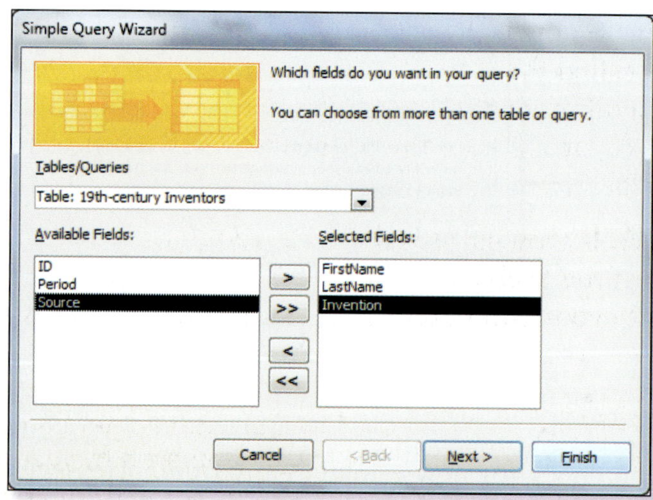

**Let's check for new e-mail.**

1. Click the **Inbox** folder in the Folder pane, if necessary, to open the folder.
2. Click the **Sync** button on the toolbar to download messages.
3. Look in the message area for any new messages.
4. Double-click a message to open and read it.
5. Close the message window.
6. Close the e-mail application window.

Sync

To quickly answer an e-mail, click the Reply button on the toolbar. The e-mail address of the person who sent you the message is automatically placed in the To box. The Subject box automatically fills in. Just key your reply and send it!

### Exploring a Web Page

The World Wide Web, usually just called the Web, is a subset of the Internet. The Web consists of Web servers that store multimedia documents, called Web pages, which can contain text, pictures, sound, and animation. A group of related Web pages stored together is called a website. The primary Web page at a website is called its home page.

You use application software called a Web browser to view Web pages. The two most popular Web browsers are *Microsoft Internet Explorer* and *Mozilla Firefox*. Other popular Web browsers include *Google Chrome* and *Apple Safari*.

The Apply It! activities in this project assume that you are using the *Internet Explorer* browser. If you are using a different browser, your teacher may modify the steps.

When you open the *Internet Explorer* browser, the browser's starting Web page, called the browser home page, is visible in the browser window. To view a different Web page, you key its address, called a Uniform Resource Locator, or URL, in the browser's Address bar and tap the ENTER key or click the Go button.

The Web browser uses the URL to send a request to a Web server for a copy of the Web page. The Web server responds by sending the Web page copy to your computer. You see the page in the browser window.

Stay safe when using the Internet or Web! View only those Web pages approved by your teacher or a parent or guardian, never enter any personal information on a Web page, and never exchange personal information with others you meet on the Internet.

The form looks fantastic! Now you are ready to enter the remaining records.

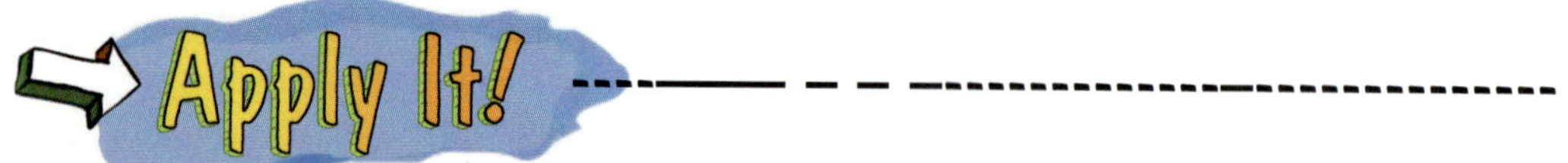


**Let's use the Inventors Data Entry form to enter the remaining records for the *19th-century Inventors* table.**

1. Using the following data, enter the remaining records.

| First Name | Last Name | Period | Invention | Source 1 |
|---|---|---|---|---|
| Sarah (Madame C.J.) | Walker | 1867-1919 | African-American hair care and cosmetics | The Black Inventor Online Museum |
| Levi | Strauss | 1826-1902 | Blue jeans | PBS: The West |
| George | Ferris | 1859-1896 | Ferris wheel | Rensselaer Alumni Hall of Fame |
| Elias | Howe | 1819-1867 | Sewing machine | Library of Congress: America's Story |
| Eli | Whitney | 1765-1825 | Cotton gin | Eli Whitney Museum website |
| John | Deere | 1804-1886 | Steel plow | John Deere company website |

2. Close the form when finished and open the table in Datasheet view.
3. Resize the columns as necessary and save the table's layout changes.

Your table should look similar to this.

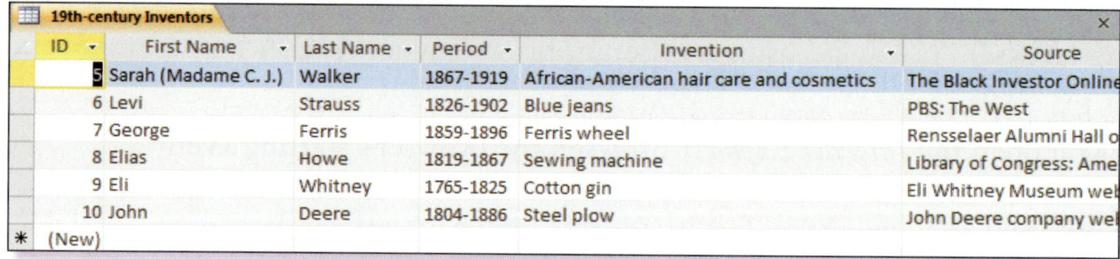

19th-century Inventors

| ID | First Name | Last Name | Period | Invention | Source |
|---|---|---|---|---|---|
| 5 | Sarah (Madame C. J.) | Walker | 1867-1919 | African-American hair care and cosmetics | The Black Investor Online |
| 6 | Levi | Strauss | 1826-1902 | Blue jeans | PBS: The West |
| 7 | George | Ferris | 1859-1896 | Ferris wheel | Rensselaer Alumni Hall o |
| 8 | Elias | Howe | 1819-1867 | Sewing machine | Library of Congress: Ame |
| 9 | Eli | Whitney | 1765-1825 | Cotton gin | Eli Whitney Museum wel |
| 10 | John | Deere | 1804-1886 | Steel plow | John Deere company wel |
| (New) | | | | | |

4. Close the table.

Great! Now let's query the data to view only the first and last names and invention data.

Web pages are connected by hyperlinks. A Web page hyperlink, often called a link, is text or a picture that you click with the mouse to *jump* to another page.

**Let's start our Web browser and view a Web page.**

1. Double-click the Web browser icon on the desktop or use the Start menu to open the Web browser. Your teacher will help you find your Web browser icon, if necessary.
2. Key the URL www.cengage.com/school/keyboarding/lwcorange in the Address bar and tap the ENTER key.
3. Click the **Links** option.
4. Click the **Getting Started** link.
5. Click the links to learn about the history of computers.

You can click the Back and Forward buttons on the Web browser's toolbar to revisit recently viewed Web pages. Try it!

When you find a Web page that you want to return to at another time, you can save it as a favorite. A Web favorite or bookmark uses the URL and name of a Web page you visit frequently to create a link to the page. To create a favorite, click Favorites on the menu bar; then click Add to Favorites.

**Let's save the Learning with Computers Web page as a favorite.**

1. Click the **Back** button to view the Learning with Computers Orange Web page.
2. Click **Favorites** on the menu bar and click **Add to Favorites**.
3. Click the **OK** button in the Add Favorite dialog box to save the favorite.

The next time you want to visit the Learning with Computers Orange home page, just click Favorites on the menu bar and then click the page's favorite in the Favorites list.

Web pages are full of useful information. But you should carefully review any information you find on the Web and make certain you can confirm the information from multiple sources before you use it.

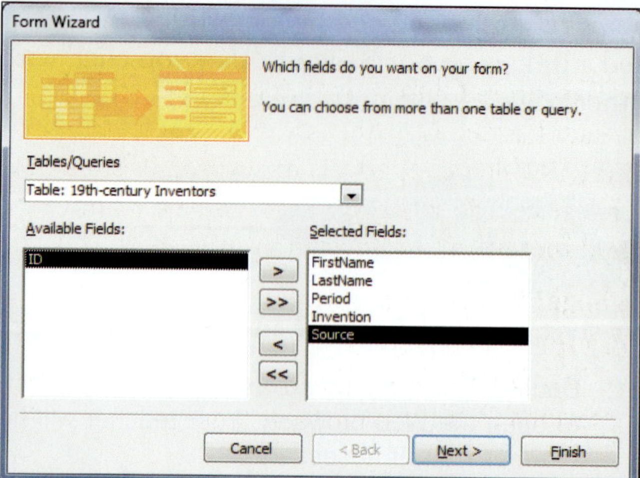


3. Click **Form Wizard** to open the first Form Wizard dialog box. In the first Form Wizard dialog box, you specify the fields you want in the form from a list of available fields in the table. The name of the preselected table appears in the Tables/Queries list.
4. Double-click the ***FirstName***, ***LastName***, ***Period***, ***Invention***, and ***Source*** field names in the Available Fields list to add them to the Selected Fields list.
5. Click the **Next** button to go to the next wizard step.

You specify a layout for the form in the second wizard step. The *Columnar* layout is the default layout.

6. Explore the different layouts and then click the **Columnar** option button. Click the **Next** button to accept the default *Columnar* layout and go to the next step.

Forms created with the Form Wizard can have different styles.

7. Explore the different form styles and then click the **Access 2007** style.
8. Click the **Next** button.

In the final Form Wizard step, you key a name for your form and specify whether you want to open the form in Form or Design view. By default, the form opens in Form view.

9. Key **Inventors Data Entry** as the form name and click the **Finish** button. The new form opens in Form view ready for you to enter your records!

Your new form should look like this.

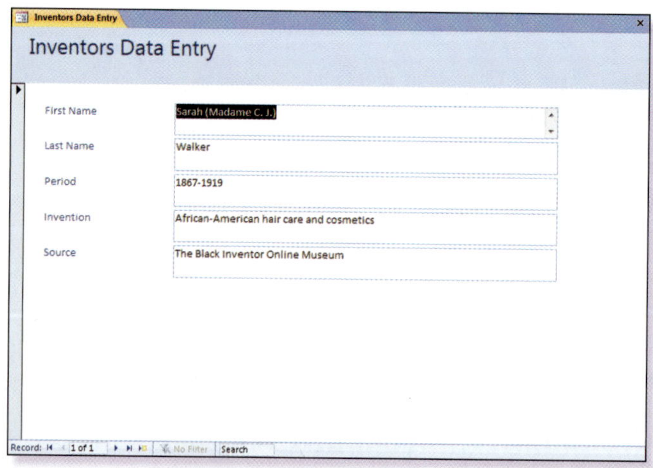

### Career Day Activities

The Explorers Club sponsors regular Career Day activities for its members. For each Career Day activity, you will join Luis, Ray, Julie, and Lin to learn about possible occupations in several different career areas. You will use your research to write a brief summary about what you have learned, print your summary, and save it in your Career Day folder.

You begin by opening your Web browser, visiting the Learning with Computers Web page (www.cengage.com/school/keyboarding/lwcorange), and clicking the Career Day link to review general information about occupations in different career areas.

**Let's check out the Career Day information.**

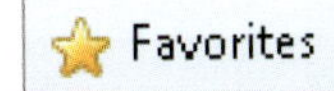


1. Click the **Favorites** button on the Favorites bar to open the Favorites Center.
2. Click your **Learning with Computers** favorite to load the Web page in your browser.
3. Click the **Career Day** link and follow the Career Cluster links to review general information about occupations in different career areas.
4. Close the browser.

Congratulations! You are ready to begin exploring!

4. Click the **Next** button to go to the next wizard step. You specify a layout for the form in the second wizard step. The *Columnar* layout is the default layout.
5. Explore the different layouts. Then click the **Columnar** option button and click the **Next** button to accept the default *Columnar* layout and go to the last wizard step, in which you name the form and open it.
6. Key **Inventors Data Entry** in the What title do you want for your form? text box and click the **Finish** button. The new form opens in Form view and contains the data for the first record already entered.

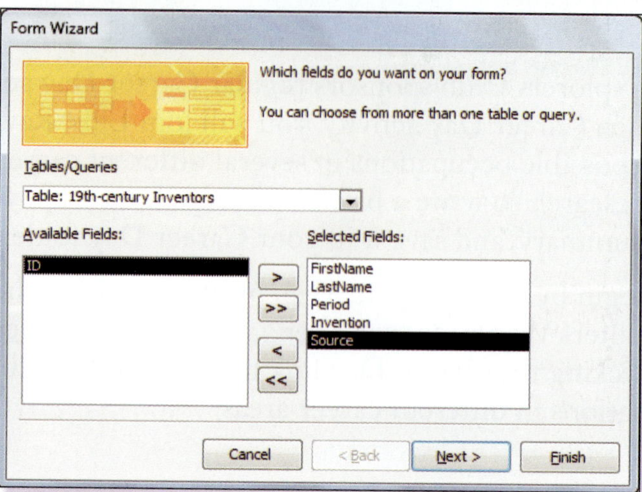

Your new form should look like this.

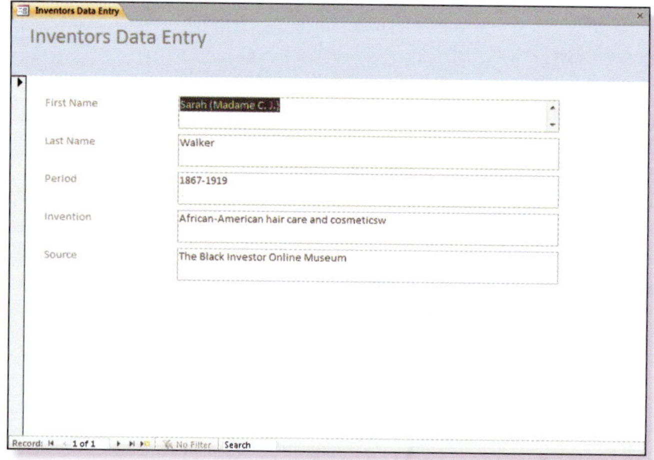


### Using the Form Wizard in *Access 2007*

The Form Wizard lets you select the fields you want to see in the form.

**Let's use the Form Wizard to create a data entry form that shows only the *FirstName*, *LastName*, *Period*, *Invention*, and *Source* fields. Before you begin, the *19th-century Reformers* table should be selected in the Navigation Pane.**

Create | Forms | More Forms

1. Click the **Create** tab and locate the **Forms** group.
2. Click the **More Forms** button in the Forms group to see a gallery of form options.

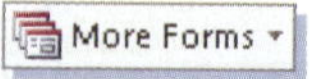

# WORD PROCESSING

***Welcome to the Explorers Club! Get ready to learn more about the colonists, writers, patriots, explorers, and conservationists who helped form the United States.***

We will:

- Raft the Mississippi with Mark Twain.
- Live in the Thirteen English Colonies.
- Cross the Missouri with Lewis and Clark.
- Explore the Writers of Concord.
- Reenact the Founding of Our Nation.
- Celebrate the Creation of Yosemite National Park.

Along the way, you will learn to use a word processing application called *Word* to create and format letters as well as multipage reports that include tables, footnotes, end-of-report citations, and tabbed columns. You will also learn how to create exciting infographics using newspaper columns, bulleted and numbered lists, colored fonts, symbols, clip art, text boxes, page borders, and WordArt. Let's get started!

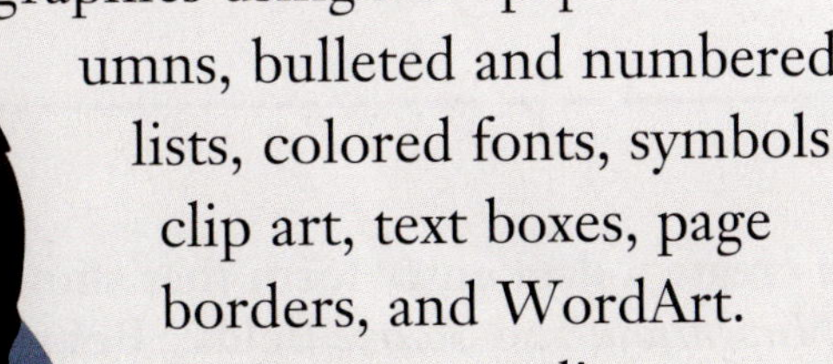

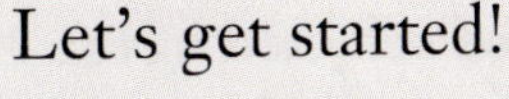

Your modified table in Datasheet view should now look similar to this.

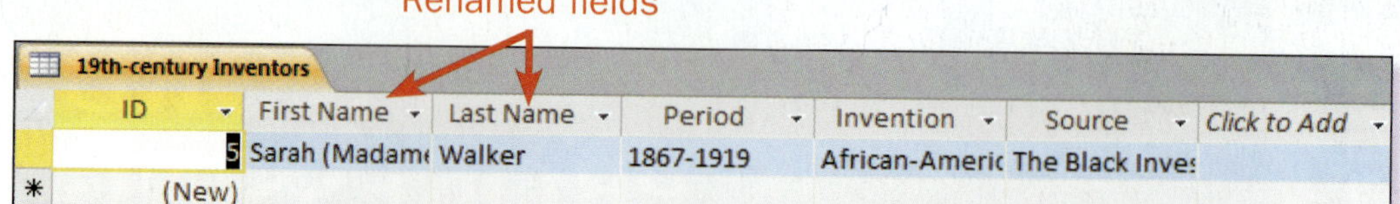


6. Close the table.

That was easy! Next, let's create a data entry form for the *19th-century Inventors* table using the Form Wizard.

## Creating a Form Using the Form Wizard

*Access* has some great fun-to-use tools called wizards. A wizard is a step-by-step series of dialog boxes that guide you through a process, such as creating a form. In Project 17, you learned how to use the Form tool to quickly create a data entry form containing all of the fields in a table.

When you want a data entry form that contains only some of a table's fields, you can use the Form Wizard to create it.

**Using the Form Wizard in *Access 2010***

The Form Wizard lets you select the fields you want to see in the form.

**Let's use the Form Wizard to create a data entry form that shows only the *FirstName*, *LastName*, *Period*, *Invention*, and *Source* fields. Before you begin, the *19th-century Inventors* table should be selected in the Navigation Pane.**

Create | Forms | Form Wizard

1. Click the **Create** tab and locate the **Forms** group.
2. Click the **Form Wizard** button in the Forms group to launch the Form Wizard. You select the underlying table, if necessary, and then select the fields to be included in the form in the first wizard step.

Form Wizard

3. Double-click the ***First Name***, ***Last Name***, ***Period***, ***Invention***, and ***Source*** field names in the Available Fields list to add them to the Selected Fields list.

# Rafting the Mississippi with Mark Twain

## Explorers' Guide

**Data files:** Mark Twain
Mississippi River

**Objectives:**
In this project, you will:
- open and save an existing document
- switch editing views and turn on formatting marks
- insert, delete, and select text
- check spelling and grammar and use the thesaurus
- preview and print a document
- create and save a new document

## Our Exploration Assignment:

### Opening, editing, and saving a document

As a steamboat steams its way down the Mississippi River, the riverboat leadsman calls out "Quarter twain!" "Half twain!" "Mark twain!" "Mark Twain" means that the water is deep enough for safe passage. The Explorers Club is learning about Mark Twain, the nineteenth-century American author and humorist who used his experiences growing up on the banks of the Mississippi to create some of fiction's greatest characters. Luis has keyed his Mark Twain research notes into a *Word* document. Can you help him make a few changes to the document? Thanks! Just follow the Trail Markers to open, rename, and save a document; switch between editing views and turn on the view of formatting marks; insert, delete, and select text; check spelling and grammar; use the thesaurus; and preview and print the document. Then you will create, name, and save a new document.

LIBRARY OF CONGRESS

**Let's add data to the first row (record) in our table and let *Access* set the Data Type property and assign each field a temporary name.**

1. Key **Sarah (Madame C. J.)** in the first field in record 1 and tap the TAB key to move the insertion point to the next field to the right.
2. Key **Walker** and tap the TAB key.
3. Key **1867-1919** and tap the TAB key.
4. Key **African-American hair care and cosmetics** and tap the TAB key.
5. Key **The Black Inventor Online Museum** and tap the Down arrow to save the record.

Temporary field names

Table1

| ID | Field1 | Field2 | Field3 | Field4 | Field5 | Click to Add |
|---|---|---|---|---|---|---|
| 5 | Sarah (Madam | Walker | 1867-1919 | African-Americ | The Black Inve | |
| (New) | | | | | | |

The first row contains all of the data for the first record. Now you can replace each field's temporary name with a more meaningful name.

**Let's rename the fields in our new table and then switch to Design view and add captions to two fields.**

1. Double-click the **Field1** column header to select the field name; then key **FirstName**.
2. Double-click the **Field2** column header; then key **LastName**.
3. Using steps 1 and 2 as your guide, rename the remaining fields as follows:
   Field3=Period
   Field4=Invention
   Field5=Source
4. Tap the ENTER key after keying the Source field name; then save the table as *19th-century Inventors* and switch to Design view.
5. Add the **First Name** caption property to the FirstName field and the **Last Name** caption property to the LastName field; then save the table and switch back to Datasheet view.

In *Access 2010*, you can add fields by double-clicking the Click to Add column header to view a list of Data Type properties; then you can click a Data Type property in the list to set the property and insert the temporary field name in the column header. Once the field is defined, you can key text or numbers in the field. Try it!

**Let's turn on your computer and use the *Windows* Start menu to start the *Word* application.**

1. Turn on your computer, if necessary.
2. Click the **Start** button on the taskbar.
3. Point to **All Programs** on the Start menu.
4. Click the ***Microsoft Office*** folder.
5. Click ***Microsoft Word 2010*** or ***Microsoft Office Word 2007*** to open the application.

Great! Now let's review the *Word* window and then open and save an existing document.

If you have a *Microsoft Word* icon on your desktop, double-click it to start the application. If your computer is on a network, follow the log-on process outlined by your teacher.

**ERGONOMICS TIP**

Remember your computer ergonomics checklist! Sit correctly at your computer keyboard, keep your elbows relaxed and at your sides, keep your wrists low but not resting on the keyboard frame, and keep your feet flat on the floor. Fantastic! Let's go to work!

## Opening and Saving an Existing Document

Check out the *Word* application window that opens on your screen. It contains super features you can use to open, edit, and save existing documents or create and save new ones.

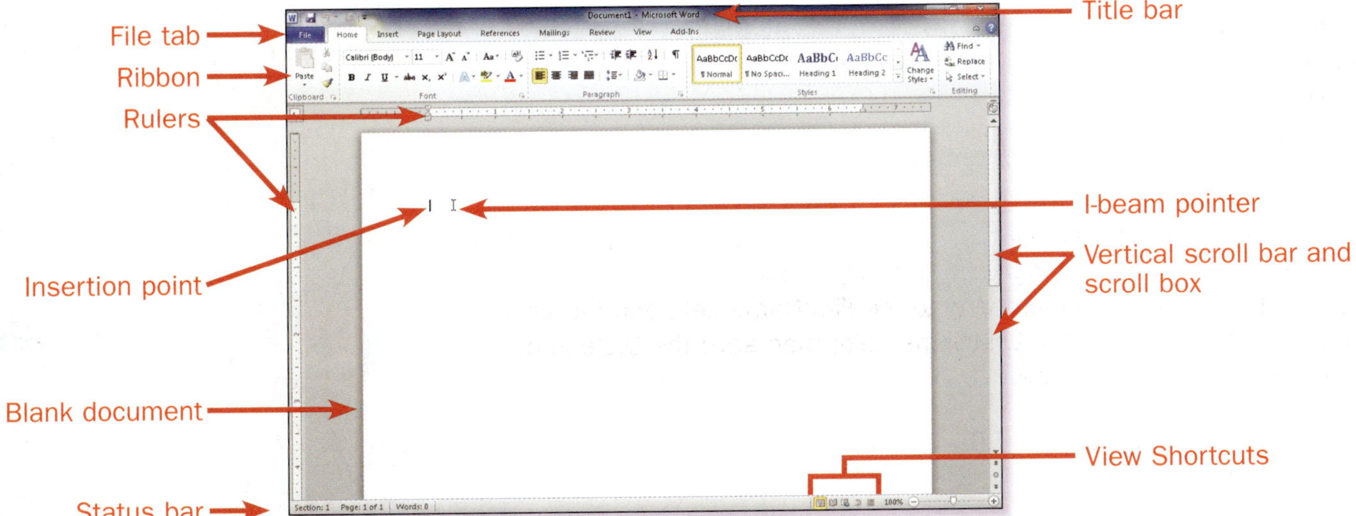

**Begin by starting the *Access* application and creating, naming, and saving a new database containing an empty table.**

1. Start the *Access* application and create a new database containing an empty table. Save the new database as *inventors18 solution*.

Way to go! Next, you add fields to the empty table and allow *Access* to automatically set field properties.

**ERGONOMICS TIP**

Wait! Before you begin, turn back to the Getting Started project in this book and find your computer ergonomics checklist. Use the checklist to check your posture—then you are ready to go!

## Adding Fields to an Empty Table in Datasheet View

In Project 17, you learned how to modify an empty table by adding fields and setting field properties in Design view. When you want to quickly add fields to an empty table, you can name table fields and allow *Access* to set field properties in Datasheet view.

As you enter data for the first record in the table, *Access* sets the Data Type property and other default properties for the data type based on what you enter in each field. For example, if you enter text in a field, *Access* sets the field's Data Type property as Text. If you enter a date in the field, *Access* sets the field's data type as Date/Time.

*Access* also gives each field a temporary name, such as *Field1* or *Field2*, as you move to the next field to the right. You can rename each field in Datasheet view.

Now you are ready to enter the field names in the table in Datasheet view.

You can switch to Design view and modify field properties or add or delete fields. *Warning!* Be careful adding or deleting fields or changing field properties after you enter data in a table. Design changes to your table might result in a loss of data or records with missing data.

| ***Word* Feature** | **Description** |
|---|---|
| **title bar** | contains the name of your document; the name of the application in which you are working and the application Minimize, Restore Down, Maximize, and Close buttons |
| **File tab (*Word 2010*)** | displays Backstage view, which contains commands you can use to create, open, save, and print a document |
| **Office Button (*Word 2007*)** | contains a menu with commands you can use to create, open, save, and print a document |
| **Quick Access Toolbar** | a customizable toolbar positioned above or below the Ribbon that contains, by default, the Save, Undo, and Repeat/Redo buttons |
| **Ribbon** | contains tabbed groups of command buttons you can click to perform a variety of document tasks |
| **rulers** | used to identify the keying position in a document and to set tabs |
| **insertion point** | vertical line that indicates the keying position in a document |
| **I-beam pointer** | the mouse pointer shape used to position the insertion point in a text area |
| **scroll bars and scroll box** | used to view different parts of a document |
| **status bar** | a customizable bar at the bottom of the *Word* window that can contain information about the open document as well as the location of the insertion point, the View Shortcuts, the Zoom button, the Zoom Slider, and other information |
| **View Shortcuts** | buttons on the right side of the status bar used to switch between editing views, such as the Print Layout and Draft views |

Each time you start *Word*, a new blank document with the temporary name *Document 1* opens. You can key in the new document and then save it with its own unique name. If you open an existing document without keying in *Document 1*, the blank *Document 1* automatically closes.

Now that you are familiar with the *Word* window, you are ready to open and edit an existing document.

# Project 18

Database

# U.S. Inventors and Inventions

## Explorers' Guide

**Data file:** none

**Objectives:**

In this project, you will:

- add fields to an empty table in Datasheet view
- create a form using the Form Wizard
- create a query using the Simple Query Wizard
- create a report using the Report Wizard

## Our Exploration Assignment:

**Creating a new database containing an empty table; adding table fields and setting table properties in Datasheet view; and using the *Access* wizards to create a form, query, and report**

The Explorers Club members are going to see the *U.S. Inventors and Inventions* exhibit at the local science and technology museum. Before going on the field trip, Luis needs to quickly organize his research notes about 19th-century U.S. inventors and inventions. Can you give him a hand? Terrific! First, you will create a new database with an empty table. Then you will follow the Trail Markers to add table fields and set field properties in Datasheet view and use *Access* wizards to create a form, a query, and a report.

AP PHOTO/MIKE DERER

**Let's open Luis's document and save it with a new name. You open a document by clicking Open on the File tab (*Word 2010*) or the Office Button menu (*Word 2007*) to open the Open dialog box.**

1. Locate the **File** tab or **Office Button** to the left of the Home tab on the Ribbon.
2. Click the **File** tab to open Backstage view or click the **Office Button** to display the Office Button menu.

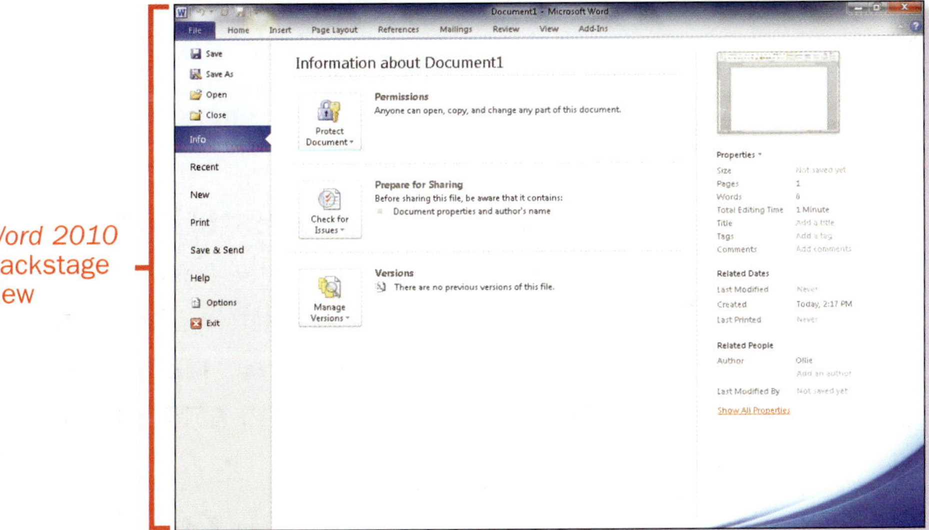


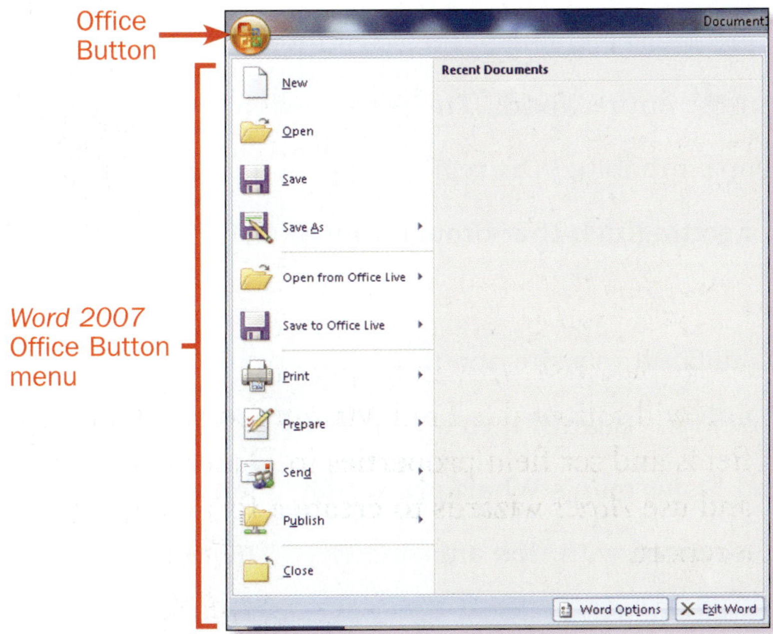

# Project 17 Keyboarding

## 17a Build Skill

Key each line twice. Double-space between 2-line groups.

For additional practice:
**MicroType 5**
Skill Building, Lesson E

1 He bought the house at 5036 Hill on June 24, 1987.
2 We met on May 19, 28, and 31 from 6:45 until 7:50.
3 Her identification number is 42091; mine is 35768.
4 Please call 706.128.3503 on May 4 or 9 to confirm.
5 Miguel wrote Check Numbers 286, 297, 340, and 351.
6 The June 15 quiz covered pages 290 and 370 to 462.
7 Jon paid Invoice Nos. 316 and 395 on May 18, 2004.

gwam 20" | 3 | 6 | 9 | 12 | 15 | 18 | 21 | 24 | 27 | 30 |

## 17b Speed Building

1. Key a 1' timing on paragraph 1.
2. Determine the number of words you keyed.
3. Key another 1' timing on paragraph 1. Try to go two words a minute faster.
4. Repeat steps 1–3 for paragraph 2.
5. Key a 2' timing on paragraphs 1–2 combined.
6. Determine the number of words you keyed.

**A** **all letters used** gwam 2'

San Francisco is one of the most interesting areas to visit 6
throughout the entire world. The history of this city is unique. Even 13
though people inhabited the region prior to the gold rush, it was the 19
prospect of getting rich that brought about the rapid growth of the 26
city. 28

It is difficult to write about just one thing that this exquisite 34
city is known for. Beautiful views, cable cars, the Golden Gate 41
Bridge, and Fisherman's Wharf are simply a few of the many things 47
that are associated with this amazing city. The city is also known 54
for the diversity of its people. 57

gwam 2' | 1 | 2 | 3 | 4 | 5 | 6 |

3. Click **Open** to open the Open dialog box.
4. Switch to the folder that contains your data files. Your teacher will tell you the name and location of your data files folder, if necessary.
5. Double-click the *Mark Twain* filename to open the document.

The *Mark Twain* document on your screen should look like this.

Mark Twain

Mark Twain, whose real name was Samuel Langhorne Clemens, was a nineteenth-century writer. He used exaggeration and regional dialects to add humor to his writing. Twain was a great storyteller. He created a vivid picture of small-town life along the banks of the Mississippi River. He often gently poked fun att society in his writings and lectures. But he also used humor to to highlight serious problems created by slavery, racim, business greed, and political corruption.

Twain's first novel was *The Gilded Age* (1873), a satire political and corruption, that he wrote with essayist Charles Dudley Warner. Next, Twain wrote *The Adventures of Tom Sawyer* (1876), a novel about the misadventures of a mischievous young boy and his friends in a small town on the banks of the Mississippi River. *Tom Sawyer* was followed by *The Prince and the Pauper* (1882) and the nonfiction *Life on the Mississippi* (1883), which is based on Twain's boyhood recollections. In 1884, he wrote his masterpiece, *The Adventures of Huckleberry Finn*. Many consider this book too be the first modern American novel.[1]

As you work in these projects, you will save each data file with a new name before you begin to work in it. In addition, you must tell *Word* where to save the document: to your hard drive; to a network drive; or to some other location, such as a flash drive.

You can name and save a document and specify its location in the Save As dialog box. Open the dialog box by clicking the File tab or Office Button and clicking Save As.

It is very important that you frequently save any changes as you key in or edit a document. To save a document without renaming it or changing its location, click the Save button on the Quick Access Toolbar.

Here's a time-saving tip! The *first time* you save a new document, click the Save button on the Quick Access Toolbar to open the Save As dialog box. Try it!

**Let's rename and save the *Mark Twain* document.**

1. Click the **File** tab or the **Office Button**.
2. Click **Save As** to open the Save As dialog box.
3. Switch to the folder in which you will save your work. Ask your teacher which folder to use, if necessary.
4. Key *Mark Twain1* followed by your initials in the File name text box.

# Exploring *Across the Curriculum*

## Social Studies: Research and Write

Nineteenth-century reformers such as Robert Gould Shaw and Sarah Moore Grimke often shared an interest in social reform with other members of their families. Use data in the *Famous Reformers* table in the *reformers17* database together with library and online resources to learn more about either Robert Gould Shaw or Sarah Moore Grimke and their families. Then create a three-level multilevel list in *Word* you can use to (1) give an oral report to your classmates or (2) write a two-page bound report with a title page and endnotes.

## Getting Help

Start *Access*, if necessary, and click the Microsoft Access Help icon to open the Help window. Key **Data Type Property** in the search box and tap the ENTER key to research the different field data types. Write down a brief description of each data type. Create a *PowerPoint* presentation that briefly describes each data type. Format and animate the presentation as desired. With permission, run the slide show to describe different field data types to a classmate.

## Career Day

Now that you have explored potential careers in various fields, let's take a survey to see how your personal interests match up with potential careers. Open your Web browser, visit the Learning with Computers Web page (www.cengage.com/school/keyboarding/lwcorange), and click the Career Day link. Then follow your teacher's instructions to download and complete a career interest survey. Save your completed survey in your Career Day folder.

## Your Personal Journal

Open your personal journal document. Insert today's date and two blank lines. Think about what you have learned about the efforts of America's nineteenth-century reformers. How did their accomplishments affect people's lives today? Update your journal with one or two paragraphs that answer this question. Spell-check, save, and close your journal.

**Online Enrichment Games**  www.cengage.com/school/keyboarding/lwcorange

Solution files location (your location and folder name may be different)

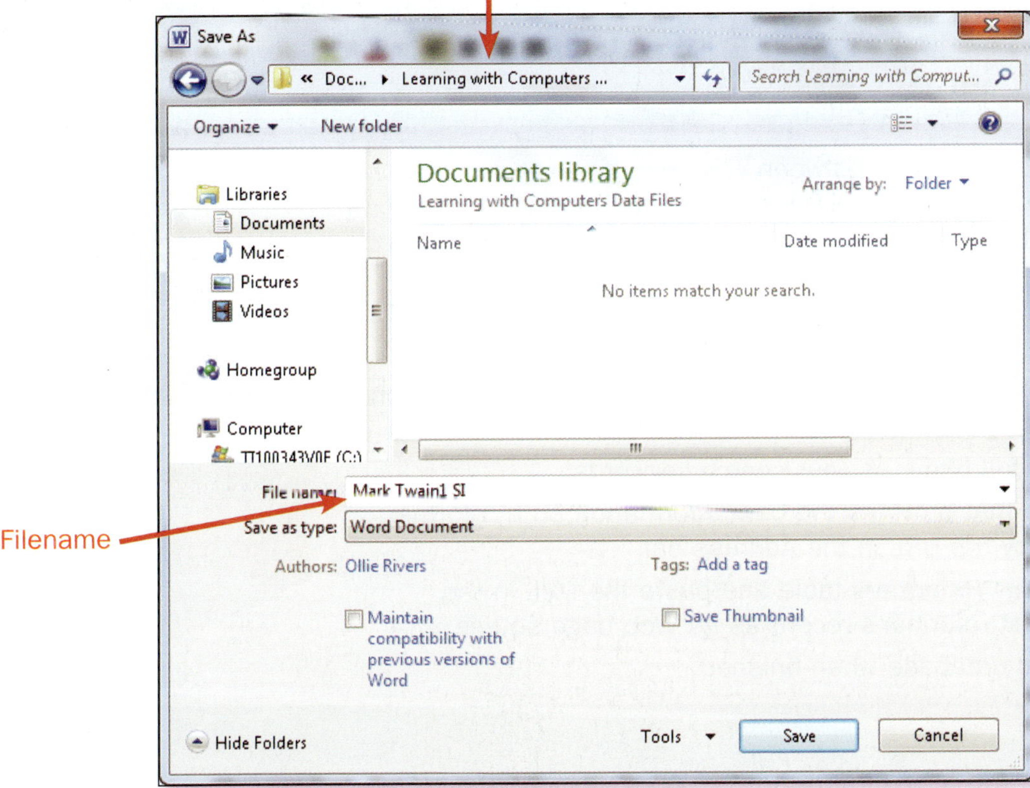


Filename

5. Click the dialog box **Save** button.

Terrific! *Word* has multiple views in which you can edit a document. Let's practice switching between editing views.

## Switching Editing Views and Turning on Formatting Marks

As you key in or edit a *Word* document, you can use editing views to view the document on the screen in different ways. The two commonly used editing views are Print Layout view and Draft view.

The *Word* application automatically opens in Print Layout view, which allows you to see the top, bottom, left, and right edges of the page. Draft view hides the page edges.

# Exploring Across the Curriculum

## Internet/Web

You can work back and forth between your Web browser and a database table to copy and paste hyperlink sources in a field in the table. Open the *reformers17* database and open the *Famous Reformers* table in Datasheet view. Open your Web browser and use a favorite or bookmark to view the Learning with Computers Web page (www.cengage.com/school/keyboarding/lwcorange). Click the **Links** option and click **Project 17**.

1. Use the Google link to find Web page sources with useful information on at least five reformers listed in the *Famous Reformers* table.
2. Use the reformer's full name as your search keywords.
3. View the Web page that provides the best information on a reformer; then select and copy the URL in the Address bar.
4. Switch to the *Famous Reformers* table and paste the URL in the *Source 1* field in that reformer's record as its Web page source.
5. Close the table and database when finished.

## Language Arts: Words to Know

Look up the meaning of the following terms in a classroom dictionary, CD-ROM dictionary or encyclopedia, or online dictionary.

| | | | |
|---|---|---|---|
| utopian | abolitionist | suffragette | Second Great Awakening |
| temperance movement | labor movement | Underground Railroad | New Harmony |

Create a new database with an empty table and save it as *definitions17*. Add the following fields to the new table in Design view and set the field properties.

| Field Name | Data Type | Field Size | Caption |
|---|---|---|---|
| ID | AutoNumber | Long Integer | ID |
| Term | Text | 25 | None |
| Definition | Text | 50 | None |

Leave the *ID* field as the primary key. Save the table as *Terms and Definitions* and then close it. Use the Form tool to create a form and enter the terms and definitions in the table using the form. *Remember—each definition can be no longer than 50 characters!* Open the table in Datasheet view, resize the columns to fit, and close the table. Then close the database.

Explore More

To switch between Print Layout and Draft views, click a button in the View Shortcuts on the right side of the status bar. To locate a button in the View Shortcuts, you can use a ScreenTip. Unless otherwise instructed, you will work in Print Layout view to key, select, replace, and delete text.

A great tool you can use to become familiar with toolbar buttons or other screen elements is ScreenTips. A ScreenTip is a small flag that shows the name of buttons and other screen elements when you place the mouse pointer on the button or screen element.

As you work in these projects, use ScreenTips as necessary to become familiar with the *Word* window elements, such as the Ribbon.

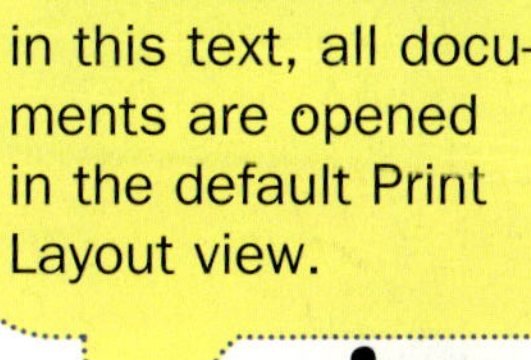

In the illustrations in this text, all documents are opened in the default Print Layout view.

You can also click the View tab on the Ribbon and then click the Print Layout or Draft View buttons in the Document Views group to switch views.

**Let's use ScreenTips and switch editing views.**

1. Use the mouse pointer and ScreenTips to locate the **Draft View** and **Print Layout View** buttons on the right side of the status bar.
2. Click the **Draft View** button in the View Shortcuts to view the document in Draft editing view. See how the top and bottom page edges are hidden.
3. Click the **Print Layout View** button in the View Shortcuts to view the document in the Print Layout editing view. The top, bottom, left, and right edges of the page are visible.

In Print Layout view, the vertical and horizontal rulers are generally visible. To turn the rulers on or off, click the View tab on the Ribbon and click the Ruler checkbox in the Show or Show/Hide group.

# Exploring On Your Own

## Reading in Action

### Standardized Test Preparation

Some standardized tests require you to read a passage and then write a short response to a question based on the passage. To practice for a standardized test, read the following passage and write a short response to this question: Why might utopian communities such as Brook Farm have failed?

Utopian communities were created as small societies where people could live together in harmony and practice an idealistic, simple lifestyle. At Brook Farm, under the leadership of philosopher Amos Bronson Alcott, everyone had to take baths with cold water. They could not wear cotton, even in summer, because cotton was picked by slave labor. Alcott insisted that animals not be exploited in any way, so horses or oxen could not be used to plow the fields. Alcott was often away on lecture tours, leaving his wife and children to run the farm.

## Math in Action

### Finding Probability

If you were to pick one person at random from the list in the *Famous Reformers* table, what is the probability that you would pick someone who was concerned with women's suffrage?

Probability of an event ($E$) =

$$\frac{\text{number of favorable outcomes}}{\text{number of possible outcomes}}$$

There are nine favorable outcomes because there are nine people concerned with women's suffrage. There are 37 people on the list, so there are 37 possible outcomes.

$$P(E) = \frac{9}{37} = 0.2432 = 24.32\%$$

There is a 24.32% probability of choosing someone concerned with women's suffrage.

Now you try it!

What is the probability of randomly choosing a person from the *Famous Reformers* table who was concerned with abolition? What is the probability of choosing someone concerned with either women's suffrage or abolition?

**Formatting Marks**

As you key text in a document, *Word* inserts special nonprinting characters called formatting marks. For example, *Word* automatically inserts a dot each time you tap the Space Bar to insert a space between words and sentences. Each time you tap the ENTER key to create a new line, *Word* inserts a paragraph formatting mark to indicate the end of the current paragraph.

In *Word*, the term *paragraph* is used to identify text that is followed by a paragraph formatting mark. Therefore, a *Word* document paragraph may be a blank line, a single word, multiple words, a single sentence, or multiple sentences—whatever precedes the paragraph formatting mark *Word* inserts when you tap the ENTER key. You will learn more about *Word paragraph formatting* in a later project.

Viewing nonprinting dots and paragraph formatting marks can help you find extra spaces between words or find the end of a paragraph. Turn the view of formatting marks on or off by clicking the Home tab on the Ribbon and clicking the Show/Hide ¶ button in the Paragraph group.

You can also turn the view of formatting marks on or off in the Word Options dialog box. Click the File tab and click Options (*Word 2010*) or click the Office Button and click the Word Options button on the submenu (*Word 2007*) to open the Word Options dialog box. Click Display in the left pane to view the formatting mark options in the right pane.

**Let's turn on the view of formatting marks in the *Mark Twain1* document.**

Home | Paragraph | Show/Hide ¶

1. Click the **Home** tab on the Ribbon, if necessary, and locate the **Paragraph** group.
2. Use ScreenTips to locate the **Show/Hide ¶** button in the Paragraph group.
3. Click the **Show/Hide ¶** button. ¶
4. Look closely to see the dots (spaces) between the words and the paragraph mark symbols (a *Word* paragraph) at the end of each paragraph.

# Exploring On Your Own

## Blaze Your Own Trail

You have learned several new skills in this project. Now blaze your own trail by practicing these skills on your own!

1. Create a new database with an empty table and save it as *utopian17 solution*.
2. Modify the table in Design view to add the following fields to the table.

| Field Name | Type | Size | Caption | Default Value | Required |
|---|---|---|---|---|---|
| ID | AutoNumber | | Record ID | | Yes |
| SocietyName | Text | 20 | Name | | Yes |
| Location | Text | 15 | | | No |
| Founder | Text | 20 | | | Yes |
| YearFounded | Text | 4 | Year Founded | | Yes |
| YearDisbanded | Text | 4 | Year Disbanded | | Yes |
| Source | Text | 35 | | "Encyclopedia.com" | No |

3. Leave the *ID* field as the primary key.
4. Save the table as *Utopian Societies*; then switch to Datasheet view, review the table, and close it.
5. Use the Form tool to create a new data entry form and save it as *Utopian Societies Data Entry*. Add the following records to the table using the form. Then view the datasheet and resize the columns to fit. Save the layout changes to the table.

| Name | Location | Founder | Year Founded | Year Disbanded |
|---|---|---|---|---|
| Amana Society | Iowa | Christian Metz | 1855 | 1932 |
| Bishop Hill | Illinois | Erik Jansson | 1846 | 1861 |
| Brook Farm | Massachusetts | George Ripley | 1841 | 1847 |
| Fruitlands | Massachusetts | Amos Bronson Alcott | 1843 | 1844 |
| Harmonie | Indiana | George Rapp | 1814 | 1825 |
| Hopedale | Massachusetts | Adin Ballou | 1841 | 1857 |
| New Harmony | Indiana | Robert Owen | 1825 | 1827 |
| Oneida Community | New York | John H. Noyes | 1848 | 1878 |

6. Use the Report Tool to create a list of all records in the table.
7. Save the report as *List of Utopian Societies* and then close the report.
8. Create a query in Design view to list the records for utopian societies that disbanded after 1850. Show the *SocietyName* and *YearDisbanded* fields in the query results. Save the query as *Disbanded After 1850* and then switch to Datasheet view to run the query. Resize the columns, if necessary, and save the layout changes to the query.
9. With permission, preview and print the query datasheet and close the database.

The *Mark Twain1* document with visible nonprinting characters on your screen should look like this.

Paragraph formatting marks

Mark·Twain¶

Mark·Twain,·whose·real·name·was·Samuel·Langhorne·Clemens,·was·a·nineteenth-century·writer.··He·used·exaggeration·and·regional·dialects·to·add·humor·to·his·writing.··Twain·was·a·great·storyteller.··He·created·a·vivid·picture·of·small-town·life·along·the·banks·of·the·Mississippi·River.··He·often·gently·poked·fun·att·society·in·his·writings·and·lectures.··But·he·also·used·humor·to·to·highlight·serious·problems·created·by·slavery,·racim,·business·greed,·and·political·corruption.¶

Twain's·first·novel·was·*The·Gilded·Age*·(1873),·a·satire·political·and·corruption,·that·he·wrote·with·essayist·Charles·Dudley·Warner.··Next,·Twain·wrote·*The·Adventures·of·Tom·Sawyer*·(1876),·a·novel·about·the·misadventures·of·a·mischievous·young·boy·and·his·friends·in·a·small·town·on·the·banks·of·the·Mississippi·River.··*Tom·Sawyer*·was·followed·by·*The·Prince·and·the·Pauper*·(1882)·and·the·nonfiction·*Life·on·the·Mississippi*·(1883),·which·is·based·on·Twain's·boyhood·recollections.··In·1884,·he·wrote·his·masterpiece,·*The·Adventures·of·Huckleberry·Finn*.··Many·consider·this·book·too·be·the·first·modern·American·novel.¶

Space formatting marks

For Projects 1–6, you may turn the view of formatting marks on or off. Document illustrations will show the formatting marks.

Now you are ready to make some changes to the document.

## Inserting, Deleting, and Selecting Text

Each time you place the mouse pointer in a text area of your document, it changes shape to become the I-beam pointer. You use the I-beam pointer to position the insertion point in the document. You can also position the insertion point by tapping the arrow keys.

*Warning!* Scrolling a document does not reposition the insertion point! It just changes your view of the document.

# Project Skills Review

| | |
|---|---|
| **Save a table, form, or report object** | Click the **Save** button on the Quick Access Toolbar. Click the **File** tab and click **Save Object As** or click the **Office Button**, point to **Save As**, and click **Save Object As**. |
| **Create a report using the Report Tool** | Click the **Report** button in the Reports group on the **Create** tab.   |
| **Create a query in Design view** | *Access 2010*: click the **Query Design** button in the Queries group on the **Create** tab. *Access 2007*: click the **Query Design** button in the Other group on the **Create** tab.     |

**Let's practice repositioning the insertion point with the I-beam pointer and the arrow keys.**

1. Move the mouse pointer over the text to view the I-beam pointer and then click anywhere in the document to position the insertion point.
2. Use the I-beam pointer to move the insertion point to a new location by clicking at a different place in the document.
3. Tap the **Up** arrow, **Down** arrow, **Left** arrow, and **Right** arrow keys to move the insertion point up a line, down a line, to the left one character, and to the right one character, respectively.
4. Continue practicing moving the insertion point with the I-beam pointer and the arrow keys as necessary.

### Inserting and Deleting Text

Two words—*of* and *greed*—are missing from the first sentence of the second body paragraph in the *Mark Twain1* document. You can move the insertion point to the correct position in the document and insert the missing text.

**Let's reposition the insertion point and insert the missing text.**

1. Use the I-beam pointer or arrow keys to move the insertion point exactly in front of the word *political* in the first sentence of the second body paragraph.

   satire|political·

2. Key **of** and tap the Space Bar.
3. Move the insertion point exactly at the end of the word *political* and tap the Space Bar.
4. Key **greed**.
5. Click the **Save** button on the Quick Access Toolbar to save the changes to the document.

Your inserted text should now look like this.

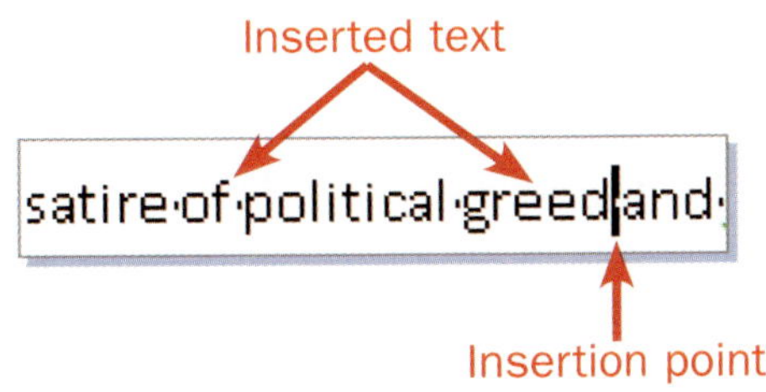

# Project Skills Review

You learned a lot in this project! We are very impressed with your progress. Let's take a few minutes to review the skills that you learned.

| Skill | How to | |
|---|---|---|
| **Start *Access* and then create, name, and save a new database** | *Access 2010*: click the **Blank database** icon in Backstage view; key the filename, browse for the solution files folder, and save the database; and then click the **Create** button in Backstage view. *Access 2007*: click the **Blank Database** icon in the New Blank Database pane in the Getting Started with Access page; key the filename, browse for the solution files folder, save the database; and then click the **Create** button. |   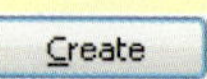 |
| **Add table fields and set properties in Design view** | Select the table name in the Navigation Pane and click the **Design View** button face in the Views group on the **Home** or **Table Tools Fields** or **Datasheet** tabs. Move back and forth between the table design grid and Field Properties pane to name fields, set the data type, and set field properties. |  |
| **Switch object views** | Click the **View** button face in the Views group on the active Ribbon tab. Click a button in the View Shortcuts on the status bar. | 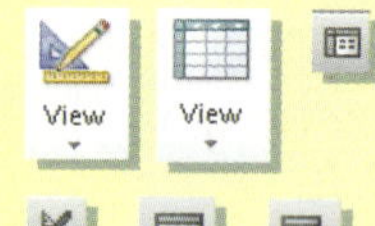 |
| **Move from text box to text box in the table design grid or Field Properties pane to define field properties** | Tap the TAB, ENTER, or arrow key. Click the text box. | |
| **Set the primary key** | Select the field name and click the **Primary Key** button in the Tools group on the **Table Tools Design** tab. |  |
| **Create a data entry form using the Form tool** | Select the underlying table in the Navigation Pane. Then click the **Form** button in the Forms group on the **Create** tab. |  |
| **Add records to a table using a form** | Open the form in Form view and key data in a field's text box; use the TAB key, SHIFT + TAB keys, ENTER key, or arrow keys to move from field to field. Use the record navigation bar at the bottom of the form to navigate between records. | |

Great job! A few more corrections still need to be made. You can use the BACKSPACE and DELETE keys to delete text to the left or right of the insertion point.

- If the text to be deleted is to the left of the insertion point, tap the BACKSPACE key.
- If the text is to the right of the insertion point, tap the DELETE key.

Another way to quickly move the insertion point in a *Word* document is to use a keyboard shortcut, a set of keystrokes you use to perform a task.

- To move the insertion point to the top of the document, tap the CTRL + HOME keys.
- To move the insertion point to the bottom of the document, tap the CTRL + END keys.

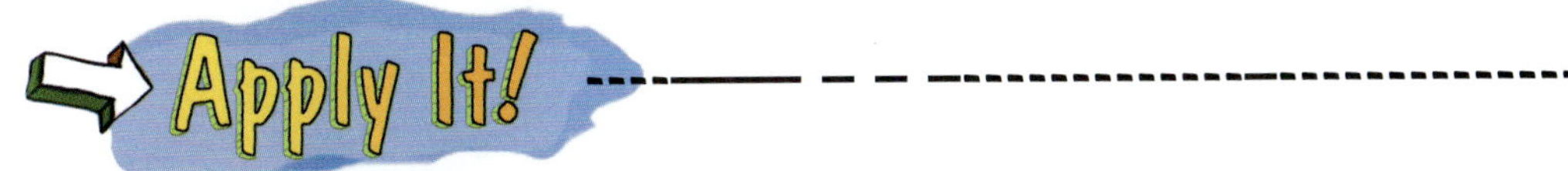


**Let's use the DELETE and BACKSPACE keys to delete text.**

1. Move the insertion point exactly at the end of the word *att* in the fifth sentence of the first body paragraph. fun·att|society·
2. Tap the BACKSPACE key to remove the extra *t*.
3. Tap the CTRL + END keys to move the insertion point to the end of the document.
4. Use the **Up** and **Right** arrow keys to move the insertion point so it is exactly between the two letters *o* in the word *too* in the next to last sentence on the page. this·book·to|o·be·
5. Tap the DELETE key to remove the extra *o*.
6. Tap the CTRL + HOME keys to move the insertion point to the top of the document.
7. Click the **Save** button on the Quick Access Toolbar.

Great! Next, you will select text and replace it by keying new text. You will also select and delete text.

You set these query criteria by keying = (equals) and > (greater than) symbols and other criteria in each field's Criteria box *on the same line* in the grid.

Adding query criteria on the same line across the grid means that all of the criteria must be met before a record is included in the query results.

Did you know you can use the Report tool to create a simple report based on a query? Just select the query name in the Navigation Pane and click the Report button in the Reports group on the Create tab. Try it!

**Let's key the query criteria in the Criteria boxes for the *Died* and *Concern* fields on the same Criteria line in the grid to indicate that records must meet both query criteria to be included in the query results.**

1. Click the **Criteria** box in the *Died* field (column).
2. Key **>1920** to specify only those records for 19th-century reformers who were alive after 1920. *Do not forget to key the greater than sign.*
3. Tap the ENTER key. *Access automatically adds quotation marks around 1920 and moves the insertion point into the Concern field's* **Criteria** *box.*

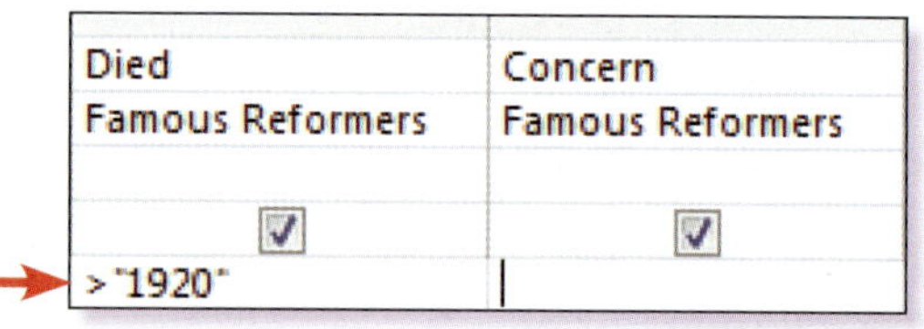


Query criteria for Died field

4. Key **=Women's suffrage** in the *Concern* field's Criteria box to specify only those records for 19th-century reformers whose social concern was Women's suffrage. *Do not forget to key the equals sign.*
5. Tap the **Down** arrow. *Access adds quotation marks around Women's suffrage and moves the insertion point down to the next box.*
6. Click the **Save** button on the Quick Access Toolbar to save the query. 
7. Key **Nineteenth Amendment** as the query name and click **OK**.
8. Click the **Datasheet View** button in the View Shortcuts on the status bar to switch to Datasheet view and run the query. Only two of the women's suffrage reformers listed in the table—Alice Stone Blackwell and Carrie Chapman Catt—lived to see the ratification of the Nineteenth Amendment. 

Your query datasheet should look like this.

Nineteenth Amendment

| First Name | Middle Name/ | Last Name | Born | Died | Social Concern |
|---|---|---|---|---|---|
| Alice | Stone | Blackwell | 1857 | 1950 | Women's suffrage |
| Carrie | Chapman | Catt | 1859 | 1947 | Women's suffrage |
| * | | | | | |

9. Close the query datasheet and other open objects and close the database.

Congratulations! Julie's data is organized and ready for the next Explorers Club meeting.

### Selecting Text

You have learned how to insert new text and delete text a character at a time using the BACKSPACE and DELETE keys. But when you need to replace or delete one or more words, you should select the text and then key new text to replace the selected text or tap the DELETE key to delete it.

*Word* offers many ways to select text; learning different selection methods will help you work more efficiently in your documents. An easy way to select text is to drag the I-beam pointer across it. You can also use the mouse pointer by itself or in combination with the CTRL and SHIFT keys to select text.

Check out this list of very useful ways to select text.

| Selection | Action |
|---|---|
| **A single word and its following space** | Double-click the word. |
| **A single line** | Move the mouse pointer to the white area to the left of the line and click. |
| **A sentence and its following spaces** | Move the I-beam into the sentence, tap and hold the CTRL key, and click the sentence. |
| **A complete paragraph** | Move the I-beam into the paragraph and triple-click. |
| **An entire document** | Move the mouse pointer into white area to the left of the text and triple-click. |
| **From the insertion point to the end of the document** | Tap the CTRL + SHIFT + END keys. |
| **From the insertion point to the top of the document** | Tap the CTRL + SHIFT + HOME keys. |
| **A large area of text** | Move the insertion point to the beginning of the selection, tap and hold the SHIFT key, and click where the selection ends. |
| **Nonadjacent characters, words, or phrases** | Make your first selection; then tap and hold the CTRL key while you click or drag to make additional selections. |

You can deselect text by clicking anywhere in your document or by tapping an arrow key.

**Let's specify the fields for the query.**

1. Scroll the table list window at the top of the query design grid to view all of the fields in the table. Note that the list shows field names and not field captions.

Table list window

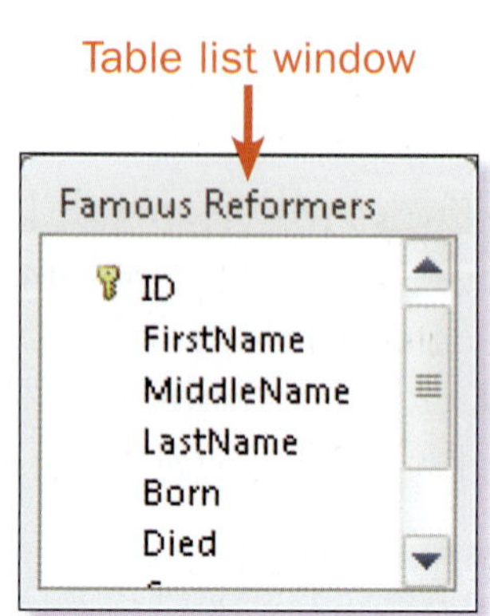


Next, you want to specify which fields from the table will be included in the query datasheet when you run the query. Fields you add to the bottom of the design grid will appear in the query datasheet. Double-click a field name to add that field to the design grid.

Julie wants to see the data in the *FirstName*, *MiddleName*, *LastName*, *Born*, *Died*, and *Concern* fields when she runs the query.

2. Double-click the *FirstName* field in the table list. The field is added to the design grid.
3. Continue by adding the *MiddleName*, *LastName*, *Born*, *Died*, and *Concern* fields to the grid.

**CHECKPOINT**

Your design grid should look like this.

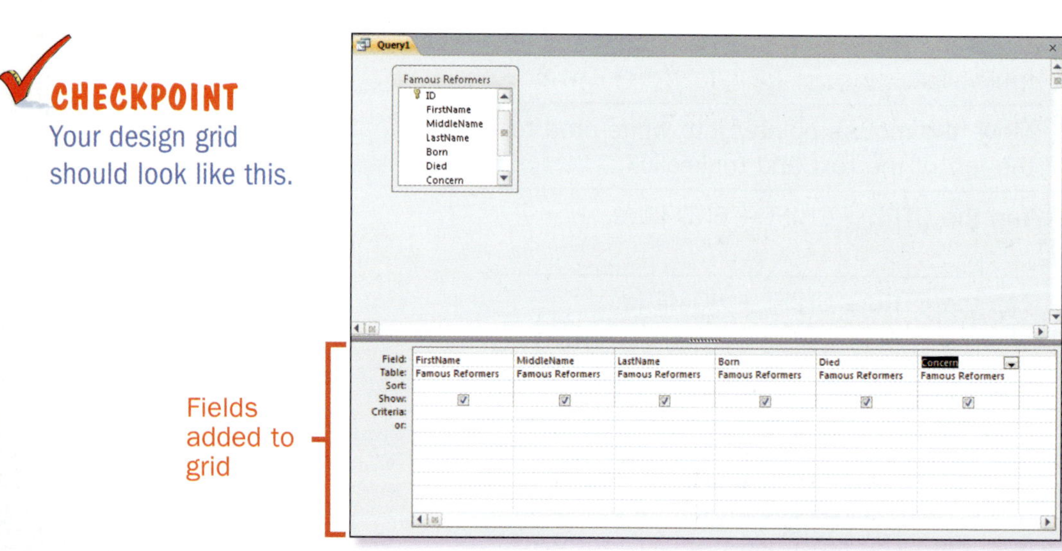


Fields added to grid

The next step is to set the query criteria to select only those records that have *Women's suffrage* in the *Concern* field *and* a date greater than 1920 in the *Died* field.

**Let's select the word *great* and key a new word, then select and delete three words all at one time.**

1. Double-click the word **great** in the second sentence of the first body paragraph. The word and its following, or trailing, space are selected.

was a great

2. Key **grand**.
3. Double-click the word **gently** in the fourth sentence of the first body paragraph.
4. Tap and hold the CTRL key and double-click the words **business** and **political** in the next sentence.
5. Release the CTRL key. All three words are selected.
6. Tap the DELETE key.
7. Save the document.

storyteller. He created a vivid picture of small-town life along the banks of the Mississippi River. He often gently poked fun at society in his writings and lectures. But he also used humor to to highlight serious problems created by slavery, racim, business greed, and political corruption.¶

Excellent! You are now ready to check the spelling and grammar in the *Mark Twain1* document and replace a word using the thesaurus.

Do not worry if you accidentally delete the wrong text! Just click the Undo button on the Quick Access Toolbar to quickly undo the delete action. To redo the undone action, click the Repeat (Redo) button on the Quick Access Toolbar.

## Checking Spelling and Grammar and Using the Thesaurus

You must check the spelling and grammar in all of your documents using *Word's* built-in dictionary and grammar checker. But remember, *Word* may not find all of your errors; for example, if you key *too* when you meant to key *two*, *Word* may not find the error. You still must read your document carefully!

To check the spelling and grammar of an entire document, click the Review tab on the Ribbon and then click the Spelling and Grammar button in the Proofing group.

## Creating a Select Query in *Access 2007*

One way to create a query is to click the Create tab and then click the Query Design button in the Other group to open the query design grid and the Show Table dialog box.

You select the table you want to query in the Show Table dialog box and then add fields from the table to the query design grid.

**Let's create a select query to find all of the records for women's suffrage reformers who were born in the 1800s and died after 1920.**

Create | Other | Query Design

1. Make certain the *Famous Reformers* table is selected in the Navigation Pane.
2. Click the **Create** tab, if necessary, and locate the **Other** group.
3. Click the **Query Design** button in the Other group. The query design grid and Show Table dialog box open.

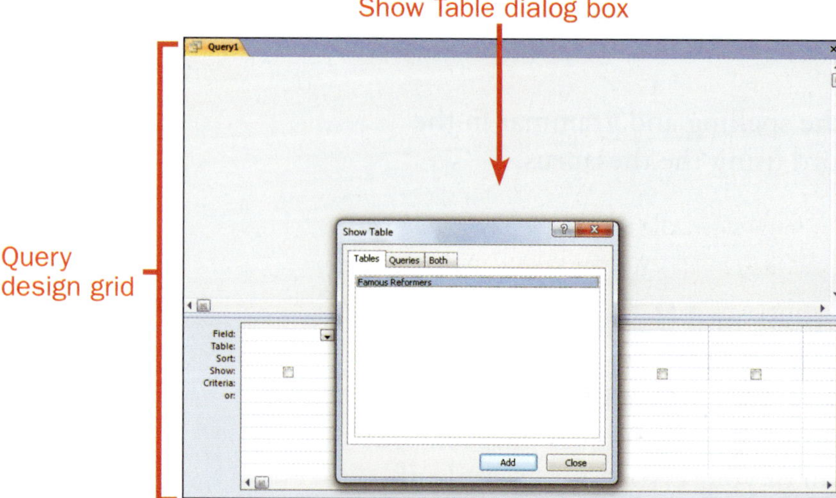


4. Double-click the *Famous Reformers* table in the Tables tab in the Show Table dialog box to add the *Famous Reformers* table to the top of the query design grid.
5. Close the Show Table dialog box. The *Famous Reformers* table field list is added in a small window at the top of the grid.

Now you are ready to set the query criteria.

### Setting Query Criteria

After you specify the fields for a query, you can set the conditions, or criteria, that control which records are listed in the query.

As you key text in a document or when you open an existing document, *Word* adds a wavy red line under a suspected misspelled word and a wavy green line under a word or phrase that may be a grammar error.

Right-click the word or phrase; then use the shortcut menu to correct the suspected error, if necessary.

**Let's use the shortcut menu to correct the spelling and grammar errors in the *Mark Twain1* document.**

1. Tap the CTRL + HOME keys, if necessary, to position the insertion point at the top of the document.
2. Right-click the second word **to** with the wavy red underline in the fourth sentence of the first body paragraph.
3. Click **Delete Repeated Word** on the shortcut menu.
4. Right-click the misspelled word **racim** with the wavy red underline in the next sentence and click **racism** on the shortcut menu.
5. Right-click the word **that** with the wavy green underline in the first sentence of the second body paragraph.
6. Click **corruption**, **which**.
7. Save the document.

### The Thesaurus

Use *Word's* built-in thesaurus to replace a selected word with a synonym or an antonym. A synonym is a word with the same or similar meaning. An antonym is a word that has the opposite meaning.

You can find synonyms and antonyms for a word by right-clicking the word and pointing to Synonyms on the shortcut menu. A list of synonyms and antonyms appears. Simply click a synonym or antonym to replace the current word.

To open the Research task pane and search for more synonyms or antonyms, point to Synonyms and click Thesaurus on the shortcut menu.

You can also open the Research task pane by clicking the Review tab on the Ribbon and then clicking the Thesaurus button in the Proofing group.

## Creating a Select Query in Design View

In August 1920, the Nineteenth Amendment to the U.S. Constitution was ratified, giving women the right to vote. Julie wants to know which of the women's suffrage reformers born in the 1800s lived long enough to see the ratification of the Nineteenth Amendment.

As you learned in Project 16, you can create a select query to find a subset of data in a table. You will query the *Famous Reformers* table to find the data Julie needs.

### Creating a Select Query in *Access 2010*

One way to create a select query is to click the Create tab and then click the Query Design button in the Queries group to open the query design grid and the Show Table dialog box.

You select the table you want to query in the Show Table dialog box and then add fields from the table to the query design grid.

**Let's create a select query to find all of the records for women's suffrage reformers who were born in the 1800s and died after 1920.**

Create | Queries | Query Design

1. Make certain the *Famous Reformers* table is selected in the Navigation Pane.
2. Click the **Create** tab, if necessary, and locate the **Queries** group.
3. Click the **Query Design** button in the Queries group. The query design grid and Show Table dialog box open.
4. Double-click the *Famous Reformers* table in the Tables tab in the Show Table dialog box to add the *Famous Reformers* table to the top of the query design grid.
5. Close the Show Table dialog box. The *Famous Reformers* table field list is added in a small window at the top of the grid.

Query Design

Show Table dialog box

Query design grid

Now you are ready to set the query criteria.

**Let's replace the word *recollections* in the fifth sentence of the second body paragraph with the word *memories* using the thesaurus and the shortcut menu.**

1. Right-click the word **recollections** in the fifth sentence of the second body paragraph, point to **Synonyms**, and click **memories**.
2. Save the document.

Outstanding! You have made all of the changes to Luis's document, and now you are ready to preview and print it.

## Previewing and Printing a Document

Previewing a document allows you to see what your document will look like on the printed page—before you print it! Previewing a document before it is printed is very important because it helps you avoid wasting paper and printer toner or ink. If the document does not look right, just make your changes and preview it again. When all necessary changes are made, you can print the document.

**Previewing and Printing a Document in *Word 2010***

If you are using *Word 2010*, you can click the Print tab on the File tab to preview the document, set print options, and then print the document. ***Make sure you ask your teacher for permission before you print any documents in this text!***

**Let's preview the document.**

1. Click the **File** tab. File
2. Click the **Print** tab to display print options and a preview of your document.
3. Observe the document preview.

You can also switch to Print Preview by clicking the View button arrow in the Views group on the Home tab or by clicking the Print Preview button in the View Shortcuts on the status bar.

To create a report using the Report tool, select a table in the Navigation Pane. Then click the Create tab and click the Report button in the Reports group.

**Let's create a simple report using the Report tool, save the report, and switch to Print Preview.**

Create | Reports | Report

1. Make certain the *Famous Reformers* table is selected in the Navigation Pane.
2. Click the **Create** tab, if necessary, and locate the **Reports** group.
3. Click the **Report** button in the Reports group to create a basic report.
4. Click the **Save** button on the Quick Access Toolbar. 
5. Key **Famous Reformers Report** in the Report Name text box and click the **OK** button.
6. Click the **Print Preview** button in the View Shortcuts on the status bar.

**CHECKPOINT**
Your report in Print Preview should look similar to this.

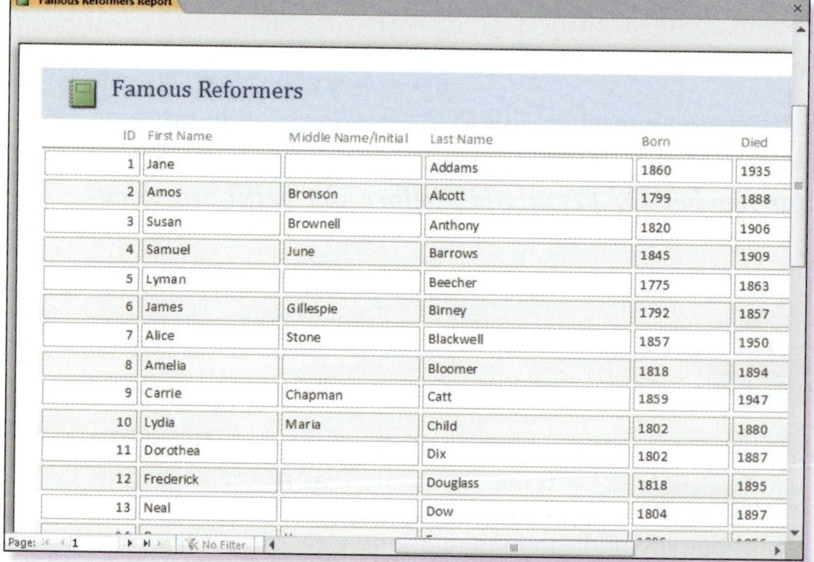

Famous Reformers Report

Famous Reformers

| ID | First Name | Middle Name/Initial | Last Name | Born | Died |
|---|---|---|---|---|---|
| 1 | Jane | | Addams | 1860 | 1935 |
| 2 | Amos | Bronson | Alcott | 1799 | 1888 |
| 3 | Susan | Brownell | Anthony | 1820 | 1906 |
| 4 | Samuel | June | Barrows | 1845 | 1909 |
| 5 | Lyman | | Beecher | 1775 | 1863 |
| 6 | James | Gillespie | Birney | 1792 | 1857 |
| 7 | Alice | Stone | Blackwell | 1857 | 1950 |
| 8 | Amelia | | Bloomer | 1818 | 1894 |
| 9 | Carrie | Chapman | Catt | 1859 | 1947 |
| 10 | Lydia | Maria | Child | 1802 | 1880 |
| 11 | Dorothea | | Dix | 1802 | 1887 |
| 12 | Frederick | | Douglass | 1818 | 1895 |
| 13 | Neal | | Dow | 1804 | 1897 |

7. With your teacher's permission, print the report and then close it.

Terrific! Julie wants some specific information from the *Famous Reformers* table. Let's query the table to find the information.

Your previewed *Word 2010* document should look similar to this.

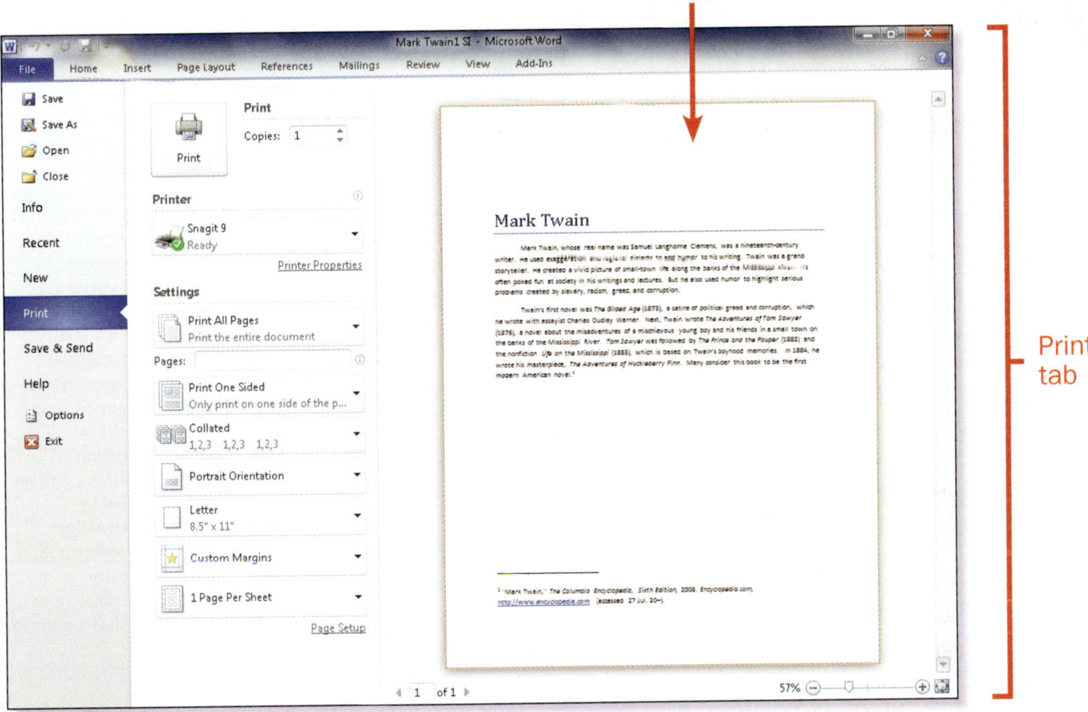


4. With permission, click the **Print** button in the Print group to the left of the document preview.

When you are finished with your document, you can close it by clicking Close on the File tab or by clicking the Close button in the upper-right corner of the *Word* window. If you have only one document open, clicking the Close button also closes the *Word* software.

5. Click **Close** on the File tab to close the *Mark Twain1* document and leave the *Word* software open.

You can also preview and print a document by clicking the Print Preview or Quick Print buttons, if available, on the customized Quick Access Toolbar.

Fantastic! Now you are ready to move on to Trail Marker 6 and create a new document.

**Previewing and Printing a Document in *Word 2007***

To Print Preview a document, click the Office Button, point to Print, and click Print Preview on the submenu. You can click the Print button on the Print Preview tab on the Ribbon to print your document.

After your document is printed, you can close Print Preview by clicking the Close Preview button on the Print Preview tab.

***Make sure you ask your teacher for permission before you print any documents in this text!***

You can close a document by clicking the Close button on the title bar.

**CHECKPOINT**

Your *Famous Reformers* datasheet should look similar to this.

Famous Reformers

| ID | First Name | Middle Name/ | Last Name | Born | Died | Social Concern | Source1 | Source2 |
|---|---|---|---|---|---|---|---|---|
| 1 | Jane | | Addams | 1860 | 1935 | Poverty | | The Reforme |
| 2 | Amos | Bronson | Alcott | 1799 | 1888 | Education reform | | The Reforme |
| 3 | Susan | Brownell | Anthony | 1820 | 1906 | Women's suffrage | | The Reforme |
| 4 | Samuel | June | Barrows | 1845 | 1909 | Prison reform | | The Reforme |
| 5 | Lyman | | Beecher | 1775 | 1863 | Religious revival | | The Reforme |
| 6 | James | Gillespie | Birney | 1792 | 1857 | Abolition | | The Reforme |
| 7 | Alice | Stone | Blackwell | 1857 | 1950 | Women's suffrage | | The Reforme |
| 8 | Amelia | | Bloomer | 1818 | 1894 | Women's suffrage | | The Reforme |
| 9 | Carrie | Chapman | Catt | 1859 | 1947 | Women's suffrage | | The Reforme |
| 10 | Lydia | Maria | Child | 1802 | 1880 | Abolition | | The Reforme |
| 11 | Dorothea | | Dix | 1802 | 1887 | Mental illness | | The Reforme |
| 12 | Frederick | | Douglass | 1818 | 1895 | Abolition | | The Reforme |
| 13 | Neal | | Dow | 1804 | 1897 | Temperance | | The Reforme |
| 14 | George | Henry | Evans | 1805 | 1856 | Labor reform | | The Reforme |
| 15 | Charles | Grandison | Finney | 1792 | 1875 | Religious revival | | The Reforme |
| 16 | William | Lloyd | Garrison | 1805 | 1879 | Abolition | | The Reforme |
| 17 | Sarah | Moore | Grimke | 1792 | 1873 | Abolition | | The Reforme |
| 18 | Josiah | | Henson | 1789 | 1883 | Abolition | | The Reforme |
| 19 | Julia | Ward | Howe | 1819 | 1910 | Women's suffrage | | The Reforme |
| 20 | Samuel | Gridley | Howe | 1801 | 1876 | Abolition | | The Reforme |
| 21 | Mary | Harris | Jones | 1837 | 1930 | Labor reform | | The Reforme |
| 22 | Juliette | Gordon | Low | 1860 | 1927 | Education reform | | The Reforme |
| 23 | Josephine | Shaw | Lowell | 1843 | 1905 | Poverty | | The Reforme |
| 24 | Horace | | Mann | 1796 | 1859 | Education reform | | The Reforme |
| 25 | Lucretia | Coffin | Mott | 1793 | 1880 | Women's suffrage | | The Reforme |

Record: 1 of 37 No Filter Search

5. Close the table.

What a terrific effort! All of the records are entered in the table. Now let's create a report that lists all of the data in each record.

Don't worry if you forget to save a table after you change the datasheet column widths. *Access* will prompt you to save the table when you close it!

4 TRAIL MARKER

## Creating a Report Using the Report Tool

A quick way to create a simple report object, like the one you reviewed in Project 16, is to use the Report tool. The Report tool creates a report for a selected table and then opens the report in Layout view.

Like the form you created earlier, *Access* displays the report in Layout view and the Report Layout Tools tabs appears on the Ribbon. To quickly switch to Print Preview, click the Print Preview button in the View Shortcuts on the status bar.

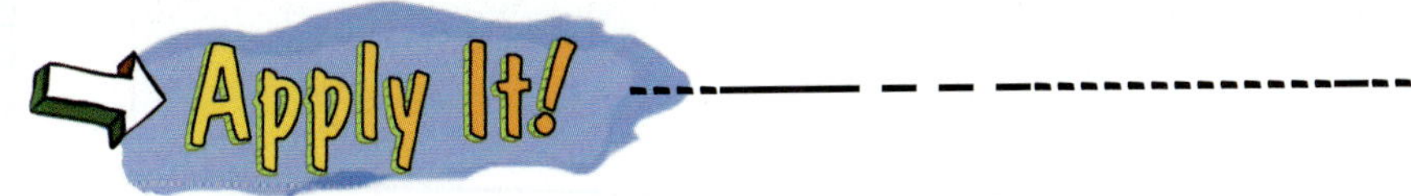


**Let's preview, print, and close the *Mark Twain1* document.**

1. Click the **Office Button**, point to **Print**, and click **Print Preview** in the submenu.

Your *Word 2007* document displayed in Print Preview should look similar to this.

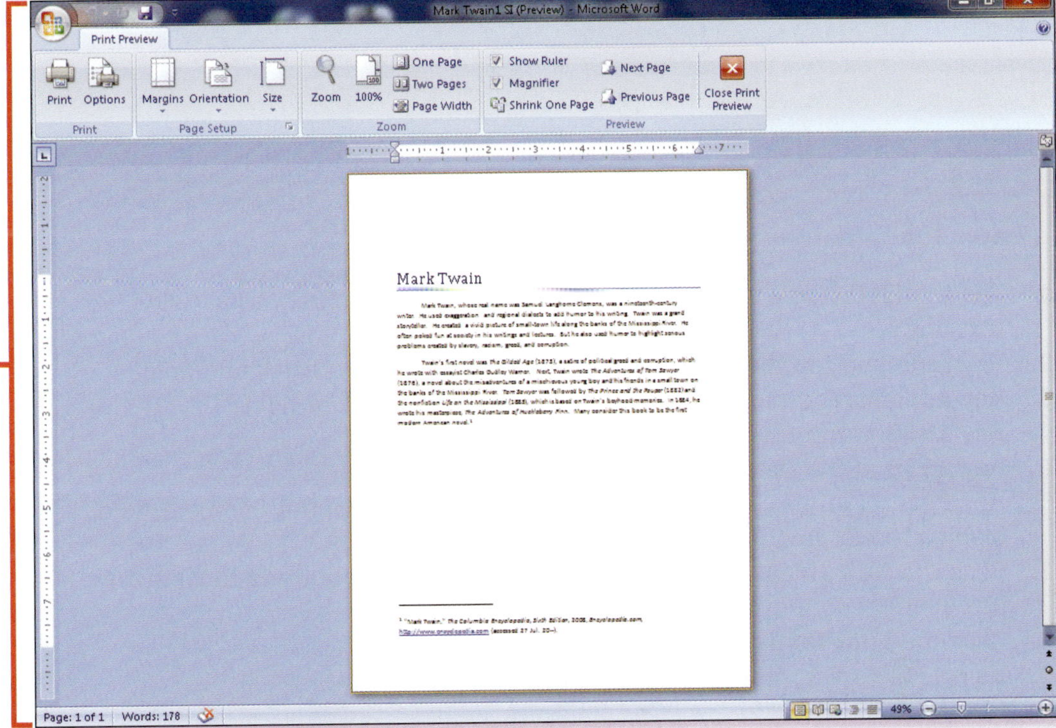


Print Preview

2. Use the mouse pointer and ScreenTips to locate the **Print** and **Close Print Preview** buttons on the Print Preview tab on the Ribbon.
3. With permission, click the **Print** button.
4. Click the **Close Print Preview** button.

Print | Close Print Preview

When you are finished with a document, you can close it by clicking Close on the Office Button menu or by clicking the Close button. Clicking the Close button when you have only one document open also closes the *Word* software.

5. Click the **Office Button** and click **Close** to close the *Mark Twain1* document and leave the *Word* software open.

Excellent! Now that you have finished editing Luis's document, you will create a new document—your very own personal journal!

You can navigate from field to field in the form as you enter the data just like you do in a datasheet by tapping the ENTER key, TAB key, SHIFT + TAB keys, or arrow key.

Don't forget! Each time you move to a new record, the record you add or edit in Form view is automatically saved.

**Let's enter Julie's data using the form.**

1. Tap the ENTER key to move the insertion point to the *First Name* field text box.
2. Key **Jane** and tap the ENTER key twice to move to the *Last Name* field.
3. Key **Addams** and tap the ENTER key to move to the *Born* field.
4. Key **1860** in the *Born* field and tap the ENTER key.
5. Key **1935** in the *Died* field and tap the ENTER key.
6. Key **Poverty** in the *Social Concern* field. For now, leave the *Source 1* field blank. The *Source 2* field contains a default value.
7. Click the **New (blank) record** button in the navigation buttons to view a new blank record in the form.
8. Click the **First Name** text box.
9. Using Julie's list, enter the remaining records.
10. Close the form.

You can open the table in Datasheet view to see the data you just entered.

**Now let's open the updated table, widen its columns, and save it.**

1. Double-click the *Famous Reformers* table name in the Navigation Pane to open the table in Datasheet view. The records you entered using the data entry form appear in the table's datasheet.
2. Double-click or drag the right boundary of the *field* selectors (column headers) to resize the columns as necessary.
3. Double-check your data entry against Julie's data.
4. Click the **Save** button on the Quick Access Toolbar to save the layout changes to the table. 

## Creating and Saving a New Document

When you close the *Mark Twain1* document by clicking Close on the File tab or Office Button menu, you will see the *Word* application null screen window, which indicates that *Word* is still open but there is no open document. To continue working in *Word*, you must open another document or create a new blank one.

To create a new blank document, click the File tab or Office Button and click New to view a number of model documents, called templates, which you can use to create a new document. The default template for a new blank document is called Blank document.

You can also double-click the Blank Document icon to create a new document.

### Creating and Saving a New Document in Word 2010

Clicking New on the File tab in *Word 2010* displays icons for the available templates installed with the *Word* software and templates that can be downloaded from the Microsoft Office.com website. The default Blank Document template is automatically selected. *Warning! Never download templates or other files from a website or Internet-connected server at school without your teacher's permission. At home, be sure to ask permission before downloading any Web-based files.*

| First Name | Middle Name | Last Name | Born | Died | Social Concern |
|---|---|---|---|---|---|
| Jane | | Addams | 1860 | 1935 | Poverty |
| Amos | Bronson | Alcott | 1799 | 1888 | Education reform |
| Susan | Brownell | Anthony | 1820 | 1906 | Women's suffrage |
| Samuel | June | Barrows | 1845 | 1909 | Prison reform |
| Lyman | | Beecher | 1775 | 1863 | Religious revival |
| James | Gillespie | Birney | 1792 | 1857 | Abolition |
| Alice | Stone | Blackwell | 1857 | 1950 | Women's suffrage |
| Amelia | | Bloomer | 1818 | 1894 | Women's suffrage |
| Carrie | Chapman | Catt | 1859 | 1947 | Women's suffrage |
| Lydia | Maria | Child | 1802 | 1880 | Abolition |
| Dorothea | | Dix | 1802 | 1887 | Mental illness |
| Frederick | | Douglass | 1818 | 1895 | Abolition |
| Neal | | Dow | 1804 | 1897 | Temperance |
| George | Henry | Evans | 1805 | 1856 | Labor reform |
| Charles | Grandison | Finney | 1792 | 1875 | Religious revival |
| William | Lloyd | Garrison | 1805 | 1879 | Abolition |
| Sarah | Moore | Grimke | 1792 | 1873 | Abolition |
| Josiah | | Henson | 1789 | 1883 | Abolition |
| Julia | Ward | Howe | 1819 | 1910 | Women's suffrage |
| Samuel | Gridley | Howe | 1801 | 1876 | Abolition |
| Mary | Harris | Jones | 1837 | 1930 | Labor reform |
| Juliette | Gordon | Low | 1860 | 1927 | Education reform |
| Josephine | Shaw | Lowell | 1843 | 1905 | Poverty |
| Horace | | Mann | 1796 | 1859 | Education reform |
| Lucretia | Coffin | Mott | 1793 | 1880 | Women's suffrage |
| John | Humphrey | Noyes | 1811 | 1886 | Utopian society |
| George | | Ripley | 1802 | 1880 | Utopian society |
| Robert | Gould | Shaw | 1837 | 1863 | Abolition |
| Anna | Howard | Shaw | 1847 | 1919 | Women's suffrage |
| Elizabeth | Cady | Stanton | 1815 | 1902 | Women's suffrage |
| Lucy | | Stone | 1818 | 1893 | Women's suffrage |
| Harriet | Beecher | Stowe | 1811 | 1896 | Abolition |
| Sojourner | | Truth | 1797 | 1883 | Abolition |
| Harriet | | Tubman | 1820 | 1913 | Abolition |
| Ida | B. | Wells-Barnett | 1862 | 1931 | Social justice |
| Emma | | Willard | 1787 | 1870 | Education reform |
| Enoch | Cobb | Wines | 1806 | 1879 | Prison reform |

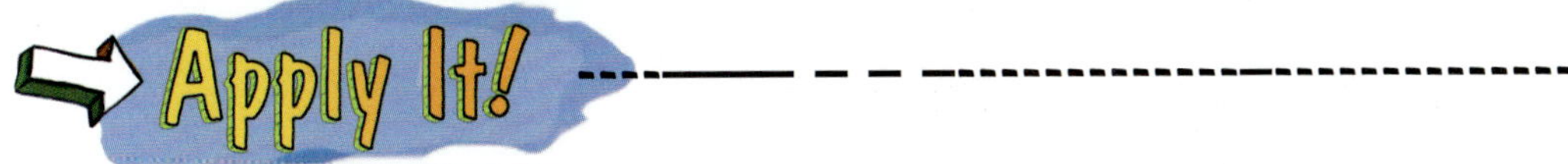


**Let's create a new document based on the Blank document template and then save it with a unique name in the folder specified by your teacher.**

1. Click the **File** tab. File
2. Click **New** to view the available templates in Backstage view.

Default template

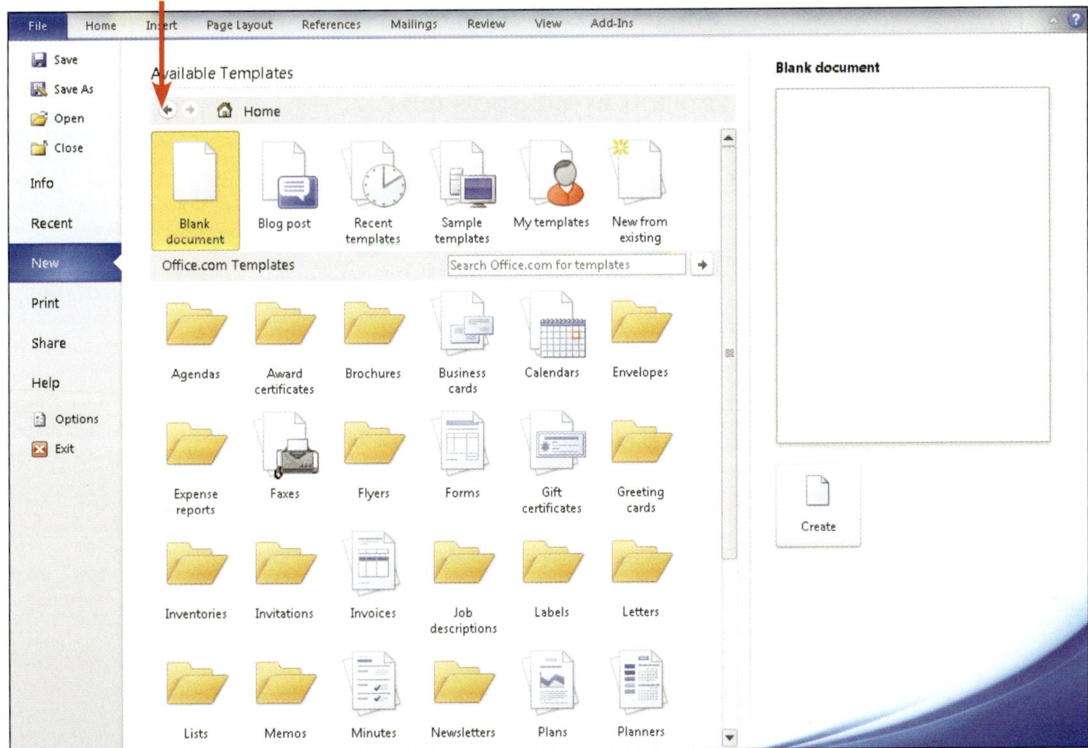


3. Click the **Create** button to create the new blank document based on the selected Blank Document template. Create
4. Save the document as **My Personal Journal** followed by your initials.

Great! Now let's add today's date and a brief paragraph to the document. Begin the first entry in your personal journal by inserting today's date instead of keying it.

### Creating and Saving a New Document in *Word 2007*

Clicking the New command on the Office Button menu opens the New Document window that contains icons for the default Blank template, recently used templates, and a category list of additional templates. The default Blank document is automatically selected.

**Let's use the Form tool to create and save a simple data entry form for the *Famous Reformers* table.**

Create | Forms | Form

1. Click the *Famous Reformers* table in the Navigation Pane, if necessary, to select the table.
2. Click the **Create** tab and locate the **Forms** group.
3. Click the **Form** button in the Forms group to create the simple data entry form.

*Access* displays the form in Layout view, and the Form Layout Tools tabs (Design, Arrange, and Format) appear on the Ribbon. You can use Layout view to change the order of the fields or make other changes to the layout of the form.

4. Click the **Save** button on the Quick Access Toolbar to open the Save As dialog box.
5. Key **Famous Reformers Data Entry Form** in the Form Name text box and click **OK**. To enter data in the form, you must switch to Form view.
6. Click the **Form View** button in the View Shortcuts to switch to Form view.
7. Scroll horizontally to the left, if necessary, to more clearly see the field names in the form.

Your data entry form in Form view should look similar to this.

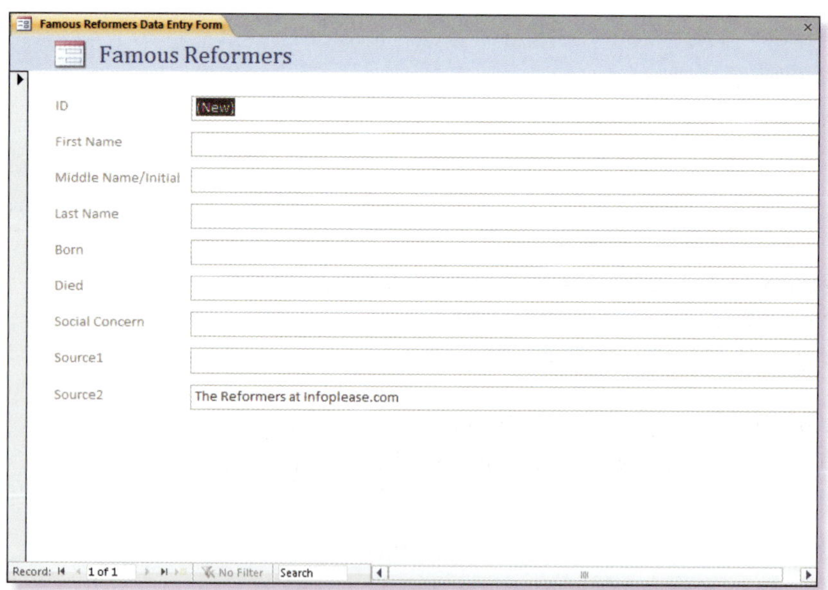


Excellent! Now let's use the form to enter Julie's data. Here is Julie's list of famous nineteenth-century social reformers.

**Let's create a new document based on the Blank document template and then save it with a unique name in the folder specified by your teacher.**

1. Click the **Office Button**.
2. Click **New** to open the New Document dialog box. The Blank document template icon is selected by default.

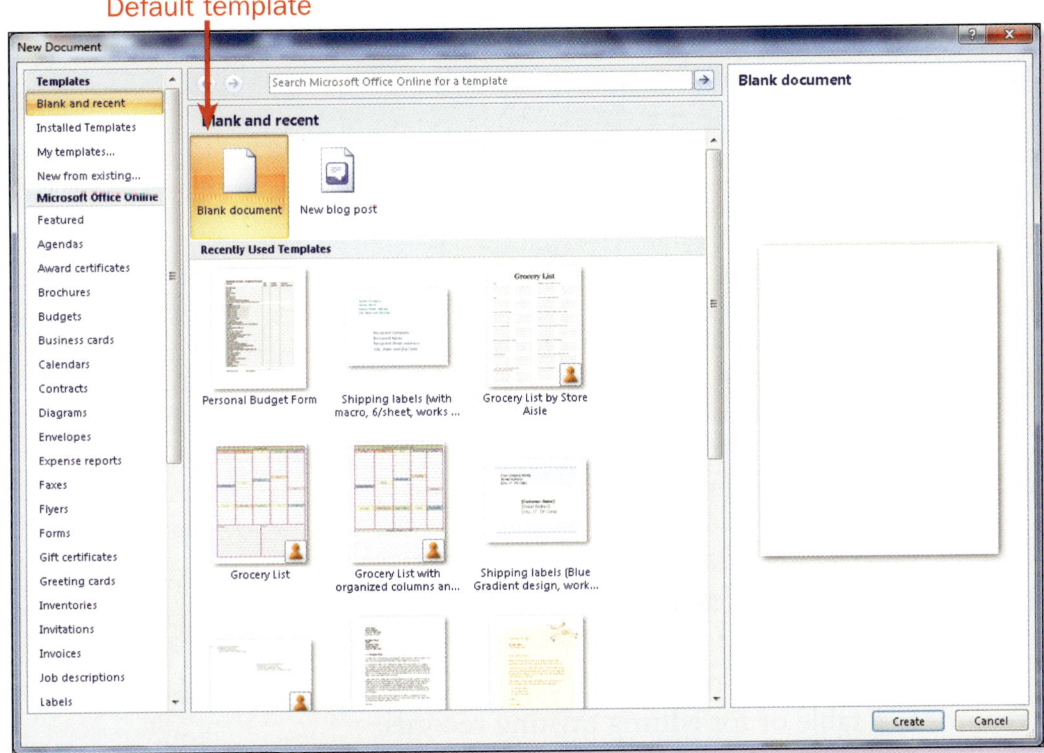


3. Click the **Create** button to create the new blank document based on the default Blank document template.
4. Save the document as **My Personal Journal** followed by your initials.

Super! Now let's add today's date and a brief paragraph to the document. Begin the first entry in your personal journal by inserting today's date instead of keying it.

### Inserting a Date

Insert a date by clicking the Insert tab on the Ribbon and clicking the Insert Date and Time button in the Text group to open the Date and Time dialog box. This dialog box offers you different date and time formats.

**Let's review the primary key set by *Access*, save the table, and close it.**

> Table Tools
> Design | Tools | Primary Key

1. Click the **ID** field in the table design grid, if necessary. The primary key icon appears in the Field selector button to the left of the field name, and the Primary Key button in the Tools group on the Table Tools Design tab is active.
2. Click the **Save** button on the Quick Access Toolbar to save the changes to the table's design.
3. Click the **Datasheet View** button in the View Shortcuts on the status bar to switch to Datasheet view. The field names now appear in the column headers.
4. Close the table.

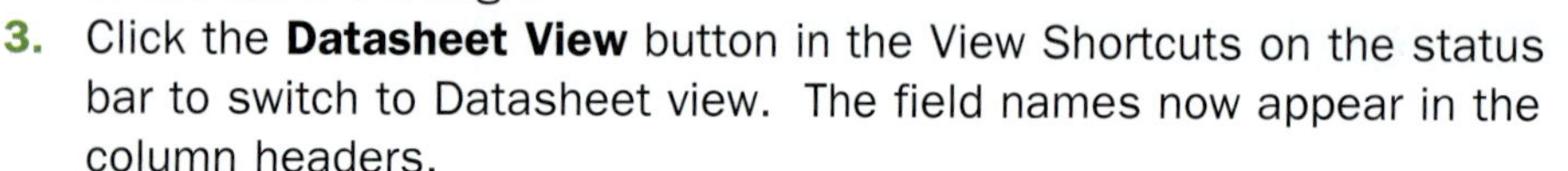

When working in a table in Design view, the default option for the View button face is Datasheet view. When working in Datasheet view, the default option for the View button face is Design view.

Great! Now let's create a data entry form and enter Julie's data.

## Creating a Form Using the Form Tool

In Project 16, you learned that a form object is an easy-to-use tool for adding new records to a table or for editing existing records. To quickly create a basic data entry form for the *Famous Reformers* table, you can use the Form tool. First, select the table in the Navigation Pane, if necessary; then click the Create tab and click the Form button in the Forms group.

The Form tool creates a simple data entry form, like the one you reviewed in Project 16, which lists all of the fields in a selected table. After you create the form, you can save it by clicking the Save button on the Quick Access Toolbar or the Save Object command on the File tab or Office Button Save As submenu.

**Let's insert today's date and a short paragraph in your journal.**

Insert | Text | Insert Date and Time

1. Click the **Insert** tab on the Ribbon and locate the **Text** group.
2. Click the **Insert Date and Time** button in the Text group to open the Date and Time dialog box.

Date & Time

3. Click the third date format in the list.
4. Click the **Update automatically** checkbox to remove the check mark, if necessary.

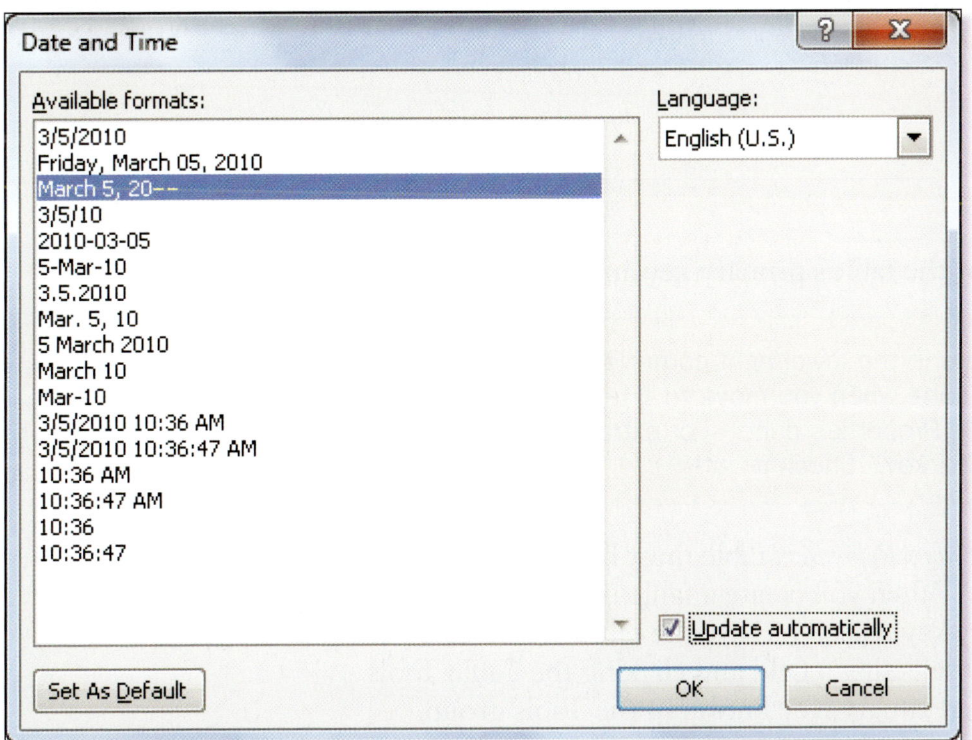


5. Click **OK**.
6. Tap the ENTER key twice to insert two paragraph marks or lines below the date.

Super! As you key text in the document, the insertion point moves across the line to the right until there is no more room on the line; then the text moves to the next line as you continue keying. This process is called wordwrap.

As you key your first personal journal entry, let *Word* wrap your text to the next line when necessary! Just tap the ENTER key to create a new *Word* paragraph.

8. Click the **Required** text box arrow and click **Yes** to require data entry in the *FirstName* field.
9. Click the next empty text box in the Field Name column in the table design grid.
10. Using the data from Julie's notes and the previous steps as a guide, define the remaining fields.

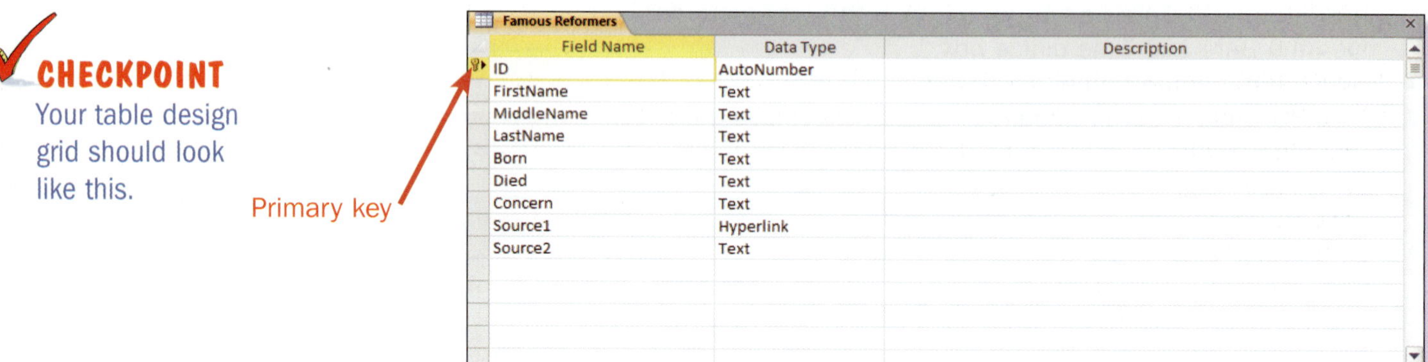


Super! Now you need to review the table's primary key and save the table.

A Help tip appears in the lower-right corner of the Field Properties pane when you move to a text box in the Fields or Field Properties pane. For extra Help, you can tap the F1 key. Check it out!

Each record you enter in the *Famous Reformers* table must have a unique identifier called its primary key. When you create a table in Design view, you can let *Access* set the primary key when you save the table or you can manually set the primary key by selecting a field and clicking the Table Tools Design tab and then clicking the Primary Key button in the Tools group.

After you modify your table in Design view, you can save your changes to the table by clicking the Save button on the Quick Access Toolbar. In *Access 2010*, you can also click the File tab and click Save (same name and location) or Save Object As (new name and/or location). In *Access 2007*, click the Office Button, click Save or point to Save As, and click Save Object As.

**Let's key a short paragraph, save the document, and close it and the *Word* application.**

1. Key three or four sentences about how Mark Twain used humor as a tool for social commentary.
2. Notice that the insertion point and the text move to the right as you key and that *Word* automatically wraps the text to the next line when necessary.
3. Use the I-beam or another method to select and change or delete words as necessary.
4. Save the document.
5. With your teacher's permission, preview and print the document.
6. Click the **Close** button on the title bar to close the document and the *Word* application.

*Word* automatically checks a document for unsaved changes when you close it. If the document has unsaved changes, a warning dialog box opens. Click Yes to save the changes before the document closes, click No if you do not want to save the changes, and click Cancel to stop the Close process.

Before you begin to add fields to a table and set field properties, think carefully about the data to be stored in the table; then write down each field name, the type and size of the data to be entered in the field, and any other field properties you want to set.

**Let's add fields to our table and set their field properties.**

1. Tap the Down arrow to move the insertion point to the next blank text box in the Field Name column in the table design grid.
2. Key **FirstName** in the text box in the Field Name column and tap the TAB key. The default Text data type is automatically selected.
3. Select the contents of the Field Size text box in the Field Properties pane using the I-beam pointer.
4. Key **10**.
5. Tap the ENTER key three times to move the insertion point into the Caption text box in the Field Properties pane.
6. Key **First Name** as the caption.

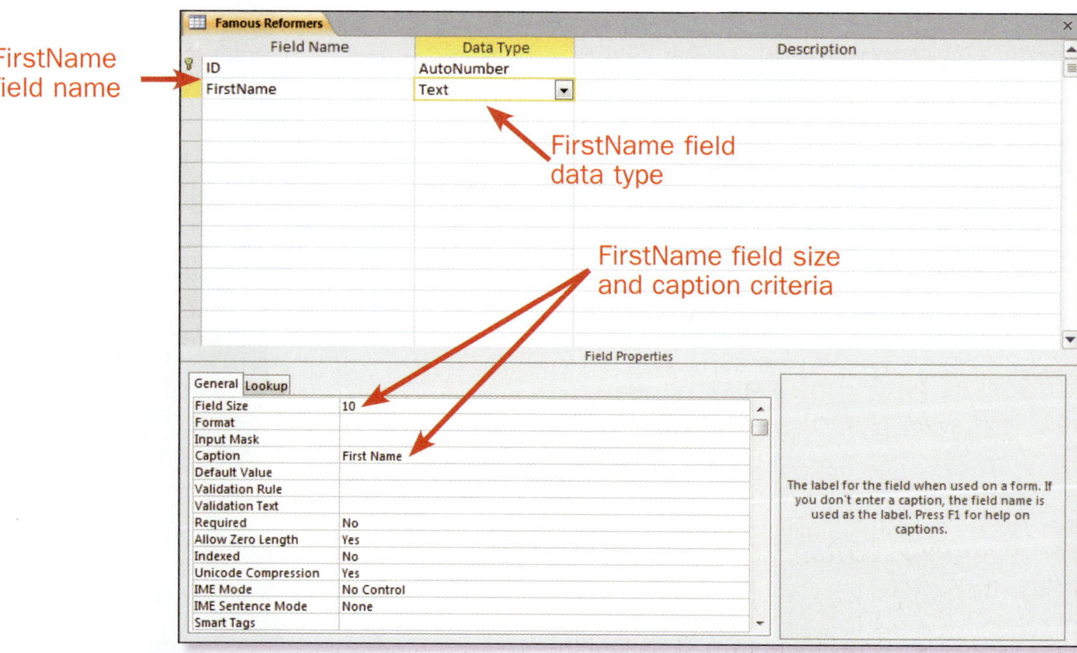


7. Tap the ENTER key four times to move down and select the **Required** text box in the Field Properties pane.

# Project Skills Review

You learned a lot in this project! We are very impressed with your progress. Let's take a few minutes to review the skills that you learned.

| | |
|---|---|
| **Open an existing document** | Click thc **File** tab or **Office Button** and click **Open**. |
| | Click the **Open** button, if available, on the **Quick Access Toolbar**. |
| **Save a document for the first time or with a new name or location** | Click the **File** tab or **Office Button** and click **Save As**. |
| **Switch between editing views** | Click a button in the **View Shortcuts** on the status bar. |
| | Click the **View** tab on the Ribbon and click a button in the Document Views group. Print Layout, Full Screen Reading, Web Layout, Outline, Draft |
| **View formatting marks** | Click the **Home** tab on the Ribbon and click the **Show/Hide ¶** button in the Paragraph group. |
| **Undo an action** | Click the **Undo** button on the **Quick Access Toolbar**. |
| **Check spelling and grammar** | Right-click the misspelled word and click the correctly spelled word on the shortcut menu. |
| **Replace an existing word with a different word** | Right-click a word, point to Synonyms, and click the replacement word or Thesaurus. |
| **Save a document with the same name and in the same location** | Click the **File** tab or **Office Button** and click **Save**. |
| | Click the **Save** button on the **Quick Access Toolbar**. |
| **Preview a document before you print it** | Click the **File** tab and click **Print**. |
| | Click the **Office Button**, point to **Print**, and click **Print Preview**. |
| | Click the **Print Preview** button, if available, on the **Quick Access Toolbar**. |

| Field Property | Description |
|---|---|
| Field Name | a descriptive name up to 64 characters |
| Data Type | the kind of data, such as text or an AutoNumber, to be stored in the field |
| Field Size | the number of characters that can be keyed in the field |
| Caption | text, instead of the field name, that appears in the datasheet or form |
| Default Value | text or a value that automatically appears in the field |
| Required | whether data must be entered in a field before a record can be saved |

*Access* automatically inserts the ID field with the AutoNumber data type when you create the database using the Blank Database icon. You will enter the remaining fields by working back and forth between two areas of the *Access* window—the table design grid and the Field Properties pane.

In the table design grid, you set the Field Name and Data Type properties. The default data type for each field is *Text*. To change the data type, click the field's Data Type arrow and click a different data type.

In the Field Properties pane below the table design grid, you specify the field's other properties: Field Size, Caption, and Default Value.

Here are Julie's notes about the fields and field properties in the new table.

| Field Name | Type | Size | Caption | Default Value | Required |
|---|---|---|---|---|---|
| FirstName | Text | 10 | First Name | | Yes |
| MiddleName | Text | 10 | Middle Name/Initial | | No |
| LastName | Text | 15 | Last Name | | Yes |
| Born | Text | 4 | | | No |
| Died | Text | 4 | | | No |
| Concern | Text | 20 | Social Concern | | Yes |
| Source1 | Hyperlink | | Source 1 | | No |
| Source 2 | Text | 35 | Source 2 | "The Reformers at Infoplease.com" | No |

You can move the insertion point from text box to text box in the table design grid or the Field Properties pane by clicking a text box or by tapping the TAB, ENTER, or arrow key.

Look carefully at the Required property for each field. Because each reformer's first and last name and social concern are the most important data, Julie wants to make sure this data is always entered before the record can be saved. That is why she set the Required property to *Yes* for this data.

# Project Skills Review

|  |  |
|---|---|
| **Print a document** | Click the **File** tab, click **Print**, and then click the Print button. |
| | Click the **Office Button**, point to **Print**, and click **Print** or **Quick Print** on the submenu. |
| | When previewing a document in Print Preview, click the **Print** button in the **Print** group on the **Print Preview** tab on the Ribbon.  |
| | Click the **Quick Print** button, if available, on the **Quick Access Toolbar**. |
| **Create a new blank document** | Click the **File** tab or **Office Button** and click **New**.  |
| | Click the **New** button, if available, on the **Quick Access Toolbar**. |
| **Insert a formatted date** | Click the **Insert** tab on the Ribbon and click the **Insert Date and Time** button in the Text group. 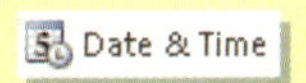 |
| **Close a document** | Click the **File** tab or **Office Button** and click **Close**. 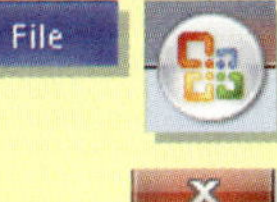 |
| | Click the **Close** button on the title bar. |

3. Key **Famous Reformers** in the Table Name text box and click **OK**.

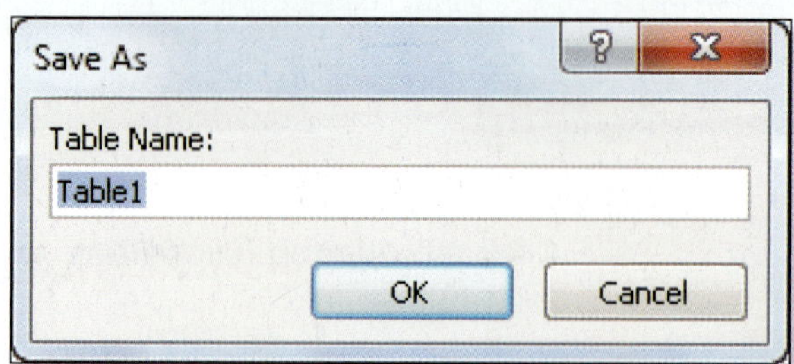


The table appears in Design view, and the Table Tools Design tab appears on the Ribbon. Now you are ready to define fields in the table.

**CHECKPOINT**

Your table in Design view should look like this.

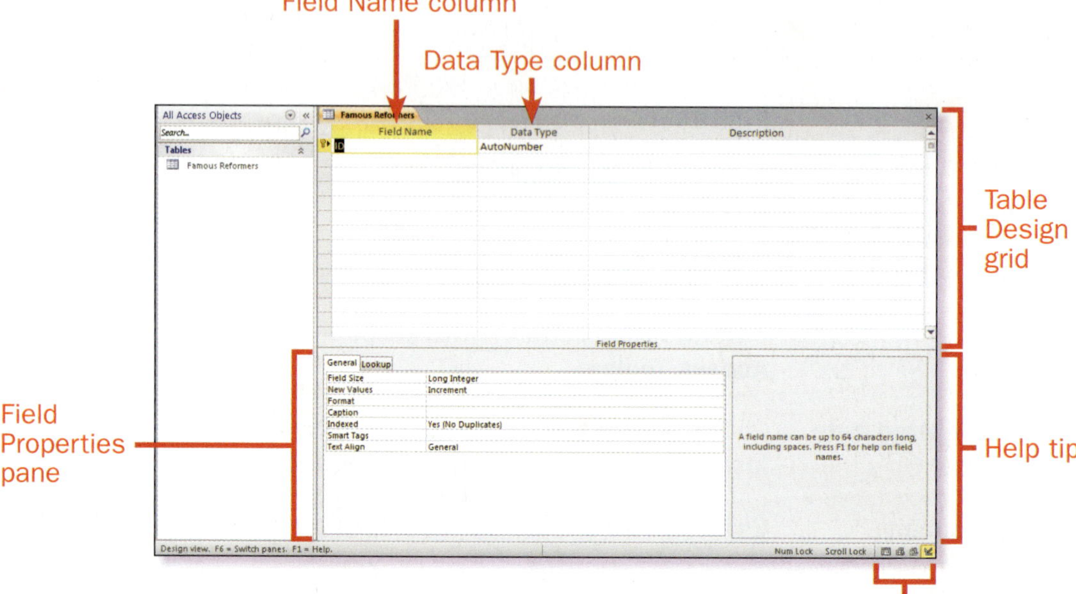


To define a field in Design view, you set the field's special characteristics, called field properties. For example, you name the field; specify what type of data can be keyed in the field; and specify how many characters can be keyed in the field by setting the Field Name, Data type, and Field Size properties, respectively.

A field can have many different properties; but in this project, you will set only the following field properties:

- Field Name, Data type, and Field Size properties for every field
- Caption, Default Value, and Required properties as needed

The following table indicates the field properties you will set for fields in this Trail Marker.

You can also name table fields in Datasheet view. You key a field name in each column header in a table's datasheet and allow *Access* to define the properties for each field based on the type of data you enter. You learn how to name table fields in Datasheet view in Project 18.

# Exploring On Your Own

## Blaze Your Own Trail

You have learned several new skills in this project. Now blaze your own trail by practicing these skills on your own! Start *Word*, if necessary; then open the *Mississippi River* document and save it as *Mississippi River1*. Make the following corrections to the document using the I-beam and the keyboard to position the insertion point and using appropriate selection methods. Display the formatting marks, if necessary.

1. Use the BACKSPACE key to delete the extra *t* in the word *itt* in the third sentence in the first body paragraph.
2. Use the DELETE key to delete the extra *o* in the word *too* in the first sentence in the second body paragraph.
3. Insert the word **the** before and the word **of** after the word *development* in the first sentence of the third body paragraph.
4. Select the state name *Illinois* in *Ste. Genevieve, Illinois* in the next to last sentence of the second body paragraph and replace it with **Missouri**.
5. Use the CTRL + HOME keys to move the insertion point to the top of the document and then use the shortcut menu to check the spelling and grammar.
6. Use the shortcut menu and the thesaurus to replace the word *bustling* in the second sentence in the third paragraph with an appropriate synonym.
7. Save the document and, with permission, preview and print it; then close it.

## Reading in Action

### Organizing Facts

To help you remember specific facts about works by Mark Twain, create a three-column chart. Use these column headings: *Book, Year Published*, and *Details About the Book*. Use the information in the *Mark Twain1* document and other resources about Twain to complete the chart.

## Math in Action

### Using Algebra to Solve Problems

A steamboat travels 10 to 20 miles per hour. Memphis and St. Louis are about 300 miles apart. How long would it take a steamboat going from Memphis to St. Louis at an average speed of 20 mph to meet a steamboat going from St. Louis to Memphis at an average speed of 10 mph?

Let $x$ = # of hours until the steamboats meet.

Every hour that passes brings the faster boat 20 miles closer and the slower boat 10 miles closer to closing the 300-mile distance.

$20x + 10x = 300$

$30x = 300$

$x = 10$ hours until the steamboats meet

Now you try it!

How long would it take these steamboats to meet if both were going 25 mph? if one was going 15 mph and the other was going 10 mph?

The empty table in your new database should look similar to this.

Empty table opened in Datasheet view in the workspace

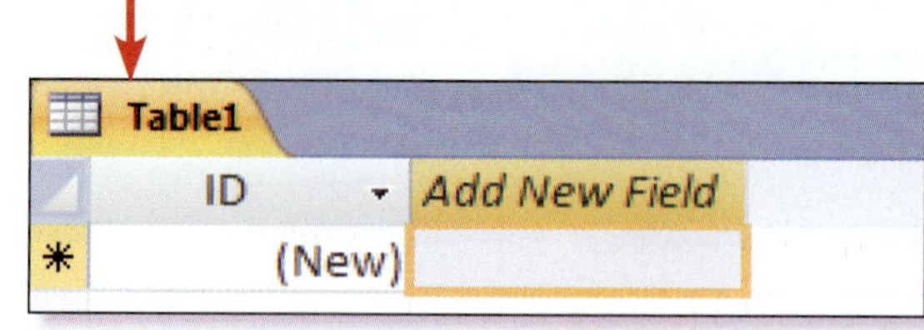


Good job! Now let's modify the table that will contain Julie's data.

## Modifying a Table in Design View

In Project 16, you learned about table objects and how to open them in Datasheet view to look at and manipulate the data stored in the tables. In this project, you will modify the table for Julie's research data in Design view, which allows you to define each table field and its properties.

To modify a table in Design view, select the table object in the Navigation Pane, if necessary, and then click the Home tab and click the Design View button face in the Views group.

If the table is open in Datasheet view, you can also click the Table Tools Fields tab (*Access 2010*) or the Table Tools Datasheet tab (*Access 2007*) and then click the Design View button face in the Views group.

If you are working with a new table, you must name and save it before it opens in Design view.

Like *Word*, *Excel*, and *PowerPoint*, *Access* provides View Shortcuts buttons on the status bar, which include the Datasheet View and Design View buttons. You can also switch between Datasheet and Design views by right-clicking a table in the Navigation Pane and clicking Design View on the shortcut menu. Try these methods!

**Let's name and save our table as we switch to Design view. Before you begin, the blank table should be open in Datasheet view.**

Home | Views | Design View

1. Click the **Home** tab, if necessary, and locate the **Views** group.
2. Click the **Design View** button face in the Views group.
   The Save As dialog box opens, which contains the temporary name *Table1*.

# Exploring *Across the Curriculum*

## Internet/Web

Open your Web browser and use a favorite or bookmark to view the Learning with Computers Web page (www.cengage.com/school/keyboarding/lwcorange). Click the **Links** option. Click **Project 1**. Follow the links to learn more about the interesting life of Samuel Langhorne Clemens, who wrote as Mark Twain. Where and when was he born? What was life like for Clemens as a young boy? What work did he do on the Mississippi River? What took Clemens to the American West, and what did he do there? How did he choose his pseudonym, Mark Twain? What are some of his most important stories and novels? Take notes about what you learn.

1. Create a new blank document and save it as *Clemens1*.
2. Insert today's date at the top of the document followed by your name on the second line below the date.
3. Insert two blank lines.
4. Key at least four paragraphs describing the life and work of Samuel L. Clemens.
5. Use a shortcut menu to check the document's spelling and grammar.
6. Use a shortcut menu and the Thesaurus to replace a word with a synonym.
7. Save the document and, with permission, preview and print it; then close it.

## Wisdom Language Arts: Words to Know

Look up the meaning of the following words, terms, or phrases in a classroom dictionary, CD-ROM dictionary or encyclopedia, or online dictionary.

| anecdote | dialect | Gilded Age | humorist |
|---|---|---|---|
| paddleboat | pseudonym | tall tale | vernacular |

Create a new document and save it as *definitions1* followed by your initials. Insert today's date at the top of the document and your name on the second line below the date; then insert two blank lines. Key each term on one line and its definition on the next line. Insert a blank line between each definition and the next term. Use a shortcut menu to check the document's spelling and grammar. Save the document and, with permission, preview and print it; then close it.

Explore More

### Creating a New Database in *Access 2007*

When you start *Access*, the templates in a specific category, such as Featured Online Templates, are visible in a scrollable Templates pane in the Getting Started with Access page.

To view the templates in different categories, such as Business or Personal, click a category in the Template Categories pane on the left side of the Getting Started with Access page.

To create a new database with an empty table, click the Blank Database icon in the New Blank Database section on the Getting Started with Access page.

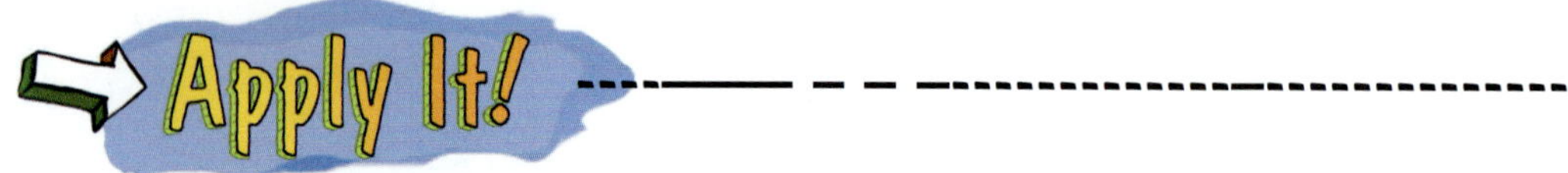


**Let's create a new database and save it to our solutions folder.**

1. Click the **Blank Database** icon in the New Blank Database pane in the Getting Started with Access page. The File Name text box and Browse icon appear in the Blank Database pane in the lower-right corner of the page.

2. Key ***reformers17 solution*** in the File Name text box and click the **Browse** icon to open the File New Database dialog box.

3. Switch to the folder that contains your solution files and click **OK** to save the database file. The path to the *reformers17 solution* database appears below the File Name text box in the lower-right corner of the page.

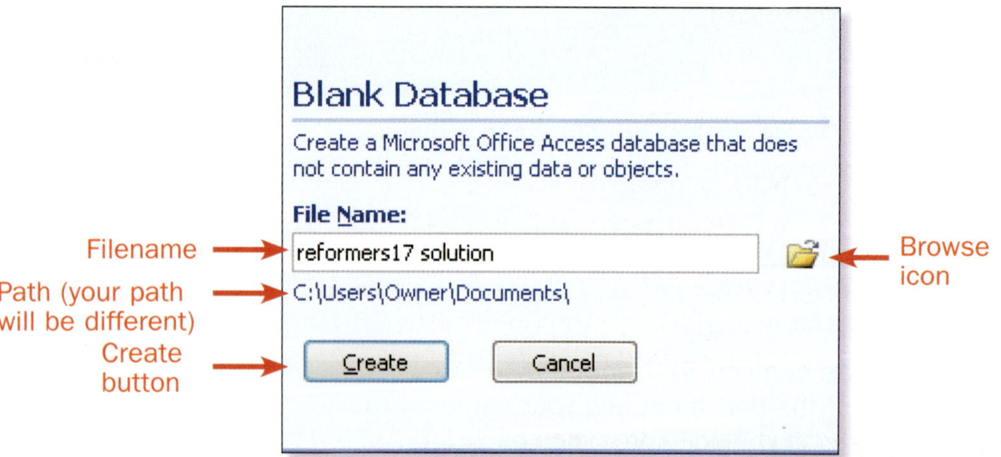


4. Click the **Create** button below the File Name text box and path to open the new database containing the empty table.

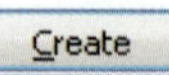

# Exploring *Across the Curriculum*

## Social Studies: Research and Write

Use library, classroom, CD-ROM, or online resources (including maps) to research life along the Mississippi River during the nineteenth century. Then imagine that you and your friends are growing up during this period in a small town along the Mississippi River. What would you see, hear, smell, and do during a typical summer day? Create a new document and key three or four paragraphs describing a typical summer day in your life along the Mississippi. Use a shortcut menu to check the document's spelling and grammar. Use a shortcut menu and the Thesaurus to replace a word with a synonym. Save the document and, with permission, preview and print it; then close it.

## Getting Help

Click the Microsoft Word Help icon below the *Word* application Close button to open the *Word* Help window. Key **document theme** in the search text box and click the Search button to research how to apply a document theme. Then create a new document, insert today's date, and key two paragraphs describing the *Word* window. Apply a theme to the document; spell-check, save, preview, and (with permission) print; and close it.

## Career Day

Mark Twain's beloved Mississippi River is one of the most valuable natural resources in the United States. If you are interested in protecting the country's natural resources, such as the Mississippi River and the land that borders it, you might enjoy a career that focuses on resource preservation in agriculture, food production, timber, minerals, or other natural resources. Using library, printed, or online resources, identify three interesting careers that involve natural resource management and preservation. Write a brief summary of each career, print your summary, and save it in your Career Day folder.

Explore More

**Let's create a new database based on the Blank database template and save it in our solutions folder.**

1. Click the **Blank database** icon to select it, if necessary.
2. Key ***reformers17 solution*** in the File Name text box in the lower-right corner of Backstage view and then click the **Browse** icon to open the File New Database dialog box.
3. Switch to the folder that contains your solution files and click **OK** to save the new database file. The path to the database file appears below the File Name text box in the lower-right corner of Backstage view.

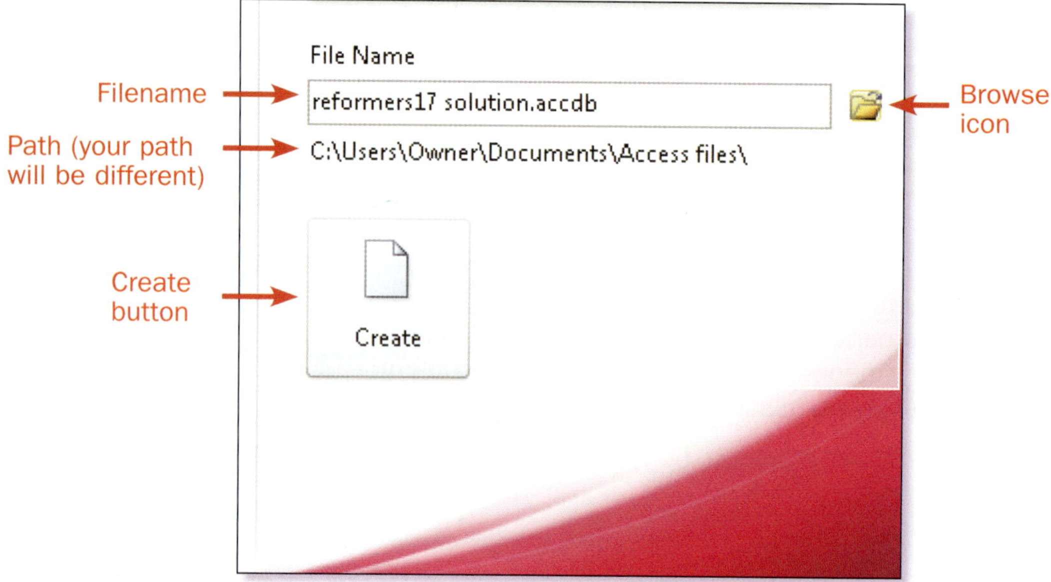


4. Click the **Create** button below the File Name text box and path to open the new database containing an empty table. The empty table opens in Datasheet view in the workspace.

The empty table in your new database should look similar to this.

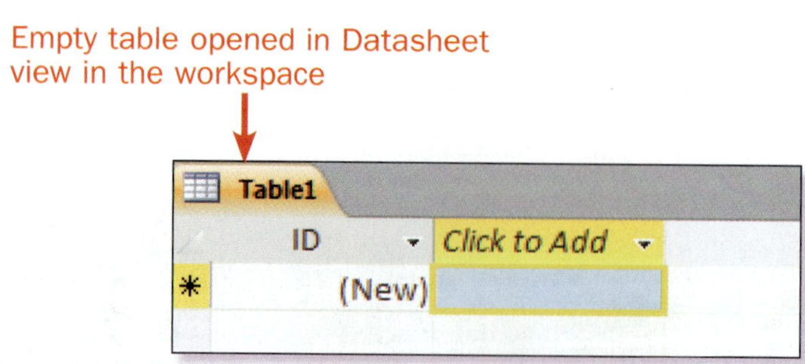


Fantastic! In Trail Marker 2, you add fields to the empty table.

# Exploring *Across the Curriculum*

## Your Personal Journal

Open your *My Personal Journal* document. Insert today's date and two blank lines. In *The Adventures of Tom Sawyer*, Tom Sawyer comes up with a way to paint a fence without doing the work himself. Write a paragraph explaining what he did. If you have not read the book, use your imagination—just like Tom did—to write your answer. Use a shortcut menu to check the spelling and grammar. Then save and close your journal document.

## Online Enrichment Games

www.cengage.com/school/keyboarding/lwcorange

**Begin by starting the *Access* application.**

1. Start the *Access* application using the Start menu or a desktop shortcut.

Super! Now let's create, name, and save a new database.

**ERGONOMICS TIP**

Remember to sit straight at your computer and keyboard so that the B key lines up with your navel.

## Creating, Naming, and Saving a New Database

*Access* provides a number of templates, or models, on which to base a new database. Sample templates might contain multiple tables, forms, and reports. You can also use a template to create a new database file that contains an empty table.

Unlike creating a new file in *Word*, *Excel*, or *PowerPoint*, in *Access*, you must save a new database before you can work in it. When you create a new database, you save the database using the File Name text box and a Browse icon that appear in the lower-right corner of the File tab in *Access 2010* or the Getting Started with Access page in *Access 2007*.

### Creating a New Database in *Access 2010*

Icons for the *Access* templates available to you appear in Backstage view when you start *Access* or when you click New on the File tab. Available templates include the Blank database template and recently used templates, sample templates, and customized templates. By default, the Blank database template icon is selected.

You will also see a search box and arrow in Backstage view that allow you to search online at Office.com for additional database templates.

# Project 1 Keyboarding

## 1a Home-Row Review

Key each line twice. Double-space between 2-line groups.

**TECHNIQUE TIP**

- body erect
- sit back in chair
- fingers curved and upright

1 f d s a j k l ; | ;l kj fd sa | ;l kj fd sa | asdf jkl;;

2 ;; aa ll ss dd kk ff jj | aa dd jj ;; ss ff kk ll dd

3 kak kak | jdj jdj | lfl lfl | s;s s;s | djd djd | fkf fkf | ll

4 ad ad | dad dad | lad lad | ask ask | fad fad | fall fall | as

5 as a lad as a lad | ask dad ask dad | fall ad fall ad;

## 1b Speed Check

1. Key a 1' timing on paragraph 1.
2. Determine the number of words you keyed.
3. Key another 1' timing on paragraph 1. Try to go two words a minute faster.
4. Repeat steps 1–3 for paragraph 2.
5. Key a 2' timing on paragraphs 1–2 combined.
6. Determine the number of words keyed.

For additional practice:
**MicroType 5**
New Key Review, Alphabetic Lesson 1

**A** **all letters used** *gwam* 2'

Who was Shakespeare? Few would even question that he 5
was one of the greatest individuals to ever write a play. His works 12
have endured the test of time. Productions of his literary works 19
continue to take place on the stage of theaters all over the world. 26
Shakespeare was an expert at creating comedies and tragedies, both 33
of which often leave the audience in tears. 37

Few of those who put pen to paper have been as successful 43
at creating such prized characters for their readers. Each character 50
he created has a life of its own. It is entirely possible that more 57
students know about the tragedy that Romeo and Juliet experienced 64
than know about the one that took place at Pearl Harbor. 69

*gwam* 2' | 1 | 2 | 3 | 4 | 5 | 6 |

# Working for Social Reform

## Explorers' Guide

**Data file:** none

**Objectives:**
In this project, you will:
- create, name, and save a new database
- modify a table in Design view
- create a form using the Form tool
- create a report using the Report tool
- create a select query in Design view

## Our Exploration Assignment:

**Creating a new database and then creating a table, a form, a report, and query objects**

The Explorers Club is learning about the men and women who led the nineteenth-century American reform movements to abolish slavery, protect workers, improve education, ensure social justice, and promote universal suffrage. Can you help Julie use a new database to organize her notes on the reform movement leaders? Fantastic! Just follow the Trail Markers to name and save a new database, modify a table in Design view, and save it. Then you use the Form tool to create a data entry form and use the form to add records to the table. You publish the table's data in a simple report using the Report tool and then create a query in Design view that answers the question "Which of the women's suffrage reformers born in the 1800s lived to see the ratification of the Nineteenth Amendment to the U.S. Constitution, which granted women the right to vote?"

Social Justice!

NORTH WIND PICTURE ARCHIVES VIA AP IMAGES

# Living in the Thirteen English Colonies

## Explorers' Guide

**Data files:** colonies list
colonies

**Objectives:**
In this project, you will:
- create a three-level multilevel list
- change document margins
- apply paragraph formatting
- apply character formatting
- follow proofreaders' marks

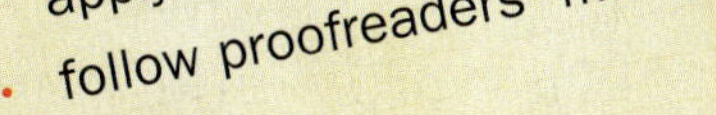

PETER NEWARK PICTURES/THE BRIDGEMAN ART LIBRARY INTERNATIONAL

## Our Exploration Assignment:

**Creating a three-level multilevel list and following proofreaders' marks to format a single-page unbound report**

The Explorers Club is learning about colonial America. Ray has created two documents: a list of his research notes about the original thirteen colonies and a report based on those notes. He needs your help to make both documents more attractive and easier to read. Follow the Trail Markers to create a three-level multilevel list; change document margins; apply paragraph formatting by changing horizontal alignment and line spacing; apply character formatting by changing font, font size, and case; and follow proofreaders' marks to format a single-page unbound report.

# Project 16 Keyboarding

## 16a Numeric Keypad Review

Use the calculator accessory and numeric keypad to complete the drills shown at the right. The answers are shown in blue. The answers to the division problems are rounded to two places.

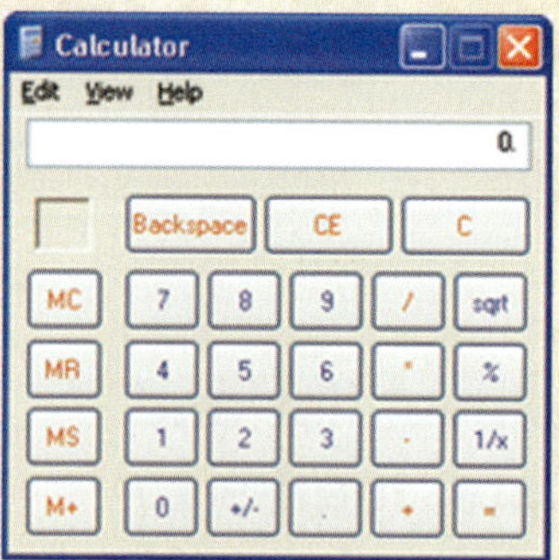

**Drill 1 – Addition**

| A | B | C | D | E |
|---|---|---|---|---|
| 186 | 495 | 297 | 756 | 397 |
| +379 | +310 | +214 | + 48 | +171 |
| 565 | 805 | 511 | 804 | 568 |

**Drill 2 – Subtraction**

| A | B | C | D | E |
|---|---|---|---|---|
| 879 | 835 | 436 | 908 | 705 |
| −214 | −167 | −210 | −314 | −267 |
| 665 | 668 | 226 | 594 | 438 |

**Drill 3 – Multiplication**

| A | B | C | D | E |
|---|---|---|---|---|
| 71 | 46 | 57 | 20 | 498 |
| × 3 | × 13 | × 45 | × 61 | × 27 |
| 213 | 598 | 2,565 | 1,220 | 13,446 |

**Drill 4 – Division**

| A | B | C | D | E |
|---|---|---|---|---|
| 102 | 143.41 | 354.82 | 115.51 | 226.43 |
| 7)714 | 32)4,589 | 17)6,032 | 65)7,508 | 14)3,170 |

## 16b Build Skill

Key each line twice. Double-space between 2-line groups.

For additional practice:
**MicroType 5**
Numeric Keypad, Lessons 3-4

**Alphabet sentences**

1 Zeb or Jack Gore explained why seven of them quit.

2 Jorge F. Bevins quickly swam the dozen extra laps.

3 Jackie Wilson helped Mary fix the big quartz vase.

4 Jewel amazed Vic by escaping quickly from the box.

**Speed sentences**

5 Laurie may fish off the big dock down by the lake.

6 Rodney kept the shamrock in the box by the mantle.

7 The eight busy men did the problems for the girls.

8 The chair by the chapel in the city is an antique.

**Start the *Word* application, if necessary; then open an existing document and save it with a new name.**

1. Start the *Word* application.
2. Open the *colonies list* document and save it as *colonies list2*.

Nicely done! Now let's format Ray's notes in the *colonies list2* document as a three-level multilevel list.

**ERGONOMICS TIP**

Looking at your screen for long periods of time can tire your eyes! Remember to rest them every 20 minutes by looking away from the screen for 20 seconds to focus on an object at least 20 feet away. That's better! Back to work!

## Creating a Three-Level Multilevel List

A multilevel list is used to organize ideas and topics for an oral presentation or a written report. A three-level multilevel list has Level 1 main topics, Level 2 subtopics, and Level 3 details that support a subtopic.

Level 1 main topics begin at the left margin; Level 2 subtopics are indented, or *moved* inward from the left margin, below the main topics; and Level 3 details are indented below the subtopics. Each level is numbered or lettered according to a set system. This is the most common numbering system for a three-level multilevel list:

**I)** Level 1 main topics begin with Roman numerals
- **A)** Level 2 subtopics begin with uppercase letters
  - **1)** Level 3 details begin with numbers

Did you know? The most efficient way to create a document in *Word* is to key all of the text first, then select and format the text!

# Exploring *Across the Curriculum*

## Social Studies: Research and Write and Map It!

Work with a classmate to use library or online resources to locate a map of the United States as it looked in 1860 and a map of the Colorado Territory that was formed in 1861 from portions of the New Mexico, Kansas, Utah, and Nebraska territories. Then use the 1860 map as a guide to draw your own 1860 U.S. map. Draw a dotted-line boundary on the map to represent where the Colorado Territory was formed. Using the data from the *states16* and *1860states16* databases, note the state or territory names and statehood dates on each state and territory, color-code the Union and Confederate states, and draw a colored border around each slave state that did not secede.

## Getting Help

Click the Microsoft Access Help icon to open the Help window. Key **check spelling** in the search box and tap the ENTER key to research how to check the spelling of data in a datasheet. Then open the *states16* database you updated in this project. Using what you learned, open the *States* table in Datasheet view and check the spelling. Make any necessary corrections. Do not add any proper names to the dictionary. Close the table and close the database.

## Career Day

All across the 50 states, the demand for health professionals continues to grow. Using library, printed, or online resources, identify three interesting occupations in the health sciences. Write a brief summary of each occupation, print your summary, and save it in your Career Day folder.

## Your Personal Journal

Open your personal journal document. Insert today's date and two blank lines. Think about what you have learned about your state; then write one or two paragraphs that describe your state and its origins. Spell-check, save, and close your journal.

**Online Enrichment Games**  www.cengage.com/school/keyboarding/lwcorange

Ray's *colonies list2* document has a title paragraph and a list of paragraphs that includes main topics, subtopics, and details. To format Ray's list as a three-level multilevel list, you can use the Multilevel List feature. By using the Multilevel List feature, you will not have to key the Roman numerals, letters, or numbers or indent the text—*Word* will do all of the work for you!

First, select all of the paragraphs below the title paragraph using the CTRL + SHIFT + END keyboard shortcut. Next, click the Home tab and click the Multilevel List button in the Paragraph group to view a gallery of numbering options. You can also open the Define new Multilevel list dialog box and customize a multilevel list.

Remember to click the Show/Hide ¶ button if you want to see the formatting marks.

Home | Paragraph | Multilevel List

**Let's select all of the paragraphs below the title paragraph, then open the Define new Multilevel list dialog box and customize the numbering for multilevel list Levels 1–3. *Do not* customize the numbering for Levels 4–9.**

1. Move the insertion point immediately in front of *Introduction: Reasons for Colonization*. Press the CTRL + SHIFT + END keys to select all of the paragraphs from the insertion point to the end of the document.

The·Thirteen·Colonies¶
Introduction:·Reasons·for·Colonization¶
Religious·and·political·freedom¶
Puritans·and·the·Great·Migration¶
French·Huguenots·and·Catholics¶
Economic·gain¶
The·Thirteen·Original·Colonies·by·Region¶
New·England·Colonies·(1620-1636)¶
Connecticut,·Massachusetts,·New·Hampshire,·and·Rhode·Island¶
Religious·and·political·freedom¶
Middle·Colonies·(1664-1776)¶
Delaware,·New·Jersey,·New·York,·and·Pennsylvania¶
Farming,·trade,·religious·freedom·and·tolerance¶
Southern·Colonies·(1607-1733)¶
Georgia,·Maryland,·North·Carolina,·South·Carolina,·and·Virginia¶
Wealthy·landowners¶
Debtors·and·small·farmers¶
Religious·freedom·and·tolerance¶

2. Click the **Home** tab, if necessary, and locate the **Paragraph** group.
3. Click the **Multilevel List** button in the Paragraph group to view the numbering options gallery.
4. Click **Define New Multilevel List** at the bottom of the gallery to open the Define new Multilevel list dialog box.

# Exploring Across the Curriculum

## Internet/Web

Open your Web browser and use a favorite or bookmark to view the Learning with Computers Web page (www.cengage.com/school/keyboarding/lwcorange). Click the **Links** option and click **Project 16**. Click the Google link and perform a Boolean search for government Web pages for your state using the name of your state and .gov as the search keywords. (Remember to add the plus sign before your state name and before .gov.) Find interesting and fun facts about your state and take notes about what you learn.

1. Using your research notes and the data in the *states16* and *1860states16* databases, create a *PowerPoint* presentation you can use to present your research.
2. Cite your sources at the end of the presentation.
3. Format the presentation as desired using a customized theme, slide transitions, clip art, movies, sound, and animation.

## Language Arts: Words to Know

Look up the meaning of the following terms in a classroom dictionary, CD-ROM dictionary or encyclopedia, or online dictionary.

| database | field | query | record |
|---|---|---|---|

Open the *definitions16* database. Open the *Technical Terms* table and enter a brief definition for each record in the *Definition* field. Use no more than 50 characters for the definitions. Print Preview the datasheet and, with your teacher's permission, print it. Close Print Preview and close the database.

Explore More

5. Set the numbering system in the Define new Multilevel list dialog box.
   - Click **1** in the Level list, if necessary.
   - Click the **Number style** drop-down arrow and click **I, II, III,....** Uppercase Roman numerals are selected for Level 1.
   - Click **2** in the Level list.
   - Click the **Number style** for this level arrow and click **A, B, C,....**
   - Click **3** in the Level list.
   - Click the **Number style for this level** arrow and click **1, 2, 3, ....**

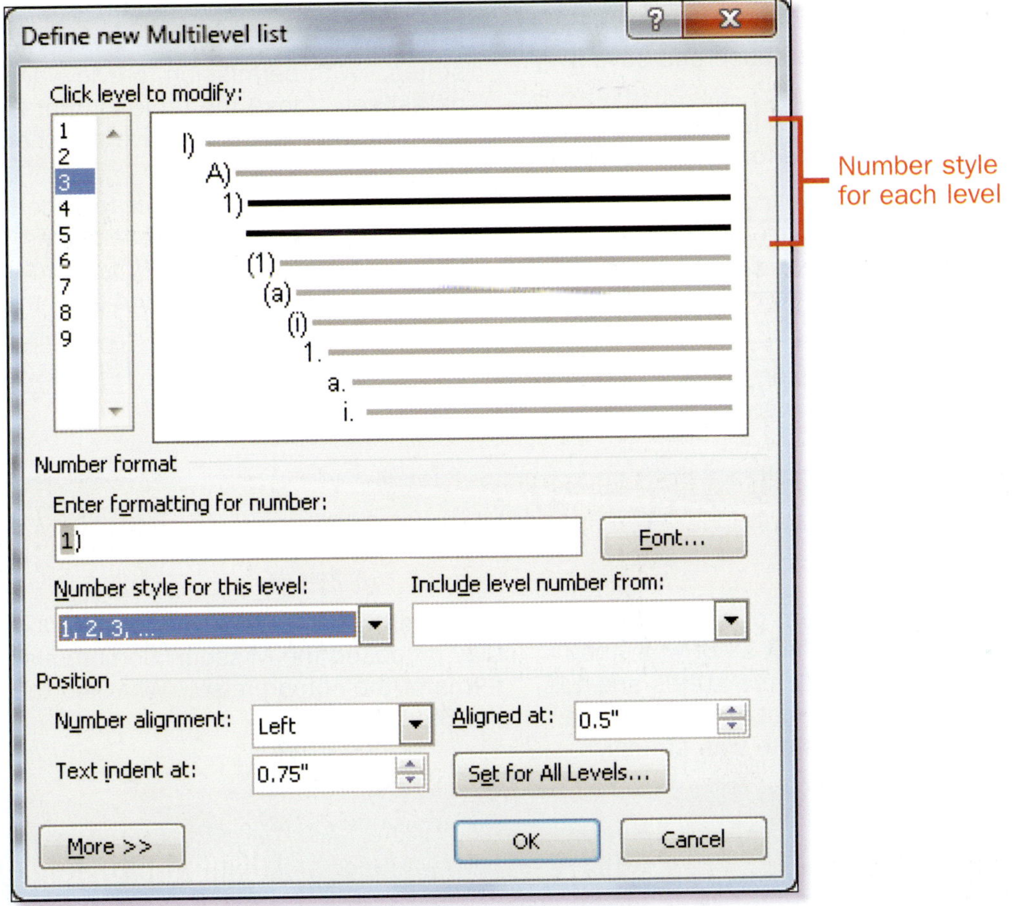


6. Click **OK**. Deselect the list and save the document.

# Exploring On Your Own

## Blaze Your Own Trail

You have learned several new skills in this project. Now blaze your own trail by practicing these skills on your own!

1. Open the *1860states16* database and save it as *1860states16 solution*.
2. Open the *States or Territories* table in Datasheet view and add the following record for Alabama.

| Name | State or Territory | Slave or Free | Union or Confederate | Date Seceded | Source |
|---|---|---|---|---|---|
| Alabama | State | Slave | Confederate | 1/11/1861 | www.pbs.org |

3. Find the Missouri record using the Find and Replace dialog box and change the *Slave or Free* data to **Slave**.
4. Sort the data in ascending alphabetical order by the *Name* field; then locate and delete the Montana record. Save the table.
5. Filter the data to show only the Confederate states. With permission, preview and print the datasheet. Close the table in Print Preview and click **No** when asked to save the changes to the table design.
6. Four slave states chose not to secede from the Union. To see a list of these states, run the *Union Slave States* query. Then with your teacher's permission, preview and print the query datasheet.
7. Close the query, close the *1860states16* database, and close *Access*.

## Reading in Action

### Identifying Supporting Details

A *compromise* is the settlement of an argument in which all sides get some but not all of what they want. In 1819, there were 11 free states and 11 slave states. Missouri's application to Congress to join the Union as a slave state was strongly opposed by the North. To end the debate, Henry Clay proposed the Missouri Compromise. Find the terms of the compromise. What did the North and the South get?

## Math in Action

### Using the Distance Formula

A car leaves Boston at the same time a train leaves New York. The car is traveling at 60 miles per hour. The train is traveling at 40 miles per hour. How long will it take the car and the train to cross paths if Boston and New York are 220 miles apart?

First, find the relative speed of the car and the train by adding each of their speeds. This is how much closer they get to each other every hour.

60 miles per hour + 40 miles per hour = 100 miles per hour

Use the distance formula to find how long it will take for the car to meet the train.

$$\text{time} = \frac{\text{distance}}{\text{speed}} = \frac{220 \text{ miles}}{100 \text{ miles per hour}}$$

= 2.2 hours until the car and train cross paths

Now you try it!

How long would it take the car and train to meet if they were both traveling at 55 miles per hour? What if they were both traveling 65 miles per hour but started 650 miles apart?

CHECKPOINT

Your multilevel list should look like this.

Level 1 topics in multilevel list

The·Thirteen·Colonies¶
I)→Introduction:·Reasons·for·Colonization¶
II)→Religious·and·political·freedom¶
III)→Puritans·and·the·Great·Migration¶
IV)→French·Huguenots·and·Catholics¶
V)→Economic·gain¶
VI)→The·Thirteen·Original·Colonies·by·Region¶
VII)→New·England·Colonies·(1620-1636)¶
VIII)→Connecticut,·Massachusetts,·New·Hampshire,·and·Rhode·Island¶
IX)→Religious·and·political·freedom¶
X)→Middle·Colonies·(1664-1776)¶
XI)→Delaware,·New·Jersey,·New·York,·and·Pennsylvania¶
XII)→Farming,·trade,·religious·freedom·and·tolerance¶
XIII)→Southern·Colonies·(1607-1733)¶
XIV)→Georgia,·Maryland,·North·Carolina,·South·Carolina,·and·Virginia¶
XV)→Wealthy·landowners¶
XVI)→Debtors·and·small·farmers¶
XVII)→Religious·freedom·and·tolerance¶

By default, *Word* formats all of the selected paragraphs as Level 1 main topics. Clicking the Increase Indent button in the Paragraph group indents or demotes the selected topic to the next lower multilevel list level.

To move or promote a topic to the next highest multilevel list level, click the Decrease Indent button in the Paragraph group. *Word* automatically applies the correct multilevel list number or letter to the demoted or promoted topic.

To demote or promote topics efficiently, select multiple topics using the CTRL key and then demote or promote them all at once by clicking the Increase Indent or Decrease Indent button.

Check out Appendix A in the back of this book for an example of a three-level multilevel list and other document formats!

Another way to create a multilevel list (or outline) is to click the Outline view button in the View Shortcuts on the status bar to switch to Outline view. Then demote and promote selected text by clicking buttons in the Outline Tools group on the Outlining tab. Try it!

## Apply It!

**Let's demote multiple topics to multilevel list Levels 2 and 3.**

Home | Paragraph | Increase Indent

1. Select the *Religious and political freedom* paragraph. Then press and hold the CTRL key and select the following paragraphs: *Economic gain, New England Colonies (1620-1636), Middle Colonies (1664-1776),* and *Southern Colonies (1607-1733).* Release the CTRL key.

# Project Skills Review

**Find specific data in Datasheet view**

Click the **Find** button in the Find group on the **Home** tab.

**Sort a table or query**

Click a field to identify the sort criteria and then click the **Ascending** or **Descending** button in the Sort & Filter group on the **Home** tab.

Ascending

Descending

**Filter a table or query by selection**

Click a field to identify the filter criteria. Click the **Selection** button in the Sort & Filter group on the **Home** tab and then click a filter option.

Selection

**Toggle a filter on or off**

Click the **Toggle Filter** button in the Sort & Filter group on the **Home** tab or click the **Filter indicator** in the **record navigation bar**.

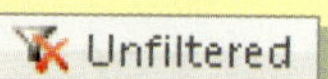


**Clear a filter**

Right-click any field in the filtered data and click **Clear Filter From [Field]**.
Click the **Filter** symbol in the filtered column header and click **Clear Filter From [Field]**.

**Print Preview a datasheet**

*Access 2010*: click the **File** tab, click **Print**, and click **Print Preview**.
*Access 2007*: click the **Office Button**, point to **Print**, and click **Print Preview**.

**Print a datasheet**

Click the **Print** button in the Print group on the **Print Preview** tab.

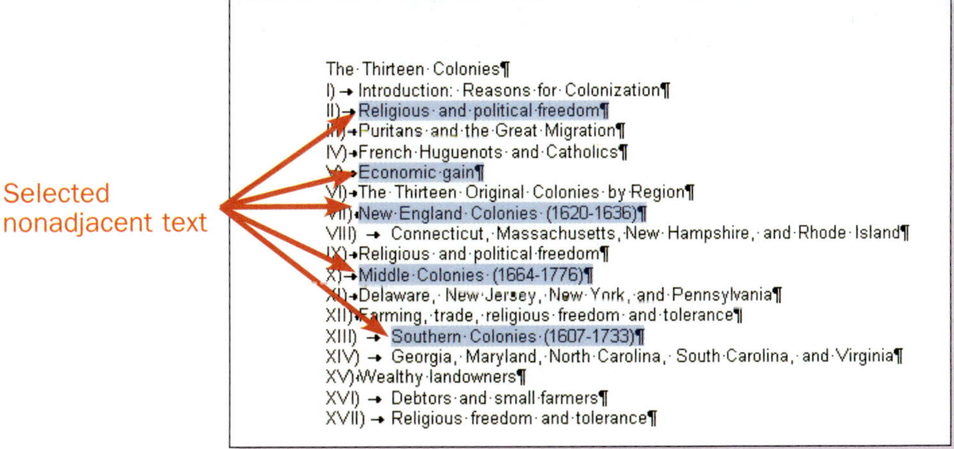


2. Click the **Increase Indent** button in the Paragraph group and deselect the text. The selected paragraphs are demoted to multilevel list Level 2 subtopics. 
3. Select the *Puritans and the Great Migration* paragraph. Press and hold the CTRL key and select the *French Huguenots and Catholics* paragraph. Release the CTRL key.
4. Click the **Increase Indent** button in the Paragraph group *twice*. The selected paragraphs are demoted to multilevel list Level 3 details.
5. Select all of the remaining paragraphs *except* the Level 1 main topics (*Introduction: Reasons for Colonization and The Thirteen Original Colonies by Region*) and the Level 2 subtopics; then demote the paragraphs you selected to Level 3 details.
6. Deselect the Level 3 details.

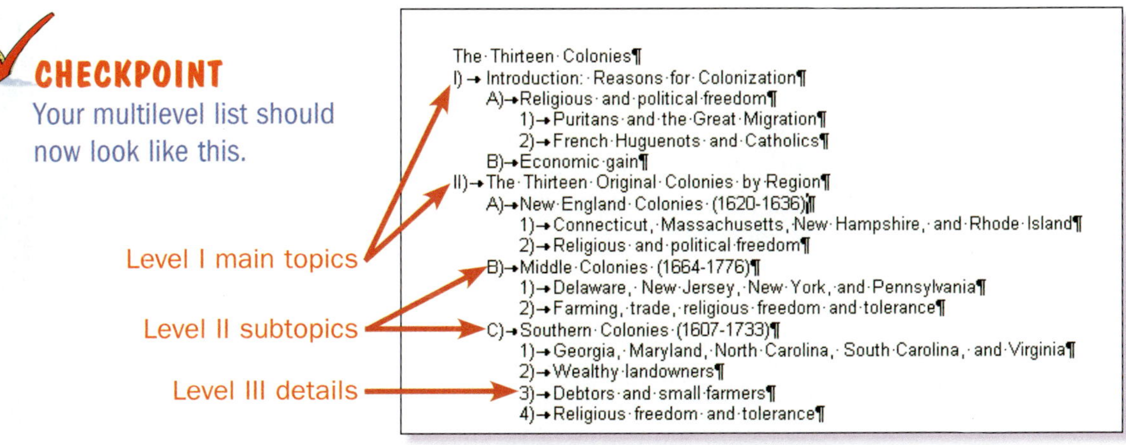


Terrific! Next, you will position the document's text more attractively on the page by setting the document's margins.

# Project Skills Review

You learned a lot in this project! We are very impressed with your progress. Let's take a few minutes to review the skills that you learned.

| | |
|---|---|
| **Open a database file** | *Access 2010*: click **Open** on the **File** tab. *Access 2007*: click the **More** link in the Open Recent Database list on the right side of the **Getting Started with Access** page. |
| **Open a database object in the workspace:**<br>• **a table in Datasheet view**<br>• **a query in Datasheet view**<br>• **a form in Form view**<br>• **a report in Report view** | Double-click the object's name in the Navigation Pane. |
| **Switch to Print Preview when viewing a report in Report view** | Click the **Print Preview** button in the View Shortcuts on the status bar. |
| **Close an open database object** | Click the workspace **Close** button. |
| **Navigate a datasheet** | Use the I-beam, mouse pointer, keyboard, and navigation buttons to move from record to record and field to field. |
| **Edit a record in Datasheet view** | Open the table in Datasheet view. Select a field and key new data. Move to a different record to save the changes to the record. |
| **Add a new record to a table in Datasheet view** | Open the table in Datasheet view. Click the **New (blank) record** button in the **record navigation bar**. Enter the data for each field. Move to a different record to save the new record. |
| **Delete a record in Datasheet view** | Open the table in Datasheet view. Click the **record selector** for the record to be deleted. Click the **Delete (Del)** button in the Records group on the **Home** tab or tap the DELETE key. |

## Changing Document Margins

A margin is the amount of white space between the edge of the top, bottom, left, and right sides of a page and the keyed text. Different types of documents require different sized margins. For example, a multilevel list document should have 2-inch top, left, and right margins and a 1-inch bottom margin.

By default, *Word* automatically sets 1-inch top and bottom margins and 1-inch left and right margins for each new document. You can change a document's margins, when necessary, by clicking the Page Layout tab and then clicking the Margins button in the Page Setup group to view a gallery of margin setting options. You can also set custom margins by clicking Custom Margins at the bottom of the gallery.

The fastest way to move from option to option in a dialog box is by tapping the TAB key. Try it!

**Let's change the margins for the *colonies list2* document to 2-inch top, left, and right margins and a 1-inch bottom margin.**

Page Layout | Page Setup | Margins

1. Click the **Page Layout** tab on the Ribbon and locate the **Page Setup** group.
2. Click the **Margins** button in the Page Setup group to view a gallery of margin options.

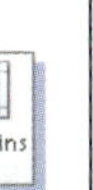


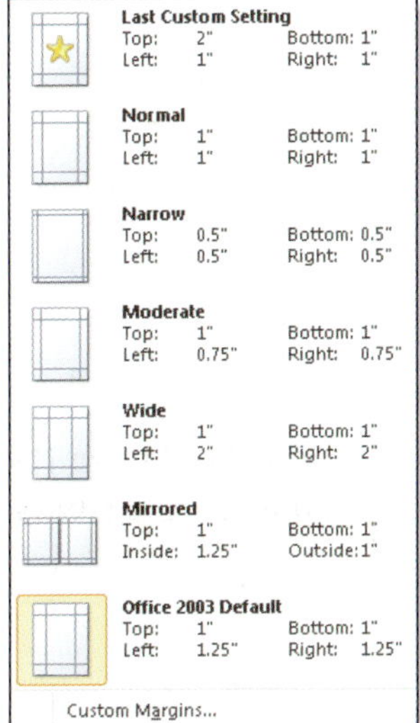

3. Click the **datasheet** with the zoom pointer to magnify the datasheet.
4. Click the **datasheet** with the zoom pointer to reduce the magnification.
5. With permission, click the **Print** button in the Print group on the Print Preview tab to print the query datasheet.

6. Click the workspace **Close** button to close the query in Print Preview.

7. Click the workspace **Close** button to close the *States* table.

Remember that you created a filter for the U.S. Region column, which alters the table's design. You must choose to save the new table design with the filter or close the table without saving it.

8. Click **No** in the confirmation dialog box to close the table datasheet without saving the changes to the table's design.
9. Close *Access* and the *states16 solution* database.

Good job updating Ray's database!

3. Click **Custom Margins** to open the Page Setup dialog box and set these custom margins for the multilevel list:
   - Key **2** in the Top, Left, and Right text boxes.
   - Leave **1** in the Bottom text box.

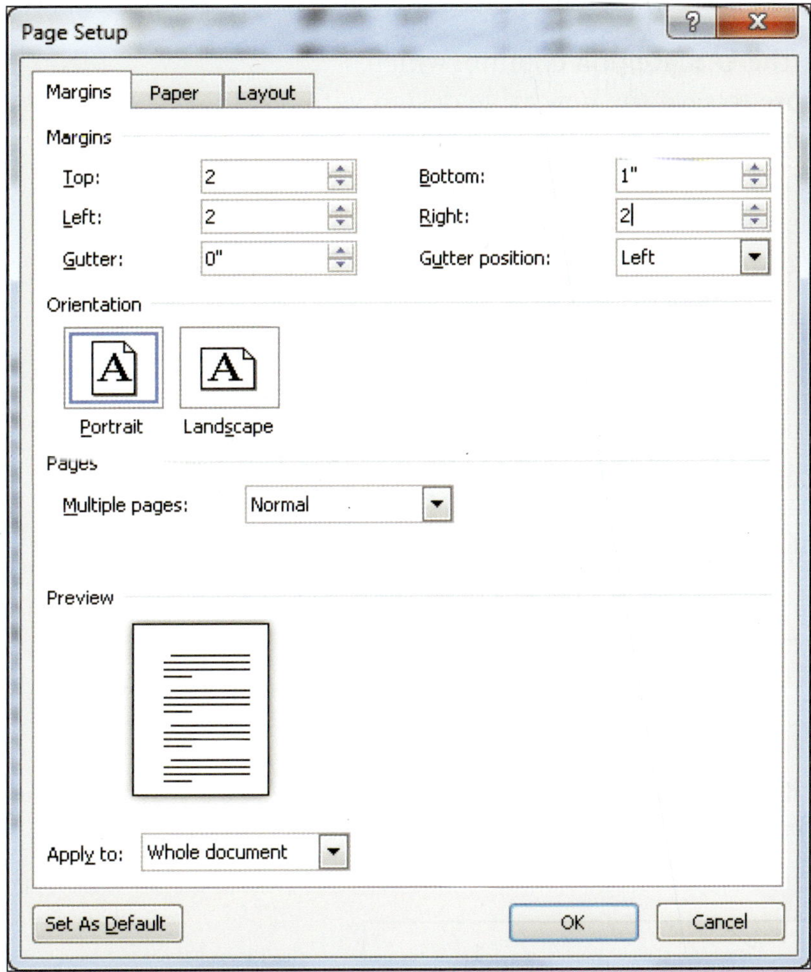


4. Click **OK** and save the document.

Fantastic! Next, you will change the multilevel list title's horizontal alignment and change the multilevel list's line spacing.

Here's another way to open the Page Setup dialog box. Click the Page Layout tab and click the Dialog Box Launcher icon in the bottom right corner of the Page Setup group. Try it!

6. With permission, click the **Print** button in the Print group on the Print Preview tab to print the query datasheet.
7. Click the workspace **Close** button to close the query in Print Preview.

8. Click the workspace **Close** button to close the *States* table.

Remember that you created a filter for the U.S. Region column, which alters the table's design. You must choose to save the new table design with the filter or close the table without saving it.

9. Click **No** in the confirmation dialog box to close the table datasheet without saving the changes to the table's design.
10. Close *Access* and the *states16 solution* database.

Congratulations on updating Ray's database!

**Previewing a Datasheet in *Access 2007***

You can preview and print a datasheet much like you preview and print an *Excel* worksheet by clicking Print Preview on the Office Button Print submenu. When you Print Preview a datasheet, the datasheet opens in Print Preview in the workspace and the Print Preview tab appears on the Ribbon.

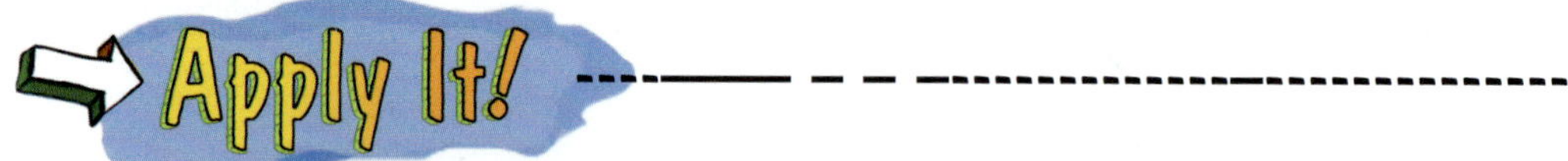


**Let's preview the datasheet.**

1. Click the **Office Button**, point to **Print**, and click **Print Preview**.
2. Move the mouse pointer over the previewed datasheet; the mouse pointer becomes a zoom pointer.

Statehood After January 1, 1850 4/29/20--

| State Name | Statehood |
|---|---|
| California | 9/9/1850 |
| Minnesota | 5/11/1858 |
| Oregon | 2/14/1859 |
| Kansas | 1/29/1861 |
| West Virginia | 6/20/1863 |
| Nevada | 10/31/1864 |
| Nebraska | 3/1/1867 |
| Colorado | 8/1/1876 |
| South Dakota | 11/2/1889 |
| North Dakota | 11/2/1889 |
| Montana | 11/8/1889 |
| Washington | 11/11/1889 |
| Idaho | 7/3/1890 |
| Wyoming | 7/10/1890 |
| Utah | 1/4/1896 |
| Oklahoma | 11/16/1907 |
| New Mexico | 1/6/1912 |
| Arizona | 2/14/1912 |
| Alaska | 1/3/1959 |
| Hawaii | 8/21/1959 |

## Applying Paragraph Formatting

A multilevel list's title paragraph should be centered between the left and right margins and should use default spacing. In Project 1, you learned that *Word* uses a special formatting definition for a paragraph—all of the text that precedes a paragraph mark. When you position text on the page by indenting paragraphs, aligning paragraphs horizontally between the left and right margins, or setting paragraph line spacing, you are applying paragraph formatting.

To select a single paragraph for paragraph formatting, simply move the insertion point into the paragraph. To apply paragraph formatting to multiple paragraphs, you must select them with the I-beam pointer or another selection method.

Selected paragraphs can be aligned horizontally between the left and right margins at the center, left, or right side of the page by clicking the Home tab and then clicking the Align Text Left, Center, or Align Text Right button in the Paragraph group.

Line spacing specifies the amount of white space between the lines of text. The default *Word* line and paragraph spacing is 1.15 line spacing with 10 points of extra white space following each paragraph.

You can also apply paragraph formatting to change indents, horizontal alignment, and line spacing in the Paragraph dialog box. To open the dialog box, click the Home tab and then click the Dialog Box Launcher icon in the bottom right corner of the Paragraph group.

**Let's center the multilevel list's title paragraph and change the line and paragraph spacing for its body paragraphs.**

Home | Paragraph | Center

Home | Paragraph | Line and Paragraph Spacing

Page Layout | Paragraph | Spacing After

1. Click the **Home** tab on the Ribbon and locate the **Paragraph** group.
2. Click the title paragraph at the top of the page to position the insertion point inside the paragraph and select it for paragraph formatting.
3. Click the **Center** button in the Paragraph group to center the entire paragraph between the left and right margins. 
4. Click immediately in front of the title paragraph.
5. Tap the CTRL + SHIFT + END keys to select all of the paragraphs from the insertion point to the end of the document.
6. Click the **Line and Paragraph Spacing** button in the Paragraph group and click **1.15**. 
7. Click the **Page Layout** tab and locate the **Paragraph** group.
8. Key **10 pt** in the Spacing After text box in the Paragraph group and press ENTER.
9. Deselect the text and save the document.

## Previewing and Printing a Datasheet

A printed datasheet is a great tool you can use to visually verify your data entry.

### Previewing a Datasheet in *Access 2010*

You can preview and print a datasheet much like you preview and print an *Excel* worksheet by clicking the File tab to switch to Backstage view and then clicking Print to view print options.

When you click the Print Preview option, the datasheet is previewed in the workspace and the Print Preview tab appears on the Ribbon.

**Let's preview the datasheet.**

1. Click the **File** tab and click **Print**.
2. Click **Print Preview** to preview the datasheet in the workspace.
3. Move the mouse pointer over the previewed datasheet; the mouse pointer becomes a zoom pointer.

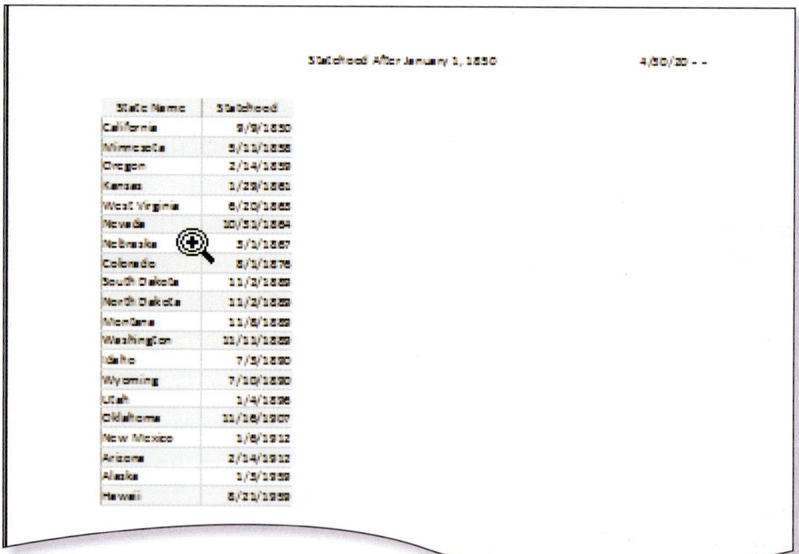

Statehood After January 1, 1850 4/30/20 - -

| State Name | Statehood |
|---|---|
| California | 9/9/1850 |
| Minnesota | 5/11/1858 |
| Oregon | 2/14/1859 |
| Kansas | 1/29/1861 |
| West Virginia | 6/20/1863 |
| Nevada | 10/31/1864 |
| Nebraska | 3/1/1867 |
| Colorado | 8/1/1876 |
| South Dakota | 11/2/1889 |
| North Dakota | 11/2/1889 |
| Montana | 11/8/1889 |
| Washington | 11/11/1889 |
| Idaho | 7/3/1890 |
| Wyoming | 7/10/1890 |
| Utah | 1/4/1896 |
| Oklahoma | 11/16/1907 |
| New Mexico | 1/6/1912 |
| Arizona | 2/14/1912 |
| Alaska | 1/3/1959 |
| Hawaii | 8/21/1959 |

4. Click the **datasheet** with the zoom pointer to magnify the datasheet.
5. Click the **datasheet** with the zoom pointer to reduce the magnification.

Your multilevel list should now look like this.

The Thirteen Colonies

I) Introduction: Reasons for Colonization
  A) Religious and political freedom
    1) Puritans and the Great Migration
    2) French Huguenots and Catholics
  B) Economic gain
II) The Thirteen Original Colonies by Region
  A) New England Colonies (1620-1636)
    1) Connecticut, Massachusetts, New Hampshire, and Rhode Island
    2) Religious and political freedom
  B) Middle Colonies (1664-1776)
    1) Delaware, New Jersey, New York, and Pennsylvania
    2) Farming, trade, religious freedom and tolerance
  C) Southern Colonies (1607-1733)
    1) Georgia, Maryland, North Carolina, South Carolina, and Virginia
    2) Wealthy landowners
    3) Debtors and small farmers
    4) Religious freedom and tolerance

Excellent! Next, let's make the multilevel list more attractive and easier to read by changing the text font's shape, size, and case.

## Applying Character Formatting

Changing the appearance of one or more characters, or letters, is called character formatting and includes changing the font, font size, and case.

### Font and Font Size

A font or typeface is the way letters and numbers are shaped. Commonly used fonts include Calibri, Times New Roman, and Arial. Other available fonts depend on which fonts are installed on your computer. Font size is measured in points; the larger the point size, the larger the text.

To change multiple character formats at one time, open the Font dialog box by clicking the Home tab and then clicking the Dialog Box Launcher icon in the bottom right corner of the Font group. Then apply font size, font face, font color, font styles, and other character formats to the selected text.

### Running a Query

As you learned earlier in this project, a query is a question you ask about the data in a table. Like filtering, opening a query object is another great way to find specific data. Opening a query object is commonly called running a query.

**Let's run the *Statehood After January 1, 1850* query.**

1. Double-click the *Statehood After January 1, 1850* query name in the Navigation Pane to run the query. Notice that the query datasheet now contains 20 records including Hawaii, which was just added to the table.

Your query should look like this.

States | Statehood After January 1, 1850

| State Name | Statehood |
|---|---|
| California | 9/9/1850 |
| Minnesota | 5/11/1858 |
| Oregon | 2/14/1859 |
| Kansas | 1/29/1861 |
| West Virginia | 6/20/1863 |
| Nevada | 10/31/1864 |
| Nebraska | 3/1/1867 |
| Colorado | 8/1/1876 |
| South Dakota | 11/2/1889 |
| North Dakota | 11/2/1889 |
| Montana | 11/8/1889 |
| Washington | 11/11/1889 |
| Idaho | 7/3/1890 |
| Wyoming | 7/10/1890 |
| Utah | 1/4/1896 |
| Oklahoma | 11/16/1907 |
| New Mexico | 1/6/1912 |
| Arizona | 2/14/1912 |
| Alaska | 1/3/1959 |
| Hawaii | 8/21/1959 |
| * | |

Query displays updated records

Did you know that you can also sort and filter the results of a query? Try it! If you do not want the sort order or filter to be saved as part of the query design, click No when you close the Print Preview window or the query datasheet.

Leave the query datasheet open for the next Trail Marker, where you will preview and, with permission, print it.

To change the font and font size for an entire document, select all of the text in the document by pressing the CTRL + A keyboard shortcut keys or by clicking the Home tab, clicking the Select button in the Editing group, and then clicking Select All.

Next, click the Home tab, if necessary; click the Font and Font Size box arrows in the Font group; and click a new font and font size.

*Word* has a great feature called Live Preview that allows you to see how text in your document will look with different formatting *before* you apply it! For example, just point to a font or font size in the drop-down list and see the changes in your document. To apply the formatting, click the font or font size option in the list.

*Word* automatically uses the Calibri 11-point font for body text in all new documents you create.

Home | Font | Font or Font Size

**Ray's *colonies list2* document is currently formatted with the Arial 10-point font. Let's select the entire *colonies list2* document and change the font and font size to the default Calibri 11 point.**

1. Press the CTRL + A keys to select the entire document.
2. Click the **Home** tab, if necessary, and locate the **Font** group.
3. Click the **Font** box arrow in the Font group and point to **Calibri** to preview the new font in your document. Scroll the font list, if necessary, to see the font name.
4. Click **Calibri** to apply the new font. Calibri (Body)
5. Click the **Font Size** box arrow and point to **11** to preview the new font size.
6. Click **11** to apply the font size. 11
7. Deselect the text and save the document.

### Text Case

Text case refers to the look of the letters or characters. Letters or characters can be uppercase (capitals) or lowercase (non-capital letters). *Word* also has other text cases that you can apply to text.

You can select the text and choose one of several case options by clicking the Home tab and then clicking the Change Case button in the Font group.

A filter symbol also appears to the right of the field name in the column (field) header. You can point to the filter icon in the column header to view a ScreenTip about the applied filter. To see a menu of sorting and filtering options, click the filter symbol.

**Let's review the filter ScreenTip, toggle the filter off and on, and then remove the filter.**

**Home | Sort & Filter | Toggle Filter**

1. Point to the **filter** icon in the U.S. Region column header to view the ScreenTip.

| ID | State Name | Abbrev. | Statehood | Entity of Origin | U.S. Region | Capital | Est. 2 |
|---|---|---|---|---|---|---|---|
| 19 | Indiana | IN | 12/11/1816 | Indiana Territory | Midwest | | |
| 29 | Iowa | IA | 12/28/1846 | Iowa Territory | Midwest | Des Moines | |



2. Click **Filter indicator (Filtered)** in the record navigation pane to toggle the filter off and view all of the records.
3. Click **Filter indicator (Unfiltered)** in the record navigation pane to toggle the filter on.
4. Click the **filter** symbol for the U.S. Region column to select the fields in the column and to view a menu of sorting and filtering options.
5. Click **Clear Filter From U.S. Region** on the shortcut menu.

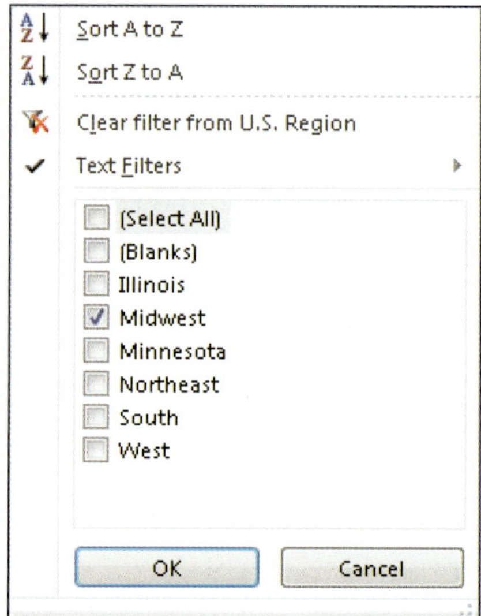


Outstanding! Next, you run a query.

You can also toggle a filter on or off by clicking the Home tab and then clicking the Toggle Filter button in the Sort & Filter group. Try it!

**Let's change the case of the title and Level 1 paragraphs from Title Case to UPPERCASE.**

Home | Font | Change Case

1. Select the title at the top of the page; then use the CTRL key to select both Level 1 topics.
2. Click the **Home** tab, if necessary, and locate the **Font** group.
3. Click the **Change Case** button in the Font group to view a gallery of case options.
4. Click **UPPERCASE** to apply the formatting and deselect the text.

**CHECKPOINT**
Your multilevel list's title and Level 1 topics should now look like this.

THE THIRTEEN COLONIES¶

I)→ INTRODUCTION: REASONS FOR COLONIZATION¶
A)→Religious and political freedom¶
1)→Puritans and the Great Migration¶
2)→French Huguenots and Catholics¶
B)→Economic gain¶
II)→THE THIRTEEN ORIGINAL COLONIES BY REGION¶
A)→New England Colonies (1620-1636)¶
1)→Connecticut, Massachusetts, New Hampshire, and Rhode Island¶
2)→Religious and political freedom¶
B)→Middle Colonies (1664-1776)¶
1)→Delaware, New Jersey, New York, and Pennsylvania¶
2)→Farming, trade, religious freedom and tolerance¶
C)→Southern Colonies (1607-1733)¶
1)→Georgia, Maryland, North Carolina, South Carolina, and Virginia¶
2)→Wealthy landowners¶
3)→Debtors and small farmers¶
4)→Religious freedom and tolerance¶

5. Save and close the document.

Congratulations! Ray's multilevel list is ready to go. Next, you need to format the report Ray wrote based on his multilevel list. Ray indicated formatting changes with notes and proofreaders' marks.

## Following Proofreaders' Marks

Proofreading each document you create to look for errors or formatting changes is very important. Ray proofread his report document and used proofreaders' marks to show mistakes such as missing words, spaces, and punctuation. He also marked changes to the font and font size, margins, the main heading's style; line spacing, and other formatting. Here are Ray's marked changes.

- To see all of the records again, you can toggle the filter off by clicking the Toggle Filter button in the Sort & Filter group. To view the filtered records again, just click the Toggle Filter button to toggle the filter on.

A table can have multiple filters. You can permanently remove a filter from a field by right-clicking the field in any record and clicking Clear Filter From (Field) on the shortcut menu. You can click the Advanced button in the Sort & Filter group and click Clear All Filters to permanently remove all of a table's filters.

*Warning! Applying a filter to a table changes the table's design to add the filter. When you close the table, you are prompted to save the design changes. In this project, you will remove the filter before you close the table.*

You can also filter a table using common preset filters by clicking a shortcut menu command or by clicking the Home tab and clicking the Filter button in the Sort & Filter group.

**Let's filter the records and then remove the filter.**

**Home | Sort & Filter | Selection**

1. Click the **U.S. Region** field for the Indiana record, record 19.
2. Click the **Selection** button in the Sort & Filter group to view the filter options.
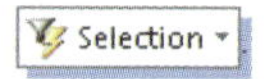

3. Click **Equals "Midwest"** in the menu. The records for the ten Midwestern states appear in the datasheet. The first record is selected, and the Current Record box in the record navigation bar indicates record 1 of 10.

Your filtered data should look like this.

Filtered records

States

| ID | State Name | Abbrev. | Statehood | Entity of Origin | U.S. Region | Capital | Est. 2 |
|---|---|---|---|---|---|---|---|
| 19 | Indiana | IN | 12/11/1816 | Indiana Territory | Midwest | Indianapolis | |
| 29 | Iowa | IA | 12/28/1846 | Iowa Territory | Midwest | Des Moines | |
| 34 | Kansas | KS | 1/29/1861 | Kansas Territory | Midwest | Topeka | |
| 26 | Michigan | MI | 1/26/1837 | Michigan Territory | Midwest | Lansing | |
| 24 | Missouri | MO | 8/10/1821 | Missouri Territory | Midwest | Jefferson City | |
| 37 | Nebraska | NE | 3/1/1867 | Nebraska Territory | Midwest | Lincoln | |
| 40 | North Dakota | ND | 11/2/1889 | Dakota Territory | Midwest | North Dakota | |
| 17 | Ohio | OH | 3/1/1803 | Northwest Territory | Midwest | Columbus | |
| 39 | South Dakota | SD | 11/2/1889 | Dakota Territory | Midwest | Pierre | |
| 30 | Wisconsin | WI | 5/29/1848 | Wisconsin Territory | Midwest | Madison | |
| (New) | | | | | | | |

When a filter is applied, the Filter indicator in the record navigation bar at the bottom of the datasheet contains the filter icon or symbol and the word *Filtered*. You can click the Filter indicator to turn the filter off or on.

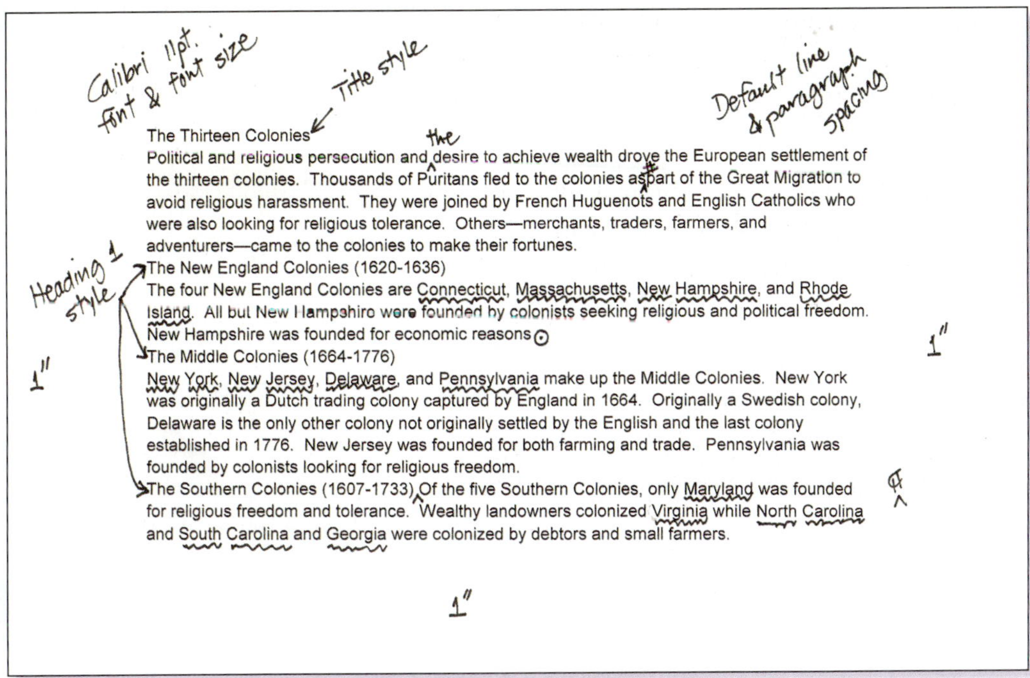


Ray's notes indicate the correct layout for a single-page unbound report:

- A 2-inch top margin and 1-inch left, right, and bottom margins are used.
- The text is formatted with the Calibri font and 11-point font size.
- The main heading or title is left-aligned and formatted with the Title style.
- Paragraph headings are left-aligned and formatted with the Heading 1 style.
- The body text paragraphs are left-aligned and formatted with the 1.15 default line spacing and 10 points of white space default paragraph spacing.
- The thirteen colony names are bolded for emphasis.

A style is a collection of different formats you can apply all at one time. Styles include paragraph styles you apply to entire paragraphs, such as report titles and paragraph headings, and character styles you apply to individual characters, single words, or multiple selected words.

**Let's sort the data and then save the sort order.**

Home | Sort & Filter | Ascending

1. Click the **State Name** field *in any record* to select this field as the sort criteria.
2. Click the **Home** tab, if necessary, and locate the **Sort & Filter** group.
3. Click the **Ascending** button in the Sort & Filter group. Ascending
4. Click the **Save** button on the Quick Access Toolbar to save the table in the current sort order.

**CHECKPOINT**
Your sorted datasheet should look like this.

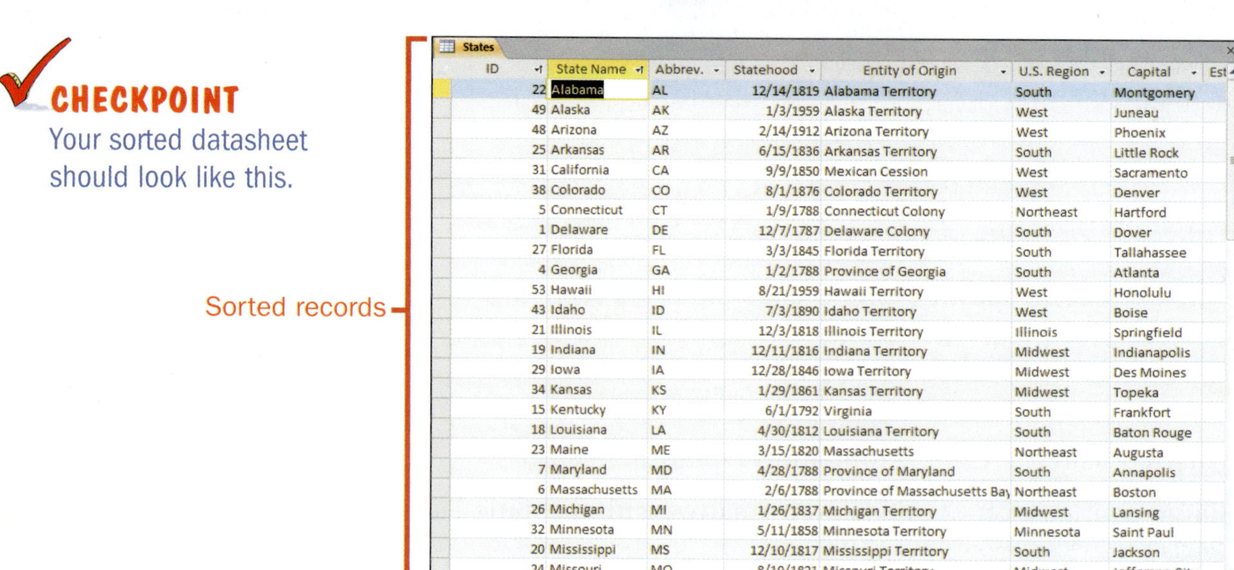


| ID | State Name | Abbrev. | Statehood | Entity of Origin | U.S. Region | Capital | Est |
|---|---|---|---|---|---|---|---|
| 22 | Alabama | AL | 12/14/1819 | Alabama Territory | South | Montgomery | |
| 49 | Alaska | AK | 1/3/1959 | Alaska Territory | West | Juneau | |
| 48 | Arizona | AZ | 2/14/1912 | Arizona Territory | West | Phoenix | |
| 25 | Arkansas | AR | 6/15/1836 | Arkansas Territory | South | Little Rock | |
| 31 | California | CA | 9/9/1850 | Mexican Cession | West | Sacramento | |
| 38 | Colorado | CO | 8/1/1876 | Colorado Territory | West | Denver | |
| 5 | Connecticut | CT | 1/9/1788 | Connecticut Colony | Northeast | Hartford | |
| 1 | Delaware | DE | 12/7/1787 | Delaware Colony | South | Dover | |
| 27 | Florida | FL | 3/3/1845 | Florida Territory | South | Tallahassee | |
| 4 | Georgia | GA | 1/2/1788 | Province of Georgia | South | Atlanta | |
| 53 | Hawaii | HI | 8/21/1959 | Hawaii Territory | West | Honolulu | |
| 43 | Idaho | ID | 7/3/1890 | Idaho Territory | West | Boise | |
| 21 | Illinois | IL | 12/3/1818 | Illinois Territory | Illinois | Springfield | |
| 19 | Indiana | IN | 12/11/1816 | Indiana Territory | Midwest | Indianapolis | |
| 29 | Iowa | IA | 12/28/1846 | Iowa Territory | Midwest | Des Moines | |
| 34 | Kansas | KS | 1/29/1861 | Kansas Territory | Midwest | Topeka | |
| 15 | Kentucky | KY | 6/1/1792 | Virginia | South | Frankfort | |
| 18 | Louisiana | LA | 4/30/1812 | Louisiana Territory | South | Baton Rouge | |
| 23 | Maine | ME | 3/15/1820 | Massachusetts | Northeast | Augusta | |
| 7 | Maryland | MD | 4/28/1788 | Province of Maryland | South | Annapolis | |
| 6 | Massachusetts | MA | 2/6/1788 | Province of Massachusetts Ba) | Northeast | Boston | |
| 26 | Michigan | MI | 1/26/1837 | Michigan Territory | Midwest | Lansing | |
| 32 | Minnesota | MN | 5/11/1858 | Minnesota Territory | Minnesota | Saint Paul | |
| 20 | Mississippi | MS | 12/10/1817 | Mississippi Territory | South | Jackson | |
| 24 | Missouri | MO | 8/10/1821 | Missouri Territory | Midwest | Jefferson City | |

Now let's filter the data to see the records for states in the Midwest region.

**Filtering Data**

In the *Excel* unit, you learned how to filter a data range to see specific records. You can also filter a table in Datasheet view to find all of the records that have the same data in a specific field. This is called filtering by selection.

For example, suppose you want to see only the records for all states in the Midwest region. You can filter the table to show only those records that have *Midwest* in the *U.S. Region* field. Just move the insertion point into the *U.S. Region* field for *any record* where the field contains *Midwest*. This selects the data on which the records are to be filtered.

- Click the Home tab and click the Selection button in the Sort & Filter group to view a menu of filter by selection options. The options you see on the menu will vary depending on the type of data you are filtering.

You can apply paragraph styles, such as the Title style and Heading 1 style, to selected text by clicking the Home tab and clicking a style from the Styles gallery in the Styles group. To remove paragraph style formatting from selected text, click Clear Formatting below the styles gallery or click the Home tab and click the Clear Formatting button in the Font group.

To select an entire paragraph for formatting, simply move the insertion point into the paragraph. Try it!

*Word* also provides three font styles—Bold, Italic, and Underline—which are commonly used to add emphasis to individual characters, entire words, or phrases and are part of character formatting.

**The Bold style makes text darker.** *The Italic style slants text to the right.*

The default Underline style adds a line underneath words and spaces.

You can apply a font style to and remove it from selected text by clicking the Home tab and then clicking the Bold, Italic, or Underline buttons in the Font group.

To select a single word for the Bold, Underline, or Italic font style, just move the insertion point into the word. Then apply the style you want. Try it!

## Apply It!

Page Layout|Page Setup|Margins

Home|Font|Font or Font Size

Home|Paragraph|Line and Paragraph Spacing

Page Layout|Paragraph|Spacing After

**Let's follow Ray's notes and proofreaders' marks as shown in Figure 2-10 to format his report document. First, you will change the margins, change the font and font size, and change the line and paragraph spacing.**

1. Open the *colonies* document and save it as *colonies2*.
2. Click the **Page Layout** tab and locate the **Page Setup** group.
3. Click the **Margins** button and click **Custom Margins**. Change the document's margins to 2-inch top and 1-inch left, right, and bottom margins.
4. Tap the CTRL + A keys to select all of the text in the document.
5. Click the **Home** tab and locate the **Font** group.
6. Click the **Font** button in the Font group and click **Calibri**.
7. Click the **Font Size** button in the Font group and click **11**.
8. Locate the **Paragraph** group on the **Home** tab.
9. Click the **Line and Paragraph Spacing** button in the Paragraph group and click **1.15**.
10. Click the **Page Layout** tab and locate the **Paragraph** group.
11. Key **10 pt** in the Spacing After text box in the Paragraph group.
12. Deselect the text.

**Let's delete a record.**

**Home | Records | Delete (Del)**

1. Tap the CTRL + HOME keys.
2. Click the *State Name* field for the first record; open the **Find and Replace** dialog box and find a record for Michigan (ID=26).
3. Click the **Find Next** button to find a second record for Michigan (ID=52).
4. Cancel the **Find and Replace** dialog box.
5. Click the **record selector** for the second Michigan record (ID=52) to select the entire record.
6. Click the **Home** tab, if necessary, and locate the **Records** group.
7. Click the **Delete (Del)** button face in the Records group; then click **Yes** in the confirmation dialog box to confirm the deletion.

X Delete

The duplicate Michigan record is deleted. The *States* table again has 50 records.

Another way to delete a selected record is to right-click the record selector and click Delete Record on the shortcut menu. You can also tap the DELETE key to delete a selected record.

Outstanding! Now let's learn how to sort and filter a table in Datasheet view.

## Sorting, Filtering, and Querying Data

You can sort records in a datasheet just like you sort data in an *Excel* data range. First, move the insertion point into the field you want to sort; then click the Home tab and click the Ascending or Descending buttons in the Sort & Filter group.

To keep the records in the new sorted order, save the table before you close it. If you want to keep the records in their original order, close the table *without* saving it. The *States* data would be easier to work with if you viewed it in ascending alphabetical order by state name.

Your report should now look like this.

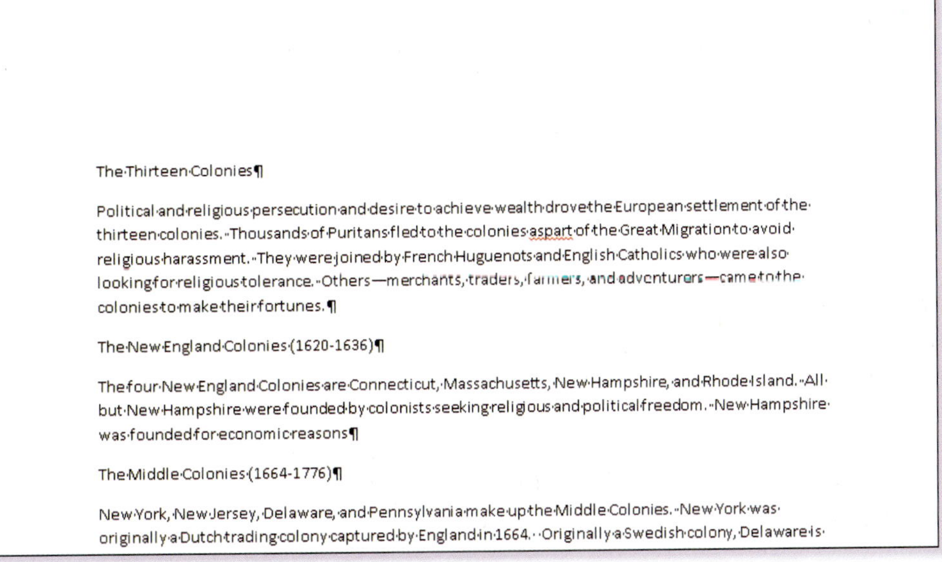

The·Thirteen·Colonies¶

Political·and·religious·persecution·and·desire·to·achieve·wealth·drove·the·European·settlement·of·the·thirteen·colonies.··Thousands·of·Puritans·fled·to·the·colonies·aspart·of·the·Great·Migration·to·avoid·religious·harassment.··They·were·joined·by·French·Huguenots·and·English·Catholics·who·were·also·looking·for·religious·tolerance.··Others—merchants,·traders,·farmers,·and·adventurers—came·to·the·colonies·to·make·their·fortunes.¶

The·New·England·Colonies·(1620-1636)¶

The·four·New·England·Colonies·are·Connecticut,·Massachusetts,·New·Hampshire,·and·Rhode·Island.··All·but·New·Hampshire·were·founded·by·colonists·seeking·religious·and·political·freedom.··New·Hampshire·was·founded·for·economic·reasons¶

The·Middle·Colonies·(1664-1776)¶

New·York,·New·Jersey,·Delaware,·and·Pennsylvania·make·up·the·Middle·Colonies.··New·York·was·originally·a·Dutch·trading·colony·captured·by·England·in·1664.··Originally·a·Swedish·colony,·Delaware·is·

Now you are ready to apply styles to the main and paragraph headings and then insert missing words, spaces, and punctuation.

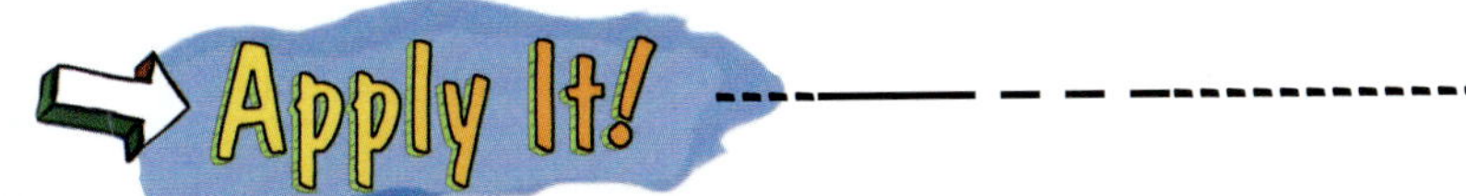


**Let's apply the Title and Heading 1 styles and insert missing words, spaces, and punctuation.**

**Home | Styles | More**

**Home | Font | Bold**

1. Move the insertion point into the report's main heading, The Thirteen Colonies, to select the paragraph.
2. Click the **Home** tab, if necessary, and locate the **Styles** group.
3. Click the **More** button in the Styles group, if necessary, to view the styles gallery.
4. Point to the **Title style** icon to live preview the style applied to the main heading; then click the **Title style** icon to apply the style.
5. Scroll to view the last paragraph, if necessary, and move the insertion point between the closing parenthesis and the word *Of* in the first line.
6. Tap the enter key to separate the paragraph heading from its following body text paragraph.
7. Select the entire first paragraph heading using the mouse pointer and the selection bar to the left of the paragraph.

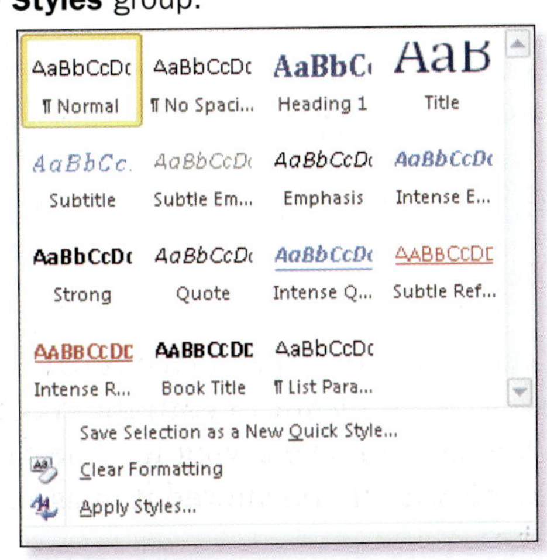

You now must add a record for a missing state—Hawaii—using the following notes from Ray:

| State Name | Abbrev. | Statehood | Entity of Origin |
|---|---|---|---|
| Hawaii | HI | 8/21/1959 | Hawaii Territory |
| **U.S. Region** | **Capital** | **Est. 2015 Pop.** | **Area in Sq. Mi.** |
| West | Honolulu | 1,553,000 | 10,931 |

**Let's add a new record for Hawaii. You will add the data for all of the fields except Source 1 and Source 2. These fields are set up to automatically contain the same information for each new record. The fields for the population and area data are preformatted to contain the thousands separator, so you do not key the comma.**

1. Click the **New (Blank) record** navigation button to move to the blank row at the bottom of the datasheet.
2. Tap the TAB key to move the insertion point into the *State Name* field.
3. Key **Hawaii** in the *State Name* field and tap the TAB key. *Access assigns the next AutoNumber. The pencil symbol in the record selector tells you that you are editing the record and that the changes* have not *been saved.*

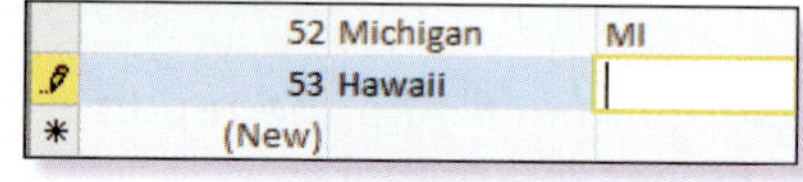


4. Key **HI** in the *Abbrev.* field and tap the TAB key.
5. Use Ray's notes to add the remaining data for Hawaii. *Do not key the thousands separator for the population or area data.*
6. Tap the **Down** arrow to move off the record and save it.

Fantastic! Now let's delete a duplicate record.

### Deleting a Record

To delete a record, first select it by clicking its record selector. Then click the Home tab and click the Delete button in the Records group or tap the DELETE key.

When you delete a record with an AutoNumber ID field, all of the remaining records keep their AutoNumber ID; the AutoNumber ID of the deleted record is not reused.

8. Tap and hold the CTRL key and select the remaining two paragraph headings.
9. Click the **Home** tab, if necessary, and click the **More** button in the Styles group to display the styles gallery.
10. Point to the **Heading 1** style icon to live preview the style applied to the selected paragraph headings; then click the **Heading 1** style icon.
11. Follow Ray's proofreaders' marks in Figure 2-10 to:
    - insert the missing word *the* before the word *desire*
    - insert the missing space between *aspart*
    - insert the missing punctuation following *economic reasons*
12. Use the CTRL key to select the names of the thirteen colonies *the first time they appear in the report*: **Connecticut, Massachusetts, New Hampshire, Rhode Island, New York, New Jersey, Delaware, Pennsylvania, Maryland, Virginia, North Carolina, South Carolina,** and **Georgia**.
13. Click the **Home** tab, if necessary, and locate the **Font** group.
14. Click the **Bold** button in the Font group; then deselect the text.

**CHECKPOINT**

Well done! Ray's formatted document should now look like this.

## The Thirteen Colonies¶

Political and religious persecution and the desire to achieve wealth drove the European settlement of the thirteen colonies. Thousands of Puritans fled to the colonies as part of the Great Migration to avoid religious harassment. They were joined by French Huguenots and English Catholics who were also looking for religious tolerance. Others—merchants, traders, farmers, and adventurers—came to the colonies to make their fortunes.¶

### The New England Colonies (1620-1636)¶

The four New England Colonies are **Connecticut**, **Massachusetts**, **New Hampshire**, and **Rhode Island**. All but New Hampshire were founded by colonists seeking religious and political freedom. New Hampshire was founded for economic reasons.¶

### The Middle Colonies (1664-1776)¶

**New York**, **New Jersey**, **Delaware**, and **Pennsylvania** make up the Middle Colonies. New York was originally a Dutch trading colony captured by England in 1664. Originally a Swedish colony, Delaware is the only other colony not originally settled by the English and the last colony established in 1776. New Jersey was founded for both farming and trade. Pennsylvania was founded by colonists looking for religious freedom.¶

### The Southern Colonies (1607-1733)¶

Of the five Southern Colonies, only **Maryland** was founded for religious freedom and tolerance. Wealthy landowners colonized **Virginia** while **North Carolina** and **South Carolina** and **Georgia** were colonized by debtors and small farmers.¶

15. Save and close the document.

In this and the remaining projects in this unit, there are no instructions to preview and print your documents. Your teacher will tell you which documents to print.

5. Click the **Find Next** button to find the record for Ohio.
6. Close the **Find and Replace** dialog box and tap the TAB key twice to select the contents of the *Statehood* field in the Ohio record (record 17).
7. Key **03** and look carefully at the field. The *Statehood* field is formatted to automatically insert the forward slashes in the date and to accept two characters for the month, two characters for the day, and four characters for the year.

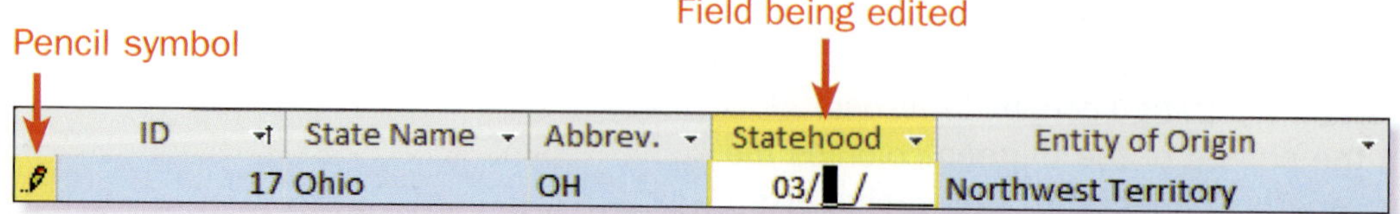


8. Continue by keying **01** and **1803** in the appropriate positions in the formatted date. Look at the record selector for the record. It still has a pencil symbol, meaning that the change to the record is not yet saved.

| ID | State Name | Abbrev. | Statehood | Entity of Origin |
|---|---|---|---|---|
| 17 | Ohio | OH | 03/01/1803 | Northwest Territory |

9. Tap the **Down** arrow key to move to the next record. The change to the Ohio record is saved. The leading zeroes in the month **03** and the day **01** are dropped.

Well done! Next, let's add two new records.

**Adding Records**

Each record in a table must have a unique identifying number. In the *States* table, this number appears in the first column, the *ID* field. When you add a new record to the *States* table, *Access* automatically assigns it a unique record number called an AutoNumber. *Access* assigns the next unused AutoNumber as you add records. The AutoNumbers for deleted records are not reused.

For example, look carefully at the *ID* field in the *States* datasheet. The *ID* field contains consecutive numbers from 1–49, then number 52. Two records—originally numbered 50 and 51—have already been deleted from the table. When Ray added the next record for Michigan, *Access* assigned the next unused AutoNumber—52.

*Remember!* An AutoNumber is used to uniquely identify each record rather than to indicate the total number of records in the table. Look in the Current Record text box in the navigation buttons to see the total number of records in the table.

# Project Skills Review

You learned a lot in this project! We are very impressed with your progress. Let's take a few minutes to review the skills that you learned.

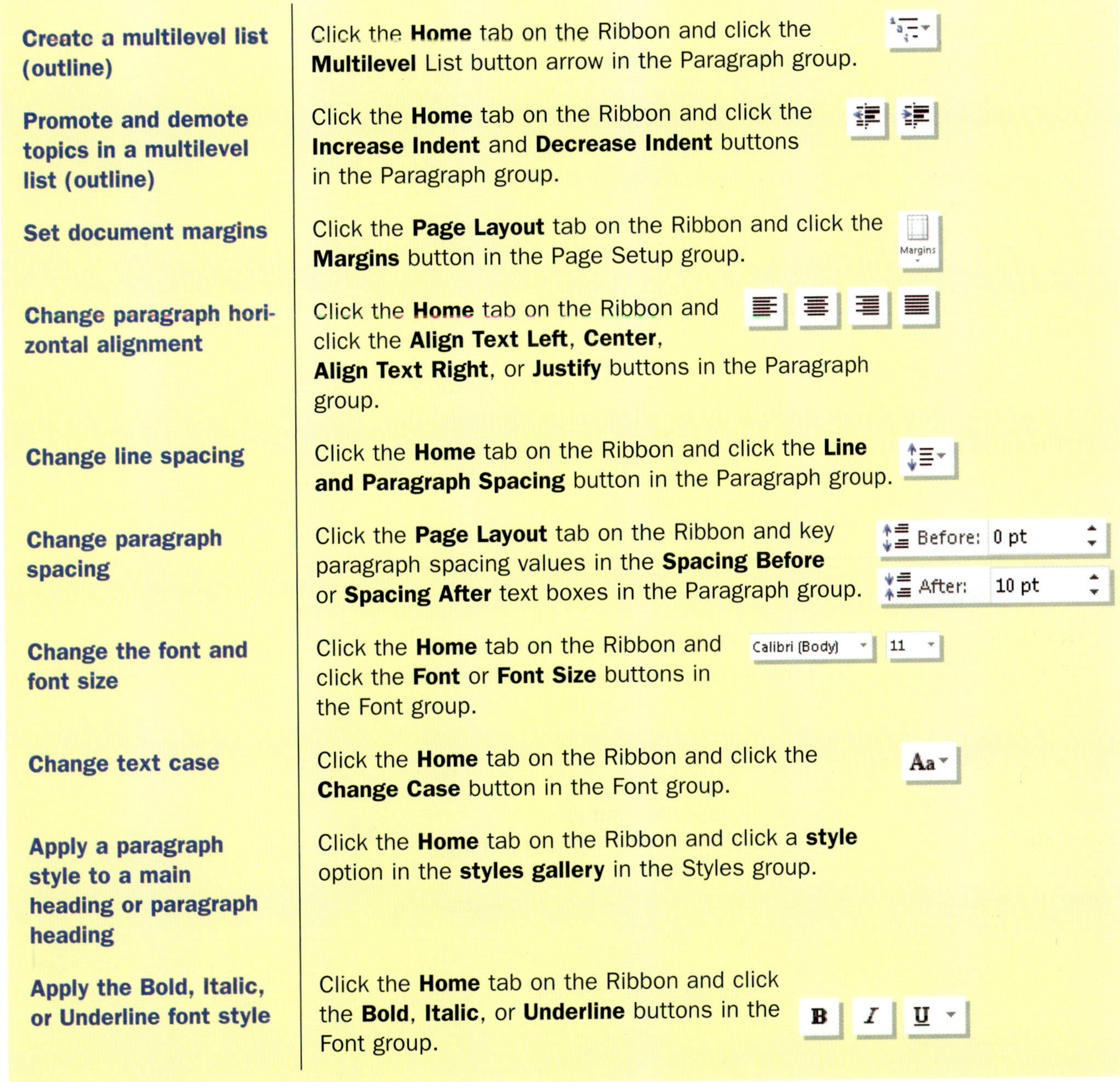

| Skill | How to |
|---|---|
| **Create a multilevel list (outline)** | Click the **Home** tab on the Ribbon and click the **Multilevel** List button arrow in the Paragraph group. |
| **Promote and demote topics in a multilevel list (outline)** | Click the **Home** tab on the Ribbon and click the **Increase Indent** and **Decrease Indent** buttons in the Paragraph group. |
| **Set document margins** | Click the **Page Layout** tab on the Ribbon and click the **Margins** button in the Page Setup group. |
| **Change paragraph horizontal alignment** | Click the **Home** tab on the Ribbon and click the **Align Text Left**, **Center**, **Align Text Right**, or **Justify** buttons in the Paragraph group. |
| **Change line spacing** | Click the **Home** tab on the Ribbon and click the **Line and Paragraph Spacing** button in the Paragraph group. |
| **Change paragraph spacing** | Click the **Page Layout** tab on the Ribbon and key paragraph spacing values in the **Spacing Before** or **Spacing After** text boxes in the Paragraph group. |
| **Change the font and font size** | Click the **Home** tab on the Ribbon and click the **Font** or **Font Size** buttons in the Font group. |
| **Change text case** | Click the **Home** tab on the Ribbon and click the **Change Case** button in the Font group. |
| **Apply a paragraph style to a main heading or paragraph heading** | Click the **Home** tab on the Ribbon and click a **style** option in the **styles gallery** in the Styles group. |
| **Apply the Bold, Italic, or Underline font style** | Click the **Home** tab on the Ribbon and click the **Bold**, **Italic**, or **Underline** buttons in the Font group. |

4. Tap the **Down** arrow key three times to move to the *Statehood* field in the fourth record.
5. Tap the SHIFT + TAB keys twice to move to the *State Name* field in the same record.
6. Move the I-beam to the *Entity of Origin* field in the next record and click to position the insertion point in the field.
7. Click the *U.S. Region* **field selector** to select the entire *U.S. Region* column.
8. Click the **record selector** for any record (row) to select the entire row.
9. Tap the CTRL + HOME keys.
10. Click the **Last record** button in the navigation buttons to move to the last record.
11. Click the **Previous record** button in the navigation buttons to move to the previous record.
12. Key **10** in the Record number box in the navigation buttons and tap the ENTER key to move to the 10th record.
13. Tap the CTRL + HOME keys.

Super! Now let's edit a record.

### Editing a Record

To select the entire contents of a field, you can move the mouse pointer to the left edge of the field where it becomes a large white plus sign selection pointer. Click the field with the large white plus pointer to select its contents.

**Let's find the record for Ohio and edit it to change the statehood date. Before you begin, make sure you are looking at the *States* table in Datasheet view.**

Home | Find | Find

1. Click the *State Name* field in any record to position the insertion point in the field.
2. Click the **Home** tab, if necessary, and locate the **Find** group.
3. Click the **Find** button in the Find group to open the Find and Replace dialog box.
4. Key **Ohio** in the Find What text box. The Current Field (or State Name in *Access 2007*) option appears in the Look In list.

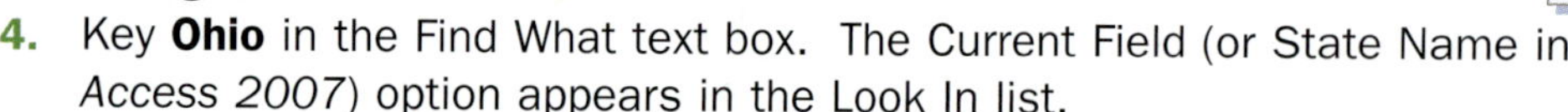

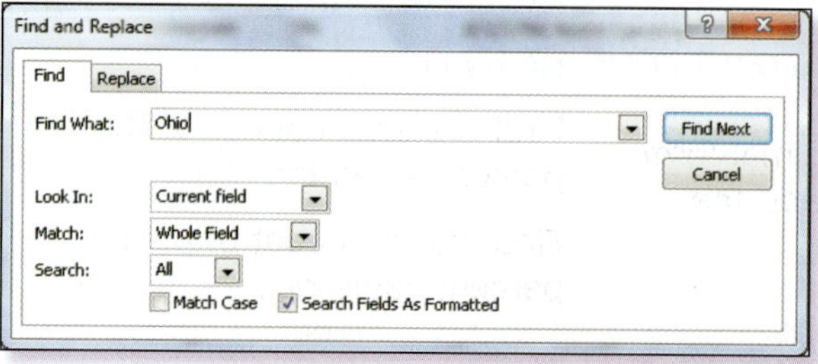

# Exploring On Your Own

## Blaze Your Own Trail

You have learned several new skills in this project. Now blaze your own trail by practicing these skills on your own! Research one of the thirteen original English colonies. Who were the first Europeans to settle the area? When was the colony settled? What were the characteristics of the early colony? Take notes and organize them into a multilevel list you can use to write a single-page unbound report. Then complete Parts 1, 2, and 3 as instructed by your teacher.

**Part 1:** Create a new document and save it as *list2*.

1. Change the document's margins to the appropriate margins for a multilevel list.
2. Key a centered, uppercase title; tap the ENTER key; and key your brief research notes in a list.
3. Select the body text below the title and format it as a multilevel list. Use the I, II, III, A, B, C, 1, 2, 3 number system for Levels 1, 2, and 3, respectively. Demote the subtopics and details using the Increase Indent button.
4. Select the Level 1 topics and change the case to UPPERCASE, if necessary.
5. Check the spelling and grammar; then save and close the document.

**Part 2:** Create a new blank document and save it as *report2*.

1. Set the correct margins for a single-page unbound report.
2. Key a main heading and key a single-page report about the colony, using your multilevel list as your guide.
3. Format your report by applying the Title style to the main heading and the Heading 1 style to paragraph headings; use the default 1.15 line spacing with 10 points of spacing after each paragraph.
4. Check the spelling and grammar; then save the document and close it.

**Part 3:** With permission, reopen the documents and preview and print them. Ask a classmate to proofread the documents carefully and use proofreaders' marks to note any changes you should make. Then follow the proofreaders' marks to edit the documents. Save the documents with a new name and close them.

## Reading in Action — Organization of Details

Details can be organized in chronological order (the order in which events occurred), order of importance, or spatial order (the physical arrangement of places). Read the *colonies2* document. Find an example of spatial order and an example of order of importance in the document.

## Math in Action — Finding Percentages

States have a sales tax they charge on goods. How much does a $12 box of tea cost if there is a 7.25 percent sales tax?

Convert the sales tax percentage to decimal form. Multiply the decimal by the price; then add the product to the original price.

$7.25\% \div 100 = 0.0725$

(\$12 * 0.0725) + \$12 = \$0.87 + \$12 = \$12.87

Now you try it!

Find the total cost of a $20 box of tea with an 8.5 percent sales tax.

Find the total cost of an $8 box of tea with a 5.25 percent sales tax.

## Editing, Adding, and Deleting Records

You can navigate a datasheet very much like you navigated an *Excel* worksheet. For example, you can:

- click the field selector (column header) to select the entire column
- click the record selector (row header) to select the entire row
- tap the CTRL + HOME keys to select the first field in the first record (the top of the table)
- tap the CTRL + END keys to select the last field in the last record (the end of the table)
- use the I-beam to position the insertion point in a field or to select field contents
- select the contents of a field by clicking the field's left boundary with the large white mouse pointer
- move right and left from field to field in the same record using the TAB key, ENTER key, SHIFT + TAB keys, or arrow key
- move up and down from record to record using the Up or Down arrow key

You also can add, edit, and delete records in a table datasheet, much like you added, edited, and deleted data in an *Excel* worksheet.

When you are working in a specific record, several different symbols can appear in its row header. For example, the black right-pointing arrow symbol indicates the current record, and a pencil symbol indicates unsaved changes you have made to a record. To save the changes, just move to a different record.

The Quick Access Toolbar and the Mini Toolbar you learned about in earlier units are also available in *Access*.

**Let's navigate through the datasheet to view different records and fields. Before you begin, make certain the *States* datasheet is open in the workspace.**

1. Tap the CTRL + END keys to move to the last field (Source 2) in the last record.
2. Tap the CTRL + HOME keys to move to the ID field in the first record.
3. Tap the TAB key three times to move to the *Statehood* field in the same record.

# Exploring *Across the Curriculum*

## Internet/Web

A Web search engine, such as Google or Bing, uses software, called a spider or robot, to locate and index Web pages. A Web directory, such as Yahoo!, is an online search tool that lists links to websites by category.

Open your Web browser and use a favorite or bookmark to view the Learning with Computers Web page (www.cengage.com/school/keyboarding/lwcorange). Click the **Links** option and click **Project 2**. Click the **Google** and **Yahoo!** links to open each search tool's Web page.

Key the keywords *"Benjamin Franklin" + inventor* in the Search text box on each search tool's page. *Do not forget to key the opening and closing quotation marks and the plus sign.* The quotation marks indicate that both words must be found together on the Web page; the plus sign indicates that the page must also contain the word that follows the plus sign. Click the **Search** button to find a list of Web pages that describe Franklin as an inventor. Take notes about what you learn.

**Part 1:** Create a new blank document and save it as *Franklin list2*. Use it to create a properly formatted three-level multilevel list based on your notes.

**Part 2:** Create a second new document and save it as *Franklin2*. Use your multilevel list to create a properly formatted single-page unbound report describing Franklin as an inventor. Remember to check the spelling and grammar in your documents before you save and close them. With permission, ask a classmate to proofread your documents and note corrections.

## Social Studies: Research and Write

Work with a classmate to use library, classroom, or online resources to research the lives of the following famous colonial women: Anne Hutchinson, Abigail Adams, Margaret Corbin, Sybilla Masters, Anne Putnam, Mercy Otis Warren, Deborah Read Franklin, and Phillis Wheatley. Then complete Parts 1, 2, and 3 as assigned by your teacher. Remember to spell-check your documents before you save and close them. Ask a classmate to proofread you documents and note corrections.

**Part 1:** Create a new document and key a title and your research notes. Format the document as a three-level multilevel list.

**Part 2:** Create a properly formatted single-page unbound report based on your multilevel list.

**Part 3:** Use your multilevel list or report to give an oral report to your class about the lives of these famous colonial women.

Explore More

**CHECKPOINT**
Your workspace should look similar to this.

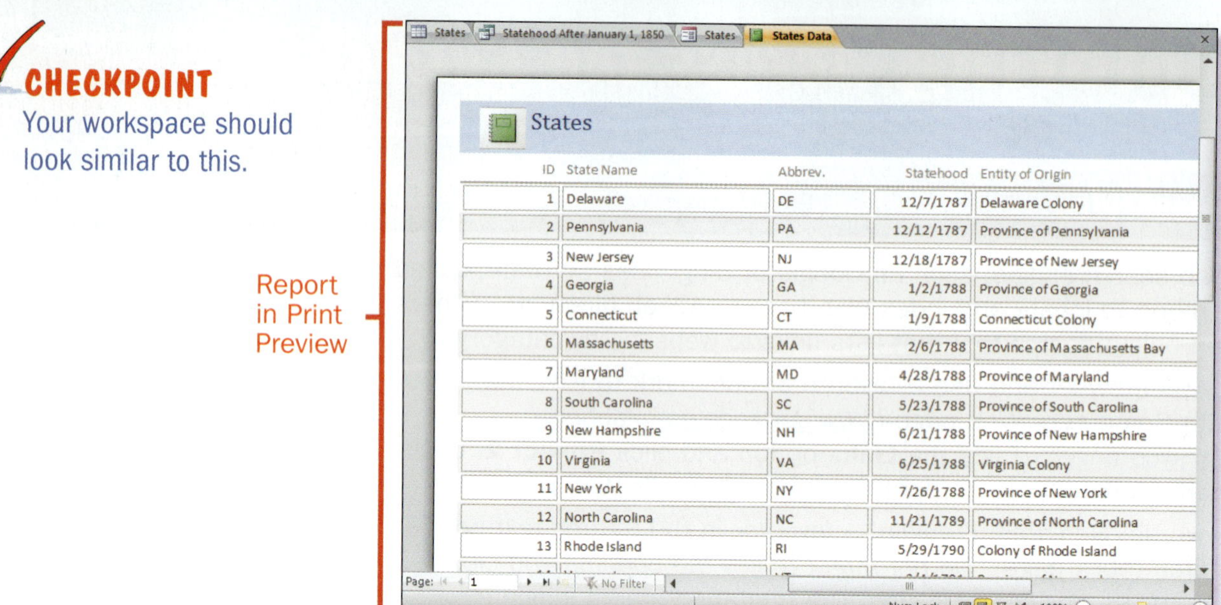


States

| ID | State Name | Abbrev. | Statehood | Entity of Origin |
|---|---|---|---|---|
| 1 | Delaware | DE | 12/7/1787 | Delaware Colony |
| 2 | Pennsylvania | PA | 12/12/1787 | Province of Pennsylvania |
| 3 | New Jersey | NJ | 12/18/1787 | Province of New Jersey |
| 4 | Georgia | GA | 1/2/1788 | Province of Georgia |
| 5 | Connecticut | CT | 1/9/1788 | Connecticut Colony |
| 6 | Massachusetts | MA | 2/6/1788 | Province of Massachusetts Bay |
| 7 | Maryland | MD | 4/28/1788 | Province of Maryland |
| 8 | South Carolina | SC | 5/23/1788 | Province of South Carolina |
| 9 | New Hampshire | NH | 6/21/1788 | Province of New Hampshire |
| 10 | Virginia | VA | 6/25/1788 | Virginia Colony |
| 11 | New York | NY | 7/26/1788 | Province of New York |
| 12 | North Carolina | NC | 11/21/1789 | Province of North Carolina |
| 13 | Rhode Island | RI | 5/29/1790 | Colony of Rhode Island |

Terrific! You have finished checking out all of the objects in the *states16 solution* database. Now let's close the open objects.

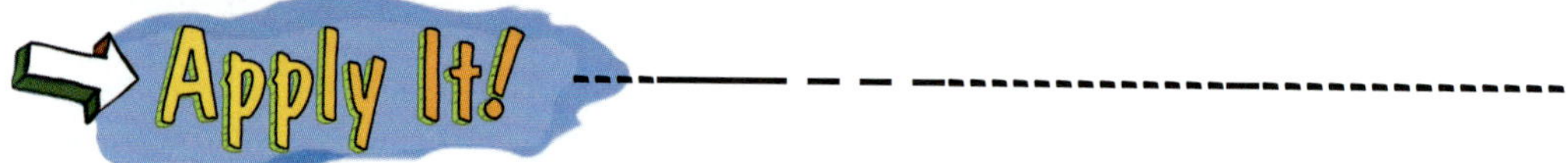


**Let's close the report, form, and query objects.**

1. Click the ***States Data*** report's workspace tab, if necessary, and then click the workspace **Close** button. ×
2. Click the ***States Data Entry Form*** workspace tab, if necessary, and then click the workspace **Close** button. ×
3. Right-click the ***Statehood After January 1, 1850*** workspace tab and click **Close**.

Now that you are more familiar with the objects in the *states16 solution* database, you are ready to make a few changes to the data in the *States* table. You will make your changes in the datasheet.

Remember, an *Access* database is a relational database that can contain multiple table, query, form, and report objects all saved together in *one* file.

# Exploring Across the Curriculum

## Language Arts: Words to Know

Look up the meaning of the following words, terms, or phrases in a classroom dictionary, CD-ROM dictionary or encyclopedia, or online dictionary.

| charter | Enlightenment | Great Awakening | Great Migration |
|---|---|---|---|
| privateer | proprietors | Puritans | taxation |

Create a new document. Save the document as *definitions2* followed by your initials. Change the margins to a 2-inch top margin and 1-inch left, right, and bottom margins. Key **Terms and Definitions** as the main heading at the top of the document. Then key each term on one line and its definition on the next line. Insert a blank line between each definition and the next term. Select all of the terms using the CTRL key and change the font to Arial 12-point Bold. Select the main heading and apply the Title style. Check the spelling and grammar; then save and close the document.

## Getting Help

Click the *Word* Help icon to open the *Word* Help window. Key **keyboard shortcuts** in the search text box and click the Search button to find at least five keyboard shortcuts you can use to apply paragraph and character formatting, such as line spacing or the Bold font style. Then open the *colonies2* document and practice what you learned. Close the document without saving it.

## Career Day

Transporting people, materials, and goods across the thirteen colonies was often a difficult undertaking. Today's modern transportation infrastructure permits the rapid movement of people, materials, and goods across the United States and the world. Using library, printed, or online resources, identify three interesting careers that involve planning, management, and technical support for tomorrow's evolving transportation infrastructure. Write a brief summary of each career, print your summary, and save it in your Career Day folder.

Explore More

CHECKPOINT

Your workspace should now look similar to this.

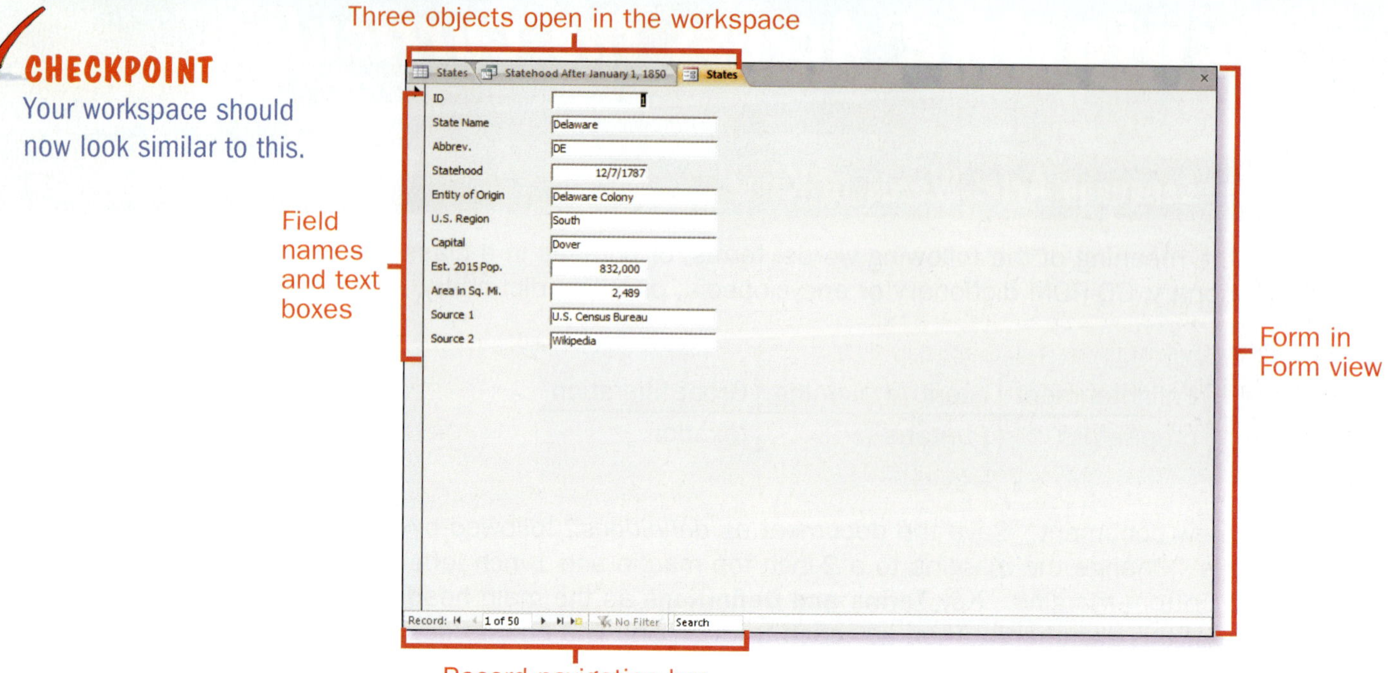


Now let's open the *States Data* report in the workspace.

**Report Objects**

A report is a hard copy or printout of a table's records. You can create a report that shows some or all of the data in a table.

Double-clicking a report object in the Navigation Pane opens the report in the workspace in Report view. You can switch to Print Preview by clicking the Print Preview button in the View Shortcuts on the status bar.

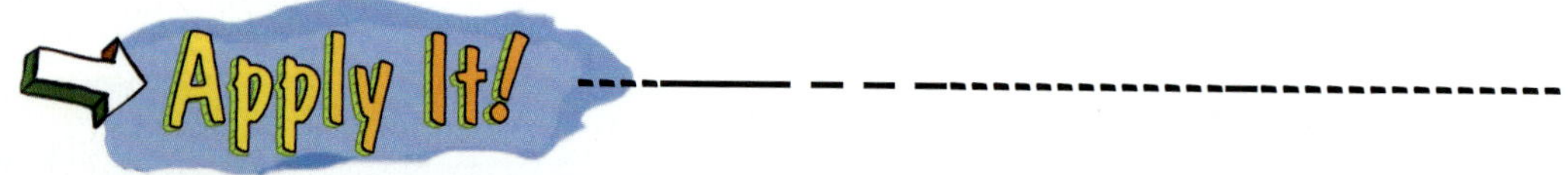


**Let's open the *States Data* report in Report view.**

1. Double-click the ***States Data*** report in the Reports category in the Navigation Pane to open the report in Report view. The *States Data* report uses data from the *States* table to create a list of each record and the data in each field in the record.
2. Click the **Print Preview** button in the View Shortcuts on the status bar. 
3. Scroll the report vertically and horizontally to view all of the records.

# Exploring Across the Curriculum

## Your Personal Journal

Open your personal journal document. Insert today's date. Think about why people were willing to come to a new land. Write a diary entry from the point of view of an early settler, giving your reasons for coming to a colony in the New World. Check the spelling and grammar; then save and close your journal document.

## Online Enrichment Games

www.cengage.com/school/keyboarding/lwcorange

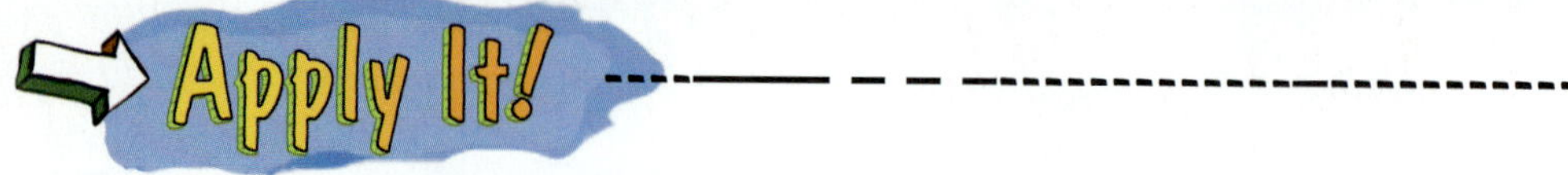


**Let's review the query.**

1. Double-click the *Statehood After January 1, 1850* query name in the Navigation Pane to open the query object in query Datasheet view.

Notice that the query datasheet now shows the name and statehood date for 19 states granted statehood after January 1, 1850. The workspace area now has two objects in Datasheet View: the *States* (table object) and *Statehood After January 1, 1850* (query object). Next, you open and review a form object.

### Form Objects

A form is used to add a new record or to edit data in an existing record. You likely have completed a *paper form* to join a club or to register for a special activity at school. A database form is an electronic version of a paper form.

A form opens in the workspace in Form view and lists all of the fields in a record. Each field has a text box you can use to enter data for a new record or to edit data in an existing record.

Like a datasheet, a form has a record navigation bar with a set of navigation buttons you can click to navigate through existing records or to create a new record. Unlike a datasheet, you can see only one record at a time in a form.

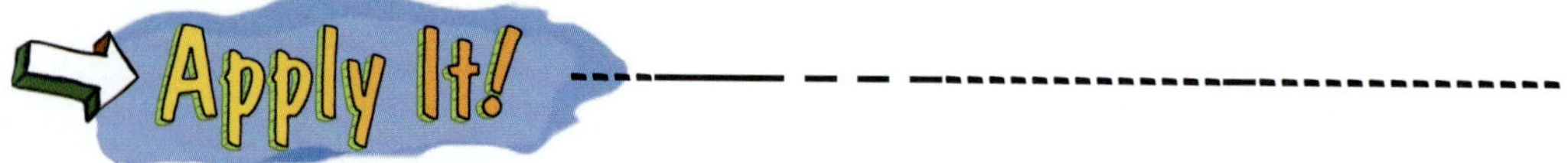


**Let's open the *States Data Entry Form* in Form view in the workspace.**

1. Double-click the ***States Data Entry Form*** name in the Forms category in the Navigation Pane to open the form in Form view. The workspace now has three tabbed documents.
2. Locate the field names, the text boxes containing data for a record, and the form's navigation buttons.

# Project 2

## 2a Review h, e, i, r

Key each line twice. Double-space between 2-line groups.

**h**

1 jh jh | hjh hjh | ha ha | hs hs | hd hd | hf hf | hj hj | hk hk;

2 ash ash | has has | had; had; | half half | lashes lashes;

**e**

3 de de | ede ede | el el | ea ea | es es | ek ek | ef ef | ej ej;

4 ease ease | keel keel | seed seed | jell jell | lead lead;

**i**

5 ki ki | iki iki | i; i; | il il | ik ik | ij ij | ia ia | id id;

6 if if | hi hi | lid lid | fill fill | hike hike | like like;

**r**

7 fr fr | rfr rfr | rd rd | rj rj | rs rs | rk rk | ra ra | rl rl;

8 read read | risk risk | raid raid | here here | dear dear;

**TECHNIQUE TIP**

Keep your fingers curved and upright.

## 2b Technique: ENTER

Key each line twice single-spaced; double-space between 2-line groups.

1 I won.

2 Jonah left.

3 Kay won a medal.

4 Helen read two books.

5 Roberto bought a baseball.

## 2c Build Skills

Key each line twice single-spaced; double-space between 2-line groups.

For additional practice:
**MicroType 5**
New Key Review, Alphabetic Lessons 3-4

1 He may go to the city to fix the bus for the city.

2 The six girls paid for the auto to go to the city.

3 She is to go with them to the city to see the dog.

4 Diane may go to the dock to visit the eight girls.

5 He is to go to the city with us to sign the forms.

*gwam* 20" | 3 | 6 | 9 | 12 | 15 | 18 | 21 | 24 | 27 | 30 |

**Let's open the *States* table in Datasheet view and then check out its records and fields.**

1. Double-click the ***States*** table name in the Navigation Pane to open the table in Datasheet view in the workspace.

Fields

Close button

Records

Table in Datasheet view

| ID | State Name | Abbrev. | Statehood | Entity of Origin | U.S. Region | Capital | Est |
|---|---|---|---|---|---|---|---|
| 1 | Delaware | DE | 12/7/1787 | Delaware Colony | South | Dover | |
| 2 | Pennsylvania | PA | 12/12/1787 | Province of Pennsylvania | Northeast | Harrisburg | |
| 3 | New Jersey | NJ | 12/18/1787 | Province of New Jersey | Northeast | Trenton | |
| 4 | Georgia | GA | 1/2/1788 | Province of Georgia | South | Atlanta | |
| 5 | Connecticut | CT | 1/9/1788 | Connecticut Colony | Northeast | Hartford | |
| 6 | Massachusetts | MA | 2/6/1788 | Province of Massachusetts Bay | Northeast | Boston | |
| 7 | Maryland | MD | 4/28/1788 | Province of Maryland | South | Annapolis | |
| 8 | South Carolina | SC | 5/23/1788 | Province of South Carolina | South | Columbia | |
| 9 | New Hampshire | NH | 6/21/1788 | Province of New Hampshire | Northeast | Concord | |
| 10 | Virginia | VA | 6/25/1788 | Virginia Colony | South | Richmond | |
| 11 | New York | NY | 7/26/1788 | Province of New York | Northeast | Albany | |
| 12 | North Carolina | NC | 11/21/1789 | Province of North Carolina | South | Raleigh | |
| 13 | Rhode Island | RI | 5/29/1790 | Colony of Rhode Island | Northeast | Providence | |
| 14 | Vermont | VT | 3/4/1791 | Province of New York | Northeast | Montpelier | |
| 15 | Kentucky | KY | 6/1/1792 | Virginia | South | Frankfort | |
| 16 | Tennessee | TN | 6/1/1796 | North Carolina | South | Nashville | |
| 17 | Ohio | OH | 3/1/1705 | Northwest Territory | Midwest | Columbus | |
| 18 | Louisiana | LA | 4/30/1812 | Louisiana Territory | South | Baton Rouge | |
| 19 | Indiana | IN | 12/11/1816 | Indiana Territory | Midwest | Indianapolis | |
| 20 | Mississippi | MS | 12/10/1817 | Mississippi Territory | South | Jackson | |
| 21 | Illinois | IL | 12/3/1818 | Illinois Territory | Illinois | Springfield | |
| 22 | Alabama | AL | 12/14/1819 | Alabama Territory | South | Montgomery | |
| 23 | Maine | ME | 3/15/1820 | Massachusetts | Northeast | Augusta | |
| 24 | Missouri | MO | 8/10/1821 | Missouri Territory | Midwest | Jefferson City | |
| 25 | Arkansas | AR | 6/15/1836 | Arkansas Territory | South | Little Rock | |

Record: 1 of 50 No Filter Search

Record navigation bar

2. Scroll the datasheet vertically to see all 50 records.
3. Scroll the datasheet horizontally to see all ten fields in each record.
4. Use ScreenTips to identify the **First record**, **Previous record**, **Next record**, **Last record**, **New (blank) record** buttons and the **Current Record** box, the **Filter indicator**, and the **Search** box in the record navigation bar at the bottom of the datasheet.

You can close a datasheet by clicking its Close button in the top right corner of the workspace. You can also close a datasheet by right-clicking the datasheet's workspace tab and clicking Close on the shortcut menu. Try it!

Next, let's view a query object in the *states16 solution* database.

## Query Objects

A query asks a question of a table object. The *Statehood After January 1, 1850* query in the *states16* database asks the question "Which states were granted statehood after January 1, 1850?" of the *States* table.

# Crossing the Missouri with Lewis and Clark

## Explorers' Guide

**Data file:** Lewis and Clark

**Objectives:**

In this project, you will:

- find and replace text
- select similarly formatted text
- paint formats
- move and duplicate text
- insert page breaks, section breaks, and page numbers
- insert footnotes

## Our Exploration Assignment:

**Formatting a multipage unbound report with footnotes**

Just imagine what Meriwether Lewis and William Clark must have felt as they crossed the Continental Divide and saw the Pacific Ocean for the first time! The Explorers Club is learning about one of the great American adventures—the Lewis and Clark Expedition. Can you help Julie finish her report about Lewis and Clark in time for the next Explorers Club meeting? Great! Just follow the Trail Markers to find and replace text, move and duplicate text, paint formats onto unformatted text, cite Julie's sources with footnotes, insert page and section breaks, and insert page numbers.

© GREG VAUGHN / ALAMY

In a datasheet, the data is organized in rows and columns, similar to an *Excel* worksheet.

- Each *row* in the datasheet is called a record; a record contains all of the data for a single item in the table.
- Each *column* in the datasheet is called a field; a field contains a specific type of data in each record.

For example, each record in the *States* table contains the following fields:

| Field | Data |
|---|---|
| **ID** | unique identifying number |
| **State Name** | name of a state |
| **Abbrev.** | U.S.P.S abbreviation |
| **Statehood** | date statehood was attained |
| **Entity of Origin** | original entity from which the state was formed |
| **U.S. Region** | regional section of the U.S. in which the state is located |
| **Capital** | state's capital city |
| **Est. 2015 Pop.** | estimated state population in 2015 |
| **Area in Sq. Mi.** | total area of the state in square miles |
| **Source 1 and Source 2** | data sources |

Contextual Ribbon tabs (tabs that appear only when needed) are also available in *Access*. For example, when a table is open in Datasheet view, the Table Tools tabs are added to the Ribbon.

At the bottom of the datasheet in the record navigation bar are the navigation buttons that allow you to view specific records: first, previous, next, last, or a specific record by number.

You can also create a new record, filter the records, and search for a specific record using the record navigation bar.

Like an *Excel* worksheet, a datasheet can be scrolled both vertically and horizontally to see all of the rows (records) and columns (fields).

Database objects are often referred to by just their name and object type.

You can right-click a table name in the Navigation Pane and click Open to open the table in Datasheet view. Check it out!

**Begin by opening the *Lewis and Clark* document and saving it with a new name.**

1. Open the *Lewis and Clark* document and save it as *Lewis and Clark3*.
2. Change the top margin to 2 inches and the left, right, and bottom margins to 1 inch.
3. Select all of the text in the document and:
   - change the font to Calibri 11 point
   - change the line spacing to 1.15
   - add 10 points of spacing after each paragraph
   - apply the Title style to the main heading
4. Save the document.

Page Layout | Page Setup | Margins

Home | Paragraph | Line and Paragraph Spacing

Page Layout | Paragraph | Spacing After

Home | Styles | More

Very nice! Next, let's find existing text and replace both the text and the formatting.

**ERGONOMICS TIP**

Are your feet flat on the floor, and is your back is resting against the back of the chair? Good! Let's go!

## Finding and Replacing Text

When you edit a document, you may want to find specific words or phrases that you decide to delete or replace with new text. You can also search for text and change its formatting—for example, by replacing one font style with another.

To find a word in a document to format or replace, click the Find or Replace button in the Editing group on the Home tab. In *Word 2010*, clicking the Find button opens the Navigation Pane. The Navigation Pane is a task pane you can use to find body text or heading text in your document.

Clicking the *Word 2010* Replace button or the *Word 2007* Find or Replace button opens the Find and Replace dialog box. Use options on the Find tab in the Find and Replace dialog box to locate specific text. Use options on the Replace tab to find specific text and then replace it with other text.

Click the More button in the Find and Replace dialog box to set additional search criteria, such as matching case.

| Database Object | Description |
| --- | --- |
| **table** | An object that contains data |
| **query** | An object used to answer a question about the data in a table |
| **form** | An object used to enter or edit table data |
| **report** | An object used to preview and print table data |

Objects are organized in the Navigation Pane by category. You can display the objects in a single category or all categories. To change the view of objects in the Navigation Pane, click the arrow on the Navigation Pane title bar and click a view option.

You can open multiple objects; each open object is represented by a tabbed document in the workspace to the right of the Navigation Pane.

If you cannot see all four objects (a table, query, form, and report) in the Navigation Pane, complete the following Apply It! steps. If your screen looks like the previous Checkpoint figure, skip the steps.

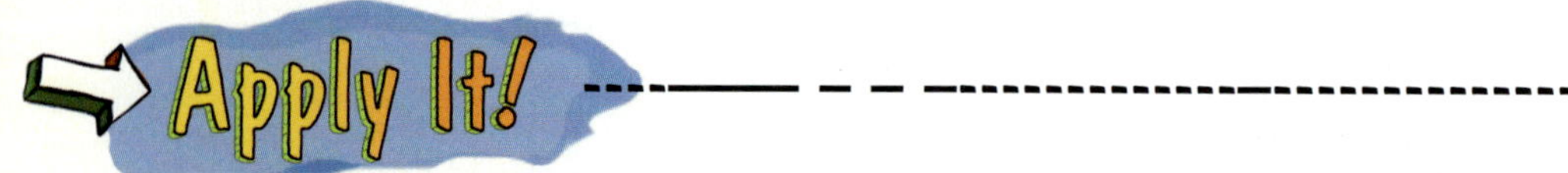


**Let's show all four database objects in the Navigation Pane.**

1. Click the **arrow** on the Navigation Pane title bar to view a menu of object categories and display options.

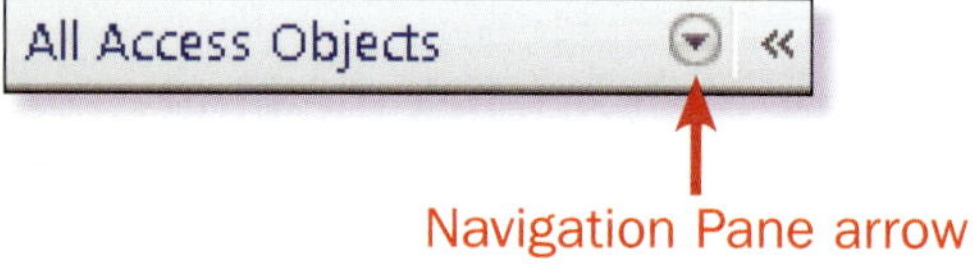


2. Click **All Access Objects**. Your Navigation Pane should now look like the previous Checkpoint figure.

### Table Objects

You can view the data stored in the table by opening the table's datasheet in Datasheet view in the workspace to the right of the Navigation Pane. Double-click a table name in the Navigation Pane to open its datasheet in Datasheet view.

*Warning!* Clicking the Replace All button in the Find and Replace dialog box without first carefully setting the More button search options can return some surprising results!

**Let's find the phrase Louis and Clark Expedition and replace it with the italicized phrase *Lewis and Clark Expedition*.**

Home | Editing | Replace

1. Tap the CTRL + HOME keys to move the insertion point to the top of the document, if necessary.
2. Click the **Home** tab, if necessary, and locate the **Editing** group.
3. Click the **Replace** button in the Editing group to open the Replace tab in the Find and Replace dialog box.
4. Key **Louis and Clark Expedition** in the Find what text box and tap the TAB key.
5. Key **Lewis and Clark Expedition** in the Replace with text box.
6. Click the **More** button to expand the dialog box, if necessary; then click the **Replace with** text box to reposition the insertion point. The More button becomes the Less button used to collapse the dialog box. *Warning! If the insertion point is not in the Replace with text box, the italic formatting will be applied to the wrong text!*
7. Click the **Format** button at the bottom of the dialog box and click **Font** to open the Replace Font dialog box.
8. Click **Italic** in the Font style list and click **OK**.
9. Click the **Less** button to collapse the dialog box. Observe the formatting indicator below the Replace with text box indicating the formatting to be applied.

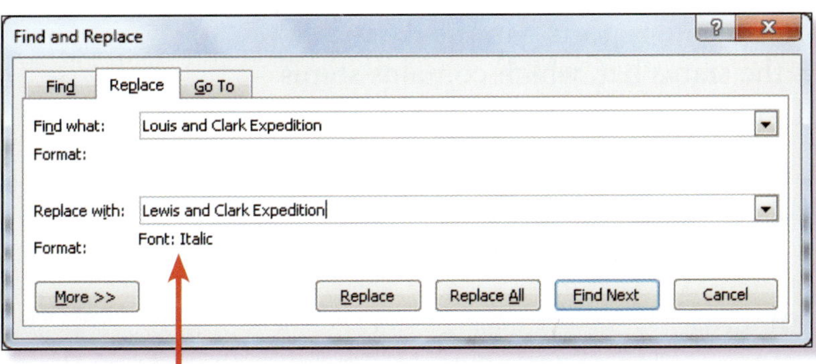


Formatting indicator

10. Click the **Find Next** button to locate and select the first instance of the phrase Louis and Clark Expedition.
11. Click the **Replace** button. The phrase is replaced by the italicized phrase *Lewis and Clark Expedition*. No more instances are found. Click **OK** in the confirmation dialog box. Leave the Find and Replace dialog box open.

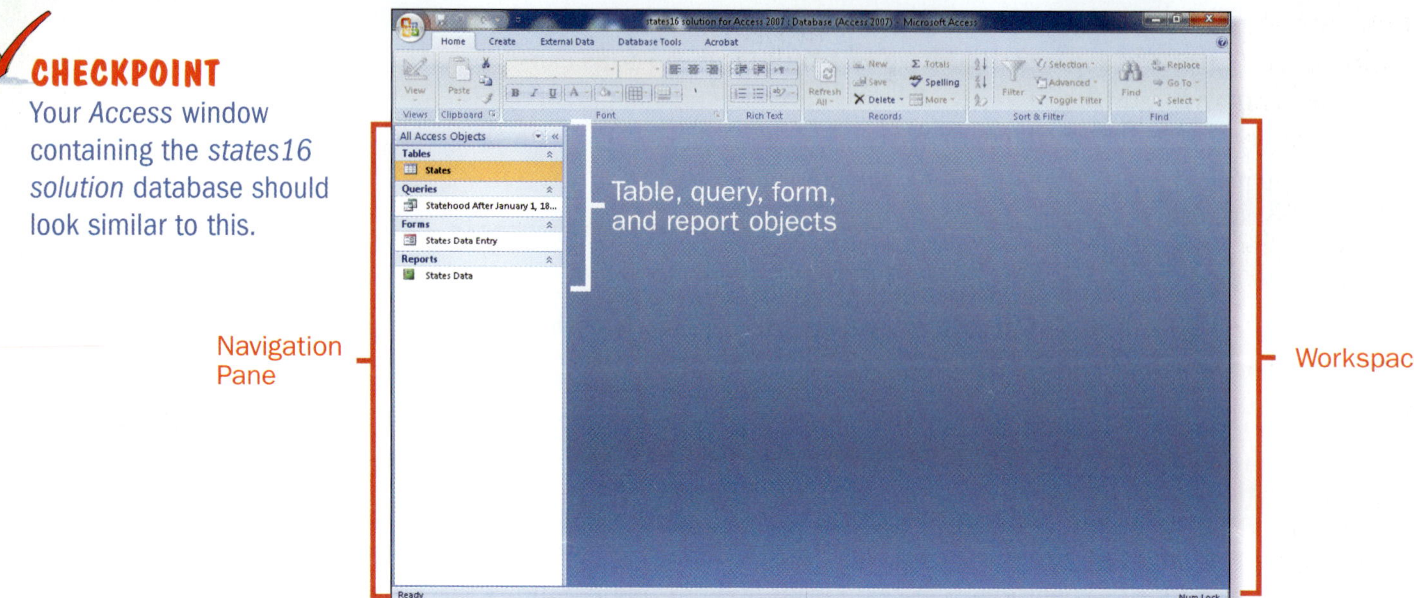


**CHECKPOINT**
Your *Access* window containing the *states16 solution* database should look similar to this.

### The *Access* Ribbon and Navigation Pane

As you work in *Access*, you will see the familiar Ribbon you worked with in *Word*, *Excel*, and *PowerPoint*. Some of the Ribbon tabs and buttons, such as the Home tab and the Paste button, are the same; however, most of the Ribbon tabs and buttons are specific to *Access*. Remember to use ScreenTips as necessary to learn names of the new *Access* buttons while you work with an *Access* database!

The Quick Access Toolbar and the Mini Toolbar you learned about in earlier units are also available in *Access*. On the left side of the *Access* window, below the Ribbon, is the Navigation Pane. The Navigation Pane contains a list of the objects—tables, queries, forms, and reports—in the database. At the bottom of the *Access* window is the status bar, which contains status messages and the View Shortcuts.

Next, let's use the Navigation Pane to check out the different database objects inside the *states16 solution* database.

## Checking Out Database Objects

An *Access* database is a *single* file that can contain many different objects. Ray's *states16 solution* database contains three objects: a table, a form, and a report.

The Find and Replace dialog box remembers your last search and formatting options. To avoid accidentally applying the Italic font style the next time you use Find and Replace, it is a good idea to clear the formatting options before you close the dialog box.

**Let's clear the Italic font style formatting option in the Find and Replace dialog box to avoid errors the next time you use the dialog box.**

1. Click in the **Replace with** text box, if necessary, to position the insertion point.
2. Click the **More** button to expand the dialog box; then click the **No Formatting** button at the bottom of the dialog box to clear the formatting option.
3. Click the **Less** button to collapse the dialog box and then click the **Close** button to close it.
4. Save the document.

Your replaced and formatted text should look like this.

Replaced and formatted text

soldier, *William Clark,* to co-lead the expedition. The expedition, which we now call the *Lewis and Clark Expedition,* became one of the great adventures of all time.¶

Good job! Next, let's select all of the text formatted with the Italic font style and reformat it with the Bold font style.

## Selecting Similarly Formatted Text

2 TRAIL MARKER

When you want to make a global formatting change—for example, to change all italicized text to bolded text—you can set options in the Find and Replace dialog box and allow *Word* to search for and change the formatting.

But a faster way to find all of the text formatted the same way is to select it using a shortcut menu. Simply right-click a sample of the formatted text you want to change, point to Styles, and click Select Text with Similar Formatting. Then reformat all of the selected text at one time with buttons in the Font group on the Home tab.

**CHECKPOINT**

Your *Access* window containing the *states16 solution* database should look similar to this.

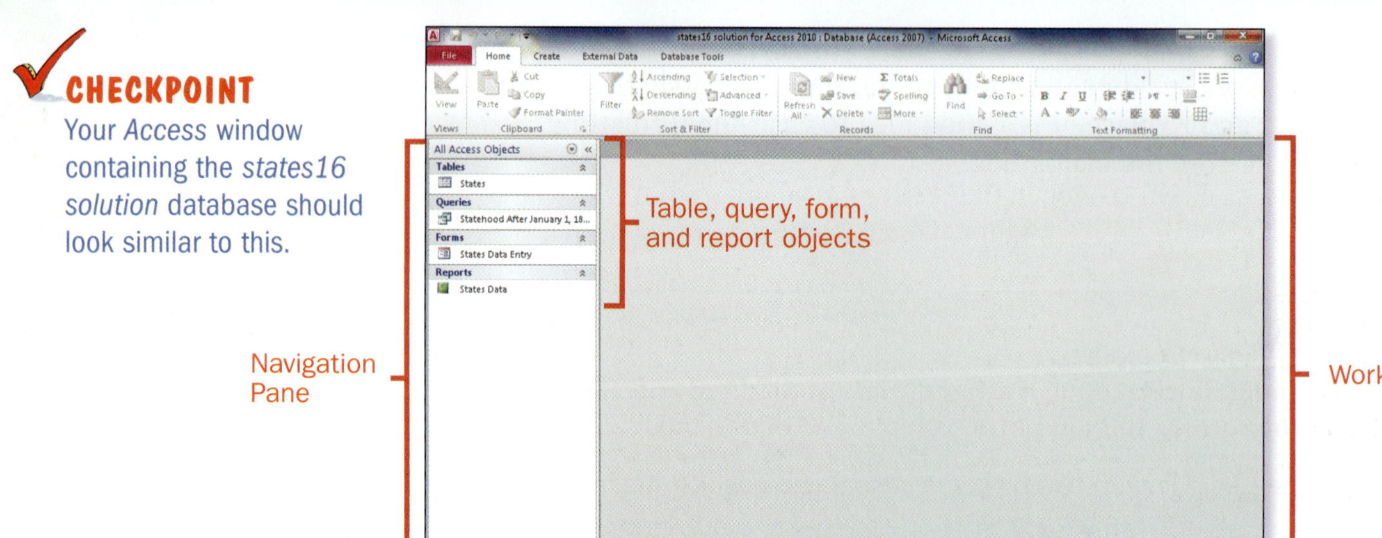


Now you are ready to review the *Access* Ribbon and learn about the Navigation Pane.

**Opening and Saving an *Access 2007* Database**

You can open and save an *Access 2007* database much like a *Word* document or an *Excel* workbook.

Unlike *Word*, *Excel*, or *PowerPoint*, in which you can open multiple documents, workbooks, or presentations, respectively, you can have only one *Access* database open at a time in the same instance or copy of *Access*.

**Let's open Ray's database and save it with a new name.**

1. Click the **More** link in the Open Recent Database list on the right side of the Getting Started with Access page to open the Open dialog box. More...
2. Switch to the folder that contains your data files and open the *states16 for Access 2007* database.
3. Click the **Office Button**, point to **Save As**, and click **Access 2007 Database** in the submenu to open the Save As dialog box.
4. Switch to the location where your solution files are stored and save the database as *states16 solution*.

**Let's use a shortcut menu to select all italicized text and then remove the Italic font style and apply the Bold font style.**

Home | Font | Italic or Bold

1. Tap the CTRL + HOME keys, if necessary, to move the insertion point to the top of the document; then scroll to see the first instance of italicized text: *Meriwether Lewis.*
2. Right-click the italicized text, point to **Styles**, and click **Select Text with Similar Formatting** in the shortcut menu below the styles gallery.
3. Scroll the document, if necessary, to see that all three instances of italicized text are selected.
4. Click the **Home** tab, if necessary, and locate the **Font** group; then click the **Italic** button in the Font group to remove the Italic font style.
5. Click the **Bold** button in the Font group to apply the Bold font style.
6. Deselect the text.

**CHECKPOINT**

The Italic font style is removed and the Bold font style is applied to all of the selected text.

Italicized text reformatted with the Bold font style

At more than 800,000 square miles, the Louisiana Purchase almost doubled the size of the United States. After the U.S. Senate ratified the treaty authorizing the Louisiana Purchase, Jefferson assigned his own private secretary, **Meriwether Lewis**, to take charge of an expedition to explore the Louisiana Purchase territories. That expedition was then called the Corps of Discovery. Lewis chose his friend and fellow soldier, **William Clark**, to co-lead the expedition. The expedition, which we now call the **Lewis and Clark Expedition**, became one of the great adventures of all time.¶

Super! Now let's paint formatting onto unformatted text.

## Painting Formats

The Format Painter is a great tool for copying, or *painting*, formats from formatted text to unformatted text. To use the Format Painter, first move the insertion point into the text that is already formatted. Then click the Home tab and click the Format Painter button in the Clipboard group.

When the Format Painter is turned on, the I-beam has a paintbrush icon. Drag the I-beam across the text or click a single word that you want to format.

To use the Format Painter on more than one text selection, double-click the Format Painter button. Then click it again to turn the Format Painter off when you are finished.

## Opening an Existing Database

A database is used to organize related data in a structured way. One common example of a database is the Yellow Pages telephone book! The Yellow Pages organizes the same type of data—business type, name, address, and telephone number—in ascending alphabetical order for each type of business listed.

Database files that are stored on electronic media, such as your hard drive, a flash drive, or a network drive, are called electronic databases. Electronic databases allow you to easily add, edit, delete, and reorganize data. An example of a simple electronic database is an *Excel* worksheet *data range* like the ones you sorted or filtered in the *Excel* unit.

You use the *Access* application to create a more complex type of electronic database, called a relational database. A relational database is a *single* file that contains multiple related items called database objects. For example, a relational database stores its data in a single table object or in multiple linked table objects. Other *Access* database objects include reports, forms, and queries. You will learn more about database tables, forms, reports, and queries as you work in this unit.

### Opening and Saving an *Access 2010* Database

You can open and save an *Access 2010* database much like a *Word* document or an *Excel* workbook.

**Let's open Ray's database and save it with a new name.**

1. Click **Open** on the File tab to open the Open dialog box.
2. Switch to the location where your data files are stored and double-click the *states16 for Access 2010* filename to open the database.
3. Click the **File** tab and click **Save Database As** to open the Save As dialog box. File
4. Switch to the location where your solution files are stored and save the database as *states16 solution*.

As you learned in Project 2, a paragraph heading is a short phrase that introduces a paragraph. The *Lewis and Clark3* document has two paragraph headings: William Clark and Meriwether Lewis. Remember to format paragraph headings with the Heading 1 style.

**Let's format the William Clark paragraph heading by applying the Heading 1 style and then copy the formatting to the Meriwether Lewis paragraph heading using the Format Painter.**

**Home | Styles | More**

**Home | Clipboard | Format Painter**

1. Select the paragraph heading **William Clark** on the first page.
2. Click the **Home** tab and locate the **Styles** group; then click the **Heading 1 style** icon in the styles gallery. If the Heading 1 style icon is not visible, click the **More** button to expand the gallery to view the icon.

3. Deselect the text but leave the insertion point in the paragraph heading. Leaving the insertion point in the William Clark formatted heading tells the Format Painter which formats to copy.
4. Click the **Home** tab, if necessary, and locate the **Clipboard** group; then click the **Format Painter** button in the Clipboard group to turn on the Format Painter.
5. Scroll to view the **Meriwether Lewis** paragraph heading and move the mouse pointer immediately to the left of the heading text. The mouse pointer is now the Format Painter pointer, and I-beam pointer with a paint brush icon.
6. Drag across the paragraph heading with the Format Painter mouse pointer to paint the copied Heading 1 format.
7. Deselect the text and save the document.

Format Painter icon

Meriwether·Lewis¶

Your formatted paragraph headings should now look like this.

Formatted paragraph headings

**William·Clark¶**
William· Clark·was·also·born·on·a·plantation· a·few·years·before·Lewis,·in·1770.· ·As·a·teenager,·Clark· lived·on·the·Kentucky·frontier·adding· backcountry·and·frontier· skills· to·his· already·honed· skills· as·a· gentleman·of·the·Virginia· plantation· class:·riding,· hunting,· and·politics.· ·Like·Lewis,·Clark·served·in·both· the·militia· and·regular· army.· ·It·was·during· his·time·in· the·army·that·he·met·and·became·friends·with· Lewis.· ·Clark·left·the·army·to·manage·his· family's· plantation· in· 1796.· ·In·1803,· he·sold· the·plantation· and· joined· Lewis·in·the·adventure·of·a·lifetime.¶

**Meriwether·Lewis¶**
As·a·young· boy,· Meriwether·Lewis·lived· for·a·few·years·on·the·Georgia· frontier·developing· his· frontier· survival· skills.· · Returning·to·Virginia· as·a·teenager,·Lewis·began·his· education· and·assumed·the· responsibility· of·managing· the· family· plantation.· ·In·1794,·Lewis·became·a·soldier· in·the·state·militia· and· then·in·the·regular·army,·rising· to·the·rank·of·captain.· ·He·gained· a·reputation· for·competence·and·honesty· and,·in·1801,·President·Thomas·Jefferson·asked·him· to·serve·as·his·private·secretary.· ·It·is·possible· that· Jefferson·already·had·Lewis·in·mind· to·lead·a·westward·expedition· because·for·the·next·two·years,· Jefferson·had·Lewis·study·with· some·of·the·foremost·scientists·in· the·country· to·get·ready· for·the·

Outstanding! Both paragraph headings are now formatted with the Heading 1 style. The next step is to move and duplicate text using buttons in the Clipboard group and using and drag and drop.

## Starting Out with *Access 2007*

Begin by starting the *Access* application.

1. Click the **Start** button on the taskbar, point to **All Programs**, point to the ***Microsoft Office*** folder, and click ***Microsoft Office Access 2007*** to open the application.

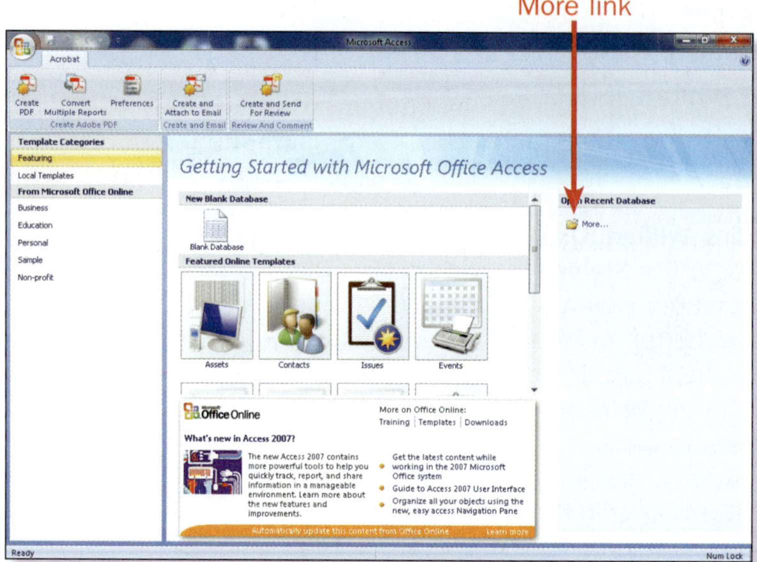


Good job! Look at the *Access* window. The *Access* application *does not* start with a blank document like *Word*, *Excel*, or *PowerPoint*. When you open *Access* from the Start menu or a desktop icon, the Getting Started with Access page opens.

From the Getting Started with Access page, you can:

- create a new empty or blank database using the Blank database template
- create a new empty database using a sample template or a template downloaded from the Web
- open an existing database

In Trail Marker 1, you open an existing database and save it with a new name in a new location.

Is the glare from uncovered windows making it difficult for you to see items on your screen? Minimize the glare by covering windows with blinds or curtains.

## Moving and Duplicating Text

Moving text from one place to another in a document is called cutting and pasting the text, and duplicating text is called copying and pasting. You can cut, copy, and paste text by clicking buttons in the Clipboard group on the Home tab. You can also open the Clipboard task pane to paste cut or copied text and use the mouse pointer to move or copy text.

### Using the Cut and Paste Buttons

To move text to a different place in the document, select the text; then click the Home tab and click the Cut button in the Clipboard group. Move the insertion point to the location in the document where you want the cut text to appear and click the Paste button in the Clipboard group.

To duplicate selected text, click the Copy button in the Clipboard group, move the insertion point to where you want the duplicate text to appear, and click the Paste button.

Text that you cut or copy using the Clipboard group buttons is temporarily stored in a special place in your computer's memory called the Office Clipboard. You can store up to 24 cut or copied items on the Office Clipboard and paste them one at a time or all at once using features in the Clipboard task pane. Items remain on the Office Clipboard until you clear them or until you close *Word*.

The Clipboard task pane might open automatically when more than one cut or copied item is stored on the Office Clipboard. To manually open the Clipboard task pane, click the Dialog Box Launcher icon in the Clipboard group.

**Let's use the Copy and Cut buttons and the Office Clipboard to copy and cut text.**

Home | Clipboard | Cut or Copy

1. Double-click the word **Virginia** where it appears in the third line of the William Clark body text paragraph.
2. Click the **Home** tab, if necessary, and locate the **Clipboard** group; then click the **Copy** button in the Clipboard group to copy the text to the Office Clipboard. 

**Starting Out with *Access 2010***

Begin by starting the *Access* application.

1. Click the **Start** button on the taskbar, click **All Programs**, click the ***Microsoft Office*** folder, and click ***Microsoft Access 2010***.

Good job! Look at the *Access* window. The *Access* application *does not* start with a blank document like *Word*, *Excel*, or *PowerPoint*. *Access 2010* opens in Backstage view, and the File tab is active.

Backstage view

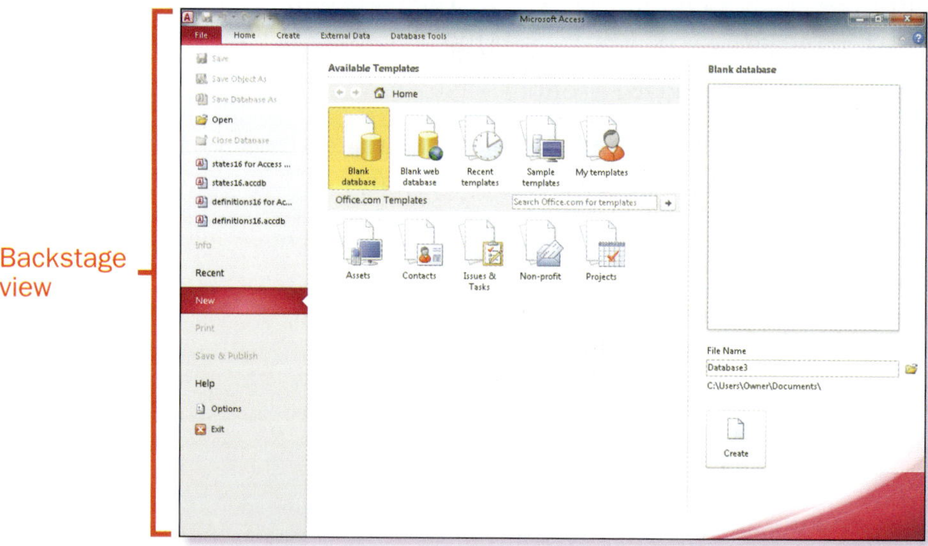

From *Access 2010* Backstage view, you can:

- create a new empty or blank database using the Blank database template
- create a new empty database using a sample template or a template downloaded from the Microsoft Office.com website
- open an existing database

In Trail Marker 1, you open an existing database and save it with a new name in a new location.

If you have a desktop icon for *Access 2010* or *Access 2007*, just double-click it to open the application.

3. Select the **Meriwether Lewis** paragraph heading and following body text paragraph.
4. Click the **Cut** button in the Clipboard group to place the text on the Office Clipboard.
5. If the Clipboard task pane does not automatically open, click the **Dialog Box Launcher** icon in the Clipboard group.

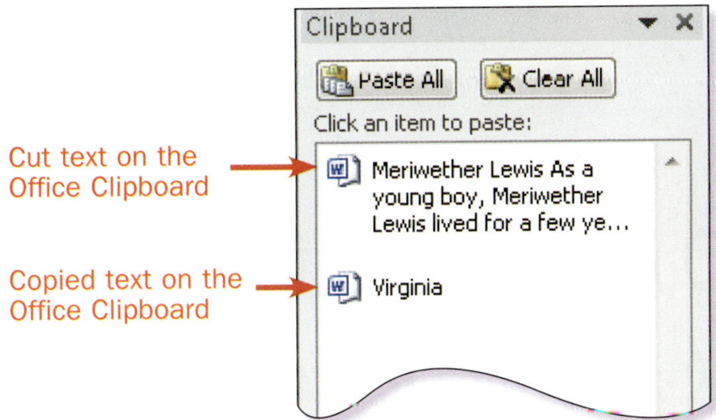


6. Move the insertion point in front of the paragraph heading **William Clark**.
7. Click the **Meriwether Lewis** text or icon in the Clipboard task pane to paste the cut paragraph into the new location.
8. Move the insertion point immediately in front of the word *plantation* in the first sentence in the William Clark body text paragraph.
9. Click the **Virginia** text or icon in the Clipboard task pane to paste the copied word at the new location.
10. Click the **Clear All** button in the Clipboard task pane to clear the contents and then click the **Close** button on the task pane title bar.
11. Save the document.

### Using Drag and Drop

Moving and copying text using just the mouse pointer is called drag and drop. First, select the text; then place the mouse pointer on the selected text, hold down the left mouse button, and drag the text to a new location to move or cut it. You will see a dashed-line insertion point that moves with the mouse pointer as you drag the text to a new location.

If a paragraph is followed by a blank line, you can select both the text and the blank line, then use drag and drop to move or copy both at one time.

Unlike using the Cut, Copy, and Paste buttons, using drag and drop to move or duplicate text *does not* temporarily store the text on the Office Clipboard. If you accidentally drop selected text in the wrong place, just click the Undo button on the Quick Access Toolbar and try again!

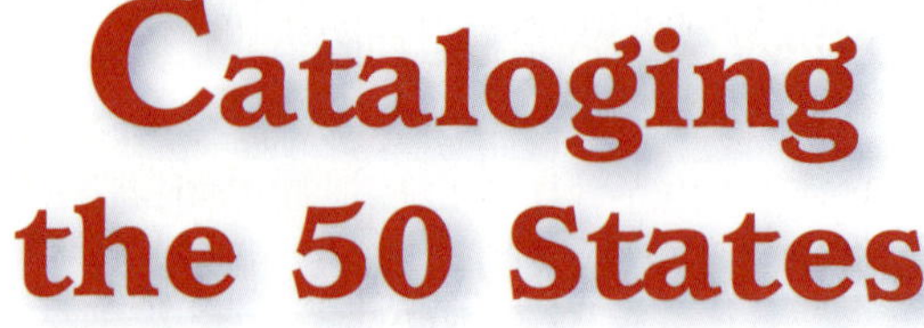


## Explorers' Guide

**Data files:** states16
1860states16
definitions16

**Objectives:**
In this project, you will:

- open an existing database
- check out database objects
- edit, add, and delete records
- sort, filter, and query data
- preview and print a datasheet

## Our Exploration Assignment:

**Review database objects; update a table; sort, filter, and query data; then preview and print a query datasheet**

Do you know the capital of Iowa? Or which two states have the largest and smallest areas? Or which were the first and last states to gain statehood? The Explorers Club is learning the answers to these and other questions about the 50 states. Ray has saved his research in a database. Can you help him update the data, answer some questions using the data, and then preview and print a portion of the data before the next meeting? Great! Just follow the Trail Markers to open an existing database and check out the database objects; add, edit, and delete records; sort, filter, and query data; and then preview and print the query datasheet.

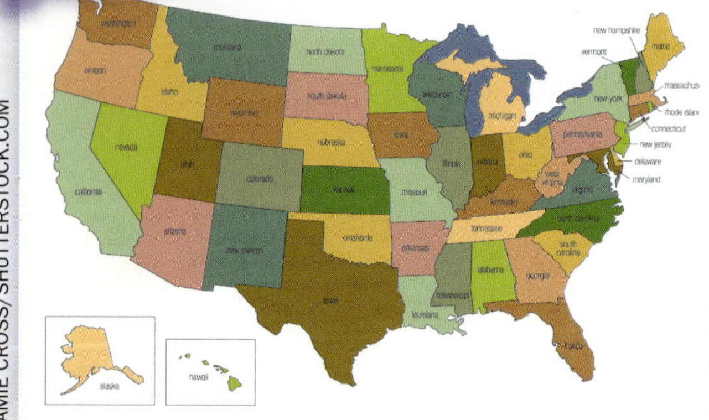
JAMIE CROSS/SHUTTERSTOCK.COM

**Let's move the last sentence in the Meriwether Lewis descriptive paragraph so that it becomes the first sentence.**

1. Use the I-beam to select the sentence **Lewis was born on his parents' Virginia plantation in 1774.** at the end of the Meriwether Lewis body text paragraph.
2. Move the mouse pointer into the selected sentence; then hold down the left mouse button. Notice the dashed-line insertion point to the left of the mouse pointer tip and the square box at the base of the mouse pointer. These symbols tell you that you can now move the selected text by dragging it to a new location.
3. Slowly drag upward until the dashed-line insertion pointer is positioned immediately in front of the word *As* in the first line of the Meriwether Lewis body text paragraph.
4. Release the mouse button, deselect the text, and insert two spaces following **1774**.
5. Use the BACKSPACE or DELETE key to remove the two extra spaces at the end of the Meriwether Lewis body text paragraph.
6. Save the document.

Move pointer with insertion point

Repositioned move pointer and insertion point

Your Meriwether Lewis heading and body text paragraph should now look like this.

**Meriwether·Lewis¶**

Lewis·was·born·on·his·parents'·Virginia·plantation·in·1774.··As·a·young·boy,·Meriwether·Lewis·lived·for·a·few·years·on·the·Georgia·frontier·developing·his·frontier·survival·skills.··Returning·to·Virginia·as·a·teenager,·Lewis·began·his·education·and·assumed·the·responsibility·of·managing·the·family·plantation.··In·1794,·Lewis·became·a·soldier·in·the·state·militia·and·then·in·the·regular·army,·rising·to·the·rank·of·captain.··He·gained·a·reputation·for·competence·and·honesty·and,·in·1801,·President·Thomas·Jefferson·asked·him·to·serve·as·his·private·secretary.··It·is·possible·that·Jefferson·already·had·Lewis·in·mind·to·lead·a·westward·expedition·because·for·the·next·two·years,·Jefferson·had·Lewis·study·with·some·of·the·foremost·scientists·in·the·country·to·get·ready·for·the·expedition.··In·the·spring·of·1803,·Lewis·was·ready·for·his·great·adventure.¶

To copy text using drag and drop, tap and hold the CTRL key as you drag the selected text to a new location. *Warning!* After you drag the selected text to a new location, be careful to release the mouse button *before* you release the CTRL key. *If you release the CTRL key first, the text will be moved instead of copied.*

Outstanding! Now let's change the margins on the second page and insert page numbers.

# DATABASE

***It is important to be able to store and access your research data quickly and easily. A great way to do this is to create databases. Join Ray, Luis, Julie, and me to work with databases to:***

- Catalog the Fifty States.
- Work for Social Reform.
- Organize Data About U.S. Inventors and Inventions.

We will create our databases using an application called *Access*. You will learn how to use *Access* to review data about the fifty states; catalog data about the leaders of the nineteenth-century U.S. social reform movements; and organize data about U.S. inventors and their inventions that changed the world in which you live. You will open and create database files and create tables to contain your data. Then you will learn how to add and edit the data in a datasheet or by using a special data entry form. After you have entered all your data, you learn some neat ways to find just the facts you want by sorting, filtering, querying, and printing the data. Hurry! We can't wait!

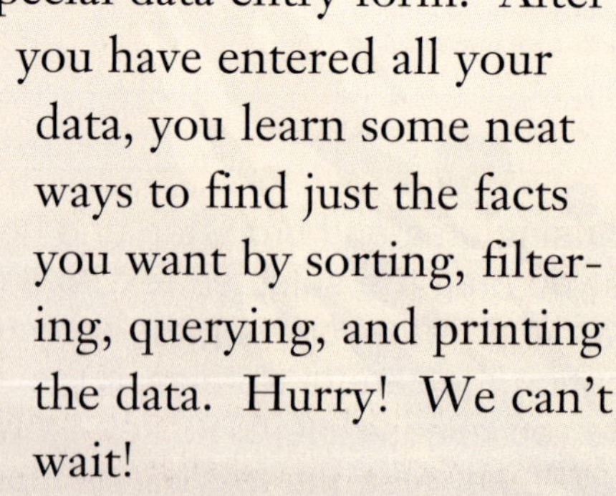

## Inserting Page Breaks, Section Breaks, and Page Numbers

When you create multipage reports, such as the *Lewis and Clark3* report, you must make sure the text breaks correctly between pages. Multipage reports also have page numbers.

### Page Breaks

A page break—where one page ends and another page begins—may be either a soft page break inserted automatically by *Word* or a hard page break inserted manually by you. When a page is full, *Word* automatically inserts a soft page break and moves the remaining text to the next page.

Each time you delete text, change the margins, or apply formatting that changes the amount of text that fits on a page, *Word* automatically adjusts the position of the soft page breaks in a process called repagination.

You can change a document's pagination by manually inserting hard page breaks anywhere you want them. To insert a hard page break, move the insertion point to the location where you want the page break to occur, click the Insert tab, and then click the Page Break button in the Pages group. You can also tap the CTRL + ENTER keys to insert a hard page break at the position of the insertion point.

*Warning! Word* cannot move or delete a hard page break when it repaginates a document. If you add or delete text or change the formatting so that the amount of text on a page changes, you must manually move or delete your hard page breaks.

In Draft view, a soft page break is shown with a single dotted line across the page and a hard page break is shown with a single dotted line and the words *Page Break.*

The best way to check the effects of repagination on a document that contains both hard and soft page breaks is to preview it!

### Section Breaks

A section break is a special type of break that allows you to change the layout of text, such as margins and columns, for a single page in a multipage document. In Draft and Print Layout views, a section break is shown by a double-dotted line with the words *Section Break* and the type of section break in parentheses.

# Day 3 – Total Care Veterinary Clinic

On Day 3 of your internship, Ms. Davis asks you to work with Beverly, the receptionist, who is on a tight deadline to update a slide show for Dr. Wilson to give next week at a local business conference. Beverly hands you a list of tasks she needs you to finish by the end of the day. To save time, she asks you to begin by creating a new presentation and applying an appropriate customized theme. Then you are to reuse slides from the presentation Dr. Wilson gave at last year's business conference.

She asks you to add appropriate audio, clip art, transitions, and animation to the slides. She also wants you to insert a summary slide with hyperlinks to the other slides, then add brief speaker notes to the summary slide.

### TO DO TODAY

1. Create a new presentation and apply a theme
2. Reuse slides from another presentation
3. Format the slides with audio, clip art, transitions, and animation
4. Insert a summary slide with hyperlinks to other slides
5. Add speaker notes to the summary slide

## Task #1 – Create a New Presentation

1. Start *PowerPoint* and save the blank presentation as *Orange Day 3 Presentation sol*.
2. Apply the customized theme of your choice.

## Task #2 – Reuse Slides

1. Open the Reuse Slides pane, open the *Orange Day 3 Previous data file* presentation, and insert all of the slides into your new presentation.
2. Delete the slide 1 blank title slide.
3. Add **Total Care Veterinary Clinic** as footer text, the current date, and slides numbers to all slides except the Title Slide.

## Task #3 – Format the Slides

1. Select slide 5 and remove the background graphics; then insert the clip art of your choice as the slide's background.
2. Insert the audio clip of your choice on the Title Slide layout in Slide Master view. Set the clip to play automatically and hide the audio icon during the slide show.
3. Apply the slide transition effect of your choice to all of the slides.
4. Animate the title text on slides 2–4 with the animation effect of your choice. Set the animation to play automatically after the previous action.
5. Run the slide show and make any adjustments you think appropriate for an effective presentation.

## Task #4 – Insert a Summary Slide

1. Insert a new Title and Content slide as slide 2 and key **Summary** as the slide title.
2. Use copy and paste to add the slide title text from the remaining slides as bulleted text on the summary slide.
3. Select each bulleted text item and use it to create a hyperlink to the related slide.
4. Add return action buttons to each of the linked-to slides that return to the summary slide.
5. Run the slide show and test the hyperlinks and action buttons.

## Task #5 – Add Speaker Notes

1. Add the following speaker notes to slide 2: **Hi! I'm Dr. Dave Wilson, and I would like to tell you about the services we offer at the Total Care Veterinary Clinic.**
2. With permission, print the slide 2 notes page.
3. Save and close the presentation.

To insert a section break, click the Page Layout tab and then click the Insert Page and Section Breaks button in the Page Setup group. Click the break option you want from the gallery.

The *first page* of an unbound multipage report has a 2-inch top margin; the *remaining pages* have a 1-inch top margin. All pages have 1-inch left, right, and bottom margins.

To change the top margin for the second page of the *Lewis and Clark3* document, you must replace the existing soft page break on the first page with a Next page section break. This will break the page and start a new section on the next page. Then you can set the top margin for the new section.

**Let's insert a Next page section break and change the top margin for the second page of the *Lewis and Clark3* document.**

Page Layout | Page Setup | Insert Page and Section Breaks

Page Layout | Page Setup | Margins

1. Move the insertion point immediately in front of the paragraph heading **William Clark**.
2. Click the **Page Layout** tab and locate the **Page Setup** group.
3. Click the **Insert Page and Section Breaks** button in the Page Setup group to view the page and section break options gallery.

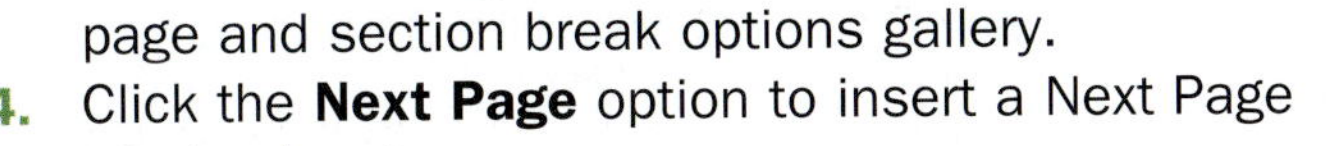


4. Click the **Next Page** option to insert a Next Page section break.
5. Scroll to view the bottom of the first page to view the Next page section break.
6. Move the insertion point to the top of the second page, if necessary, into Section 2.
7. Set the top, bottom, left, and right margins to 1 inch.
8. Observe the 1-inch top margin on the second page.
9. Tap the CTRL + HOME keys to view the top of page 1 to see the original 2-inch top margin; then save the document.

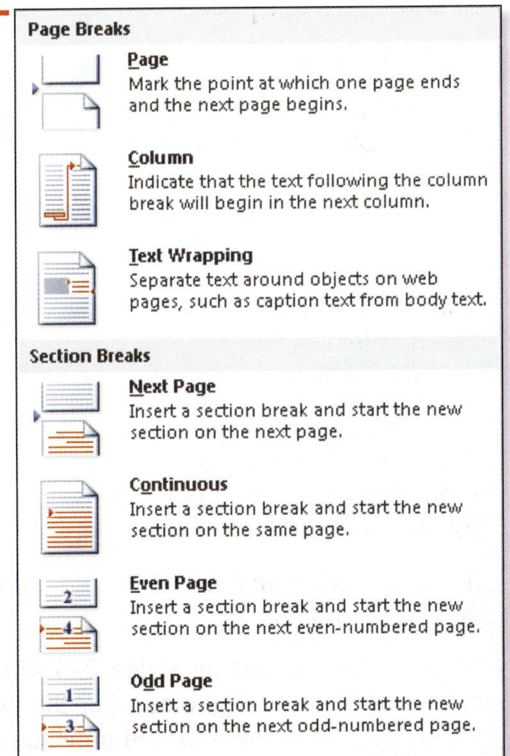


Page and section break options

# Project 15



## 15a Numeric Keypad Review

Use the numeric keypad and calculator accessory to complete the addition drills shown at the right. The answers are shown in blue.

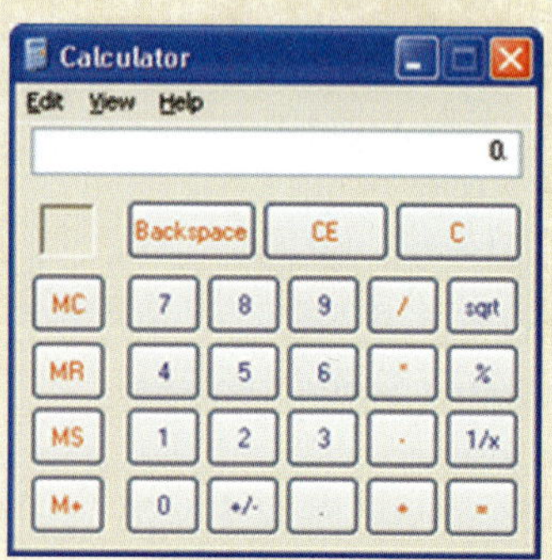

**Drill 1 – 4/5/6**

| A | B | C | D | E |
|---|---|---|---|---|
| 44 | 45 | 546 | 446 | 555 |
| 55 | 56 | 465 | 454 | 546 |
| 66 | 64 | 654 | 465 | 564 |
| 165 | 165 | 1,665 | 1,365 | 1,665 |

**Drill 2 – 7/8/9**

| A | B | C | D | E |
|---|---|---|---|---|
| 779 | 879 | 997 | 798 | 779 |
| 878 | 789 | 898 | 879 | 899 |
| 797 | 978 | 979 | 987 | 878 |
| 2,454 | 2,646 | 2,874 | 2,664 | 2,556 |

**Drill 3 – 1/2/3**

| A | B | C | D | E |
|---|---|---|---|---|
| 123 | 113 | 322 | 212 | 112 |
| 132 | 323 | 132 | 331 | 223 |
| 312 | 231 | 113 | 213 | 313 |
| 567 | 667 | 567 | 756 | 648 |

## 15b Build Skill

Key each line twice. Double-space between 2-line groups.

For additional practice:
**MicroType 5**
Numeric Keypad, Lessons 1–2

**Alphabet sentences**

1 Jack Betz will give us the equipment for six days.
2 Jack Vance helped Maryann with six bags of quartz.
3 Levi Lentz packed my bag with six quarts of juice.
4 Kevin can fix the unique jade owl as my big prize.

**Speed sentences**

5 A box with the forms is on the mantle by the bowl.
6 The small ornament on their door is an ivory duck.
7 The sorority may do the work for the city auditor.
8 She owns the big dock, but they own the lake land.

Remember! You can see the Section number and Page number location of the insertion point on the left side of the status bar. If this information is not visible on your screen, right-click the status bar and click Section and/or Page Number. Check it out!

When you work in headers or footers, the contextual Header & Footer Tools Design tab is added to the Ribbon.

**Page Numbers**

A multipage report, such as the *Lewis and Clark3* document, has page numbers in the top right corner of each page *except* the first page. Page numbers are inserted at the top of the page in a header or at the bottom of a page in a footer.

To insert a page number in the upper-right corner in a header, click the Insert tab and click the Page Number button in the Header & Footer group. Point to Top of Page on the menu to view a list of top-of-page page numbering options; then click a page numbering option.

**Let's insert a right-aligned page number in a header on all pages except the first page.**

Insert | Header & Footer | Insert Page Number

Header & Footer Tools Design | Options | Different First Page

1. Click the **Insert** tab and locate the **Header & Footer** group.
2. Click the **Insert Page Number** button in the Header & Footer group and point to **Top of Page** to view the page numbering options. Page Number

Page numbering options

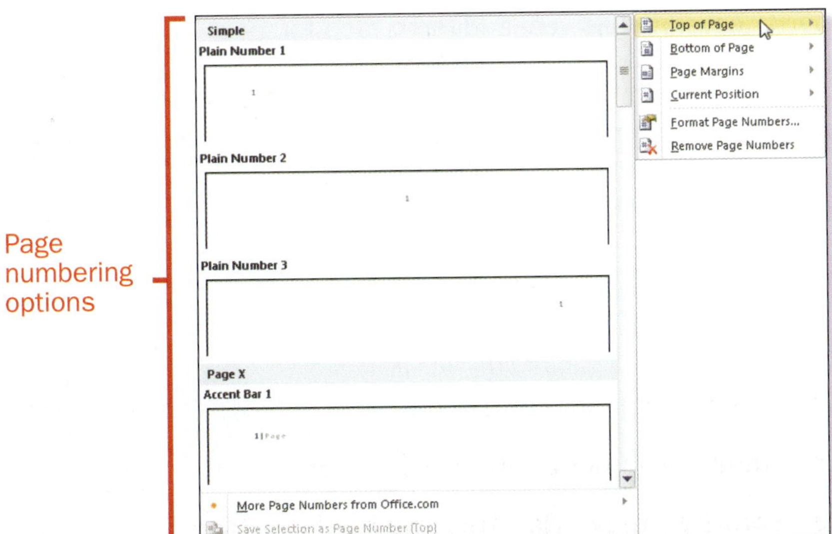

# Exploring Across the Curriculum

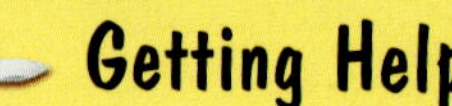

## Getting Help

Click the Microsoft PowerPoint Help icon below the *PowerPoint* application Close button to open the *PowerPoint* Help window. Key **send *PowerPoint* handouts to *Word* for printing** in the search box and tap the ENTER key to research how to send a presentation's handouts to *Microsoft Word* to create a *Word* document that can be formatted and then printed. Then open the *Iditarod15* presentation you completed in this project. Use your research to send the presentation to *Word*. Preview the new *Word* document and then close it without saving. Close the presentation without saving it.

## Career Day

Public safety and security professionals also use software tools, such as *Word*, *Excel*, and *PowerPoint*, in the performance of their duties. Using library, printed, or online resources, identify three interesting careers in fields of public safety, corrections, or security. Write a brief summary of each career, print your summary, and save it in your Career Day folder.

## Your Personal Journal

Open your personal journal document. Insert today's date and two blank lines. Imagine that you are a reporter covering this year's Iditarod race for your local newspaper. Write a two- or three-paragraph story about the race. Spell-check, save, and close your journal.

**Online Enrichment Games**  www.cengage.com/school/keyboarding/lwcorange

3. Click the **Plain Number 3** option. Notice that the page number 1 is inserted at the right margin in the header on page 1. The first page (Section 1) should not be numbered.
4. Click the contextual **Header & Footer Tools Design** tab that appears on the Ribbon and locate the **Options** group.
5. Click the **Different First Page** checkbox in the Options group to insert a check mark, which removes the page number from the first page of the report.

Different First Page

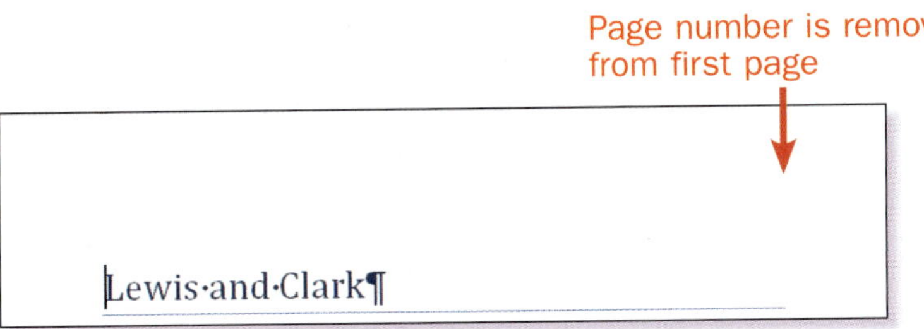


6. Double-click the text area below the header to activate it and close the header area.
7. Scroll the document to view the page number 2 in the header on page 2.

The top of your document's second page should look like this.

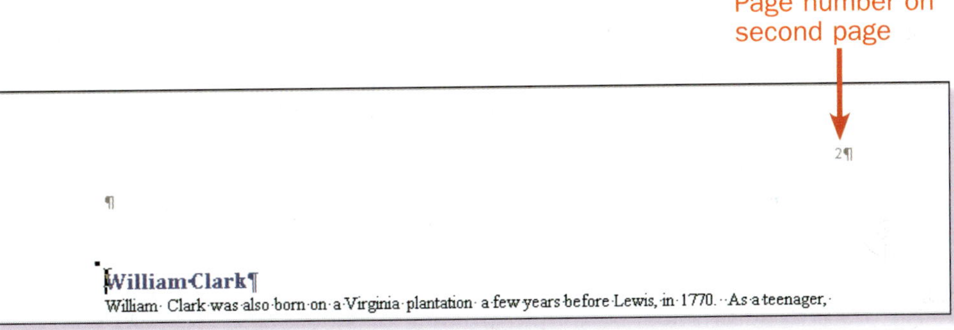


8. Tap the CTRL + HOME keys and save the document.

Fantastic! Now let's cite Julie's sources with footnotes.

## Inserting Footnotes

You must cite the sources, or the origin of the facts and ideas you use in a report, by providing the name and date of the source and the author's name, if possible, in footnotes at the bottom of the same page as the referenced text or as endnotes on a separate page at the end of the report. In this project, you insert footnotes to cite Julie's sources.

## Language Arts: Words to Know

Look up the meaning of the following terms in a classroom dictionary, CD-ROM dictionary or encyclopedia, or online dictionary.

| Balto | frostbite | husky | Iditarod Trail |
|---|---|---|---|
| musher | mushing | Nome | sled dog |

Create a new presentation. Save it as *definitions15*. Key **Iditarod** as the title and **Definitions** as the subtitle on the Title Slide. Apply the theme of your choice. Insert eight new Title and Content slides.

Key a single term in the title placeholder and the related definition in the bulleted-list placeholder on each of the eight slides. Add slide numbers to all slides *except* the Title Slide. Create a summary slide for the first four Title and Content slides. Create a second summary slide for the last four Title and Content slides. Add the slide transitions of your choice; then save and close the presentation.

## Science: Research, Write, and Present

Work with a classmate to use library or online resources to learn more about the characteristics, care, and training of sled dogs. Record your research on three worksheets named **Characteristics**, **Care**, and **Training** in an *Excel* workbook. Use grouping to enter and format common information, such as a title, on all three worksheets. Remember to ungroup the worksheets!

Create a new presentation and apply the customized theme of your choice. Add three Title Only slides; then copy and paste the data from your three worksheets on the slides: (1) as a *PowerPoint* table, (2) as an embedded workbook object, and (3) as a picture object. Format the objects as desired. Cite your sources on Title and Content slides. Create a summary slide as a new slide 2 and use the summary slide bulleted list text to create hyperlinks to each related slide. Add action buttons that link back to slide 2. Run the slide show. Save and close the presentation.

Explore More

Check out Appendix A to see the citation formats for different types of sources: books, magazines, journals, and Web pages. Remember! The content of books, magazines, journals, and Web pages is protected by copyright law. If you copy information directly from another source, you must enclose the information in quotation marks and cite the source.

A footnote has two parts: the note reference mark and the footnote text. When you insert a footnote, *Word* automatically inserts a note reference mark at the insertion point, a short line called the note separator line near the bottom of the page, and the note reference marks and note text below the note separator line.

*Word* automatically numbers multiple footnotes sequentially as 1, 2, 3, and so forth or i, ii, iii, and so forth.

To insert a footnote, move the insertion point to the end of the text to be cited. Then click the References tab and click the Insert Footnote button in the Footnotes group.

In Draft view, footnotes and endnotes are keyed in a notes pane. In Print Layout view, footnotes and endnotes are keyed on the page in which they appear.

You will insert the footnotes in the *Lewis and Clark3* document in Print Layout view.

To delete a footnote, just select its note reference mark and tap the DELETE key. Try it!

**Let's cite Julie's sources with footnotes.**

References | Footnotes | Insert Footnote

1. Move the insertion point to the end of the first body paragraph on page 1.
2. Click the **References** tab and locate the **Footnotes** group.
3. Click the **Insert Footnote** button in the Footnotes group. The superscript note reference mark [1] appears at the end of the paragraph, and the note separator line and the same note reference mark appear at the bottom of the page.

# Exploring Across the Curriculum

## Internet/Web

Open your Web browser and use a favorite or bookmark to view the Learning with Computers Web page (www.cengage.com/school/keyboarding/lwcorange). Click the **Links** option and Click **Project 15**. Click the links to learn more about The Iditarod Sled Dog Race. What critical 1925 event inspired the race? Who or what does the race honor? Where does the race get its name? In what year was the first race run? How many times has the race been held? Who won the last five races?

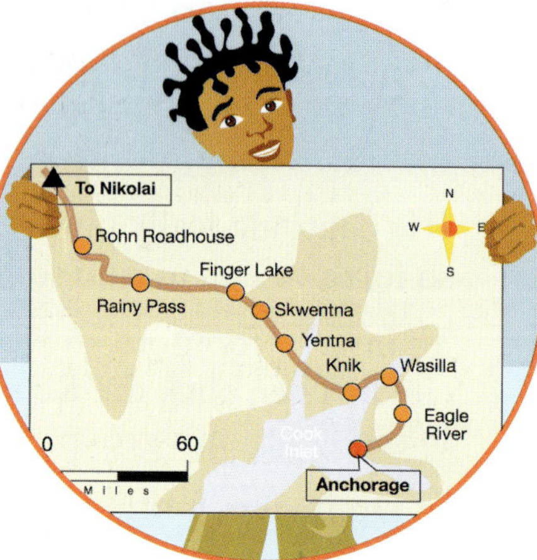


1. Create a new workbook and save it as *Iditarod history15*.
2. Rename the Sheet1 sheet tab as **Race Facts**.
3. Add an appropriate worksheet title and column names; then in the worksheet, record the facts you learned about the history of the Iditarod.
4. Create a new presentation and save it as *Iditarod facts15*.
5. Apply the customized theme of your choice.
6. Add an appropriate title and subtitle to the Title Slide.
7. Insert two Title Only slides and cite your sources on Title and Content slides at the end of the presentation.
8. Make certain that both the *Iditarod history15* workbook and the *Iditarod facts15* presentation are open.
9. Select and copy all of the data on the *Race Facts* worksheet and paste it on the first Title Only slide as an embedded workbook object and on the second Title Only slide as a picture object.
10. Add appropriate slide titles to the two slides and format the objects as desired.
11. List your slides on a summary slide as the new slide 2 titled **About the Iditarod**.
12. Use the slide 2 text to create hyperlinks to the appropriate slides and add action buttons that link back to slide 2.
13. Add your own speaker notes to slide 2.
14. Run the slide show and navigate using the hyperlinks and action buttons.
15. Save the presentation.

Explore More

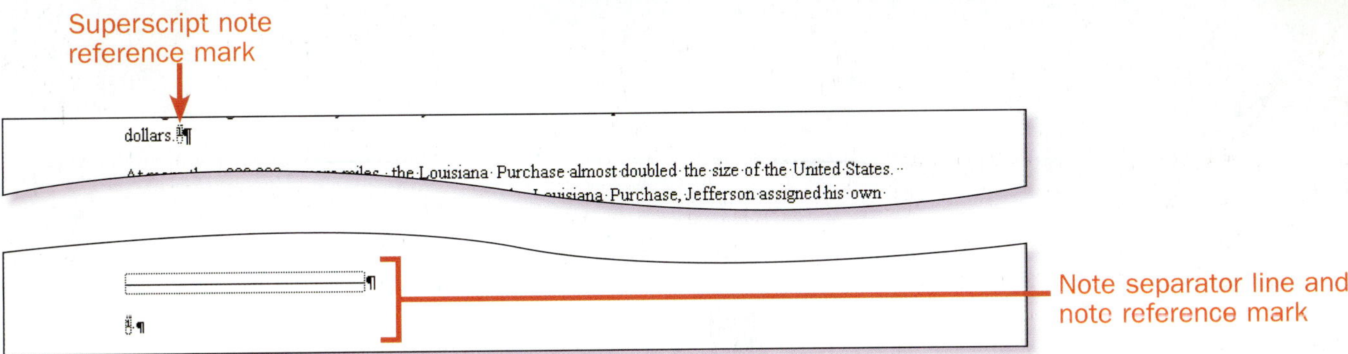


4. Key the first footnote text exactly as follows:
   **Jon Kukla, *A Wilderness So Immense* (New York: Alfred A. Knopf, 2003), p. 265.**
5. Move the insertion point immediately following the sentence that ends *his frontier survival skills*. in the Meriwether Lewis body text paragraph.
6. Click the **Insert Footnote** button in the Footnotes group.
7. Key the second footnote as follows:
   **Stephen Ambrose, *Undaunted Courage: Meriwether Lewis, Thomas Jefferson, and the Opening of the American West* (New York: Simon & Schuster, 1996), p. 24.**
8. Move the insertion point to the end of the William Clark paragraph. Insert footnote 3. Allow *Word* to automatically format the hyperlink.
   **"William Clark: Biography," *National Park Service: The Lewis and Clark Journey of Discovery* http://nps.gov/jeff/LewisClark2/CorpsofDiscovery/TheLeaders/Clark/Clark.htm (accessed 10 October 20–).**
9. Save and close the document.

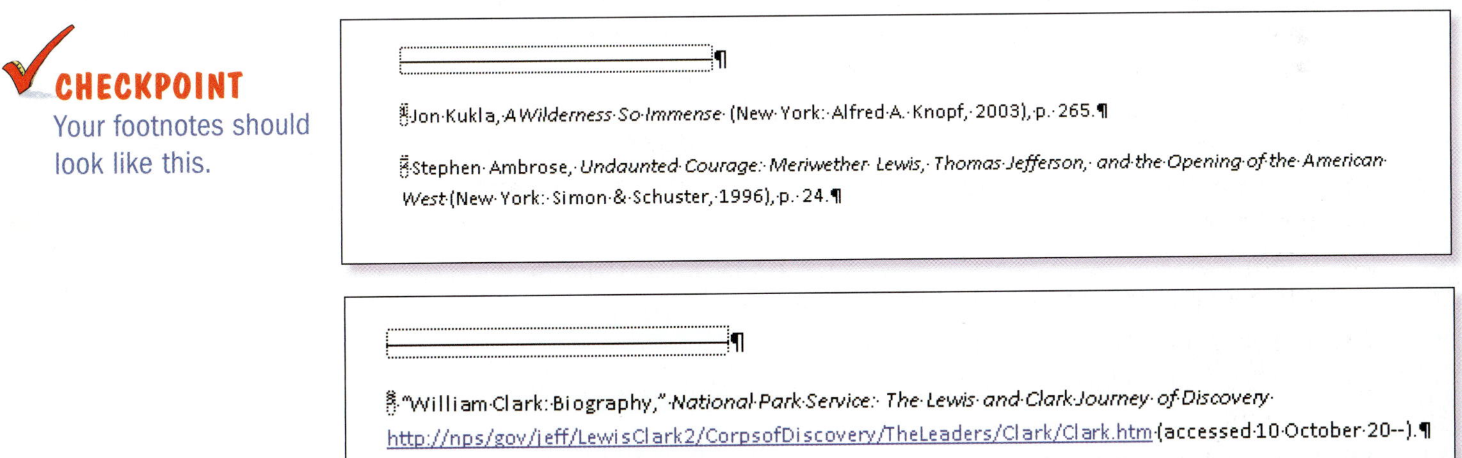


Jon Kukla, *A Wilderness So Immense* (New York: Alfred A. Knopf, 2003), p. 265.

Stephen Ambrose, *Undaunted Courage: Meriwether Lewis, Thomas Jefferson, and the Opening of the American West* (New York: Simon & Schuster, 1996), p. 24.

"William Clark: Biography," *National Park Service: The Lewis and Clark Journey of Discovery* http://nps/gov/jeff/LewisClark2/CorpsofDiscovery/TheLeaders/Clark/Clark.htm (accessed 10 October 20--).

Congratulations! Julie's *Lewis and Clark3* document looks great!

# Exploring On Your Own

## Blaze Your Own Trail

Blaze your own trail by practicing newly learned skills on your own!

**Part 1**

1. Open the *mushers* workbook and save it as *mushers15*.
2. Group the *Famous Women Mushers* and *Famous Men Mushers* worksheets.
3. Enter **The Iditarod Trail Sled Dog Race** in cell A1 and center the contents of cell A1 across the range A1:B1.
4. Apply the **Bold** font style and change the font size to 14. *Then ungroup the worksheets* and save the workbook.

**Part 2**

1. Open the *famous mushers* presentation and save it as *famous mushers15*. Apply the customized theme of your choice and add slide numbers, your name, and today's date as a fixed date to each slide *except* the Title Slide.
2. Replace *Student Name* with your name on the Title Slide; then view **slide 2**.
3. Switch to the *Famous Women Mushers* worksheet, select the range **A1:B7**, copy the range, and paste it as a *PowerPoint* table on slide 2 in the *famous mushers15* presentation.
4. Switch to the *Famous Men Mushers* worksheet, copy the range **A1:B7**, and paste it on slide 3 as a picture object.
5. Switch to the *Iditarod Winners* worksheet, copy the embedded chart, and paste it on slide 4 as an embedded chart object.
6. Close the workbook and close *Excel*. Then reposition, resize, and format the three pasted objects as desired.
7. Insert a new Title and Content slide as slide 2 and use it to create a summary slide with text hyperlinks to slides 3–6. Key **Summary** as the title on the new summary slide.
8. Add action buttons on slides 3–5 that return to **slide 2**. Create speaker notes for the new **slide 2**.
9. View the notes page for slide 2 and, with permission, preview and print it. Run the slide show; then save and close.

## Reading in Action

### Reading Informational Material

When you read informational material, look for answers to the questions *who*, *what*, *when*, *where*, *why*, and *how*. Read the slides in *Iditarod15* and takes notes that answer these questions. You may have more than one answer to some questions.

## Math in Action

### Using Distance and Rate to Calculate Time

Sled dogs race through 1,100 miles in the Iditarod. How long would it take a team to finish the race if they traveled at an average speed of 4 miles per hour?

$$\frac{1{,}100 \text{ miles}}{4 \text{ miles per hour}} = 275 \text{ hours} = 11 \text{ days } 11 \text{ hours}$$

Now you try it!

How long would it take a team of sled dogs to finish the race if they traveled at an average speed of 5 miles per hour? What if they traveled at an average speed of 5.5 miles per hour?

# Project Skills Review

You learned a lot in this project! We are very impressed with your progress. Let's take a few minutes to review the skills that you learned.

| | |
|---|---|
| **Find and replace text** | Click the **Find** or **Replace** buttons in the Editing group on the **Home** tab. Find Replace |
| **Select similarly formatted text** | Right-click formatted text, point to **Styles**, click **Select Text with Similar Formatting**. |
| **Paint formats from formatted text to unformatted text** | Click the **Format Painter** button in the Clipboard group on the **Home** tab. |
| **Cut, copy, and paste text** | Click the **Cut**, **Copy**, or **Paste** button in the Clipboard group on the **Home** tab. Select text and drag the text to a new location to move it.Select text, tap and hold the CTRL key, and drag the text to a new location to copy it. Paste |
| **Insert a hard page break** | Click the **Page Break** button in the Pages group on the **Insert** tab. Tap the CTRL + ENTER keys. Click the **Insert Page and Section Break** button in the Page Setup group on the **Page Layout** tab. Page Break Breaks |
| **Insert a Next Page section break** | Click the **Insert Page and Section Breaks** button in the Page Setup group on the **Page Layout** tab. Then click **Next Page** in the Section Breaks portion of the gallery to insert a new page and a new section. Breaks |
| **Insert page numbers in a header** | Click the **Insert Page Number** button in the Header & Footer group on the **Insert** tab, point to **Top of Page**, and click a numbering option. Page Number |
| **Insert footnotes** | Click the **Insert Footnote** button in the Footnotes group on the **References** tab. AB[1] Insert Footnote |

# Project Skills Review

You learned a lot in this project! We are very impressed with your progress. Let's take a few minutes to review the skills that you learned.

| **Group and ungroup worksheets** | Use the SHIFT + click method to group (select) adjacent worksheets; use the CTRL + click method to group (select) nonadjacent worksheets. Right-click a grouped worksheet and click **Ungroup Sheets**. | |
|---|---|---|
| **Paste *Excel* worksheet data as a *PowerPoint* table** | In *Excel*: click the **Copy** button in the Clipboard group on the **Home** tab. In *PowerPoint*: click the **Paste** button face in the Clipboard group on the **Home** tab. |  |
| **Apply a table style** | Click the **More** button in the Table Styles group on the **Table Tools Design** tab to view the styles gallery. |  |
| **Change the font color for table text** | Click the **Text Fill** button in the Table Styles group on the **Table Tools Design** tab. |  |
| **Paste *Excel* worksheet data as a picture** | In *Excel*: click the **Copy** button on the Clipboard group on the **Home** tab. In *PowerPoint 2010*: click the **Paste** button arrow in the Clipboard group on the **Home** tab and click the **Picture** icon in the Paste Options group. In *PowerPoint 2007*: click the **Paste** button arrow in the **Clipboard** group on the **Home** tab and click **Paste Special**. |  |
| **Paste *Excel* chart as an embedded workbook object** | In *Excel*: click the **Copy** button on the Clipboard group on the **Home** tab. In *PowerPoint 2010*: click the **Paste** button arrow in the Clipboard group on the **Home** tab and click the **Use Destination Theme & Embed Workbook** icon in the Paste Options group. In *PowerPoint 2007*: click the **Paste** button face in the Clipboard group on the **Home** tab. Then click the **Paste Options** icon and click **Excel Chart (Entire Workbook)**. |  |
| **Insert a summary slide** | Insert a Title and Content slide and then copy and paste the titles from other slides into a bulleted list on the new Title and Content slide. | |
| **Create text and action button hyperlinks** | Text hyperlink: select the text and then click the **Insert Hyperlink** button in the Links group on the **Insert** tab. Action button hyperlink: click the **Shapes** button in the Illustrations group on the **Insert** tab and draw an action button shape. |  |
| **Create and view speaker notes** | Key text in the notes pane below the slide pane. Click the **Notes Page** button in the Presentation Views group on the **View** tab. |  |

# Exploring On Your Own

## Blaze Your Own Trail

Blaze your own trail by practicing your new skills! Use classroom, library, CD-ROM, or online resources to learn more about the Louisiana Purchase. Where was the area called Louisiana that was claimed by the French? What was the Louisiana Purchase? When did it occur? What happened to the United States because of the Louisiana Purchase? Take notes about what you learn. Then create a new document and save it as *Louisiana Purchase3*.

1. Key the main heading **The Louisiana Purchase** and use your research notes to key several paragraphs about the Louisiana Purchase. Add at least two paragraph headings. Format the document appropriately, including margins and the main and paragraph headings, as a multi-page unbound report.
2. Use Find and Replace as necessary to find and replace text and formatting.
3. Use the Format Painter to paint formatting. Move and duplicate text as necessary using the Cut, Copy, and Paste buttons or using drag and drop. *After formatting, your document should be no more than two pages long.*
4. Use the Italic font style to add emphasis to multiple important words; then select all of the text formatted with the Italic font style using a shortcut menu. Remove the Italic font style and apply the Bold font style.
5. Cite your sources using footnotes.
6. Use a Next Page section break to create both a page break and a section break between the first and second page. Set a 1-inch top margin for the second page. Insert page numbers on all pages *except* the first page.
7. Check the spelling and grammar; then save and close the document.

## Reading in Action — Understanding Cause and Effect

Read the first page of the *Lewis and Clark3* document. The first event set in motion other events. Use a cause-and-effect graphic organizer to take notes about the events. One cause may have more than one effect. Effects, in turn, become causes of other events.

## Math in Action — Finding the Volume of a Cylinder

Lewis and Clark carried gunpowder in canisters. How much gunpowder could a cylinder hold if the cylinder was 4 feet high and had a base with a radius of 2 feet?

Volume = $\pi r^2 h$

$\pi$ is approximately 3.14, r is the radius of the base of the cylinder, and h is the height of the cylinder.

$V = \pi \times (2\text{ ft})^2 \times 4\text{ ft} = 3.14 \times 4\text{ ft}^2 \times 4\text{ ft} = 50.24\text{ ft}^3$ of gunpowder

Now you try it!

How much gunpowder could fit inside a cylinder 3 feet high with a radius of 5 feet? a cylinder 5 feet high with a radius of 3 feet?

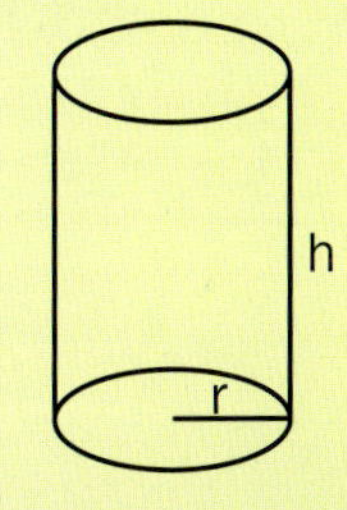

Speaker notes are also keyed in the text placeholder on notes pages. To view the notes pages, click the Views tab and then click the Notes Page button in the Presentation Views group.

**Let's add speaker notes in the slide 2 notes pane and then preview the notes page.**

**View | Presentation Views | Notes Page**

1. View **slide 2** and click inside the notes pane below the slide pane to position the insertion point.
2. Key the following text:
   **The Iditarod Trail Sled Dog Race is held annually in early March. The formal starting point is Anchorage, Alaska. But the race actually begins at Mile 0 at Wasilla, Alaska, just outside Anchorage.**
3. Click the **View** tab and locate the **Presentation Views** group.
4. Click the **Notes Page** button in the Presentation Views group to view the notes page for slide 2.

You can preview and print individual notes pages as necessary. *Remember!* Do not print your notes pages unless your teacher instructs you to do so.

5. Switch back to Normal view; then save and close the presentation.

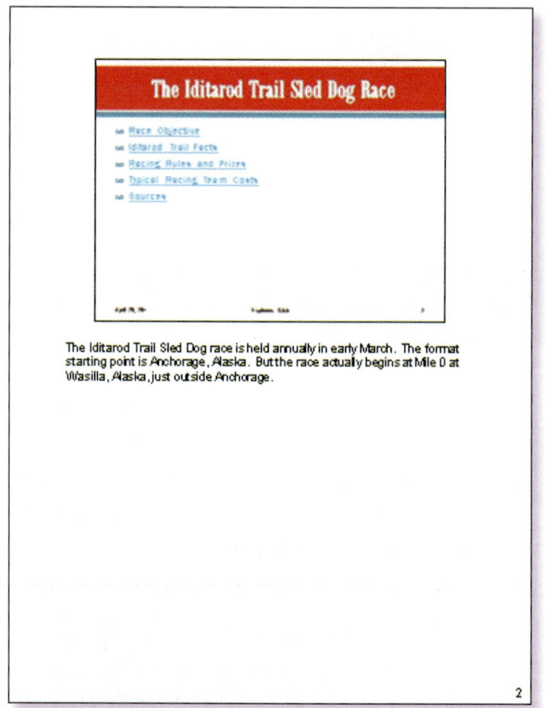


Congratulations! Luis's workbook and presentation are ready to go!

# Exploring *Across the Curriculum*

## Internet/Web

Open your Web browser and use a favorite or bookmark to view the Learning with Computers Web page (www.cengage.com/school/keyboarding/lwcorange). Click the **Links** option and click **Project 3**. Click the links to learn more about the Lewis and Clark Expedition. What was the purpose of the expedition? What was the path of the expedition? How long did the expedition take? Who guided the expedition into unknown territory? What important discoveries were made as a result of the expedition? Take notes about what you learn. Then create a new document and save it as *expedition3*.

1. Key the main heading **Lewis and Clark Expedition** followed by several paragraphs describing the expedition based on your notes. Add two paragraph headings. Format your document appropriately, including margins and main and paragraph headings, as an unbound report.
2. Move and duplicate text, as necessary, using the Cut, Copy, and Paste buttons or drag and drop.
3. Use Find and Replace, as necessary, to locate and replace text and formatting. Use the Format Painter to paint formats.
4. Cite your sources with footnotes. *After formatting, your document should be no more than two pages long.*
5. Use a Next Page section break to create a page break and a section break between the first and second page. Set 1-inch top, left, right, and bottom margins for the second page.
6. Insert page numbers on all pages *except* the first page.
7. Check the spelling and grammar; then save and close the document.

## Social Studies: Research and Write

Work with a classmate to use library, classroom, or online resources, including maps, to research the timeline and path of the Lewis and Clark Expedition from St. Louis to the Pacific Ocean and back. On a map of the United States, plot the path of the expedition through the 11 states, starting at and returning to St. Louis, Missouri. Note at least five significant dates and events along the path.

Explore More

Your selected action button should look similar to this.

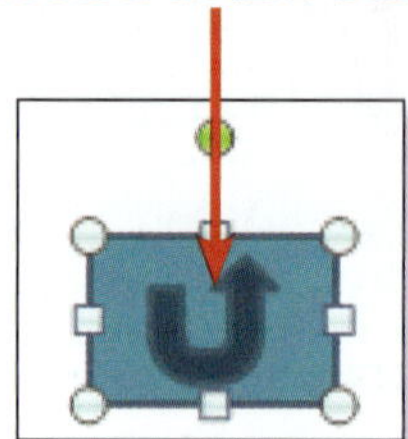

13. Tap CTRL + C to copy the action button and then paste it in the lower-right corners of slides 4–6.
14. Deselect the last pasted action button and save the presentation.

Well done! Each time you click an action button, you will jump back to slide 2. Now you are ready to run the slide show and test the hyperlinks.

**Let's run the slide show and navigate using hyperlinks and action buttons.**

1. View **slide 1** and run the slide show.
2. Click the mouse button to advance to **slide 2**.
3. Click the **Race Objective** hyperlink to jump to slide 3.
4. Point to the **action button** in the lower-right corner of slide 3. The mouse pointer becomes a pointing hand.
5. Click the **action button** to jump back to slide 2. The **Race Objectives** hyperlink has changed color, which indicates that you have already clicked it.
6. Continue by clicking the hyperlinks on slide 2 to jump to a specific slide and then clicking the action button to jump back to slide 2.
7. Tap the ESC key when you have finished checking the hyperlinks and action buttons.

Fantastic! Now let's add speaker notes to slide 2.

## Adding Speaker Notes

You can add speaker notes for additional information you want to tell your audience as you advance your slides during a slide show. Speaker notes are keyed in the notes pane below the slide pane and printed as separate notes pages. Each notes page contains both a miniature of the slide and the note text.

# Exploring Across the Curriculum

## Language Arts: Words to Know

Look up the meaning of the following terms in a classroom dictionary, CD-ROM dictionary or encyclopedia, or online dictionary.

| Corps of Discovery | fauna | flora | geographer |
|---|---|---|---|
| Mandan | Missouri River | northwest passage | Shoshone |

Create a new document. Save the document as *definitions3* followed by your initials. Set a 2-inch top margin and 1-inch left and right margins. Key **Terms and Definitions** as a main heading at the top of the document and format the main heading using the Title style. Key each term on one line and its definition on the following line below the main heading. Insert a blank line between each definition and the next term. Select all of the terms using the CTRL key and apply the Underline font style. Select all of the definitions using the CTRL key and apply the Italic font style.

Insert a section break near the bottom of the first page to force the remaining text to a second page. Change the top, left, right, and bottom margins for the second page to 1-inch. Insert a page number on just the second page. Select all underlined text using a shortcut menu and then remove the Underline font style and apply the Bold font style. Check the spelling and grammar; then save and close the document.

## Getting Help

The Word Options dialog box is very important. It contains different preferences you can set to control how many of the *Word* features work. Click the File tab and click Options or click the Office Button and click Word Options to open the Word Options dialog box. Then review the preferences you can change. *Do not make any changes unless directed to do so by your teacher.*

Explore More

When you draw or select an action button shape, the Drawing Tools Format tab appears on the Ribbon. You can use buttons on the tab to change the shape's style, fill, and outline and to apply special effects to the shape. Check it out!

In the shapes gallery, click an action button shape at the bottom of the gallery and draw the shape on the slide. When you release the mouse button, the Action Settings dialog box opens. You assign the hyperlink's target or destination to the shape in this dialog box. Action button colors are controlled by the theme applied to the presentation.

**Let's create action button hyperlinks on slides 3–6 that jump back to slide 2. To save time, create the first action button on slide 3 and then copy and paste it on slides 4–6.**

Insert | Illustrations | Shapes

1. View **slide 3**.
2. Click the **Insert** tab, if necessary, and locate the **Illustrations** group.
3. Click the **Shapes** button in the Illustrations group to display the shapes gallery; then locate the **Action Button** shapes category at the bottom of the gallery.

4. Use ScreenTips to locate the **Action Button: Return** icon in the gallery.
5. Click the **Action Button: Return** shape. The mouse pointer becomes a crosshair drawing pointer.
6. Move the drawing pointer to the lower-right corner of the slide.
7. Drag down and to the right approximately 1/2 inch to draw the button.
8. Release the mouse button to open the Action Settings dialog box.
9. Click the **Hyperlink to** arrow.
10. Click **Slide** to open the Hyperlink to Slide dialog box.
11. Click **2. The Iditarod Trail Sled Dog Race** in the Slide title list and click **OK** to return to the Actions Settings dialog box.
12. Click **OK**. The selected action button is now linked to slide 2.

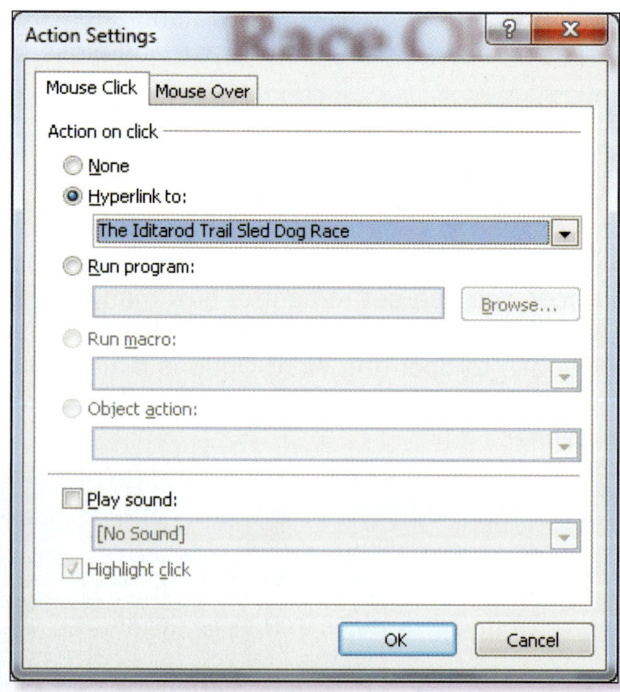

# Exploring Across the Curriculum

## Career Day

The history surrounding the Lewis and Clark Expedition provides a number of states, cities, and towns from Missouri to the Pacific Northwest for generating hospitality and tourism revenues. The hospitality and tourism industry includes the marketing and management of lodging, restaurant, and recreation services. Using library, printed, or online resources, identify three interesting occupations in the hospitality and tourism industry. Write a brief summary of each occupation, print your summary, and save it in your Career Day folder.

## Your Personal Journal

Open your personal journal document. Insert today's date. Key two or three paragraphs explaining how the decision by Monroe and Livingston to purchase all of the French territories called Louisiana—instead of just New Orleans—changed the United States. Check the spelling and grammar; then save and close your journal document.

**Online Enrichment Games**  www.cengage.com/school/keyboarding/lwcorange

6. Click **OK** and deselect the placeholder. The Race Objective bulleted list text is now a different color and underlined, indicating a hyperlink to slide 3.
7. Run the slide show for slide 2 to test the hyperlink.
8. Move the mouse pointer to the Race Objective hyperlink. The mouse pointer becomes a pointing hand.
9. Click the **Race Objective** hyperlink to view slide 3.
10. Tap the ESC key to stop the slide show.
11. View **slide 2**. The Race Objective hyperlink is now a different color, indicating that the hyperlink has been clicked.
12. Using the previous steps as your guide, create the following hyperlinks on slide 2:
    - **Iditarod Trail Facts** to slide 4
    - **Racing Rules and Prizes** text to slide 5
    - **Typical Racing Team Costs** text to slide 6
    - **Sources** to slide 7

Your slide 2 should look similar to this.

The Iditarod Trail Sled Dog Race

- Race Objective
- Iditarod Trail Facts
- Racing Rules and Prizes
- Typical Racing Team Costs
- Sources

April 26, 20-- Explorers Club 2

13. Deselect the placeholder and save the presentation.

Fantastic! Next, create action button hyperlinks that jump back to slide 2 on slides 3–6.

### Action Button Hyperlinks

You can also create hyperlinks by drawing action buttons. An action button is a predesigned button shape you draw with the mouse pointer. To draw an action button, click the Insert tab and then click the Shapes button in the Illustrations group to view the shapes gallery.

# Project 3



## 3a Review o, t, n, g

Key each line twice. Double-space between 2-line groups.

### TECHNIQUE TIP

Use a down-and-in spacing motion.

**o**

1 l o l o | olo olo | loj loj | olko olko | dojo dojo | os os;

2 sold sold | loan loan | foot foot | hook hook | load load;

**t**

3 f t f t | tft tft | thft thft | tjft tjft | trft trft | tft;

4 take take | tire tire | heat heat | hot hot | after after;

**n**

5 j n j n | njn njn | hjn hjn | nhk nhk | knjs knjs; | jnj jn;

6 not not | noon noon | nine nine | done done | found found;

**g**

7 f g f g | gfg gfg | gtg gtg | tgfg tgfg | ghfg ghfg | dg df;

8 eggs eggs | gate gate | frog frog | gone gone | good good;

## 3b Technique: ENTER

Key each line twice single-spaced; double-space between 2-line groups.

1 Dave bought a new camera.

2 Julian competed in the finals.

3 Steve wanted to buy the video game.

4 Vanna enjoyed the hike in the mountains.

5 Keith may not make the varsity baseball team.

## 3c Build Skill

Key each line twice single-spaced; double-space between 2-line groups.

For additional practice: **MicroType 5** New Key Review, Alphabetic Lessons 6–7

1 The sign is on the mantle by the antique ornament.

2 Pamela kept the food for the fish by the fishbowl.

3 I paid the man by the dock for the bushel of corn.

4 The box with a shamrock and an iris is by the car.

5 To the right of the big lake is the dismal shanty.

gwam 20" | 3 | 6 | 9 | 12 | 15 | 18 | 21 | 24 | 27 | 30 |

For example, slides are often advanced *sequentially* during a slide show—from slide 1 to slide 2 to slide 3 and so forth. But you can also advance slides or return to previous slides *in any order* you choose by using hyperlinks.

You can also use hyperlinks in a slide show to jump to a slide in a different presentation, to open another file type such as an *Excel* workbook, and to start your Web browser and load a Web page. Hyperlinks can also be created using clip art, pictures, and shapes.

**Text Hyperlinks**

To create text hyperlinks, select the text, click the Insert tab, and then click the Insert Hyperlink button in the Links group to open the Insert Hyperlink dialog box. In the Insert Hyperlink dialog box, you specify the target or destination of the hyperlink. The text hyperlink colors are controlled by the theme applied to the presentation.

You can also create hyperlinks by pressing the CTRL + K keys to open the Insert Hyperlink dialog box.

**Let's use the bulleted list text on slide 2 to create text hyperlinks to the related slides in the same presentation.**

Insert | Links | Insert Hyperlink

1. View **slide 2**, if necessary, and select the **Race Objective** text.
2. Click the **Insert** tab and locate the **Links** group.
3. Click the **Insert Hyperlink** button in the Links group to open the Insert Hyperlink dialog box.
4. Click the **Place in This Document** button in the Link to pane.
5. Click **3. Race Objective** in the Select a place in this document pane.

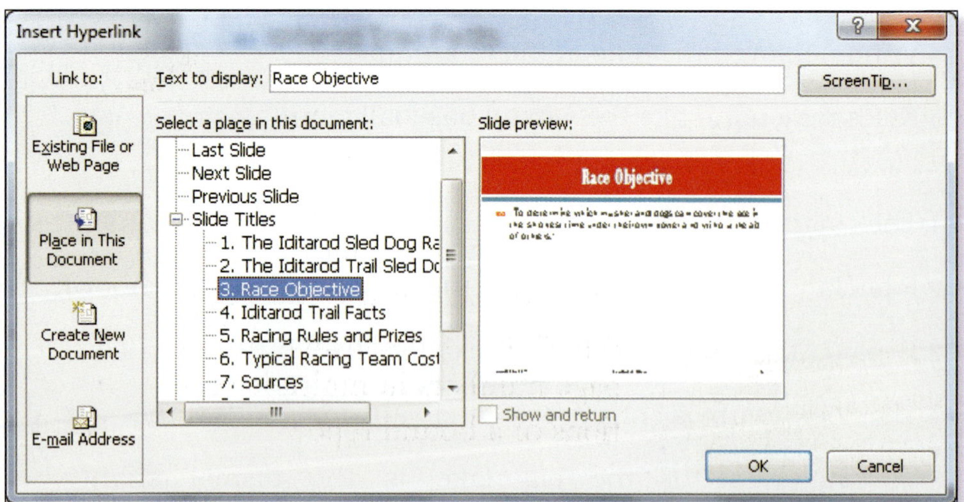

# Exploring the Writers of Concord

## Explorers' Guide

**Data file:** writers

**Objectives:**
In this project, you will:
- explore additional keyboard shortcuts
- use Full Screen Reading view
- create and format a table
- create a report cover page
- cite sources on a separate page
- paginate a multipage bound report

© ANDREW O'BRIEN / ALAMY

## Our Exploration Assignment:

**Adding a title page and formatting sections of a multipage bound report**

The Explorers Club is learning about influential nineteenth-century writers and philosophers who shared ties to Concord, Massachusetts. Luis has started a report about the writers of Concord. Can you help him finish the report? Fantastic! Just follow the Trail Markers to explore using additional keyboard shortcuts, add a report title or cover page, create and format a table, cite sources as endnotes on a separate page at the end of the report, and set margins and insert page numbers in multiple sections of a bound report.

3. Key **The Iditarod Trail Sled Dog Race** as the title on the new slide 2.
4. View **slide 3**, drag to select the slide title text, and tap the CTRL + C keys to copy the title.
5. View **slide 2**, click the Content placeholder, tap the CTRL + V keys to paste the copied slide title as bulleted text, and tap the ENTER key.

The Iditarod Trail Sled Dog Race

- Race Objective
-

6. Using steps 4 and 5 as your guide, copy and paste the titles from slides 4–7 to slide 2.
7. Deselect the slide 2 bulleted list placeholder and save the presentation.

**CHECKPOINT**
Your new slide 2 should look similar to this.

The Iditarod Trail Sled Dog Race

- Race Objective
- Iditarod Trail Facts
- Racing Rules and Prizes
- Typical Racing Team Costs
- Sources

Terrific! Next, you will create hyperlinks you can click to navigate during a slide show.

## Creating Text and Action Button Hyperlinks

As you learned in the Getting Started project, a hyperlink is clickable text, a picture, or an icon that allows you to jump to another Web page. You have been using hyperlinks to jump from one Web page to another in your Web browser. You can also use hyperlinks to jump to a different *Word* document, *Excel* worksheet or workbook, or *PowerPoint* presentation or slide.

**Begin by opening Luis's document and saving it with a new name.**

1. Open the *writers* document and save it as *writers4*.

OK! Let's get started by exploring new ways to use keyboard shortcuts.

**ERGONOMICS TIP**

Wait! Check the position of your index finger on the mouse! Make certain it is resting lightly on the mouse button; do not hold your finger above the button between clicks.

## Exploring Additional Keyboard Shortcuts

Using keyboard shortcuts to select and format text and perform other *Word* tasks allows you to work in your documents more efficiently. Why? Because your hands are already on the keyboard! You can save time by not reaching for the mouse and moving the mouse pointer across the screen!

In earlier projects, you learned how to use keyboard shortcuts such as the CTRL + HOME keys to reposition the insertion point. You can also use the keyboard to navigate the Ribbon tabs and groups, create new documents, open existing documents, save and print documents, move and duplicate text, apply character and paragraph formatting, check spelling and grammar, and perform many other tasks.

Although it would be difficult to remember all of the many, many keyboard shortcuts, it is important to learn and practice those that help you perform common tasks. Let's see how using keyboard shortcuts to perform common selection and formatting tasks can save you time.

You can find a useful list of *Word* keyboard shortcuts by searching *Word* Help for keyboard shortcuts topics.

Your slide 5 should look similar to this.

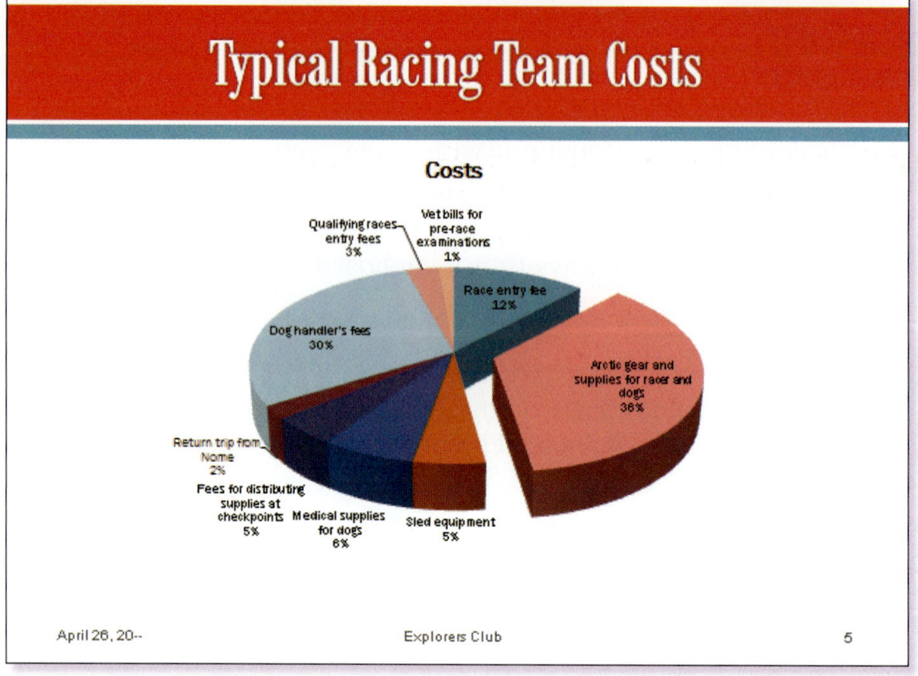


Wow! What a great-looking slide! Now let's insert a new slide that summarizes all of the slides in the presentation.

## Creating a Summary Slide Using Copy and Paste

The second slide in a presentation—sometimes called a summary slide—is often used to list the topics to be covered in the remaining slides. Like a book's table of contents that lists the titles of each chapter, a summary slide often lists the titles of each remaining slide.

To create a summary slide, you can insert a Title and Content slide and key a slide title, then copy each remaining slide's title and paste it as a bullet in the content pane.

**Let's use copy and paste to create a summary slide.**

Home | Slides | New Slide

1. Click between slide 1 and slide 2 in the Slides tab to indicate where the new slide will be inserted.
2. Insert a new Title and Content slide as slide 2.

**Let's use keyboard shortcuts to position the insertion point, select text, align text horizontally, apply the Heading 1 style, repeat the last formatting action, and save the changes to the document.**

1. Tap the CTRL + HOME keys, if necessary, to move the insertion point to the beginning of the main heading at the top of the document.
   - Tap and hold down the SHIFT key as you tap the END key to select the entire main heading line; then release the SHIFT key.
   - Tap the CTRL + L keys to left-align the main heading.
   - Apply the Title style using the mouse (there is no keyboard shortcut for this style).
2. Tap the CTRL + END keys to move the insertion point to the end of the main heading on the last page of the document.
   - Tap and hold down the SHIFT key as you tap the HOME key to select the entire main heading.
   - Apply the Title style using the mouse.
   - Tap the CTRL + HOME keys to return to the top of the first page.
3. Use the arrow keys to move the insertion point to the beginning of the first paragraph heading, **Louisa May Alcott (1832-1888)**.
   - Tap the SHIFT + END keys to select the paragraph heading.
   - Tap the ALT + CTRL + 1 keys to apply the Heading 1 style.
4. Use the arrow keys to move the insertion point to the beginning of the second paragraph heading, **Henry David Thoreau (1817-1862)**.
   - Tap the SHIFT + END keys to select the paragraph heading.
   - Tap the CTRL + Y keys to repeat the previous formatting (applying the Heading 1 style).
5. Using steps 2 and 3 as your guide, select and format the remaining two paragraph headings using the keyboard shortcuts.
6. Tap the CTRL + S keys to save the document.

Wow! That was terrific! Now let's practice additional keyboard shortcuts.

Here's a great idea! Create a short list of the keyboard shortcuts you frequently use and keep the list handy for easy reference!

**Let's display the underlying data for the chart and change the Race entry fee value from $1,850 to $2,000. Because we pasted the chart as an embedded workbook object, no change will be made to the original *racing data 15* workbook.**

Chart Tools Design | Data | Edit Data

1. Select the chart on slide 5, if necessary, and observe that the data label for the Race entry fee is currently $1,850.
2. Click the **Chart Tools Design** tab and locate the **Data** group.
3. Click the **Edit Data** button in the Data group to display the underlying data in an *Excel* workbook entitled *Chart in Microsoft PowerPoint*. The presentation and workbook containing the underlying data are tiled vertically on the screen.

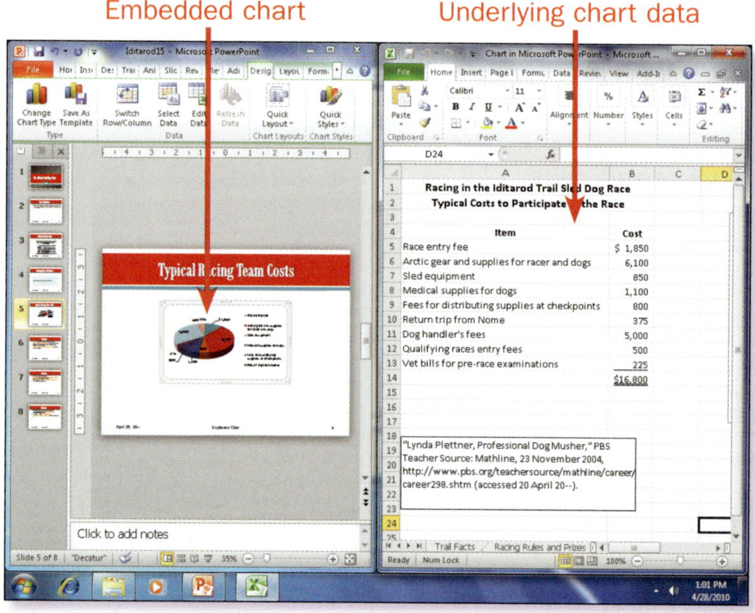


4. Click the workbook's **title bar** to activate the workbook, if necessary; then click cell **B5** and enter **2,000**.
5. Close the *Chart in Microsoft PowerPoint* workbook.
6. Observe that the chart is updated to reflect the new value for the Race entry fee.
7. Resize the chart object with the mouse to view the entire legend and reposition the chart attractively on the slide.
8. Explode a pie slice of your choice using the mouse.
9. Using buttons on the Chart Tools Design, Layout, and Format tabs, modify the chart to change its layout, add **Costs** as the chart title, recolor a data marker, and make other desired formatting changes.
10. Deselect the chart and save the presentation.

**Let's use keyboard shortcuts to move the third paragraph so that it becomes the second paragraph, apply font styles to keywords, and spell-check the document.**

1. Use the arrow keys to move the insertion point to the beginning of the first sentence in the third body text paragraph.
   - Tap and hold the SHIFT key as you tap the END key and then tap the Down arrow key four times to select the entire paragraph. Release the SHIFT key.
   - Tap the CTRL + X keys to cut the selected paragraph.
   - Use the arrow keys to move the insertion point to the beginning of the first sentence in the second body text paragraph.
   - Tap the CTRL + V keys to paste the cut paragraph at the new location.
2. Use the CTRL key and the mouse pointer to select the following book titles located in the paragraphs on the first and second report pages: *Little Women, Walden, Life in the Woods*, and *The Scarlet Letter*.
   - Tap the CTRL + I keys to apply the Italic font style.
   - Tap the CTRL + HOME keys.
3. Tap the F7 key to open the Spelling and Grammar dialog box and correct the two spelling errors in the body text: the words *revoluton* and *ownd*. Click **OK** to close the dialog box.
4. Tap the CTRL + HOME keys; then tap the CTRL + S keys to save the document.

Good job! Now let's check out the changes we made in our document by switching to Full Screen Reading view.

## Using Full Screen Reading View

In an earlier project, you learned how to switch between the Print Layout and Draft editing views and how to preview your document. Another useful *Word* view is Full Screen Reading view, which allows you to more easily read a document on your computer screen.

Like Print Layout view and Draft view, you can switch to Full Screen Reading view by clicking a button in the View Shortcuts on the status bar or by clicking the View tab and clicking a button in the Document Views group.

In Full Screen Reading view, you can set options to view one or multiple pages, scroll to view additional pages, highlight or edit text, add comments for other reviewers, temporarily increase the text size for easier reading, save, print, and more.

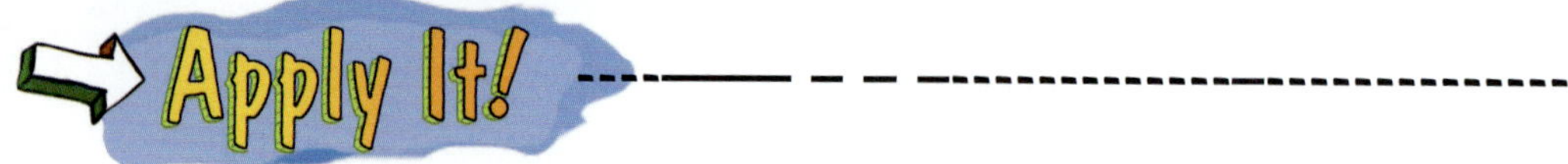


Home | Clipboard | Copy or Paste

**Let's copy the embedded chart on the *Racing Team Costs* worksheet and paste it on slide 5 as an embedded chart object using Paste Options.**

1. Switch to the workbook and click the *Racing Team Costs* sheet tab.
2. Click the embedded chart to select it and then click the **Copy** button face in the Clipboard group. Close the Clipboard task pane, if necessary. 
3. Switch to the presentation and view **slide 5**.
4. In *PowerPoint 2010*, click the **Paste** button arrow in the Clipboard group and click the **Use Destination Theme & Embed Workbook** icon in the Paste Options group. 

PowerPoint 2010 Paste Options

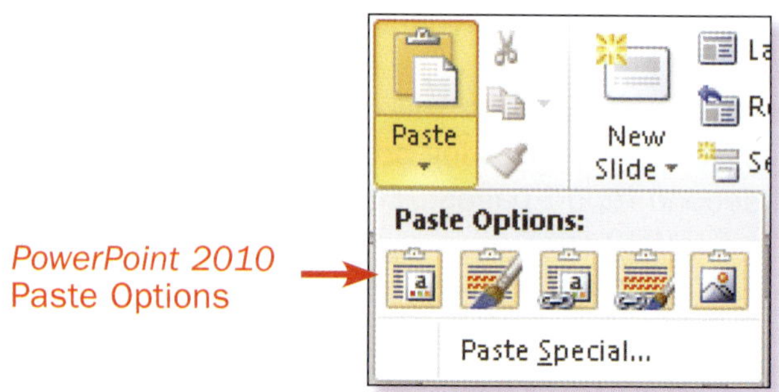


5. In *PowerPoint 2007*, click the **Paste** button face in the Clipboard group; then click the **Paste Options** icon below the chart and click **Excel Chart (Entire workbook)** in the menu.  

PowerPoint 2007 Paste Options

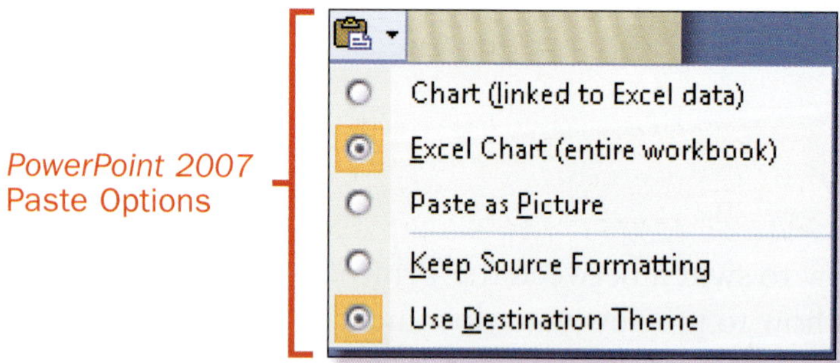


6. Switch to the workbook; deselect the chart and then save and close the workbook.

Now let's see how you can change the chart's underlying data without changing the original workbook.

**Let's switch to Full Screen Reading view and check out the changes we made to the *writers4* document in the previous Trail Marker.**

1. Click the **Full Screen Reading** button in the View Shortcuts on the status bar. 
2. If pages 1–2 are not visible, click the **View Options** button in the upper-right corner of the screen and click **Show Two Pages** in the options gallery.

**CHECKPOINT**

Screens 1–2 of your document in Full Screen Reading view should look like this.

Document in Full Screen Reading view

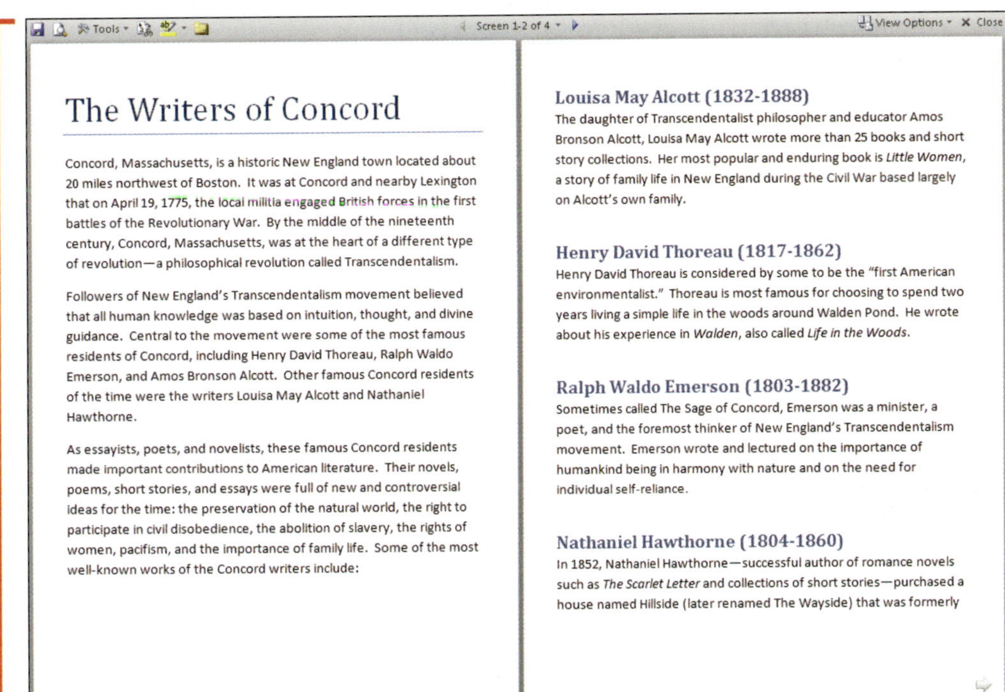

Tools · Screen 1-2 of 4 · View Options · Close

# The Writers of Concord

Concord, Massachusetts, is a historic New England town located about 20 miles northwest of Boston. It was at Concord and nearby Lexington that on April 19, 1775, the local militia engaged British forces in the first battles of the Revolutionary War. By the middle of the nineteenth century, Concord, Massachusetts, was at the heart of a different type of revolution—a philosophical revolution called Transcendentalism.

Followers of New England's Transcendentalism movement believed that all human knowledge was based on intuition, thought, and divine guidance. Central to the movement were some of the most famous residents of Concord, including Henry David Thoreau, Ralph Waldo Emerson, and Amos Bronson Alcott. Other famous Concord residents of the time were the writers Louisa May Alcott and Nathaniel Hawthorne.

As essayists, poets, and novelists, these famous Concord residents made important contributions to American literature. Their novels, poems, short stories, and essays were full of new and controversial ideas for the time: the preservation of the natural world, the right to participate in civil disobedience, the abolition of slavery, the rights of women, pacifism, and the importance of family life. Some of the most well-known works of the Concord writers include:

## Louisa May Alcott (1832-1888)

The daughter of Transcendentalist philosopher and educator Amos Bronson Alcott, Louisa May Alcott wrote more than 25 books and short story collections. Her most popular and enduring book is *Little Women*, a story of family life in New England during the Civil War based largely on Alcott's own family.

## Henry David Thoreau (1817-1862)

Henry David Thoreau is considered by some to be the "first American environmentalist." Thoreau is most famous for choosing to spend two years living a simple life in the woods around Walden Pond. He wrote about his experience in *Walden*, also called *Life in the Woods*.

## Ralph Waldo Emerson (1803-1882)

Sometimes called The Sage of Concord, Emerson was a minister, a poet, and the foremost thinker of New England's Transcendentalism movement. Emerson wrote and lectured on the importance of humankind being in harmony with nature and on the need for individual self-reliance.

## Nathaniel Hawthorne (1804-1860)

In 1852, Nathaniel Hawthorne—successful author of romance novels such as *The Scarlet Letter* and collections of short stories—purchased a house named Hillside (later renamed The Wayside) that was formerly

3. Read your document carefully to make certain all of the changes from Trail Marker 1 were made correctly.

You can scroll the view of multipage document screens by clicking a navigation arrow at the top of the Full Screen Reading window or a navigation arrow in the lower-left or lower-right corner of each screen.

**CHECKPOINT**

Your slide 4 should look similar to this.

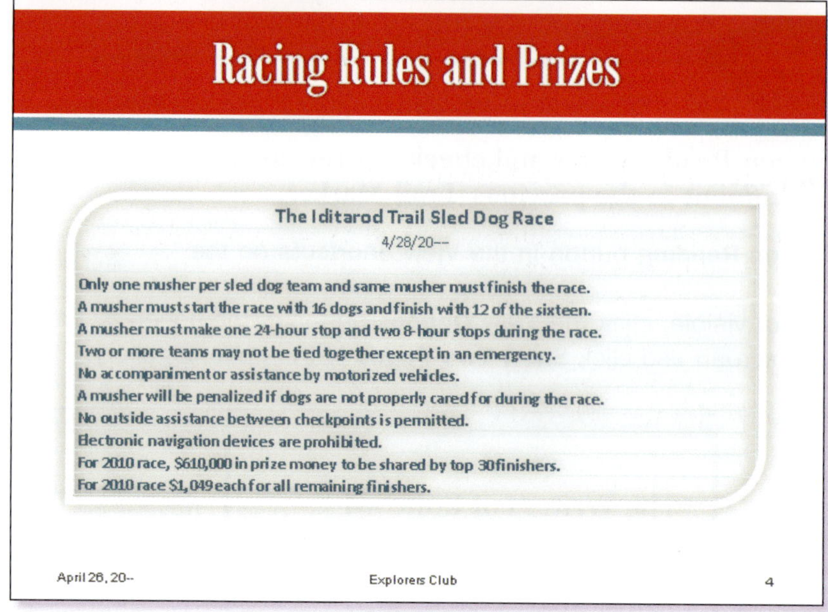


Great! Now let's copy and paste the *Excel* chart on the *Racing Team Costs* worksheet as an embedded object and then format it.

**Pasting an *Excel* Chart as an Embedded Object**

By default, an *Excel* chart is pasted on a slide as a *PowerPoint* chart you can format and edit just like an *Excel* chart; however, you cannot access and change the underlying data on which the chart is based.

If you want to be able to access and change the chart's underlying data while working in *PowerPoint*, you must paste the copied *Excel* chart as an embedded or linked object.

- If you paste the *Excel* chart as a linked object, changes to the underlying data must be made in the original workbook. This is a good option if the data in the workbook frequently changes and you want the chart on the slide to have the most current data each time you open the presentation.
- However, if you want to access and change the underlying data for the chart in the presentation *only* (without making changes to the data in the original workbook), you must paste the chart as an embedded object.

You can paste an *Excel* chart as an embedded object using options in the Paste Special dialog box or using Paste Options.

**Let's navigate between pages of the *writers4* document.**

1. Click the **Next Screen** or right-pointing navigation arrow at the top of the Full Screen Reading window to view screens 3–4.
2. Click the navigation arrow in the lower-left corner of screen 3 to view screens 1–2.

You can turn on document editing by clicking the View Options button at the top of the Full Screen Reading view and clicking Allow Typing.

**Let's turn on text editing and select and edit text.**

1. Click the **View Options** button at the top of the Full Screen Reading window and click **Allow Typing**, if necessary, to turn on text editing. The insertion point is now visible in the text, and you can select, key, and format text.
2. Select the word **Transcendentalism** at the end of the first body paragraph on screen 1.
3. Tap the CTRL + B keys to apply the Bold font style; then deselect the text.

The Writers of Concord

Concord, Massachusetts, is a historic New England town located about 20 miles northwest of Boston. It was at Concord and nearby Lexington that on April 19, 1775, the local militia engaged British forces in the first battles of the Revolutionary War. By the middle of the nineteenth century, Concord, Massachusetts, was at the heart of a different type of revolution—a philosophical revolution called **Transcendentalism**.

Text edited in Full Screen Reading view

4. Click the **View Options** button at the top of the Full Screen Reading window and click **Allow Typing** to turn off text editing. The insertion point is no longer available in the text; text editing is turned off.

Similar to previewing your document in Backstage view or Print Preview, you can see how your document will look when printed in Full Screen Reading view.

**Let's copy the data on the *Racing Rules and Prizes* worksheet, paste it on slide 4 as a picture object, and then recolor the picture and apply a picture style.**

**Home|Clipboard|Copy or Paste**

**Picture Tools Format|Picture Styles|Color or Recolor**

**Picture Tools Format|Picture Styles|More**

1. Switch to the workbook; tap the ESC key to clear the Clipboard and tap the CTRL + HOME keys to activate cell A1.
2. Click the ***Racing Rules and Prizes*** sheet tab.
3. Select the range **A1:A13** and click the **Copy** button in the Clipboard group.
4. Switch to the presentation and view **slide 4**.

5. Click the **Paste** button arrow in the Clipboard group and click **Paste Special** to open the Paste Special dialog box.
6. Click the **Paste** option button, if necessary, and click **Picture (Enhanced Metafile)** in the As list.

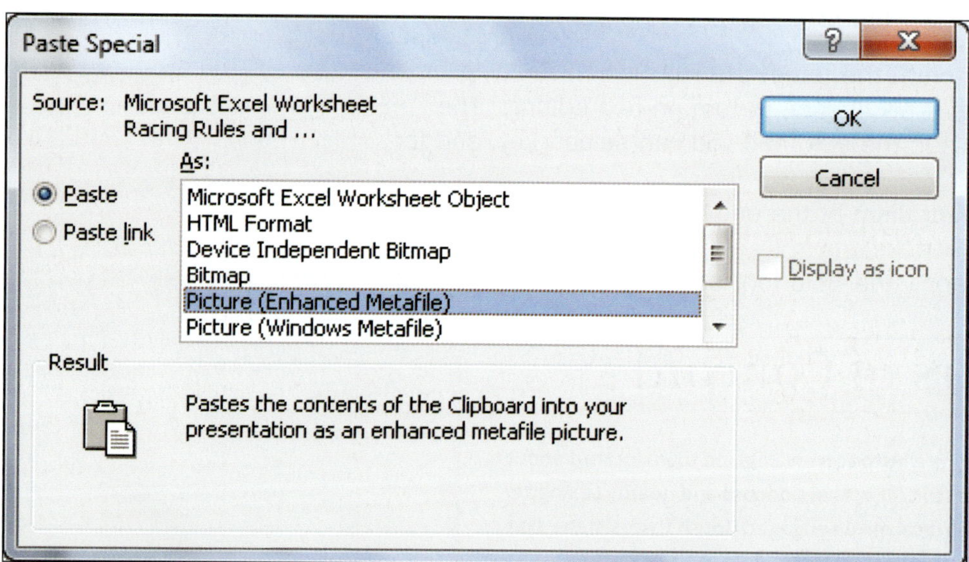


7. Click **OK** to insert the picture in the center of the slide.

As you learned in previous projects, inserting or selecting a picture object adds the Picture Tools Format tab to the Ribbon; the tab contains buttons you can use to format the picture.

8. Click the **Picture Tools Format** tab, if necessary, and then recolor the picture, change its style, and make other formatting changes as desired.
9. Resize and reposition the picture as desired; then deselect the picture and save the presentation.

**Let's see how the *writers4* document will look if printed now, without additional changes.**

1. Click the **View Options** button at the top of the Full Screen Reading window and click **Show Printed Page**. You are now previewing Page 1–2 of 3.

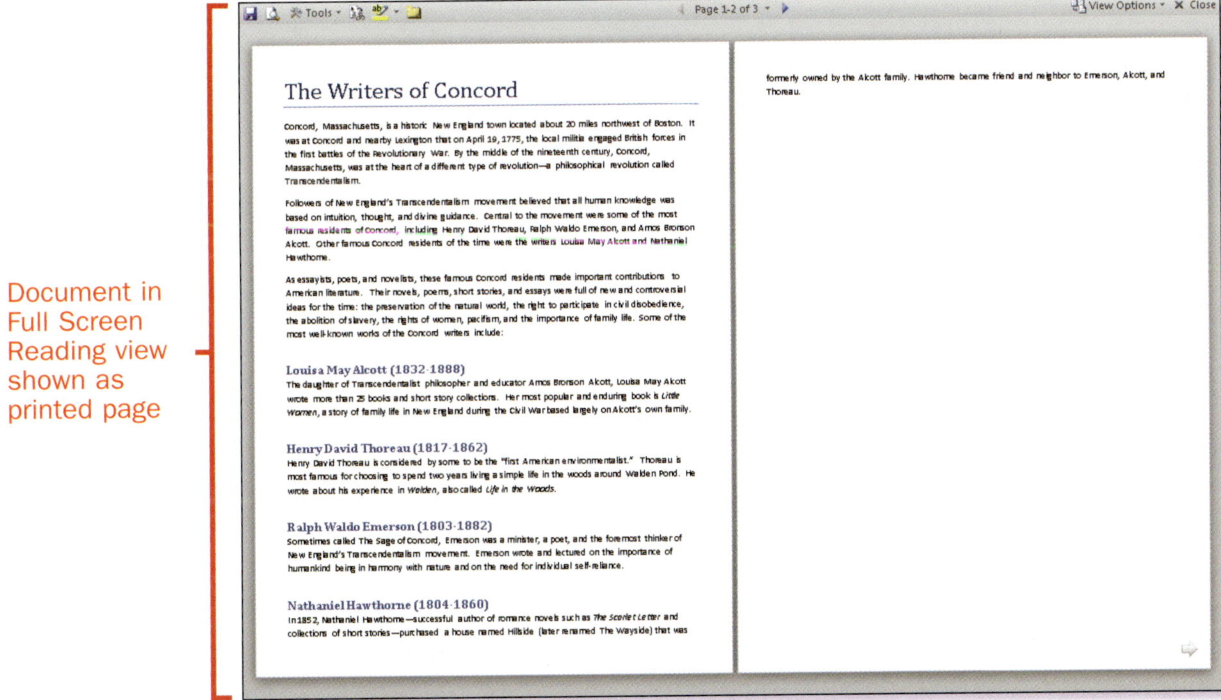


The Writers of Concord

Concord, Massachusetts, is a historic New England town located about 20 miles northwest of Boston. It was at Concord and nearby Lexington that on April 19, 1775, the local militia engaged British forces in the first battles of the Revolutionary War. By the middle of the nineteenth century, Concord, Massachusetts, was at the heart of a different type of revolution—a philosophical revolution called Transcendentalism.

Followers of New England's Transcendentalism movement believed that all human knowledge was based on intuition, thought, and divine guidance. Central to the movement were some of the most famous residents of Concord, including Henry David Thoreau, Ralph Waldo Emerson, and Amos Bronson Alcott. Other famous Concord residents of the time were the writers Louisa May Alcott and Nathaniel Hawthorne.

As essayists, poets, and novelists, these famous Concord residents made important contributions to American literature. Their novels, poems, short stories, and essays were full of new and controversial ideas for the time: the preservation of the natural world, the right to participate in civil disobedience, the abolition of slavery, the rights of women, pacifism, and the importance of family life. Some of the most well-known works of the Concord writers include:

Louisa May Alcott (1832-1888)
The daughter of Transcendentalist philosopher and educator Amos Bronson Alcott, Louisa May Alcott wrote more than 25 books and short story collections. Her most popular and enduring book is *Little Women*, a story of family life in New England during the Civil War based largely on Alcott's own family.

Henry David Thoreau (1817-1862)
Henry David Thoreau is considered by some to be the "first American environmentalist." Thoreau is most famous for choosing to spend two years living a simple life in the woods around Walden Pond. He wrote about his experience in *Walden*, also called *Life in the Woods*.

Ralph Waldo Emerson (1803-1882)
Sometimes called The Sage of Concord, Emerson was a minister, a poet, and the foremost thinker of New England's Transcendentalism movement. Emerson wrote and lectured on the importance of humankind being in harmony with nature and on the need for individual self-reliance.

Nathaniel Hawthorne (1804-1860)
In 1852, Nathaniel Hawthorne—successful author of romance novels such as *The Scarlet Letter* and collections of short stories—purchased a house named Hillside (later renamed The Wayside) that was

formerly owned by the Alcott family. Hawthorne became friend and neighbor to Emerson, Alcott, and Thoreau.

2. Click the **View Options** button at the top of the Full Screen Reading window and click **Show Printed Page** to turn off the feature.
3. Click the **Close** button at the top of the Full Screen Reading window to close it and return to Print Layout view.
4. Save the document.

Fantastic! You have learned how to use another helpful tool for viewing, editing, previewing, and printing your document. Next, let's continue editing the *writers4* document by organizing data in a table.

7. Select the four lines below the date and convert the lines to a bulleted list.
8. Reposition the table object attractively on the slide.
9. Deselect the table and then save the presentation.

Your slide 3 should now look similar to this.

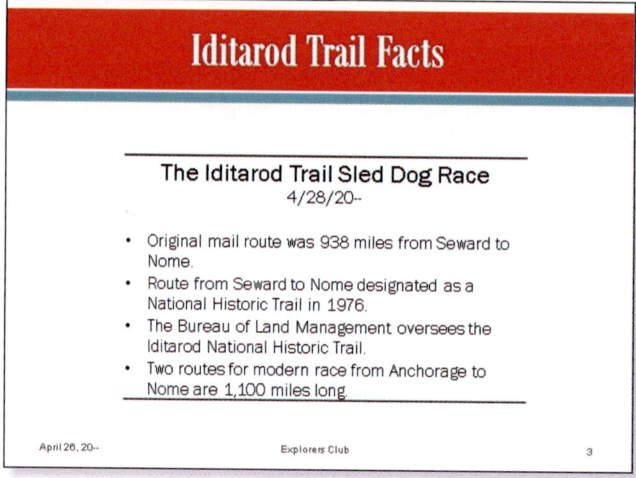


Terrific! Next, let's copy and paste the data from the *Racing Rules and Prizes* worksheet.

**Pasting *Excel* Worksheet Data as a Picture**

If you do not need to format or edit the data, paste the data as a picture. One way to paste *Excel* worksheet data as a picture instead of a *PowerPoint* table is to click the Paste button arrow and click Paste Special to open the Paste Special dialog box. In the dialog box, you can select an alternative paste option, such as Enhanced Metafile (picture).

In *PowerPoint 2010*, you can click the Paste button arrow and click the Picture icon in the Paste Options group. As an alternative, you can paste the data as a *PowerPoint* table and then click the Paste Options icon below the table and click the Picture icon in the Paste Options group to convert the table to a picture. Try using Paste Options!

A Metafile picture object can be resized and repositioned, and its fill and line color and size can be changed just like a shape you draw, but the data itself *cannot* be changed.

## Creating and Formatting a Table

A table is a grid of vertical columns and horizontal rows. You key your text in the cells at the intersection of a column and row. Tables are used to organize data in a document.

To create a table, click the Insert tab and click the Table button in the Tables group; then drag down and across the column and row grid to select the number of columns and rows you want in the table.

When you create a table, *Word* adds the Table Tools Design and Layout contextual tabs to the Ribbon.

- Click buttons on the Table Tools Design tab to apply and modify table styles or to draw a table using the mouse pointer.
- Click buttons on the Table Tools Layout tab to add or remove rows and columns, to align text in cells, and to open the Table Properties dialog box.

**Let's insert a table with two columns and three rows, called a 2 x 3 table.**

Insert | Tables | Table

1. Move the insertion point to the end of the last sentence that ends *writers include:* in the third body text paragraph.
2. Click the **Insert** tab and locate the **Tables** group.
3. Click the **Table** button in the Tables group to view a grid of columns and rows.
4. Drag across to select two columns and down to select three rows. The top of the grid shows **2 x 3 Table**, and live preview shows a 2 x 3 table in the document.
5. Release the mouse button to insert the table.
6. Observe the **Table Tools Design** and **Table Tools Layout** contextual tabs on the Ribbon.

The new 2 x 3 table in your document should look like this.

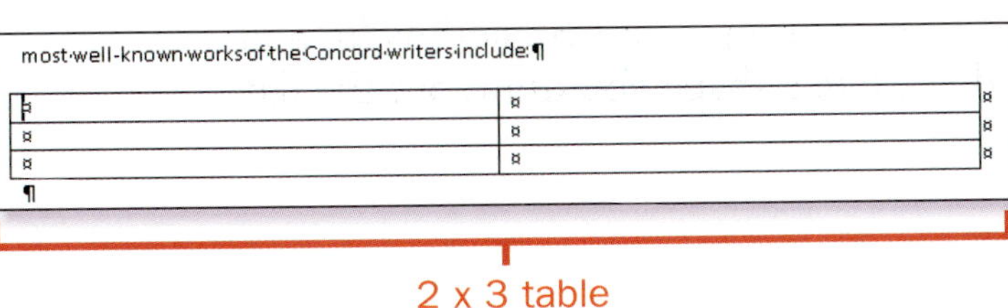


2 x 3 table

Now you need to edit the table. To edit the table, click it to activate it and then click buttons on the Table Tools Design and Layout tabs or the Home tab.

Table Tools Design | Table Styles | More

Table Tools Design | WordArt Styles | Text Fill

Home | Font | Bold or Font Size

Home | Paragraph | Bullets

**Let's activate the table, format the table object, and format the text inside the table.**

1. Click the table to activate it.

Selected table

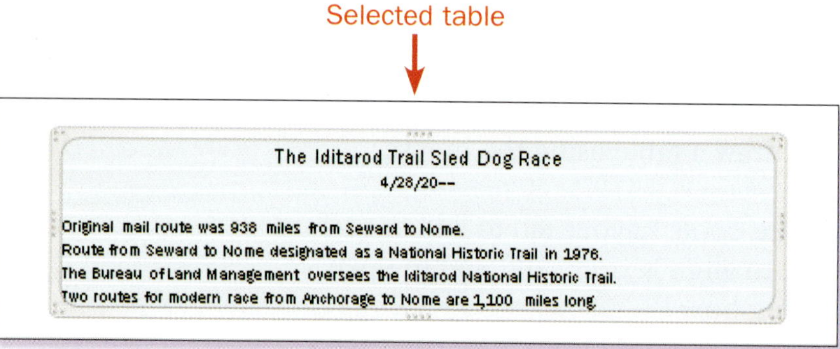


2. Click the **Table Tools Design** tab and locate the **Table Styles** group.
3. Click the **More** button in the Table Styles group to display a gallery of table styles.
4. Use live preview to review different table styles; then click the style of your choice.
5. Click the **Text Fill** button arrow in the WordArt Styles group to view the color grid; then click the color of your choice on the Theme Colors grid.
6. Select all of the text in the table and apply the **Bold** font style; then increase the font size to make the table text easier to read. The table object will resize to accommodate the new font size.

Table styles gallery

By default, *Word* adds a dark printable border to a table and its cells. You can modify or remove the border by clicking the Table Tools Design tab and clicking the Borders button in the Table Styles group to view the border options gallery.

You can change the width of the columns or the table's horizontal position on the page in the Table Properties dialog box. Open the dialog box by clicking the Table Tools Design tab and then clicking the Properties button in the Table group.

Gridlines help you see the table cells when there is no printable border. You can toggle the view of a table's gridlines on or off by clicking the Table Tools Layout tab and then clicking the View Gridlines button in the Table group.

Change table column widths by dragging a column marker on the Horizontal Ruler. Align a table horizontally by selecting the entire table and then clicking an alignment button In the Paragraph group on the Home tab. Try it!

The new table should be centered horizontally between the left and right margins and single-spaced, and its columns should be 1.75 inches wide. Its printable border should be removed. Begin by using the move handle and the mouse to select the entire table.

A quick way to select the entire table is to move the mouse pointer over the table until the table's move handle appears in the upper-left corner, then click the move handle.

**Let's select and modify the table.**

**Table Tools Layout | Cell Size | Table Column Width**

**Table Tools Design | Table Styles | Borders**

1. Move the mouse pointer to the table's move handle located above the upper-left corner of the table. The mouse pointer becomes a move pointer.
2. Click the move handle to select the entire table.
3. Click the **Table Tools Layout** tab and locate the **Cell Size** group.
4. Key **1.75** in the Table Column Width text box in the Cell Size group and tap ENTER. The table's columns are resized.

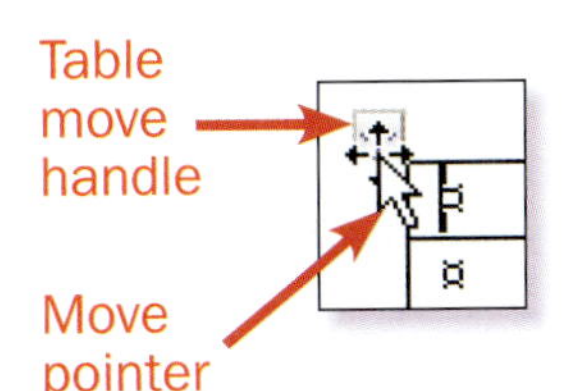


1.33"

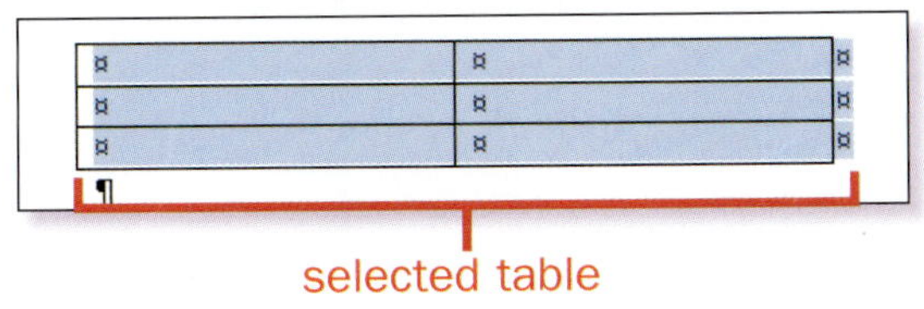

selected table

### Pasting *Excel* Data as a *PowerPoint* Table

By default, when you click the Paste button face in the Clipboard group on the Home tab, the data copied from an *Excel* worksheet is pasted into a *PowerPoint* table. Working with a *PowerPoint* table is much like working with a *Word* table.

When you paste data in a *PowerPoint* table or when you select a *PowerPoint* table, the Table Tools Design and Layout tabs appear on the Ribbon.

The *PowerPoint* Paste Options icon might appear below and to the right of the pasted *Excel* data; you can click this icon to view a menu of paste options. You will use the Paste Options later in this Trail Marker.

**Let's copy the data on the *Trail Facts* worksheet and paste it on slide 3 as a *PowerPoint* table.**

Home | Clipboard | Copy or Paste

1. Activate the *Trail Facts* worksheet, if necessary; then click the **Home** tab, if necessary, and locate the **Clipboard** group.
2. Select the range **A1:A7** and click the **Copy** button face in the Clipboard group. 
3. Switch to the *Iditarod15* presentation.
4. View **slide 3**; click the **Home** tab, if necessary, and locate the **Clipboard** group.
5. Click the **Paste** button face in the Clipboard group to paste the copied data as a *PowerPoint* table. Observe the Table Tools Design and Layout tabs on the Ribbon. 

6. Deselect the table and save the presentation.

**CHECKPOINT**

Your slide 3 should look similar to this.

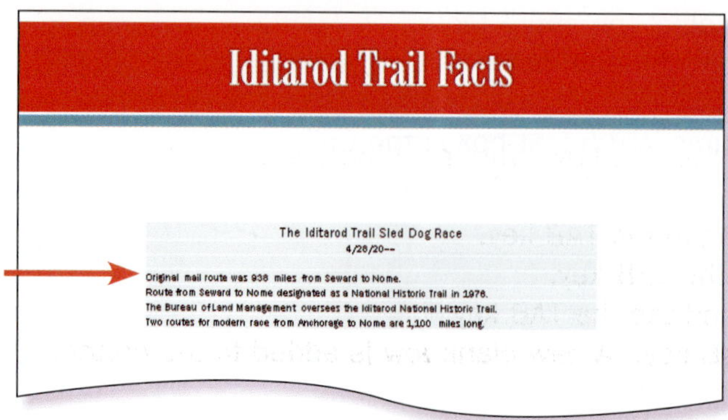


*Excel* data pasted as *PowerPoint* table

5. Tap the CTRL + E shortcut keys to center the table on the page horizontally.
6. Click the **Table Tools Design** tab and locate the **Table Styles** group.
7. Click the **Borders** button arrow in the Table Styles group to view the gallery of border options.
8. Click the **No Border** option to remove the border. The table's gridlines are now visible.
9. Click the first cell in the first row to position the insertion point.

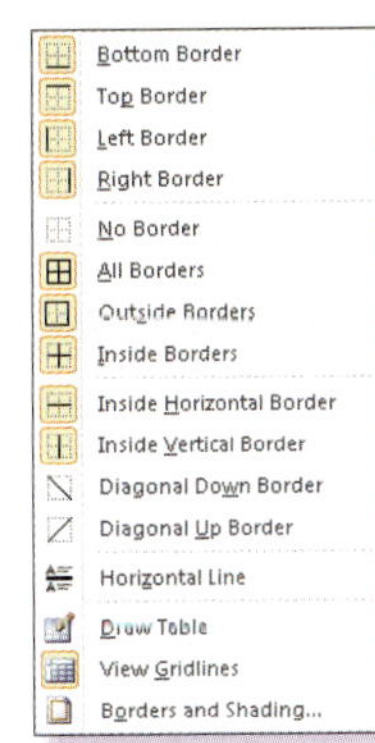


**CHECKPOINT**
Your modified table with visible gridlines should look like this.

Insertion point in first cell

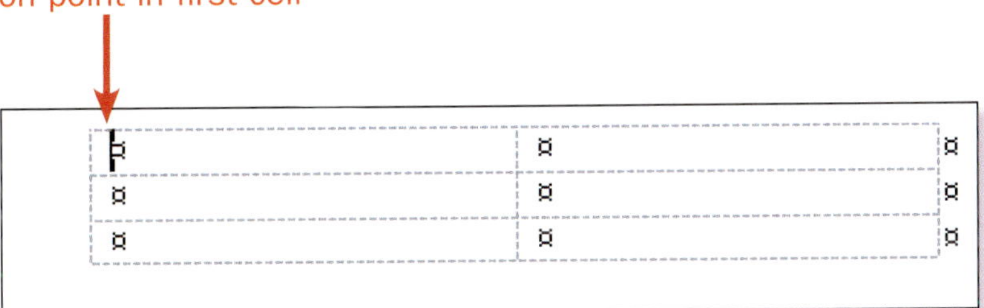

Super! Now you are ready to add text to the table.

Before you begin keying in the table, make sure the insertion point is in the first cell in the first row. Then move the insertion point from cell to cell by:

- tapping the TAB key to move to a cell to the right
- tapping the SHIFT + TAB keys to move to a cell to the left
- tapping the arrow keys to move up or down a row
- clicking a cell with the I-beam

**Let's add column names, author names, and book titles to the table and then format the table's text.**

1. Verify that the insertion point is in the first cell in the first row; then key **Author** and tap the TAB key.
2. Key **Famous Work** and tap the TAB key. The insertion point moves to the first cell in the second row.
3. Key **Louisa May Alcott** and tap the TAB key.
4. Key **Little Women** and tap the TAB key.
5. Key **Henry David Thoreau** and tap the TAB key.
6. Key **Walden** and tap the TAB key. A new blank row is added to the bottom of the table.

**CHECKPOINT**

The top of your two worksheets should look like this.

New worksheet title and date

| | A |
|---|---|
| 1 | **The Iditarod Trail Sled Dog Race** |
| 2 | 4/28/20-- |

What a great job! Now you are ready to copy the data from the workbook and paste it on slides in the presentation.

TRAIL MARKER

## Copying and Pasting from *Excel* to *PowerPoint*

Luis has already added slides to the *Iditarod15* presentation. You will copy data from the *Trail Facts* and *Racing Rules and Prizes* worksheets, switch to the *PowerPoint* presentation, and then use the *PowerPoint* Paste button in the Clipboard group on the Home tab to paste the data onto the slides as a *PowerPoint* table, a picture object, or an embedded workbook object.

The choice to paste the data as a *PowerPoint* table, or as a picture, or as an *Excel* embedded or linked workbook object depends on whether and how you want to edit the *Excel* data after it is pasted.

- Pasting as a default *PowerPoint* table allows you to edit the table's content using *PowerPoint* features; however, the changes you make do not affect the original workbook.
- Pasting as a picture allows you to format the picture, such as changing the picture style or recoloring the picture, but you cannot change the picture's contents and your changes do not affect the original workbook.
- Pasting as an embedded workbook object allows you to access and edit data in the workbook object without changing the original workbook.
- Pasting as a linked workbook object requires that all changes be made in the original workbook.

Next, you will practice pasting worksheet data or chart using three paste options: as a *PowerPoint* table, as a picture object, and as an embedded workbook object.

7. Key **Nathaniel Hawthorne** and tap the TAB key.
8. Key **The Scarlet Letter** and tap the TAB key.
9. Key **Ralph Waldo Emerson** and tap the TAB key.
10. Key **Nature**. *After you key the last entry, do not tap the TAB key to add another row to the bottom of the table.*

| Author | Famous Work |
|---|---|
| Louisa May Alcott | Little Women |
| Henry David Thoreau | Walden |
| Nathaniel Hawthorne | The Scarlett Letter |
| Ralph Waldo Emerson | Nature |

Now you are ready to select and format the text you keyed in the table.

To format table contents, first select table cells, rows, and columns or the entire table using the mouse pointer. Here are five great ways to select in a table:

1. Select a single cell—move the small black arrow selection pointer just into the cell at the left boundary and click.
2. Select a row—move the large white arrow selection pointer just outside the left boundary of the row and click.
3. Select a column—move the small black arrow selection pointer to the top of the column and click.
4. Select multiple cells, rows, or columns—drag the selection pointer across the cells, rows, or columns.
5. Select the entire table by selecting all of the rows or all of the columns.

*Warning!* Tapping the ENTER key in a cell inserts a new paragraph in the cell. If you accidentally insert a new paragraph in a cell, just tap the BACKSPACE key to remove it.

**Let's apply the Bold font style to the column names, center the author names and book titles in their cells, and apply the Italic font style to the book titles. Use keyboard shortcuts where possible.**

1. Scroll to view the first table row, if necessary.
2. Move the mouse pointer to the left side of the first row and click to select the entire row.
3. Tap the CTRL + B keys to apply the Bold font style to the column names in the first row.
4. Move the mouse pointer just above the first column to see the black selection arrow; then tap and hold down the mouse button and drag across both columns to select them.
5. Tap the CTRL + E keys to center the column headings, author names, and book titles.
6. Move the mouse pointer just inside the second cell in the second column (*Little Women*) and drag down slowly to select all of the book titles.
7. Tap the CTRL + I keys to apply the Italic font style.
8. Click the blank line below the table and tap the DELETE key to delete it.

As long as the worksheets are grouped, every action you take will affect all of the grouped worksheets! *Warning!* Remember to ungroup your worksheets when you have finished making your changes.

When you ungroup worksheets, only one worksheet remains active. To ungroup the worksheets, right-click a grouped sheet tab and click Ungroup Sheets.

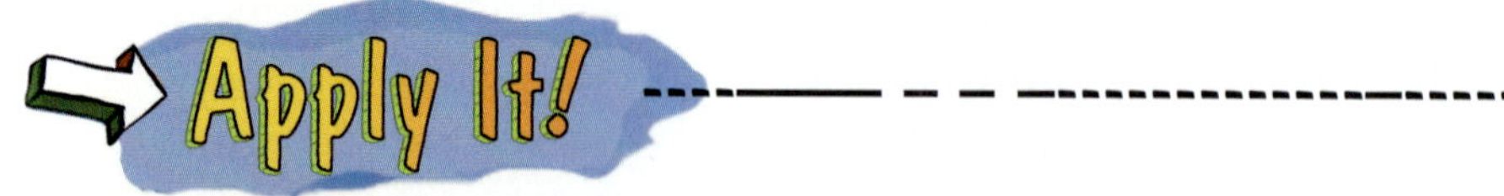


**Let's group the *Trail Facts* and *Racing Rules and Prizes* worksheets using the SHIFT key; add text, a function, and formatting; and ungroup the worksheets when you are finished.**

1. Click the *Trail Facts* sheet tab, if necessary.
2. Tap and hold the SHIFT key and click the *Racing Rules and Prizes* sheet tab. Look at the title bar to see the word *[Group]* following the workbook name. This means that multiple worksheets are selected.

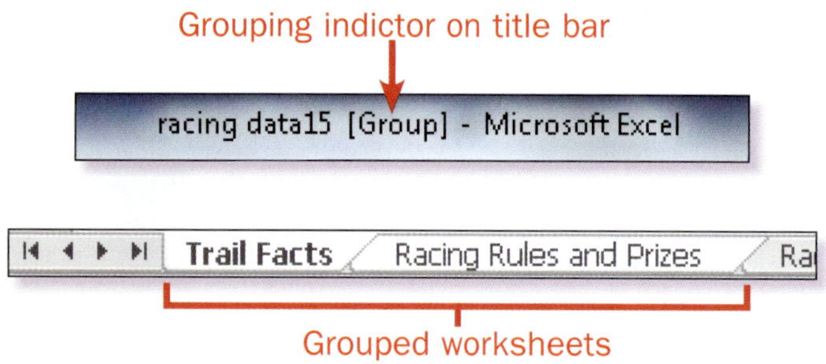


3. Enter **The Iditarod Trail Sled Dog Race** in cell A1 on the *Trail Facts* sheet tab.
4. Activate cell **A1** and center the contents in the cell, apply the **Bold** font style, and change the font size to **14**.
5. Activate cell **A2** and enter the TODAY function using Function AutoComplete; center the date in the cell.
6. Activate cell **A1**.
7. Right-click the *Trail Facts* sheet tab and click **Ungroup Sheets**. The sheets are ungrouped; the word *[Group]* is removed from the title bar; only the *Trail Facts* worksheet is active.
8. Click the *Racing Rules and Prizes* sheet tab to verify that the formatted title and today's date appear in cells A1 and A2.
9. Click the *Trail Facts* sheet tab and save the workbook.

Your table should look now like this.

| Author¤ | Famous·Work¤ |
|---|---|
| Louisa·May·Alcott¤ | *Little·Women¤* |
| Henry·David·Thoreau¤ | *Walden¤* |
| Nathaniel·Hawthorne¤ | *The·Scarlett·Letter¤* |
| Ralph·Waldo·Emerson¤ | *Nature¤* |

Formatted table contents

Your table looks great! Now let's add a cover page to the report.

## Creating a Report Cover Page

Reports often have a title page, also called a cover page, with the name of the report, the writer's name, other information (such as a school or organization name), and the current date.

To quickly create a cover page, click the Insert tab on the Ribbon. Then click the Cover Page button in the Pages group and click a cover page style from the gallery.

The cover pages in the gallery are preformatted and contain fields in which you key information about the report.

**Let's create a cover page.**

Insert | Pages | Cover Page

1. Tap the CTRL + HOME keys to move the insertion point to the top of the document, if necessary.
2. Click the **Insert** tab and locate the **Pages** group.
3. Click the **Cover Page** button in the Pages group to display a gallery of preformatted cover page options.

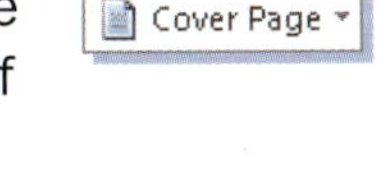


4. Click the **Sideline** cover page option in the gallery. Scroll to view the option near the bottom of the gallery.
5. Select and delete the **Company field placeholder**.
6. Select the **[Type the document title] field place holder**, if necessary, and key **The Writers of Concord** in the placeholder.
7. Select the **[Type the document subtitle] field placeholder** and key **Explorers Club** in the placeholder.

Built-In

Alphabet | Annual | Austere | Austin | Conservative | Contrast

More Cover Pages from Office.com

Remove Current Cover Page

Save Selection to Cover Page Gallery...

Gallery of cover page options

**Begin by opening Luis's presentation and saving it with a new name. Then open Luis's workbook and save it with a new name.**

1. Open the *Iditarod* presentation and save it as *Iditarod15*.
2. Apply the customized theme of your choice and add *Explorers Club*, today's date as a fixed date, and slide numbers to all of the slides.
3. Then start *Excel*, open the *racing data* workbook, and save it as *racing data15*.

Leave both the presentation and workbook open; then begin by modifying the workbook.

**ERGONOMICS TIP**

Are you sitting up straight? To avoid muscle strain, sit up with your back against your chair as you work at the computer.

## Grouping, Formatting, and Ungrouping Worksheets

The *racing data15* workbook has three worksheets: *Trail Facts*, *Racing Rules* and *Prizes, and Racing Team Costs*. Each worksheet contains interesting information about the Iditarod Trail and the sled dog race.

Luis wants to add the same title and the date in cells A1 and A2 on two of the worksheets: *Trail Facts* and *Racing Rules* and *Prizes*. Instead of entering and formatting the title and entering the TODAY function *one worksheet at a time*, you can group the worksheets by selecting them. Then on one of the grouped (or selected) worksheets, you can enter and format the title and then enter the function—your changes are automatically made to the other grouped worksheet! What a time-saver!

You can group adjacent worksheets by using the SHIFT + click method. Use the CTRL + click method to group nonadjacent worksheets. When you group worksheets, the sheet tabs for each grouped worksheet are white, indicating the worksheets are active, and the word [Group] in brackets appears on the title bar following the workbook name.

8. Select the contents of the Author field placeholder near the bottom of the cover page and key **Luis Gonzales**.
9. Select the **Pick the date field placeholder**.
10. Click the **placeholder arrow** to view the calendar.
11. Click the **Today** button in the calendar to insert today's date.
12. Click outside the box that contains the placeholders and zoom the document to view the cover page and the first report page.

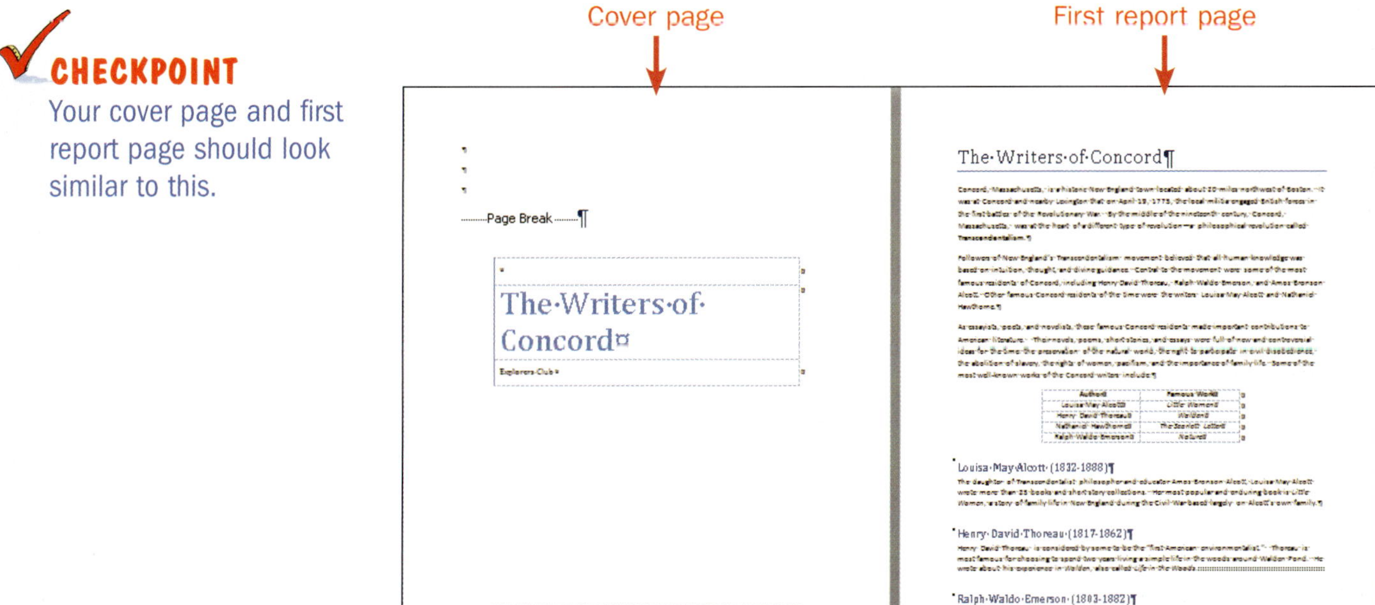


13. Zoom the document back to 100% and scroll to view the first report page.

Wonderful! Now let's cite Luis's sources with endnotes.

## Citing Sources on a Separate Page

Luis wants you to cite his sources as references on the last page at the end of *writers4* document. You can position the insertion point below the formatted main heading using the Click and Type feature.

Click and Type allows you to quickly position the insertion point in a blank area of a page in Print Layout view. Simply move the Click and Type pointer (the I-beam pointer with an alignment icon) to a blank area on the page and double-click to position the insertion point at that location.

# Racing the Iditarod Trail

## Explorers' Guide

**Data files:** racing data, mushers (workbook), Iditarod, famous mushers (presentation)

**Objectives:**
In this project, you will:
- group, format, and ungroup worksheets
- copy and paste from Excel to PowerPoint
- create a summary slide using copy and paste
- create text and action button hyperlinks
- add speaker notes

KIRK GEISLER/SHUTTERSTOCK.COM

## Our Exploration Assignment:

**Adding *Excel* worksheet data, an *Excel* chart, and a summary slide to a presentation; navigating during a slide show using hyperlinks**

Imagine being pulled across 1,100 miles of wilderness by powerful dogs in temperatures up to 60 degrees below zero! Wow! That's what the racers, called mushers, experience when they and their dog sled teams participate in the annual Iditarod Trail Sled Dog Race from Anchorage to Nome, Alaska. Luis entered some research data about the Iditarod Trail and race in an *Excel* workbook and created an accompanying *PowerPoint* presentation. Now he needs your help to add some finishing touches to his worksheets, copy and paste his Excel data into the presentation, and add interest and fun to the presentation. Follow the Trail Markers to group, format, and ungroup worksheets; copy and paste *Excel* worksheet data and a chart on slides; use copy and paste to create a summary slide; create text and action button hyperlinks; and add speaker notes.

**Let's cite Luis's sources on the References page at the end of the document.**

1. Scroll to view the last page of the report, the References page.
2. Position the **Click and Type pointer** (the I-beam pointer with a left alignment icon) at the left margin below the formatted main heading and double-click to position the insertion point.
3. Key the following citation and tap the ENTER key.
   **Ellis, Robert. *The New England Transcendental Movement* (Boston: Wilson Press, 2003) p. 32.**
4. Key the following citation and tap the ENTER key.
   **"Henry David Thoreau." *Wikipedia*. 11 August 2009. http://en.wikipedia.org/wiki/Henry_David_Thoreau. (accessed 10 November 20--).**
5. Key the following citation and tap the ENTER key.
   **"Ralph Waldo Emerson." *PBS Thomas Hampson: I Hear America Singing*. http://www.pbs.org/wnet/ihas/poet/emerson.html. (accessed 10 November 20–).**
6. Key the following citation and tap the ENTER key.
   **"The Wayside Authors: Hawthorne." *National Park Service*. http://www.nps.gov/mima/wayside/Hawth.htm. (accessed 10 November 20--).**

Luis's citations should look like this.

# References¶

Ellis, Robert. *The New England Transcendental Movement* (Boston: Wilson Press, 2003). p. 32.¶

"Henry David Thoreau." *Wikipedia*. 11 August 2009. http://en.wikipedia.org/wiki/Henry_David_Thoreau. (accessed 10 November 20--).¶

"Ralph Waldo Emerson." *PBS Thomas Hampson: I Hear America Singing*. http://www.pbs.org/wnet/ihas/poet/emerson.html. (accessed 10 November 20--).¶

"The Wayside Authors: Hawthorne." *National Park Service*. http://www.nps.gov/mima/wayside/Hawth.htm. (accessed 10 November 20--).¶

Super! Now you are ready to paginate your document as a multipage bound report.

# Project 14 Keyboarding

## 14a Build Skill

Key each line twice. Double-space between 2-line groups.

**TECHNIQUE TIP**

Reach out with the little finger and tap the enter key quickly. Return your finger to the home key.

N No one knew Nathan N. Nevins was not here at noon.
O I told Jose and Brook not to mop the floors today.
P Philippe paid for the pepper and paprika for Pepe.
Q Quinton quit questioning the adequacy of the quiz.
R Jerry corrects the four problems before departing.
S Steven and I saw Sam at Sally's session on Sunday.
T Tim bottled the water after talking with the maid.
U He urged us to put the rugs under the four trucks.
V Vivian Von Vogt took the vivid van to the village.
W Wesley will work on the walnut wall for two weeks.
X Six tax experts explained the existence of the tax exams.
Y Jay may be ready to pay you your money on Tuesday.
Z Zelda was puzzled by the sizzling heat at the zoo.

gwam 30" | 2 | 4 | 6 | 8 | 10 | 12 | 14 | 16 | 18 | 20 |

## 14b Technique: ENTER

Key two 30" timed writings on each line.

For additional practice:
**MicroType 5**
Skill Building, Lesson D

1 Jay kept the turkey.
2 Pamela may be able to go.
3 You can see the next game too.
4 Mike will be out of town on Friday.
5 Shawn and I can take the exam next week.
6 Nancy will bring your new computer next week.
7 The new version of the video game will be on sale.

gwam 30" | 2 | 4 | 6 | 8 | 10 | 12 | 14 | 16 | 18 | 20 |

## Paginating a Multipage Bound Report

The *writers4* document now has four pages: a cover page and three report pages. To properly paginate the document, you must divide it into three sections: Section 1 (the cover page and the first page of the report), Section 2 (the second page of the report), and Section 3 (the separate References page).

Not all of the sections will have the same margins, and the page numbering will begin in Section 2 starting with report page number 2. To correctly paginate the document using the appropriate margins and page numbering, divide the document into the three sections by inserting section breaks.

Remember! The Section: indicator on the status bar tells you which document section contains the insertion point. Check it out!

### Setting Margins for a Multipage Bound Report

Reports with three pages or more, such as the *writers4* document, are usually bound at the left margin with a plastic clip or another binding. A bound report must have additional white space, called a gutter, added to a margin for the binding. You can create a 0.5-inch left gutter in two ways:

- Add 0.5 inch to the document's left margin.
- Set the Left Gutter option in the Margins tab in the Page Setup dialog box to 0.5 inch.

In this project, you will add 0.5 inch to the left margin for the gutter.

Here are the margins and page number settings for each section you need in the *writers4* document.

| | | |
|---|---|---|
| **Section 1** | Cover page and first report page | 2-inch top margin, 1.5-inch left margin, 1-inch right and bottom margins, no page number |
| **Section 2** | Second report page | 1-inch top margin, 1.5-inch left margin, 1-inch right and bottom margins, page number 2 |
| **Section 3** | References page | 2-inch top margin, 1.5-inch left margin, 1-inch right and bottom margins, page number 3 |

# Exploring *Across the Curriculum*

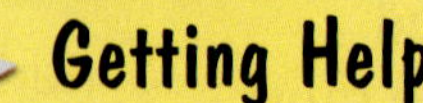

## Getting Help

Click the Microsoft PowerPoint Help icon below the *PowerPoint* application Close button to open the *PowerPoint* Help window. Key **Handout Master** in the search box and tap the ENTER key to research how to control content on your audience handouts by modifying the Handout Master. Then open the presentation of your choice and modify the Handout Master. Preview your audience handouts; then close the presentation, saving it with a new name.

## Career Day

The California Gold Rush created a population explosion in California, turning towns such as San Francisco into cities and resulting in a building boom. If you think that planning, designing, and building homes and office buildings for America's cities sounds interesting, you might enjoy an occupation in architecture and construction. Using library, printed, or online resources, identify three interesting occupations in architecture and building. Write a brief summary of each occupation, print your summary, and save it in your Career Day folder.

## Your Personal Journal

Open your personal journal document. Insert today's date and two blank lines. Imagine that you were helping to build Sutter's Mill on January 24, 1848, and witnessed Marshall's discovery of gold. Write two or three paragraphs describing how your life might change as a result of Marshall's discovery. Spell-check, save, and close your journal.

## Online Enrichment Games

www.cengage.com/school/keyboarding/lwcorange

**Let's set the margins, including a gutter, for Section 1, which contains the cover page and the first page of the report by using the Page Setup dialog box. Then let's create Sections 2 and 3 and reset the margins for each section.**

1. Tap the CTRL + HOME keys to move the insertion point to the top of the cover page.
2. Set a custom 2-inch top margin and 1.5-inch left margin and 1-inch right and bottom margins.

Page Layout | Page Setup | Margins

Now let's create Sections 2 and 3 and reset their margins.

3. Move the insertion point to the top of the second report page.
4. Insert a **Continuous** section break to create the new Section 2.
5. Look at the status bar to verify that the section indicator is Section: 2; then open the Page Setup dialog box and change the top margin to 1 inch.
6. Move the insertion point in front of the word *References* above the endnotes on the third report page.
7. Insert a **Continuous** section break to create Section 3.
8. Look at the status bar to verify that the section indicator is Section 3; then open the Page Setup dialog box and change the top margin to 2 inches.

Page Layout | Page Setup | Insert Page and Section Breaks

Well done! Now that you have set the correct margins for the three document sections, you need to insert page numbers in Sections 2 and 3. Remember, only Sections 2 and 3 require page numbers. Page numbers should not appear in Section 1—the cover page and the first page of the report.

**Inserting Page Numbers**

Page numbers in a multipage report are inserted in a header in the upper-right corner of all pages except the cover page and the first report page. A quick way to open the header area for a section is to move the insertion point into the first page of a section and then double-click the white area above the first line of text.

To specify the starting page number, click the Page Number button in the Header and Footer group and click Format Page Numbers to open the Page Number Format dialog box. Click the Start as option button and key the starting page number in the text box. The Header & Footer Tools Design tab appears on the Ribbon when the header or footer area is active.

*Warning! Word* automatically links or duplicates headers across sections; when you key text in a header for one section, the header automatically appears for all sections. To prevent the unwanted duplication of headers, you must unlink a header from the previous section's header. To do this, click the Link to Previous button in the Navigation group to turn off the linking.

# Exploring *Across the Curriculum*

## Language Arts: Words to Know

Look up the meaning of the following terms in a classroom dictionary, CD-ROM dictionary or encyclopedia, or online dictionary.

| forty-niner | High Sierra | Levi Strauss | nugget |
|---|---|---|---|
| Overland Trail | panning | sluice | Sutter's Mill |

Create a new presentation. Save it as *definitions14*. Key **Gold Rush** as the title and **Definitions** as the subtitle on the Title Slide. Apply the theme with the customized color scheme of your choice. Insert four slides using the Title and Content slide layout. Key **Terms** as the title. Click the table icon in the content placeholder to create a table with two columns and two rows on each slide. (*Hint:* You can navigate and key in a *PowerPoint* table just like you do in a *Word* table.) Key two terms and two definitions in the table on each slide. Add slide transitions of your choice. Run the slide show using the control buttons or shortcut menu; then save and close the presentation.

## Social Studies Research, Write, and Present

Work with a classmate to use classroom, library, CD-ROM, or online resources to learn about the role the following people played during the California Gold Rush: John Charles Fremont; Samuel Brannan; Lotta Crabtree; Domenico Ghirardelli; Leland Stanford, Sr.; and John Studebaker. Then create a new presentation. Apply the theme and customized color scheme of your choice. Add an appropriate title and subtitle to the Title Slide. Insert Title and Content slides or other slides as necessary to describe each person. Cite your sources on Title and Content slides at the end of the presentation. Insert SmartArt graphics, add slide transitions of your choice, and apply custom animation to the SmartArt graphics. Remove the background graphics from a slide and then insert a picture or clip art of your choice as the background on the slide. Insert today's date as an automatically updating date, your name as footer text, and slide numbers on all slides *except* the Title Slide. Run the slide show using the control buttons or a shortcut menu; then save and close the presentation.

Explore More

**Let's display the Section 2 header area, unlink it from the Section 1 header, and insert page numbers for Sections 2 and 3.**

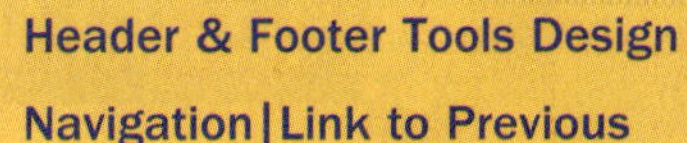


Header & Footer Tools Design | Header & Footer | Page Number

1. Move the insertion point into Section 2 at the top of page 3.
2. Double-click the white area above the text to open the Header area for the first page of Section 2 and to display the Header & Footer Tools Design tab on the Ribbon.

The first step is to unlink Section 2 from Section 1. Then you insert the Plain Number 3 page number style in the Section 2 header.

3. Click the **Link to Previous** button in the Navigation group to turn off the linking between document sections.
4. Click the **Page Number** button in the Header & Footer group and click **Format Page Numbers** to open the Page Number Format dialog box.
5. Click the **Start at** option button and key **2** in the text box.

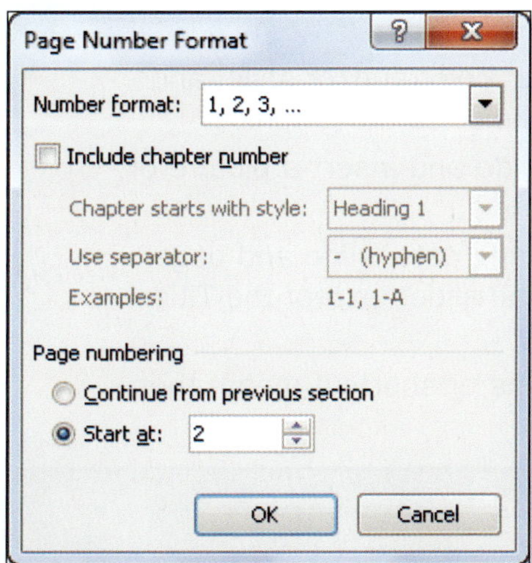


6. Click **OK** to change the page number to 2.
7. Click the **Page Number** button in the Header & Footer group, point to **Top of Page**, and click **Plain Number 3** in the gallery. The page number 2 is inserted in the header.

8. Click the **Next Section** button in the Navigation group to verify that the page number is page 3.

9. Click the **Close Header and Footer** button in the Close group to close the header area.

10. Zoom the document to see all four pages.

# Exploring *Across the Curriculum*

## Internet/Web

Open your Web browser and use a favorite or bookmark to view the Learning with Computers Web page (www.cengage.com/school/keyboarding/lwcorange). Click the **Links** option and click **Project 14**. Click the links to research the history of the California Gold Rush. Take notes about what you learn.

1. Create a new presentation and save it as *gold rush history14*.
2. Apply the theme of your choice or apply a theme from another presentation.
3. Add an appropriate title and subtitle to the Title Slide. Insert slides with different layouts, such as Title and Content, Title Only, or Blank slides, to present what you learned.
4. Cite your sources on Title and Content slides at the end of your presentation.
5. Add the slide transitions of your choice.
6. Add SmartArt graphics, modify the graphics' color and/or style, and then apply the custom animation of your choice to the graphics.
7. Remove the background graphics from a slide and insert a picture or clip art of your choice as the slide background.
8. Add today's date as an automatically updating date, slide and page numbers, and your name as footer text to all slides *except* the Title Slide.
9. Run the slide show using the control buttons or shortcut menu; then save and close the presentation.

Explore More

**CHECKPOINT** Your report's pages should look like this.

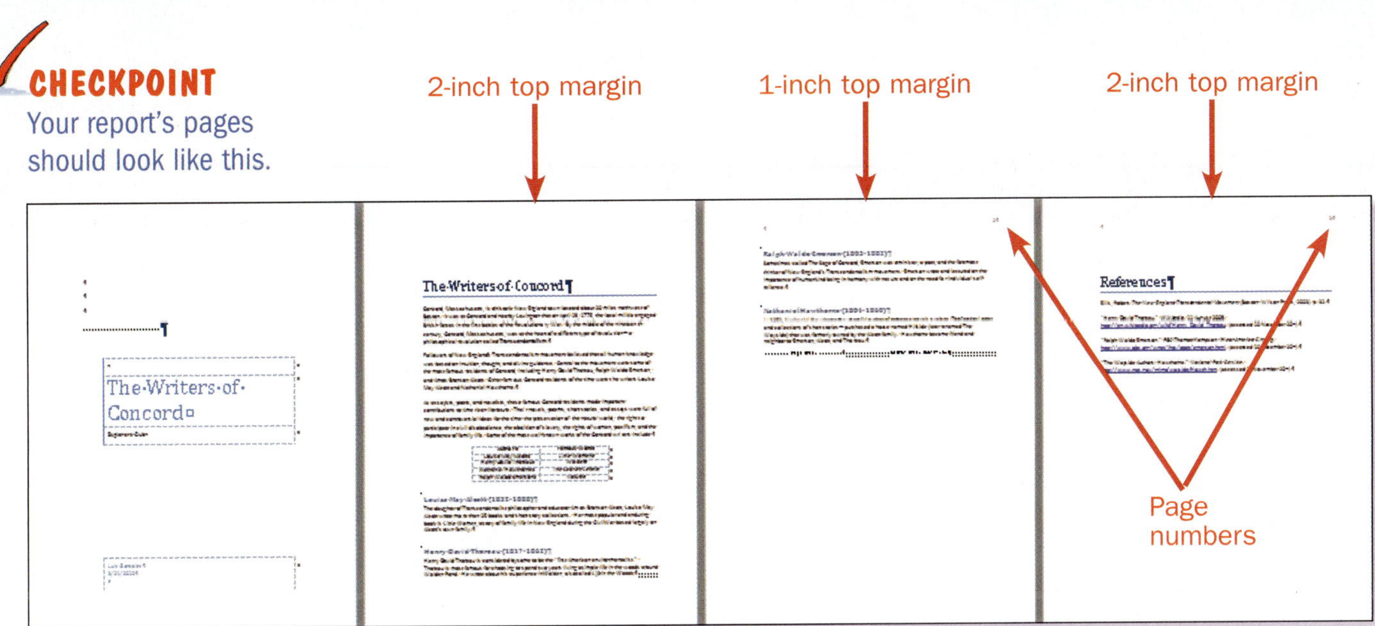


Pages one and two do not have page numbers. Pages three and four have page number 2 and page number 3 to indicate the second and third pages of the report, respectively. The first report page and the References page have a 2-inch top margin; the second page of the report has a 1-inch top margin.

11. Zoom back to 100%.
12. Save the document and close it.

What an amazing job! Luis's *writers4* document looks terrific!

# Exploring On Your Own

## Blaze Your Own Trail

Use library or online resources to learn more about gold. What is gold? Why do people value gold so highly? What are some fun facts about gold? Take notes about what you learn.

1. Create a new presentation and save it as *gold14*.
2. Apply the theme from the *custom theme* data file.
3. Add a title and subtitle of your choice on the Title Slide.
4. Add a Title and Content slide and key a portion of your notes in a bulleted list; then convert the list to a SmartArt graphic for a list.
5. Add a Title Only slide, insert a SmartArt graphic of your choice, and key text based on your research notes into the graphic.
6. Modify the SmartArt graphics' style or color as desired.
7. Cite your sources on Title and Content slides. Then insert the slide from the *source* data file following your source citation slides.
8. Insert a Blank slide at the end of the presentation, insert the *gold* photo data file as the slide's background, and remove any background graphics from the slide.
9. Add the slide transitions of your choice to all of the slides and the custom animation of your choice to the SmartArt graphics.
10. Add your name as footer text, page numbers, and today's date as an automatically updating date to all slides *except* the Title Slide.
11. Run the slide show using the control buttons and shortcut menu. Then save and close the presentation.

## Reading in Action

### Writing a Summary Statement

A summary statement gives the important facts and specific details about a topic. A good summary includes information that answers the questions *who*, *what*, *when*, *where*, and *why*. Write a summary statement about the Gold Rush, using the information provided in the slides in *gold rush14*.

## Math in Action

### Using a Conversion Factor

A *conversion factor* is a ratio that is used to convert measurements into different units. Assume that the price of a valuable product is $400 per ounce. How much money is 4.5 ounces of the product worth?

$$4.5 \text{ ounces} \times \frac{\$400}{1 \text{ ounce}} = (4.5)(\$400) = \$1{,}800$$

To find how much of the commodity you can buy with a given amount of money, use this conversion factor:

$$(\text{amount of \$}) \times \frac{1 \text{ ounce}}{\$400} = \text{ounces of the product}$$

Now you try it!

How much money would 6 ounces of the product be worth if the price is $350 per ounce? How much could you buy with $6000 if the price is $250 per ounce?

# Project Skills Review

You learned a lot in this project! We are very impressed with your progress. Let's take a few minutes to review the skills that you learned.

**Use keyboard shortcuts to perform common tasks**

Move the insertion point to the top of the document: CTRL + HOME
Select a line: SHIFT + END
Left-align selected text: CTRL + L
Apply Heading 1 style: ALT + CTRL + 1
Repeat the previous action: CTRL + Y
Save a document with the same name in the same location: CTRL + S
Cut, copy, and paste text: CTRL + X, CTRL + C, CTRL + V, respectively
Spell-check the document: F7
Apply font styles: CTRL + B, CTRL + I, CTRL + U
Center horizontally: CTRL + E
Change line spacing to single spacing: CTRL + 1

**Switch to Full Screen Reading view**

Click the **Full Screen Reading** button in the **View Shortcuts**. Click the **Full Screen Reading** button in the Document Views group on the **View** tab.

Full Screen Reading

**Navigate between screens in Full Screen Reading view**

Click the **Next Screen** or **Previous Screen** arrow at the top of the Full Screen Reading view window or click a navigation arrow in the lower-left or lower-right corner of a screen.

**Turn various Full Screen Reading view options on or off**

Click the **View Options** button in the upper-right corner of the Full Screen Reading window and click an option in the gallery

**Create a table**

Click the **Table** button in the Tables group on the **Insert** tab and then drag down and across the grid.

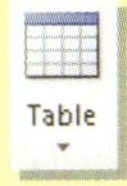


**Change table column widths**

Select the column(s) and then key the desired width in the **Table Column Width** text box in the Cell Size group on the **Table Tools Layout** tab.

1.33"

# Project Skills Review

You learned a lot in this project! We are very impressed with your progress. Let's take a few minutes to review the skills that you learned.

| | |
|---|---|
| **Convert a bulleted list to a SmartArt graphic** | Click the **Convert to SmartArt Graphic** button in the Paragraph group on the **Home** tab. |
| **Insert a SmartArt graphic** | Click the **Insert SmartArt Graphic** button in the Illustrations group on the **Insert** tab. SmartArt |
| **Modify a SmartArt graphic** | Click buttons on the **SmartArt Tools Design** and **SmartArt Tools Format** tabs. |
| **Insert a picture as a slide's background** | Click the **Background Styles** button in the Background group on the **Design** tab; then click **Format Background**. Background Styles |
| **Apply, modify, and preview custom animation effects** | Click various buttons on the **Animations** tab. Preview Preview Start: On Click Duration: 00.50 Animation Painter Custom Animation |
| **Use the slide show menu or controls to navigate during a slide show** | During a slide show, right-click the screen and click a menu command. During a slide show, move the mouse pointer to the lower-left area of the screen, if necessary, to display the controls (Previous Slide, Pen Pointer, Menu, and Next Slide) and click a control. |

# Project Skills Review

| Skill | How To |
|---|---|
| **Add, edit, or delete a printable table border** | Click the **Borders** button in the Table Styles group on the **Table Tools Design** tab. |
| **Navigate a table** | Tap the TAB, SHIFT + TAB, and arrow keys. |
| **Create a report cover (title) page** | Click the **Cover Page** button in the **Pages** group on the **Insert** tab. |
| **Set custom margins including a gutter** | Click the **Margins** button in the Page Setup group on the **Page Layout** tab and click **Custom Margins**. |
| **Insert a Continuous section break** | Click the **Insert Page and Section Breaks** button in the Page Setup group on the **Page Layout** tab and click **Continuous** in the Section Breaks area. |
| **Unlink a header from the previous section's header** | Click the **Link to Previous** button in the Navigation group on the **Header & Footer Tools Design** tab. |
| **Insert page numbers in a header** | Click the **Page Number** button in the Header & Footer group in the **Header & Footer Tools Design** tab.   |
| **Format page numbers** | Click **Format Page Numbers** in the **Page Number** button gallery |

8. Click the **Pen Pointer** button and click **Highlighter** to change the pen pointer to a highlighter pointer.
9. Draw across the **James W. Marshall** name in the SmartArt graphic to highlight it. *Do not worry if your highlight line is not straight.* Tap the ESC key to turn off the pen pointer.

Text highlighted during slide show

10. Click the **Menu** control button to display the slide show menu with commands for navigating during a slide show.

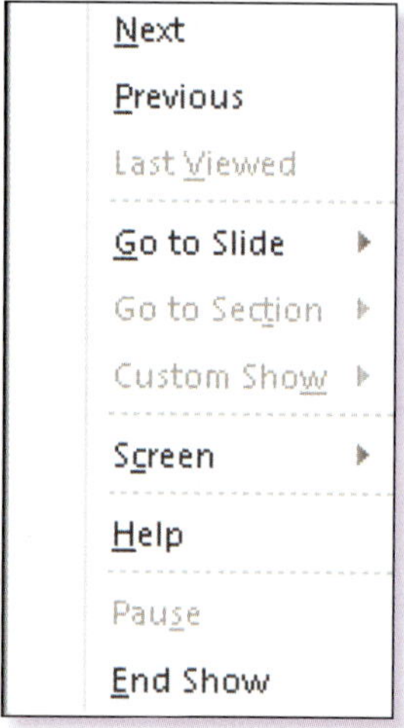


You can advance to the next slide, return to the previous slide or last slide viewed, go to a specific slide, temporarily change the screen to all black or all white, get online help, and end the slide show using this menu.

11. Point to **Go to Slide** and click **1 "Gold! Boys! Gold!"** to view slide 1.
12. Click the **Menu** button and click **End Show**. A Confirmation dialog box opens asking if you want to keep or discard your pen pointer annotations.
13. Click the **Discard** button and then save and close the presentation.

Congratulations! Julie's presentation is ready to go!

# Exploring *On Your Own*

## Blaze Your Own Trail

Blaze your own trail by practicing your new skills! Use classroom, library, or online resources to research the following landmarks in Concord, Massachusetts: Old North Bridge, Orchard House, The Wayside, Walden Pond, Bullet Hole House, and First Parish in Concord. Take notes about what you learn; then create a multipage bound report that has a title page, at least two report pages based on your notes, and a References page.

1. Cite your sources on a separate References page.
2. Switch to Full Screen Reading view, turn on text editing, and use keyboard shortcut keys to apply paragraph and character formatting and to spell-check your document. Then turn off text editing and switch back to Print Layout view.
3. Organize some data in your report using a borderless, formatted two-column table.
4. Add a cover page.
5. Create three sections using section breaks: Section 1 (cover page and first report page), Section 2 (second report page), and Section 3 (References page). Set the appropriate margins for each section of the report, including a 0.5-inch gutter. Insert page numbers in the appropriate sections.
6. Save and close the document.

## *Reading* in Action — Main Ideas and Details

Read the *writers4* document. What was Transcendentalism? What subjects did the Concord writers write about? Find answers to these questions. Put your notes in a graphic organizer that lists main ideas and details.

## *Math* in Action — Solving Problems with Logic

Hawthorne, Emerson, and Thoreau each wrote one of these books—*Nature, The Scarlet Letter, and Walden*. Which book did each author write? Use logic based on this information: Hawthorne did not like nature. Thoreau admired the author of *The Scarlet Letter*, but he did not get along with the author of *Nature*.

Solution:
Thoreau had opinions about the authors of *The Scarlet Letter* and *Nature*, so he could not be the author of those books; he must be the author of *Walden*. Hawthorne did not like nature, and Thoreau wrote *Walden*, so Hawthorne must have authored *The Scarlet Letter*. Therefore, Emerson is the author of *Nature*.

Now you try it!
Alex, Curt, and Ivan play for the baseball teams in New York, Detroit, and Boston. Curt always plays his best games against Detroit. Curt and Ivan have never been able to beat the New York team. Which team does each player play for? Explain your answer.

**Let's use the Slide Show toolbar to advance to the next slide, return to the previous slide, turn on the pen pointer and change its ink color, and view the slide show menu.**

1. Click **slide 1**, if necessary, and run the slide show.
2. If you do not see the control buttons, move the mouse pointer across the screen to the left to display the buttons.

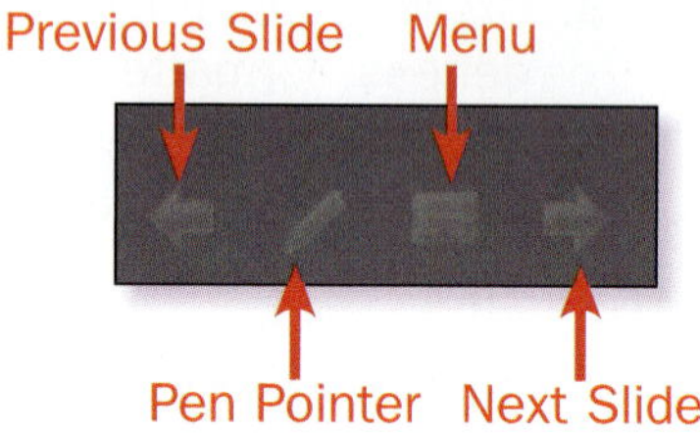


3. Click the **Next Slide** control button to advance to slide 2, then slide 3, and then slide 4.
4. Click the **Previous Slide** control button to return to slide 3.
5. Click the **Pen Pointer** control button to view the menu options for the pen pointer.
6. Point to **Ink Color** and click the **Orange** color in the Standard Color grid, if necessary, to select the ink color. The mouse pointer becomes a small pen pointer.
7. Move the pen pointer above and to the left of the slide's title; then draw a freestyle circle around the title. *Do not worry if your circle is not smooth.* Tap the ESC key to turn off the pen pointer.

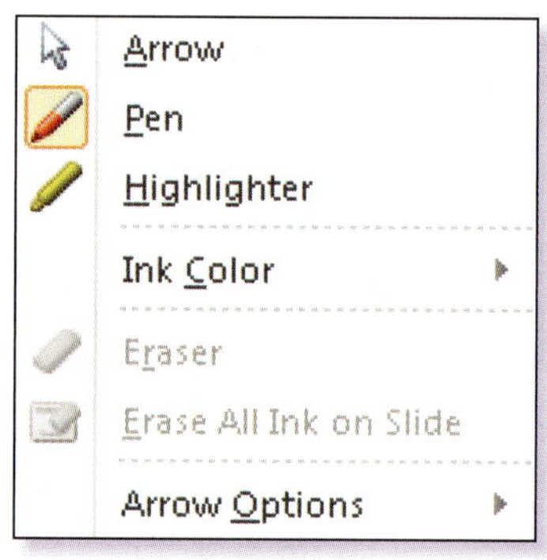


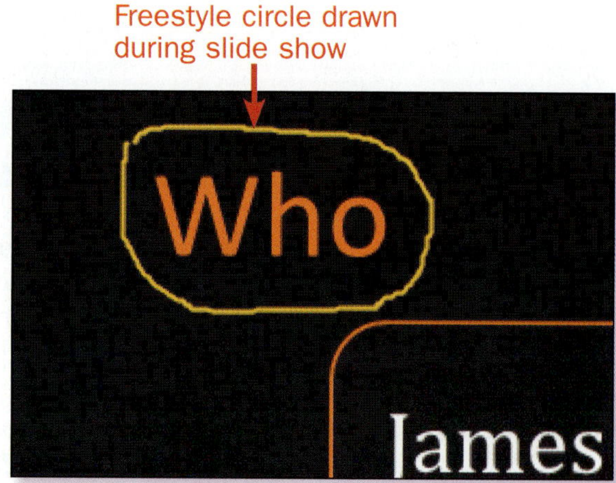

# Exploring *Across the Curriculum*

## Internet/Web

Open your Web browser and use a favorite or bookmark to view the Learning with Computers Web page (www.cengage.com/school/keyboarding/lwcorange). Click the **Links** option and click **Project 4**. Click the links to learn more about the writers of Concord and their relationship to the nineteenth-century philosophical movement called Transcendentalism. What were the basic ideas behind this movement? How did Transcendentalism affect the lives of writers of Concord, such as Amos Bronson Alcott, Louisa May Alcott, Henry David Thoreau, Ralph Waldo Emerson, and Nathaniel Hawthorne? Take notes about what you learn.

1. Create a multipage bound report that has a cover page, at least two report pages based on your notes, and a References page for your source citations.
2. Use paragraph headings and use a borderless table to organize some data.
3. Use keyboard shortcuts as desired to select and format the document.
4. Cite your sources on the References page.
5. Set the appropriate margins for each section of the report, including a 0.5-inch gutter.
6. Insert page numbers for the sections that contain the report pages and the References page.
7. Spell-check, save, and close the document.

**Let's apply a slide transition effect and add footer text, slide numbers, and today's date.**

1. Apply the slide transition effect of your choice to all of the slides.
2. Open the Header and Footer dialog box and key **Julie Wilson** as footer text, add today's date as a fixed date with the month spelled out, and add slide numbers to all slides *except* the Title Slide.

The top left corner of your slide 2 should look similar to this.

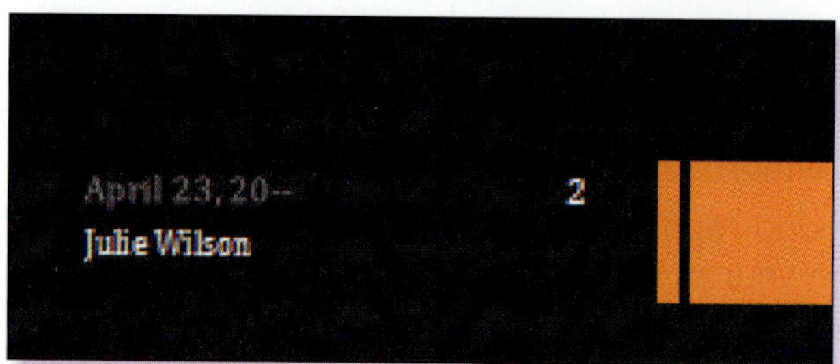


Fantastic! Now let's run the slide show and navigate with buttons on the Slide Show toolbar.

## Using the Slide Show Controls

When you run a slide show, four control buttons appear in the lower-left corner of the screen. You can click these buttons to return to the previous slide, advance to the next slide, display a menu, and turn on a pen pointer that uses different styles and ink colors.

The pen pointer can be used to draw or highlight annotations on a slide during a slide show. You can also change the ink color for the pen pointer. To turn off the pen pointer, just tap the ESC key or click Arrow on the Pen Pointer menu. You can choose to keep or discard your pen point annotations when you exit the slide show.

# Exploring Across the Curriculum

## Language Arts: Words to Know

Look up the meaning of the following terms in a classroom dictionary, CD-ROM dictionary or encyclopedia, or online dictionary.

| | | | |
|---|---|---|---|
| Amos Bronson Alcott | Margaret Fuller | Margaret Sidney | philosophy |
| "Sage of Concord" | self-reliance | Transcendentalism | Walden Pond |

Create a new document. Save the document as *definitions4*. Change the margins to a 2-inch top margin and 1-inch left, right, and bottom margins. Key **Terms and Definitions** as the main heading and use keyboard shortcuts to select and center the main heading. Insert two blank lines; then starting on the second blank line below the main heading, key each term on one line and its definition on the following line. Insert a blank line between each definition and the next term. Select all of the terms and use a keyboard shortcut to apply the Bold font style. Select all of the definitions and use a keyboard shortcut to apply the Italic font style. Spell-check, save, and close the document.

## Language Arts: Research and Write

Use classroom, library, or online resources to research the life of Louisa May Alcott, the nineteenth-century author of the semiautobiographical novel *Little Women*. Also locate and read a synopsis of *Little Women*. Then compare Miss Alcott's family life with that of the characters in *Little Women*. How are their lives the same? How are they different? Who or what were the major influences in Miss Alcott's life? How do these influences compare to those for the family in *Little Women*? Which character in *Little Women* is most like Miss Alcott? Why?

Then write a correctly formatted multipage bound report that answers these questions. Add a cover page to the report, use paragraph headings, and cite your sources on a separate References page. Use keyboard shortcuts to apply character and paragraph formatting. Set the appropriate margins for each section of the report and insert page numbers in all sections except Section 1 (the title page and the first report page).

Explore More

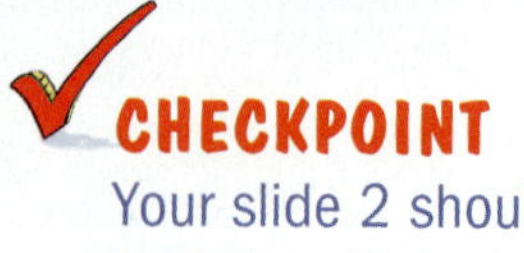

**CHECKPOINT**
Your slide 2 should look like this.

Animation sequence tag

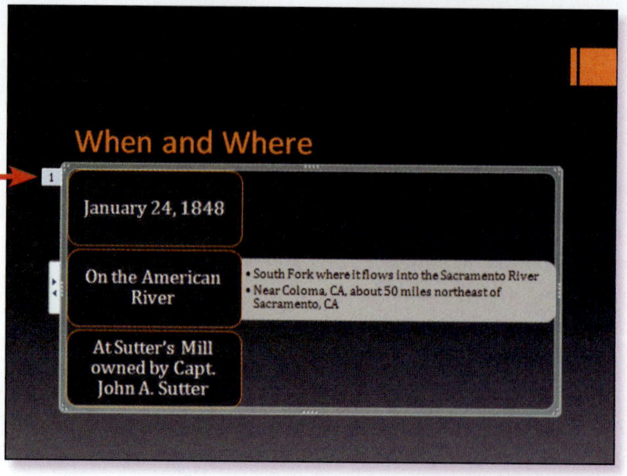

When and Where
1
January 24, 1848
On the American River
• South Fork where it flows into the Sacramento River
• Near Coloma, CA, about 50 miles northeast of Sacramento, CA
At Sutter's Mill owned by Capt. John A. Sutter

Now you are ready to customize the animation effect.

## Apply It!

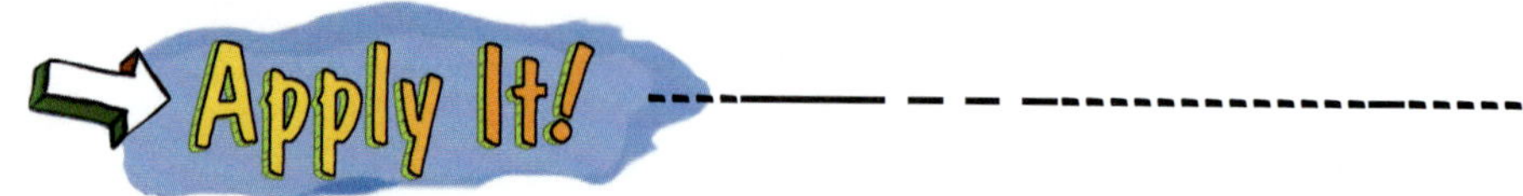

**Let's customize the slide 2 SmartArt graphic animation by specifying that animation start automatically after any previous slide animation and set a medium speed, then apply the same customized animation effect to slide 3.**

1. Click the **Start** arrow in the Custom Animation task pane to view the start options.
2. Click **After Previous**.
3. Click the **Speed** arrow in the Custom Animation task pane.
4. Click **Slow**.
5. Click the **Slide Show** button in the Custom Animation task pane to view the customized animation effect.
6. Using the previous steps as a guide, apply the customized animation effect to the SmartArt graphic on slide 3.
7. Close the Custom Animation task pane.
8. Run the slide show from slide 2 to view the animation.
9. Save the presentation.

Custom Animation
Add Effect
Remove
Modify: Wedge
Start:
After Previous
Property:
Speed:
Slow
0
Diagram 3

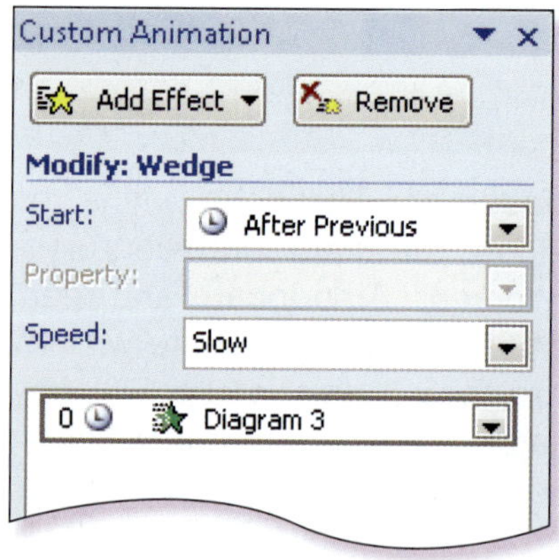

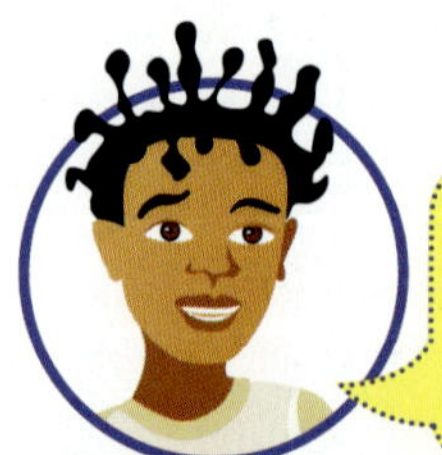

Another way to preview an animation effect is to click the Play button near the bottom of the Custom Animation task pane. Try it!

Terrific! Adding transition effects and slide footers will wrap up our work on Julie's presentation.

# Exploring Across the Curriculum

## Getting Help

Click the Microsoft Word Help icon to open the Help window. Search *Word* Help for a list of keyboard shortcuts. Select ten keyboard shortcuts not covered in this project and practice using them.

## Career Day

Great advances in the sciences and engineering took place during the nineteenth century, such as the development of the steam engine, telephone, and elevator and the discovery of germs. Using library, printed, or online resources, identify three interesting occupations in the fields of science and engineering. Write a brief summary of each occupation, print your summary, and save it in your Career Day folder.

## Your Personal Journal

Open your personal journal document. Insert today's date. If you could travel back in time to nineteenth-century New England, which of the Concord writers would you most like to meet? What questions would you like to ask this writer? Write a conversation you might have with the writer. Spell-check, save, and close your journal document.

**Online Enrichment Games**  www.cengage.com/school/keyboarding/lwcorange

**Let's apply an Entrance animation effect to the SmartArt graphic on slide 2.**

> **Animations | Animations | Custom Animation**

> **Animations | Preview | Preview Animations**

1. Activate **slide 2** and click the **SmartArt graphic** to select it and display the drawing canvas.
2. Click the **Animations** tab and locate the **Animations** group.
3. Click the **Custom Animation** button in the Animations group to open the Custom Animation task pane to the right of the Slide pane.
4. Click the **Add Effect** button in the Custom Animation task pane and point to Entrance to see a list of Entrance animation effects.

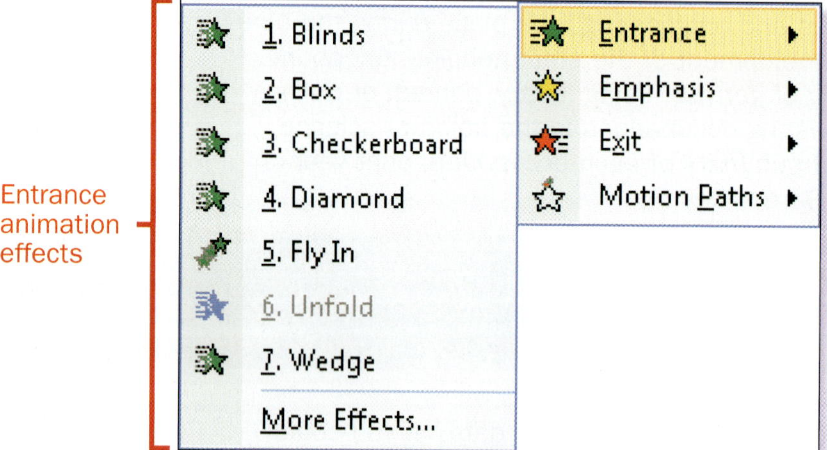


5. Click **Wedge** to apply the animation effect to the SmartArt graphic.

The AutoPreview feature automatically previews the animation effect immediately after it is applied. Nonprinting numbered sequence tags appear to the left of the bulleted list placeholder. These numbers indicate the current animation sequence from first to last.

6. Click the **Preview Animations** button in the Preview group to replay the Zoom animation effect.

# Project 4

## 4a Review Left Shift, Period, u, c

Key each line twice. Double-space between 2-line groups.

### TECHNIQUE TIP

To key capital letters with the right hand:

1. Hold down the Left Shift with the little finger on the left hand.
2. Tap the letter with the right hand.
3. Return finger(s) to home keys.

**left shift**

1 j J j J | l L l L | n N n N | k K k K | h H h H | i I i I | oO

2 Hal Hal | Jason Jason | Nate Nate | Jose Jose | Kent Kent;

**period**

3 l . l . | .l. .l. | lo. lo. | .o. .o. | .li. .li. | .l. .l.;

4 Ill. Ill. | Okla. Okla. | Ind. Ind. | Kans. Kans. | Oreg.;

**u**

5 j u j u | ujn ujn | uhn uhn | juh juh | uns uns | kun kun | ju

6 fun fun | use use | hut hut | just just | unusual unusual;

**c**

7 d c d c | edc edc | fec fec | rcd rcd | ecga ecga | ctc ctc;

8 ace ace | luck luck | case case | rock rock | clown clown;

## 4b Build Skill

Key each line twice single-spaced; double-space between 2-line groups.

For additional practice:
**MicroType 5**
New Key Review, Alphabetic Lessons 8–10

**Balanced-hand words**

1 auto burn dusk kept form half rich pale sign maid;
2 panel quake; right shelf chair; eight elbow giant;
3 enrich handle eighty bushel chapels turkey suspend

**Balanced-hand phrases**

4 by the end | pay the man | if they fix the | go to work
5 make the sign | right problem | key to the map | to risk
6 with the neighbor | work with the city | sign the maps

**Balanced-hand sentences**

7 Pay the girl by the city dock for the six bushels.
8 The girls paid for their gowns for the big social.
9 The city officials kept the fox in the big kennel.
10 Jay and Hal may go with us to visit the neighbors.

**Let's paint the animation from the SmartArt graphic on slide 2 to the SmartArt graphic on slide 3.**

Animations | Advanced Animation | Animation Painter

1. Click the **Animation Painter** button in the Advanced Animation group; then click **slide 3** and click the **SmartArt graphic** to paint the customized animations to the slide 3 SmartArt graphic. Animation Painter
2. Run the slide show for slide 2 and slide 3 to view the SmartArt graphics' animation.
3. Tap the ESC key to return to Normal view and save the presentation.

Terrific! Now you are ready to wrap up the presentation by applying a transition effect and adding slide footers.

**Applying Customized Animation Effects in *PowerPoint 2007***

To create a custom animation effect and apply it to a slide object, click the Custom Animation button in the Animations group on the Animations tab to open the Custom Animation task pane. Then set customization options for the selected slide object, such as the specific effects, duration, playing speed, and playing sequence or order.

When you apply an animation effect to a slide object, the AutoPreview feature, which is turned on by default, automatically plays the animation effect. You can also click the Preview Animations button in the Preview group on the Animations tab to preview the animation effect.

The Animation Pane displays a sequential list of the animation effects applied to a slide. You can display or hide the Animation Pane by clicking the Animations tab and then clicking the Animation Pane button in the Advanced Animation group. You can customize an animation effect, reorder one or more effects, and remove one or more effects with options in the Animation Pane. Check it out!

To quickly apply a predefined animation effect, click the Animation button arrow in the Animations group on the Animations tab to display a gallery of predefined animation effect options. You can use live preview to preview a predefined animation effect, then click an effect to apply it to the selected slide object.

# Reenacting the Founding of Our Nation

## Explorers' Guide

**Data files:** **letter body**
**Johnson text**

**Objectives:**
In this project, you will:
- create a personal-business letter
- insert a file into an open document
- organize data in tabbed columns
- add an envelope to a letter document
- prepare a sheet of return address labels

© POODLESROCK/CORBIS

## Our Exploration Assignment:

**Creating a personal-business letter, an envelope, and labels**

Thomas Jefferson! John and Abigail Adams! Benjamin Franklin! George Washington! Explorers Club members are going to portray famous patriots of the American Revolution during the *Celebration of American History* program at school. Julie wants to write a letter to the director of a local theater group asking for tips on makeup and costumes. Can you help Julie write her letter? Great! Follow the Trail Markers to learn how to create and format a personal-business letter, insert a saved file into an open document, organize data in tabbed columns, add an envelope to a letter, and create a sheet of return address labels.

You can modify the animation by clicking the Effect Options button in the Animation group and then clicking an option. The types of options available, such as animating the graphic object 'As One Object' or 'One by One,' will vary depending on the effect you are applying and the type of object being animated.

For example, the default options for the Zoom animation applied to a SmartArt graphic is to zoom from the object's center and to animate as one object.

You can also specify whether the animation should begin automatically or on a mouse click, what the duration of the animation will be, and when to start the animation with buttons in the Timing group on the Animations tab.

**Let's customize the slide 2 SmartArt graphic animation by specifying that animation start automatically after any previous slide animation and set a three-second duration, then paint the customized animation effect to the SmartArt graphic on slide 3.**

1. Click the **SmartArt graphic** on slide 2, if necessary.
2. Click the **Animations** tab, if necessary, and locate the **Animation**, **Timing**, **Preview**, and **Advanced Animation** groups.
3. Click the **Animation Timing** button arrow in the Timing group to view the options for starting the animation. (Start: On Click)
4. Click **After Previous**.
5. Key **3** in the Animation Duration text box in the Timing group to change the duration of the animation to three seconds. (Duration: 00.50)
6. Click the **Preview Animations** button face in the Preview group to preview the customized animation to see the change in the duration of the animation's playing time. (Preview)

Animations | Animation | Effect Options

Animations | Timing | Animation Timing

Animations | Timing | Animation Duration

Animations | Preview | Preview Animations

The Animation Painter button, like the Format Painter button you learned to use in *Word* and *Excel*, copies the animation effect from one object to another.

- To copy an animation effect and then paint the effect on a single slide object, click the Animation Painter once.
- To copy an animation effect to multiple slide objects, double-click the Animation Painter button to turn the feature on and leave it on while you paint the effect on multiple slide objects. When you are finished painting the animation effect, click the Animation Painter button or tap the ESC key to turn the feature off.

**Begin by creating and saving a new document for your personal-business letter.**

1. Create a new blank document, if necessary, and save it as *theater letter5*.

Great! Let's get started with Julie's letter.

**ERGONOMICS TIP**

Are your fingers stiff and shoulders tight after working at the computer for a while? Do not forget to relax by stretching your fingers and rolling your shoulders forward and back several times.

## Creating a Personal-Business Letter

Julie's letter asking for makeup and costume tips is a formal letter written about a personal topic, called a personal-business letter.

A personal-business letter has seven basic parts, including the:

1. return address (sender's address)
2. date
3. letter address (receiver's name and address)
4. salutation (greeting)
5. body (message)
6. complimentary closing
7. writer's name

Check out Appendix A in the back of this book to see an example of a personal-business letter!

In a personal-business letter that follows the block format style, all letter parts begin at the left margin, the salutation is followed by a colon (:), and the complimentary closing is followed by a comma (,). The margin settings for a personal-business letter are a 2-inch top margin and 1-inch bottom, left, and right margins.

**Let's add an animation effect to the SmartArt graphic on slide 2.**

Animations | Animation | More

Animations | Preview | Preview Animations

1. Activate **slide 2** and click the **SmartArt graphic** to select it and display the drawing canvas.
2. Click the **Animations** tab and locate the **Animation** group.
3. Click the **More** button in the Animation group to view a gallery of predefined or sample animation effects by category. 
4. Use live preview to preview animation effects from the four different categories.
5. Click the **Zoom** animation effect in the Entrance Effect category to apply it to the SmartArt graphic and play the animation. Observe the sequence tag to the left of the graphic.
6. Locate the **Preview** group.
7. Click the **Preview Animations** button face in the Preview group to replay the Zoom animation effect; then deselect the placeholder.

Preview

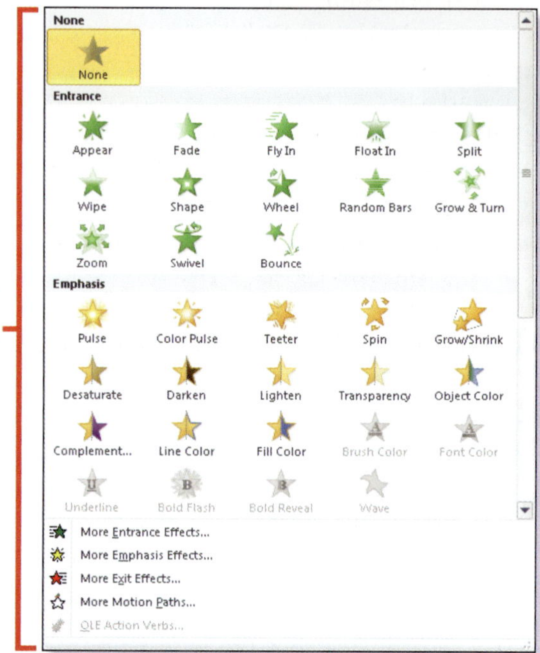


Gallery of animation options

Your slide 2 should look like this.

Animation sequence tag

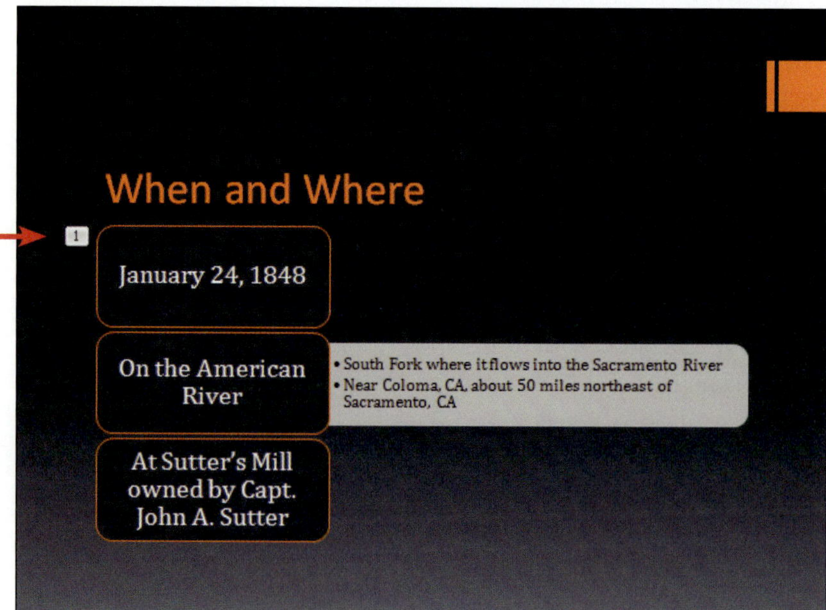

**Let's start Julie's personal-business letter by setting the margins and then keying all of the letter parts *except* the body.**

Page Layout|Margins|Custom Margins

1. Set a 2-inch top margin and 1-inch left, right, and bottom margins; then key the following return address at the top of the page at the left margin.
   **1925 Rocky Hill Drive**
   **Madison, WI 53707-1925**
2. Key today's date with the month spelled out on the next line following the return address and then insert two blank lines.
3. Key the following letter (delivery) address and follow it with two blank lines.
   **Ms. Janice Hollingsworth**
   **Director**
   **Actors Alliance Theater Group**
   **9645 West Henderson Street**
   **Madison, WI 53778-9645**
4. Key **Dear Ms. Hollingsworth:** as the salutation and tap the ENTER key.
5. Key **Sincerely,** as the complimentary closing and insert two blank lines. *Do not forget to key the comma.*
6. Key **Julie Wilson** as the writer's name and save the document.

Now you need to remove the extra spacing following some of the return and letter address paragraphs.

In previous projects, you learned that you can remove the extra paragraph spacing following each paragraph by keying a zero value in the Spacing After box in the Paragraph group in the Page Layout tab.

Another way to remove the extra 10 points of spacing after a paragraph is to click the Home tab, click the Line and Paragraph Spacing button in the Paragraph group, and click Remove Space After Paragraph.

**Let's remove the extra paragraph spacing from the return and letter addresses.**

Home|Paragraph|Line and Paragraph Spacing

1. Select the first line of the two-line return address at the top of the document.
2. Click the **Home** tab, if necessary, and locate the **Paragraph** group.

Like audio and video, however, take care when adding animation effects to your slides. Excessive animation might be distracting to your audience.

**Applying Customized Animation Effects in *PowerPoint 2010***

You can apply one of several animation effects and then customize the effect by changing its direction or sequence, specifying a trigger to start the effect, setting timing for the effect, and previewing it before applying it to the slide object.

You can add an animation effect to a slide object by selecting the slide object and then clicking the Animations tab and clicking an animation effect in the animations gallery.

When you apply an animation effect to a slide object, the AutoPreview feature, which is turned on by default, automatically plays the animation effect. Nonprinting numbered sequence tags appear to the left of each animated object on the slide. These numbers indicate the current animation sequence from first to last.

You can also manually preview the animation by clicking the Animations tab and then clicking the top of the Preview Animations button in the Preview group or by running the slide show.

You can add Entrance, Emphasis, Exit, and Motion Path effects to the same slide object. Try it!

When you have multiple objects on a slide, such as several shapes, you can open the Selection and Visibility pane to view a list of all of the objects on the slide. Click an object in the pane to quickly select the object on the slide. You can also show or hide slide objects or reorder them with options in the pane. To open the Selection and Visibility Pane, click the Home tab and then click the Arrange button in the Drawing group and click Selection Pane.

3. Click the **Line and Paragraph Spacing** button in the Paragraph group to view line and paragraph spacing options. In *Word 2010*, point to **Remove Space After Paragraph** to live-preview the removal of the extra paragraph spacing. Live preview is not available for this command in *Word 2007*.
4. Click **Remove Space After Paragraph**. The extra paragraph spacing is removed.
5. Select the first four lines of the five-line letter address.
6. Click the **Line and Paragraph Spacing** button in the Paragraph group.
7. Click **Remove Space After Paragraph**. The extra paragraph spacing is removed.
8. Deselect the text and save the document.

**CHECKPOINT**
Your partially completed letter should look like this.

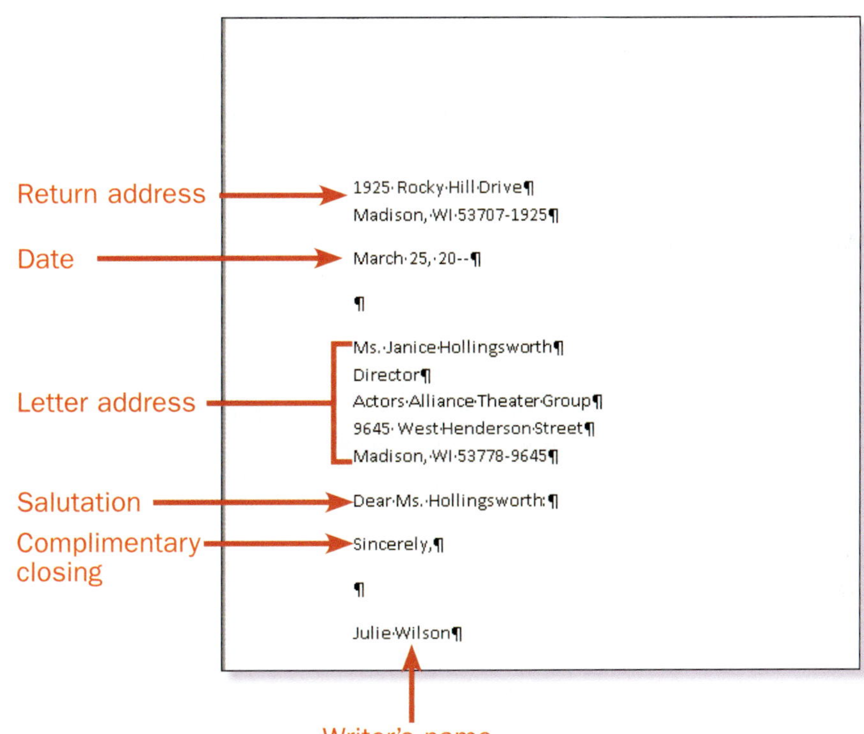


Super! Now let's add the body of the letter. Instead of keying the text, you can insert it from a saved document.

4. Click **Format Background** to open the Format Background dialog box.
5. Click **Fill** in the left pane, if necessary, to view Fill options.
6. Click the **Picture or texture fill** option button to view the picture or fill options.
7. Click the **Insert from File** button to open the Insert Picture dialog box.
8. Switch to the folder that contains your data files and double-click the *miners* filename.
9. Click the **Hide background graphics** option button or checkbox.
10. Click **Close** to insert the picture, which covers the entire slide; then save the presentation.

Your slide 8 should look like this.

© BUREAU OF LAND MANAGEMENT

Fantastic! Now let's apply a customized animation effect to the two SmartArt graphic objects.

## Applying Customized Animation Effects

An animation effect adds motion to selected slide objects, such as title text, bulleted or numbered text, a picture, SmartArt, or a shape. The four categories of animation effects are Entrance, Emphasis, Exit, and Motion Path.

- Entrance—specifies how a slide object first appears on a slide.
- Emphasis—draws attention to a slide object.
- Exit—specifies how a slide object leaves a slide.
- Motion Path—defines the movement of a slide object across a slide.

## Inserting a File into an Open Document

When you want to use some of the text from one document in another document, you can open both documents, select and copy the text from the first document, and then paste it into the other document.

But when you want to use *all* of the text from a saved document, just position the insertion point where you want the new text to be inserted; then click the Insert tab and click the Insert Object button arrow in the Text group. Next, click Text from File to open the Insert File dialog box; then locate, select, and insert the saved document using the dialog box options.

If you accidentally insert a saved document in the wrong place, just click the Undo button on the Quick Access Toolbar, reposition the insertion point, and try again!

Julie wrote two paragraphs for the body of her letter to Ms. Hollingsworth and saved the document as *letter body*.

**Let's insert the complete *letter body* document into the *theater letter5* document.**

Insert | Text | Insert Object

1. Move the insertion point immediately in front of the complimentary closing *Sincerely,*.
2. Click the **Insert** tab and locate the **Text** group.
3. Click the **Insert Object** button arrow in the Text group to display insertion options.

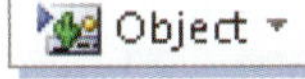


4. Click **Text from File** to open the Insert File dialog box.
5. Switch to the folder that contains your data files and double-click the *letter body* filename.
6. Tap the ENTER key and save the document.

The SmartArt graphics on slides 2 and 3 should now look similar to this.

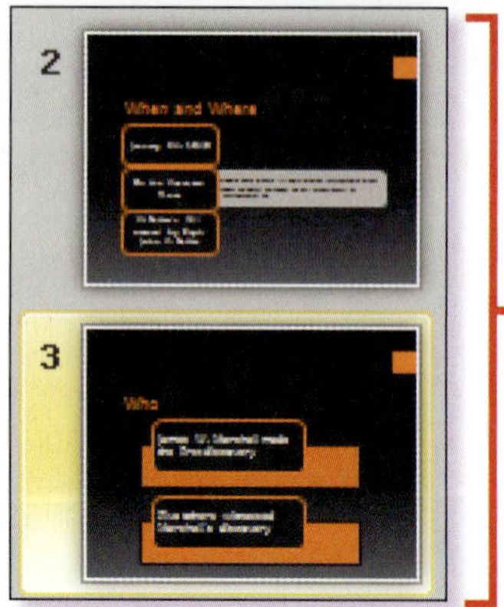

Recolored SmartArt graphics

Great! Now let's use a picture as the background for the last slide in the presentation.

## Inserting a Picture as the Slide Background

You have already learned how to remove a slide's background graphics. You can also use special fill effects—such as patterns or a picture—to change a slide's background.

Another quick way to open the Format Background dialog box and remove a slide's background graphics or use special fill effects as the background is to right-click a slide and click Format Background on the shortcut menu. Try it!

**Let's insert a photograph of miners who are working a placer mine as the background on slide 8. They are using a sloping pan to wash away the sediment to find gold.**

**Design | Background | Background Styles**

1. Insert a new **slide 8** at the end of the presentation using the Blank slide layout.
2. Click the **Design** tab and locate the **Background** group.
3. Click the **Background Styles** button in the Background group to view the styles gallery. Background Styles

Gallery of background styles

**CHECKPOINT**

Your letter's inserted body text should look like this.

File inserted as the letter's body text

Dear·Ms.·Hollingsworth:¶

The·Explorers·Club·is·going·to·participate·in·the·*Celebration·of·American·History*·program·at·our·school·next·month.··During·the·program,·five·of·our·members·will·portray·the·following·five·people·involved·in·America's·struggle·for·independence.¶

Can·someone·in·your·actors'·group·spend·two·or·three·hours·next·week·to·give·us·tips·on·applying·stage·makeup·and·creating·our·costumes?··We·would·be·happy·to·note·your·group's·support·on·the·program·flyers·and·ads.··Please·contact·me·by·phone·at·608-555-6578·or·by·e-mail·at·juliew@odzok.com·if·your·group·can·help.¶

Fantastic! Next, you will add two tabbed columns to the body of the letter.

## Organizing Data in Tabbed Columns

In Project 4, you learned how to use a table to organize data in a grid of columns and rows. Another way to organize data is in tabbed columns. Tabbed columns are created with tab stops and tab formatting marks.

A tab stop is an icon on the Horizontal Ruler that indicates a specific keying position on a line. To align text at a tab stop, tap the TAB key to move the insertion point to the tab stop position and then key the text. Each time you tap the TAB key, *Word* inserts a tab formatting mark. Here are the four main types of tab stops and their icons.

| | | |
|---|---|---|
| **Left tab** | Indents text from the left margin or left-aligns text columns | └ |
| **Right tab** | Right-aligns text columns or aligns dates and other text at the right margin | ┘ |
| **Center tab** | Centers headings over text columns | ┴ |
| **Decimal tab** | Aligns numbers on the decimal point | ┴. |

Tab stops are also used to align text at the right margin and to move the first line of a paragraph inward from the left margin.

### Modifying a SmartArt Graphic

The SmartArt Tools Design and Format tabs appear on the Ribbon when you insert or select a SmartArt graphic. You can use buttons on the SmartArt Tools Design tab to change the layout, apply a style, change colors, or add another shape to a SmartArt graphic. The SmartArt Tools Format tab contains buttons you can use to edit the graphic's shapes and text.

**Let's change the colors in the SmartArt graphic objects on slides 2 and 3.**

SmartArt Tools Design | SmartArt Styles | Change Colors

1. Activate **slide 2** and click the **SmartArt graphic** object to display it on the drawing canvas.
2. Click the **SmartArt Tools Design** tab and locate the **SmartArt Styles** group.
3. Click the **Change Colors** button in the SmartArt Styles group to display a gallery of style color options.

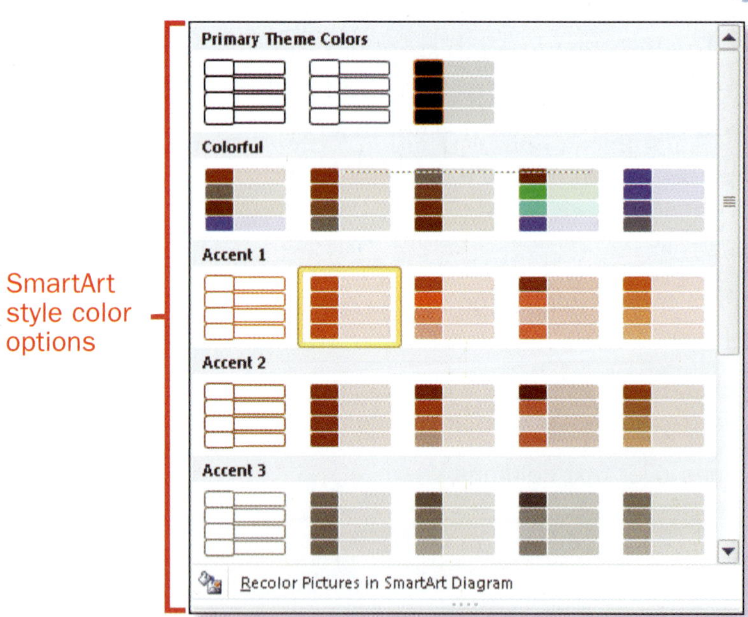


SmartArt style color options

4. Live-preview different color options; then click the **Dark 2 Fill** option (the third option in the Primary Theme Colors group).
5. Activate **slide 3**, click the **SmartArt graphic**, and change its color combination to Dark 2 Fill.
6. Deselect the SmartArt graphic and save the presentation.

*Word* automatically sets default Left tab stops every 0.5 inch on the Horizontal Ruler. You can set custom Left, Right, Center, or Decimal tab stops at any position on the Horizontal Ruler.

To set a tab stop, click the tab indicator button to the left of the Horizontal Ruler to select the type of tab stop you want. Then click the Horizontal Ruler where you want to position the tab stop.

When a custom tab stop is set on the Horizontal Ruler, all of the default Left tab stops to the left of it are automatically removed.

Julie wants to add one tabbed column for the names of patriots and another tabbed column for the Explorers Club members who will portray them.

**Let's set Center tab stops and key the column headings. Then let's set Left tab stops and key the names that go in each column.**

1. Move the insertion point to the end of the first body text paragraph and tap the ENTER key.
2. Click the **tab indicator** button to the left of the Horizontal Ruler until the Center tab stop icon appears.
3. Move the mouse pointer to the 1.75-inch position on the Horizontal Ruler and click to insert a Center tab stop.
4. Set a Center tab stop at the 3.5-inch position.
5. Tap the TAB key and key **Famous Person**.
6. Tap the TAB key, key **Member**, and tap the ENTER key. Each column heading is centered at its tab stop.

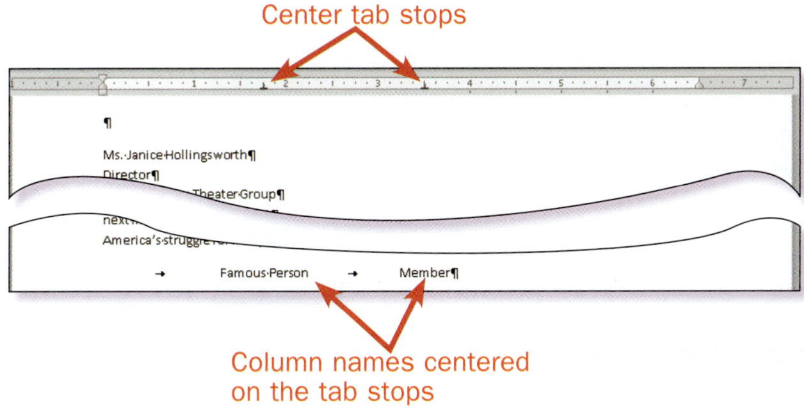

You can enter text in a SmartArt graphic by keying the text in the graphic's Text pane or by keying inside individual shapes within the graphic. You can also cut or copy existing text and paste it in a SmartArt graphic.

To display the SmartArt Text pane, click the Text pane control on the left side of the graphic. Try it!

**Let's add text to the SmartArt graphic.**

Home | Font | Font Size

1. Click the **[TEXT]** text box inside the first rectangle shape in the SmartArt graphic to position the insertion point.
2. Key **James W. Marshall made the first discovery**. *Do not key the period.* The rectangle shape automatically resizes to fit all of the text.
3. Click the **[TEXT]** text box inside the second rectangle shape and key **Five others witnessed Marshall's discovery**. *Do not key the period.*
4. Click the **boundary** of the last [TEXT] text box and tap the DELETE key to delete it from the graphic.
5. Tap and hold the CTRL key and click the boundary of the remaining rectangle shapes as necessary to select the shapes and their contents.
6. Change the font size to 28 point and then tap the ESC key twice to deselect the graphic and close the drawing canvas.
7. Save the presentation.

**CHECKPOINT**
Your slide 3 and SmartArt graphic should look similar to this.

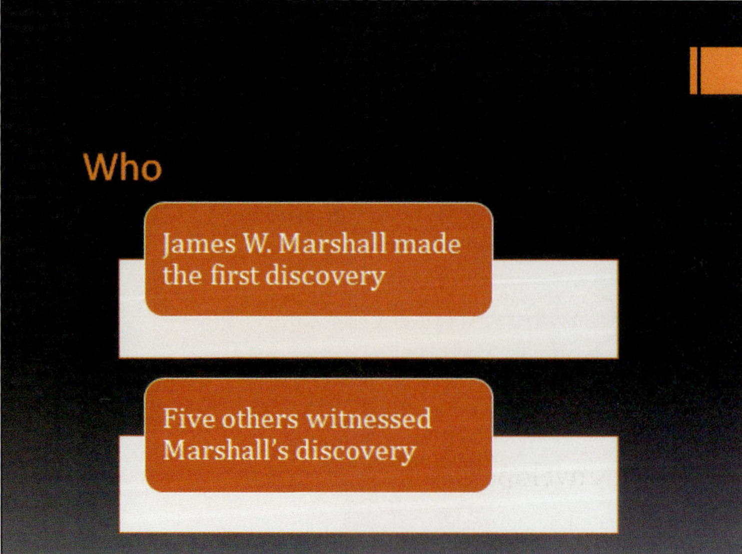

When you tap the ENTER key to create a new paragraph, *Word* remembers the Center tab stops you set for the previous paragraph (the column headings). You want to use different tab stops for the names, so you must remove these Center tab stops by dragging them off the Horizontal Ruler, then set Left tab stops for the new paragraph.

7. Point to the first **Center** tab stop on the Horizontal Ruler. Press and hold the mouse button and drag the tab stop downward off the ruler.
8. Drag the remaining Center tab stop off the ruler.

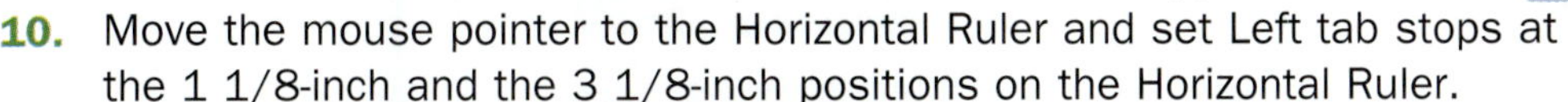

9. Click the **tab indicator** button until the Left tab icon appears.
10. Move the mouse pointer to the Horizontal Ruler and set Left tab stops at the 1 1/8-inch and the 3 1/8-inch positions on the Horizontal Ruler.
11. Tap the TAB key and key **Richard Henry Lee**; tap the TAB key and key **Steve Huang**; tap the ENTER key. Continue keying the rest of the column text as shown.

| | |
|---|---|
| **Thomas Jefferson** | **Luis Gonzales** |
| **John Adams** | **Jeff Stevens** |
| **Benjamin Franklin** | **Ray Jackson** |
| **Abigail Adams** | **Julie Wilson** |

12. Apply the **Bold** font style to the column headings.
13. Select the tabbed columns, change the line spacing to single, and remove the extra 10 points of spacing from the column heading paragraph and the first three paragraphs below the column headings.

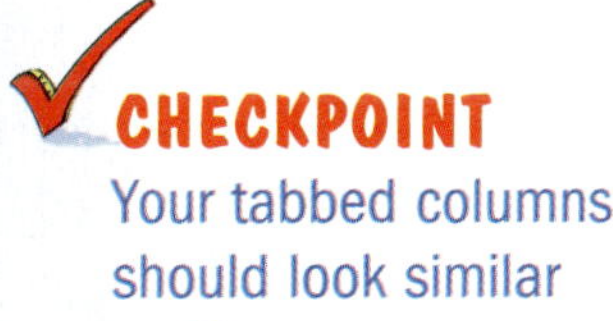

**CHECKPOINT**

Your tabbed columns should look similar to this.

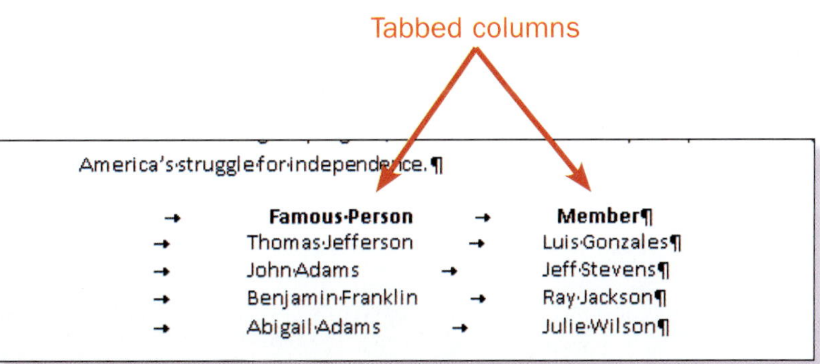

You can also set and clear tab stops in the Tabs dialog box. Double-click any tab stop on the Horizontal Ruler or click the Dialog Box Launcher icon in the Paragraph group on the Page Layout tab to open the Page Setup dialog box and then click the dialog box Tabs button.

Super! Now you are ready to add an envelope to the *theater letter5* document.

6. Click the **Vertical Box List** icon in the center pane to preview the graphic in the right pane.

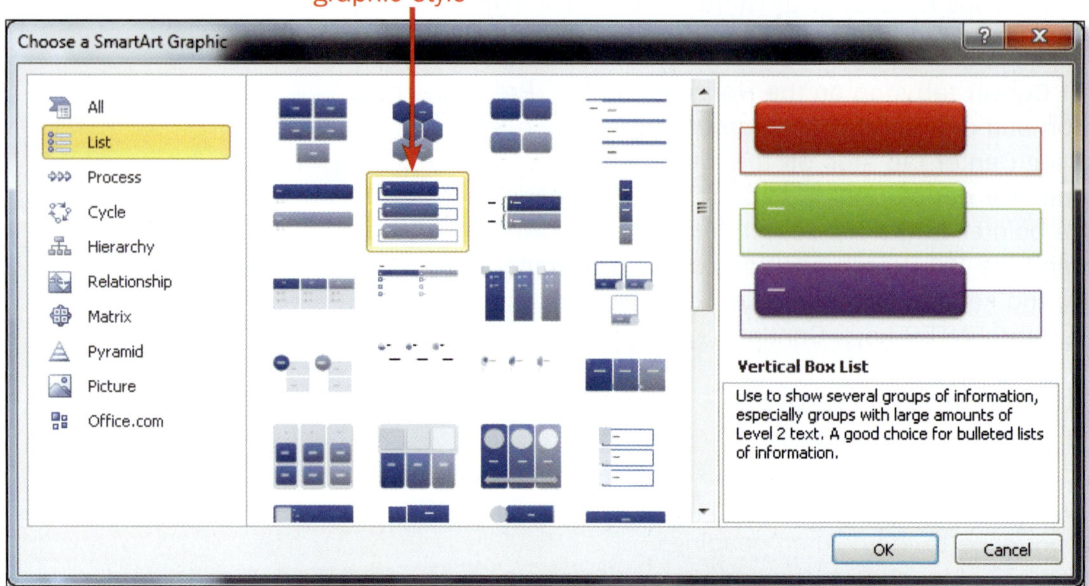


7. Click **OK** to insert the graphic and display the SmartArt Tools Design and Format tabs on the Ribbon.
8. Drag the drawing canvas down until you can see the slide title.

**CHECKPOINT**

Your slide 3 with the repositioned Vertical Box List SmartArt graphic on the drawing canvas should look similar to this.

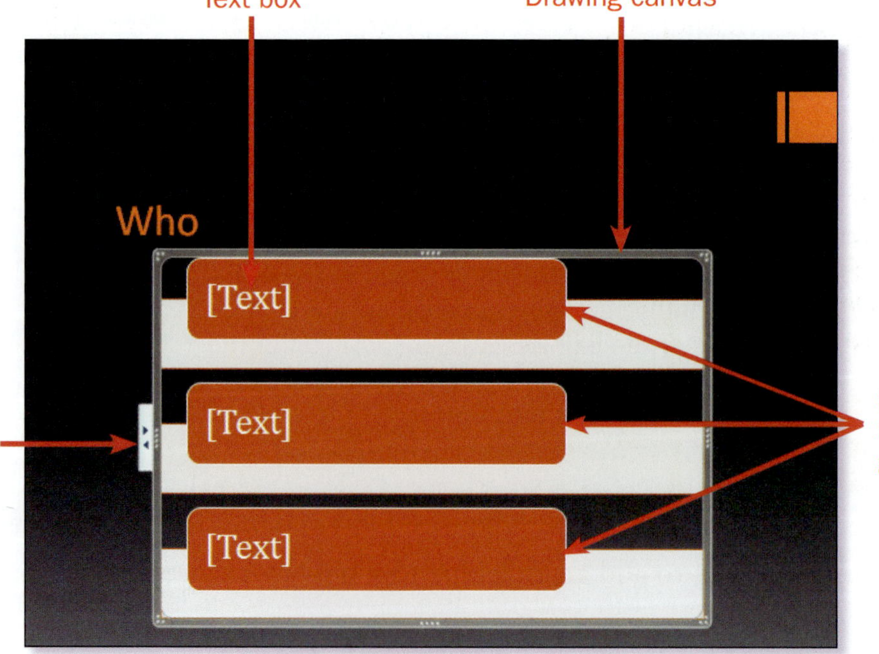

## Adding an Envelope to a Letter Document

When you key a personal-business letter, you always include the address of the person to whom you are writing. When you create an envelope, *Word* can automatically use that address as the envelope's delivery address. Just identify the letter address by selecting it. Then create the envelope by clicking the Mailings tab and clicking the Create Envelopes button in the Create group to open the Envelopes and Labels dialog box.

You must also specify which size envelope to use. For a personal-business letter, use a Size 10 envelope. Finally, you can print just the envelope or you can add it to the letter document and print them both together.

According to the U.S. Postal Service guidelines, an envelope's delivery address should be keyed in all UPPERCASE letters *without* punctuation. This format allows an envelope to be processed more efficiently by the Postal Service's equipment. If you use the selection method to identify the delivery address, you should edit it for case and punctuation.

**Let's add an envelope to the *theater letter5* document.**

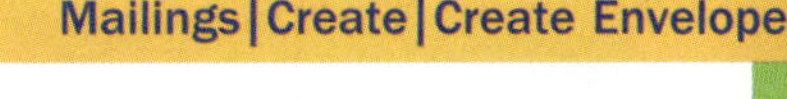


1. Select the letter address.
2. Click the **Mailings** tab and locate the **Create** group.
3. Click the **Create Envelopes** button in the Create group to open the Envelopes tab in the Envelopes and Labels dialog box.
4. Click the **Envelopes** tab, if necessary.
   The selected letter address is automatically inserted in the Delivery address text box.

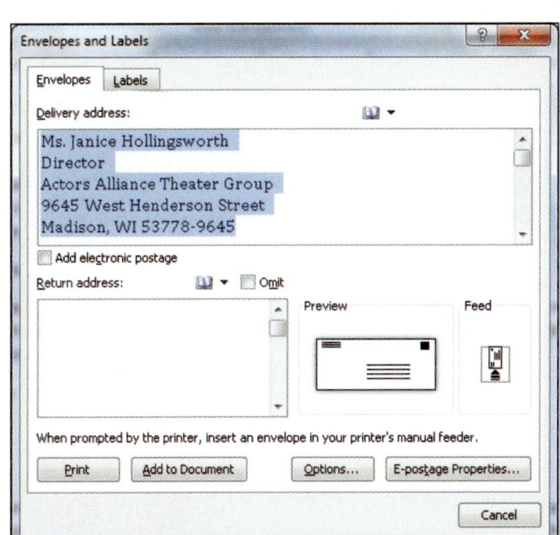

4. Use live preview to see how the bulleted list appears when converted to different SmartArt graphic style; then click the **Vertical Block List** style icon (the second icon in the first row).
5. Click outside the slide in the slide work area or tap the ESC key to close the drawing canvas and deselect the SmartArt graphic object.

Your slide 2 with the Vertical Block List SmartArt graphic should look similar to this.

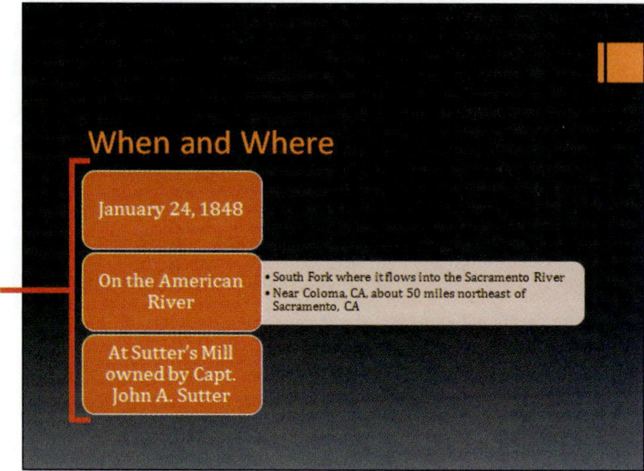


SmartArt graphic

Now let's insert a SmartArt graphic.

### Inserting a SmartArt Graphic and Adding Text

To insert a SmartArt graphic, click the Insert tab and then click the Insert SmartArt Graphic button in the Illustrations group.

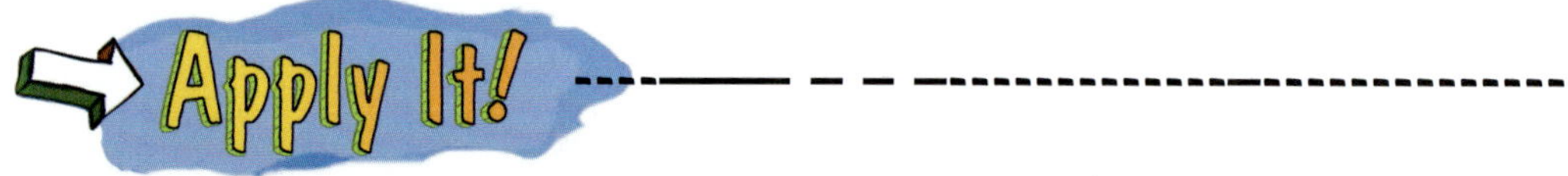


**Let's insert a new slide 3 and then insert a SmartArt graphic.**

1. Insert a new slide 3 using the Title Only layout.
2. Key **Who** as the slide's title.
3. Click the **Insert** tab and locate the **Illustrations** group.
4. Click the **Insert SmartArt Graphic** button to open the Choose a SmartArt Graphic dialog box.
5. Click **List** in the left pane to view a gallery of SmartArt list style graphics in the center pane.

5. Right-click the selected text in the Delivery address text box and click Font to open the Font dialog box.
6. Click the **All caps** checkbox in the Effects group and click **OK**.
7. Delete the period after *MS* and the comma after *MADISON* in the delivery address.
8. Click the **Return address** text box and key the following return address:

   **Julie Wilson**
   **1925 Rocky Hill Drive**
   **Madison, WI 53707-1925**

9. Click the **Options** button near the bottom of the dialog box and then click the **Envelope Options** tab, if necessary.
10. Click the **Envelope size** drop-down arrow and click **Size 10 (4 1/8 x 9 1/2 in)**, if necessary.
11. Click **OK** in the **Envelope Options** dialog box.
12. Click the **Add to Document** button; click **No** if asked to save the new return address as the default return address.
13. Zoom the envelope and letter documents so that you can view both at once.

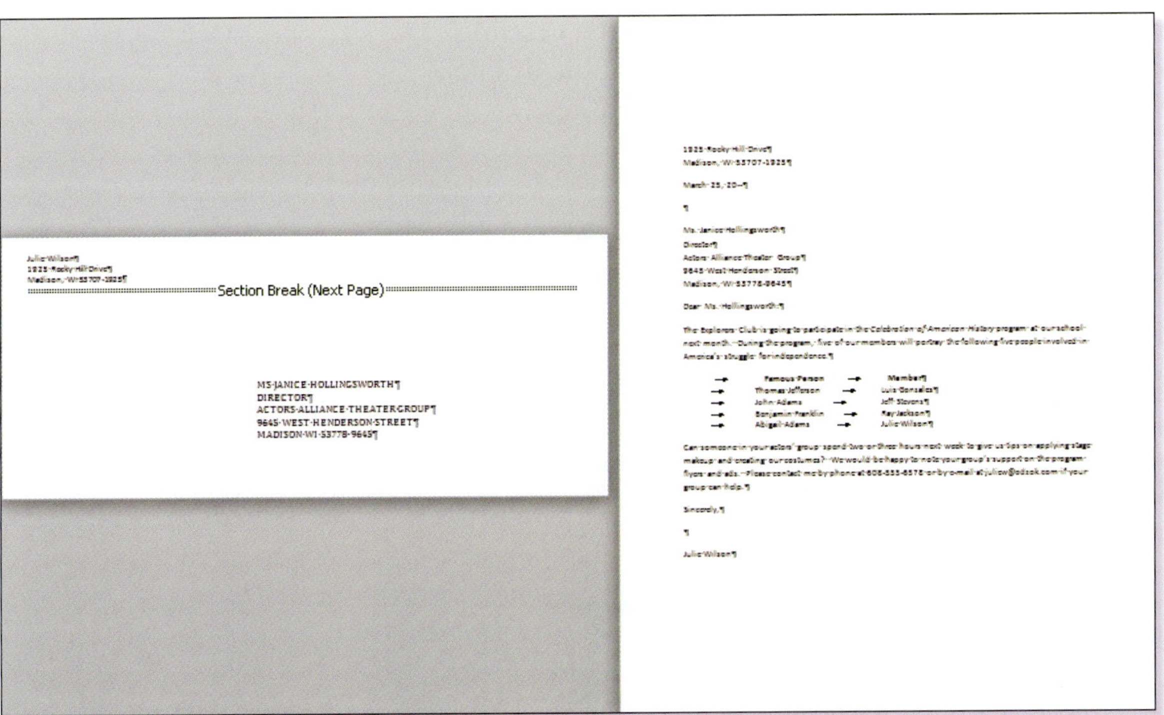


14. Zoom back to **100%**; then save and close the document.

Great job! Now Julie needs you to create a sheet of address labels with her return address that she can use on envelopes in the future.

## Creating and Modifying SmartArt Graphics

SmartArt objects are predesigned graphics you can insert to express your ideas or present facts. SmartArt categories allow you to:

- show an organizational hierarchy or the steps in a decision
- present items in a list
- illustrate various types of relationships
- illustrate the steps in a process or a continuous cycle

### Converting a Bulleted List to a SmartArt Graphic

In *PowerPoint*, you can convert a bulleted list to a SmartArt graphic by clicking inside the bulleted list placeholder to select the placeholder, then clicking the Home tab and clicking the Convert to SmartArt Graphic button in the Paragraph group.

When you select a SmartArt graphic, the graphic appears on the drawing canvas. You can close the drawing canvas and deselect the graphic by clicking the slide work area outside the slide or by tapping the ESC key.

**Let's convert the slide 2 bulleted list to a SmartArt graphic.**

**Home | Paragraph | Convert to SmartArt Graphic**

1. Activate **slide 2** and click the bulleted list placeholder to activate it.
2. Click the **Home** tab, if necessary, and locate the **Paragraph** group.
3. Click the **Convert to SmartArt Graphic** button in the Paragraph group to view a gallery of SmartArt list styles. 

SmartArt list style gallery

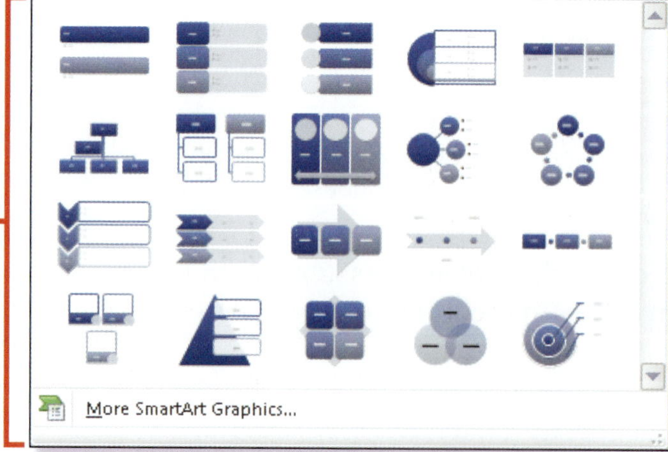

## Preparing a Sheet of Return Address Labels

You have probably created labels by hand and then placed the labels on envelopes, file folders, and schoolwork. Most labels, such as address labels, are attached to a sheet that you can feed through a printer. You can key text for one label or for the whole sheet of labels in *Word* just like you key text for an envelope—with options in the Envelopes and Labels dialog box.

In the Labels tab in the Envelope and Labels dialog box, you specify the type of label you want and key the text for the label. You can either send the information directly to the printer or create a new document to be printed later. *For the label activities in this project, you will create a new document. Then you will print the labels on plain paper if your teacher tells you to do so.*

**Let's create a sheet of return address labels containing Julie's address.**

Mailings | Create | Labels

1. Create a new blank document, if necessary, and save it as *labels5*.
2. Click **Mailings** tab, if necessary, and then click the **Labels** button in the Create group to open the Labels tab in the Envelopes and Labels dialog box.

3. Key Julie's return address in the Address text box.

   **Julie Wilson**
   **1925 Rocky Hill Drive**
   **Madison, WI 53707-1925**

4. Verify that the **Full page of the same label** option in the Print section is selected.
5. Click the **Options** button to open the Label Options dialog box.
6. Click the **Label vendors** arrow and click **Avery US Letter** in the vendors' list, if necessary.
7. Scroll the **Product number** list box to find the 5260 style; then click **5260 Easy Peel Address Labels** or **5260** and click **OK**.
8. Click the **New Document** button to create a new labels document.

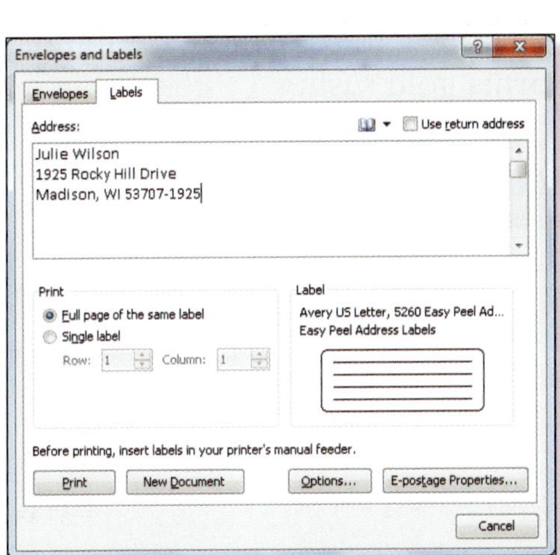

**Begin by creating Julie's presentation and applying a custom theme from an existing presentation. Then reuse slides from a different presentation.**

Home | Slides | New Slide

1. Create a new presentation and save it as *gold rush14*.
2. Key **"Gold! Boys! Gold!"** (don't forget to key the quotation marks) as the title and key **Explorers Club** and **Julie Wilson** as the subtitles on the Title Slide.
3. Apply the theme from the *custom theme* data file to the new presentation.
4. Display the **Reuse Slides** pane and insert all of the slides from the *gold rush* data file into your new presentation following the Title Slide.
5. View slide 3 and resize the picture from its center point so that the slide title "What" is visible; then change the picture's style.
6. View slide 1 and close the Reuse Slides pane.

Super! Now let's use SmartArt graphics to illustrate facts about the California gold rush.

Do your feet reach the floor when you sit in your computer chair? If not, make sure you use some kind of footrest.

Another quick way to zoom a document is to click the View tab and then click a button in the Zoom group.

9. Click the **View** tab and locate the **Zoom** group.
10. Click the **One Page** button in the Zoom group to zoom the document so that you can see the entire page.

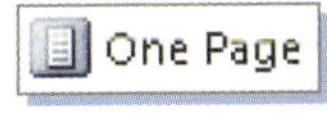


| | | |
|---|---|---|
| Julie Wilson<br>1925 Rocky Hill Drive<br>Madison, WI 53707-1925 | Julie Wilson<br>1925 Rocky Hill Drive<br>Madison, WI 53707-1925 | Julie Wilson<br>1925 Rocky Hill Drive<br>Madison, WI 53707-1925 |
| Julie Wilson<br>1925 Rocky Hill Drive<br>Madison, WI 53707-1925 | Julie Wilson<br>1925 Rocky Hill Drive<br>Madison, WI 53707-1925 | Julie Wilson<br>1925 Rocky Hill Drive<br>Madison, WI 53707-1925 |
| Julie Wilson<br>1925 Rocky Hill Drive<br>Madison, WI 53707-1925 | Julie Wilson<br>1925 Rocky Hill Drive<br>Madison, WI 53707-1925 | Julie Wilson<br>1925 Rocky Hill Drive<br>Madison, WI 53707-1925 |
| Julie Wilson<br>1925 Rocky Hill Drive<br>Madison, WI 53707-1925 | Julie Wilson<br>1925 Rocky Hill Drive<br>Madison, WI 53707-1925 | Julie Wilson<br>1925 Rocky Hill Drive<br>Madison, WI 53707-1925 |
| Julie Wilson<br>1925 Rocky Hill Drive<br>Madison, WI 53707-1925 | Julie Wilson<br>1925 Rocky Hill Drive<br>Madison, WI 53707-1925 | Julie Wilson<br>1925 Rocky Hill Drive<br>Madison, WI 53707-1925 |
| Julie Wilson<br>1925 Rocky Hill Drive<br>Madison, WI 53707-1925 | Julie Wilson<br>1925 Rocky Hill Drive<br>Madison, WI 53707-1925 | Julie Wilson<br>1925 Rocky Hill Drive<br>Madison, WI 53707-1925 |
| Julie Wilson<br>1925 Rocky Hill Drive<br>Madison, WI 53707-1925 | Julie Wilson<br>1925 Rocky Hill Drive<br>Madison, WI 53707-1925 | Julie Wilson<br>1925 Rocky Hill Drive<br>Madison, WI 53707-1925 |
| Julie Wilson<br>1925 Rocky Hill Drive<br>Madison, WI 53707-1925 | Julie Wilson<br>1925 Rocky Hill Drive<br>Madison, WI 53707-1925 | Julie Wilson<br>1925 Rocky Hill Drive<br>Madison, WI 53707-1925 |
| Julie Wilson<br>1925 Rocky Hill Drive<br>Madison, WI 53707-1925 | Julie Wilson<br>1925 Rocky Hill Drive<br>Madison, WI 53707-1925 | Julie Wilson<br>1925 Rocky Hill Drive<br>Madison, WI 53707-1925 |
| Julie Wilson<br>1925 Rocky Hill Drive<br>Madison, WI 53707-1925 | Julie Wilson<br>1925 Rocky Hill Drive<br>Madison, WI 53707-1925 | Julie Wilson<br>1925 Rocky Hill Drive<br>Madison, WI 53707-1925 |

11. Click the **100%** button in the Zoom group to zoom back to 100%.
12. Save and close the document.

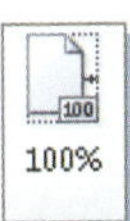


Outstanding! Julie's letter, envelope, and labels are ready!

# Rushing to California

## Explorers' Guide

Data files: gold rush
custom theme
source
miners.jpg
gold.jpg

Objectives:
In this project, you will:
- create and modify SmartArt graphics
- insert a picture as the slide background
- apply customized animation effects
- use the Slide Show controls

© NORTH WIND / NORTH WIND PICTURE ARCHIVES – ALL RIGHTS RESERVED.

## Our Exploration Assignment:

**Creating a presentation containing SmartArt and custom animation and running the slide show**

"Gold! Boys! Gold!" shouted a witness to the first discovery of gold in California—the event that changed the western United States forever. Explorers Club members are participating in the Gold Rush Days celebration at school. Julie is working on a presentation about the first discovery of California gold, and she needs your help. Follow the Trail Markers to convert a bulleted list to a SmartArt graphic, insert a Title Only slide, and create a SmartArt graphic; modify SmartArt graphics; insert a picture as a slide's background; add custom animation to SmartArt graphics; and use Slide Show controls during a slide show.

# Project Skills Review

You learned a lot in this project! We are very impressed with your progress. Let's take a few minutes to review the skills that you learned.

| | |
|---|---|
| **Remove extra paragraph spacing** | Click the **Line and Paragraph Spacing** button in the Paragraph group on the **Home** tab and then click **Remove Spacing After Paragraph**. |
| **Insert a file** | Click the **Insert Object** button in the Text group on the **Insert** tab. |
| **Set tab stops** | Select the type of tab stop using the tab indicator and then click at the tab stop position on the Horizontal Ruler. |
| **Create an envelope** | Click the **Create Envelopes** button in the Create group on the **Mailings** tab. |
| **Create labels** | Click the **Labels** button in the Create group on the **Mailings** tab. |
| **Zoom a document to one page or to 100%** | Click the **One Page** or **100%** button in the Zoom group on the **View** tab. |

# Project 13 Keyboarding

## 13a Build Skill

Key each line twice. Double-space between 2-line groups.

**Alphabet sentences**

1 Fran Vasquez put down the six jackets by my glove.
2 Javy quickly swam the dozen extra laps before Gus.
3 Jacki Vizquel played six ball games for the Twins.
4 Jack Gable explained most of his very low quizzes.
5 Before leaving, Jexon quickly swam the dozen laps.

gwam 20" | 3 | 6 | 9 | 12 | 15 | 18 | 21 | 24 | 27 | 30 |

1. Key a 1' timing on paragraph 1.
2. Determine the number of words you keyed.
3. Key another 1' timing on paragraph 1. Try to go two words a minute faster.
4. Repeat steps 1–3 for paragraph 2.
5. Key a 2' timing on paragraphs 1–2 combined.
6. Determine the number of words you keyed.

For additional practice:
**MicroType 5**
Skill Building, Lesson C

**A** **all letters used** gwam 2'

Austria is a rather small country located between Germany 6
and Italy. The best-known city in this country is Vienna. Over the 13
years this city has been known for its contributions to the culture 20
in the area. It is especially known for its performing arts. Another 27
place that has played an important part in the exquisite culture of 33
the region is the city of Salzburg. 37

Salzburg is also recognized for its music. Just as important, 43
however, is that the city is the birthplace of Wolfgang Amadeus 50
Mozart. Mozart was one of the greatest composers of all time. 56
Perhaps no other composer had an earlier start at his professional 63
endeavors than did Mozart. It is thought that he began playing at 70
the age of four and began composing at the age of five. 75

gwam 2' | 1 | 2 | 3 | 4 | 5 | 6 |

# Exploring *On Your Own*

## Blaze Your Own Trail

You have learned several new skills in this project. Now blaze your own trail by practicing these skills on your own! Complete each part as instructed by your teacher.

**Part 1**

1. Create a new blank document.
2. Create a sheet of 5260 return address labels using your name and address; save the labels as *my labels5*.

**Part 2:**

1. Create a new blank document and save it as *Johnson letter5*.
2. Set the appropriate margins for a personal-business letter.
3. Add your return address and insert today's date.
4. Address the letter to:

   **Mr. David Johnson**
   **Johnson Theatrical Costumes**
   **3500 West Jensen Avenue**
   **Madison, WI 53782-3500**

5. Add the salutation **Dear Mr. Johnson**, leave space for the body text, add the complimentary closing **Sincerely,** and add your name as the writer's name.
6. Insert the *Johnson text* data file as the body text of the letter.
7. Key the following tabbed columns between the body paragraphs. Set Center tab stops at 2 and 3.5 inches for the column headings. Set a Left tab stop at 1.5 inches and a Center tab stop at 3.5 inches for the costume names and sizes. Bold the column names.

| **Costume** | **Size** |
|---|---|
| Thomas Jefferson | 12 |
| Abigail Adams | 10 |
| Benjamin Franklin | 12 |

8. Add a Size 10 envelope to the letter with the delivery address in UPPERCASE characters and no punctuation. Do not add a return address.
9. Spell-check, save, and close the document.

## Reading in Action — Understanding Purpose and Audience

Read *theater letter5*. Name the purpose and the audience of the letter. What information supports the purpose? Why is the tone appropriate for the audience?

## Math in Action — Using Functions

Functions use variables to help show the mathematical relationship between different elements. Use a function to figure out the relationship between the number of pages of a letter and the number of words in the letter. If there are 250 words per page, how many pages will your letter be if it is 500 words?

$y$ = number of pages, $x$ = number of words in the letter

Function: $y = x \div 250$

$y$ = 500 words ÷ 250 words per page = 2 pages

Now you try it! How many pages will your letter be if you write 1,250 words? if you write 625 words?

# Exploring Across the Curriculum

## Getting Help

Click the Microsoft PowerPoint Help icon below the *PowerPoint* application Close button to open the *PowerPoint* Help window. Key **saving a custom theme** in the search box and tap the ENTER key to research how to save a custom theme for later use. Then create a new presentation with a custom theme. Use the slides to present the instructions for creating and saving a custom theme. With your teacher's permission, run the slide show to explain the process to your classmates. *Do not save the custom theme unless instructed to do so by your teacher.*

## Career Day

Businesses, universities, and government agencies that work to develop new scientific breakthroughs often use marketing professionals to plan, manage, and perform the activities needed to communicate with others about their work. Using library, printed, or online resources, identify three interesting careers in marketing. Write a brief summary of each occupation, print your summary, and save it in your Career Day folder.

## Your Personal Journal

Open your personal journal document. Insert today's date and two blank lines. Think about the *PowerPoint* presentations you created in this project. Then write two or three paragraphs explaining how running an unattended slide show could be useful in presenting facts and ideas to an audience. Spell-check, save, and close your journal.

**Online Enrichment Games**  www.cengage.com/school/keyboarding/lwcorange

# Exploring *Across the Curriculum*

## Internet/Web

To learn more about the people who helped draft the Declaration of Independence, you can use the Web. Open your Web browser and use a favorite or bookmark to view the Learning with Computers Web page (www.cengage.com/school/keyboarding/lwcorange). Click the **Links** option and click **Project 5**. Click the links to learn more about the part that John Adams, Thomas Jefferson, Robert R. Livingston, Roger Sherman, Benjamin Franklin, and others played in drafting the Declaration of Independence. Take notes about what you learn.

1. Write a personal-business letter to your teacher asking for permission to present your research to the class. Use two tabbed columns to list each person researched and an interesting fact about that person. Remember to spell-check your letter.
2. Add a Size 10 envelope to the letter addressed to your teacher at your school's address; use your personal return address.

## Language Arts: Words to Know

Look up the meaning of the following terms in a classroom dictionary, CD-ROM dictionary or encyclopedia, or online dictionary.

| *Common Sense* | Continental Congress | despotism | Loyalist |
|---|---|---|---|
| Patriot | preamble | tyranny | unalienable rights |

Create a new document. Save the document as *definitions5*. Key your name at the top of the document. Tap the ENTER key twice. Use the TAB key and tab stops to create one column for the term and the second column for its brief definition. Set Center tabs at the 1.0-inch and 3.0-inch positions on the Horizontal Ruler; key the column headings **Term** and **Definition**. Apply the Bold font style to the column headings.

Remember to drag the Center tabs off the ruler *for the new paragraph* created when you tap the ENTER key. Set Left tabs at the 0.75-inch and 2.0-inch positions on the ruler; key each term in the first column and its brief definition in the second column. Spell-check, save, and close the document.

Explore More

# Exploring Across the Curriculum

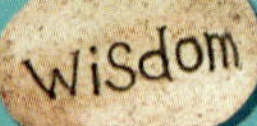

## Language Arts: Words to Know

Look up the meaning of the following terms in a classroom dictionary, CD-ROM dictionary or encyclopedia, or online dictionary.

| electron | molecule | neutron | nucleus |
|---|---|---|---|
| particle | proton | quark | subatomic |

Create a new presentation. Save it as *definitions13*. Key **Atoms** as the title and **Definitions** as the subtitle on the Title Slide. Apply the theme from another presentation. Add slide numbers to all slides *except* the Title Slide. Insert four Title and Content slides. Key **Terms** as the title on each slide. Key *two terms and their definitions on each slide*, creating a two-item bulleted list. Apply the transition effect of your choice. Set slide timings and set up the slide show to run unattended in a continuous loop. Run the slide show and save and close the presentation.

## Science: Research, Write, and Present

Working with a classmate, use classroom, library, CD-ROM, or online sources to learn more about the following scientists who made discoveries associated with matter and energy: Andre Marie Ampere, Anders Celsius, Marie Curie, Michael Faraday, Albert Einstein, Lise Meitner, Sir Isaac Newton, and Nikola Tesla. Then create a new presentation to create a slide show about what you have learned.

Apply a theme from an existing presentation of your choice. Insert at least two slides from the *notes* presentation. Insert Title and Content slides to cite your sources. Add your name as the slide footer and add slide numbers to all slides *except* the Title Slide. Apply the transition effect of your choice, set slide timings, and set up the show to run unattended in a continuous loop. Save and close the presentation.

Explore More

# Exploring Across the Curriculum

## Social Studies: Research and Write

Use classroom, library, or online resources to learn more about what the colonists who remained Loyalists thought about the Declaration of Independence. Take notes about what you learn. Then review the format for a *modified-block* style letter in Appendix A in the back of this book.

Create a new document and use it to write a personal letter in the modified-block style to a friend or classmate. Imagine that you are a Massachusetts Loyalist and have just heard that the Second Continental Congress has ratified the Declaration of Independence. Write at least two body paragraphs in your letter describing what you think and how you feel about the new Declaration of Independence. Create a Size 10 envelope with your return address and add it to the letter. Spell-check, save, and close the document.

## Getting Help

Open the Word Help window. Key **tab stops** in the search box. Use the **Help** links to research how to set Right and Decimal tab stops and tab stops with leaders. Then create a new blank document. Set Center tab stops at 1-inch and 3-inch positions for column headings and key **Snack** and **Cost** as the heading text. Tap the ENTER key. Set a Left stop at the 0.5-inch position for the snack name and set a Decimal tab stop at the 3-inch position for the snack cost. Use the TAB key and in two tabbed columns, key the names of five of your favorite snacks and their cost in dollars and cents. Save the document as *decimal tabs* and close it.

Create another new document. Set Center tab stops at the 0.75-inch position and 2-inch position. Using the TAB key to position the insertion point, key *Name* and *Phone Number* as the column headings. Tap the ENTER key. Set a Left tab stop at the 0.25-inch position for a name and a Right tab stop *with a dotted tab leader* at the 2.5-inch position for a phone number. Using the TAB key to position the insertion point, in two tabbed columns, key fictitious names and telephone numbers for five people. Save the document as *tab leaders* and close it.

Explore More

# Exploring Across the Curriculum

## Internet/Web

You can learn more about atoms and how different types of energy are generated by using the Web. Open your Web browser and use a favorite or bookmark to view the Learning with Computers Web page (www.cengage.com/school/keyboarding/lwcorange). Click the **Links** option and click **Project 13**. Click the links to learn more about the role atoms play in generating electrical, nuclear, and radiant energy. Take notes about what you learn.

1. Create a new presentation and save it as *atoms and energy13*.
2. Apply the theme from the presentation of your choice.
3. Add an appropriate title and subtitle on the Title Slide.
4. Insert at least two slides from the *notes* presentation.
5. Manually insert additional Title and Content, Title Only, or other slides as necessary to present what you learned about atoms and energy. Cite your sources on Title and Content slides at the end of your presentation.
6. Modify the slide master to change the font and horizontal alignment of the title text and the first-level bullet graphic and color.
7. Insert the motion clip and sound file of your choice on the Title Slide.
8. Add today's date, slide numbers, and your name as the footer on all of the slides in the presentation *except* the Title Slide.
9. Apply the predefined animation effect of your choice, set slide timings, and set up the slide show to run unattended in a continuous loop.
10. Run the slide show; then save and close the presentation.

Explore More

# Exploring *Across the Curriculum*

## Career Day

Members of the Explorers Club enjoy playing famous American Revolutionary patriots in the school program. If you like performing, writing, or communicating facts and ideas to others, you might enjoy a career in the performing arts, journalism, or communications. Using library, printed, or online resources, identify three interesting careers in communications, journalism, or the performing arts. Write a brief summary of each career, print your summary, and save it in your Career Day folder.

## Your Personal Journal

Open your personal journal document. Insert today's date and two blank lines. Imagine that you are a representative from the Virginia colony to the Second Continental Congress. Would you vote to ratify the Declaration of Independence? Why or why not? Explain your answers to these questions in two or three paragraphs. Spell-check, save, and close your journal.

**Online Enrichment Games**  www.cengage.com/school/keyboarding/lwcorange

# Exploring *On Your Own*

## *Math in Action*

### Finding the Volume of a Sphere

Volume tells us how much space an object occupies. We can determine the approximate volume of Earth if we know the radius of Earth, which is the mean distance between the center of Earth and Earth's surface. This distance is 3,959 miles.

Formula: Volume of a sphere (V) = $\frac{4}{3}\pi r^3$

$V = \frac{4}{3}(3.14)(3{,}959 \text{ miles})^3$

$= (4.186)(62{,}052{,}103{,}079 \text{ miles}^3)$

$= 259{,}750{,}103{,}489 \text{ miles}^3$

Now you try it!

Find the approximate volume of the Moon if its mean radius is 1,080 miles.

Find the approximate volume of Mars if its mean radius is 2,100 miles.

# Project 5 Keyboarding

## 5a Review w, Right Shift, b, y

Key each line twice. Double-space between 2-line groups.

**w**

1 sw sw | sws sws | swj swj | wks wks | lws lws | hsw hsw | s;w;

2 was was | wide wide | wait wait | work work | which which;

**right shift**

3 aA aA | sS sS | dD dD | fF fF | gG gG | eE eE | rR rR | tT tT | wW

4 Drew Drew | Wade Wade | Tara Tara | Diana Diana | Tai Tai;

**b**

5 fb fb | bfb bfb | rbf rbf | fbrb fbrb | fbjb fbjb | fbo fbob

6 bat bat | Abe Abe | able able | bubble bubble | stub stub;

**y**

7 jy jy | yjy yjy | jyn jyn | y; y; | fy fy | jujy jujy | fy fy;

8 yes yes | days days | gray gray | Ryan Ryan | youth youth;

To key capital letters with the left hand:

- Hold down the Right Shift with the right little finger.
- Tap the letter with the left hand.
- Return finger(s) to home keys.

## 5b Build Skill

Key each line twice single-spaced; double-space between 2-line groups.

For additional practice:
**MicroType 5**
New Key Review, Alphabetic Lessons 11–12

**balanced-hand sentences**

1 Turn down the lane by the lake to see the bicycle.

2 Pamela may hand signal to the big tug by the dock.

3 The six girls in the sorority may pay for the bus.

4 It is right for the man to aid them with the sign.

5 I am to pay the six men if they do the work right.

6 He paid the men for the work they did on the dock.

7 Six of the eight firms may make a bid for the bus.

8 Orlando may keep the turkeys in a box by the dock.

*gwam* *20"* | 3 | 6 | 9 | 12 | 15 | 18 | 21 | 24 | 27 | 30 |

# Exploring *On Your Own*

## Blaze Your Own Trail

You have learned several new skills in this project. Now blaze your own trail by practicing these skills on your own! Create a new presentation and save it as *energy13*.

1. Key **Sources of Renewable Energy**, **Explorers Club**, and your name as the title and subtitles on the Title Slide.
2. Reuse all of the slides from the *renewable energy* data file following the Title Slide using the Reuse Slides pane.
3. Apply the customized theme from the *matter and energy* data file.
4. Modify the slide master to change the bullet graphic for the first-level bullets using the graphic of your choice.
5. Insert a motion clip and an audio file of your choice on the Title Slide. Recolor the motion clip and change its style. Hide the audio icon during the slide show and set it to play automatically.
6. View **slides 2 and 3** in Normal view and remove the background graphics.
7. Add today's date as a fixed date with the month spelled out, your name as the footer text, and the slide number to all of the slides in the presentation *except* the Title Slide.
8. Apply the transition effects of your choice.
9. Set ten-second slide timings and set up the slide show to run unattended in a continuous loop.
10. Run the presentation, letting it loop at least twice, and then save and close it.

## Reading in Action

### Reading for Details

In the *atoms13* presentation, slides 4 through 7 state general definitions and explanations for atoms and molecules. Read these slides; then use the information to answer the following questions.

1. The atomic number of carbon is 6. How many protons and electrons does carbon have?
   a. 2 protons and 4 electrons
   b. 3 protons and 3 electrons
   c. 6 protons and 6 electrons
   d. 12 protons and 6 electrons
2. The chemical formula for salt is NaCl. What atoms make up one molecule of salt?
   a. one atom of NaCl
   b. one atom of Na and two atoms of Cl
   c. two atoms of Na and two atoms of Cl
   d. one atom of Na and one atom of Cl

# Creating Yosemite National Park

## Explorers' Guide

Data files: handout
flyer

Objectives:
In this project, you will:

- create an infographic
- use bulleted and numbered lists
- add special text effects
- insert clip art and text boxes
- add a page border
- add a footer

CHEE-ONN LEONG/SHUTTERSTOCK.COM

## Our Exploration Assignment:

### Creating an infographic

The Explorers Club is learning about John Muir and the early twentieth-century conservation movement that led to the creation of Yosemite National Park and other federally protected lands. Luis is working on a handout for the next meeting and needs your help to make it more attractive and fun. Just follow the Trail Markers to change page orientation; place text in newsletter columns; itemize text in bulleted or numbered lists; use symbols, styles, drop caps, and other special font effects; insert, resize, and reposition clip art; insert and reposition text boxes; apply borders and shading; and add a footer.

# Project Skills Review

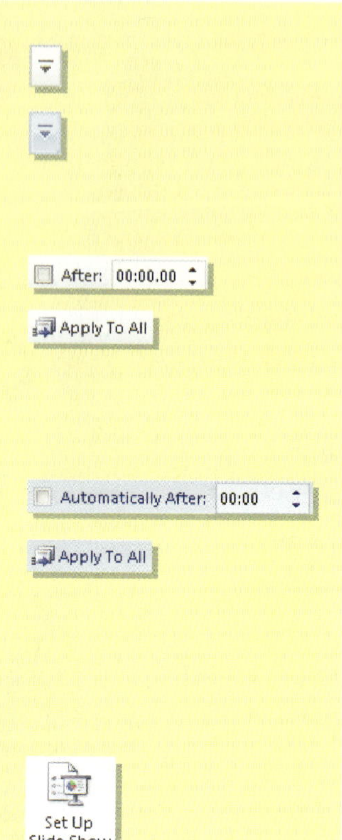


| | |
|---|---|
| **Add transition effects** | In *PowerPoint 2010*, click the **More** button in the Transition to This Slide group on the **Transitions** tab. In *PowerPoint 2007*, click the **More** button in the Transition to This Slide group on the **Animations** tab. |
| **Set slide timings** | In *PowerPoint 2010*, click the **Advance Slide: After** checkbox in the Timing group on the **Transitions** tab. Key the timing in seconds in the Automatically After text box. Click the **Apply to All** button in the Timing group.<br>In *PowerPoint 2007*, click the **Advance Slide: Automatically After** checkbox in the Transition to This Slide group on the **Animations** tab. Key the timing in seconds in the Automatically After text box. Click the **Apply to All** button in the Transition to This Slide group. |
| **Set up a slide show** | Click the **Set Up Show** button in the Set Up group on the **Slide Show** tab. |

**Begin by opening a document and saving it with a new name.**

1. Open the *handout* data file and save it as *handout6*.

Now you are ready to create Luis's meeting handout.

**ERGONOMICS TIP**

Are you looking straight ahead? Remember that your monitor should be directly in front of you so that you do not have to turn your head to see the screen.

## Creating an Infographic

An infographic combines text, pictures, and drawings to convey a message. Examples of infographic documents include newsletters, flyers, and meeting handouts. Let's begin modifying Luis's meeting handout by changing its page orientation and placing some of the body text into newsletter columns.

### Changing Page Orientation

Page orientation specifies how you want *Word* to print text on a page—horizontally or vertically. You can specify horizontal or vertical orientation by clicking the Page Layout tab and then clicking the Page Orientation button in the Page Setup group.

To print the text in a wide, horizontal format, set up the page in Landscape orientation; to print the text vertically, set up the page in Portrait orientation.

Did you know that you can mix Portrait and Landscape orientation in a multipage document? Just use a Next page section break to separate Portrait and Landscape pages!

# Project Skills Review

You learned a lot in this project! We are very impressed with your progress. Let's take a few minutes to review the skills that you learned.

| Skill | Steps | |
|---|---|---|
| **Apply a theme from another presentation** | Click the **More** button in the Themes group on the **Design** tab to expand the themes gallery and then click **Browse for Themes**. |  |
| **Reuse slides from another presentation** | Click the **New Slide** button arrow in the Slides group on the **Home** tab and click **Reuse Slides**. | New Slide |
| **Modify clips and shapes** | Click buttons on the **Picture Tools Format** tab. Click buttons on the **Drawing Tools Format** tab. | |
| **Switch to Slide Master View** | Click the **Slide Master** button in the Master Views or Presentation Views group on the **View** tab. |  |
| **Modify a bullet graphic** | Click the **Bullets** button arrow in the Paragraph group on the **Home** tab. | 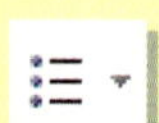 |
| **Insert slide footers** | Click the **Header & Footer** button in the Text group on the **Insert** tab. |  |
| **Add video and audio to slides** | In *PowerPoint 2010*, click the **Insert Video** or **Insert Audio** button in the Media group on the **Insert** tab. In *PowerPoint 2007*, click the **Movie from File** or **Sound from File** button in the Media Clips group on the **Insert** tab. |  |
| **Hide the audio icon during a slide show** | In *PowerPoint 2010*, click the **Hide During Show** checkbox in the Audio Options group on the **Audio Tools Playback** tab. In *PowerPoint 2007*, click the **Hide During Show** checkbox in the Sound Options group on the **Sound Tools Options** tab. | 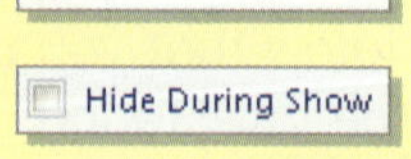 |

**Let's change the document's page orientation to Landscape, then zoom the document to Page Width to see the change.**

Page Layout|Page Setup|Page Orientation

View|Zoom|Page Width

1. Click the **Page Layout** tab and locate the **Page Setup** group.
2. Click the **Page Orientation** button in the Page Setup group to view the orientation options.
3. Click **Landscape**.

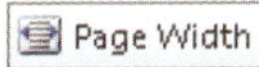


Zooming a document in Landscape orientation to Page Width allows you to view a page without scrolling horizontally.

4. Click the **View** tab and locate the **Zoom** group.
5. Click the **Page Width** button in the Zoom group to view the left and right edges of the document in Landscape orientation.

Page Width

Great job! Now let's put part of the text in the handout into two columns.

**Creating Newsletter Columns**

In a *Word* document, vertical columns of text, like those you see in your local newspaper, are sometimes called newspaper-style or newsletter columns. To format text in newsletter columns, first select the text. Then click the Page Layout tab and click the Columns button in the Page Setup group. Next click the number of columns you want from the Columns gallery. *Word* automatically inserts a Continuous section break for the selected text and places it in the columns.

You can click More Columns in the Columns gallery to open the Columns dialog box and set custom column widths. Try it!

Because text automatically fills columns from left to right, you may want to control where a column ends by inserting a manual or hard column break. Tap the CTRL + SHIFT + ENTER keys to quickly insert a hard column break.

**Let's set up the *atoms13* slide show to run unattended in a continuous loop.**

Slide Show|Set Up|Set Up Show

1. Click the **Slide Show** tab and locate the **Set Up** group.
2. Click the **Set Up Show** button to open the Set Up Show dialog box.
3. Click the **Browsed at a kiosk (full screen)** option button in the Show type section.
4. Note that the Loop continuously until 'Esc' checkbox in the Show options section contains a check mark.
5. Note that the Using timings, if present option is selected in the Advance slides section.

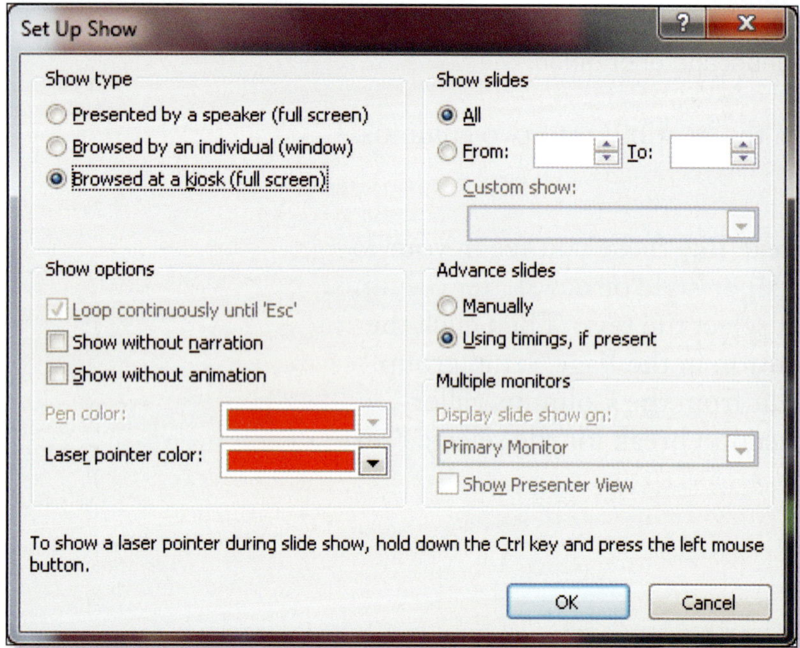


6. Click the **OK** button.
7. Run the slide show from slide 1 and let it loop twice; then save and close the presentation.

Congratulations! Ray's slide show is ready for the next Explorers Club meeting!

**Let's format part of the body text as two newsletter columns.**

**Page Layout | Page Setup | Columns**

1. Move the insertion point to the beginning of the **John Muir** paragraph heading below the title.
2. Tap and hold the SHIFT key and click at the end of the **President Theodore Roosevelt** body paragraph to select the text from the insertion point.

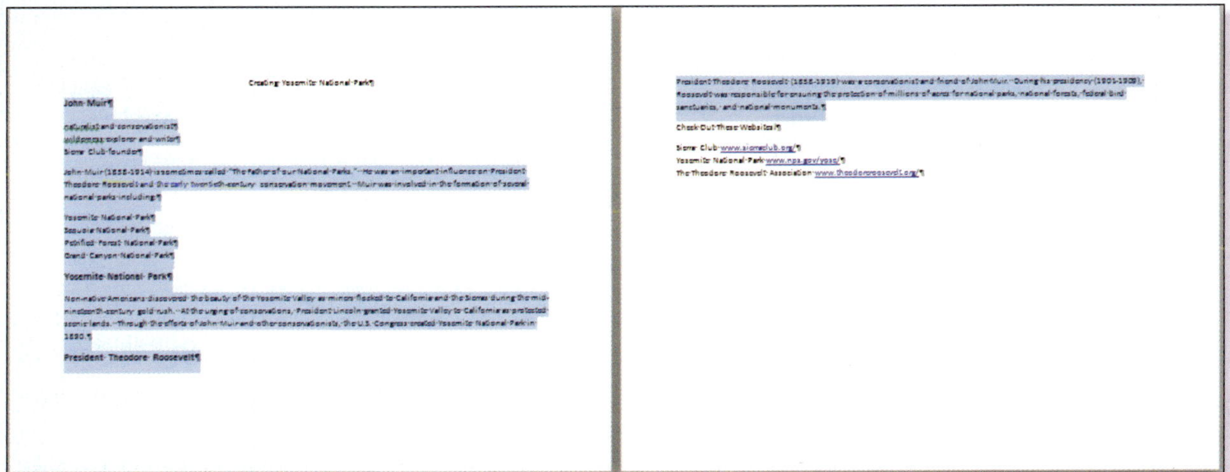
Creating Yosemite National Park

**John Muir**

naturalist and conservationist
wilderness explorer and writer
Sierra Club founder

Yosemite National Park
Sequoia National Park
Petrified Forest National Park
Grand Canyon National Park

**Yosemite National Park**

**President Theodore Roosevelt**

Check Out These Websites

Sierra Club www.sierraclub.org/
Yosemite National Park www.nps.gov/yose/
The Theodore Roosevelt Association www.theodoreroosevelt.org/

3. Click the **Page Layout** tab and locate the **Page Setup** group.
4. Click the **Columns** button in the Page Setup group to view the gallery of columns options.
5. Click the **Two** option in the gallery to arrange the selected text in two newsletter columns.
6. Deselect the text and save the document.

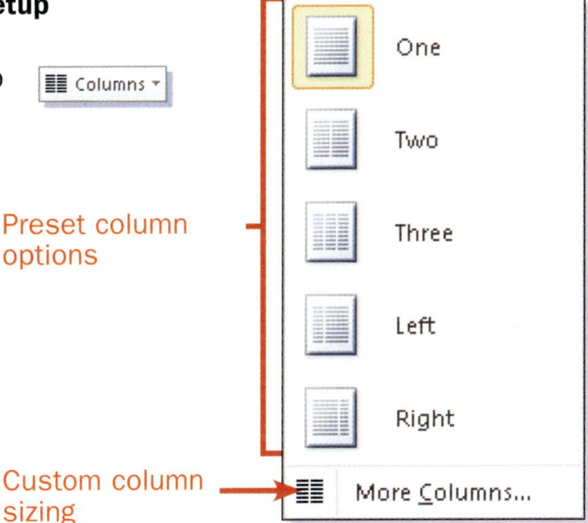

Animations | Transition to This Slide | Automatically After

Animations | Transition to This Slide | Apply to All

**Let's set ten-second slide timings for all of the slides.**

1. Click the **Animations** tab, if necessary, and locate the **Transition to This Slide** group.
2. Click the **Automatically After** checkbox in the Advance Slide section of the Transition to This Slide group to insert a check mark. Leaving the check mark in the On Mouse Click checkbox allows you to set up the slide show to run either manually or automatically.
3. Select the contents of the Automatically After text box and key **10**.
4. Click the **Apply To All** button in the Transition to This Slide group to add the ten-second slide timings to each slide.
5. Run the slide show from slide 1. *Do not try to advance the slides manually. Just sit back and watch the show!*

Automatically After: 00:00

Apply To All

Excellent! Now let's set up the slide show to run unattended.

Remember to set your timings so that the audience has plenty of time to read each slide.

**Setting Up a Slide Show**

Ray wants to be able to run the slide show unattended—without manually advancing the slides—on a computer while members are arriving at the next Explorers Club meeting. He also wants the slide show to run over and over from beginning to end in a continuous loop.

To set up a slide show to run unattended in a continuous loop based on previously set slide timings, set options in the Set Up Show dialog box. Open the dialog box by clicking the Slide Show tab and then clicking the Set Up Slide Show button in the Set Up group.

Your newsletter columns should look like this.

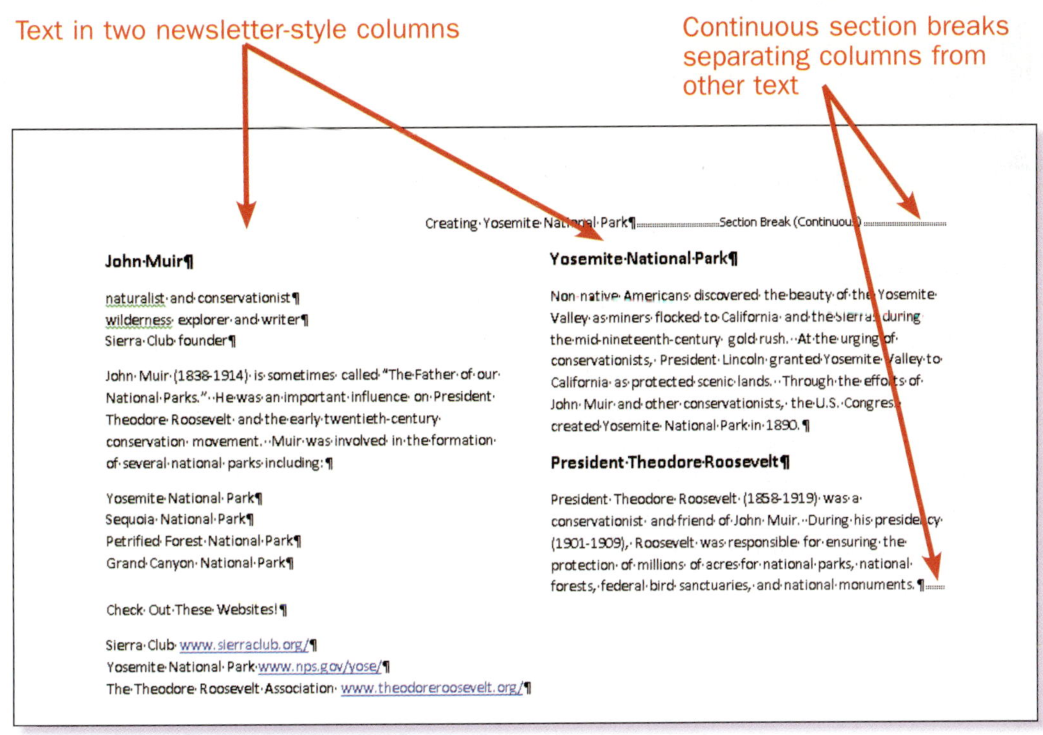


Creating Yosemite National Park Section Break (Continuous)

**John Muir**

naturalist and conservationist
wilderness explorer and writer
Sierra Club founder

John Muir (1838-1914) is sometimes called "The Father of our National Parks." He was an important influence on President Theodore Roosevelt and the early twentieth-century conservation movement. Muir was involved in the formation of several national parks including:

Yosemite National Park
Sequoia National Park
Petrified Forest National Park
Grand Canyon National Park

Check Out These Websites!

Sierra Club www.sierraclub.org/
Yosemite National Park www.nps.gov/yose/
The Theodore Roosevelt Association www.theodoreroosevelt.org/

**Yosemite National Park**

Non native Americans discovered the beauty of the Yosemite Valley as miners flocked to California and the Sierras during the mid-nineteenth-century gold rush. At the urging of conservationists, President Lincoln granted Yosemite Valley to California as protected scenic lands. Through the efforts of John Muir and other conservationists, the U.S. Congress created Yosemite National Park in 1890.

**President Theodore Roosevelt**

President Theodore Roosevelt (1858-1919) was a conservationist and friend of John Muir. During his presidency (1901-1909), Roosevelt was responsible for ensuring the protection of millions of acres for national parks, national forests, federal bird sanctuaries, and national monuments.

Super! Next, let's organize text in bulleted and numbered lists.

## Using Bulleted and Numbered Lists

To organize a list of items in a document, use a bulleted or numbered list of two or more short paragraphs.

- A bulleted list, also called an unordered list, begins each paragraph with a bullet graphic.
- A numbered list, also called an ordered list, begins each paragraph with a number in sequence, such as 1, 2, 3.

To create a bulleted or numbered list from existing paragraphs, select the paragraphs and click the Home tab; then click the Bullets button or Numbering button in the Paragraph group.

Like other paragraph formatting, you can use live preview to see how a bullet graphic or numbering scheme will look before you apply it to your selected paragraphs.

You can quickly convert a bulleted list to a numbered list and vice versa. Just select the list and click either the Bullets or Numbering button. Try it!

*Be careful using sound, movies, and animation!* These special effects should be used sparingly and only when they support your presentation's message. Too much sound or animation can annoy an audience.

Wow! What a fun and useful presentation! Now you are ready to set slide timings.

### Setting Slide Timings

Ray wants to run the *atoms13* slide show automatically as he discusses each slide. Slide timings specify the amount of time, usually in seconds, between slides as they advance automatically.

### Setting Slide Timings in *PowerPoint 2010*

To set slide timings for a slide show that will run unattended, click the Transitions tab and then click the Advance Slide After checkbox in the Timing group and set the amount of time in seconds between each slide.

**Let's set ten-second slide timings for all of the slides.**

Transitions | Timing | Advance Slide After

Transitions | Timing | Apply to All

1. Click the **Transitions** tab, if necessary, and locate the **Timing** group.
2. Click the **Advance Slide After** checkbox in the Timing group (After: 00:00.00) to insert a check mark. Leaving the check mark in the On Mouse Click checkbox allows you to set up the slide show to run either manually or automatically.
3. Select the contents of the Advance Slide After text box and key **10**.
4. Click the **Apply To All** button in the Timing group to add the ten-second slide timings to each slide. (Apply To All)
5. Run the slide show from slide 1. *Do not try to advance the slides manually. Just sit back and watch the show!*

Great! Now let's set up the slide show to run unattended.

### Setting Slide Timings in *PowerPoint 2007*

To set slide timings for a slide show that will run unattended, you can click the Animations tab and then click the Advance Slide Automatically option in the Transition to This Slide group.

**Let's format the three short paragraphs below the John Muir paragraph heading as a bulleted list, then format the list of national parks as a numbered list.**

**Home | Paragraph | Bullets or Numbering**

1. Select the three short paragraphs beginning with *naturalist and conservationist* and ending with *Sierra Club founder*.
2. Click the **Home** tab and locate the **Paragraph** group.
3. Click the **Bullets** button arrow in the Paragraph group to view a gallery of bullet options.

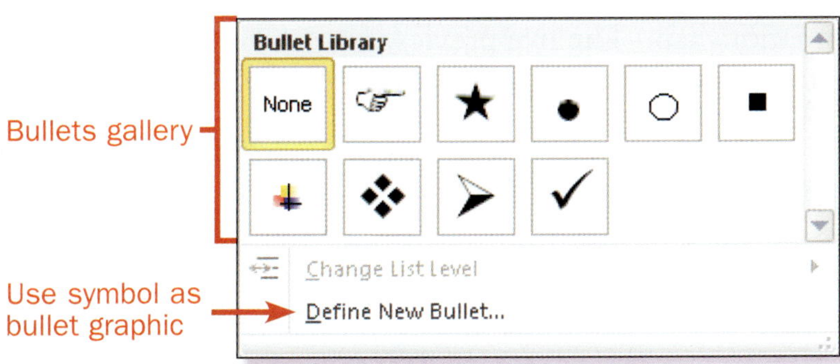


4. Use live preview to check out different bullet graphic options; then click the bullet option of your choice.
5. Select the list of national parks beginning with *Yosemite National Park* and ending with *Grand Canyon National Park*.
6. Click the **Numbering** button arrow in the Paragraph group to view the gallery of numbering options.
7. Use live preview to check out different numbering options; then click the numbering option of your choice.
8. Deselect the paragraphs and save the document.

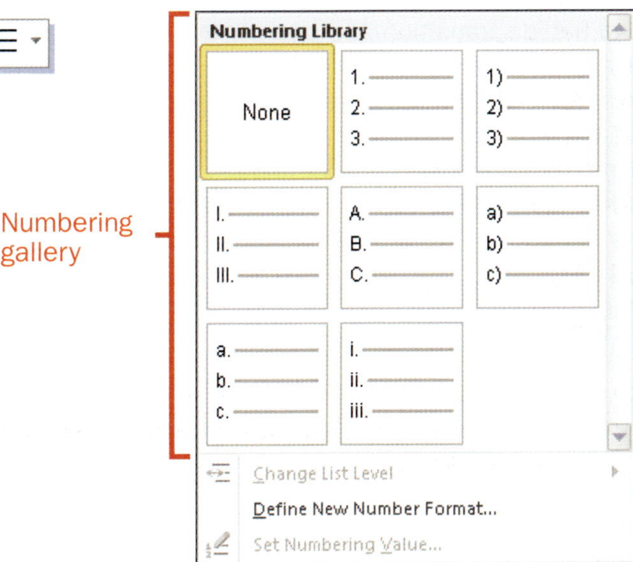

4. Point to a slide transition and live-preview the movement applied to slide 2.
5. Continue by previewing several additional slide transitions; then click the slide transition of your choice.
6. Click the **Apply To All** button in the Timing group to apply the slide transition to all slides.
7. Run the slide show from slide 1; then return to Normal view and save the presentation.

Nice work! Now you are ready to set up Ray's slide show to run unattended during the Explorers Club meeting. You begin by setting slide timings.

**Applying a Slide Transition Effect in *PowerPoint 2007***

You can choose a slide transition from the slide transitions gallery in the Transition to This Slide group on the Animations tab. The live preview feature allows you to explore several slide transitions before you apply the one of your choice.

**Animations | Transition to This Slide | More**

**Animations | Transition to This Slide | Apply to All**

**Let's explore several slide transitions using slide 2 and then apply a slide transition to all of the slides.**

1. View **slide 2** in the slide pane.
2. Click the **Animations** tab, if necessary, and locate the **Transition to This Slide** group.
3. Click the **More** button in the Transition to This Slide group to expand the slide transition gallery.
4. Point to a slide transition and preview the motion effect applied to slide 2.
5. Continue by previewing several additional slide transitions.
6. Click the slide transition of your choice.
7. Click the **Apply to All** button in the Transition to This Slide group to apply the slide transition to all slides.
8. Run the slide show from slide 1; then save the presentation.

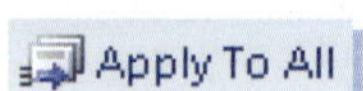


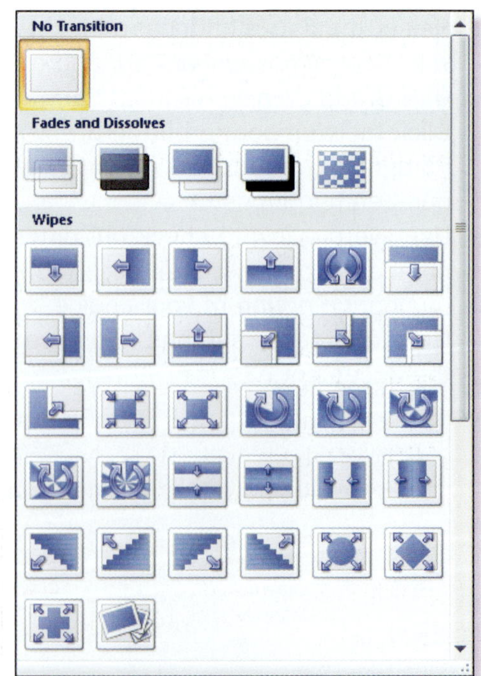

**CHECKPOINT**

The bulleted and numbered lists on your screen should look similar to this.

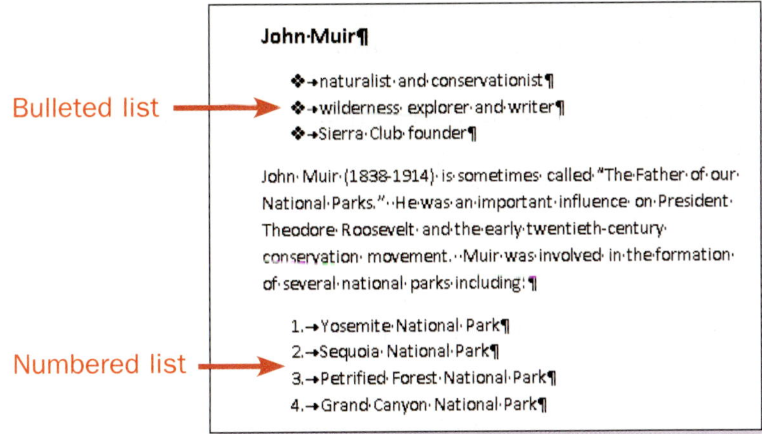


John Muir

- naturalist and conservationist
- wilderness explorer and writer
- Sierra Club founder

John Muir (1838-1914) is sometimes called "The Father of our National Parks." He was an important influence on President Theodore Roosevelt and the early twentieth-century conservation movement. Muir was involved in the formation of several national parks including:

1. Yosemite National Park
2. Sequoia National Park
3. Petrified Forest National Park
4. Grand Canyon National Park

A symbol is a special character you can insert in your text. The © symbol means *copyright* and the ™ symbol means *trademark*.

Some symbols—📫 or 🗁 or 💻—are used to represent physical things. Other symbols, such as arrows or stars, can make an infographic more interesting.

You can customize a bulleted list by inserting symbols for the bullet graphic. To customize a bullet graphic, click Define New Bullet at the bottom of the Bullets gallery to open the Define New Bullet dialog box. Then select the bullet graphic you want to modify and customize it with a symbol from the Symbols dialog box.

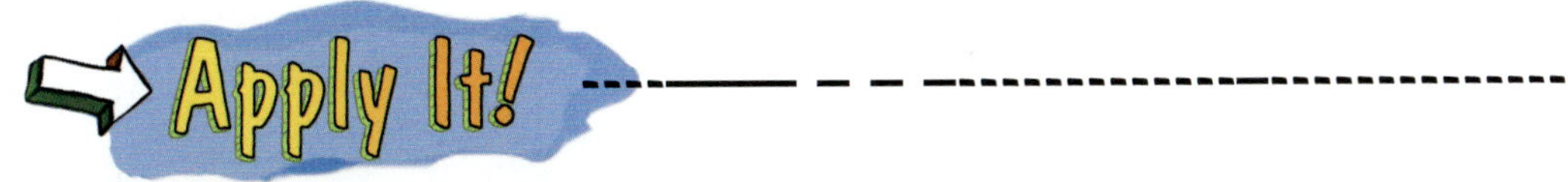


**Let's customize the bulleted list by replacing the bullets with a Wingding symbol.**

Home | Paragraph | Bullets

1. Select the bulleted list.
2. Click the **Bullets** button arrow in the Paragraph group and click **Define New Bullet** to open the Define New Bullet dialog box.

3. Click the **Symbol** button to open the Symbol dialog box.
4. Click the **Font** arrow and scroll to view the Wingdings font, if necessary.
5. Click **Wingdings** and scroll to view the Wingdings symbols.
6. Click a five-pointed star symbol to select it, click **OK** twice, and deselect the list. Each bullet is replaced with the five-pointed star symbol.

**CHECKPOINT**

Your bulleted list should look like this.

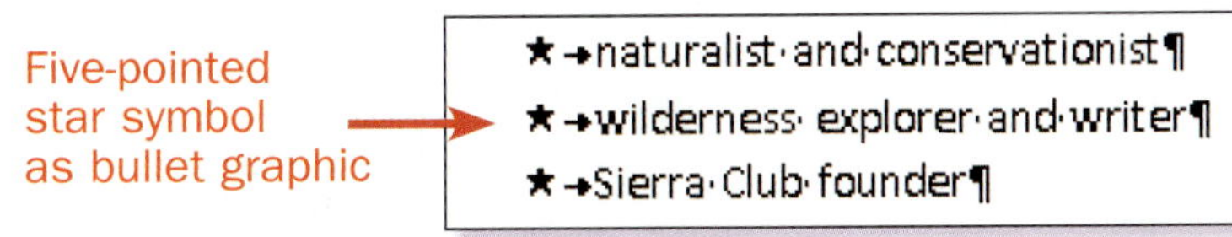


★ naturalist and conservationist
★ wilderness explorer and writer
★ Sierra Club founder

Large audio and video files are *linked* to a presentation, not inserted in it. If you move your presentation to a different computer, make sure you also move copies of any linked video or audio files. Check out linked versus embedded audio and video files in *PowerPoint* Help.

Very nice! Next, let's add some fun to the presentation with slide transition effects and set up the slide show to run unattended.

## Adding Transition Effects and Setting Up a Slide Show

To make your presentation more fun and exciting, you can add a slide transition effect. A slide transition effect adds movement that appears as one slide leaves the screen and another one takes its place during a slide show.

**Applying a Slide Transition Effect in *PowerPoint 2010***

You can click the Transitions tab and then click a slide transition from the slide transitions gallery in the Transition to This Slide group. You can also use live preview to explore several slide transitions.

**Let's explore several slide transitions using slide 2 and then apply a slide transition to all of the slides.**

Transitions | Transition to This Slide | More

Transitions | Timing | Apply To All

1. View **slide 2** in the slide pane.
2. Click the **Transitions** tab, if necessary, and locate the **Transition to This Slide** and **Timing** groups.
3. Click the **More** button to expand the slide transitions gallery.

Slide transitions gallery

Subtle
None Cut Fade Push Wipe Split Reveal Random Bars
Shape Uncover Cover Flash
Exciting
Dissolve Checkerboard Blinds Clock Ripple Honeycomb Glitter Vortex
Shred Switch Flip Gallery Cube Doors Box Zoom
Dynamic Content
Pan Ferris Wheel Conveyor Rotate Window Orbit Fly Through

You can insert a symbol anywhere in your document at the position of the insertion point by clicking the Insert tab and then clicking the Symbol button in the Symbols group. Try it!

## Adding Special Text Effects

In previous projects, you learned how to apply the Title and Heading 1 styles to selected text to add emphasis to the text and make your document more interesting to the reader. The Styles gallery also offers a number of other styles you can use to add emphasis to text.

**Let's apply a heading style to the three primary paragraph headings and change the font size.**

Home | Styles | More

1. Use the CTRL key to select the nonadjacent paragraph headings **John Muir**, **Yosemite National Park**, and **President Theodore Roosevelt**.
2. Click the **Home** tab, if necessary, and locate the **Styles** group.
3. Click the **More** button in the Styles group and click the **Intense Emphasis** style. (Use ScreenTips, if necessary, to locate the style.)
4. Click the **Font Size** button arrow in the Font group and click **14**. 11
5. Deselect the paragraph headings.

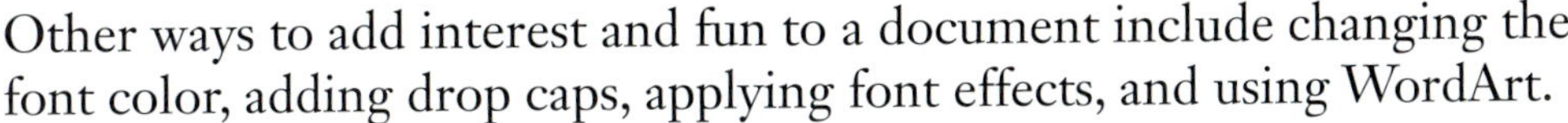

Other ways to add interest and fun to a document include changing the font color, adding drop caps, applying font effects, and using WordArt.

**Drop Caps**

Chapters in some books begin with a large capital letter, called a drop cap. To turn the first letter of the first word in a paragraph into a capital letter that "drops down" two or three lines, move the insertion point into the paragraph and click the Drop Cap button in the Text group on the Insert tab.

Here's a great way to clear all formatting from selected text. Click the More button in the Styles group on the Home tab to view the styles gallery; then click Clear Formatting. To reapply the formatting, click the Undo button on the Quick Access Toolbar. Try it!

**Let's add a motion clip to the Title Slide.**

Insert | Media Clips | Movie from File

Picture Tools Format | Adjust | Recolor

1. Activate slide 1, if necessary; then click the **Insert** tab and locate the **Media Clips** group.
2. Click the **Movie from File** button arrow in the Media Clips group to view the menu.
3. Click **Movie from Clip Organizer**. The Clip Art task pane opens; it contains movies and motion clips organized in the Clip Organizer.
4. Search for appropriate clips using the keyword **atoms**.
5. Click the motion clip of your choice to insert it on the Title Slide. The Picture Tools Format tab appears on the Ribbon. You can use buttons on the tab to format set options of the motion clip.
6. Resize and recolor the clip, if desired, and drag it to the lower-left area of the Title Slide; then deselect it.

Movie

Next, you add an audio clip to the Title Slide. When you add or select a sound icon, the Sound Tools Format tab appears on the Ribbon.

**Now let's add an audio clip that play automatically when the Title Slide is viewed during a slide show. You will hide the sound icon so that it is not visible during the slide show.**

Insert | Media Clips | Sound from File

Sound Tools Options | Sound Options | Hide During Show

1. Verify that the Title Slide is the active slide; then click the **Insert** tab and locate the **Media Clips** group.
2. Click the **Sound from File** button arrow in the Media Clips group to view sound effect options.
3. Click **Sound from Clip Organizer** to view the list of sound files in the Clip Art task pane.
4. Scroll the list and click any sound file to insert a sound icon on the Title Slide.
5. Click the **Automatically** button in the confirmation dialog box to allow the sound to play automatically when the Title Slide is viewed.
6. Click the **Sound Tools Options** tab, if necessary, and locate the **Sound Options** group.
7. Click the **Hide During Show** checkbox to insert a check mark.
8. Deselect the sound icon and close the Clip Art task pane.
9. Run the slide show from slide 1 to hear the sound and see the animation in the motion clip; then save the presentation.

Sound

Hide During Show

**Let's apply a drop cap effect to the first letter in the first sentence of each descriptive paragraph.**

**Insert | Text | Drop Cap**

1. Click in the **John Muir** body paragraph to position the insertion point in the paragraph.
2. Click the **Insert** tab and locate the **Text** group.
3. Click the **Drop Cap** button in the Text group to view a gallery of drop cap options.
4. Click the **Dropped** option. The first letter in the paragraph is enlarged and dropped along the left margin of the paragraph.
5. Click in the **Yosemite National Park** body paragraph and tap the CTRL + Y keys to repeat the drop cap formatting.
6. Click in the **President Theodore Roosevelt** body paragraph and tap the CTRL + Y keys to repeat the drop cap formatting and then deselect the text.

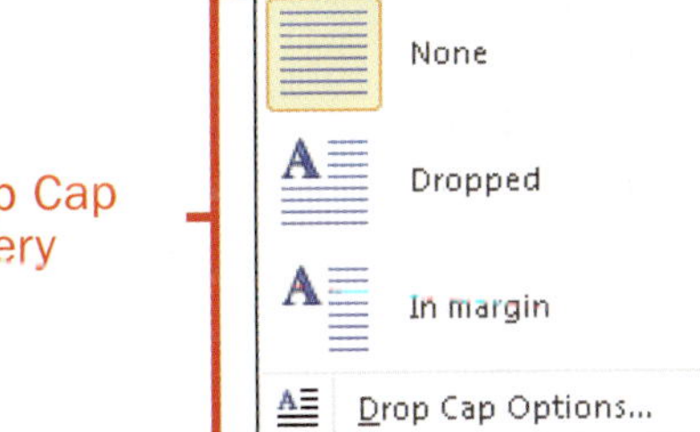


Drop Cap gallery

Creating the drop caps changes the text flow in the columns. You need to move the Yosemite National Park paragraph heading back to the top of the second column.

7. Move the insertion point in immediately in front of the Yosemite National Park paragraph heading at the bottom of the first column.
8. Tap the CTRL + SHIFT +ENTER keys to insert a hard column break and force the paragraph heading to the top of the second column.

Your paragraph headings and dropped caps should look like this.

Dropped caps

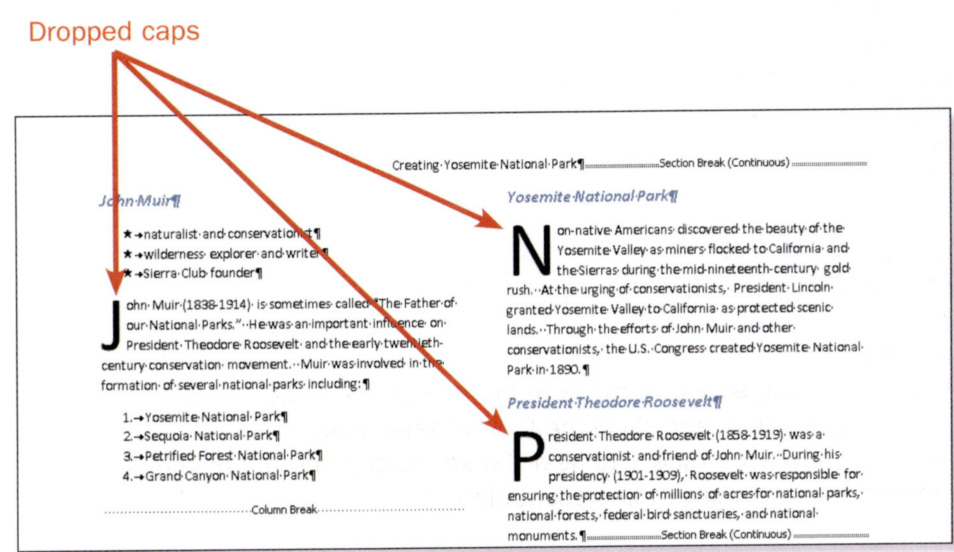

3. Click the **Insert Audio** button arrow in the Media group to view the audio options.
4. Click **Clip Art Audio** to view installed audio files in the Clip Art task pane.
5. Scroll the list and double-click the audio file of your choice to add the effect and a sound icon to the Title Slide.

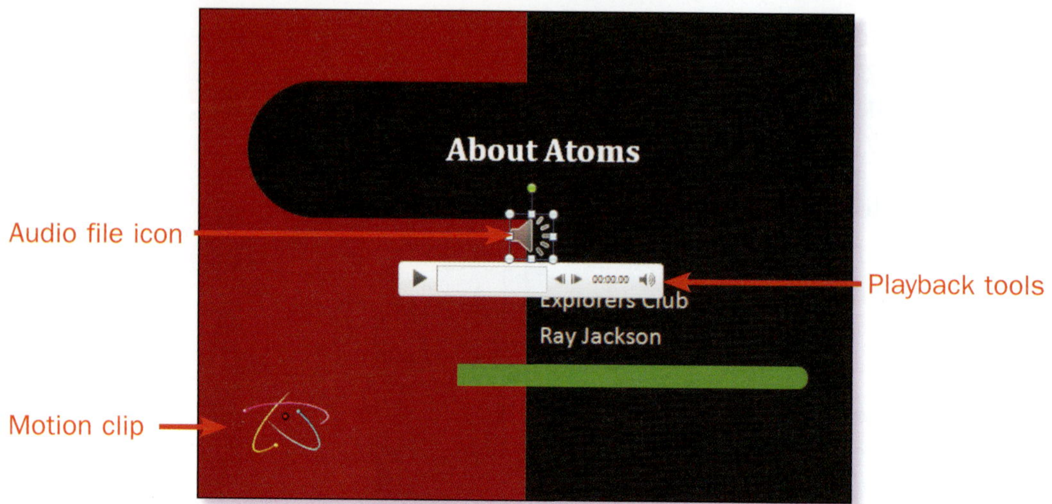


The audio file icon is inserted in the center of the Title Slide, and the Audio Tools Format and Playback tabs appear on the Ribbon. Playback tools appear below the audio icon. You can format or set options for the audio file with buttons on the Audio Tools Format and Playback tabs. Use the Playback tools to play or pause the sound effect.

6. Click the **Audio Tools Playback** tab and locate the **Audio Options** group.
7. Click the **Start** button arrow in the Audio Options group and click **Automatically**.
8. Click the **Hide During Show** checkbox in the Audio Options group to insert a check mark.
9. Deselect the sound icon and close the Clip Art task pane.
10. Run the slide show for slide 1 to hear the sound effect and view the motion clip animation; then return to Normal view and save the presentation.

Well done! In Trail Marker 6, you will add slide transitions and set up a slide show.

**Inserting Video and Audio in *PowerPoint 2007***

When you insert a motion clip, the Picture Tools Format tab appears on the Ribbon. When you insert a sound clip, the Sound Tools Options tab appears on the Ribbon. You can use buttons on these tabs to format or set options for the sound clip.

A document theme is a color-coordinated set of formats; each new document is automatically formatted with the default Office theme color set. You can dress up a handout or flyer by changing the document's theme and available color set. Click the Page Layout tab and then click the Themes button in the Themes group to explore available themes. Check it out!

### Font Effects

*Word*'s font effects allow you to change the look of text in a number of ways including Superscript or Subscript, ALL CAPS, Shadow, and SMALL CAPS. Apply a font effect by clicking an Effects checkbox in the Font dialog box.

**Home | Font | Dialog Box Launcher**

**Let's format a paragraph with the Small caps effect.**

1. Select the *Check Out These Websites!* paragraph.
2. Click the **Home** tab and locate the **Font** group.
3. Click the **Dialog Box Launcher** icon in the Font group to open the Font dialog box.
   - Click the **Small caps** checkbox to insert a check mark.
   - Click the **Bold** font style.
   - Click the **Font** color arrow and click **Blue** in the Standard Colors grid.
4. Click **OK**, deselect the text, and save the document.

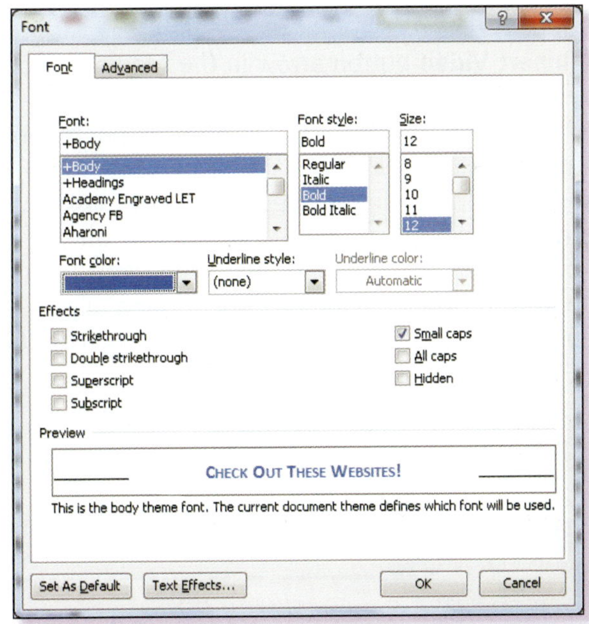

Your formatted text should now look like this.

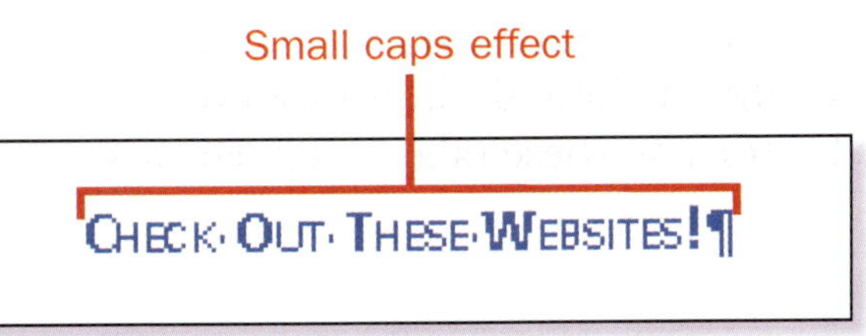

## Adding Video and Audio to Slides

Video includes movies and animated clip art called motion clips, while audio includes music and other sound effects. Audio and video can add fun to a slide show.

### Adding Video and Audio in *PowerPoint 2010*

Movies and audio can be set to play automatically when a slide is viewed during a slide show, or they can be set to play manually when the person running the slide show clicks an icon on the slide. Motion clip animation plays automatically during a slide show.

**Let's add a motion clip to the Title Slide.**

Insert | Media | Insert Video

1. Activate **slide 1**, if necessary; then click the **Insert** tab and locate the **Media** group.
2. Click the **Insert Video** button arrow in the Media group to view video options.
3. Click **Clip Art Video** to open the Clip Art task pane containing installed motion clips.
4. Search for appropriate clips using the keyword **atoms**.
5. Click the motion clip of your choice to insert it on the Title Slide. The Picture Tools Format tab appears on the Ribbon. You can use buttons on the tab to format or set options for the motion clip.
6. Resize and recolor the clip, if desired, and drag it to the lower-left area of the Title Slide; then deselect it.

Next, you add an audio clip to the Title Slide.

**Now let's insert an audio clip that plays automatically when the Title Slide is viewed during a slide show. You will hide the sound icon so that it is not visible during the slide show.**

Insert | Media | Insert Audio

Audio Tools Playback | Audio Options | Start

1. Verify that the Title Slide is the active slide.
2. Click the **Insert** tab and locate the **Media** group.

## WordArt

To create an interesting, colorful, and fun text effect, you can format existing text as WordArt. To create WordArt from existing text, select the text, click the Insert tab, and click the WordArt button in the Text group in either *Word 2010* or *Word 2007*.

### Using WordArt in *Word 2010*

When you create a WordArt text effect in *Word 2010*, the selected and formatted text is placed in a drawing shape, called a text box, which "floats" above the underlying document text. You can move or copy the floating text box shape using drag and drop.

You can also move a selected floating WordArt text box to position it a short space up, down, left, or right by tapping one of the arrow keys in a process called nudging.

When the text box shape is selected, the Drawing Tools Format tab appears on the Ribbon. You can click buttons on this tab to format the text box and its contents.

**Let's use the title text to create a WordArt object and then reposition the object on the page using drag and drop and nudging.**

Insert | Text | WordArt

1. Select the title paragraph **Creating Yosemite National Park**.
2. Click the **Insert** tab and locate the **Text** group.
3. Click the **WordArt** button in the Text group to display a gallery of WordArt styles.

4. Click the first **WordArt style** in the fourth row to create the WordArt text in a text box shape.
5. Move the mouse pointer to the boundary of the text box. The mouse pointer becomes a move pointer.

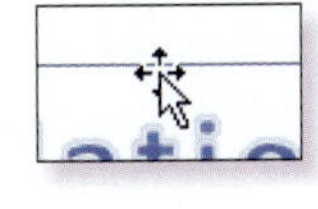

6. Drag the text box up and to the right until it is approximately centered between the left and right margins and no longer overlaps the handout text.
7. Nudge the selected text box to the left or right using the arrow keys as necessary to position it more precisely.
8. Click in the document to deselect the text box.

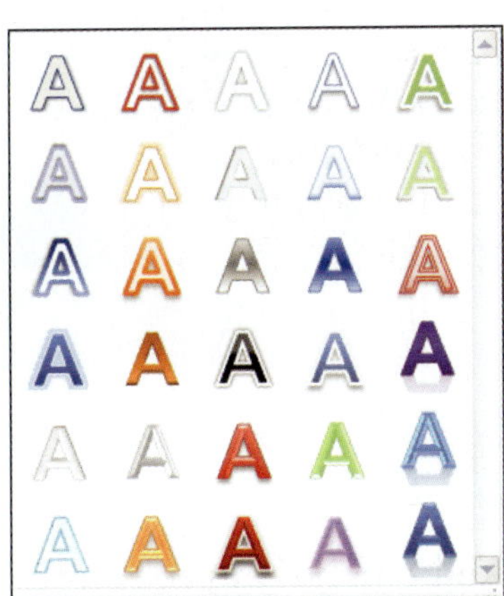

3. Click the **Date and time** checkbox, if necessary, to insert a check mark; then click the **Fixed** option.
4. Key today's date with the month spelled out in the text box.
5. Click the **Slide number** checkbox to insert a check mark.
6. Click the **Footer** checkbox to insert a check mark, if necessary.
7. Key **Explorers Club** in the text box.
8. Click the **Don't show on title slide** checkbox to insert a check mark.

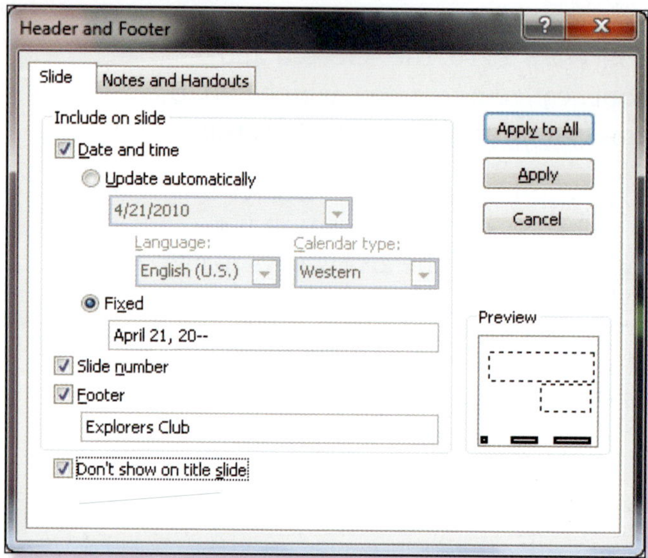


9. Click the **Apply to All** button.
10. Scroll the slides to see that the Title Slide does not have the footer text, slide number, or date but that all of the remaining slides do. Then save the presentation.

**CHECKPOINT**

The bottom of your slide 2 should look similar to this.

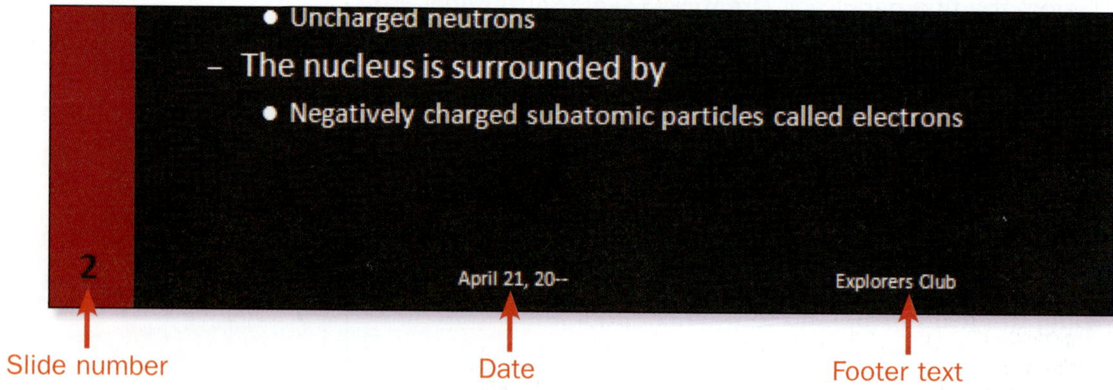


Outstanding! Let's add interest to the *atoms13* presentation with video and audio.

Your WordArt title should look similar to this.

Creating·Yosemite·National·Park

Very nice! Now let's move to Trail Marker 4 and insert clip art and text boxes.

**Using WordArt in *Word 2007***

When you click the WordArt button in the Text group on the Insert tab in *Word 2007*, the selected text is converted to a WordArt object.

By default, a *Word 2007* WordArt object is positioned in line with the text. When a WordArt object is positioned in line with the text, the object can only be repositioned horizontally on the page by clicking the Align Text Left, Center, or Align Text Right buttons in the Paragraph group on the Home tab.

Positioning a WordArt object in front of the text as a floating object allows you to move or copy the objects using drag and drop. You can "float" a WordArt object by changing its text wrapping formatting.

A *Word 2007* WordArt object is sized, colored, and shaped with buttons on the WordArt Tools Format tab that appears automatically on the Ribbon when you create or select a WordArt object.

To convert an in line WordArt object to a floating object, click the Text Wrapping button in the Arrange group on the WordArt Tools Format tab, which appears automatically when you select a WordArt object. Then select the In Front of Text or Behind Text option.

Insert | Text | WordArt

**Let's use the title text to create a WordArt object.**

1. Select the title paragraph **Creating Yosemite National Park**.
2. Click the **Insert** tab on the Ribbon and locate the **Text** group.
3. Click the **WordArt** button in the Text group to display a gallery of WordArt styles. WordArt

3. Click the **Bullets** button arrow in the Paragraph group to view a gallery of button graphic options.

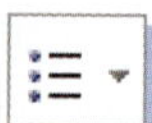

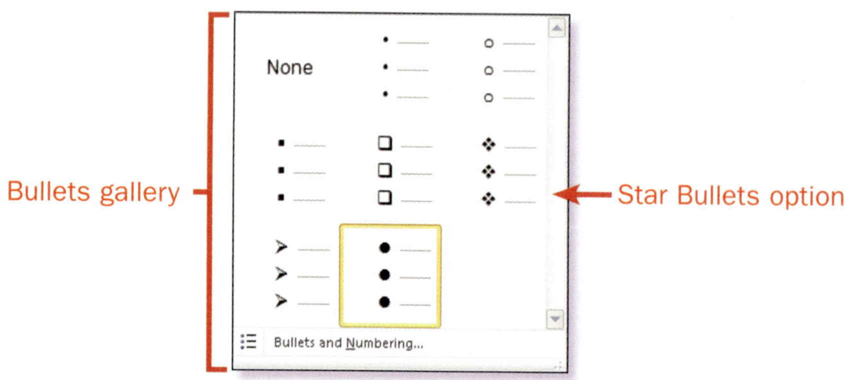


4. Click the **Star Bullets** option in the second row.
5. Deselect the placeholder and click the **Slide Master** tab to return to Slide Master view. The Title and Content slides' first-level bullet is now a star shape.
6. Click the **Close Master View** button in the Close group on the Slide Master View tab to return to Normal view.

7. Scroll the slides to verify the change to the first-level bullet graphic. Then return to slide 1.

Next, let's add footer text, slide numbers, and today's date to the slides.

**Inserting Slide Footers**

You can insert footer text, slide numbers, or a date on selected slides, on all slides, or on all slides *except* the Title Slide. A date can be inserted as a fixed date or as a date that automatically changes to the current date each time the presentation is opened.

As you learned when you reviewed the slide master, the position of the footer text, slide numbers, or date is controlled by slide master placeholders. To insert a footer, slide numbers, or a date, you can click the Insert tab and click buttons in the Text group.

**Let's insert today's date, slide numbers, and footer text on all slides *except* the Title Slide. Before you begin, make sure you are viewing slide 1 in Normal view.**

Insert | Text | Header & Footer

1. Click the **Insert** tab and locate the **Text** group.
2. Click the **Header & Footer** button in the Text group to open the Header and Footer dialog box.

4. Click the **fifth WordArt style** in the second row of the gallery to open the Edit WordArt dialog box.
5. Click **OK** to accept the default font and font size.
6. Click the **WordArt object** to select it, if necessary, and tap the CTRL + E keys to center the object horizontally.
7. Deselect the object.

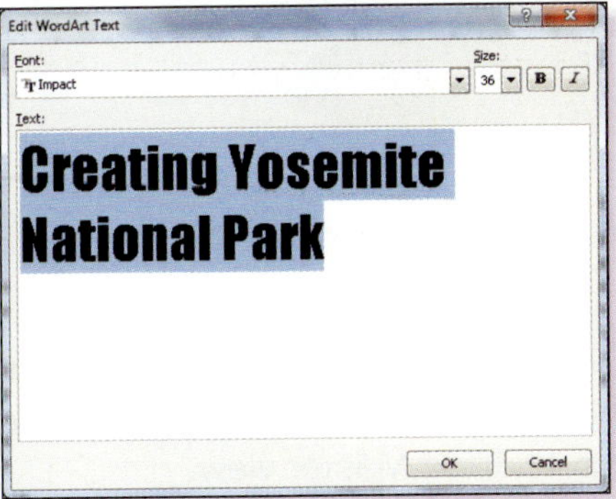

Your WordArt title object should look similar to this.

Creating Yosemite National Park

Very nice! Now let's insert clip art and text boxes.

## Inserting Clip Art and Text Boxes

Pictures and drawings that come with the *Office* applications, such as *Word* and *PowerPoint*, are called clip art. You can use clip art to make the handout more fun to read. You can use a text box to reposition text anywhere in the document.

### Clip Art

You can search for existing clip art by clicking the Insert tab and then clicking the Clip Art button in the Illustrations group to open the Clip Art task pane. In the Clip Art task pane, key a keyword to specify the clip art you need and search for it.

Another way to insert clip art is to insert a clip you already have saved on your computer. Click the Insert tab and then click the Insert Picture from File button in the Illustrations group to open the Insert Picture dialog box. Open the folder containing your clip art files and insert a clip.

**Let's switch to Slide Master view.**

View | Presentation Views | Slide Master View

1. View **slide 1**, if necessary.
2. Click the **View** tab and locate the **Presentation Views** group.
3. Click the **Slide Master View** button in the Presentation Views group to switch to Slide Master view.
4. Click the **slide master** (slide 1) in the left pane, if necessary, to view the slide master in the right pane.
5. Look carefully at the placeholders on the slide master and related slide layouts, including the date, a footer, and slide number placeholders. The position of footer text, slide numbers, or a date is controlled by these placeholders.

Slide Master

You can click Bullets and Numbering in the Bullets gallery to open the Bullets and Numbering dialog box and search for a new bullet graphic or customize the selected bullet graphic. Try it!

### Modifying the Bullet Graphic in Slide Master View

Modifying a presentation's slide master is a good choice when you want to change the formatting of an element on all slides in the presentation. For example, the theme applied to each Title and Content slide in the *atoms13* presentation has a specific graphic for each first-level bullet.

If you want to change the bulleted list graphic's shape, size, or color on *all* Title and Content slides, make the change *just once* on the slide master. Any new Title and Content slides that you insert will use the modified bullet graphic.

**Let's modify the first-level bullet graphic for Title and Content slides.**

Home | Paragraph | Bullets

1. Move the I-beam immediately in front of the first-level bullet text **Click to edit Master text styles** and click to position the insertion point. (The insertion point will be between the bullet graphic and the text.)
2. Click the **Home** tab and locate the **Paragraph** group.

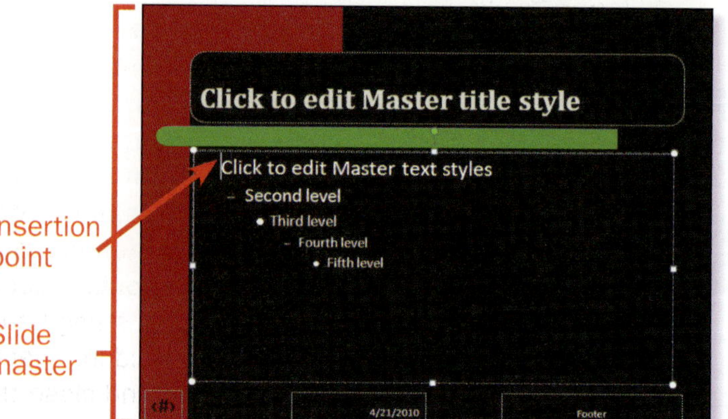

Clip art that is too big can be resized by dragging a sizing handle—one of the circles or squares you see on the outside border of the selected clip art. To resize clip art proportionally, drag a corner sizing handle. To resize clip art from the center while maintaining its proportions, tap and hold down the CTRL key while dragging a corner sizing handle.

By default, clip art is inserted in line with text. Inline objects can be aligned horizontally with the Align Text Left, Center, and Align Text Right buttons in the Paragraph group on the Home tab.

If you want to position clip art in front of or behind text or allow the text to wrap around it, you must convert the inline clip art into a floating object that can be repositioned on the page using drag and drop.

When you select a clip or picture, the Picture Tools Format tab appears on the Ribbon. You can click the Picture Tools Format tab and then click the Text Wrapping button in the Arrange group to view a gallery of text wrapping options.

Clicking a text wrapping option, such as Square, Tight, or In Front of Text, converts the clip or picture into a floating object and applies the designated wrapping option.

**Let's search for and insert a picture of a park. Then we'll resize it, convert it to a floating object, and reposition it. Your teacher may modify these steps if you do not have appropriate clip art installed or an Internet connection.**

Insert | Illustrations | Clip Art

1. Move the insertion point in front of the paragraph mark at the end of the second column and tap the ENTER key.
2. Click the **Insert** tab and locate the **Illustrations** group.
3. Click the **Clip Art** button in the Illustrations group to open the Clip Art task pane.

Clip Art

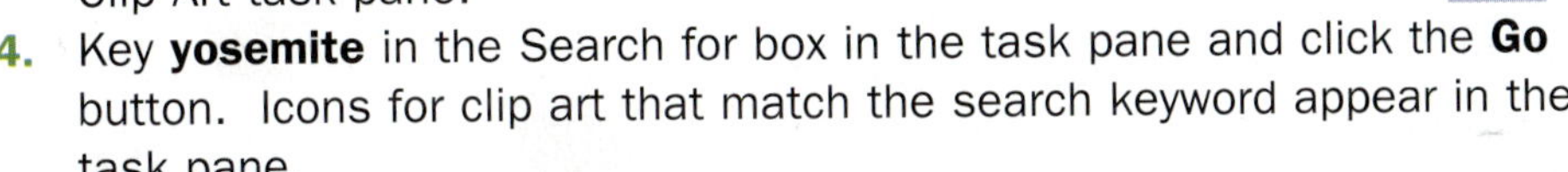

4. Key **yosemite** in the Search for box in the task pane and click the **Go** button. Icons for clip art that match the search keyword appear in the task pane.
5. Scroll the task pane to view clip art icons; then click the icon for the clip you want to insert in the document at the insertion point.
6. Click the inserted clip to select it, if necessary, and then move the mouse pointer to the sizing handle in the upper-left corner of the picture. The mouse pointer changes its shape to a double-headed arrow sizing pointer.
7. Tap and hold the CTRL key and drag the sizing handle downward until the picture is small enough to fit in the President Theodore Roosevelt body text paragraph. Release the CTRL key and close the Clip Art task pane.

You can view and edit a presentation's slide master by switching to Slide Master view. Click the View tab and click the Slide Master button in the Master Views or Presentation Views group to switch to Slide Master view.

The Slide Master tab automatically appears when you switch to Slide Master view. Check it out!

**Switching to Slide Master View in *PowerPoint 2010***

In Slide Master view, the pane on the left side of your screen contains the slide master thumbnail (slide 1) and related slide layout thumbnails for the theme applied to the presentation. Changing an element on the slide master also changes that element on the related slide layouts.

Click the View tab and then click the Slide Master View button in the Master Views group to switch to Slide Master view.

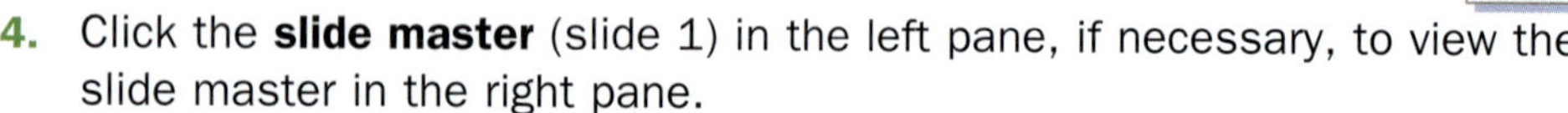

**Let's switch to Slide Master view.**

View | Master Views | Slide Master View

1. View **slide 1**, if necessary, in the slide pane.
2. Click the **View** tab and locate the **Master Views** group.
3. Click the **Slide Master View** button in the Master Views group to switch to Slide Master view.
4. Click the **slide master** (slide 1) in the left pane, if necessary, to view the slide master in the right pane.
5. Look carefully at the placeholders on the slide master and related slide layouts, including the date, a footer, and slide number placeholders. The position of footer text, slide numbers, or a date is controlled by these placeholders.

Slide Master

Now you are ready to modify the bullet graphic on the Title and Content slides.

**Switching to Slide Master View in *PowerPoint 2007***

Slide Master view shows the slide master (slide 1) and related slide layout thumbnails in a pane on the left side of your screen. Clicking a thumbnail displays an enlarged version in the right pane. When you change an element on the slide master, such as the alignment of the title placeholder, the element is also changed on the related slide layouts.

Click the View tab and then click the Slide Master View button in the Presentation Views group to switch to Slide Master view.

8. Click the clip to select it, if necessary, to display the **Picture Tools Format** tab on the Ribbon; then click the Picture Tools Format tab, if necessary.
9. Click the **Wrap Text** or **Text Wrapping** button in the Arrange group on the Picture Tools Format tab.
10. Click **Square** in the gallery of text wrapping options; then move the mouse pointer to the clip. Scroll to the top of the document, if necessary, to see the floating object. The mouse pointer shape changes to a move pointer. (Hint: You might have to scroll the document to locate the floating clip.)
11. Drag the clip into the President Theodore Roosevelt body paragraph so that the text wraps attractively around it. You might choose to resize the clip as you determine its text wrapping position.
12. Deselect the clip by clicking anywhere in the document and save the document.

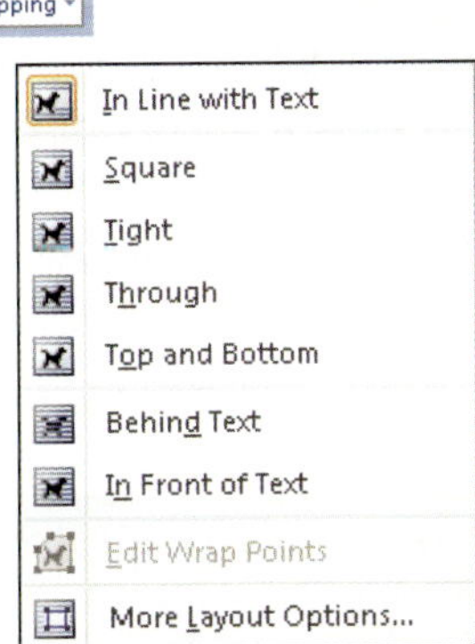

Your repositioned clip should look similar to this.

*President·Theodore·Roosevelt¶*

President·Theodore·Roosevelt·(1858-1919)·was·a· conservationist· and·friend·of·John·Muir.·· During·his·presidency·(1901-1909),· Roosevelt·was·responsible·for·ensuring·the· protection·of·millions·of·acres·for·national·parks,· national·forests,·federal·bird·sanctuaries,·and· national·monuments.¶

*Word* also offers a variety of tools, such as shapes and SmartArt, that you can use to draw illustrations using the mouse pointer. You can select a shape or SmartArt object to draw by clicking the Insert tab and then clicking the Shapes or SmartArt buttons in the Illustrations group. Check it out!

### Inserting Text Boxes

As you learned earlier in this project, a text box is a floating container for text. You create a text box by clicking the Text Box button in the Text group on the Insert tab. You can create a blank text box and then key in it or paste text into it.

7. Click **slide 6** in the Slides tab to make it the active slide.
8. Click the **Hydrogen shape** to select the grouped Hydrogen and Oxygen shapes.
9. Click the **Shape Effects** button in the Shape Styles group to view a gallery of effects options. 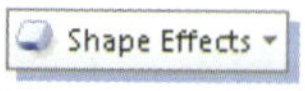
10. Point to **Glow** to view a gallery of Glow options.
11. Use live preview to view different Glow options; then click the **Red 18 pt glow, Accent color 2** option.

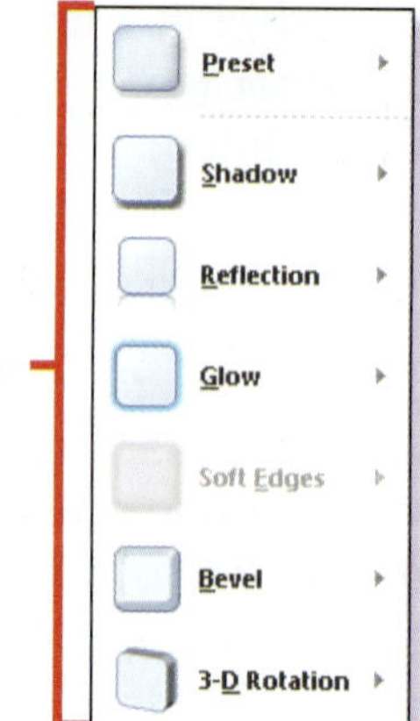


Effects options gallery

Shapes with glow effect

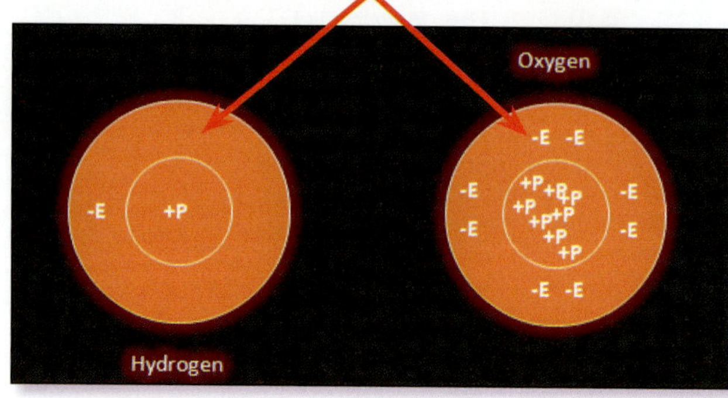


12. Deselect the grouped object.

The background graphics on the slides make it difficult to read the content on slides 9 and 10. To wrap up the changes to the reused slides, you should hide the background graphics on slides 9 and 10.

13. Select slide 9 and hide the background graphics; then select slide 10 and hide the background graphics.
14. Activate slide 1 and save the presentation.

Great! Next, let's see how you can control formatting using the slide master and add slide footers.

## Working with the Slide Master and Slide Footers

The slide master is a special hidden slide that controls the appearance of slides. Information about theme formatting elements, such as font, placeholder position, background color, and graphics, is stored in a presentation's slide master. When necessary, you can modify a presentation's slide master to change font sizes, font styles, font colors, and horizontal alignment and to change placeholder size and position.

Let's place the text at the bottom of the page in a text box; then reposition the text box with the mouse pointer and format it with a heavy blue border.

Insert | Text | Text Box

1. Select the CHECK OUT THESE WEBSITES! text and the following URLs.
2. Tap the CTRL + X keys to cut the text to the Office Clipboard.
3. Click the **Insert** tab and locate the **Text** group.
4. Click the **Text Box** button in the Text group to view a gallery of text box options.

Text Box gallery

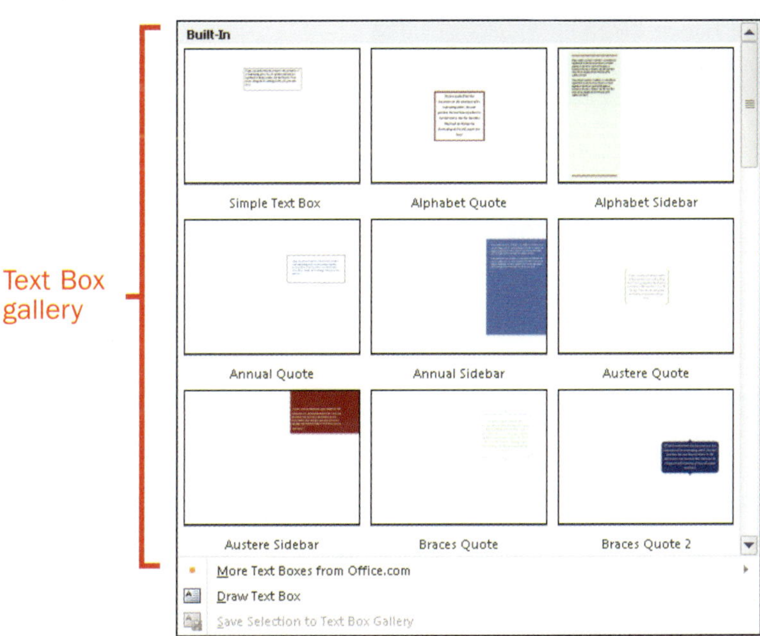


5. Click the **Simple Text Box** option to insert it at the bottom of the page.
6. Tap the CTRL + V keys to paste the cut text into the text box and tap the BACKSPACE key to remove the last blank line in the text box. When a text box is selected, the Drawing Tools Format tab (*Word 2010*) or the Text Box Tools Format tab (*Word 2007*) opens on the Ribbon.
7. Select the **CHECK OUT THESE WEBSITES!** text inside the text box and tap the CTRL + E keys to center the text in the text box.
8. Click the **Drawing Tools Format** tab and locate the **Shape Styles** or click the **Text Box Tools Format** tab and locate the **Text Box Styles** group.
9. Click the **More** button in the Shape Styles or Text Box Styles group or in the Text Box Styles group to view a gallery of text box styles.
10. Use live preview to preview different styles; then click the text box style of your choice.
11. Drag the text box up and to the left to position it below the left column; deselect the text box; delete any blank lines that create a second page, if necessary; and then save the document.

CHECKPOINT

Your slide 3 should look similar to this.

Modified clip

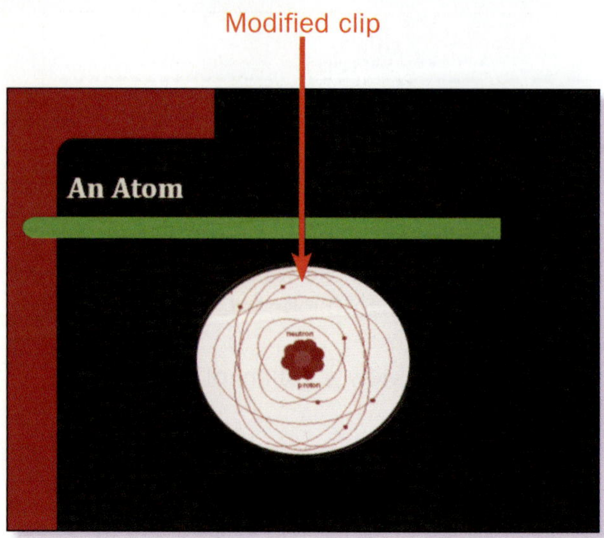


Reused slides 4 and 6 contain shapes. You can modify a shape's color, style, and position and add special effects by clicking buttons on the Drawing Tools Format tab.

**Drawing Tools Format|Shape Styles|More**

**Drawing Tools Format|Shape Styles|Shape Effects**

**Design|Background|Hide Background Graphics**

**Let's modify the shapes on slide 4 to change their style and modify the shape on slide 6 to add a glow effect.**

1. Click **slide 4** in the Slides tab to make it the active slide.
2. Click the **Proton shape** to select it and view the Drawing Tools Format tab.
3. Click the **Drawing Tools Format** tab and locate the **Shape Styles** group.
4. Click the **More** button in the Shape Styles group to view a gallery of shape styles. 
5. Use live preview to sample various styles; then click the shape style of your choice.
6. Apply the same style to the Electron shape.

Shape Styles gallery

Shapes with new style

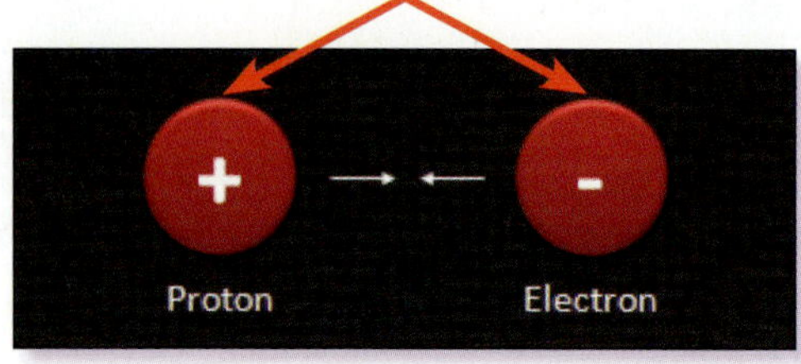

Your text box should look similar to this.

Column Break

CHECK·OUT·THESE·WEBSITES!¶

Sierra·Club·www.sierraclub.org/¶
Yosemite·National·Park·www.nps.gov/yose/¶
The·Theodore·Roosevelt·Association·
www.theodoreroosevelt.org/¶

## Adding a Page Border

Borders (dark lines) and shading (background fill) can be added to selected paragraphs or to a complete page by clicking the Home tab and clicking the Borders or Shading buttons in the Paragraph group.

You can also open the Borders and Shading dialog box by clicking the Page Layout tab and then clicking the Page Borders button in the Page Background group.

**Page Layout | Page Background | Page Borders**

**Let's add a 4 ½-point blue page border to the *handout6* document.**

1. Click the **Page Layout** tab, if necessary, and locate the **Page Background** group.
2. Click the **Page Borders** button in the Page Background group to open the Borders and Shading dialog box; then click the Page Border tab, if necessary.
3. Click the **Color** arrow and click **Blue** on the Standard Colors grid.
4. Click the **Width** arrow and click **4 ½ pt**.
5. Click the **top**, **bottom**, **left**, and **right** buttons, as necessary, in the Preview section to show the page border on all sides of the document.
6. Click the **Apply to** arrow and click **Whole Document**, if necessary.

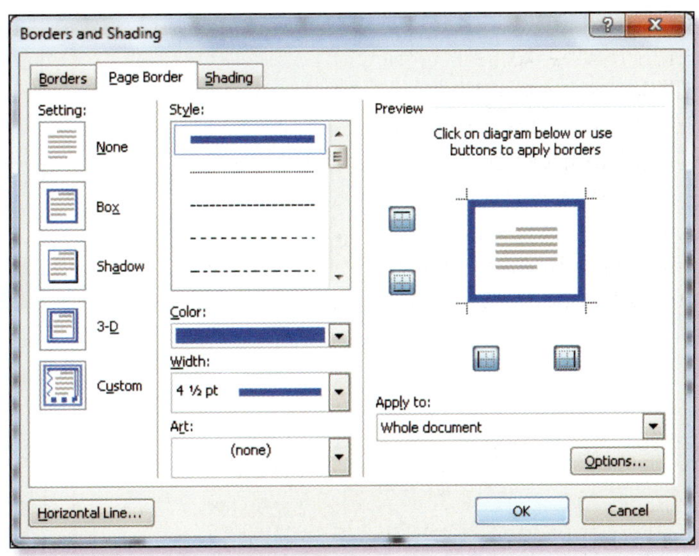

3. Click the **Picture Tools Format** tab and locate the **Adjust** and **Picture Styles** groups.
4. Click the **Color** or **Recolor** button in the Adjust group to view a gallery of recolor options.

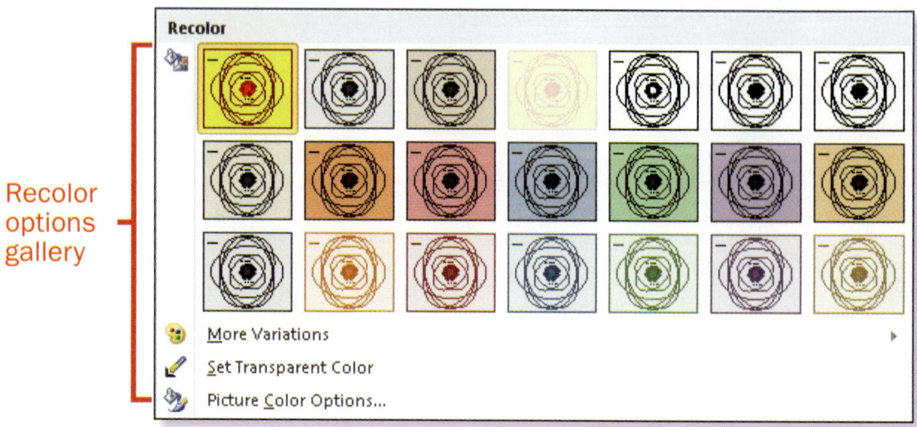


PowerPoint 2010

5. Use live preview to sample different recolor options; then click the recolor option of your choice.
6. Click the **More** button in the Picture Styles group to view a gallery of style options.
7. Use live preview to sample different style options; then click the style option of your choice.
8. Save the presentation.

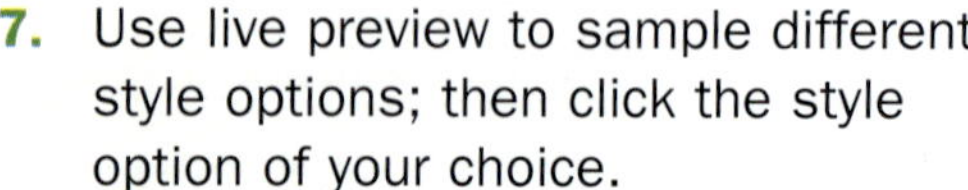

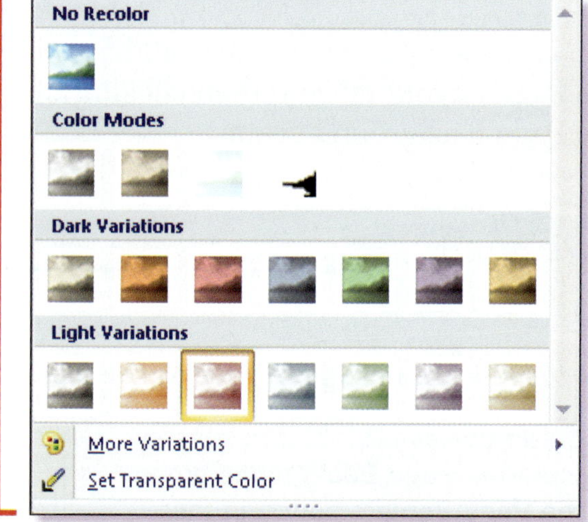


PowerPoint 2007

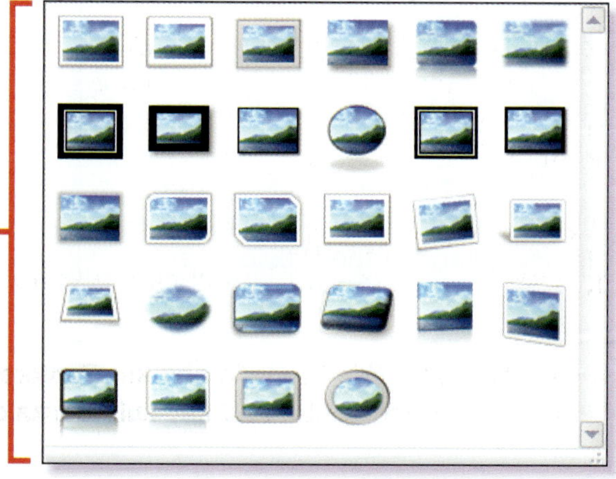

7. Click **OK** to apply a 4 ½-point blue border that appears on the top, bottom, left, and right edges of the page; then save the document.

Your *handout6* document should now look similar to this.

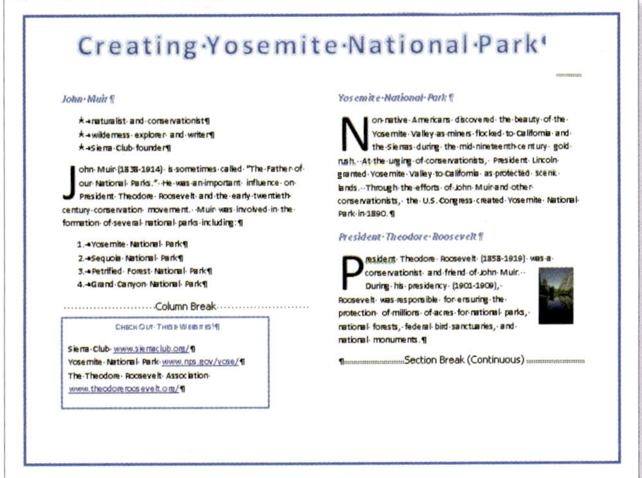

Creating Yosemite National Park

*John Muir*

- naturalist and conservationist
- wilderness explorer and writer
- Sierra Club founder

John Muir (1838-1914) is sometimes called "The Father of our National Parks." He was an important influence on President Theodore Roosevelt and the early twentieth century conservation movement. Muir was involved in the formation of several national parks including:

1. Yosemite National Park
2. Sequoia National Park
3. Petrified Forest National Park
4. Grand Canyon National Park

Column Break

CHECK OUT THESE WEBSITES!

Sierra Club www.sierraclub.org/
Yosemite National Park www.nps.gov/yose/
The Theodore Roosevelt Association www.theodoreroosevelt.org/

*Yosemite National Park*

Non-native Americans discovered the beauty of the Yosemite Valley as miners flocked to California and the Sierras during the mid-nineteenth-century gold rush. At the urging of conservationists, President Lincoln granted Yosemite Valley to California as protected scenic lands. Through the efforts of John Muir and other conservationists, the U.S. Congress created Yosemite National Park in 1890.

*President Theodore Roosevelt*

President Theodore Roosevelt (1858-1919) was a conservationist and friend of John Muir. During his presidency (1901-1909), Roosevelt was responsible for ensuring the protection of millions of acres for national parks, national forests, federal bird sanctuaries, and national monuments.

Section Break (Continuous)

Terrific! Now let's wrap up the document by adding a footer.

## Adding a Footer

The text *Explorers Club*, Luis's name, and today's date should be added at the bottom of the handout in a footer.

**Let's view the footer area, key the footer text, and insert today's date.**

**Insert | Header & Footer | Footer**

**Home | Font | Font Color**

1. Click the **Insert** tab and locate the **Header & Footer** group.
2. Click the **Footer** button in the Header & Footer group to view a gallery of footer options.
3. Click the **Blank (Three Columns)** footer option.

The footer area opens with text fields at the left margin, the center, and the right margin of the document. You click a text field to select it and key your own text.

4. Click the text field at the left margin and key **Explorers Club**.
5. Click the text field in the center and key **Luis Gonzales**.

6. Right-click a slide thumbnail in the Reuse Slides pane and click **Insert All Slides** on the shortcut menu. All of the slides from the *notes* presentation now appear in the *atoms13* presentation.
7. Save the presentation and close the Reuse Slides pane.

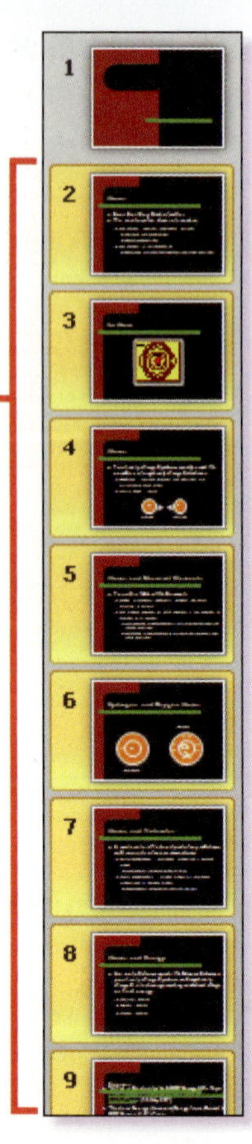

Reused slides inserted into *atoms13* presentation

Super! Some of the slides reused in the *atoms13* presentation contain clip art or shapes. Next, you will modify the clip art or shapes to change color, change style, and add a special effect.

## Modifying Clips and Shapes

When you insert or select a clip, the Picture Tools Format tab appears on the Ribbon. You can change a clip's color scheme and shape, add a border, crop it to a smaller size, position it on the slide or in relation to other objects, and perform other formatting tasks by clicking buttons on the Picture Tools Format tab.

Reused slide 3 contains a clip. You can modify the clip to make it more attractive by changing its color scheme and/or shape or by adding a border.

**Let's modify the clip on slide 3 to recolor it and apply a style.**

Picture Tools Format | Adjust | Color or Recolor

Picture Tools Format | Pictures Styles | More

1. Click **slide 3** in the Slides tab to make it the active slide.
2. Click the **clip** to select it and view the Picture Tools Format tab on the Ribbon.

6. Click the text field at the right margin and key or insert the current date in the mm/dd/yyyy format.
7. Click the **Home** tab, if necessary, and locate the **Font** group.
8. Select the footer text and click the **Font Color** button arrow in the Font group; then click **Blue** in the Standard Colors grid.
9. Double-click in the document area to close the footer area.

**CHECKPOINT**

Your *handout6* document should now look similar to this.

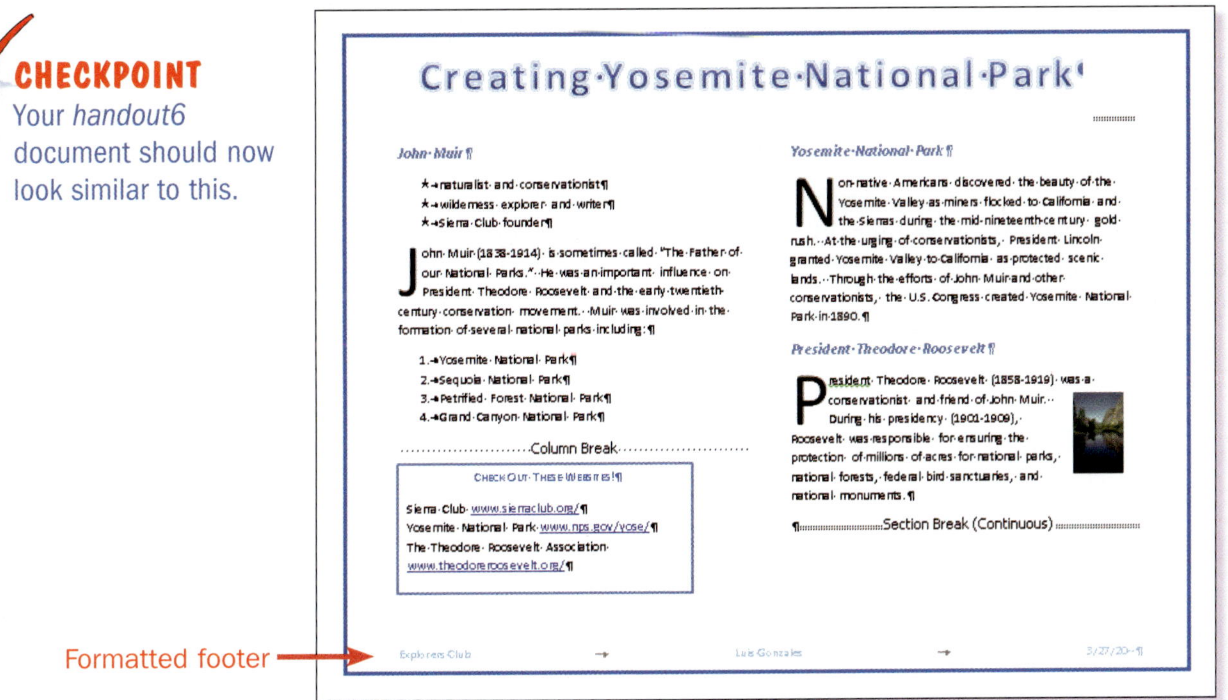


# Creating Yosemite National Park

*John Muir*

- naturalist and conservationist
- wilderness explorer and writer
- Sierra Club founder

John Muir (1838-1914) is sometimes called "The Father of our National Parks." He was an important influence on President Theodore Roosevelt and the early twentieth century conservation movement. Muir was involved in the formation of several national parks including:

1. Yosemite National Park
2. Sequoia National Park
3. Petrified Forest National Park
4. Grand Canyon National Park

Column Break

CHECK OUT THESE WEBSITES!

Sierra Club www.sierraclub.org/
Yosemite National Park www.nps.gov/yose/
The Theodore Roosevelt Association www.theodoreroosevelt.org/

*Yosemite National Park*

Non-native Americans discovered the beauty of the Yosemite Valley as miners flocked to California and the Sierras during the mid-nineteenth-century gold rush. At the urging of conservationists, President Lincoln granted Yosemite Valley to California as protected scenic lands. Through the efforts of John Muir and other conservationists, the U.S. Congress created Yosemite National Park in 1890.

*President Theodore Roosevelt*

President Theodore Roosevelt (1858-1919) was a conservationist and friend of John Muir. During his presidency (1901-1909), Roosevelt was responsible for ensuring the protection of millions of acres for national parks, national forests, federal bird sanctuaries, and national monuments.

Section Break (Continuous)

Explorers Club → Luis Gonzales → 3/27/20--

10. Save and close the document.

Congratulations! Luis's handout is ready to go!

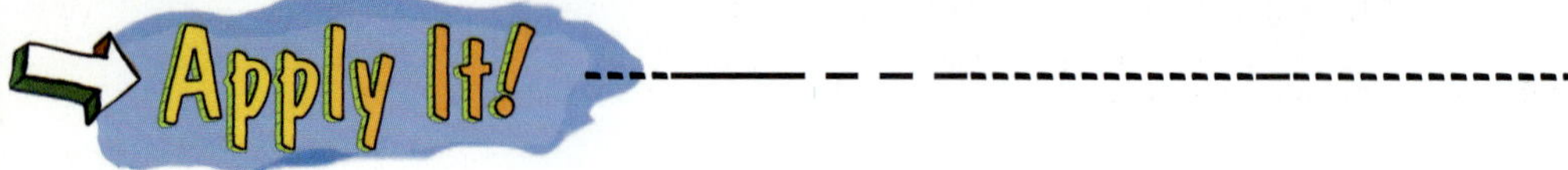


**Let's insert slides from an existing presentation into the *atoms13* presentation.**

Home | Slides | New Slide

1. Click the **Home** tab and locate the **Slides** group.
2. Click the **New Slide** button arrow in the Slides group and click **Reuse Slides** to open the Reuse Slides pane.
3. Click the **Open a PowerPoint File** link in the pane to open the Browse dialog box.
4. Switch to the folder that contains your data files and double-click the *notes* filename. The slides from the *notes* presentation appear in the Reuse Slides pane as thumbnails.

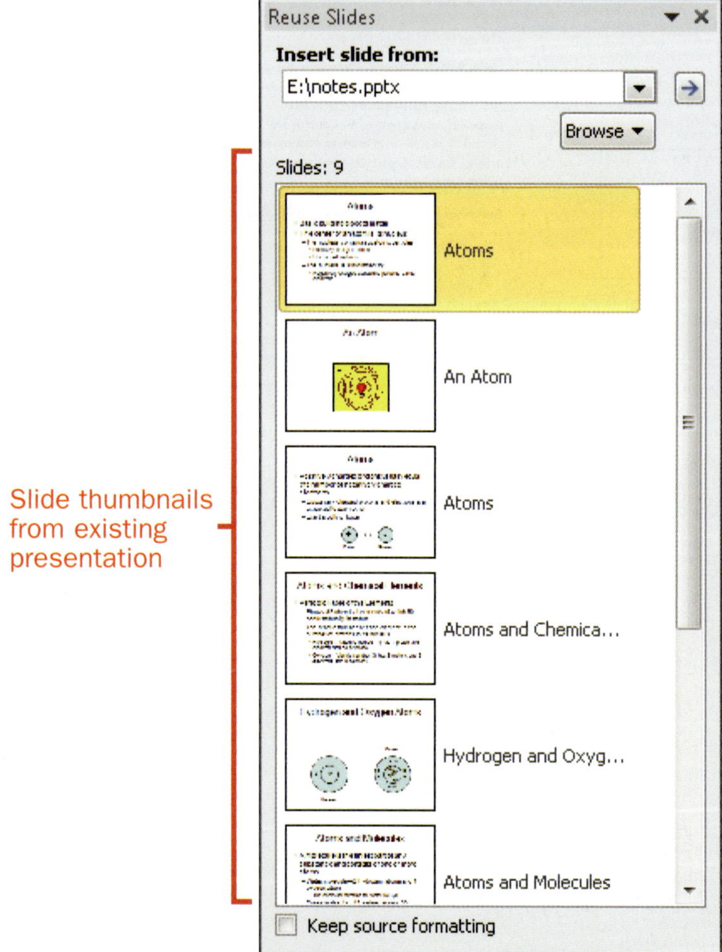


Slide thumbnails from existing presentation

5. Click the **Slides tab** below the Title Slide to indicate where the new slides should be inserted.

# Project Skills Review

You learned a lot in this project! We are very impressed with your progress. Let's take a few minutes to review the skills that you learned.

| Skill | How to | Button |
|---|---|---|
| **Change page orientation** | Click the **Page Orientation** button in the Page Setup group on the **Page Layout** tab. | Orientation |
| **Zoom a document to Page Width** | Click the **Page Width** button in the Zoom group on the **View** tab. | Page Width |
| **Create newsletter columns** | Click the **Columns** button in the Page Setup group on the **Page Layout** tab. | Columns |
| **Create bulleted or numbered lists** | Click the **Bullets** or **Numbering** button arrow in the Paragraph group on the **Home** tab. | |
| **Define a new bullet** | Click the **Bullets** button arrow in the Paragraph group on the **Home** tab and click **Define New Bullet**. | |
| **Apply the drop cap effect** | Click the **Drop Cap** button in the Text group on the **Insert** tab. | Drop Cap |
| **Open the Font dialog box** | Click the **Dialog Box Launcher** icon in the Font group on the **Home** tab. | |
| **Create a WordArt object** | Click the **WordArt** button in the Text group on the **Insert** tab. | WordArt |
| **Insert clip art using the Clip Art task pane** | Click the **Clip Art** button in the Illustrations group on the **Insert** tab. | Clip Art |
| **Convert an in line clip art object to a floating object** | Select the clip and click the **Wrap Text** or **Text Wrapping** button in the Arrange group on the **Picture Tools Format** tab. | Wrap Text; Text Wrapping |
| **Insert a text box** | Click the **Text Box** button in the Text group on the **Insert** tab. | Text Box |
| **Apply a shape or text box style** | Click the **More** button in the Shape Styles group on the **Drawing Tools Format** tab. Click the **More** button in the Text Box Styles group on the **Text Box Tools Format** tab. | |
| **Add a page border** | Click the **Page Borders** button in the Page Background group on the **Page Layout** tab. | Page Borders |
| **Add a footer** | Click the **Footer** button in the Header & Footer group on the **Insert** tab. | Footer |

3. Click **Browse for Themes** to open the Choose Theme or Themed Document dialog box.
4. Switch to the folder that contains your data files.
5. Double-click the *custom theme* filename. The theme formatting applied to the *custom theme* presentation is now applied to the *atoms13* presentation.

Your Title Slide should look like this.

Customized theme applied from an existing presentation

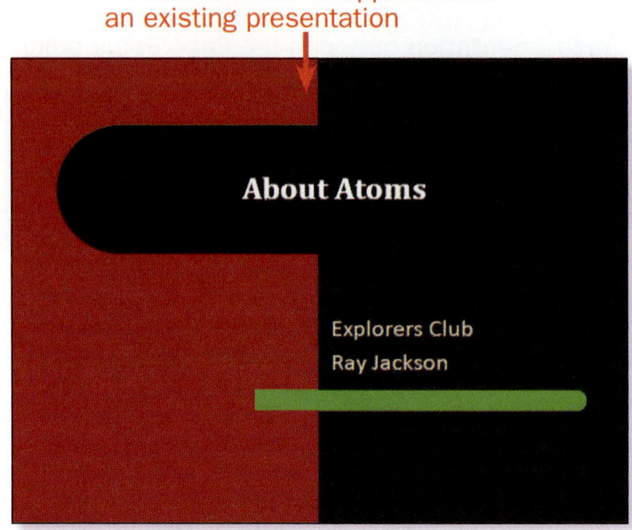


Nice job! Another way you can save time is to insert some or all of the slides from an existing presentation into your new presentation.

## Reusing Slides from Another Presentation

Ray has already added his research notes about atoms to several slides. He wants you to use these slides in the *atoms13* presentation.

You can easily insert Ray's existing slides into the *atoms13* presentation by using the Reuse Slides pane. To open the Reuse Slides pane, click the Home tab and then click the New Slide button arrow and click Reuse Slides.

You can add slides from an existing presentation to the pane and then insert one or more of them into your active presentation. By default, the inserted slides will be reformatted with the active presentation's theme.

# Exploring On Your Own

## Blaze Your Own Trail

You have learned several new skills in this project. Now blaze your own trail by practicing these skills on your own! Create an eye-catching flyer for the Explorers Club yard sale.

1. Open the *flyer* data file and save it as *flyer6*.
2. Change the page orientation to Landscape.
3. Format the title as WordArt.
4. Select the *When? Where?* and *What?* subheadings and details and create three newsletter columns. Insert a Column break to balance the text in three short columns, if necessary.
5. Paste the last sentence below the columns into a text box.
6. Center the text box below the three columns and format it with the style of your choice.
7. Add interest to the flyer with bulleted or numbered lists, symbols, pictures, heading styles, font styles, colored fonts, drop caps, special font effects, clip art, and page borders as desired. You might choose to apply a different document theme and work with that theme's color set.
8. Create a footer with *Explorers Club*, your name, and the date. Spell-check, save, and close the document.

## Reading in Action

### Using Suffixes

The word *conservation* means "the protection and preservation of something." It comes from the root word *conservare*, meaning "to keep or guard," and the suffix *-tion*, meaning "the act, condition, or result of." The suffix *-ist* means "one who practices." Use the meaning of the suffixes to write definitions of the words *preservation, preservationist, conservation, conservationist, naturalist.*

## Math in Action

### Understanding a Scatter Plot

The graph below is a scatter plot. The data points show two sets of data as ordered pairs: the number of trees per square mile and the town's population. Is there a relationship between the number of trees per square mile and the population of the town?

Draw a straight line, called a trend line, through the data so that there are about the same number of points above and below the line. A positive correlation (line goes up as you go left to right) means that trees per square mile increased as population grew; a negative correlation (line goes down) means that trees decreased as population grew.

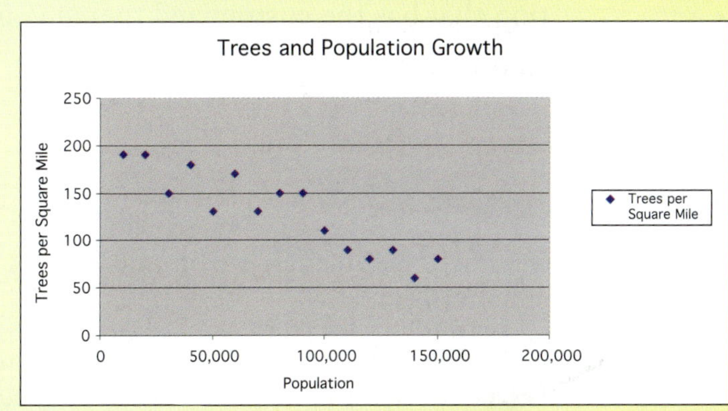

**Begin by creating and saving a new presentation. Then add the title and subtitle text to the Title Slide.**

1. Create a new blank presentation and save it as *atoms13*.
2. Key **About Atoms** as the title and **Explorers Club** and **Ray Jackson** as the subtitles on the Title Slide.

Good job! Now let's see how we can use two existing presentations to help us create a new one!

**ERGONOMICS TIP**

Are you holding your wrists in a neutral position as you key? Remember! Do not bend your wrists up or down!

## Applying a Theme from Another Presentation

In Projects 11 and 12, you learned how to dress up a presentation by applying a theme and customizing a theme's color scheme and font combination. If you already have a presentation with a customized theme that you like, you can save time by applying the customized theme from the existing presentation to your new one!

Just expand the theme gallery in the Themes group on the Design tab and click Browse for Themes to open the Choose Theme or Themed Document dialog box. Switch to the folder that contains your presentations and double-click the filename of the presentation that has the customized theme you want to apply.

**Let's apply a customized theme from an existing presentation to the *atoms13* presentation.**

Design | Themes | More

1. Click the **Design** tab and locate the **Themes** group.
2. Click the **More** button in the Themes group to expand the themes gallery. 

# Exploring *Across the Curriculum*

## Internet/Web

You can use the Web to learn about global warming. Open your Web browser and use a favorite or bookmark to view the Learning with Computers Web page (www.cengage.com/school/keyboarding/lwcorange). Click the **Links** option. Click **Project 6**. Click the links to research global warming. Take notes about what you learn.

1. Create a new document and save it as *global warming6*.
2. Use your notes to create a Landscape-oriented infographic about global warming.
3. Place some or all of the body text into newsletter columns.
4. Use WordArt clip art, bulleted or numbered lists, symbols, heading styles, font styles, borders, drop caps, colored fonts, and font effects as desired to make the infographic more interesting and fun. Save and close the document.

## Language Arts: Words to Know

Look up the meaning of the following terms in a classroom dictionary, CD-ROM dictionary or encyclopedia, or online dictionary.

| | | | |
|---|---|---|---|
| activism | conservation | environmentalist | habitat |
| National Park Service | natural resources | naturalist | Sierra Club |

Create a new document. Save the document as *definitions6*. Change the page orientation to Landscape and set the top margin to 2 inches. Key the title **Project 6 Definitions**. Bold and center the title. Then key each term on one line and the term's definition on the next line or lines. Select the title text and use it to create a WordArt text object with the style, shape, and font size of your choice. Select all of the terms and definitions and create two or three newsletter columns. Insert column breaks as necessary to create even columns. Add a page border. Spell-check, save, and close the document.

Explore More

# Project 13 Presentations and Multimedia

# Observing the Atom

## Explorers' Guide

**Data files:** **custom theme, notes, renewable energy, matter and energy**

**Objectives:**

In this project, you will:

- apply a theme from another presentation
- reuse slides from another presentation
- modify clips and shapes
- work with the slide master and slide footers
- add video and audio to slides
- add transition effects and set up a slide show

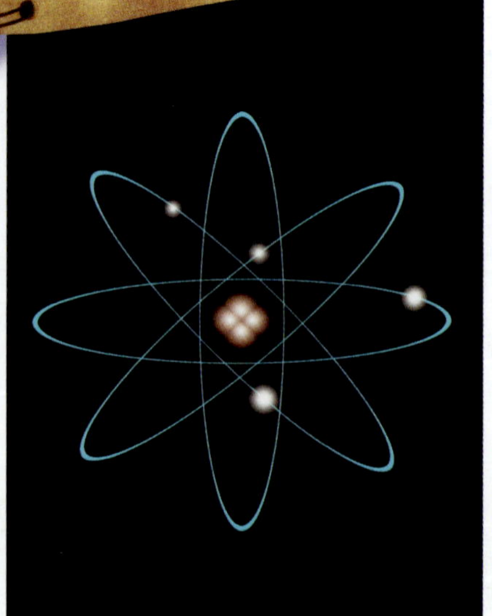

© IMAGE COPYRIGHT YURI4U80, 2009.
USED UNDER LICENSE FROM SHUTTERSTOCK.COM

## Our Exploration Assignment:

**Creating a new presentation from existing presentations, add video and audio, add transitions and timings, and set up the slide show**

Protons! Neutrons! Electrons! Quarks! The Explorers Club is continuing its study of matter and energy by learning about atoms. The members have already created some slides that Ray wants to use in his presentation. Can you help Ray get his presentation about atoms ready for the next meeting? Super! Follow the Trail Markers to apply a theme from another presentation, insert slides from another presentation using the Reuse Slides pane, work with the slide master, insert video and audio, and add transition effects. Then set slide timings and set up the slide show to run unattended in a continuous loop.

# Exploring *Across the Curriculum*

## Science: Research and Write

Use classroom, library, or online resources to research President Theodore Roosevelt and his interest in conservation. When was Theodore Roosevelt president? What event or events motivated him to lead the conservation movement? What was the outcome of his interest in conservation? Take notes about what you learn.

Use your notes to create an infographic that tells the story of President Theodore Roosevelt and conservation. Use Landscape orientation. Place the document's body text in two or three newsletter columns. Insert column breaks as necessary to create even columns. Create interesting WordArt text for the infographic. Use bulleted or numbered lists, symbols, drop caps, text boxes, borders, and font effects as desired. Insert, size, and position clip art. Add a footer with **Explorers Club**, your name, and today's date. Spell-check, save, and close the document.

## Getting Help

Click the Microsoft Word Help icon to open the *Word* Help window. Key **newsletter columns** in the search box. Follow the appropriate links to research how to manage newsletter column formatting. Open the *handout6* document you just modified and save it with a new name. Explore resizing columns, changing the number of columns, and removing columns. Close the document *without saving it*.

## Career Day

Working for the National Park Service to plan, conserve, and manage park areas and facilities offers a variety of interesting and useful public service careers. Using library, printed, or online resources, identify three interesting public service careers in government and public administration. Write a brief summary of each career, print your summary, and save it in your Career Day folder.

Explore More

# Project 12

Keyboarding

## 12a Review 5, 7, 3, 6, and 2

Key each line twice. Double-space between 2-line groups.

**TECHNIQUE TIP**

Reach up to the number keys without moving your hands away from your body.

**5**

1 f 5 f 5 | f r 5 f r 5 | f t 5 f t 5 | f5tr f5tr | f5rt f5r

2 5 and 8 and 5 and 1 and 5 and 9 and 5 and 4 and 50

**7**

3 j 7 j 7 | j u 7 j u 7 | ju7 ju7 | 78 78 | 71 71 | 79 79 | 747;

4 7 or 5 or 7 or 8 or 7 or 1 or 7 or 9 or 7 or 47 or

**3**

5 d 3 d 3 | d e 3 d e 3 | de3 de3 | 37 37 | 30 30 | 35 35 | 433;

6 a 3 b 3 c 3 d 3 e 3 f 3 g 3 h 3 i 3 j 3 k 3 l 3 m.

**6**

7 j 6 j 6 | j u 6 j u 6 | ju76 ju76 | 6jy6 6jy6 | juy6 juy6;

8 the 6 the 6 the 6 the 6 the 6 the 6 the 6 the 160;

**2**

9 s 2 s 2 | s w 2 s w 2 | xsw2 xsw2 | 2sx2 2sx2 | w2x2 w2x2;

10 20n, 21o, 22p, 23q, 24r, 25s, 26t, 27u, 28v, 29wx;

11 Flight No. 7938 left at 10:45 on October 26, 2005.

12 Checks 387, 391, and 406 were all dated August 25.

## 12b Build Skill

Key each line twice. Double-space between 2-line groups.

For additional practice:
**MicroType 5**
Numeric Keyboarding, Lessons 3–4

**Balanced-hand sentences**

1 Vivian may handle all the forms for the big firms.
2 A neighbor paid the men to fix the bicycle for us.
3 The men may pay for half of the maps for the city.
4 He may make a big profit if he owns the lake land.
5 Hans may go to the lake to work for the eight men.
6 Eight of them may form a panel to fix the problem.
7 The signs by the downtown spa may work for us too.

gwam 30" | 2 | 4 | 6 | 8 | 10 | 12 | 14 | 16 | 18 | 20 |

# Exploring Across the Curriculum

## Your Personal Journal

Open your personal journal document. Insert today's date and two blank lines. You have learned many new word processing skills in the past six projects. What word processing skills do you think will be most helpful in your school work? Why? Update your journal with one or two paragraphs that answer these questions. Spell-check, save, and close your journal.

## Online Enrichment Games  www.cengage.com/school/keyboarding/lwcorange

## Getting Help

Click the Microsoft PowerPoint Help icon below the *PowerPoint* application Close button to open the *PowerPoint* Help window. Key **gridlines and guides** in the search box and tap the ENTER key to research *PowerPoint's* gridlines and guides. Read about how to use them to align objects on a slide. Create a new presentation and change the Title Slide layout to a Blank slide. Insert clip art and draw shapes on the slide. Then display the gridlines and guides and use them to align the objects on the slide. Turn off the gridlines and guides; then close the presentation without saving it.

## Career Day

If you enjoy learning about chemistry and physics and sharing what you have learned with others, you might find a career in science education and training very rewarding. Using library, printed, or online resources, identify three interesting careers in science education and training. Write a brief summary of each career, print your summary, and save it in your Career Day folder.

## Your Personal Journal

Open your personal journal document. What is matter? How are the two components of matter—mass and volume—measured? What are some physical characteristics of matter that can be measured? How can you use your senses to describe matter? Update your journal with two or three paragraphs that answer these questions. Spell-check, save, and close your journal.

## Online Enrichment Games  www.cengage.com/school/keyboarding/lwcorange

## 6a Review m, x, p, and v

Key each line twice. Double-space between 2-line groups.

1 jm jm | mjm mjm | jmu jmu | jmn jmn | muj muj | mj nj mj nj;
m 2 make make | mark mark | math math | ream ream | fame fame;

3 sx sx | xs xs | swx swx | jsx jsx | jxk jxk | lwx lwx | cx cx;
x 4 exam exam | extra extra | expand expand | Maxine Maxine;

5 ; p; ; p; | p;p p;p | op; op; | p.p p.p | pojp pojp; | ;p ;p
p 6 page page | plan plan | cope cope | damp damp | open open;

7 fv fv; | vf vf | fbv fbf | bfv bfv | rvf rvf | jfv jfv | vf vf
v 8 five five | vain vain | move move | have have | even even;

## 6b Speed Check

1. Key a 1' timing on paragraph 1.
2. Determine the number of words you keyed.
3. Key another 1' timing on paragraph 1. Try to go two words a minute faster.
4. Repeat steps 1–3 for paragraph 2.
5. Key a 2' timing on paragraphs 1–2 combined.
6. Determine the number of words you keyed.

For additional practice:
**MicroType 5**
New Key Review, Alphabetic Lessons 14–15

**A** all letters used — gwam 2'

Each president since George Washington has had a Cabinet. 6
The Senate must approve them. It is the exception rather than the 13
rule for the president's choice to be rejected by this branch of the 20
government. In keeping with tradition, most of the Cabinet members 26
belong to the same political party as the president. 32

The purpose of the Cabinet is to provide advice to the 37
president on matters pertaining to the job of the president. The 44
person holding the office, of course, may or may not follow the 50
advice. Some presidents have frequently utilized their Cabinet. 57
Others have used it little or not at all. For example, President 63
Wilson held no Cabinet meetings at all during World War I. 69

gwam 2' | 1 | 2 | 3 | 4 | 5 | 6 |

# Exploring Across the Curriculum

## Language Arts: Words to Know

Look up the meaning of the following terms in a classroom dictionary, CD-ROM dictionary or encyclopedia, or online dictionary.

| freezing point | energy | state change | melting point |
|---|---|---|---|
| condensation point | physical property | boiling point | evaporation |

Create a new presentation. Save it as *definitions12*. Key **Changing States** as the title and **Definitions** as the subtitle on the Title slide. Apply the customized theme of your choice. Insert a Title and Content slide for each term and change its layout to Title Only. Key the name or term as the title. Then draw a text box and key the definition inside the text box. Resize, format, and position each text box as desired. Draw a shape over the text box; then change the order by sending the shape to the back. Drag the slide thumbnails in the Slides tab to reposition the slides in ascending alphabetical order by title. Run the slide show and then save and close the presentation.

## Science: Research, Write, and Present

Work with a classmate to use classroom, library, CD-ROM, or online resources to research six physical properties of matter: thermal conductivity, density, solubility, state, ductility, and malleability. Then create a new presentation to present what you learn. Apply the customized theme of your choice. Include a Title Slide and insert at least six slides with the layout of your choice to describe what you learned about the six physical properties. Use bulleted lists, clip art, pictures, text boxes, and shapes as needed to present your information. Insert Title and Content slides as necessary to cite your sources. Switch to Slide Sorter view and drag the slide thumbnails to reposition the slides in ascending alphabetical order by physical property. Run the slide show and then save and close the presentation.

Explore More

# Capstone Project Summary

Good News! It's Spring Break at last! During Spring Break, the Explorers Club members are participating in a special Career Day activity—a four-day internship at a local organization or business. Luis and Julie are interning at a catering company. Ray and Lin are interning at a Web design firm. You are interning at a veterinary clinic.

The veterinary clinic's office manager, Ms. Davis, will give your assignments to you each day. You will find these assignments at the end of each unit in this book.

## Capstone Project — Day 1

Today is your first day, and you meet with Dr. Wilson, the owner of the veterinary clinic. He gives you a tour of the clinic and describes the types of services the clinic provides to its clients, including small animal medical care and pet boarding and grooming services.

Next, Dr. Wilson introduces you to Ms. Davis, the clinic's office manager. Ms. Davis wants you to begin by helping her catch up with Dr. Wilson's reports and correspondence. She gives you a list of items that must be ready for his review by the end of the day. She asks you to:

- Create a multilevel list for Dr. Wilson's client meeting.
- Create a personal-business letter for Dr. Wilson's signature.
- Create an envelope for the personal-business letter.

## Capstone Project — Day 2

On your second day, Ms. Davis asks you to help by completing a few accounting tasks. She asks you to:

- Summarize vendor invoices in a new workbook.
- Complete next year's boarding and grooming services budget.
- Add a chart to the budget worksheet.

## Capstone Project — Day 3

On your third day, Ms. Davis asks you to work with Beverly, the receptionist, to create a slide show that Dr. Wilson can present at this year's Support Our Local Businesses conference. Beverly is on a tight deadline and asks you to:

- Create a new presentation and apply a theme.
- Reuse slides from another presentation.
- Format the slides with audio, clip art, transitions, and animation.
- Insert a summary slide with hyperlinks to other slides.
- Add speaker notes to the summary slide.

## Capstone Project — Day 4

Today is the last day of your Spring Break internship. Ms. Davis asks you to update Dr. Wilson's Address Book database and create a new database to contain client information. She needs you to:

- Add data to a table using a form.
- Sort and query the table and create a report using the Report Wizard.
- Create a new database and define table fields and field properties in Design view.
- Create a form using the Form Wizard.

# Exploring *Across the Curriculum*

## Internet/Web

Physics and chemistry are two scientific fields concerned with matter and energy. You can learn more about physics and chemistry by searching the Web. A Boolean Web search uses the word *and* or the *plus sign (+)* to include keywords in a search. For example, if you key the keywords *+physics +chemistry +.gov* in the Search text box, a search engine will find the URLs for those Web pages that contain the words *physics* and *chemistry* and the domain *.gov (government)* in the page's URL.

Open your Web browser and use a favorite or bookmark to view the Learning with Computers Web page (www.cengage.com/school/keyboarding/lwcorange). Click the **Links** option and click **Project 12**. Click the Google link. Key **+physics +chemistry +.gov** in the Google **Search** text box. *Be sure to key a space following each word; do not key a space following the plus sign*. Then click the **Google Search** button. Follow the links to learn more about government websites that support the physical sciences. Take notes about what you learn.

1. Create a new presentation and save it as *physical sciences12*.
2. Apply the customized theme of your choice.
3. Insert slides using the slide layout of your choice.
4. Add a title and subtitle text to the Title Slide.
5. Use bulleted lists, clip art, and shapes as desired to present what you learned. Remove any background graphics from slides on which the clip art, text boxes, or shapes appear. Group, distribute, and align slide objects as necessary.
6. Cite your sources on Title and Content slides at the end of your presentation.
7. Run the slide show. Then save and close the presentation.

**Explore More**

# Day 1 – Total Care Veterinary Clinic

How exciting! Today is the first day of your internship! You meet with Dr. Dave Wilson, the owner of Total Care Veterinary Clinic, who gives you a tour of the clinic and introduces you to Ms. Alana Davis, the clinic's office manager. Ms. Davis then takes you to your work area outside her office. She gives you instructions for logging on to the computer and asks you to create a new folder named *Clinic Assignments* in which to save all of your work.

Today you will help Ms. Davis by creating a multilevel list Dr. Wilson needs for a client meeting and a personal-business letter with an envelope. She gives you a list of tasks to complete by the end of the day.

### TO DO TODAY

1. Create a multilevel list for Dr. Wilson's client meeting
2. Create a personal business letter for Dr. Wilson's signature
3. Create an envelope for the personal-business letter

## Task #1 – The Multilevel List

1. Open the *Orange Day 1 Multilevel List data file* and save it as *Orange Day 1 Multilevel List sol* in the Clinic Assignments folder. With permission, print the document and then edit using proof-readers' marks. Indicate whether each paragraph should be demoted to Level II or Level III.
2. Change the document's margins to the appropriate margins for a multilevel list.
3. Select all of the text; change the font to Calibri 11 point and the line spacing to 1.15 with 10 points of spacing after each paragraph.
4. Center the **Your New Puppy** title horizontally.
5. Select the body text below the title and format it as a multilevel list. Use the I, II, III, A, B, C, 1, 2, 3 numbering. Demote Level II subtopics and Level III details based on your step 1 review.
6. Select the title and all of the Level 1 topics and change the case to UPPERCASE. Check spelling and grammar; save and close the document.

## Task #2 – The Personal-Business Letter

1. Open the *Orange Day 1 Letter data file* and save it as *Orange Day 1 Letter solution* in the Clinic Assignments folder.
2. Set the appropriate margins for a block format personal-business letter. Insert the *Orange Day 1 Contents data file* as the body of the letter. Remove any extra lines, if necessary.
3. Use drag and drop to reposition the second body text paragraph as the first body text paragraph.
4. Create a 2 x 6 table below the second body paragraph. Center the table between the left and right margins. Select the tabbed columns and remove the tab stops from the horizontal ruler.
5. Use Cut and Paste or drag and drop to move the text from the two tabbed columns into the two-column table. Resize the columns to fit by double-clicking the right boundary of each column.
6. Bold and center the column titles and then center the numbers in the Quantity column. Delete any remaining tab characters.
7. Select the blank line (paragraph formatting mark) below the table and remove the 10 points of spacing after the paragraph.
8. Check spelling and grammar; save the document.

## Task #3 – The Envelope

1. Open the *Orange Day 1 Letter solution*, if necessary, and add a size 10 envelope.
2. Use standard USPS formatting for the delivery address. Leave the return address blank. Save and, with permission, print the letter and envelope.

# Exploring On Your Own

## Blaze Your Own Trail

You have learned several new skills in this project. Now blaze your own trail by practicing these skills on your own!

1. Open the *matter* presentation and save it as *matter12*.
2. On the Title Slide, replace *Student Name* with your name.
3. Apply a different theme and customize the theme's color scheme and font combination.
4. Insert a new Title Only slide at the end of the presentation and remove its background graphics.
5. Key **Using Our Senses** as the title. Then insert clip art, text boxes, and shapes to illustrate using sight, touch, and smell to observe the physical properties of an object.
6. Distribute and align the slide objects attractively.
7. Group all of the shapes, text boxes, and clip art into one object.
8. Display the drawing guides and use them to arrange the single grouped object attractively on the slide.
9. Reposition **slide 5** (*Matter*) so that it becomes slide 2; then delete slide 4 (*Applying Physical Forces*).
10. Run the slide show; then save and close the presentation.

## Reading in Action

### Using Latin Root Words

The Latin word *materia* means "matter, physical substance." The Latin word *proprietas* means "own." Use the context clues in the *matter12* slide show and the meaning of the Latin root words to write definitions of the words *material*, *materialize*, *property*, and *proprietor*.

## Math in Action

### Converting Fahrenheit to Celsius

The states of matter can change due to forces of temperature. Water changes to ice at 32° Fahrenheit. What is the freezing temperature for water in °Celsius?

°Celsius = (°Fahrenheit – 32)(5/9)

°Fahrenheit = [(°Celsius)(9/5)] + 32

(°Fahrenheit – 32)(5/9) = (32 – 32)(.56) = 0° Celsius

Now you try it!

Water boils and becomes a gas at 100° Celsius. What is the boiling temperature of water in °Fahrenheit?

# WORKSHEETS

***Learning to solve problems by analyzing data is interesting and fun. Join Ray, Julie, Lin, and me as we use data to:***

- Explore Elements from the Periodic Table.
- Analyze Early U.S. Population Data.
- Create a Budget.
- Discover the Universe.

To complete these explorations, you will organize and analyze data using an application called *Excel*. You will learn how to create and open workbooks and how to enter data in worksheets. Then you will learn how to create formulas that let you add, subtract, and multiply numbers with a few clicks of your mouse. You will use special calculations, called functions, to find the largest, smallest, average, and total value of a group of numbers. You will also use functions to round the results of your calculations and perform a logical test on the data. You will even learn how to perform a *what-if analysis* on the data—*what* will happen to the data *if* some of the individual values change. Finally, you will learn how to turn worksheet data into attractive and useful pie and column charts. Let's go!

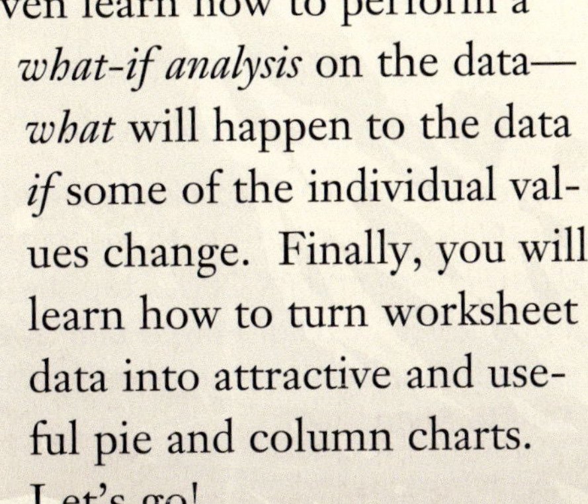

# Project Skills Review

You learned a lot in this project! We are very impressed with your progress. Let's take a few minutes to review the skills that you learned.

| | |
|---|---|
| **Customize a theme** | Click the **Theme Colors**, **Theme Fonts**, or **Theme Effects** button in the Themes group on the **Design** tab. |
| **Insert a new slide using the slide layout gallery** | Click the **New Slide** button arrow in the Slides group on the **Home** tab and click a layout in the gallery. |
| **Hide a slide's background graphics** | Click the **Hide Background Graphics** checkbox in the Background group on the **Design** tab. |
| **Insert clip art or a picture** | Click the **Clip Art** or **Insert Picture from File** button in the Illustrations group on the **Insert** tab. |
| **Draw text boxes and shapes** | Click the **Shapes** button in the Images or Illustrations group or **Text Box** button in the Text group on the **Insert** tab. |
| **Stack objects and move one object behind the other** | Draw a shape over another shape or text box. In *PowerPoint 2010*, click the **Send Backward** button in the Arrange group on the **Drawing Tools Format** tab. In *PowerPoint 2007*, click the **Send to Back** button in the Arrange group on the **Drawing Tools Format** tab. |
| **Group, distribute, and align objects on a slide** | Click the **Group** or **Align** button in the Arrange group on the **Drawing Tools Format** tab. |
| **Turn the drawing guides on or off** | Tap the ALT + F9 shortcut keys. |
| **Delete a selected slide** | In *PowerPoint 2007*, click the **Delete** button in the Slides group on the **Home** tab. In *PowerPoint 2010* or *PowerPoint 2007*, tap the DELETE key. In *PowerPoint 2010* or *PowerPoint 2007*, right-click a slide thumbnail in the Slides pane and click **Delete Slide**. |
| **Reposition a slide** | Drag a slide thumbnail to a new position in the Slides tab or in Slide Sorter view. |

# Exploring Elements from the Periodic Table

## Explorers' Guide

**Data file:** elements

**Objectives:**
In this project, you will:
- open, rename, and save a workbook
- navigate and select in a worksheet
- enter text and numbers
- format a worksheet
- sort data
- preview a worksheet and change page setup options

© IMAGE SOURCE/JUPITER IMAGES

## Our Exploration Assignment:

### Organizing data about elements and their properties

Did you know that hydrogen is the most abundant element in the universe? Or that nitrogen makes up 78 percent of Earth's air? Or that oxygen is the third most abundant element in our Sun? At the next Explorers Club meeting, members will learn about the Periodic Table of the Elements. Can you help Ray organize his notes in an *Excel* workbook for the meeting? Fantastic! Just follow the Trail Markers to learn how to open, rename, and save a workbook; navigate and select in a worksheet; enter, format, and sort data; and preview and print a worksheet.

## Deleting and Repositioning Slides

Luis reviewed the presentation and now wants you to make two changes. He wants slide 7 (*States of Water*) deleted and slide 2 (*Three Common States*) moved to the position of slide 4.

You can reposition a slide by using drag and drop in the Slides tab or Outline tab in Normal view or in Slide Sorter view.

You can delete a selected slide in Normal view or Slide Sorter view by tapping the DELETE key or by right-clicking the slide thumbnail and clicking Delete Slide.

Sometimes you may want to temporarily hide a slide instead of deleting it. To hide or unhide a slide, right-click the slide in the Slides tab and then click Hide Slide on the shortcut menu. A hidden slide is still visible in the Slides tab but does not appear in the slide show. Try it!

**Let's delete slide 7 and then reposition slide 2 using the Slides tab.**

1. Click the **slide 7** thumbnail in the Slides tab and tap the DELETE key.
2. Move the mouse pointer to **slide 2**, titled *Three Common States*.
3. Tap and hold down the mouse button and drag the slide immediately in front of **slide 5**. You will see a thin vertical line indicating where the slide will appear when you release the mouse button.
4. Release the mouse button. Slide 2 (*Three Common States*) is now slide 4.
5. Save and close the presentation.

New position for slide 2

Well done! Luis's presentation is ready for the meeting.

**Begin by starting the *Excel* application and opening a new blank workbook.**

1. Turn on your computer, if necessary.
2. Click the **Start** button on the taskbar.
3. Point to **All Programs** on the Start menu.
4. Click the ***Microsoft Office*** folder.
5. Click ***Microsoft Excel 2010*** or ***Microsoft Office Excel 2007*** to open the application.

If you have an icon on your desktop for *Excel*, just double-click it to open the application.

Terrific! You can use the *Excel* application to solve problems and analyze data by calculating totals, finding the smallest or largest value, sorting data into a specific order, or analyzing data in many other ways.

**ERGONOMICS TIP**

Need a break? Remember to take short exercise breaks when working at your computer! Stand up and stretch your muscles and shake your wrists every 30 minutes or so.

## 1 TRAIL MARKER — Opening, Renaming, and Saving a Workbook

The *Excel* window is similar to the *Word* window with a title bar, the Ribbon, the Quick Access Toolbar, and scroll bars. However, because the *Excel* application is used to analyze data and solve problems instead of creating text documents, it also has some great new features.

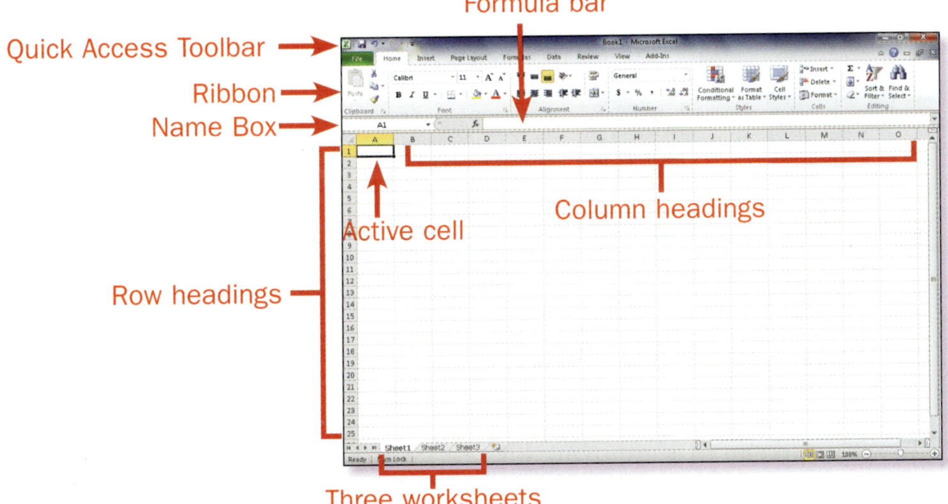

3. Click the **Drawing Tools Format** tab, if necessary; click the **Group** button in the Arrange group and click **Group**. The selected objects are now grouped into one object.

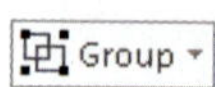


4. Tap the ALT + F9 shortcut keys to turn on the drawing guides. Dotted vertical and horizontal lines intersect at the center point of the slide.

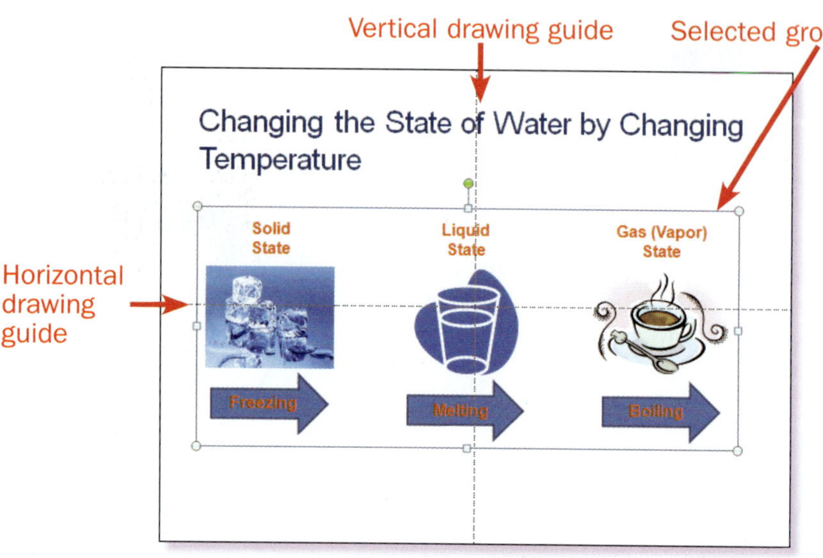


To turn on the drawing guides, you can click the Home tab and then click the Arrange button in the Drawing group, point to Align, and click Grid Settings to open the Grid and Guides dialog box. Finally, click the Display drawing guides on screen checkbox.

5. Drag or nudge the selected object until the vertical guide intersects the object's top and bottom center sizing handles.
6. Drag or nudge the selected object until the horizontal guide intersects the object's left and right sizing handles.
7. Tap the ALT + F9 shortcut keys to turn off the drawing guides.
8. Deselect the object and save the presentation.

**CHECKPOINT**

Your slide should look similar to this

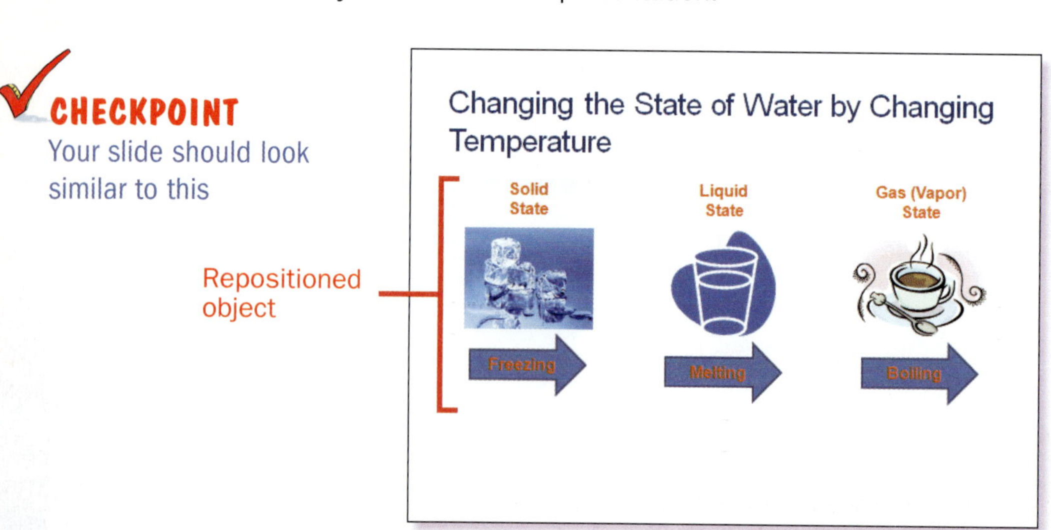


What a great-looking slide! To wrap up the presentation, let's reposition a slide and delete an unwanted slide.

Each time you start *Excel*, the application opens with a blank file called a workbook, which is temporarily named *Book1*. A workbook is a single file that contains multiple pages called worksheets. When you save a workbook, you give it a new unique name; all of the worksheets are saved together in the workbook file. By default, a new *Excel* workbook contains three worksheets named *Sheet1*, *Sheet2*, and *Sheet3*; however, it can contain up to 255 worksheets!

The term *spreadsheet* is sometimes used interchangeably with *worksheet*; however, when you work in the *Excel* application, the correct term is *worksheet*.

A worksheet has a grid of columns and rows similar to a *Word* table. Each worksheet grid is very large with 1,048,576 rows and 16,384 columns. Row headings are numbered from 1 through 1048576 and run down the left side of the worksheet. Column headings are lettered from A through XFD and run across the top of the worksheet.

The intersection of a column and row is called a cell. The active cell—the cell in which you can enter text or numbers—has a dark border around it. The cell's column heading and row heading is called a cell reference. The cell reference for the first cell in column A and row 1 is A1.

A group of adjacent cells is called a range. For example, the group of cells beginning with cell A1 and ending with cell B3 is the range A1:B3. You will use individual cell references or range references to enter data, select data, apply formatting, or create formulas to perform calculations on the data.

The Name Box, which shows the cell reference of the active cell, and the formula bar, which shows the contents of the active cell, appear immediately below the Ribbon.

To activate a worksheet, click its sheet tab—the tab at the bottom of the screen above the status bar. The default sheet tab names for the three worksheets in a new workbook are Sheet1, Sheet2, and Sheet3. You can rename each worksheet you use instead of leaving the default name. Just right-click the sheet tab and click Rename on the shortcut menu or double-click the sheet tab. Then key a new name in 32 or fewer characters (including spaces).

To create a new workbook, just click the File tab or Office Button and click New; then click the Blank workbook template icon, if necessary, and click Create. Try it!

You can open, rename, and save an existing workbook exactly like you would a *Word* document with commands on the File tab or Office Button menu. Remember! When you save a workbook, give it a unique filename that says something about its contents.

6. Select, vertically distribute, and align at their center points the remaining *Gas State* text box, the *steam* clip art, and the *Boiling* text box.
7. Deselect the objects and save the presentation.

**CHECKPOINT**
Your slide should look similar to this.

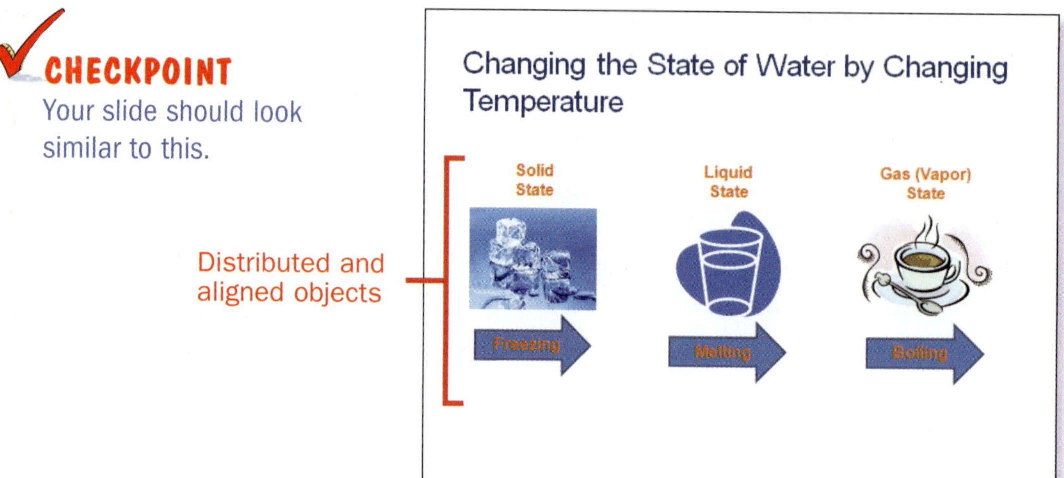


Nice work! Let's finish the slide by grouping the text boxes, clip art, and shapes into a single object, then use the vertical and horizontal drawing guides to reposition the object.

You can also display vertical and horizontal gridlines, similar to Excel worksheet gridlines, and use the gridlines to position or snap slide objects to the grid. To turn the display of gridlines on or off, click the Design tab and then click the Gridlines checkbox in the Show/Hide group.

### Using the Drawing Guides

The drawing guides are vertical and horizontal lines you can display on a slide to help you align objects. A quick way to turn the drawing guides on or off is to tap the ALT + F9 shortcut keys.

**Let's select and group all of the text boxes, clip art, and shapes, then reposition the grouped object using the drawing guides.**

Drawing Tools
Format | Arrange | Group

1. Move the mouse pointer above and to the left of the first text box.
2. Drag down and to the right to select all of the text boxes, clip art, and shapes; then release the mouse button.

**Let's open an existing workbook, rename the *Sheet1* tab, and save the workbook with a new name.**

1. Click the **File** tab or **Office Button** and click **Open** to open the Open dialog box.
2. Switch to your data files folder; double-click the *elements* workbook filename to open the workbook.
3. Click the **File** tab or **Office Button** and click **Save As** to open the Save As dialog box.
4. Switch to your solution files folder and save the workbook as *elements7*.
5. Double-click the *Sheet1* sheet tab.
6. Key **Elements** and tap the ENTER key.

Great! Now let's look at different ways to navigate and select in a worksheet. *Do not worry if you cannot read all of the worksheet cells' contents. In a later Trail Marker, you will format the worksheet to make it easier to read.*

The mouse pointer takes many different shapes in an *Excel* worksheet. You can move the mouse pointer to a Ribbon button, a column heading, the boundary between two rows, and a cell to see some of the pointer shapes. Check it out!

## Navigating and Selecting in a Worksheet

Before you can enter data in a cell, you must activate the cell using one of several methods. To activate a cell, you can:

- click a cell
- tap the TAB key or Right arrow key to activate the next cell to the right
- tap the SHIFT + TAB keys or tap the Left arrow key to activate the previous cell to the left
- tap the ENTER key to activate the next cell in the same column
- tap the Up or Down arrow key to activate the previous or next cell in the same column

3. Click the **Align** button in the Arrange group to view the alignment and distribution options and click **Align to Slide**, if necessary. This allows you to distribute the clips horizontally *in relation to the slide*.
4. Click the **Align** button in the Arrange group again and click **Distribute Horizontally** to distribute the selected clips horizontally in relation to the slide with an equal amount of spacing between each clip and between the edges of the slide and the clips.
5. Click the **Align** button in the Arrange group and click **Align Selected Objects**. This allows you to align the clips *in relation to each* other—not the slide.
6. Click the **Align** button in the Arrange group and click **Align Bottom**. The clips are aligned at their bottom points.
7. Deselect the clips.

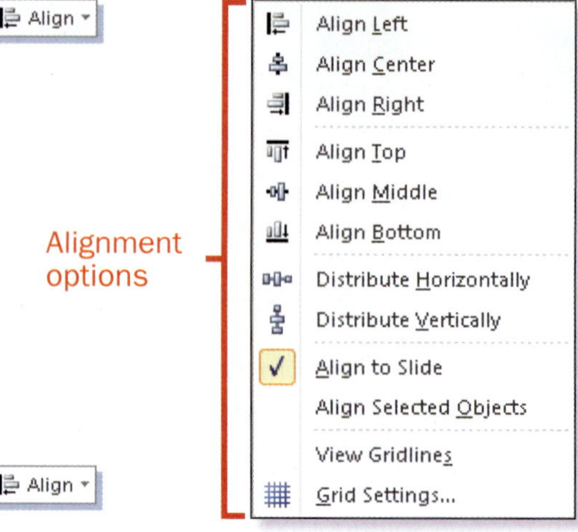

**Now let's distribute each related text box, clip art, and shape vertically *in relation to each other* and align them at their center points.**

1. Use the SHIFT key to select the *Solid State* text box, the *ice* clip art, and the *Freezing* text box and arrow.
2. Click the **Drawing Tools Format** tab, if necessary; then click the **Align** button in the Arrange group and click **Distribute Vertically** to space the objects vertically an equal distance apart.
3. Click the **Align** button in the Arrange group and click **Align Center**. The three objects are aligned at their center points.
4. Deselect the objects.

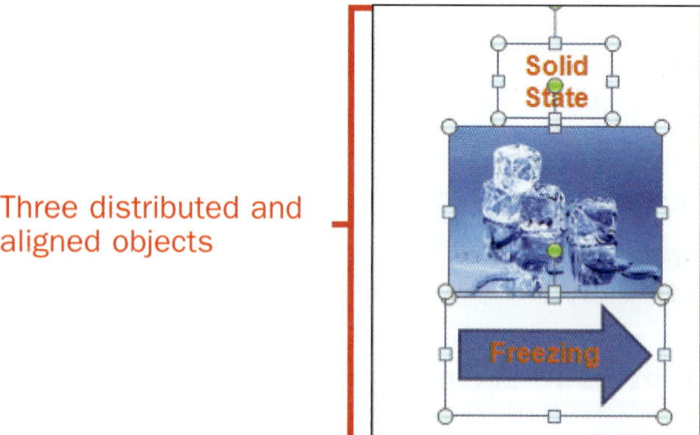


5. Select the *Liquid State* text box, the *water* clip art, and the *Melting* text box; then distribute the three objects vertically and align them at their center points.

You can use many of the keyboard shortcuts you learned in *Word* as you work in *Excel*. For example, tapping the CTRL + HOME keys in *Excel* makes the first cell at the top of the worksheet—A1, often called the home cell—the active cell.

Clicking a single cell, row heading, or column heading selects the contents of the cell, row, or column, respectively.

To select the contents of one or more ranges, multiple rows, or multiple columns, drag across the cells, row headings, or column headings with the mouse pointer.

You can also use the SHIFT + click method to select *adjacent* cells, rows, or columns; use the CTRL + click method to select *nonadjacent* cells, rows, or columns.

**Let's practice activating cells and selecting ranges.**

1. Move the large white plus sign mouse pointer to cell **C5**; then click cell **C5** to make it the active cell.
2. Move the large white plus sign mouse pointer to cell **A9**.
3. Tap and hold the mouse button and drag across the row to cell **G9**; then release the mouse button to select the range **A9:G9**.

| | | | | | | | |
|---|---|---|---|---|---|---|---|
| 8 | 4 | iron | Fe | 26 | 55.85 | 8B | 4 |
| 9 | 5 | copper | Cu | 29 | 63.55 | 1B | 4 |
| 10 | 6 | bromine | Br | 35 | 79.90 | 7A | 4 |

4. Click cell **A4**, tap and hold down the mouse button, and drag down and across to cell **D11**. Release the mouse button to select the range **A4:D11**.
5. Tap the CTRL + HOME keys to activate cell **A1**.
6. Tap and hold the SHIFT key and click cell **I13** to select the adjacent cells in the range **A1:I13**.
7. Tap the Down arrow to deselect the range.

| 3 | | | | |
|---|---|---|---|---|
| 4 | Item # | Element N | Atomic Sy | Atomic Nu |
| 5 | 1 | sodium | Na | 11 |
| 6 | 2 | nitrogen | N | 7 |
| 7 | 3 | potassiur | K | 19 |
| 8 | 4 | iron | Fe | 26 |
| 9 | 5 | copper | Cu | 29 |
| 10 | 6 | bromine | Br | 35 |
| 11 | 7 | radon | Rn | 86 |
| 12 | 8 | silicon | Si | 14 |

### Distributing and Aligning Slide Objects

Previously, you arranged the text boxes in relation to the clips by nudging them into position using the arrow keys. To more precisely arrange slide objects—clip art, text boxes, and shapes—neatly on a slide, you can distribute them so that there is an even amount of space between them in relation to each other or in relation to the slide; you can also align them vertically and horizontally in relation to each other or to the slide.

If you align objects incorrectly, don't worry. Just click the Undo button on the Quick Access Toolbar and try again!

Instead of trying to position slide objects using drag and drop, let *PowerPoint* do the work! First, select the objects; then click the Drawing Tools Format tab and click the Align button in the Arrange group to view distribution and alignment options.

- Click Align to Slide to distribute or align objects *in relation to the slide.* Click Align Selected Objects to distribute or align objects *in relation to each other.*
- Click Distribute Horizontally or Distribute Vertically to position three or more objects in relation to the slide or to each other.
- Click Align Top, Align Middle, or Align Bottom to align *horizontal* objects across the slide through their top or bottom edge or middle position. *Be careful! Using these commands to align selected vertical objects stacks them on top of each other.*
- Click Align Left, Align Center, or Align Right to align vertical objects down the slide through their left or right edge or center position. *Warning! Using these commands to align selected horizontal objects stacks them on top of each other.*

Now you are ready to more precisely arrange the objects on the slide by distributing and align the clip art, text boxes, and shapes.

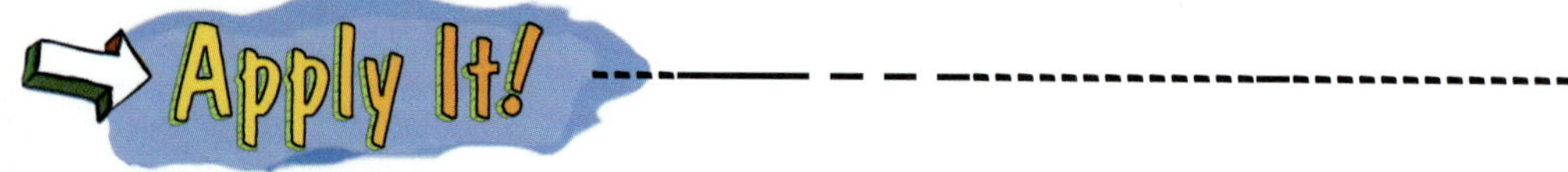


**First, let's distribute the clip art horizontally *in relation to the slide* and align all three clips at their bottom position *in relation to each other.***

Drawing Tools
Format | Arrange | Align

1. Tap and hold the SHIFT key and click each clip to select all three clips.
2. Click the **Drawing Tools Format** tab, if necessary, and locate the **Arrange** group.

8. Select the range **B5:B12**; then tap and hold the CTRL key and select the range **D5:D12** to select two *nonadjacent* ranges.

| 4 | Item # | Element N | Atomic Sy | Atomic Nu |
|---|---|---|---|---|
| 5 | 1 | sodium | Na | 11 |
| 6 | 2 | nitrogen | N | 7 |
| 7 | 3 | potassium | K | 19 |
| 8 | 4 | iron | Fe | 26 |
| 9 | 5 | copper | Cu | 29 |
| 10 | 6 | bromine | Br | 35 |
| 11 | 7 | radon | Rn | 86 |
| 12 | 8 | silicon | Si | 14 |
| 13 | | | | |

9. Click the row **6** heading to select the entire row; then click the column **H** heading to select the entire column.
10. Drag across the column headings **D:F** to select multiple columns.
11. Drag across the row headings **5:9** to select multiple rows.
12. Tap an arrow key or click a cell to deselect the rows.

Fantastic! Now you are ready to update Ray's worksheet by adding two more elements.

## Entering Text and Numbers

Entering text and numbers in a cell is a three-step process:

Step 1: Activate the cell.
Step 2: Key the text or numbers.
Step 3: Enter the data by activating a different cell.

The most common ways to enter data in a cell are by tapping the ENTER key, the TAB key, or an arrow key or by clicking another cell.

By default, text is aligned at the left of a cell and numbers are aligned at the right of a cell.

With practice, using the numeric keypad on the right side of your keyboard instead of the numbers on the top row of the keyboard can make entering numbers easier and faster. Tap the numbers on the numeric keypad just like you do on a calculator. You can also tap the decimal point and ENTER keys on the numeric keypad.

**Let's group each text box with its accompanying shape. Before you begin, make sure slide 8 (the Title Only slide) is visible in the slide pane.**

Drawing Tools
Format | Arrange | Group

1. Move the mouse pointer above and to the left of the Freezing block arrow and text box. The mouse point is a left pointing arrow or selection pointer.
2. Drag down and to the right to select both the block arrow shape and the text box in front of the block arrow shape. As you drag, make certain the blue selection color covers *both* the arrow shape and the text box. When you release the mouse button, both objects are selected.

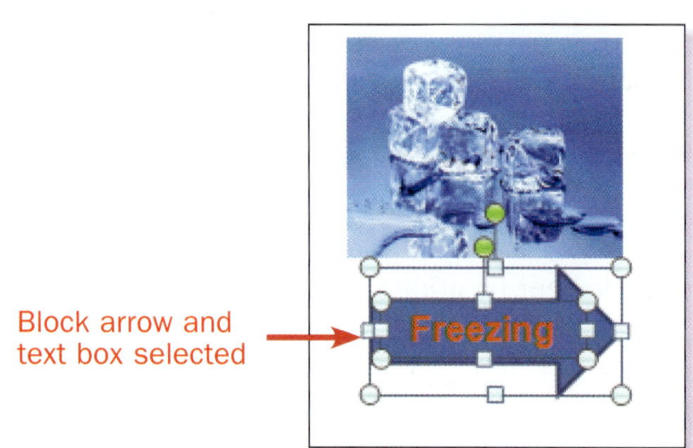


3. Click the **Drawing Tools Format** tab, if necessary, and locate the **Arrange** group.
4. Click the **Group** button in the Arrange group to view grouping options.

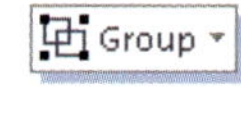

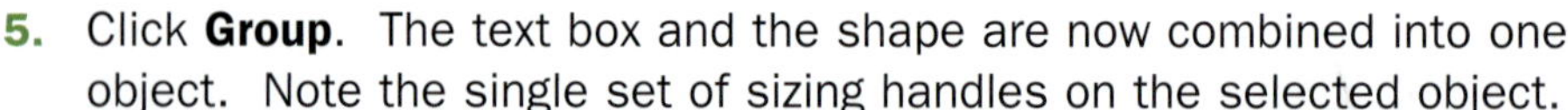

5. Click **Group**. The text box and the shape are now combined into one object. Note the single set of sizing handles on the selected object.
6. Deselect the grouped object; then using the previous steps as your guide, group the Melting text box and related block arrow and group the Boiling text box and related block arrow.
7. Deselect the objects.

You can also group, ungroup, distribute, and align selected objects by clicking the Home tab and then clicking the Arrange button in the Drawing group to view grouping and alignment options.

*Warning!* Be sure to tap the Num Lock key, if necessary, to turn on the numeric keypad before you use it to key numbers. If the Num Lock key is not turned on, the numeric keypad keys revert to their alternate use, which is to navigate the worksheet.

*Excel*'s AutoComplete feature helps you enter the same text in different cells in the same column. Suppose that a previous cell in the same column contains the text *nonmetal*. As soon as you begin to key *nonmetal* in a new cell in the same column, *Excel* automatically fills the cell with *nonmetal*.

To accept *Excel*'s AutoComplete text, just tap the ENTER or TAB key to move to the next cell. If you do not want to accept the text, just continue keying.

Here are Ray's notes about the two additional elements he wants you to add to the worksheet.

| Element Name | Atomic Symbol | Atomic Number | Atomic Mass | Group | Period | Metal, Metalloid, Nonmetal | Liquid, Gas, Solid | Interesting Fact |
|---|---|---|---|---|---|---|---|---|
| hydrogen | H | 1 | 1.01 | 1A | 1 | nonmetal | gas | most abundant element in the universe |
| helium | He | 2 | 4.00 | 8A | 1 | nonmetal | gas | lowest melting point of any element |

**Let's enter the data for the two new elements using several methods.**

1. Tap the NUM LOCK key, if necessary, to turn on the numeric keypad.
2. Click cell **A13** and key **9**; then tap the TAB key to activate cell **B13**.
3. Key **hydrogen** and tap the ENTER key and the Left arrow key, if necessary, to activate cell **A14**.
4. Key **10** and tap the TAB key.
5. Key **helium**, tap the Right arrow key, and tap the Up arrow key to activate cell **C13**.
6. Key **H** and tap the Right arrow key.
7. Key **1** using the numeric keypad and tap the ENTER key on the numeric keypad to activate cell **D14**.
8. Tap the Left arrow key to activate cell **C14** and key **He**.
9. Click cell **E13** to activate it.
10. Continue to use Ray's notes and the numeric keypad, ENTER key, TAB key, or arrow keys to enter the remaining data for the two elements; then save the workbook with the same name in the same location by clicking the **Save** button on the Quick Access Toolbar.

6. Click the **Drawing Tools Format** tab, if necessary, and locate the **Arrange** group.
7. If you are using *PowerPoint 2010*, click the **Send Backward** button in the Arrange group. If you are using *PowerPoint 2007*, click the **Send to Back** button in the Arrange group. The arrow shape is moved behind the text box so that the word *Freezing* appears inside the arrow.

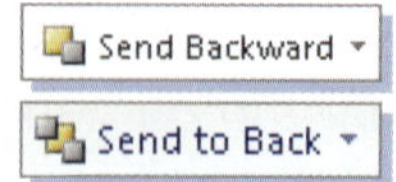


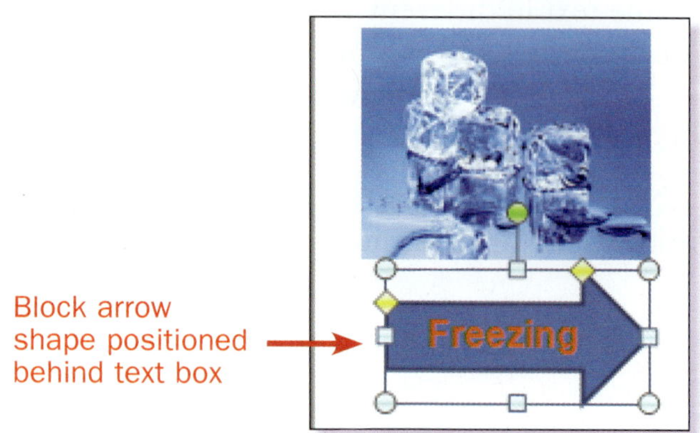


8. Copy the arrow shape twice, drag each arrow shape over the remaining two text boxes, and send the arrow shape behind the text box.

**CHECKPOINT**

Your text boxes, clip art, and shapes should now look similar to this.

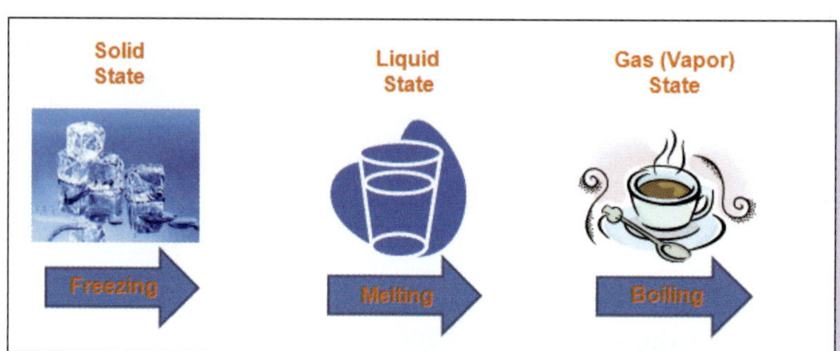


Super! Now you are ready to arrange the clip art, text boxes, and shapes more neatly on the slide.

## Grouping, Distributing, and Aligning Slide Objects

Grouping objects allows you to combine multiple objects into one object. This allows you to move or reposition all objects at one time. You can group and ungroup selected objects by clicking the Drawing Tools Format tab and then clicking the Group button in the Arrange group to view grouping options.

To keep the *Freezing*, *Melting*, and *Boiling* text boxes together with their block arrow shapes, let's group them.

**CHECKPOINT**
Your rows 13 and 14 should look like this.

Added data

| 13 | 9 hydrogen | H | 1 | 1.01 | 1A | 1 | nonmetal | gas | most abundant element in the universe |
|---|---|---|---|---|---|---|---|---|---|
| 14 | 10 helium | He | 2 | 4.00 | 8A | 1 | nonmetal | gas | lowest melting point of any element |

What a super job! Now you are ready to format the worksheet to make it easier to read.

## 4 Formatting a Worksheet

TRAIL MARKER

Formatting cell contents in *Excel* is much like formatting text in *Word*. For example, you can change the font or font size and align the contents inside the cell using the same Ribbon buttons you used in *Word*. But *Excel* also has many new formatting features, such as merging and centering text across a range of cells.

**Merging Cells, Font Styles, Horizontal Alignment, and Wrapping Text**

The Merge & Center button in the Alignment group on the Home tab allows you to merge a range of cells into one cell and then center the contents over the range. The Alignment group also contains the Wrap Text button you can click to wrap multiple lines of text inside a cell.

To apply other formatting options, such as the Italic and Bold font styles or numeric formatting, you can click buttons in the Font and Number groups on the Home tab.

Do you remember some of the keyboard shortcuts you used in *Word* to apply formatting? You can use many of those same keyboard shortcuts, such as CTRL + I and CTRL + B, to apply formatting to cell contents.

You already learned how to use the Format Painter button in the Clipboard group on the Home tab to copy and paste formats in a *Word* document. You can use it the same way in *Excel*!

You can quickly open the Format Cells dialog box by clicking the Dialog Box Launcher icon in the Font, Alignment, or Number groups on the Home tab or by tapping the CTRL + 1 keyboard shortcut keys. Try it!

### Drawing and Stacking Shapes

You can stack text boxes and shapes on top of each other and then move one of the objects in the stack to the front or back of the other objects in the stack.

You can also position a selected clip or shape in back of or in front of another clip or shape by clicking the Picture Tools Format or Drawing Tools Format tab and clicking a button in the Arrange group. Check it out!

To practice the concept of direction, you will draw a right-pointing block arrow shape on top of the *Freezing* text box and then move the arrow shape behind the text box.

Insert | Illustrations | Shapes

Drawing Tools Format | Arrange | Send Backward

**Let's draw an arrow shape on top of each text box and then position the arrow shapes behind the text boxes.**

1. Click the **Insert** tab, if necessary, and locate the **Illustrations** group.
2. Click the **Shapes** button in the Illustrations group to view a gallery of shapes.
3. Click the **Right Arrow** shape (the first arrow in the first row) in the Block Arrows group in the gallery.
4. Move the mouse pointer above and to the left of the word *Freezing*.
5. Drag down and to the right to draw a right-pointing block arrow shape just slightly larger than the text box. Release the mouse button to draw the shape.

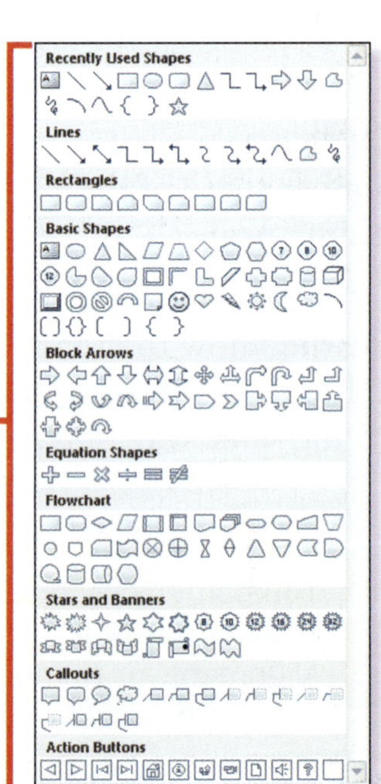


Shapes gallery

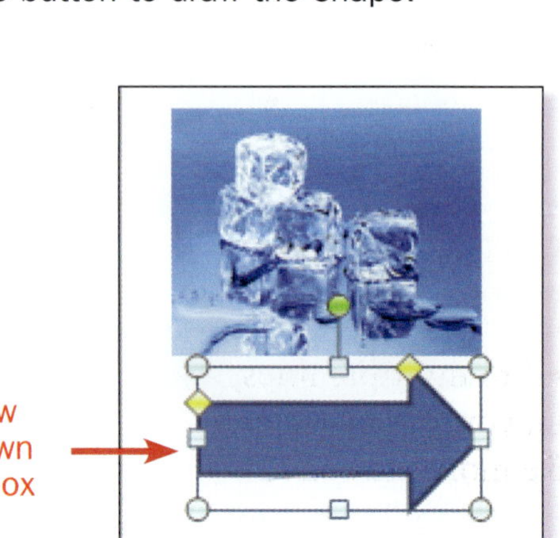

Block arrow shape drawn over text box

Home | Alignment | Merge & Center, Center, or Wrap Text

Home | Font | Bold

Home | Clipboard | Format Painter

**Let's make the *Elements* worksheet easier to read and more attractive by centering the title and subtitle text across the top of the worksheet and applying the Bold font style, centering the contents of individual cells or an entire column, applying the Italic font style to a range of cells, and wrapping text inside a cell.**

1. Click the **Home** tab, if necessary, and locate the **Clipboard**, **Font** and **Alignment** groups.
2. Select the range **A1:J1** and click the **Merge & Center** button in the Alignment group.
3. Click the **Bold** button in the Font group.

The individual cells in the range are merged into one cell, and the worksheet title is bolded and centered in the cell.

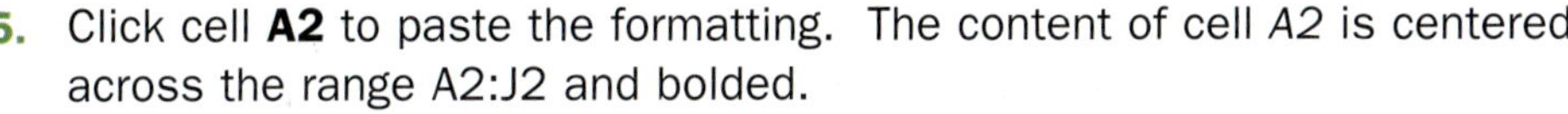

4. Click cell **A1**, if necessary, and click the **Format Painter** button in the Clipboard group to copy the formatting.
5. Click cell **A2** to paste the formatting. The content of cell *A2* is centered across the range A2:J2 and bolded.
6. Select the range **B5:B14** and tap the CTRL + I keys to apply the Italic font style.
7. Select the range **C5:G14** and click the **Center** button in the Alignment group to center-align the contents in each cell.
8. Select the range **A4:J4** and click the **Wrap Text** button in the Alignment group to wrap the long column names inside the cells.
9. Click the **Center** button in the Alignment group to center the wrapped text inside the cells.
10. Click the **Bold** button in the Font group to bold the column labels. 
11. Tap the CTRL + HOME keys to activate A1 (the home cell) and save the workbook.

The Numbering group on the Home tab contains the Accounting Number Format, Percent Style, Comma Style, Increase Decimal, and Decrease Decimal buttons. Use these buttons to format a range of numbers with dollar signs, commas, percent signs, and decimal places. Check it out!

Excellent! The too-long column names are now wrapped to multiple lines, centered inside each cell, and bolded. In the next section, you will change the column widths so that the wrapped column names are more attractive and easier to read.

**Let's select all of the text boxes and center the contents in each box. Then we'll select each text box and nudge it into position using the arrow keys.**

Home|Paragraph|Center

Insert|Text|Text Box

Home|Font|Font Color or Bold

1. Tap and hold the SHIFT key and click each text box to select all three text boxes.
2. Center the contents of all of the text boxes and deselect them.
3. Select each text box and tap the Up or Down arrow key, as necessary, to position it approximately a half inch above the clip art or pictures. Tap the Left or Right arrow key, as necessary, to align closer to the center point of its related clip art. *Do not worry if the three text boxes and clip art are not exactly aligned. You will modify the alignment in the next Trail Marker.*

Text boxes nudged into position

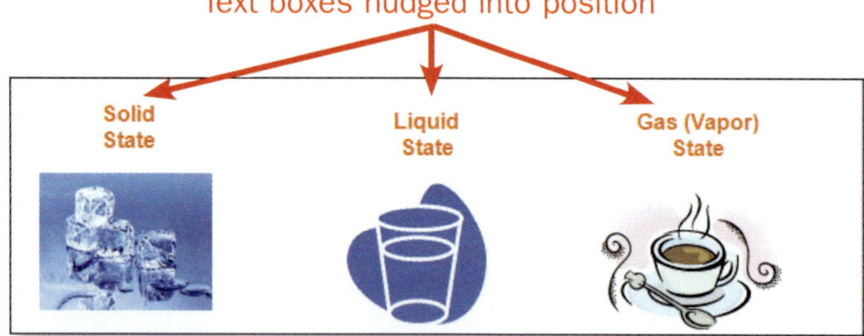


Now let's repeat these steps to create three text boxes that will go below the clip art or pictures.

4. Draw a text box, key **Freezing**, and position the text box below the *ice* clip art or picture. Center the contents, change the font color, and apply the Bold font style.
5. Select the text box and tap the CTRL + D keys twice to duplicate the selected text box.
6. Drag one text box below the *water* clip art or picture and the other text box below the steam clip art or picture.
7. In the second text box, replace *Freezing* with **Melting**; in the third text box, replace *Freezing* with **Boiling**.
8. Select each text box and nudge it up, down, left, or right until it is approximately a half inch below the center point of its related clip art or picture; then deselect the text boxes.

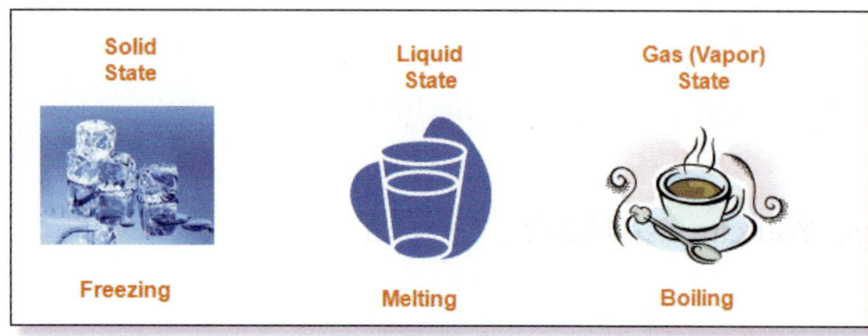

## Resizing Columns and Rows

To quickly change the column width or row height, drag a column or boundary with the resizing pointer. As you drag the boundary, a ScreenTip shows the current column width or row height.

A quick way to resize a column is to double-click a column boundary with the resizing pointer. *Excel* then resizes the column automatically *to fit* the longest cell contents in the column.

You can also change row height or column width by clicking the Format button in the Cells group on the Home tab and then clicking Row Height or Column Width.

**Let's let *Excel* automatically resize columns A–J to fit the cell contents. Then we'll resize column H to 10.0 and row 4 to 45.0.**

1. Drag across the column headings *A:J* to select all ten columns.
2. Move the mouse pointer to the column J right boundary. The mouse pointer becomes a resizing pointer.
3. Double-click the column J boundary to have *Excel* automatically resize the columns.
4. Click anywhere in the worksheet to deselect the columns.
5. Place the mouse pointer on the boundary between columns H and I.
6. Tap and hold down the mouse button to see the ScreenTip.
7. Slowly drag the boundary to the right until the ScreenTip indicates a 10.0 column width; then release the mouse button.
8. Place the mouse pointer on the boundary between rows 4 and 5.
9. Slowly drag up until the ScreenTip shows 45.0.
10. Tap the CTRL + HOME keys and save the workbook.

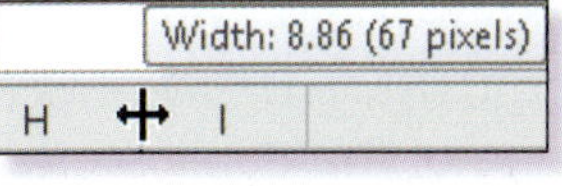

Your worksheet should look like this.

A1 — Periodic Table of the Elements

| | A | B | C | D | E | F | G | H | I | J |
|---|---|---|---|---|---|---|---|---|---|---|
| 1 | Periodic Table of the Elements | | | | | | | | | |
| 2 | Some Interesting Elements | | | | | | | | | |
| 3 | | | | | | | | | | |
| 4 | Item # | Element Name | Atomic Symbol | Atomic Number | Atomic Mass | Group | Period | Metal, Metalloid, Nonmetal | Liquid, Gas, Solid | Interesting Fact |
| 5 | 1 | *sodium* | Na | 11 | 22.99 | 1A | 3 | metal | solid | fourth most abundant element on earth |
| 6 | 2 | *nitrogen* | N | 7 | 14.01 | 5A | 2 | nonmetal | gas | makes up 78% of the Earth's air |
| 7 | 3 | *potassium* | K | 19 | 39.10 | 1A | 4 | metal | solid | essential for plant growth |
| 8 | 4 | *iron* | Fe | 26 | 55.85 | 8B | 4 | metal | solid | Earth's core may be largely iron |
| 9 | 5 | *copper* | Cu | 29 | 63.55 | 1B | 4 | metal | solid | good conductor of heat and electricity |
| 10 | 6 | *bromine* | Br | 35 | 79.90 | 7A | 4 | nonmetal | liquid | only nonmetallic liquid element |
| 11 | 7 | *radon* | Rn | 86 | 222.00 | 8A | 6 | nonmetal | gas | heaviest known gas |
| 12 | 8 | *silicon* | Si | 14 | 28.09 | 4A | 3 | metalloid | solid | one of the most useful elements |
| 13 | 9 | *hydrogen* | H | 1 | 1.01 | 1A | 1 | nonmetal | gas | most abundant element in the universe |
| 14 | 10 | *helium* | He | 2 | 4.00 | 8A | 1 | nonmetal | gas | lowest melting point of any element |
| 15 | | | | | | | | | | |

Good work! Ray wants to rearrange the data. You can use *Excel*'s powerful sorting tools to do this.

Insert | Text | Text Box

Home | Font | Font Color or Bold

**Let's draw, format, and resize text boxes. Before you begin, make sure you are viewing slide 8, the Title Only slide with clip art.**

1. Click the **Insert** tab, if necessary, and locate the **Text** group.
2. Click the **Text Box** button in the Text group and move the mouse pointer to the slide above the ice clip. The mouse pointer becomes a drawing pointer.
3. Drag down and to the right to draw a small text box above the *ice* clip.

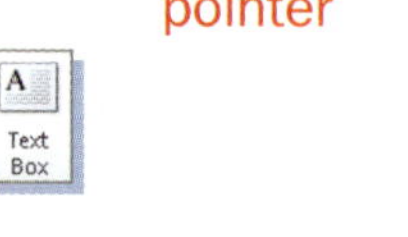

After you draw the text box, the Home tab becomes the active Ribbon tab. Remember! You can select the text in a text box and format it using buttons in the Font or Alignment group on the Home tab.

4. Key **Solid State** in the text box.
5. Select the text, change the font color to a color of your choice, and apply the Bold font style.
6. Click the text box boundary to select the text box and its contents.
7. Tap the CTRL + D keys twice to create two duplicate text boxes.
8. Drag one of the duplicate text boxes above the *water* clip art or picture.
9. Drag the other duplicate text box above the *steam* clip art or picture.
10. Edit the text box above the *water* clip art or picture to replace *Solid* with **Liquid**.
11. Edit the text box above the *steam* clip art or picture to replace *Solid* with **Gas (Vapor)**.
12. Size the text boxes, if necessary, to force the word *State* to a second line.

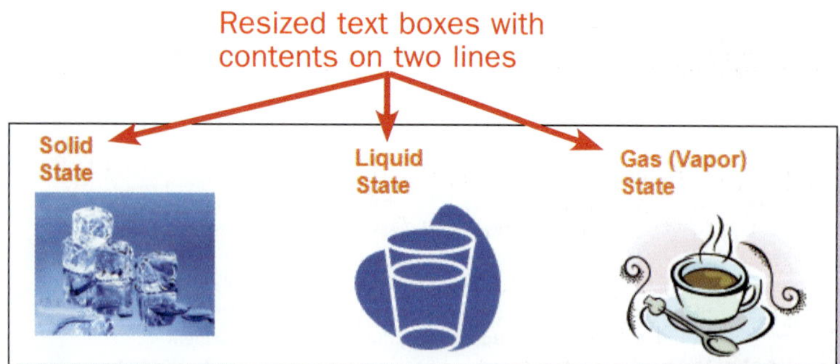


You can select multiple slide objects, such as the text boxes, by holding down the SHIFT key as you click the objects. You can nudge selected chart objects a small distance at a time by tapping an arrow key.

If you are working in *PowerPoint 2010*, you might see the Smart Guides—vertical or horizontal dashed lines—as you position multiple shapes on a slide. The Smart Guides, which are turned on by default in the Grid and Guides dialog box, show you when multiple shapes are aligned.

## Sorting Data

Sorting means to put text and numbers in ascending order (from A to Z or from 0 to 9) or descending order (from Z to A or from 9 to 0). You should arrange data to be sorted in a special way, called a data range, so that the data is easier to sort.

It is a good idea to add an item number as the first cell in each row in a data range. Then no matter how you sort the data, you can always resort it by the item number to place the data range data in its original order!

An *Excel* data range has rows of related data; the first row contains unique column names and is formatted differently than the data in the following rows. You should leave a blank row above and below a data range, a blank column to the right of a data range, and a blank column to the left of a data range that does not begin in column A. This allows *Excel* to identify the boundaries of a data range and to *automatically* select all of the rows and columns in the data range when it is sorted.

**Single Column Sort**

To quickly sort a data range by a single column, activate a cell in a column you want to sort *inside the boundaries of the data range* and click the Sort & Filter button in the Editing group on the Home tab to view sorting and filtering options.

**Let's sort the data range in ascending order by the liquid, gas, or solid data found in Column I and then return the data range to its original order.**

Home | Editing | Sort & Filter

1. Look at the data in the range A4:J14. The rows contain related data; the first row contains unique, formatted column names; the rows above and below the range are blank; and the column to the right of the range is blank. The data in the range A4:J14 is organized as an *Excel* data range.
2. Click cell **I5** to activate any cell within the data range boundaries and inside the column to be sorted.
3. Click the **Home** tab, if necessary, and locate the **Editing** group.

## Drawing Text Boxes and Shapes

You can create a text box, a container for text, by clicking the Insert tab, clicking the Text Box button in the Text group, and then:

- moving the mouse pointer to the slide; the mouse pointer becomes a drawing pointer
- dragging down and across to draw the text box
- keying text in the text box
- clicking outside the text box to deselect it

You can draw other shapes—rectangles, lines, ovals, arrows, and so forth—by clicking the Insert tab and then clicking the Shapes button in the Illustrations group to view a gallery of available shapes.

Next, click a shape in the gallery and, just like drawing a text box, drag down and to the right with the drawing pointer to draw the shape on the slide.

You can also draw and format shapes with buttons in the Drawing group on the Home tab. Check it out!

The text box or shape formatting is automatically determined by the applied theme. But you can change text box or shape formatting with buttons on the Drawing Tools Format tab that appears when a text box or shape is selected.

By default, text boxes and shapes are inserted as floating objects, and they can be repositioned using drag and drop. You can copy and paste a selected slide object—such as a text box or shape—by using the CTRL key and drag and drop or by tapping the CTRL + D keyboard shortcut keys.

Remember to drag a corner sizing handle to resize a text box or shape proportionally. Tap and hold the CTRL key and drag a corner sizing handle to resize a text box or shape proportionally from the center outward. Try it!

**Drawing and Positioning Text Boxes**

Now that you have inserted three pictures on slide 8, let's insert a text box and label above each picture. The easiest way to create three text boxes is to create the first one, then use the CTRL + D shortcut keys to copy it two times.

4. Click the **Sort & Filter** button in the Editing group to view sorting and filtering options. Because column I contains alphabetic data, the alphabetical sorting options appear.
5. Click **Sort A to Z**. *Excel* selects all of the data in the range A4:J14 and sorts it in ascending order by gas, liquid, or solid.

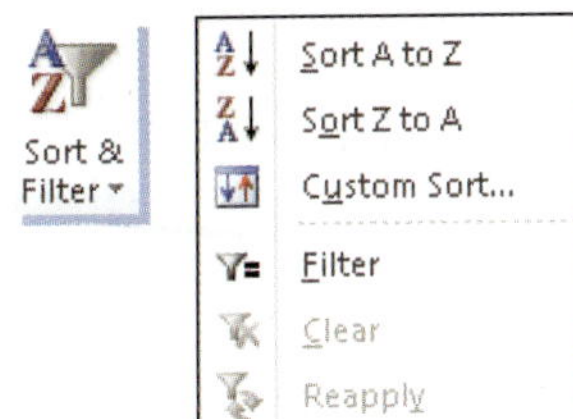


Data sorted in gas, liquid, or solid order

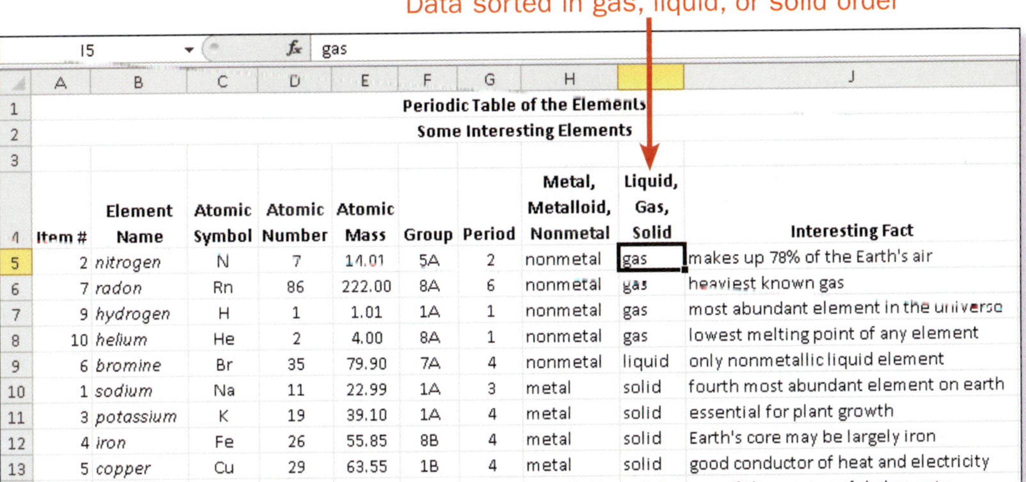

I5 | gas

| | A | B | C | D | E | F | G | H | I | J |
|---|---|---|---|---|---|---|---|---|---|---|
| 1 | | | | | | Periodic Table of the Elements | | | | |
| 2 | | | | | | Some Interesting Elements | | | | |
| 3 | | | | | | | | | | |
| 4 | Item # | Element Name | Atomic Symbol | Atomic Number | Atomic Mass | Group | Period | Metal, Metalloid, Nonmetal | Liquid, Gas, Solid | Interesting Fact |
| 5 | 2 | nitrogen | N | 7 | 14.01 | 5A | 2 | nonmetal | gas | makes up 78% of the Earth's air |
| 6 | 7 | radon | Rn | 86 | 222.00 | 8A | 6 | nonmetal | gas | heaviest known gas |
| 7 | 9 | hydrogen | H | 1 | 1.01 | 1A | 1 | nonmetal | gas | most abundant element in the universe |
| 8 | 10 | helium | He | 2 | 4.00 | 8A | 1 | nonmetal | gas | lowest melting point of any element |
| 9 | 6 | bromine | Br | 35 | 79.90 | 7A | 4 | nonmetal | liquid | only nonmetallic liquid element |
| 10 | 1 | sodium | Na | 11 | 22.99 | 1A | 3 | metal | solid | fourth most abundant element on earth |
| 11 | 3 | potassium | K | 19 | 39.10 | 1A | 4 | metal | solid | essential for plant growth |
| 12 | 4 | iron | Fe | 26 | 55.85 | 8B | 4 | metal | solid | Earth's core may be largely iron |
| 13 | 5 | copper | Cu | 29 | 63.55 | 1B | 4 | metal | solid | good conductor of heat and electricity |
| 14 | 8 | silicon | Si | 14 | 28.09 | 4A | 3 | metalloid | solid | one of the most useful elements |

Now let's return the data range to its original order by sorting the item numbers in ascending order.

6. Click cell **A6** and click the **Sort & Filter** button in the Editing group. Because column A contains numeric data, the numeric sorting options appear.
7. Click **Sort Smallest to Largest**. *Excel* selects all of the data in the data range and sorts it in ascending order by item number—placing the data in its original order.

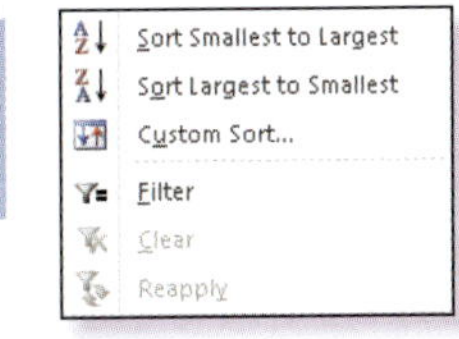


You can also click the Data tab and then click buttons in the Sort & Filter group to sort a data range or open the Sort dialog box to create a custom sort. Try it!

**Multicolumn Sort**

Sometimes you want to sort data in a more complex way, perhaps by two or three columns. For example, in a data range containing names of U.S. cities and the states in which each city is located, you may want to sort the data range first by state and then by city within each state.

To resize clip art or a picture, select it and drag a boundary sizing handle with the mouse pointer. To reposition clip art or a picture, select it and drag it to a new location using the mouse pointer.

**Let's insert, resize, and reposition pictures of ice, water, and steam.**

**Insert | Images or Illustrations | Clip Art**

1. Click **slide 8**, the Title Only slide, in the Slides tab to make it the active slide, if necessary.
2. Key **Changing the State of Water by Changing Temperature** in the title placeholder. The font size will automatically change to fit the text inside the placeholder.
3. Click the **Insert** tab and locate the **Images** or **Illustrations** group.
4. Click the **Clip Art** button in the Illustrations group to open the Clip Art task pane on the right side of the *PowerPoint* window.
5. Search for clip art or a picture using the keyword *ice*.
6. Insert the clip art or picture of your choice, resize it, and drag it to the left side of the slide.
7. Search for clip art or a picture using the keyword *water*.
8. Insert the clip art or picture of your choice, resize it, and drag it to the center of the slide.
9. Search for clip art using the keyword *steam*.
10. Insert the clip art or picture of your choice, resize it, and drag it to the right side of the slide.
11. Deselect the clip art, close the task pane, and save the presentation.

*Don't worry about the exact position of each clip; you will carefully position them on the slide in Trail Marker 5.*

Your slide should look similar to this.

Changing the State of Water by Changing Temperature

Excellent! Now let's insert and format some text boxes and shapes.

A two- or three-column custom sort is performed by setting sort criteria in the Sort dialog box. Open the Sort dialog box by clicking the Sort & Filter button in the Editing group and then clicking Custom Sort.

You set sort criteria in the Sort dialog box in decreasing order of importance, then set the primary or most important sort criteria first, set the secondary or next most important criteria second, and so forth.

Home | Editing | Sort & Filter

**Let's sort the data range first by Period in ascending order and then by Element Name in ascending order.**

1. Click any cell within the data range boundaries.
2. Click the **Sort & Filter** button in the Editing group.
3. Click **Custom Sort** to select the data range and open the Sort dialog box.
4. Click the dialog box **Sort by** arrow and click **Period**. *Excel* uses the content of the Period column to automatically set the Sort On and Order criteria.

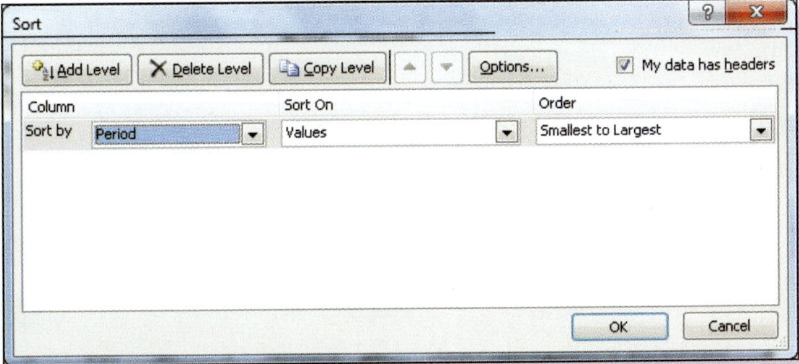


5. Click the dialog box **Add Level** button to add another set of criteria boxes.
6. Click the **Then by** arrow and click **Element Name**. Again, the Sort On and Order criteria are automatically set based on the content of the Element Name column.

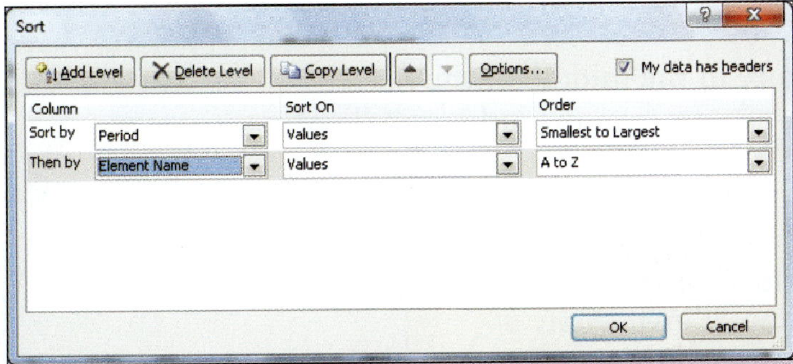


7. Click **OK**.

4. Click the **New Slide** button arrow in the Slides group to view a gallery of slide layout options. 
5. Click the **Title Only** slide layout to insert a new Title Only slide following slide 7.

Click to add title

The new slide now has only a title placeholder, but you can still see the background graphics. You can turn the background graphics off or on by clicking the Hide Background Graphics checkbox in the Background group on the Design tab.

**Let's turn off the background graphics on slide 8.**

Design | Background | Hide Background Graphics

1. Click the **Design** tab and locate the **Background** group.
2. Click the **Hide Background Graphics** checkbox in the Background group to insert a check mark.

Hide Background Graphics

3. Save the presentation.

The background graphics are removed from the current slide; all of the remaining slides still have the background graphics. Now you are ready to add a title to slide 8 and insert clip art.

TRAIL MARKER

## Inserting and Resizing Clip Art

The default Title and Content layout has icons you can click to insert a picture or clip art on the slide instead of a bulleted list. However, clip art or pictures can be inserted on any slide by clicking the Clip Art or Insert Picture from File buttons in the Images (2010) or Illustrations (2007) group.

*PowerPoint* inserts clip art or a picture in the middle of the placeholder that contains the picture or clip art icon or in the middle of a Blank or Title Only slide.

Did you know that you can recolor clip art or a picture, change its shape, or format it in a variety of ways by clicking buttons on the Picture Tools Format tab? Check it out!

The data range is sorted in ascending order by Period (the primary sort) and then in ascending order by Element Name (the secondary sort).

**CHECKPOINT**

Your sorted data should look like this.

| | A | B | C | D | E | F | G | H | I | J |
|---|---|---|---|---|---|---|---|---|---|---|
| 1 | | | | | | Periodic Table of the Elements | | | | |
| 2 | | | | | | Some Interesting Elements | | | | |
| 3 | | | | | | | | | | |
| 4 | Item # | Element Name | Atomic Symbol | Atomic Number | Atomic Mass | Group | Period | Metal, Metalloid, Nonmetal | Liquid, Gas, Solid | Interesting Fact |
| 5 | 10 | *helium* | He | 2 | 4.00 | 8A | 1 | nonmetal | gas | lowest melting point of any element |
| 6 | 9 | *hydrogen* | H | 1 | 1.01 | 1A | 1 | nonmetal | gas | most abundant element in the universe |
| 7 | 2 | *nitrogen* | N | 7 | 14.01 | 5A | 2 | nonmetal | gas | makes up 78% of the Earth's air |
| 8 | 8 | *silicon* | Si | 14 | 28.09 | 4A | 3 | metalloid | solid | one of the most useful elements |
| 9 | 1 | *sodium* | Na | 11 | 22.99 | 1A | 3 | metal | solid | fourth most abundant element on earth |
| 10 | 6 | *bromine* | Br | 35 | 79.90 | 7A | 4 | nonmetal | liquid | only nonmetallic liquid element |
| 11 | 5 | *copper* | Cu | 29 | 63.55 | 1B | 4 | metal | solid | good conductor of heat and electricity |
| 12 | 4 | *iron* | Fe | 26 | 55.85 | 8B | 4 | metal | solid | Earth's core may be largely iron |
| 13 | 3 | *potassium* | K | 19 | 39.10 | 1A | 4 | metal | solid | essential for plant growth |
| 14 | 7 | *radon* | Rn | 86 | 222.00 | 8A | 6 | nonmetal | gas | heaviest known gas |

Your worksheet looks great! Now you are ready to preview and print it!

## Previewing a Worksheet and Changing Page Setup Options

You can preview and print a worksheet just as you previewed and printed a *Word* document. To preview your worksheet, click the File tab and click Print (*Excel 2010*) or click the Office Button, point to Print, and click Print Preview (*Excel 2007*).

Unlike a *Word* document, however, it is often better to preview a worksheet *as* you change its page setup by changing the page orientation, changing margins, resizing data by scaling it up or down to fit better on the page, and so forth.

To make the *Elements* worksheet easier to read, let's change the page orientation to Landscape, scale the worksheet data to print on one page, and add a custom header and a predefined footer as we preview it. You can make all of these changes in the Page Setup dialog box.

You can add the Print Preview button to the Quick Access Toolbar in both *Excel 2010* and *Excel 2007*, then click the button to quickly switch to the Print tab or to Print Preview.

### Opening the Page Setup Dialog Box in *Excel 2010*

You can change individual page setup settings by clicking the File tab and then clicking options in the Settings group in the Print tab. To save time when you have multiple settings to change, you can open the Page Setup dialog box by clicking the Page Setup link in the Print tab, then change all of the settings.

12. Click the font combination of your choice that best suits both the Title Slide and the Title and Content slides to apply the font combination to all of the slides in the presentation.

Your Title Slide with the customized theme could look similar to this.

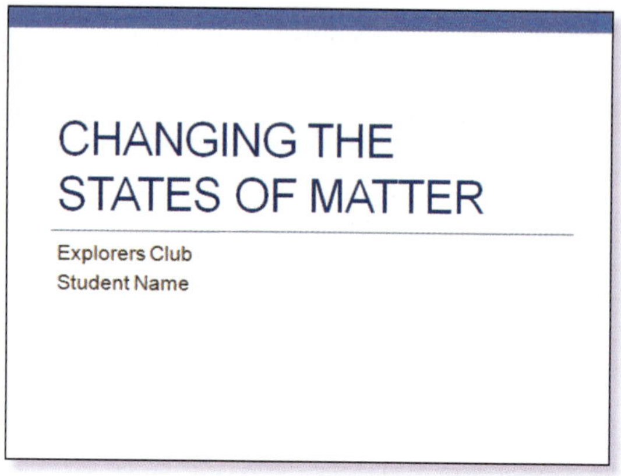

CHANGING THE STATES OF MATTER

Explorers Club
Student Name

Great job! Next, let's insert a new slide and remove the background graphics.

## Inserting a New Slide Using the Slide Layout Gallery

Luis wants to add a slide that uses pictures, drawings, and text boxes to illustrate how water changes from a solid to a liquid to a gas when its temperature increases or decreases. He wants the slide to have a title but no other placeholders.

You can insert a Title Only slide by clicking the Home tab and then clicking the New Slide button arrow in the Slides group to view a gallery of slide layout options including the Title Only option.

You can also insert a default Title and Content slide and then change its layout to Title Only. Right-click the slide, point to Layout, and click Title Only. Try it!

**Let's insert a new Title Only slide at the end of the presentation.**

Home | Slides | New Slide

1. Click the **Home** tab and locate the **Slides** group.
2. Scroll the **Slides** tab to view the last slide, slide 7.
3. Click below slide 7 in the Slides tab to insert a blinking horizontal line; this line indicates where the new slide will be inserted.

**Let's open the Page Setup dialog box.**

1. Click the **File** tab and click **Print** to view your worksheet in the Print tab.

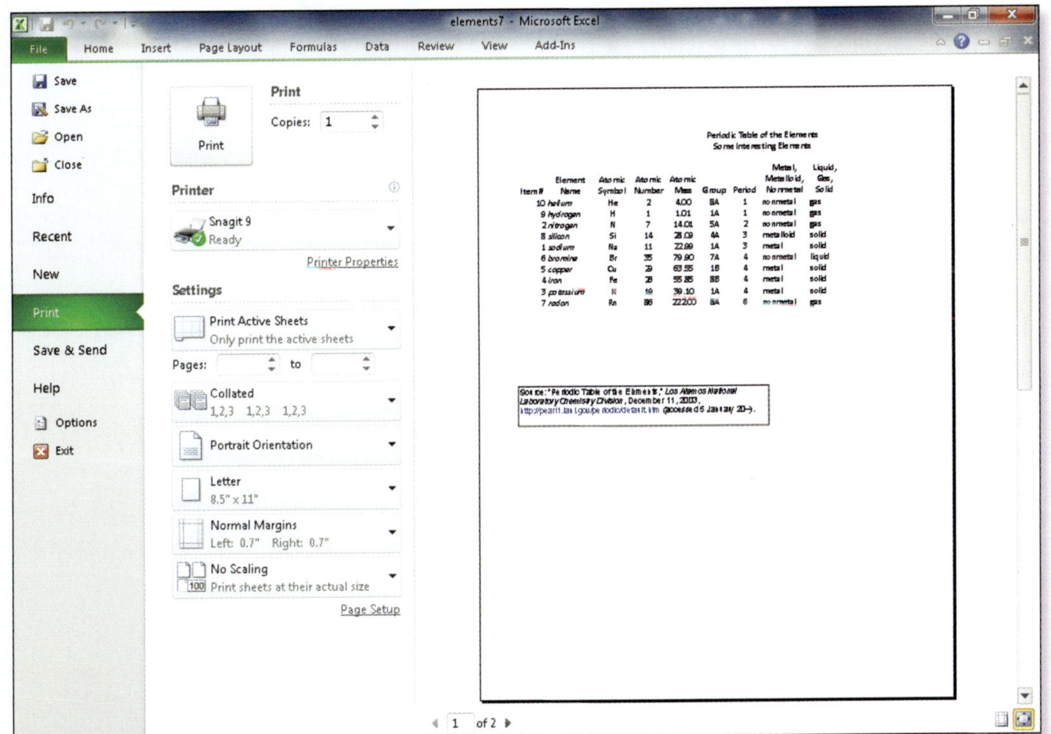


2. Locate the **Page Setup** link below the Settings options.
3. Click the **Page Setup** link to open the Page Setup dialog box.

Next, you change multiple settings in the Page Setup dialog box.

**Opening the Page Setup Dialog Box in *Excel 2007***

To change a worksheet's page setup options as you preview it, click the Page Setup button in the Print group on the Print Preview tab to open the Page Setup dialog box.

5. Click the theme of your choice to apply the theme to the slides.

You can customize a theme to change the theme's color scheme by clicking the Design tab and clicking the Theme Colors button in the Themes group to view a gallery of color scheme options; then you choose a different color scheme in the gallery.

6. Click the **Theme Colors** button in the Themes group to view the color scheme gallery.
7. Use live preview to see how different color schemes change the look of the Title Slide.
8. Click the color scheme of your choice in the color scheme gallery to apply the new color scheme.

Theme Colors gallery

You can also add interest to the slides by changing the font, font style, and font size combination used on the slides. Before you change a theme's font combination, use live preview to see how a new font combination looks when applied to a Title and Content slide in addition to the Title Slide.

9. Click the **Theme Fonts** button in the Themes group to view a gallery of font combinations.

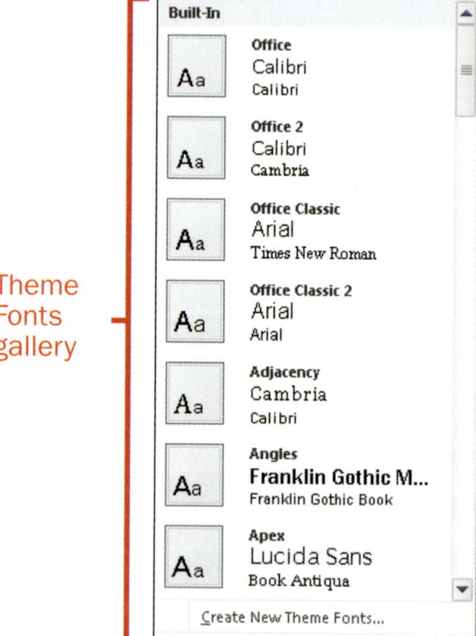

Theme Fonts gallery

10. Use live preview to see how different font combinations look when applied to the Title Slide.
11. Click a Title and Content slide, such as slide 2, in the Slides tab and use live preview to see how different font combinations look when applied to a Title and Content slide.

**Let's open the Page Setup dialog box.**

1. Click the **Office Button**, point to **Print**, and click **Print Preview**. 

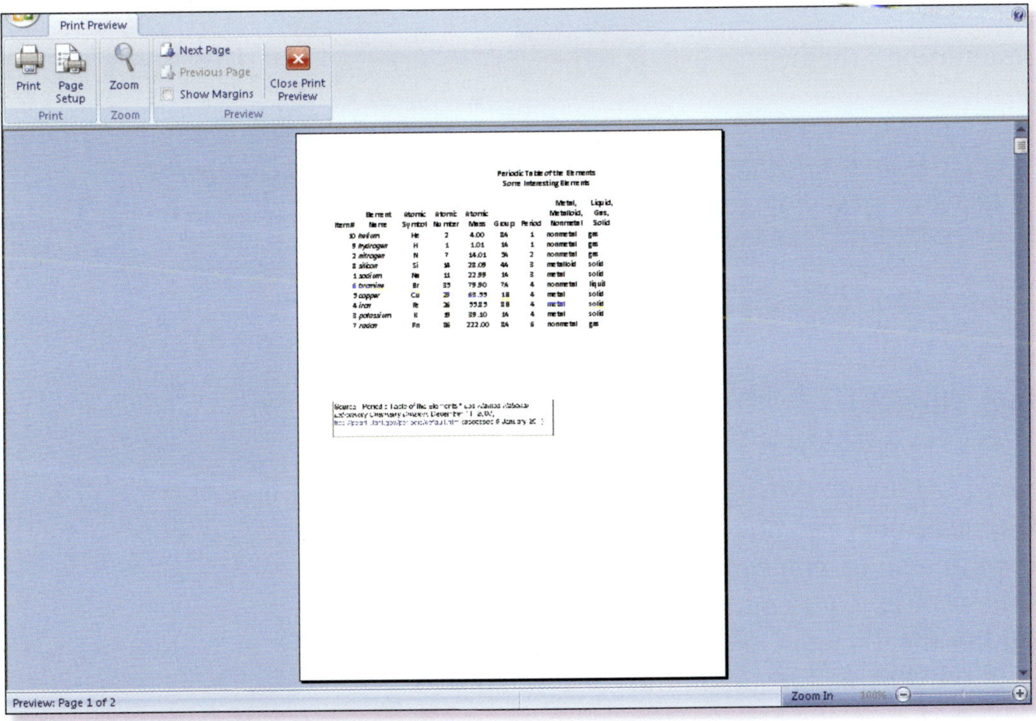


2. Locate the **Print** group on the Print Preview tab.
3. Click the **Page Setup** button to open the Page Setup dialog box.

Now you are ready to change the settings in the Page Setup dialog box.

**Changing Settings in the Page Setup Dialog box**

In the Page Setup dialog box, you can change page orientation, scale the worksheet to fit on a single page, set margins, and add headers and footers.

**Begin by opening Luis's presentation and saving it with a new name.**

1. Open the *changing states* presentation and save it as *changing states12*.
2. Replace *Student Name* with your name on the Title Slide.

Great! Now let's change the presentation's theme.

**ERGONOMICS TIP**

Can you see your screen without tilting your head up or down? If not, adjust your chair height or tilt your monitor so that you can look straight ahead at the screen.

## Applying a Customized Theme

As you learned in Project 11, a theme provides color-coordinated background, font, and accent colors and bullet graphics. To make Luis's presentation more interesting, you can apply a theme and then customize the theme's colors, fonts, and effects. You customize a theme's elements using the Theme Colors, Theme Fonts, and Theme Effects buttons in the Themes group on the Design tab.

Audiences can see slides projected on a wall or projection screen more easily if the background color is dark.

**Let's apply a theme and then customize the theme's color scheme and fonts.**

Design | Themes | More

Design | Themes | Theme Color or Theme Fonts

1. Click **Design** tab and locate the **Themes** group.
2. Click the **Title Slide** in the Slides tab, if necessary.
3. Click the **More** button in the Themes group to expand the themes gallery.
4. Use live preview to see how the Title Slide looks with different themes applied.

Let's change Page settings in the Page Setup dialog box.

1. Click the dialog box **Page** tab, if necessary.
2. Click the **Landscape** option and the **Fit to** option to print all of the data in the active worksheet on one page in Landscape orientation.

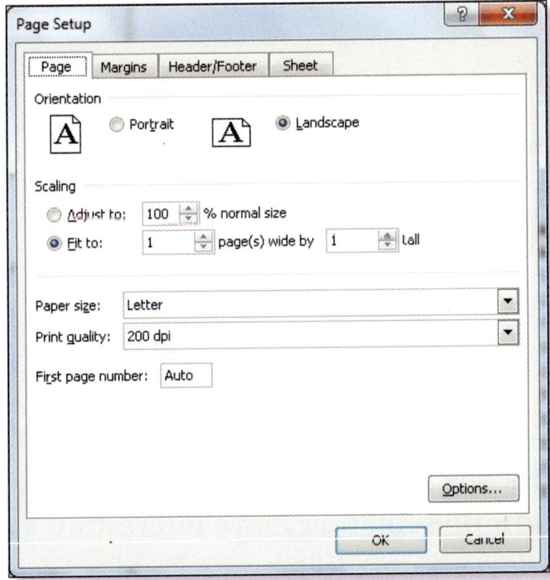


3. Click the dialog box **Margins** tab and click the **Center on page Horizontally** and **Vertically** check boxes to center the data between the margins.

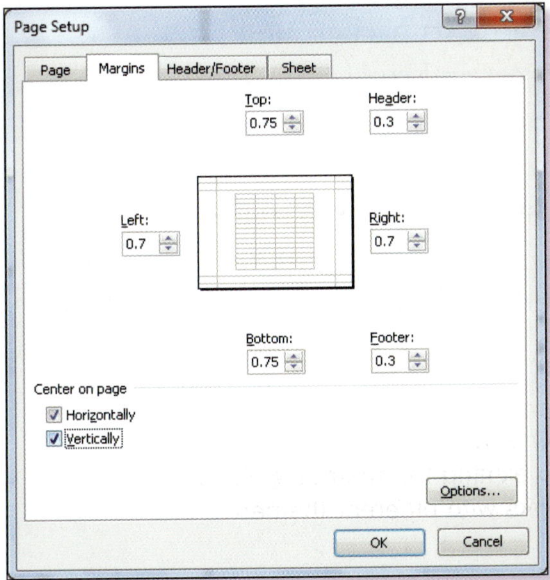

# Changing the States of Matter

## Explorers' Guide

**Data files:** changing states matter

**Objectives:**

In this project, you will:

- apply a customized theme
- insert a new slide using the slide layout gallery
- insert and resize clip art
- draw text boxes and shapes
- group, distribute, and align slide objects
- delete and reposition slides

© IMAGE SOURCE / ALAMY

## Our Exploration Assignment:

### Modifying a slide show

Explorers Club members are learning about matter and energy. Luis has created a presentation for the next meeting. Can you help him make his presentation more interesting and fun? Great! Just follow the Trail Markers to customize a presentation's theme; change a slide's layout and modify its background; insert and resize clip art; draw and format text boxes and shapes; group, distribute, and align slide objects; and reposition and delete slides.

The Header/Footer tab in the Page Setup dialog box is used to add headers and footers. *Excel* includes some common headers and footers that you can select and insert. Click the Header or Footer button arrows to see them.

You can click the Custom Header button or Custom Footer button to key custom header or footer text or to insert predefined information such as the current date.

**Let' create a custom header and insert a predefined footer.**

1. Click the **Header/Footer** tab in the dialog box.
2. Click the **Custom Header** button to open the Header dialog box.

The Custom Header dialog box has three header areas for a left-aligned header, a center-aligned header, and a right-aligned header. It also contains ten formatting buttons above the header areas. You can click these buttons to insert information into a header area.

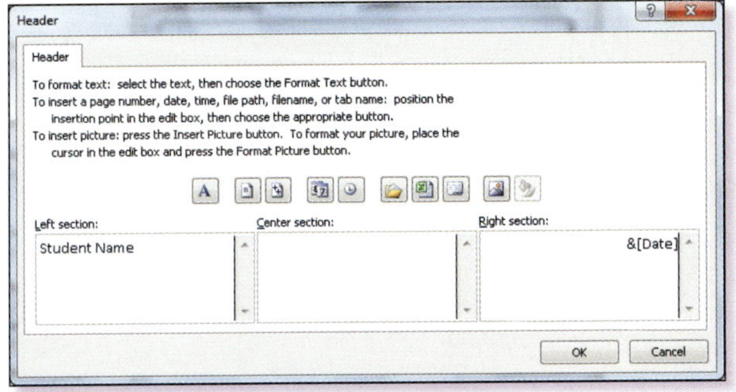


3. Key your name in the left-aligned header area.
4. Tap the TAB key twice to move the insertion point to the right-aligned header area.
5. Click the **Insert Date** button above the header area.
6. Click the **OK** button to close the Header dialog box.
7. Click the **Footer** arrow and click the *elements7* filename from the list of predefined footer options.
8. Click **OK** to add the header and footer to the worksheet. Print the worksheet as instructed by your teacher.
9. Save and close the workbook and close the *Excel* application.

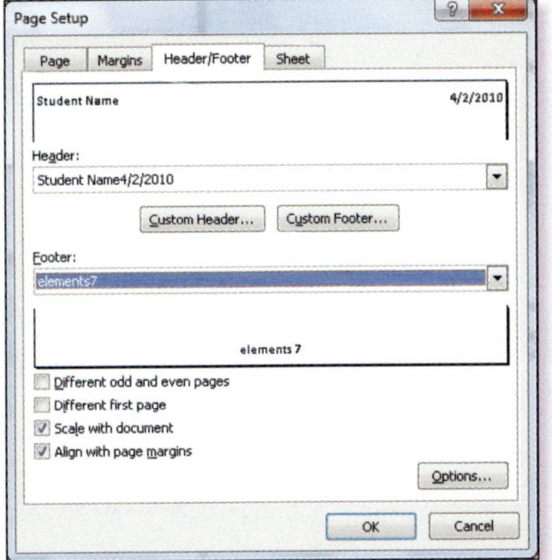

You can also open the Page Setup dialog box by clicking the Dialog Box Launcher icon in the Page Setup group on the Page Layout tab. Try it!

# Project 11



## 11a Review 8, 1, 9, 4, and 0

Key each line twice. Double-space between 2-line groups.

**TECHNIQUE TIP**

Reach up to the number keys without moving your hands away from your body.

**8**

1 k 8 k 8|k i 8 k i 8|ki8 ki8|8k8 8k8|8i8 8i8|8, 8,;

2 The blue team lost 8 out of 88, not 88 out of 888.

**1**

3 a 1 a 1|a q 1 a q 1|aq1 aq1|zaq1 zaq1|z1 z1|q1 q1;

4 Maryann keyed 18, 81, 118, 181, 811, 818, and 881.

**9**

5 l 9 l 9|l o 9 l o 9|lo9 lo9|9l9 9l9|.9. .9.|9l. 9l

6 Kay got 18 out of 19 on the quizzes and 81 out 91.

**4**

7 f 4 f 4|f r 4 f r 4|fr4 fr4|4f4 4f4|4r4 4r4|4v 4v;

8 Felipe scored 144 or 148 points out of 149 points.

**0**

9 ; 0 ; 0|; p 0 ; p 0|;p0 ;p0|0;0 0;0|?0? ?0?|0;? 0;

10 Their four missing values were 10, 80, 90, and 40.

11 Toua bowled 189; Jan bowled 140; Jason bowled 148.

12 Thomas set the dates for May 18-19 and June 10-14.

## 11b Build Skill

Key each line twice. Double-space between 2-line groups.

For additional practice: **MicroType 5** Numeric Keyboarding, Lessons 1–2

1 Gwen took a picture.

2 She may be in her office.

3 He forgot to take their money.

4 Benito won first place in his race.

5 I will have him call you when he leaves.

6 Tryouts for the play take place next Tuesday.

7 Jason and Katie plan on going to the lake to swim.

*gwam* 30" | 2 | 4 | 6 | 8 | 10 | 12 | 14 | 16 | 18 | 20 |

# Project Skills Review

You learned a lot in this project! We are very impressed with your progress. Let's take a few minutes to review the skills that you learned.

| | | |
|---|---|---|
| **Rename a sheet tab** | Double-click a sheet tab and key a new name. | |
| **Activate the home cell** | Tap CTRL + HOME. | |
| **Save a workbook** | Click the **File** tab or **Office Button** and click Save As. Click the **Save** button on the **Quick Access Toolbar**. |    |
| **Activate a cell** | Tap the ENTER, TAB, SHIFT + TAB, or arrow keys. | |
| **Merge a range of cells and center the first cell's contents across the range** | Click the **Merge & Center** button in the Alignment group on the **Home** tab. |  |
| **Apply the Bold or Italic font styles** | Click the **Bold** or **Italic** button in the Font group on the **Home** tab. | |
| **Center cell contents within the cell** | Click the **Center** button in the Alignment group on the **Home** tab. | 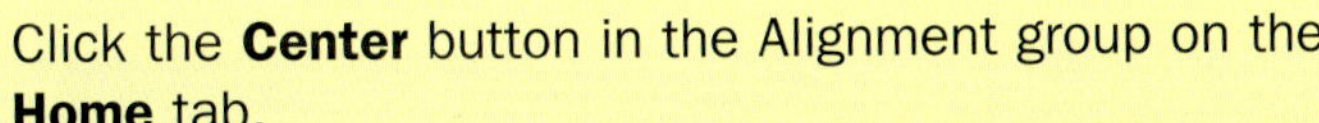  |
| **Wrap text in the cell** | Click the **Wrap Text** button in the Alignment group on the **Home** tab. |  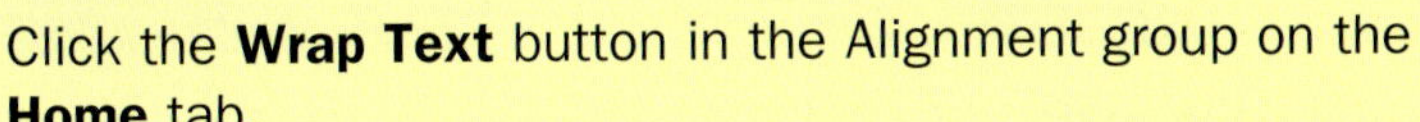  |
| **Resize column widths** | Double-click the column heading boundary with the resizing pointer. Drag a column boundary with the resizing pointer. | 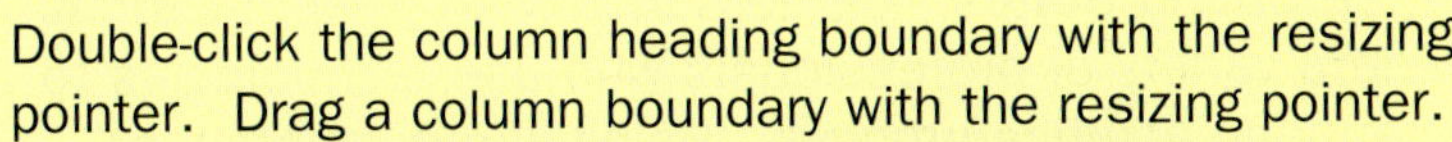 |
| **Sort worksheet data** | Click the **Sort & Filter** button in the Editing group on the **Home** tab; click **Sort A to Z** or **Sort Smallest to Largest** or click **Sort Z to A** or **Sort Largest to Smallest**. |   |
| **Create a custom sort** | Click the **Sort & Filter** button in the Editing group on the **Home** tab and then click **Custom Sort**. |  |
| **Preview and print a worksheet** | Click the **File tab** and click **Print** or click the **Office Button**, point to **Print**, and click **Print Preview**. |   |
| **Change page setup options while previewing a worksheet** | Click the **Page Setup link** in the Print tab (*Excel 2010*) or click the **Page Setup** button in the Print group on the **Print Preview** tab (*Excel 2007*). |  |
| **Print a worksheet while previewing it** | Click the **Print** button in the Print tab or on the Print Preview tab on the Ribbon. |   |

# Exploring *Across the Curriculum*

## Research, Write, and Present

Work with a classmate to use classroom, library, CD-ROM, or online resources to learn more about the early organized labor movement in the textile mills. Mill workers eventually formed unions to demand labor reform. What did the workers want? How did the mill owners react to the workers' demands? Create a new presentation and insert slides as needed to present your facts and cite your sources. Apply the theme of your choice. Run the slide show. With permission, preview and print the slides. Save and close the presentation.

## Getting Help

Click the Microsoft PowerPoint Help icon below the *PowerPoint* application Close button to open the *PowerPoint* Help window. Key **templates** in the search box and tap the ENTER key to research how to create a new presentation using *PowerPoint* templates. Then using what you have learned, create a new presentation based on the template of your choice. Close the presentation without saving it.

## Career Day

The early 19th-century textile mills in New England heralded the beginning of manufacturing in the United States. Careers in modern manufacturing are varied and include a variety of professionals who use technologies to plan and manage the manufacturing process. Using library, printed, or online resources, identify three interesting careers in manufacturing. Write a brief summary of each occupation, print your summary, and save it in your Career Day folder.

## Your Personal Journal

Open your personal journal document. Insert today's date and two blank lines. Think about what you have learned about working in a 19th-century textile mill. What was the general working environment in the mills? Who chose to work in the mills and why? If you lived in 19th-century New England, would you go to work in the mills? Why or why not? Update your journal with three or four paragraphs that answer these questions. Spell-check, save, and close your journal.

**Online Enrichment Games**  www.cengage.com/school/keyboarding/lwcorange

# Exploring On Your Own

## Blaze Your Own Trail

You have learned several new skills in this project. Now blaze your own trail by practicing these skills on your own! Open the *elements7* workbook.

1. Click the *Sheet2* tab to activate the worksheet and change the sheet tab name to **Gases**.
2. Enter the following data in the range A5:G14.

| Item # | Element Name | Atomic Symbol | Atomic Number | Atomic Mass | Group | Period |
|---|---|---|---|---|---|---|
| 1 | argon | Ar | 18 | 39.95 | 8A | 3 |
| 2 | chlorine | Cl | 17 | 35.45 | 7A | 3 |
| 3 | fluorine | F | 9 | 19.00 | 7A | 2 |
| 4 | helium | He | 2 | 4.00 | 8A | 1 |
| 5 | krypton | Kr | 36 | 83.80 | 8A | 4 |
| 6 | neon | Ne | 10 | 20.18 | 8A | 2 |
| 7 | nitrogen | N | 7 | 14.01 | 5A | 2 |
| 8 | oxygen | O | 8 | 16.00 | 6A | 2 |
| 9 | radon | Rn | 86 | 222.00 | 8A | 6 |
| 10 | xenon | Xe | 54 | 131.29 | 8A | 5 |

3. Merge and center the title over columns **A:G** and bold it.
4. Use the **Format Painter** to paint the formats from cell A1 to cell A2.
5. Select the column names; then center, bold, and wrap the column names in the cells.
6. Center the contents of the range C5:G14.
7. Bold the contents of the range B5:B14.
8. Select the nonadjacent ranges **E7:E8** and **E11:E13**. Click the **Increase Decimal** button in the Number group on the Home tab to add a decimal place, if necessary.
9. Resize the columns and rows as necessary.
10. Sort the data range in ascending alphabetical order by *Group* and then *Element Name*.
11. Preview the worksheet and open the Page Setup dialog box. Change the page orientation to Landscape. Add your name and today's date as a custom header and the filename as a predefined footer. With your teacher's permission, print the worksheet.
12. Save and close the workbook.

# Exploring Across the Curriculum

## Internet/Web

Open your Web browser and use a favorite or bookmark to view the Learning with Computers Web page (www.cengage.com/school/keyboarding/lwcorange). Click the **Links** option and click **Project 11**. Click the links to research the lives of young women, called "mill girls," who worked in the 19th-century New England textile mills in Lowell, Massachusetts. Take notes about what you learn.

1. Create a new blank presentation and save it as *mill girls11*.
2. On the Title Slide, key **Lowell Mill Girls** as the title and **Explorers Club** as the subtitle. Edit the subtitle to add your name.
3. Imagine that you are a Lowell mill girl. Using at least four Title and Content slides and text, introduce yourself, describe a day in your life, and cite your sources.
4. Apply the theme of your choice and run the slide show.
5. With your teacher's permission, preview and print your slides using the Handouts (3 slides per page) layout.
6. Save and close the presentation.

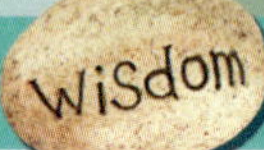


## Language Arts: Words to Know

Look up the meaning of the following terms in a classroom dictionary, CD-ROM dictionary or encyclopedia, or online dictionary.

| Industrial Revolution | labor movement | mill | mill girl |
|---|---|---|---|
| power loom | spindle | spool | textiles |

Create a new presentation. Save it as *definitions11*. On the Title Slide, key **Textile Mills** as the title and **Definitions** as the subtitle. Insert a Title and Content slide for each term. Key the name or term as the title and the definition as the bulleted text. Apply the theme of your choice. Run the slide show. With permission, preview and print the slides as handouts, six per page. Save and close the presentation.

Explore More

# Exploring *On Your Own*

## Reading in Action — Understanding the Periodic Table

The periodic table is arranged in columns, called **groups** or **families**, and rows, called **periods**. There are 7 periods and 18 labeled groups. The first period has only two elements: hydrogen (H) and helium (He). How many elements are in the second period? in the third period? Use the key or legend on the periodic table to ask and answer one question. For example, you might ask, What does the number at the bottom of each box stand for? The key tells you that the number stands for the atomic mass.

## Math in Action — Using Scientific Notation

Scientific notation is used to express large numbers in simpler terms. For example, a breath of air contains approximately 180,000,000,000,000,000 molecules of carbon dioxide. Using scientific notation, this number can be written as $1.8 \times 10^{17}$.

In this number, 17 is called the exponent and 10 is called the base. The number $10^{17}$ is read as *10 raised to the 17th power*. Writing $10^{17}$ is an abbreviated way of writing 100,000,000,000,000,000; it is 10 multiplied by itself 17 times:

10 x 10 x 10 x 10 x 10 x 10 x 10 x 10 x 10 x 10 x 10 x 10 x 10 x 10 x10 x 10 x 10) = 100,000,000,000,000,000.

Now you try it! Write the following numbers in scientific notation.

A 22.4-liter volume of gas contains Avogadro's number of molecules, which is 600,000,000,000,000,000,000,000 molecules.

An atom is 0.00000000045 inches wide. (*Hint*: Use a negative exponent to move right.)

# Exploring On Your Own

## Blaze Your Own Trail

You have learned several new skills in this project. Now blaze your own trail by practicing these skills on your own! Use classroom, library, CD-ROM, or online resources to learn more about the invention of the power loom and the role the power loom played in the Industrial Revolution.

1. Create a new presentation with a Title Slide and at least three Title and Content slides: two for your facts and one for your source citations.
2. Save the presentation as *power loom11*.
3. On the Title Slide, key **The Power Loom** as the title and **Explorers Club** as the subtitle.
4. Edit the subtitle to add your name; then key your facts and citations on the appropriate slides.
5. Apply the theme of your choice to the presentation.
6. Practice navigating your slides using the scroll bar and navigation buttons and the Slides and Outline tabs.
7. View your slides in Slide Sorter view and Notes Page view and then switch back to Normal view.
8. Run the slide show.
9. With your teacher's permission, preview and print your slides as a handout to accompany a class discussion.
10. Save and close the presentation.

## Reading in Action

### Generate Questions

As you read informational material, generate questions about the topic. Ask yourself questions that you can answer through research. Look at slide 4 in the *textile11* presentation. Write three questions that you can research about the topic of the labor force in the mills. Example: What were working conditions like in the mills?

## Math in Action

### Calculating Salaries

The Lowell mill girls earned a salary of about $0.04 per hour. The girls worked 13 hours each day, 6.5 days per week. Each month they had to pay $5 for room and board. How much money would a mill girl have at the end of one month?

Formula: [*(salary) (time)*] – *room and board*

[($0.04) (4 weeks × 6.5 days × 13 hours)] – $5.00

[($0.04) (338)] – $5.00 = $13.52 – $5.00 = $8.52

Now you try it!

How much money would a mill girl have at the end of the month if she earned $0.03 per hour and paid $1 for room and board? if she earned $0.05 per hour and paid $10 for room and board?

# Exploring Across the Curriculum

## Internet/Web

You can learn more about the Periodic Table of the Elements on the Web. Open your Web browser and use a favorite or bookmark to view the Learning with Computers Web page (www.cengage.com/school/keyboardlng/lwcorange). Click the **Links** option and click **Project 7**. Click the links to research information about the Periodic Table of the Elements—its origins and purpose and how to read it. Take notes about what you learn.

1. Create a new *Word* document and key your notes as a properly formatted three-level multilevel list.
2. Use the multilevel list to (1) write a properly formatted two-page *unbound* report with citations on a separate References page or (2) to present an oral report to your classmates about the Periodic Table of the Elements.

## Language Arts: Words to Know

Look up the meaning of the following terms in a classroom dictionary, CD-ROM dictionary or encyclopedia, or online dictionary.

| period | atomic mass | metal | atomic number |
|---|---|---|---|
| liquid | solid | gas | isotope |

Click the File tab or Office Button and click New; create a new workbook based on the Blank workbook template. Save the workbook as *definitions7*. Rename the Sheet1 sheet tab as **Definitions**. Enter the title **Periodic Table Definitions** in cell **A1**. Merge and center the title across the range A1:B1. Enter **Term** as the column name in **A3**. Enter **Definition** as the column name in **B3**. Bold the title and column names. Center the column names.

Enter the terms in the range A4:A11. Enter the term definitions in the range B4:B11. Use the resizing pointer to automatically fit the cell contents for columns A and B. Sort the data in ascending alphabetical order by term. Save, preview, set page setup options, and (with permission) print the worksheet. Close the workbook.

Explore More

# Project Skills Review

| | |
|---|---|
| **View a specific slide in the slide pane** | Drag the scroll box on the vertical scroll bar. Click the **Next Slide** or **Previous Slide** button below the vertical scroll bar. Click a slide thumbnail in the Slides tab. Click a slide icon in the Outline tab. Double-click a slide thumbnail in Slide Sorter or Notes Page view. |
| **Navigate between slides during a slide show** | Click the mouse button, tap the Right or Down arrow key, or tap the Space Bar to advance to the next slide.Tap the Left or Up arrow key to return to the previous slide. Right-click the screen or click the icon in the lower-left corner of the slide show screen and click a shortcut menu command. |
| **Preview and print presentation** | Click the **File tab** and click **Print** or click the **Office Button**, point to **Print**, and click **Print Preview**. Click the **Print** button on the Print tab or in the Print group on the **Print Preview** tab.      |

# Exploring *Across the Curriculum*

## Science: Research and Write

Use classroom, library, or online resources to learn more about hydrogen, oxygen, and carbon. How are these elements alike? How are they different? Why are these three elements so important to your world? Take notes about what you learn. Then create a new *Word* document and save it as *elements7*. Use the *elements7* workbook data and your research notes to write a properly formatted two-page *unbound* report that compares and contrasts these three elements. Cite your sources on a separate References page.

## Getting Help

Click the Microsoft Excel Help icon below the *Excel* application Close button to open the *Excel* Help window. Key **insert cells** in the search box and tap the ENTER key. Research how to insert cells, rows, and columns. Key **delete cells** in the search box and tap the ENTER key. Research how to delete cells, rows, and columns. Then open the workbook of your choice and practice what you learned. Close the workbook *without saving it*.

## Career Day

Business professionals use data stored in *Excel* workbooks in many of their business planning, organizing, and evaluating activities. Using library, printed, or online resources, identify three interesting careers in business management and administration. Write a brief summary of each career, print your summary, and save it in your Career Day folder.

## Your Personal Journal

Open your personal journal document. Insert today's date and two blank lines. Think about what you have learned about *Excel*. How could you use *Excel* to help you in school or at home? What kinds of data could you put into a worksheet? Update your journal with one or two paragraphs that describe one way you can use *Excel*. Spell-check, save, and close your journal.

**Online Enrichment Games**  www.cengage.com/school/keyboarding/lwcorange

# Project Skills Review

You learned a lot in this project! We are very impressed with your progress. Let's take a few minutes to review the skills that you learned.

| Skill | How to | |
|---|---|---|
| **Create, name, and save a new presentation** | Click the **File tab** or **Office Button** and click **New**. Click the **File tab** or **Office Button** and click **Save As**. Click the **Save** button on the Quick Access Toolbar. | File |
| **Add text to placeholders** | Click the placeholder and key the text. Tap CTRL + ENTER and key the text. | |
| **Format slide text** | Select the text and click a button in the Font group on the **Home** tab. | |
| **Insert a new slide** | Click the **New Slide** button in the Slides group on the **Home** tab. With the insertion point still in a slide placeholder, tap CTRL + ENTER. | New Slide |
| **Deactivate a placeholder** | Click the slide work area outside the slide, click the slide background, or tap the ESC key. | |
| **Move the insertion point up or down a level in a bulleted list** | Tap the TAB key or tap the SHIFT + TAB keys. | |
| **Apply a theme** | Click a theme in the themes gallery in the Themes group on the **Design** tab. Click the **More** button to expand the themes gallery. | |
| **Navigate slides** | Drag the scroll box on the vertical scroll bar.Tap the CTRL + HOME or CTRL + END keys. Click the **Previous Slide** or **Next Slide** button below the vertical scroll bar. | |
| **Switch to Slide Sorter, Reading, Notes Page, or Slide Show view** | Click buttons in the Presentation Views group on the **View** tab. Click buttons in the View Shortcuts on the status bar. | |

# Project 7 — Keyboarding

## 7a Review q, comma, z, colon

Key each line twice. Double-space between 2-line groups.

**TECHNIQUE TIP**

Reach down to the comma without moving your hands towards your body.

**q**

1 aq aq | qaq qaq | Jq Jq | Kq Kq | Lq Lq | Yq Yq | Uq Uq | Pq Pq;

2 equal equal | equip equip | quart quart | Jaques Jaques;

**comma**

3 k, k, | ,k, ,k, | ,E ,E | ,U ,U | ,Q ,Q | ,O ,O | ,N ,N | ,G ,G,

4 Pedro, Tasha, and Ben | Eli, LaToya, Erin, and Trent

**z**

5 az az | zaz zaz | aqz aqz | zoo zoo | jazz jazz | zone zone;

6 quiz quiz | buzz buzz | hazy hazy | zero zero | zinc zinc;

**colon**

7 ;: ;: | p:p p:p | :R: :R: | W:Q: W:Q: | p:C: p:C: | Z:T: Z:T

8 Ship To: Invoice No.: Dear Mr. Alou: TO: From:

## 7b Technique: Space Bar and ENTER

Key each line once. Key the lines again at a faster rate.

1 The girls left the field

2 The girls left the field with

3 The girls left the field with five

4 The girls left the field with five more

5 The girls left the field with five more dogs.

*gwam* 20" | 3 | 6 | 9 | 12 | 15 | 18 | 21 | 24 |

## 7c Build Skill

Key each line twice single-spaced; double-space between 2-line groups.

1 Jack Vasquez may work for Bill Pagel the next day.
2 Jake Win placed first by solving the complex quiz.
3 J. Zan quickly removed two boxes from the package.
4 Jewel Vikings quickly baked extra pizzas for them.
5 By solving the tax quiz, Jud Mack won first prize.

*gwam* 20" | 3 | 6 | 9 | 12 | 15 | 18 | 21 | 24 | 27 | 30 |

For additional practice:
**MicroType 5**
New Key Review, Alphabetic Lessons 17–18

The Handouts (6 slides per page) print layout is useful for proofreading your slides. The Handouts (3 slides per page) print layout is *very* useful for an audience because it has preprinted lines for writing notes!

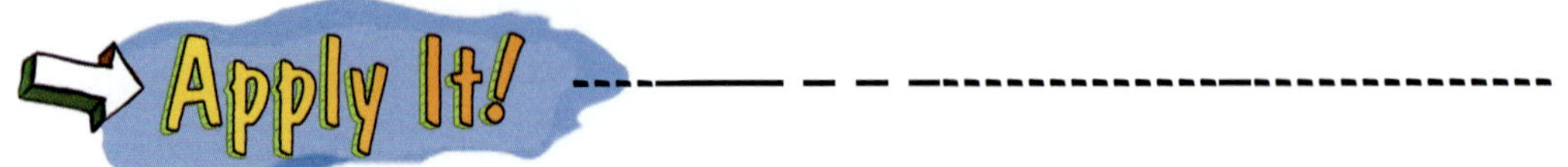


**Let's preview the presentation and then print it using the Handouts (3 slides per page) print layout.**

**Print Preview | Page Setup | Print What**

1. Click the **Office Button**, point to **Print**, and click **Print Preview**; then review groups of buttons on the Print Preview tab.
2. Click the **Print What** arrow in the Page Setup group on the Print Preview tab to view a list of print options.

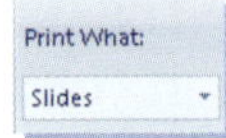


3. Click **Handouts (3 slides per page)** in the list.

Your Handouts (3 slides per page) preview should look similar to this.

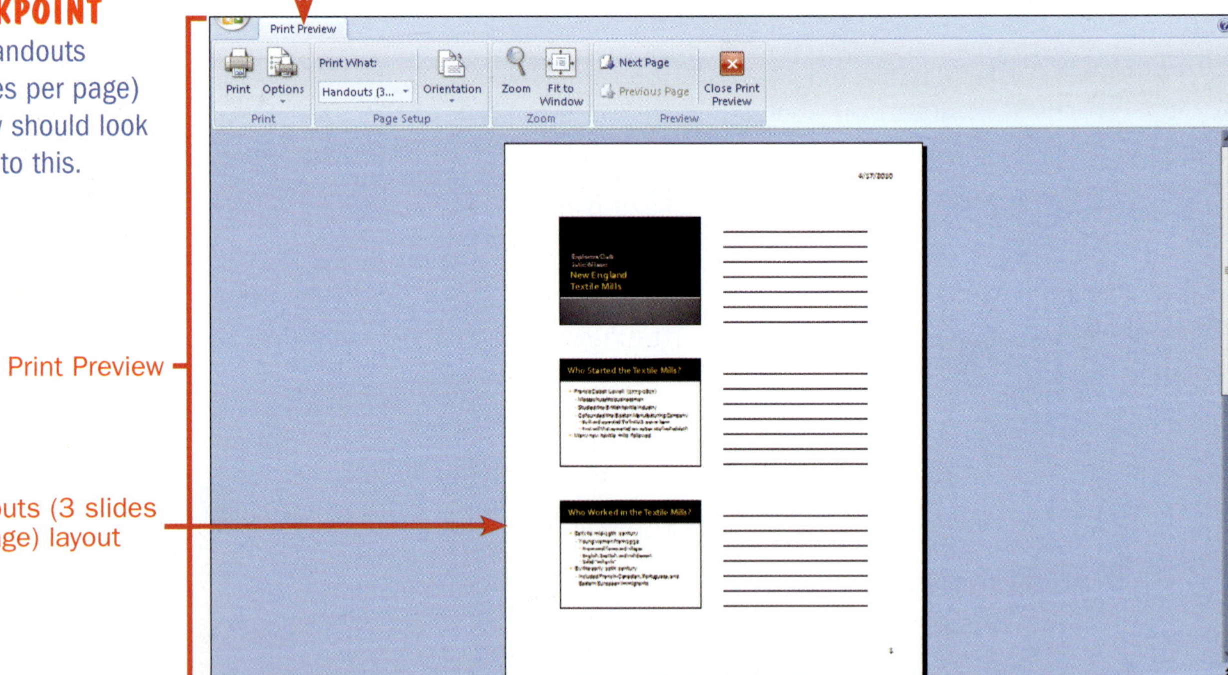


4. With permission, print your presentation.
5. Click the **Close Print Preview** button in the Preview group on the Print Preview tab; then save and close the presentation.

6. Close *PowerPoint*.

# Analyzing Early U.S. Population Data

## Explorers' Guide

Data file: **population data**

**Objectives:**

In this project, you will:

- fill a range with a series of numbers
- edit data
- filter, copy, and paste data
- enter formulas and use the SUM, MIN, MAX, and AVERAGE functions
- use the LOOKUP, TODAY, and NOW functions
- add and remove temporary subtotals

## Our Exploration Assignment:

### Analyzing Early U.S. Population Data

Did you know that the first U.S. population census was taken more than 200 years ago—in 1790? The Explorers Club is learning how the U.S. population changed from 1790 to 1880. Julie has recorded early U.S. census data in a workbook. Can you help her analyze the data and answer some questions about it? Fantastic! Follow the Trail Markers to fill a range; edit data; and filter, copy, and paste data. Then use formulas and functions to answer questions about the data and to add and remove temporary subtotals.

© NORTH WIND / NORTH WIND PICTURE ARCHIVES – ALL RIGHTS RESERVED.

**Let's preview and print the presentation in the 3 Slides print layout.**

File | Print | Slides

1. Click the **File** tab and click **Print**. File
2. Click the **Slides** button in the Settings options to view a gallery of print layout options.
3. Click the **3 Slides** option to change the print layout.

**CHECKPOINT**

Your presentation in the 3 Slides handout layout should look similar to this.

3 slides layout

Print tab in Backstage view

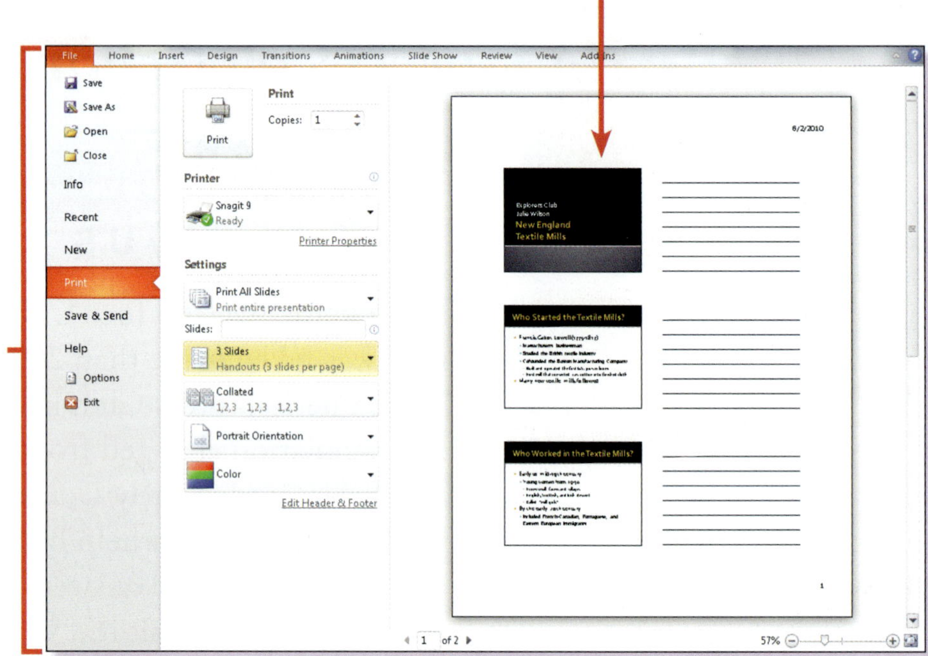


4. With permission, print your presentation.
5. Click the **Home** tab, save your presentation, and close *PowerPoint*.

Remember to ask your teacher before you print any slides in this unit.

### Previewing and Printing in *PowerPoint 2007*

Just as you did in *Word* and *Excel*, you can click Print Preview on the Office Button submenu to view your slides in Print Preview. Then you click the Print What down arrow in the Page Setup group on the Print Preview tab to select a print layout.

**Begin by opening Julie's workbook and saving it with a new name.**

1. Open the *population data* workbook.
2. Save the workbook as *population data8*.
3. Click the **1790-1830 Data** sheet tab, if necessary, to make it the active worksheet.

Great! Let's make a few changes to the worksheet and then answer Julie's questions about the data.

**ERGONOMICS TIP**

Is your monitor dirty? Remember to clean your monitor's screen to remove dust and fingerprints to avoid straining your eyes. Do you wear glasses? Remember to clean them, too!

## 1 Filling a Range with a Series of Numbers

The data in the *1790-1830 Data* worksheet is organized as a data range. In Project 7, you learned that it is a good idea to add a unique sequential identifying number to each row in a data range so that you can sort the data range in any way and then return it to its *original order* by sorting the identifying numbers in ascending numerical order.

Instead of keying each number, you can start with a number and then use AutoFill to automatically fill in all of the other rows with numbers in sequential order.

1. Enter a number in a cell. If you want to fill a range with years or numbers that increase in increments of 1 (2006, 2007 or 1, 2, 3), tap and hold down the CTRL key; otherwise, do not use the CTRL key.
2. Drag the fill handle—the small black square in the lower-right corner of an active cell—to an adjacent cell or cells.

As you drag across empty cells, you will see a ScreenTip indicating what will be filled in each cell. Releasing the mouse button fills the cells.

**Let's run the slide show. Before you begin, make sure slide 1 is the current slide and is visible in the Slide pane.**

1. Click the **Slide Show** button in the View Shortcuts on the status bar. The slide show begins with slide 1, which covers the entire screen.
2. Click the mouse button to advance to **slide 2**.
3. Tap the Right arrow key to advance to **slide 3**.
4. Use either method to advance to **slide 4** and to the end of the slide show.
5. Click the mouse button when you see the black exit screen to return to slide 1 in Normal view.

You can run a slide show from slide 1 regardless of which slide is the current slide. A quick way to start a slide show from slide 1 is to tap the F5 key. Try it!

Super! What a great job! Let's wrap up the presentation by previewing and printing the audience handouts.

## Previewing and Printing a Presentation

You can preview slides and then print each slide on its own page or print multiple slides on a single page. Printed slides are often used as handouts for a slide show audience.

### Previewing and Printing in *PowerPoint 2010*

Previewing and printing a presentation in *PowerPoint 2010* is much like previewing and printing a document in *Word* or a worksheet in *Excel*. Click the File tab and then click Print to view the presentation in Backstage view.

You can view individual slides on the Print tab by clicking the Next Page or Previous Page icons or zoom the view of your slides. When you are ready to print your presentation, you set your print options, such as which slides to print and how to arrange the slides on a page, using the Print tab Settings options.

Printing six slides per page is useful for proofreading your slides. Printing three slides per page is very useful for an audience because it has preprinted lines for writing notes!

You can use the fill handle to paste formulas, increment dates, and do other great time-saving actions while you are working in a worksheet. Check out AutoFill and the fill handle in *Excel* Help!

You can quickly select a row or column heading and insert a new row or column or delete a row or column by right-clicking row or column headings and clicking Insert or Delete, respectively, on the shortcut menu. By default, rows are automatically inserted above and columns are inserted to the left.

**Let's insert a new column A and delete the blank row 19, then add a column name in cell A5 and fill the range A6:A34 with a series of incremental numbers by using AutoFill. Next, you will fill the column names for years 1810, 1820, and 1830 by completing the pattern in the range D5:E5.**

Home | Font | Bold or Center

1. Right-click the **column A** heading and click **Insert** on the shortcut menu to insert a new column A.
2. Right-click the **row 19** heading and click **Delete** to remove the blank row.
3. Enter **Item #** in cell **A5**.
4. Activate cell **A5** and bold and center the contents.
5. Enter **1** in cell **A6**.
6. Activate cell **A6**, move the mouse pointer to the fill handle and tap and hold down the CTRL key. The mouse pointer changes shape to a small black crosshair pointer with a tiny plus sign in the upper-right corner.

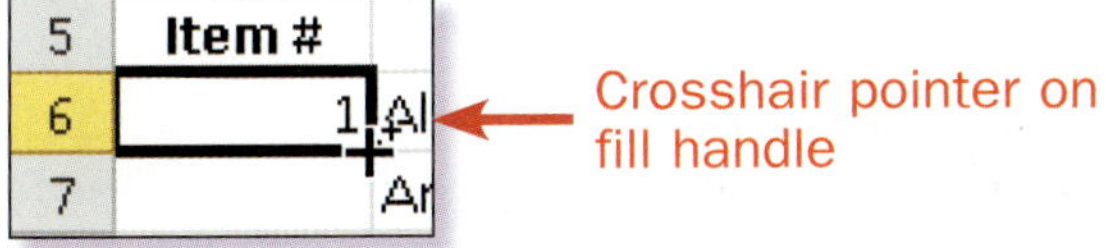


7. Drag down to cell **A34**; release the mouse button and then the CTRL key. A series of numbers from 1 to 29 fills the cells in the range A6:A34.
8. Select the range **D5:E5**.
9. Drag the selected range's fill handle to cell **H5**. *Do not use the CTRL key! Excel* recognizes the pattern of incrementing by 10 and fills the cells with the years 1810, 1820, and 1830.
10. Tap the CTRL + HOME keys and save the workbook.

**Let's use the View tab buttons to switch to Notes Page view, view the slide thumbnail and text box, and then switch back to Normal view.**

View | Presentation Views | Notes Page

1. Click the **View** tab and locate the **Presentation Views** group.
2. Click the **Notes Page** button in the Presentation Views group the notes page for slide 1.

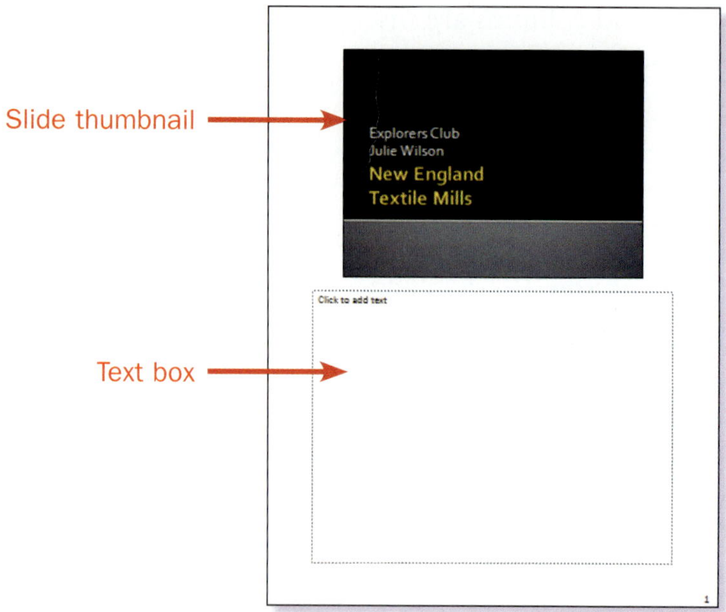


3. Double-click the slide 1 thumbnail to view the slide in Normal view.

You can use Slide Show view to see how your presentation slide show will look to others. Run a slide show starting with the *current slide* by clicking the Slide Show button in the View Shortcuts buttons on the status bar.

When your computer is connected to a projector, use Slide Show view to run the slide show by displaying each slide on a wall or projection screen. Here are some great ways to navigate between slides during a slide show:

- To advance to the next slide: click the mouse button or tap the Right or Down arrow key or Space Bar
- To return to the previous slide: tap the Left or Up arrow key
- To advance or return: right-click the screen and click Next or Previous on the shortcut menu

A slide show ends when you advance one screen beyond your final slide. To stop a slide show at any time, tap the ESC key.

To project a *PowerPoint* slide show on a wall or projection screen, the computer is connected to a special type of projector, such as an LCD projector.

Your column A and row 5 should look like this.

Row 5 column names

Column A item numbers

| 4 | | | | | | | | |
|---|---|---|---|---|---|---|---|---|
| 5 | Item # | State | Census Division | 1790 | 1800 | 1810 | 1820 | 1830 |
| 6 | 1 | Alabama | East South Central | 0 | 1250 | 9046 | 127901 | 309527 |
| 7 | 2 | Arkansas | West South Central | 0 | 0 | 1062 | 14273 | 30388 |
| 8 | 3 | Connecticut | New England | 237946 | 251002 | 261942 | 275248 | 297675 |
| 9 | 4 | Delaware | South Atlantic | 59096 | 64273 | 72674 | 74749 | 76748 |
| 10 | 5 | District of Columbia | South Atlantic | 0 | 8144 | 15471 | 23336 | 30261 |

Now let's edit some of Julie's data.

## Editing Data

In Project 7, you learned that *entering* text or numbers in a specific cell means to follow the three-step process: activate the cell, key the text or numbers, and activate another cell.

When you need to edit the contents of a cell, you can do the following:

1. Enter new text or numbers in the cell.
2. Click the formula bar with the I-beam and edit the cell contents in the formula bar.
3. Double-click the cell and edit the cell contents directly in the cell.
4. Tap the F2 key to open the cell and position the insertion point in the cell.

You can also use the I-beam to select text or numbers in the formula bar or in the active cell and then key new text or numbers.

To cancel your data entry *before* you tap the ENTER or TAB keys, just tap the ESC key!

**Let's edit the *1790-1830 Data* worksheet using the four methods.**

1. Activate cell **H16** and enter 215739 to replace the existing cell contents.
2. Activate cell **H13**; then move the mouse pointer to the formula bar, where it becomes the I-beam pointer.

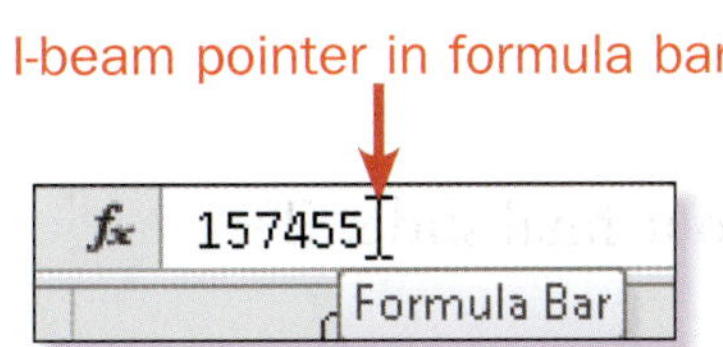

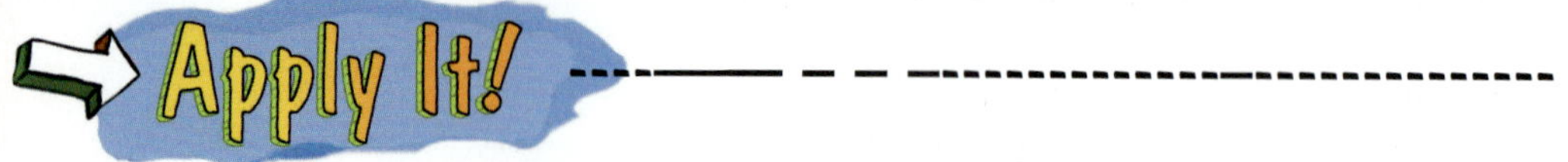


**Let's switch to Slide Sorter view, view the slide thumbnails, and then switch back to Normal view.**

1. Click the **Slide Sorter View** button on the status bar to switch to Slide Sorter view. In Slide Sorter view, you can see all of the slide thumbnails in one pane. 

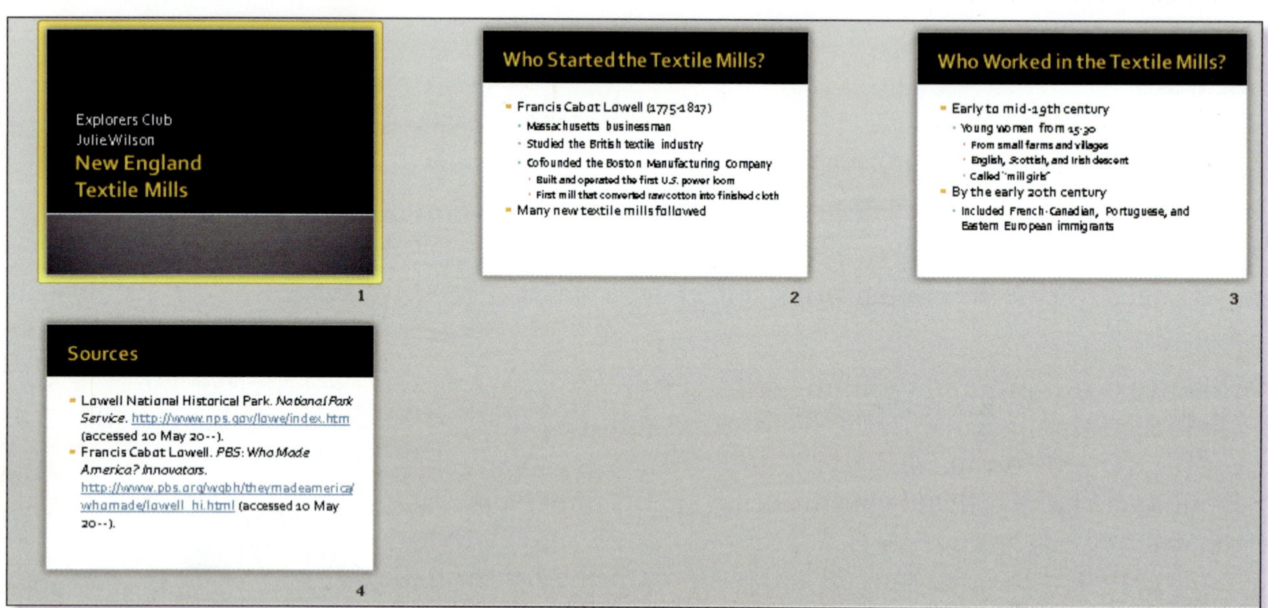


Thumbnails for all the slides in one pane

You can quickly switch back to Normal view and view any slide in the Slide pane by double-clicking a slide thumbnail.

2. Double-click the slide 1 thumbnail to switch back to Normal view and view slide 1 in the Slide pane.

Notes Page view shows a small version of each slide on a single page with a text placeholder in which you can key speaker notes. You can double-click the small slide to return to Normal view.

3. Click the end of the number 157455 in the formula bar to position the insertion point.
4. Edit the last three numbers to be **445** and tap the ENTER key.
5. Double-click cell **B11** to position the insertion point in the cell.

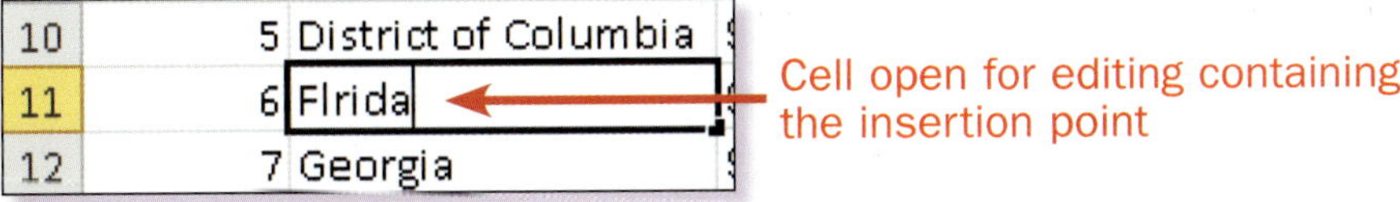


6. Edit the state name to be **Florida** and tap the ENTER key.
7. Activate cell **E31** and tap the **F2** key.

8. Edit the number to be **105602** and tap the ENTER key.
9. Tap the CTRL + HOME keys.

Fantastic! Now let's make the worksheet easier to read.

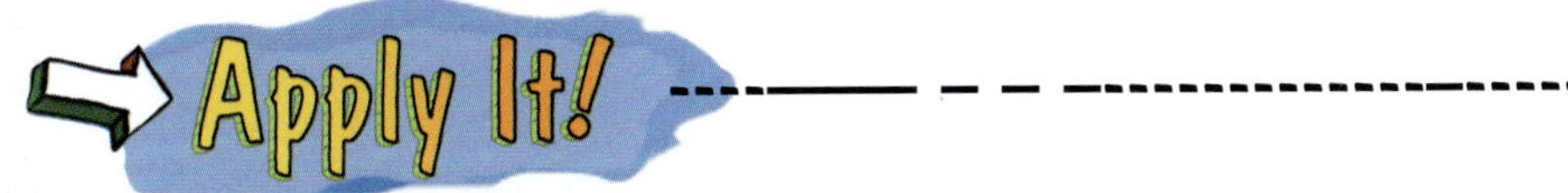


**Let's change the title font size and bold it and then format the population data with a thousands separator and no decimal places.**

Home | Font | Font Size

Home | Number | Comma Style or Decrease Decimal

1. Click the **Home** tab, if necessary, and locate the **Font** and **Number** groups.
2. Activate cell **B1:B2** and tap the CTRL + B keys to apply the Bold font style.
3. Click the **Font Size** button arrow in the Font group and click **12**.
4. Use the SHIFT + click method to select the range **D6:H34**.
5. Click the **Comma Style** button in the Number group to add a thousands separator.
6. Click the **Decrease Decimal** button in the Number group *twice* to remove the two decimal places.
7. Resize columns **D:H** to fit using the mouse pointer.
8. Tap the CTRL + HOME keys.

To delete the contents of a selected cell or range, tap the DELETE key. To clear a cell or range of its contents and/or formatting, click the Clear button in the Editing group on the Home tab and click a clear option.

5. Click the **slide 1** thumbnail to select slide 1 in the Slides tab and to show slide 1—the Title Slide—in the Slide pane.
6. Click the **Outline** tab to view the slide outline.
7. Scroll the Outline tab to see the slide 3 text and icon, if necessary.
8. Move the mouse pointer to the slide 3 icon. The mouse pointer becomes a four-headed move pointer.

Mouse pointer on slide icon

3  **Who Worked in the Textile Mills?**

- Early to mid-19th century
  - Young women from 15-30
    - From small farms and villages
    - English, Scottish, and Irish descent
    - Called "mill girls"
- By the early 20th century
  - Included French-Canadian, Portuguese, and Eastern European immigrants

9. Click the **slide 3** icon in the Outline tab to view slide 3 in the Slide pane.
10. Click the **Slides** tab to view the slide thumbnails.
11. Tap the CTRL + END keys to select slide 4 in the Slides tab and view the last slide, slide 4, in the Slide pane.
12. Tap the CTRL + HOME keys to select slide 1 in the Slides tab and view slide 1 in the Slide pane.

Reading view (Full Screen Reading view in *PowerPoint 2007*) is a great tool for proofreading your slides. You can switch to Reading or Full Screen Reading by clicking a button in the Presentation Views group on the View tab or a button in the View Shortcuts on the status bar. Try it!

In Slide Sorter view, you see miniatures or thumbnails of all of the slides in the presentation. You can then select and move slides or delete them. You can also insert new slides and apply special effects in Slide Sorter view.

Your worksheet should look like this.

| | A | B | C | D | E | F | G | H |
|---|---|---|---|---|---|---|---|---|
| 1 | | **U.S. Population by State (includes District of Columbia)** | | | | | | |
| 2 | | **For the Years 1790-1830** | | | | | | |
| 3 | | | | | | | | |
| 4 | | | | | | | | |
| 5 | **Item #** | **State** | **Census Division** | **1790** | **1800** | **1810** | **1820** | **1830** |
| 6 | 1 | Alabama | East South Central | - | 1,250 | 9,046 | 127,901 | 309,527 |
| 7 | 2 | Arkansas | West South Central | - | - | 1,062 | 14,273 | 30,388 |
| 8 | 3 | Connecticut | New England | 237,946 | 251,002 | 261,942 | 275,248 | 297,675 |
| 9 | 4 | Delaware | South Atlantic | 59,096 | 64,273 | 72,674 | 74,749 | 76,748 |
| 10 | 5 | District of Columbia | South Atlantic | - | 8,144 | 15,471 | 23,336 | 30,261 |
| 11 | 6 | Florida | South Atlantic | - | | - | - | 34,730 |
| 12 | 7 | Georgia | South Atlantic | 82,548 | 162,686 | 252,433 | 340,989 | 516,823 |
| 13 | 8 | Illinois | East North Central | - | - | 12,282 | 55,211 | 157,445 |
| 14 | 9 | Indiana | East North Central | - | 5,641 | 24,520 | 147,718 | 343,031 |
| 15 | 10 | Kentucky | East South Central | 73,677 | 220,955 | 403,511 | 564,317 | 687,917 |
| 16 | 11 | Louisiana | West South Central | - | - | 76,556 | 153,407 | 215,739 |
| 17 | 12 | Maine | New England | 96,540 | 151,719 | 228,705 | 298,335 | 399,455 |
| 18 | 13 | Maryland | South Atlantic | 319,728 | 341,548 | 380,546 | 407,530 | 447,040 |
| 19 | 14 | Massachusetts | New England | 378,787 | 422,845 | 472,040 | 523,287 | 610,408 |
| 20 | 15 | Michigan | East North Central | - | - | 4,762 | 8,896 | 31,639 |
| 21 | 16 | Mississippi | East South Central | - | 7,600 | 31,306 | 75,448 | 136,621 |
| 22 | 17 | Missouri | West North Central | - | - | 19,783 | 66,586 | 140,455 |
| 23 | 18 | New Hampshire | New England | 141,885 | 183,858 | 214,460 | 244,161 | 269,328 |
| 24 | 19 | New Jersey | Middle Atlantic | 184,139 | 211,149 | 245,562 | 277,575 | 320,823 |
| 25 | 20 | New York | Middle Atlantic | 340,120 | 589,051 | 959,049 | 1,372,812 | 1,918,608 |

## 3 Filtering, Copying, and Pasting Data

A filter is a set of criteria applied to a worksheet data range to allow you to view and work with a portion of it. For example, Julie wants to see the population only for the New England Census Division. You can filter the data range on the *1790-1830* Data worksheet to show only those rows where the Census Division is New England and hide all remaining rows in the data range.

In Project 7, you learned about the criteria for an *Excel* data range. To filter a data range, activate any cell *within the data range boundaries*. Then click the Sort & Filter button in the Editing group on the Home tab and click Filter to turn on the AutoFilter feature.

The AutoFilter feature adds filtering arrows to each cell in the data range header row that contains column names. Click a filtering arrow to see a list of filtering options; then click a specific option to filter the data range.

To scroll sheet tabs, click a first sheet, previous sheet, next sheet, or last sheet tab scrolling button to the left of the workbook's sheet tabs.

## Navigating Slides and Running a Slide Show

*PowerPoint* offers several ways for you to view and work with your slides, including Normal view, Slide Sorter view, Reading or Full Screen Reading view, Notes Page view, and Slide Show view. You can switch between views by clicking a button in the View Shortcuts on the right side of the status bar. You can also click the View tab and then click buttons in the Presentation Views group to switch to a different view.

You have been using Normal view to add and edit your slides. In Normal view, you can move from slide to slide by dragging the scroll box on the vertical scroll bar or clicking the Previous Slide or Next Slide button located below the scroll bar.

The Slides tab shows thumbnails of each slide in your presentation; you can click a slide thumbnail to view the slide in the Slide pane. The Outline tab shows your slides' text as an outline; you can click a slide icon on the Outline tab to view that slide in the Slide pane.

You can also reposition slides by dragging a slide thumbnail in the Slides tab or the slide icon in the Outline tab to a new position in the presentation. Check it out!

**Let's navigate between slides and tour the *PowerPoint* views. You will work in these views in later projects. Before you begin, make sure the Title Slide is visible in the Slide pane.**

1. Click the scroll box on the vertical scroll bar and hold down the mouse button to see the ScreenTip that shows you the current slide number, the total number of slides in the presentation, and the title of the current slide.

Slide information as you drag scroll box

2. Drag the scroll box on the vertical scroll bar downward until the ScreenTip shows the information for slide 3.
3. Release the mouse button to see slide 3 in the Slide pane.
4. Click the **Slides** tab, if necessary, to view the slide thumbnails.

Let's filter the data range on the *1790-1830 Data* worksheet.

**Home | Editing | Sort & Filter**

1. Activate *1790-1830 Data* worksheet, if necessary.
2. Click any cell inside the data range to place the active cell within the data range's boundaries.
3. Click the **Home** tab, if necessary, and locate the **Editing** group.
4. Click the **Sort & Filter** button in the Editing group and click **Filter** to turn on the AutoFilter feature. The filtering arrows now appear to the right of each column name in each cell in the header row.

Filtering arrows

| | | | | | | | | |
|---|---|---|---|---|---|---|---|---|
| 4 | | | | | | | | |
| 5 | Item | State | Census Division | 1790 | 1800 | 1810 | 1820 | 1830 |
| 6 | 1 | Alabama | East South Central | - | 1,250 | 9,046 | 127,901 | 309,527 |

5. Click the **Census Division** column name filtering arrow to see the sorting and filtering options.
6. Click the **(Select All)** checkbox to remove all of the check marks and then click the **New England** checkbox to insert a check mark.
7. Click **OK** to filter the data range to show only those rows in which New England is in the Census Division column.

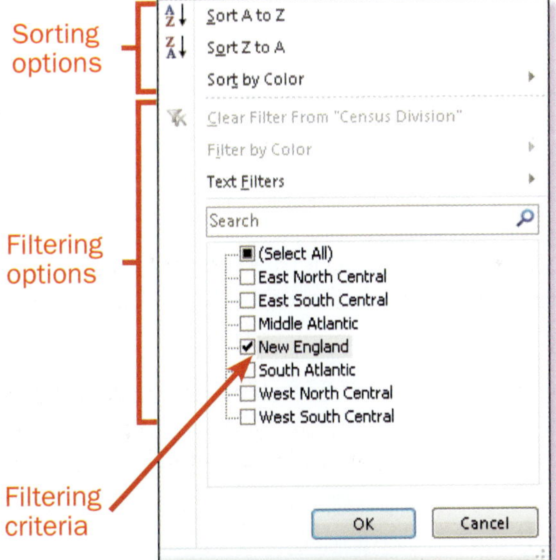


*Excel* hides all rows in the data range except those that have *New England* in the *Census Division* column. A filter symbol appears instead of the AutoFilter arrow to indicate that a filter is applied in that column.

## Applying a Theme

A theme—color-coordinated formatting that defines fonts, colors, and background color or design—changes the look of a presentation. To apply a theme, click the Design tab and then click a theme in the theme gallery in the Themes group.

To give your presentation a unified look, apply the same theme to all of the slides in your presentation.

**Let's apply a theme.**

Design | Themes | More

1. Click the **Design** tab and locate the **Themes** group.
2. Click the **More** button in the Themes group to view the themes gallery.
3. Move the mouse pointer to a theme to see a ScreenTip with the theme's name and to live-preview the theme applied to the slide behind the gallery.
4. Click the **Module** theme to apply it to the presentation.

Your Title Slide should look like this.

Title Slide with Module design template

Excellent! Now let's look at ways we can navigate the slides in Julie's presentation.

Your filtered data should look like this.

Filter symbol

| Row | Item | State | Census Division | 1790 | 1800 | 1810 | 1820 | 1830 |
|---|---|---|---|---|---|---|---|---|
| 4 | | | | | | | | |
| 5 | Item | State | Census Division | 1790 | 1800 | 1810 | 1820 | 1830 |
| 8 | 3 | Connecticut | New England | 237,946 | 251,002 | 261,942 | 275,248 | 297,675 |
| 17 | 12 | Maine | New England | 96,540 | 151,719 | 220,705 | 298,335 | 399,455 |
| 19 | 14 | Massachusetts | New England | 378,787 | 422,845 | 472,040 | 523,287 | 610,408 |
| 23 | 18 | New Hampshire | New England | 141,885 | 183,858 | 214,460 | 244,161 | 269,328 |
| 29 | 24 | Rhode Island | New England | 68,825 | 69,122 | 76,931 | 83,059 | 97,199 |
| 32 | 27 | Vermont | New England | 85,425 | 154,465 | 217,895 | 235,981 | 280,652 |

Filtered data

You can clear a filter by clicking the filter symbol for the filtered column and then clicking Clear Filter from (Column Name).

After you filter the data range to show the New England data, Julie wants the data copied and pasted on a separate worksheet. You can insert and delete worksheets by right-clicking a sheet tab and then clicking Insert or Delete on the shortcut menu.

**Let's insert and name a new worksheet and then copy the filtered data range and paste it on the new worksheet.**

**Home | Clipboard | Copy or Paste**

**Home | Editing | Sort & Filter**

1. Right-click the *1840-1880* Data sheet tab and click **Insert** on the shortcut menu to open the Insert dialog box.
2. Double-click the **Worksheet** icon in the Insert dialog box to insert a blank worksheet.
3. Change the sheet tab name to **1790-1830 New England**.
4. Activate *1790-1830 Data* worksheet.
5. Click the **Home** tab, if necessary, and locate the **Clipboard** group.
6. Select the range **B1:H32** and click the **Copy** button in the Clipboard group. *Excel* copies all rows in the range *except* the hidden rows.
7. Activate the *1790-1830 New England* worksheet.
8. Click cell **A1**, if necessary, and click the **Paste** button in the Clipboard group to paste the copied data to the new worksheet.
9. Edit cell **A1** to be **New England Population**, resize columns **A:B** to fit, and activate cell **A1** again.

Paste

Next, let's insert a slide and cite Julie's online sources for the facts about the New England textile mills. Like *Word*, when you key a Web source's URL, *PowerPoint* converts it to a hyperlink. Leave the automatic hyperlink formatting as part of your citation.

Remember to proofread and spell-check your presentation! *PowerPoint* has a spelling checker—just like *Word*. When you see a wavy red line below your text, you can correct the spelling by using a shortcut menu or spell-check the entire presentation by clicking the Spell Check button on the status bar or the Spelling button in the Proofing group on the Review tab.

**Let's create a third Title and Content slide and then view slide 1.**

1. Insert a new Title and Content slide as slide 4.
2. Tap the CTRL + ENTER keys to move the insertion point into the title placeholder.
3. Key **Sources** and tap the CTRL + ENTER keys.
4. Using the following figure as your guide, add the two source citations as first-level bullets. *Remember to italicize the website name and key the period following the parenthesis.* Deactivate the placeholder.

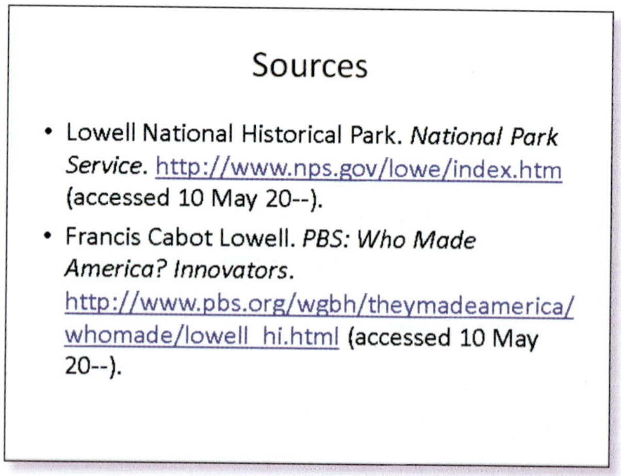

Sources

- Lowell National Historical Park. *National Park Service.* http://www.nps.gov/lowe/index.htm (accessed 10 May 20--).
- Francis Cabot Lowell. *PBS: Who Made America? Innovators.* http://www.pbs.org/wgbh/theymadeamerica/whomade/lowell_hi.html (accessed 10 May 20--).

5. Tap the CTRL + HOME keys to view slide 1; then save the presentation.

Nice job! Now let's add some fun and interest to the presentation by applying a theme.

**CHECKPOINT**
Your pasted data should look like this.

| | A | B | C | D | E | F | G |
|---|---|---|---|---|---|---|---|
| 1 | New England Population | | | | | | |
| 2 | For the Years 1790-1830 | | | | | | |
| 3 | | | | | | | |
| 4 | | | | | | | |
| 5 | State | Census Division | 1790 | 1800 | 1810 | 1820 | 1830 |
| 6 | Connecticut | New England | 237,946 | 251,002 | 261,942 | 275,248 | 297,675 |
| 7 | Maine | New England | 96,540 | 151,719 | 228,705 | 298,335 | 399,455 |
| 8 | Massachusetts | New England | 378,787 | 422,845 | 472,040 | 523,287 | 610,408 |
| 9 | New Hampshire | New England | 141,885 | 183,858 | 214,460 | 244,161 | 269,328 |
| 10 | Rhode Island | New England | 68,825 | 69,122 | 76,931 | 83,059 | 97,199 |
| 11 | Vermont | New England | 85,425 | 154,465 | 217,895 | 235,981 | 280,652 |

10. Activate the *1790-1830 Data* worksheet and deselect the range.
11. Click the **Home** tab, if necessary, and locate the **Editing** group.
12. Click the **Sort & Filter** button in the Editing group and click **Filter** to turn off AutoFilter.
13. Activate cell **A1** and save the workbook.

Excellent! Now you are ready to answer Julie's questions about the New England population data using formulas and functions.

Did you know? You can move or copy entire worksheets using drag and drop! Just drag a sheet tab to move a worksheet; tap and hold the CTRL key as you drag a sheet tab to copy it.

TRAIL MARKER

## Entering Formulas and Using the SUM, MIN, MAX, and AVERAGE Functions

A formula is an equation you enter in one cell to perform a calculation on the contents of other cells. You begin an *Excel* formula by keying an equals sign (=). This tells *Excel* that you are entering a formula. Then you key the cell references (or click the cells) on which the formula is to act *and* you key the calculation operator (+, -, *, or /) that tells *Excel* what to do: add, subtract, multiply, or divide.

10. Key **First mill that converted raw cotton into finished cloth** and tap the ENTER key.
11. Tap and hold the SHIFT key and tap the TAB key twice to promote the bullet to a first-level bullet; then release the SHIFT key.
12. Key **Many new textile mills followed.**
13. Deactivate the placeholder and save the presentation.

Your completed slide should look like this.

### Who Started the Textile Mills?

- Francis Cabot Lowell (1775-1817)
  - Massachusetts businessman
  - Studied the British textile industry
  - Cofounded the Boston Manufacturing Company
    - Built and operated the first U.S. power loom
    - First mill that converted raw cotton into finished cloth
- Many new textile mills followed

Nice work! Now let's insert a slide that summarizes who worked in the textile mills. A quick way to move the insertion point into the first placeholder on the new slide is to tap the CTRL + ENTER keyboard shortcut keys.

**Let's insert a second Title and Content slide.**

1. Click the **New Slide** button face in the Slides group.
2. Tap the CTRL + ENTER keys to position the insertion point in the **Click to add title** placeholder.
3. Key **Who Worked in the Textile Mills?** in the placeholder.
4. Tap the CTRL + ENTER keys to move the insertion point into the bulleted-list placeholder. Using the following figure as your guide, add the bulleted-list text.
5. Save the presentation.

### Who Worked in the Textile Mills?

- Early to mid-19th century
  - Young women from 15-30
    - From small farms and villages
    - English, Scottish, and Irish descent
    - Called "mill girls"
- By the early 20th century
  - Included French-Canadian, Portuguese, and Eastern European immigrants

Here are examples of basic *Excel* formulas.

| Basic Formula | What It Does |
|---|---|
| **=A1+B1 entered in cell C1** | Adds the contents of cells A1 and B1 and places the result in cell C1 |
| **=B3-C3 entered in cell D3** | Subtracts the content of cell C3 from the content of cell B3 and places the result in cell D3 |
| **=D5*E5 entered in cell F5** | Multiplies the content of cell D5 by the content of cell E5 and places the result in cell F5 |
| **=E7/F7 entered in cell G7** | Divides the content of cell E7 by the content of cell F7 and places the result in cell G7 |

A formula can also contain a function. A function is a built-in *Excel* calculation. You can use a function to perform common calculations, such as adding a range of numbers or finding the largest number in a range.

You can also use a function for a more complex calculation, such as using a specific number in a data range to find or look up other data in the data range. Here are some commonly used functions:

| | |
|---|---|
| **AVERAGE** | Finds the average value of the numbers in a range |
| **MAX** | Finds the largest number value in a range |
| **MIN** | Finds the smallest number value in a range |
| **SUM** | Calculates the total value of a range of numbers |

Julie wants to know the total New England population for each census year. Let's use three methods to build a formula: manually adding cell values, building a formula that includes the SUM function, and using the Sum (AutoSum) button.

**Keying a Formula**

To enter a formula, you first activate the cell that will contain the formula and its calculated results; then you key an equals sign (=) to tell *Excel* you are entering a formula. Next, you key the cell references that contain values for the calculation and the mathematical operators plus, minus, division, or multiplication (+, -, /, or *, respectively) needed to perform the calculation.

You can also demote or promote bullets by clicking the Home tab and then clicking the Increase Indent or Decrease Indent buttons in the Paragraph group. Try it!

Be sure to keep your bulleted text brief and limit the number of bullets on each Title and Content slide to no more than four or five first-level bullets. This helps your audience quickly scan the slide and pick out the important points.

**Let's insert a new Title and Content slide.**

Home | Slides | New Slide

1. Click the **Home** tab, if necessary, and locate the **Slides** group.
2. Click the **New Slide** button face in the Slides group to insert a new Title and Content slide as slide 2.

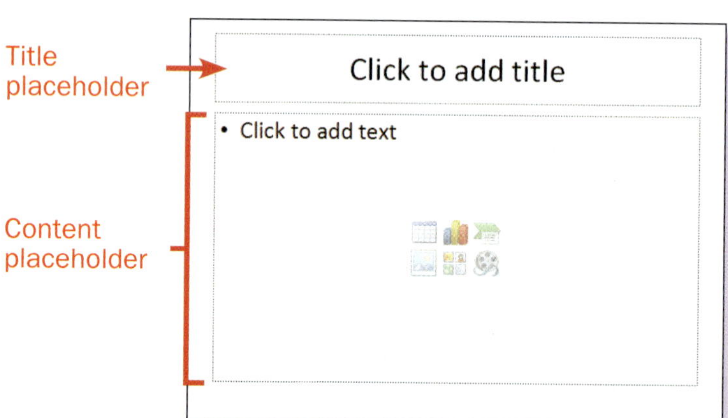


3. Click inside the **Click to add title** placeholder and key **Who Started the Textile Mills?**
4. Click inside the content placeholder to create a bulleted list.
5. Key **Francis Cabot Lowell (1775-1817)** and tap the ENTER key to move the insertion point to the next bullet.
6. Tap the TAB key to demote the bullet, key **Massachusetts businessman**, and tap the ENTER key.
7. Key **Studied the British textile industry** and tap the ENTER key.
8. Key **Cofounded the Boston Manufacturing Company** and tap the ENTER key.
9. Tap the TAB key to demote the bullet, key **Built and operated the first U.S. power loom**, and tap the ENTER key.

For example, to calculate the total population for the census year 1790 on the *1790-1830 New England* worksheet, you can activate cell C12 and then enter the formula **=C6+C7+C8+C9+C10+C11** to add the values in cells C6 through C11. What a long formula!

While this formula returns the correct result, a faster and easier way to calculate the total population for census year 1790 is to use the SUM function.

1. Activate cell **C12**.
2. Enter the formula **=SUM(C6:C11)**; the equals sign identifies the formula, and the SUM function automatically adds the values in the range C6:C11. Much better!

Function names are shown in ALL CAPS in this unit for readability. You do not have to key a function's name in ALL CAPS; *Excel* recognizes SUM, Sum, or sum as the same function.

When you use a function in a formula, you *must* include the function's name followed by a set of parentheses. The cell references or values inside the parentheses are called function arguments.

As you begin to key a function's name, the Formula AutoComplete list appears below the active cell. You can double-click a function name in the list to insert the function in your formula or continuing keying the function name. You practice using the Formula AutoComplete feature in the next section.

Home|Editing|Sum (AutoSum)

**Let's build a formula manually to calculate the total population for the 1790 census year by referencing each state's population and using the plus sign (+) calculation operator, then enter a formula by keying the SUM function and its arguments to calculate the total population for 1800.**

1. Click the *1790-1830 New England* sheet tab to activate the worksheet, if necessary.
2. Click cell **C12**.
3. Key **= C6+C7+C8+C9+C10+C11** and tap the ENTER key.

For example, another way to select a placeholder—even when it is inactive and you cannot see its boundaries—is to tap and hold the SHIFT key as you click the text inside the placeholder.

9. Tap and hold the SHIFT key and click the **New England Textile Mills** title to select the placeholder and its contents; then release the SHIFT key.
10. Change the font size to **48**.
11. Deselect the placeholder by clicking the slide work area outside the slide or by tapping the ESC key; save the presentation.

**CHECKPOINT**
Your edited Title Slide should look like this.

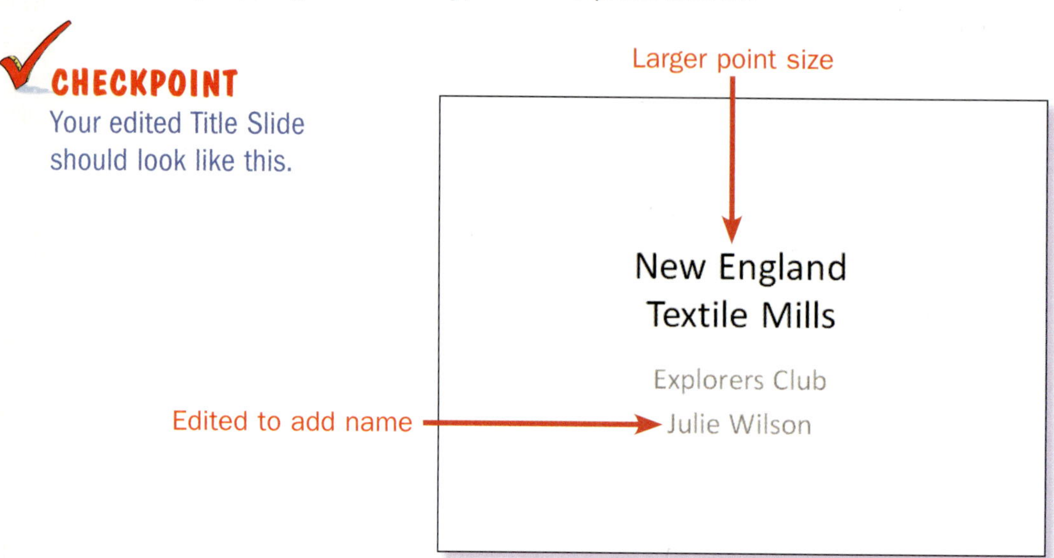


Good job! Now let's insert a new slide with a different slide layout.

## Inserting New Slides

To add a slide to the presentation, click the Home tab and then click the New Slide button face in the Slides group. The slide is inserted following the current slide and is automatically formatted with the Title and Content slide layout. If you click the New Slide button arrow, a gallery of layout options appears.

You can also right-click a slide and point to Layout to view a gallery of slide layout options. Try it!

The bulleted list on a Title and Content slide can have multiple levels of bulleted text, and each level can have a different bullet graphic. As you key the bulleted text, tap the TAB key to *demote* the text to the next level or tap the SHIFT + TAB keys to *promote* it to a previous level.

4. Click cell **C12**. The formula's result (1,009,408) appears in cell C12, and the formula appears in the formula bar.

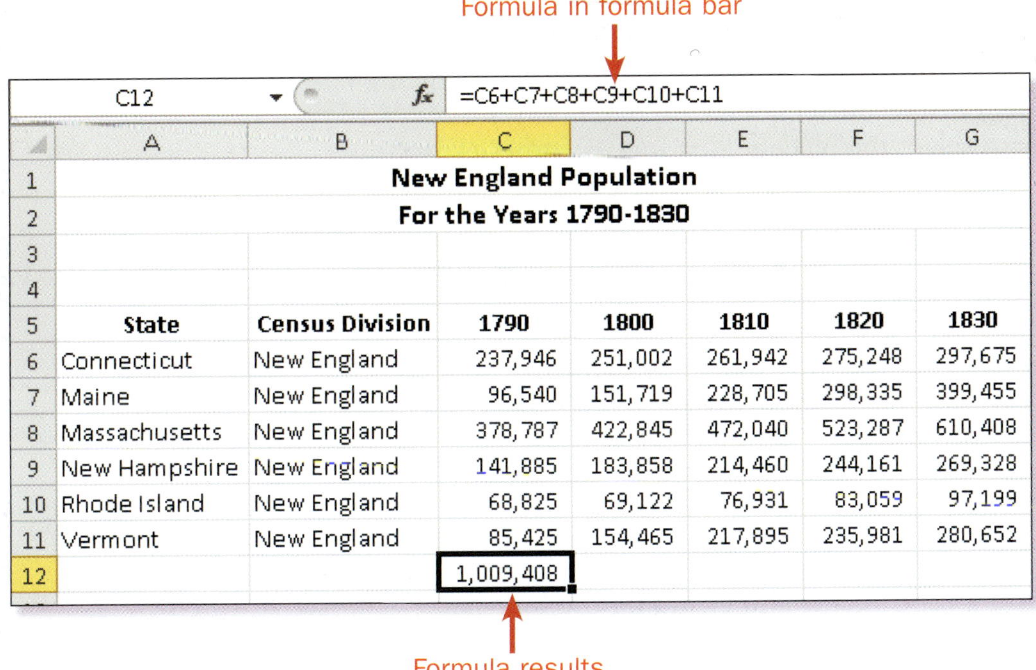


C12 | =C6+C7+C8+C9+C10+C11

| | A | B | C | D | E | F | G |
|---|---|---|---|---|---|---|---|
| 1 | New England Population | | | | | | |
| 2 | For the Years 1790-1830 | | | | | | |
| 3 | | | | | | | |
| 4 | | | | | | | |
| 5 | State | Census Division | 1790 | 1800 | 1810 | 1820 | 1830 |
| 6 | Connecticut | New England | 237,946 | 251,002 | 261,942 | 275,248 | 297,675 |
| 7 | Maine | New England | 96,540 | 151,719 | 228,705 | 298,335 | 399,455 |
| 8 | Massachusetts | New England | 378,787 | 422,845 | 472,040 | 523,287 | 610,408 |
| 9 | New Hampshire | New England | 141,885 | 183,858 | 214,460 | 244,161 | 269,328 |
| 10 | Rhode Island | New England | 68,825 | 69,122 | 76,931 | 83,059 | 97,199 |
| 11 | Vermont | New England | 85,425 | 154,465 | 217,895 | 235,981 | 280,652 |
| 12 | | | 1,009,408 | | | | |

Now see how much faster it is to use the SUM function to calculate the total population for 1800.

5. Activate cell **D12**.
6. Key **=S** and observe the Formula AutoComplete list below the active cell.
7. Continue by keying **UM(D6:D11)**; then tap the ENTER key to add the closing parenthesis and enter the formula. The SUM function quickly calculates the total population for 1800 (1,233,011).
8. If you see ####### symbols in cell D12, this means that the column is not wide enough to show the formula's calculated result; widen column **D** to fit, if necessary.

### Using the Sum (AutoSum) Button

Another way to create a formula containing the SUM function is to click the Sum (AutoSum) button in the Editing group on the Home tab. To insert a formula that contains the AVERAGE, MIN, or MAX function, click the Sum (AutoSum) button arrow and click a function name from the data range.

The Sum (AutoSum) button inserts the equals sign (=), the function name, the parentheses, and a single argument—the range of data to be added, averaged, or evaluated as the largest or smallest number.

Now that you have keyed your title and subtitle, you can format the text. To edit placeholder text, click the text with the I-beam pointer. To format placeholder text, select the text with the I-beam pointer and change the font, font size, font color, font style, and horizontal alignment using buttons in the Font and Paragraph groups on the Home tab.

If you want to format all of the text inside a placeholder the same way, just click the placeholder's boundary to select the placeholder and its contents and change the formatting.

Just like formatting text in *Word* and *Excel*, you can use live preview to review formatting before you apply it.

The default slide font is Calibri, and the default font sizes are very large. Fonts with clean lines, such as Calibri, and fonts in a large size might make it easy for an audience to read slides projected on a wall or projection screen.

Next, let's edit the subtitle by adding Julie's name and changing the font size.

**Let's edit the subtitle text.**

Home | Font | Font Size

1. Move the I-beam pointer to the end of the *Explorers Club* text and click to activate the placeholder and to position the insertion point.
2. Tap the ENTER key to move the insertion point to the center position on the next line.
3. Key **Julie Wilson**.
4. Move the mouse pointer to the placeholder's boundary; the mouse pointer becomes a selection pointer.
5. Click the placeholder boundary to select the placeholder and its contents. The boundary changes to a solid line border indicating that the placeholder and its contents are selected.
6. Click the **Home** tab, if necessary, and locate the **Font** groups.
7. Click the **Font Size** button in the Font group and point to **36** to see a live preview of the font size change; then click **36** to apply the new font size formatting.
8. Tap the ESC key to deactivate the placeholder.

18

You can use keyboard shortcuts to perform tasks in *PowerPoint* just like you did in *Word* and *Excel*. Many of the keyboard shortcuts you already learned—such as CTRL + HOME—work the same or a similar way in *PowerPoint*.

Be careful using the Sum (AutoSum) button! The Sum (AutoSum) button *guesses* at the range to use in the AVERAGE, MIN, MAX, and SUM functions' calculations! This *guess* is based on how the data is arranged above or to the left of the cell containing the function. If the *guess* is incorrect, you will have to edit the function to correct the range.

*Always verify the function's argument when you use the Sum (AutoSum) button.*

"You can also find the Sum (AutoSum) button in the Function Library group on the Formulas tab. Look for it!"

## Apply It!

**Let's use the Sum (AutoSum) button to enter formulas to calculate the remaining census years' total population.**

1. Select the range **E6:G12**. This range includes the data to be totaled and a blank cell at the bottom of each column in which to place the formula containing the SUM function.
2. Click the **Home** tab, if necessary, and locate the **Editing** group.
3. Click the **Sum** (**AutoSum**) button in the Editing group. Σ

| 1810 | 1820 | 1830 |
|---|---|---|
| 261,942 | 275,248 | 297,675 |
| 228,705 | 298,335 | 399,455 |
| 472,040 | 523,287 | 610,408 |
| 214,460 | 244,161 | 269,328 |
| 76,931 | 83,059 | 97,199 |
| 217,895 | 235,981 | 280,652 |
| | | |

Home | Editing | Sum (AutoSum)

*Excel* inserts a formula with the SUM function in each blank cell and *guesses* that the data to be totaled is in the cells immediately above the formula. It inserts the range of cells containing numbers immediately above the formula in the parentheses as each SUM function's argument.

4. Widen columns **E:G** to fit, if necessary. Then check out the formulas in the cells D12, E12, F12, and G12 and activate cell **A1**.

**CHECKPOINT**
Your worksheet with totals should look like this.

| | A | B | C | D | E | F | G |
|---|---|---|---|---|---|---|---|
| 1 | New England Population | | | | | | |
| 2 | For the Years 1790-1830 | | | | | | |
| 3 | | | | | | | |
| 4 | | | | | | | |
| 5 | State | Census Division | 1790 | 1800 | 1810 | 1820 | 1830 |
| 6 | Connecticut | New England | 237,946 | 251,002 | 261,942 | 275,248 | 297,675 |
| 7 | Maine | New England | 96,540 | 151,719 | 228,705 | 298,335 | 399,455 |
| 8 | Massachusetts | New England | 378,787 | 422,845 | 472,040 | 523,287 | 610,408 |
| 9 | New Hampshire | New England | 141,885 | 183,858 | 214,460 | 244,161 | 269,328 |
| 10 | Rhode Island | New England | 68,825 | 69,122 | 76,931 | 83,059 | 97,199 |
| 11 | Vermont | New England | 85,425 | 154,465 | 217,895 | 235,981 | 280,652 |
| 12 | | | 1,009,408 | 1,233,011 | 1,471,973 | 1,660,071 | 1,954,717 |

Calculated column totals

Because the first slide in a presentation usually contains the title and other introductory information, such as your name, *PowerPoint* automatically applies the Title Slide layout to slide 1 in a new presentation.

You can click inside a text placeholder with the I-beam pointer to position the insertion point.

As in *Word* and *Excel*, the mouse pointer becomes an I-beam pointer when placed in a slide text placeholder.

**Let's add a title and subtitle to slide 1.**

1. Click inside the **Click to add title** placeholder with the I-beam pointer. A dashed-line border appears around the placeholder, indicating that the placeholder contains the insertion point.
2. Key **New England** and tap the ENTER key.
3. Key **Textile Mills**.

4. Click inside the **Click to add subtitle** placeholder.
5. Key **Explorers Club**.
6. Click the slide work area outside the slide to deactivate the placeholder.
7. Save the presentation.

Your Title Slide should look like this.

What a great job! Now let's answer more of Julie's questions about the New England population data.

**Using the MAX, MIN, and AVERAGE Functions**

Julie wants to know the largest population in 1790, the smallest population in 1800, and the average population in 1810. To answer Julie's questions, you can enter formulas using the MAX, MIN, and AVERAGE functions.

To avoid keying errors, you will use the Formula AutoComplete list to enter the function and the mouse pointer to select each function's argument.

**Let's add Julie's questions to the worksheet and then find the answers using the MIN, MAX, and AVERAGE functions.**

1. Enter this question in cell **A14**: **What is the largest state population in 1790?**
2. Enter this question in cell **A15**: **What is the smallest state population in 1800?**
3. Enter this question in cell **A16**: **What is the average state population in 1810?**
4. Activate cell **E14**.
5. Key **=M** and double-click **MAX** in the Formula AutoComplete list that appears below the cell. The MAX function and an open parenthesis are inserted in the formula.

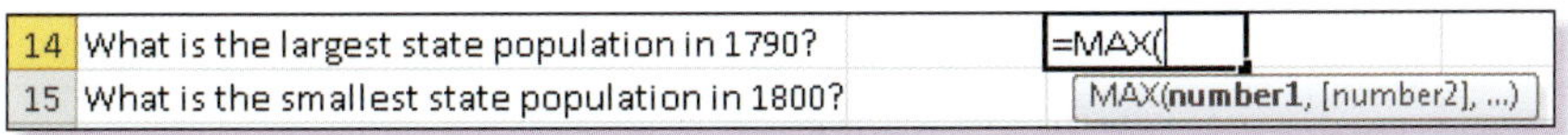


6. Select the range **C6:C11** to add the MAX function's argument.

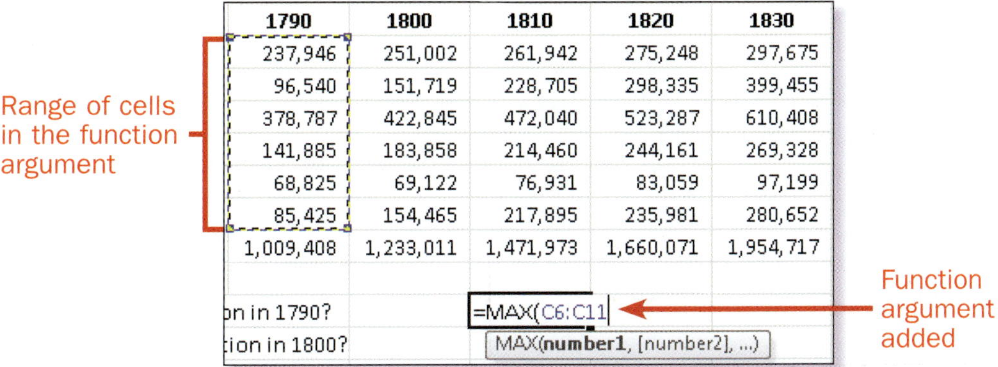

|  | 1790 | 1800 | 1810 | 1820 | 1830 |
|---|---|---|---|---|---|
| | 237,946 | 251,002 | 261,942 | 275,248 | 297,675 |
| | 96,540 | 151,719 | 228,705 | 298,335 | 399,455 |
| | 378,787 | 422,845 | 472,040 | 523,287 | 610,408 |
| | 141,885 | 183,858 | 214,460 | 244,161 | 269,328 |
| | 68,825 | 69,122 | 76,931 | 83,059 | 97,199 |
| | 85,425 | 154,465 | 217,895 | 235,981 | 280,652 |
| | 1,009,408 | 1,233,011 | 1,471,973 | 1,660,071 | 1,954,717 |
| on in 1790? | | =MAX(C6:C11 | | | |
| tion in 1800? | | MAX(number1, [number2], ...) | | | |

- Slides tab—shows a tiny version of each slide, called a thumbnail
- Notes pane—the area in which you can key additional comments about the slide
- Ribbon—tabs and groups of buttons you can click to perform various tasks
- status bar—shows the number of the slide in the slide pane and the total number of slides in the presentation; also contains the View Shortcuts and the zooming tools

You name and save a *PowerPoint* presentation just like you named and saved your *Word* documents and *Excel* workbooks, by clicking Save As on the File tab or Office Button.

Just as you did in *Word* and *Excel*, you can also click the Save button on the Quick Access Toolbar to name and save a new presentation or to resave a presentation with the same name in the same location.

**Let's name and save the presentation.**

1. Click the **Save** button on the Quick Access Toolbar to open the Save As dialog box.
2. Switch to the folder that contains your solution files, key **textile mills11** in the File name text box, and click the dialog box **Save** button.

Great! Now let's add title and subtitle text to slide 1.

## Adding and Editing Slide Text

Each slide has a specific slide layout with boxes—called place-holders—for organizing content such as text, clip art, tables, SmartArt graphics, media clips, and charts.

*PowerPoint* has many different slide layouts, including these:

- Title Slide (title and subtitle text placeholders)
- Title and Content (title text, bulleted list placeholder, and other content icons)
- Title Only (title placeholder only) layouts
- Blank (no placeholders)

7. Tap the ENTER key to add the closing parenthesis and enter the formula. Cell E14 contains the largest population number for 1790—378,787. Ignore the error message if one appears.
8. Activate cell **E15**, if necessary.
9. Key **=M**, double-click **MIN** in the Formula AutoComplete list, select the range **D6:D11** and tap the ENTER key. Cell **E15** contains the smallest population number for 1800—69,122. Ignore the error message if one appears.
10. Activate cell **E16**, if necessary.
11. Key **=AV**, double-click **AVERAGE** in the Formula AutoComplete list, select the range **E6:E11**, and tap the ENTER key. Cell E16 contains the average population number of 1810—245,329. Ignore the error message if one appears.

**CHECKPOINT**

Your questions and answers should look like this.

| 14 | What is the largest state population in 1790? | 378,787 |
|---|---|---|
| 15 | What is the smallest state population in 1800? | 69,122 |
| 16 | What is the average state population in 1810? | 245,329 |

Well done! Now let's create a more complex formula using two functions.

## 5 Using the LOOKUP, TODAY, and NOW Functions

TRAIL MARKER

The LOOKUP function uses a value in one range to find another value in a different range. For example, Julie wants to know which states had the largest and smallest populations in 1830. You can combine the LOOKUP, MAX, and MIN functions to answer that question.

Let's learn how to use the LOOKUP and MAX functions together to find the name of the state that had the largest population in 1830. The LOOKUP function has three arguments separated by commas:

1. a lookup value
2. the range in which to find the lookup value *sorted in ascending order*
3. the range in which to locate a related value

This is the formula used to find the name of the state with the largest population in 1830:

**=LOOKUP(MAX(G6:G11),G6:G11,A6:A11)**

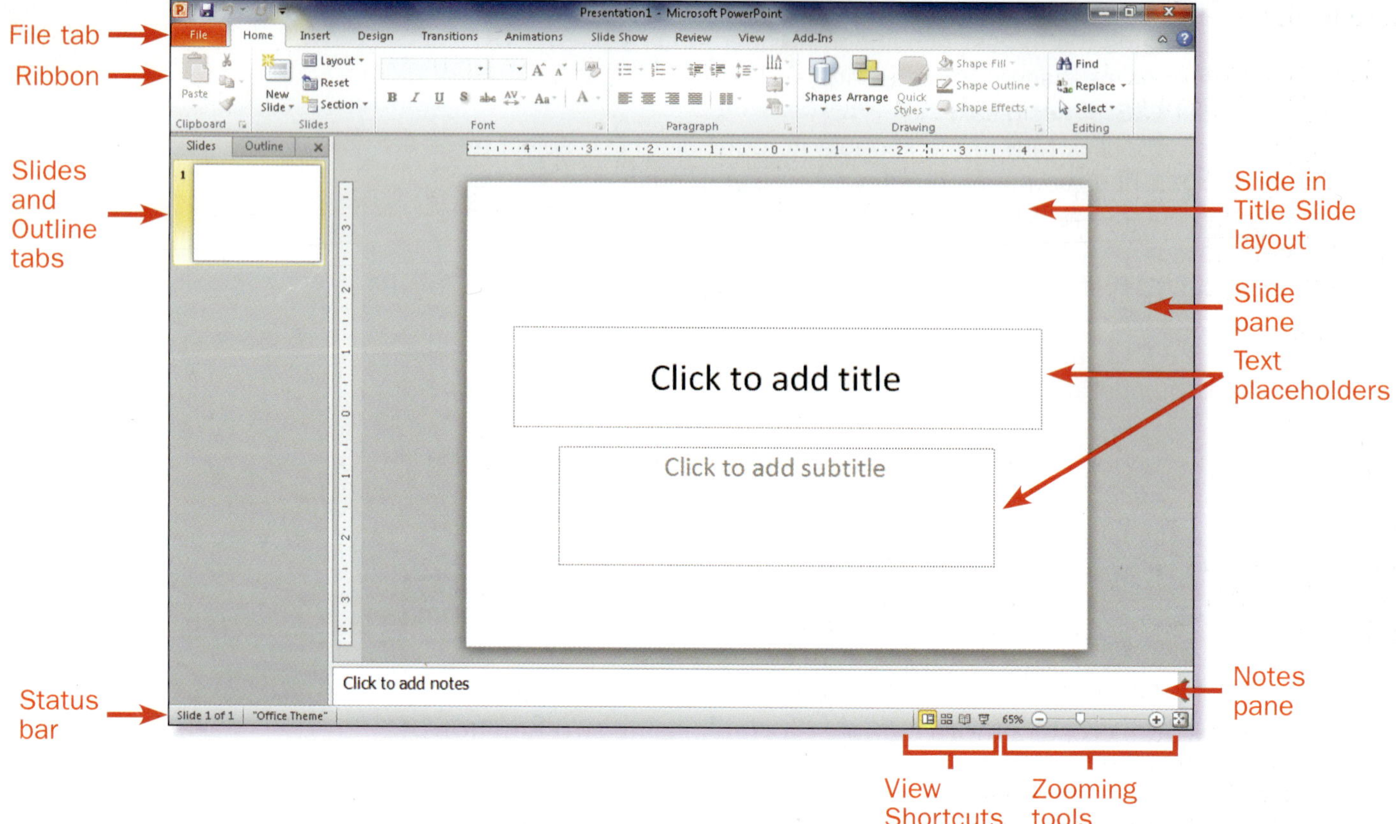


*PowerPoint* opens with a new blank file, called a presentation, which is similar to a blank *Word* document or an empty *Excel* workbook. Also just like *Word* and *Excel*, you can create a new presentation when *PowerPoint* is already open by clicking the File tab or Office Button and clicking New.

A new blank *PowerPoint* presentation contains one individual page, called a slide. Slides are numbered sequentially beginning with slide 1. You can insert additional slides as you need them. All of the slides in one presentation are saved in a single file.

Slides can contain text, graphics, video, and even sound. You can present the slides one after another, called running a slide show, by projecting the slides on a wall or projector screen. You can also print the slides for review or audience handouts.

By default, *PowerPoint* opens in Normal view, the view in which you create and edit your slides. Normal view features include the following:

- Slide pane—the area in which you add text, drawings, clip art, video, and sound to a slide
- Outline tab—used to create and view slides in an outline format

Here is how the formula works:

1. The formula finds the largest population number for the year 1830 using the MAX function (MAX(G6:G11).
2. The formula compares the results of the MAX calculation to values in the range G6:G11 to locate the row in which the largest population number for 1830 is located.
3. The formula looks across the row to find the state name in the range A6:A11.

**Let's answer Julie's last two questions by using the LOOKUP function and the MAX or MIN function together in a formula. Before we enter the formulas, let's sort the data for 1830 in ascending order by population.**

Data | Sort & Filter | Sort Smallest to Largest

1. Enter this question in cell **A17**: **Which state had the largest population in 1830?**
2. Enter this question in cell **A18**: **Which state had the smallest population in 1830?**
3. Click the **Data** tab and locate the **Sort & Filter** group. Similar to the buttons in the Editing group on the Home tab, this tab group contains buttons for sorting and filtering a data range.
4. Click any cell in column G inside the data range boundaries.
5. Click the **Sort Smallest to Largest** button in the Sort & Filter group to sort the data range in ascending order by population for the 1830 census year.
6. Activate cell **E17**.
7. Key **=LOOKUP(MAX(G6:G11),G6:G11,A6:A11)** and tap the ENTER key. *Don't forget to key the closing parenthesis after the MAX function's argument, the commas between the arguments, and the closing parenthesis at the end of the formula.* Cell E17 now contains the name of the state with the largest population in 1830—Massachusetts.
8. Activate cell **E18**, if necessary.
9. Enter **=LOOKUP(MIN(G6:G11),G6:G11,A6:A11)** and tap the ENTER key. Cell **E18** now contains the name of the state with the smallest population in 1830—Rhode Island.
10. Tap the CTRL + HOME keys and save the workbook.

Your questions and answers should now look like this.

| | | |
|---|---|---|
| 14 | What is the largest state population in 1790? | 378,787 |
| 15 | What is the smallest state population in 1800? | 69,122 |
| 16 | What is the average state population in 1810? | 245,329 |
| 17 | Which state had the largest population in 1830? | Massachusetts |
| 18 | Which state had the smallest population in 1830? | Rhode Island |

**Begin by starting the *PowerPoint* application and opening a new blank presentation.**

1. Turn on your computer, if necessary.
2. Click the **Start** button on the taskbar.
3. Point to **All Programs** on the Start menu.
4. Click the ***Microsoft Office*** folder.
5. Click ***Microsoft PowerPoint 2010*** or ***Microsoft Office PowerPoint 2007*** to open the application.

If you have an icon on your desktop for *PowerPoint*, just double-click it to open the application.

Good job! You can use the *PowerPoint* application to present facts and ideas to an audience—with a slide show and/or printed material. Let's begin by naming and saving Julie's presentation.

**ERGONOMICS TIP**

Don't forget! It is important to take several short exercise breaks when working at your computer! Ready? Stand up, stretch, and flex your fingers. Great! Back to work!

## Creating, Naming, and Saving a New Presentation

The *PowerPoint* window shares many elements with the *Word* and *Excel* windows, such as the File tab or Office Button, the Ribbon, and the status bar. Many of the File tab, Office Button, or Ribbon buttons, such as the Copy and Paste buttons in the Clipboard group on the Home tab, work the same in *PowerPoint* as they do in *Word* and *Excel*. Other Ribbon buttons and software features are designed specifically for working in *PowerPoint*.

Remember to use ScreenTips to identify new Ribbon buttons or other PowerPoint screen elements!

What a great job! Now let's add today's date using a function.

**Using the TODAY and NOW Functions**

Next, you need to add the current system date to all of the worksheets. You can do this with the TODAY or NOW function. The TODAY function inserts today's date; the NOW function inserts today's date and time; the cell containing the NOW function can be formatted to show just the date, just the time, or both the date and time.

The TODAY and NOW functions use your computer's system clock. You can see the current system date and time in the notification area on the right side of the task bar.

The SUM, MAX, and LOOKUP functions you have learned to use all require one or more function arguments. Some functions, such as TODAY and NOW, do not have a function argument; however, you must still include the parentheses!

If you forget to include a set of parentheses for the TODAY or NOW function, you will see the #NAME? error message in the cell. This means that *Excel* does not recognize the function without the empty parentheses.

The Function Library group on the Formulas tab provides buttons you can click to quickly access a function from a specific function category. The TODAY and NOW functions are located in the Date & Time category in the Function Library.

**Let's insert today's date in cell A3 on two worksheets.**

Formulas | Function Library | Date & Time

Home | Alignment | Merge & Center

Home | Number | Number Format

1. Click the *1790-1830 Data* sheet tab.
2. Click the **Formulas** tab and locate the **Function Library** group to view buttons for the specific function categories.
3. Activate cell **B3**.
4. Click the **Date & Time** button in the Function Library group to view a gallery of date and time functions. 

5. Click **TODAY** in the Date & Time gallery. The formula =TODAY() is entered in cell B3, and the Function Arguments dialog box opens. The dialog box contains a description of the TODAY function. Click **OK** to calculate the current system date.
6. Center the date across the range B3:H3.
7. Click the *1790-1830 New England* sheet tab.
8. Using steps 4–6 as your guide, insert the **NOW** function in a formula in cell **A3**.

# Working in New England's Textile Mills

## Explorers' Guide

**Data file:** none

**Objectives:**
In this project, you will:
- create, name, and save a new presentation
- add and edit slide text
- insert new slides
- apply a theme
- navigate slides and run a slide show
- preview and print a presentation

© CORBIS

## Our Exploration Assignment:

### Creating a new slide show presentation

The Explorers Club is learning about the lives of the people who worked in the 19th-century New England textile mills. Can you help Julie create a slide show for the next meeting? Great! Follow the Trail Markers to create, name, and save a new slide show; add and edit slide text; insert new slides; apply a theme; navigate slides; run a slide show; and then preview and print the slides.

9. Click the **Home** tab, if necessary, and locate the **Number** group.
10. Click the **Number Format** button arrow in the Number group and click **Long Date** to format the date with the day spelled out followed by the month spelled out, the day, and the year in four digits.
11. Center the date across the range **A3:G3**.
12. Activate cell **A1** and save the workbook.

Well done! Now Julie wants to see population subtotals for the other census divisions. Instead of filtering, copying, and pasting the data for the other census divisions, you can create temporary subtotals on the *1790-1830 Data* worksheet.

## Adding and Removing Temporary Subtotals

Julie wants to know the total population for each Census Division for 1790–1830, but she doesn't want to alter the worksheet.

You can find this information without altering the worksheet by sorting the data range on the *1790-1830 Data* worksheet by Census Division and then creating *temporary* subtotals for the population data for each division. You then easily remove the subtotals when you no longer need them.

Warning! Sorting and creating subtotals requires that the active cell be inside the boundaries of an *Excel* data range. Check out Project 7, if necessary, to review the rules for working with an *Excel* data range.

To insert temporary subtotals, click the Data tab and then click the Subtotal button in the Outline group to open the Subtotals dialog box. In the dialog box, set the subtotal criteria to tell *Excel* which data and function to use and when to use them.

*Excel* outlines a worksheet containing subtotals and provides outline level buttons (1, 2, 3, +, and -) that you can use to expand or collapse the outline.

# PRESENTATIONS AND MULTIMEDIA

***Great to see you again! Julie, Luis, Lin, and I are excited about our new explorations. Come along to:***

- Work in New England's Textile Mills.
- Change the States of Matter.
- Observe the Atom.
- Rush to California.
- Race the Iditarod Trail.

Presenting your research facts to an audience is very rewarding! You will learn how to use an application called *PowerPoint* to create slide shows to help your with your oral presentations. You will create new slide show presentations and open and modify existing presentations. You will learn to add color, animations, slide transitions, audio and video, clip art, shapes, and text boxes to enhance your slides. You will also create handouts to accompany your slide show. You will even learn how to paste data from an *Excel* worksheet into a *PowerPoint* slide! Ready! Set! Go!

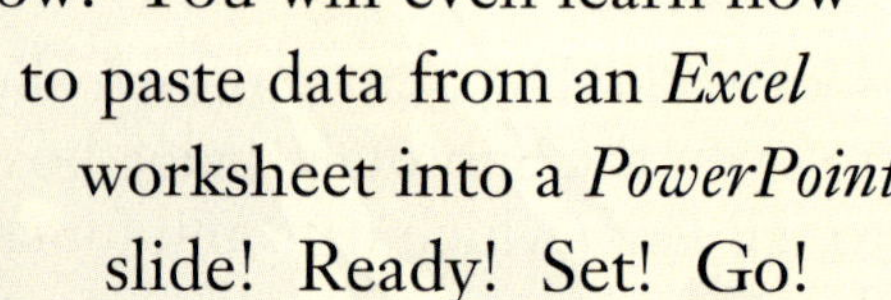

**Let's sort the data by Census Division and then insert temporary subtotals.**

Data | Outline | Subtotal

1. Activate the *1790-1830 Data* worksheet, if necessary.
2. Activate any cell in the Census Division column within the data range boundaries.
3. Sort the data range by Census Division in ascending alphabetical order to organize the data by Census Division.
4. Click the **Data** tab, if necessary, and locate the **Outline** group.
5. Click the **Subtotal** button to open the Subtotal dialog box.
6. Click the **At each change in** arrow and click **Census Division**. This tells *Excel* when to insert the subtotals.

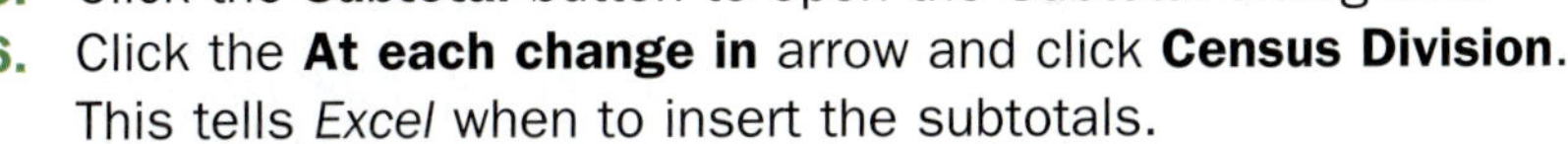


7. Click the **Use function** arrow and click **Sum**, if necessary. This tells *Excel* what calculation to perform each time the Census Division changes.
8. Scroll the **Add subtotal to** list of column names and click the **1790**, **1800**, **1810**, **1820**, and **1830** checkboxes. These check marks tell *Excel* what data to use in the subtotal calculations.
9. Remove any other check marks from the other **Add subtotal** to data range checkboxes, if necessary. By default, the **Replace current subtotals** and **Summary below data** checkboxes should already contain check marks.

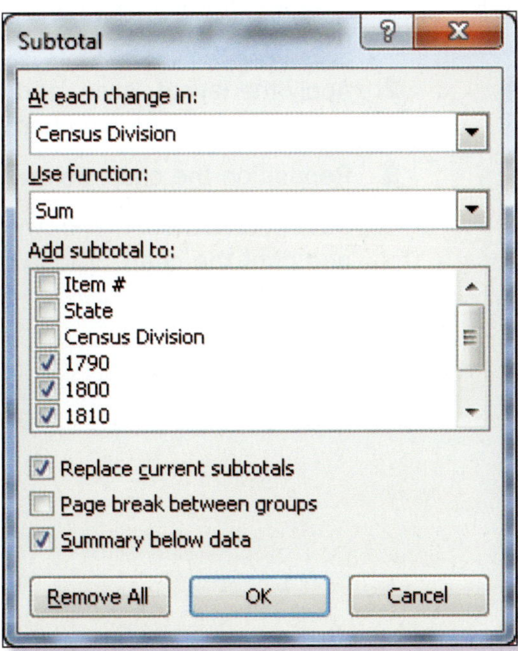


10. Click **OK**.
11. Resize the columns to fit the contents, if necessary. Subtotals are inserted, and the outlining pane appears on the left side of the worksheet.

# Day 2 – Total Care Veterinary Clinic (continued)

2. Look at the Assumptions box.
   a. The Animal Food expenses for each quarter are projected to be a percentage of Boarding Services revenues. Using the Qtr 1 Boarding Services revenues and the Animal food expense assumption, create a formula to calculate the cost of animal food for Qtr 1; copy the formula to Qtr 2–4 using an absolute reference.
   b. Grooming Staff fees for each quarter are projected to be a percentage of Grooming Services revenues. Using the Qtr 1 Grooming Services revenues and the Grooming staff fees assumption, create a formula to calculate grooming fees for Qtr 1; copy the formula to Qtr 2–4 using an absolute reference.
3. Use a function and the Formula AutoComplete feature to calculate the Total Revenues and Total Expenses for Qtr 1; then use the fill handle to copy the formulas to Qtr 2–4.
4. Create a formula to calculate the surplus or deficit value for Qtr 1; then use the fill handle to copy the formula to Qtr 2–4.
5. Select the appropriate columns; then use the Sum (AutoSum) button to calculate the Total column values for all of the data at one time.
6. Use a function to eliminate a small rounding error by adjusting the Qtr 1 Animal Food and Grooming Staff Fees formulas; then copy the formulas to Qtr 2–4.
7. Use the status bar calculations (the AutoCalculate feature) and/or manual calculations to verify your formulas' results.
8. Resize columns as necessary.
9. Save the workbook and, with permission, print the worksheet.

## Task #3 – The Boarding & Grooming Services Budget Chart

1. Open the *Orange Day 2 Budget solution* file, if necessary, and create an embedded 3-D pie chart named *Budget Expenses* to show the percentage of each expense total to the total of all expenses.
2. Apply the layout, style, and other formatting of your choice to the pie chart.
3. Reposition the chart below the data.
4. Save the workbook and, with permission, select and print the chart. Close the workbook.

12. Click cells **E10** and **F15** to view examples of the SUBTOTAL formulas.
13. Tap the CTRL + HOME keys.

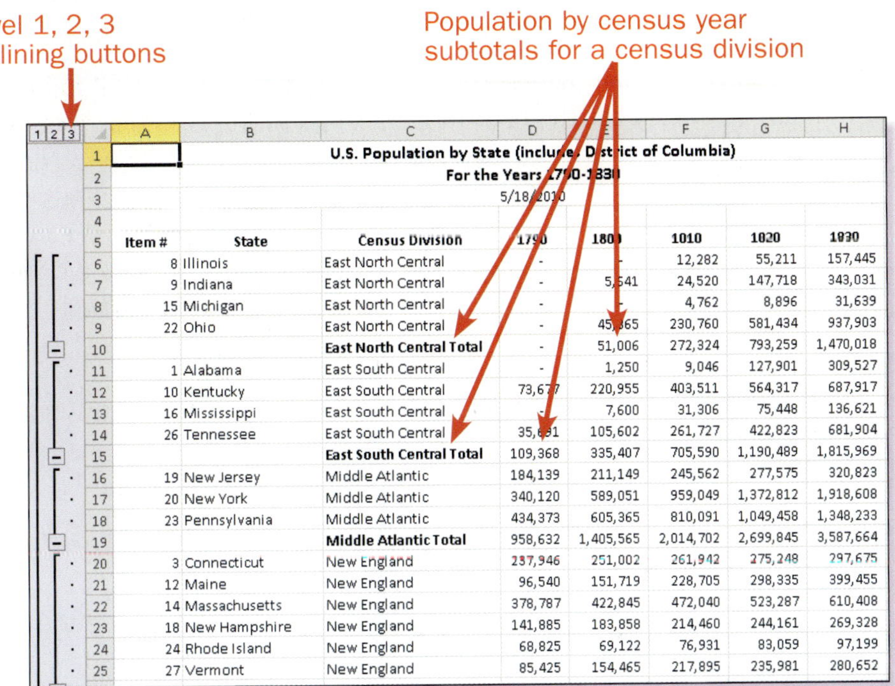


| | A | B | C | D | E | F | G | H |
|---|---|---|---|---|---|---|---|---|
| 1 | | | U.S. Population by State (includes District of Columbia) | | | | | |
| 2 | | | For the Years 1790-1830 | | | | | |
| 3 | | | 5/18/2010 | | | | | |
| 4 | | | | | | | | |
| 5 | Item # | State | Census Division | 1790 | 1800 | 1810 | 1820 | 1830 |
| 6 | 8 | Illinois | East North Central | - | - | 12,282 | 55,211 | 157,445 |
| 7 | 9 | Indiana | East North Central | - | 5,[illegible]41 | 24,520 | 147,718 | 343,031 |
| 8 | 15 | Michigan | East North Central | - | - | 4,762 | 8,896 | 31,639 |
| 9 | 22 | Ohio | East North Central | - | 45,[illegible]65 | 230,760 | 581,434 | 937,903 |
| 10 | | | **East North Central Total** | - | 51,006 | 272,324 | 793,259 | 1,470,018 |
| 11 | 1 | Alabama | East South Central | - | 1,250 | 9,046 | 127,901 | 309,527 |
| 12 | 10 | Kentucky | East South Central | 73,6[illegible]7 | 220,955 | 403,511 | 564,317 | 687,917 |
| 13 | 16 | Mississippi | East South Central | - | 7,600 | 31,306 | 75,448 | 136,621 |
| 14 | 26 | Tennessee | East South Central | 35,[illegible]91 | 105,602 | 261,727 | 422,823 | 681,904 |
| 15 | | | **East South Central Total** | 109,368 | 335,407 | 705,590 | 1,190,489 | 1,815,969 |
| 16 | 19 | New Jersey | Middle Atlantic | 184,139 | 211,149 | 245,562 | 277,575 | 320,823 |
| 17 | 20 | New York | Middle Atlantic | 340,120 | 589,051 | 959,049 | 1,372,812 | 1,918,608 |
| 18 | 23 | Pennsylvania | Middle Atlantic | 434,373 | 605,365 | 810,091 | 1,049,458 | 1,348,233 |
| 19 | | | **Middle Atlantic Total** | 958,632 | 1,405,565 | 2,014,702 | 2,699,845 | 3,587,664 |
| 20 | 3 | Connecticut | New England | 237,946 | 251,002 | 261,942 | 275,248 | 297,675 |
| 21 | 12 | Maine | New England | 96,540 | 151,719 | 228,705 | 298,335 | 399,455 |
| 22 | 14 | Massachusetts | New England | 378,787 | 422,845 | 472,040 | 523,287 | 610,408 |
| 23 | 18 | New Hampshire | New England | 141,885 | 183,858 | 214,460 | 244,161 | 269,328 |
| 24 | 24 | Rhode Island | New England | 68,825 | 69,122 | 76,931 | 83,059 | 97,199 |
| 25 | 27 | Vermont | New England | 85,425 | 154,465 | 217,895 | 235,981 | 280,652 |

The level 1, 2, and 3 outlining buttons at the top of the outlining pane expand or collapse the worksheet to show you all of the rows (3), the subtotals and the grand total (2), or just the grand total (1). Clicking a minus sign (-) collapses a group of rows, and clicking a plus sign (+) expands a group.

**Let's expand and collapse the worksheet outline, then remove the subtotals.**

1. Click the **level 2** button at the top of the outlining pane to view only the subtotals and grand total.
2. Click the **level 1** button at the top of the outlining pane to view just the grand total.
3. Click the **level 3** button at the top of the outlining pane to view all of the data.
4. Click any cell inside the data range boundaries, if necessary.
5. Click the **Subtotal** button in the Outline group to open the Subtotals dialog box.
6. Click the **Remove All** button. The subtotals, grand total, and outlining pane are removed from the worksheet.
7. Sort the **Item #** column in ascending numerical order to return the worksheet to its original order; then save and close the workbook.

Subtotal

# Day 2 – Total Care Veterinary Clinic

On Day 2 of your internship, Ms. Davis asks you to help out with some accounting tasks. But first, she asks you to help James, one of the clinic's veterinary technicians, take a supplies inventory for the boarding and grooming services area. When the inventory is finished, Ms. Davis gives you a list of accounting tasks to complete by the end of the day.

## TO DO TODAY

1. Summarize vendor invoices in a new workbook
2. Complete next year's boarding and grooming services budget
3. Add a chart to the budget worksheet

## Task #1 – The Vendor Invoices Summary

1. Start *Excel* with a new blank workbook. Rename Sheet1 as *Vendor Invoices*. Delete Sheet2 and Sheet3. Save the workbook as *Orange Day 2 Vendor Invoices sol*.
2. Open the *Orange Day 2 Vendor Inv List data Word* document. Working back and forth between the open document and workbook as necessary:
   - **a.** Enter a worksheet title in cell A1. Use the NOW() function to enter the current date in cell A2. Format the date with the Long Date format using the Date button in the Number group on the Home tab. Bold the contents of the range A1:A2 and center the range across the columns A:D.
   - **b.** Enter column headings and the invoice list data in the range A4:D13. Bold and center the column headings.
   - **c.** Format the range B5:B13 with a Date format that shows the month spelled out, the day, and the current year.
   - **d.** Use the Sum (AutoSum) button to calculate the total amount in cell D14.
   - **e.** Apply the Accounting Number Format with zero decimal places to the values in cells D5 and D14. Apply the Comma Style with zero decimal places to the values in the range D6:D13.
   - **f.** Add a Single Underline format to cell D13 and a Double Underline format to cell D14.
3. Check the spelling in the worksheet.
4. Save the workbook and, with permission, print the worksheet.
5. Close the *Word* document and close the *Excel* workbook.

## Task #2 – The Boarding & Grooming Services Budget

1. Open the *Orange Day 2 Budget data file* and save it as *Orange Day 2 Budget solution* in the Clinic Assignments folder.
   - **a.** Rename the Sheet1 sheet tab as *B & G Budget*.
   - **b.** Bold the contents of the range A1:A2 and center the contents across the range A1:F2.
   - **c.** Select the range B4:F4 and bold and center the contents.
   - **d.** Select the nonadjacent cells A5, A8, A10, A16, and A18 and bold the contents.
   - **e.** Select the nonadjacent ranges A6:A7 and A11:A15 and indent the contents two spaces from the left margin.

# Project Skills Review

You learned a lot in this project! We are very impressed with your progress. Let's take a few minutes to review the skills that you learned.

| | | |
|---|---|---|
| **Fill a range of cells with a data series** | Drag the active cell's or range's fill handle. Use the CTRL key to increment numbers by 1. | |
| **Insert or delete rows or columns** | Right-click one or more column or row headings and click **Insert** or **Delete**. | |
| **Edit data** | Enter new text or numbers in a cell. Click the **Formula Bar** with the I-beam and edit its contents. Tap the **F2** key to open the cell for editing and position the insertion point in the cell; then edit the cell's contents. | |
| **Apply formatting to cell contents** | Click a button in the **Font**, **Alignment**, or **Number** groups on the **Home** tab. | 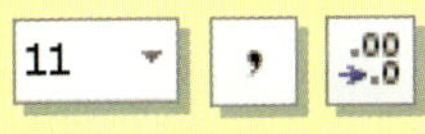 |
| **Filter data** | Click the **Sort & Filter** button in the Editing group on the **Home** tab and click **Filter**. | 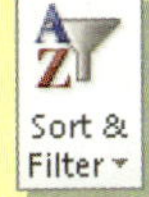  |
| **Insert a new worksheet** | Right-click a sheet tab and click **Insert**. | |
| **Use functions** | Click the **Sum** (**AutoSum**) button or button arrow in the Editing group on the **Home** tab. Click a function category button in the Function Library on the **Formulas** tab. | 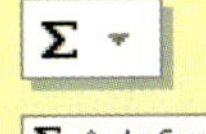  |
| **Add or remove temporary subtotals** | Click the **Subtotal** button in the Outline group on the **Data** tab. | |

# Project 10 Keyboarding

## 10a Build Skill

Key each line twice. Double-space between 2-line groups.

**TECHNIQUE TIP**

Reach out with the little finger and tap the enter key quickly. Return your finger to the home key.

A Abe ate banana bread at Anna's Cafe at 18 Parkway.

B Bob Abbott bobbled the baseball hit by Barb Banks.

C Cecelia can check the capacities for each cubicle.

D Dan added additional games and divided the squads.

E Emery recently developed three new feet exercises.

F Jeff Florez offered the fifty officials free food.

G Gregg gingerly gave the giggling girl a gold ring.

H Herb had shared half the hay with their neighbors.

I I will live in Illinois after leaving Mississippi.

J Jay, Jet, and Joy enjoyed the jet ride to Jamaica.

K Kay Kern took the kayak to Kentucky for Kent Kick.

L Will lives in Idaho; Lance Bell lives in Illinois.

M Mary Mead assumed the maximum and minimum amounts.

gwam 30" | 2 | 4 | 6 | 8 | 10 | 12 | 14 | 16 | 18 | 20 |

## 10b Technique: ENTER

Key two 30" timed writings on each line.

For additional practice:
**MicroType 5**
Skill Building, Lesson B

1 Jan left to go home.

2 They won their last game.

3 Kay's test score was terrible.

4 The next game may not be cancelled.

5 The hurricane struck Florida on Tuesday.

6 The teacher said Jane could make up the exam.

7 She may be able to catch a later flight on Friday.

gwam 30" | 2 | 4 | 6 | 8 | 10 | 12 | 14 | 16 | 18 | 20 |

# Exploring On Your Own

## Blaze Your Own Trail

You have learned several new skills in this project. Now blaze your own trail by practicing these skills on your own!

1. Open the *population data8* workbook and activate the *1840-1880 Data* worksheet.
   - Insert a new column A and enter the text **Item #,** bolded and centered, in cell **A5**.
   - Delete the blank row 6.
   - Use the fill handle to add the remaining census years in cells **F5, G5,** and **H5**; then use the fill handle to enter consecutive numbers for all of the rows containing data beginning with 1 in cell **A6**.
   - Format the population data in the range D6:H53 to apply the Comma Style and no decimal places.
2. Insert a new worksheet named *1840-1880 South Atlantic* following the *1840-1880 Data* worksheet. (*Hint*: Drag the new worksheet's sheet tab to the desired position.)
3. On the *1840-1880 Data* worksheet, use AutoFilter to filter the data to see only the South Atlantic Census Division.
4. Copy the filtered data in the range B1:H34 and paste it on the *1840-1880 South Atlantic* worksheet beginning in cell **A1**.
   - Resize the columns to fit.
   - Edit cell **A1** to be **South Atlantic Population**.
   - In cell **C15**, enter a formula that adds the population for each state (=C6+C7+C8, and so forth).
   - Use SUM function to calculate the total population for the remaining census years.
   - Use the MIN, MAX, and LOOKUP functions to answer the following questions: What is the largest population in 1840? What is the smallest population in 1860? Which state has the largest population in 1880? Which state has the smallest population in 1880?
5. Use the TODAY or NOW function to add today's date to cell A3 on both worksheets. Format the date as desired.
6. On the *1840-1880 Data* worksheet, turn off the AutoFilter and then save and close the workbook.

## Reading in Action — Multiple-Meaning Words

The Latin root of the word *argument* is *arguere*, which means "to make clear." Look up the meanings of the word *argument* in a dictionary. Write at least three definitions, using the meaning of the Latin root in each definition. Use the Latin root to help you understand the mathematical meaning of the word *argument*.

## Math in Action — Finding the Percent of Change

Determine the percent of change in population from 1820 (523,287) to 1830 (610,408) in Massachusetts. Subtract the 1820 population from the 1830 population and then divide the result by the 1820 population. Convert the decimal as a percent.

610,408 – 523,287 = 87,121

$$\frac{87{,}121}{523{,}287} = 0.166 = 17\%$$

Now you try it!

Find the percent of change in population from 1810 (472,040) to 1820 in Massachusetts. Then find the change in population from 1810 to 1830.

# Exploring *Across the Curriculum*

## Getting Help

Click the Microsoft Excel Help icon below the *Excel* application Close button to open the *Excel* Help window. Key **data table** in the search box and tap the ENTER key to research data tables and ways to show and hide a data table on a chart. Then using what you have learned, open the *universe10* workbook, select a chart, and show and hide a data table on the chart. Close the workbook without saving it.

## Career Day

Information technologies are critical tools for scientists studying the universe. Using library, printed, or online resources, identify three interesting careers in science-related information technologies. Write a brief summary of each occupation, print your summary, and save it in your Career Day folder.

## Your Personal Journal

Open your personal journal document. Insert today's date and two blank lines. Think about what you have learned about creating charts in *Excel*. Select one of the charts you created in this project. Explain what the chart shows when it is created by column orientation and by row orientation. Spell-check, save, and close your journal.

**Online Enrichment Games**  www.cengage.com/school/keyboarding/lwcorange

# Exploring *Across the Curriculum*

## Internet/Web

Open your Web browser and use a favorite or bookmark to view the Learning with Computers Web page (www.cengage.com/school/keyboarding/lwcorange). Click the **Links** option and click **Project 8**. Click the links to learn how immigration in the nineteenth century dramatically changed the U.S. population. Take notes about what you learn.

1. Create a new *Word* document.
2. Using your research and the data from the *population data8* workbook, create a three-level multilevel list you can use to present an oral report to your classmates on nineteenth-century U.S. immigration or write a properly formatted multipage bound report with a title page and sources cited on a separate References page.

## Language Arts: Words to Know

Look up the meaning of the following terms in a classroom dictionary, CD-ROM dictionary or encyclopedia, or online dictionary.

| population | demographic data | economic data | census |
|---|---|---|---|
| sampling | cohort | occupation | household |

Create a new workbook. Save the workbook as *definitions8*. Rename the Sheet1 sheet tab as **Definitions**. Enter the title **Population Definitions** in cell **A1** and today's date using the TODAY function in cell **A2**. Merge and center **A1** and **A2** across the range A1:B2, change the font size to 12 point, and apply the Bold font style.

Enter **Term** as the column name in **A4**. Enter **Definition** as the column name in **B4**. Bold the column names. Center the column names in the cells. Enter the terms in the range A5:A12. Enter the term definitions in the range B5:B12. Use the resizing pointer to automatically fit the cell contents for columns A and B. Sort the data range by term in ascending order. Save and close the workbook.

Explore More

# Exploring *Across the Curriculum*

## Internet/Web

Open your Web browser and use a favorite or bookmark to view the Learning with Computers Web page (www.cengage.com/school/keyboarding/lwcorange). Click the **Links** option and Click **Project 10**. Use the links to learn more about stars, planets, galaxies, black holes, asteroids, and other objects in the universe. Select the object or objects you find most interesting and take notes about what you learn. Create a new *Word* document and organize your notes as a three-level multilevel list you can use to (1) present an oral report to your classmates or (2) write a multipage bound report with a title page and endnotes.

## Language Arts: Words to Know

Look up the meaning of the following terms using a classroom, library, CD-ROM, or online encyclopedia or dictionary.

| asteroid | astronomy | comet | dark energy |
|---|---|---|---|
| galaxy | gravity | light year | mass |

Create a new workbook. Save the workbook as *definitions10*. Rename the Sheet1 sheet tab as **Definitions**. Enter the title **Universe Definitions** in cell **A1**. Merge and center the title across the range A1:B1. Enter **Term** as the column name in **A3**. Enter **Definition** as the column name in **B3**. Bold the title and column name. Center the column name in the cells.

Enter the terms in the range A4:A11. Enter the definitions in the range B4:B11. Use the resizing pointer to automatically fit the cell contents for columns A and B. Save and close the workbook.

## Science: Research and Write

Work with a classmate to use online resources to research current news and discoveries about our solar system and the universe. Organize your notes on a new worksheet in the *universe10* workbook. Then with your teacher's permission, report to the class on what you learned about new research or discoveries.

Explore More

# Exploring Across the Curriculum

## Social Studies: Research, Organize, and Map It!

Work with a classmate to use classroom, library, CD-ROM, or online resources to locate a map of the United States as it looked in 1880. Using the map as your guide, draw your own 1880 U.S. map. Then using data from the *population data8* workbook, (1) group states by Census Division by coloring them the same color, (2) add a Census Division legend to your map, and (3) note the 1880 census year population number on each state.

## Getting Help

Click the Microsoft Excel Help icon below the *Excel* application Close button to open the *Excel* Help window. Key **filling adjacent cells** in the search box and tap the ENTER key. Research different ways to use the fill handle to fill data in adjacent cells. Create a blank workbook. Practice the different fill methods you researched. Close the workbook without saving it.

## Career Day

Growing populations and changing demographics can lead to an increase in career opportunities in human services, services that provide care for families and human needs. Using library, printed, or online resources, identify three interesting careers in the human services. Write a brief summary of each occupation, print your summary, and save it in your Career Day folder.

## Your Personal Journal

Open your personal journal document. Insert today's date and two blank lines. Think about what you have learned about the U.S. Census. Why is it important to take a periodic census of the U.S. population? Write a persuasive paragraph in which you give two or three strong reasons for a periodic U.S. census. Support each reason with specific details. Spell-check, save, and close your journal.

**Online Enrichment Games**  www.cengage.com/school/keyboarding/lwcorange

# Exploring *On Your Own*

## Math in Action

### Using Algebra to Solve Problems

Mars and Earth are approximately 48,000,000 miles apart. A space shuttle traveling to Mars from Earth has traveled 26,000,000 miles in 1,625 hours. If the space shuttle continues traveling at this rate, how much longer will it take to reach Mars?

$$\text{Rate of change} = \frac{\textit{distance}}{\textit{time}} = \frac{26{,}000{,}000 \textit{ miles}}{1{,}625 \textit{ hours}}$$

$$= 16{,}000 \text{ miles per hour}$$

Formula: Distance Remaining ÷ Rate of Change = Time Remaining

$$\frac{22{,}000{,}000 \textit{ miles}}{16{,}000 \textit{ miles/hour}} = 1{,}375 \text{ hours remaining}$$

Now you try it!

- Find the amount of time remaining for the space shuttle to reach Mars if it travels 30,000,000 miles in 2,000 hours and continues at that rate.
- Find the remaining time if the shuttle travels 36,000,000 miles in 2,250 hours.

# Project 8



## 8a Review ?, CAPS LOCK, TAB, BACKSPACE

Key each line twice. Double-space between 2-line groups.

**TECHNIQUE TIP**

Keep your eyes on the textbook as you key.

?

1 :? :? ;? ;? Who? What? When? Where? Why? How?

2 Who is it? When is it? What is it? Who will go?

caps lock

3 Mark the YES box, the NO box, or the NOT SURE box.

4 Is Jeffrey a REPUBLICAN, a DEMOCRAT, or UNDECIDED?

tab

5 TAB→ Pepe TAB→ Jan TAB→ Carlos TAB→ Juan RETURN

6 TAB→ Nadia TAB→ Bren TAB→ Omar TAB→ Elena RETURN

backspace

7 nobackspaceopbackspacepqbackspaceqrbackspacersbackspacestbackspace

8 tubackspaceuvbackspacevwbackspacewxbackspacexybackspaceyzbackspace

## 8b Technique: TAB

Set tabs at 2.5" and 4.5". Key the text at the right.

Louisiana　Kentucky　Oregon
Baton Rouge　Frankfort　Salem

Wyoming　Wisconsin　Virginia
Cheyenne　Madison　Richmond

Vermont　Utah　Texas
Montpelier　Salt Lake City　Austin

Tennessee　South Dakota　Rhode Island
Nashville　Pierre　Providence

## 8c Build Skill

Key each line twice single-spaced; double-space between 2-line groups.

For additional practice:
**MicroType 5**
New Key Review, Alphabetic Lesson 19

**One-hand words**

1 in we no be up as on you was him are get only rate

2 case only best upon area you water oil great after

**One-hand phrases**

3 you were|at my best|get set|set rate|as few|no tax

4 water rate|my only date|my tax case|my care|as few

# Exploring On Your Own

## Blaze Your Own Trail

You have learned several new skills in this project. Now blaze your own trail by practicing these skills on your own!

1. Open the *universe10* workbook and activate *The Sun* worksheet.
2. Create an embedded 3-D pie chart using data about the Sun's components.
3. Add **The Sun** as the chart title; then drag the chart to the right of the data.
4. Edit the chart to change the data marker colors, patterns, gradient, or fill; reposition the legend to the bottom of the chart; and add data labels using the format or style of your choice.
5. Use drag and drop to explode the largest pie slice.
6. Activate the *Star Systems* worksheet.
7. Use the F11 key to create a default column chart on its own sheet that illustrates the relative mass of each host star to our Sun. (*Hint*: Remember to use the CTRL key to select nonadjacent ranges.)
8. Name the chart sheet *Stars' Relative Mass*.
9. Change the charted data orientation from *by columns* to *by rows*.
10. Replace each colored data marker with the stacked picture of the Sun located in your data files. Format the stacked Sun pictures with a 3-point black border. (*Hint:* Use the Stack fill option.)
11. Turn off the legend and insert Outside End data labels above the data markers.
12. Insert a chart title object above the chart and use the formula bar to create a linking formula on the chart sheet to link the contents of cell A2 on the *Star Systems* worksheet as the chart title.
13. Draw a text box in the upper-left corner of the chart and key **Sun picture courtesy NASA/JPL-Caltech**. Resize and format the text box as desired.
14. Save and close the workbook.

## Reading in Action

### Main Idea and Details

When you read informational passages, to find the main idea, ask yourself what the passage is about. After you have determined the main idea, look for details that tell more about the main idea. Read the following paragraphs. Then write sentences that explain the main idea and supporting details.

According to discoveries that scientists made in the 1990s, the universe is expanding. The source of this mysterious force opposing gravity is called "dark energy." This strange force of energy has a weird repulsive gravity that is pulling the universe apart.

If the repulsion from dark energy becomes stronger, the universe may be torn apart some 30 billion years from now by a "Big Rip." The universe would expand so violently that the gravity that holds the universe together would no longer hold. The galaxies, then the stars, then planets, and finally atoms would fly apart, destroying the universe. Currently, this idea is just a theory. However, discovering the properties of dark energy—its strength and its permanence—is a key goal of astronomy and physics today.

# Creating a Budget

## Explorers' Guide

**Data file:** budgeting

**Objectives:**

In this project, you will:

- add borders and fill colors and indent cell contents
- enter budget formulas
- use the ROUND function
- copy and paste formulas
- use the IF function
- perform a what-if analysis

© ART RESOURCE, NY

## Our Exploration Assignment:

### Creating a budget

When Abraham Lincoln ran for a seat in the Senate in 1858, he challenged his opponent, Stephen Douglas, to a series of debates. What issues did they debate? Who was the winner? With the help of the local historical society, which is reenacting the seven Lincoln-Douglas debates, the Explorers Club will find out. Club members will sell snacks and drinks at each debate to raise money for a field trip to Lincoln's home in Springfield, Illinois. Luis is using a worksheet to budget for the snacks and drinks, and he needs your help. Follow the Trail Markers to add cell borders and a fill color, indent cell contents, enter formulas, use the ROUND function, copy formulas, use the IF function, and perform a *what-if analysis* on the budget.

# Project Skills Review

You learned a lot in this project! We are very impressed with your progress. Let's take a few minutes to review the skills that you learned.

| Skill | Procedure | |
|---|---|---|
| **Create an embedded pie chart** | Select the worksheet data and click the **Pie** button in the Charts group on the **Insert** tab. |  |
| **Resize or reposition an embedded chart** | Drag a sizing handle on the selected chart's border. Drag the chart to a new location. | |
| **Use Chart Tips** | Move the mouse pointer over individual chart objects or elements. | |
| **Select an individual chart object for formatting** | Select the chart by clicking the chart area; then click the individual chart object. | |
| **Format a chart or an individual chart object** | Click buttons on the **Chart Tools Layout, Design, or Format** tab. Right-click a chart object and click **Format (Object)** on the shortcut menu. | |
| **Create a default column chart on its own chart sheet** | Select the worksheet data and tap the F11 key. | |
| **Switch the data orientation for a chart** | Click the **Switch Row/Column** button in the Data group on the **Chart Tools Design** tab. |  |
| **Insert data labels** | Click the **Data Labels** button in the Labels group on the **Chart Tools Layout** tab. |  |
| **Turn the legend on or off or format it** | Click the **Legend** button in the Labels group on the **Chart Tools Layout** tab. |  |
| **Insert a text box** | Click the **Text Box** button in the Insert group on the **Chart Tools Layout** tab. |  |
| **Format a text box** | Click buttons in the **Shape Styles** group on the **Drawing Tools Format** tab. | |
| **Link a chart title to a cell on the underlying worksheet** | In *Excel 2010*, edit the chart title formula in the formula bar on the chart sheet to remove the default Chart Title text; in *Excel 2007*, key an equal sign in the formula bar. Then activate the underlying worksheet, click the appropriate cell, and tap the ENTER key. | |

**Begin by opening Luis's workbook and saving it with a new name. Then add today's date and time using a function.**

Formulas | Function Library | Date & Time

Home | Number | Number Format

Home | Alignment | Merge & Center

1. Open the *budgeting* workbook, save it as *budgeting9*, and activate the *Snacks and Drinks Budget* worksheet, if necessary.
2. Using the Function Library, enter the NOW function in cell **A3**; then format the date in the Long Date format and merge and center the date across the range A3:I3.

Super! Now let's make areas of the worksheet stand out by adding outline borders and the white fill color to a range of cells. Then we will indent row names to make the worksheet easier to read.

**ERGONOMICS TIP**

Can you easily reach the mouse? Remember to keep the mouse next to your keyboard so you do not have to strain to reach it.

1 TRAIL MARKER

## Adding Borders and Fill Colors and Indenting Cell Contents

Luis's *Snacks and Drinks Budget* worksheet contains information you will use to create the budget calculations. This information is in the area of the worksheet labeled *Assumptions*, which begins in cell A30. To draw attention to the assumptions data, Luis wants to add an outside border around the data and use color to fill the cells within the border.

To add a border, select the cell or cells, click the Home tab, and click the Borders button arrow in the Font group; then click a border style.

To add a fill color, click the Fill Color button arrow in the Font group and then click a color on the color grid.

**CHECKPOINT**

Your completed chart should look similar to this.

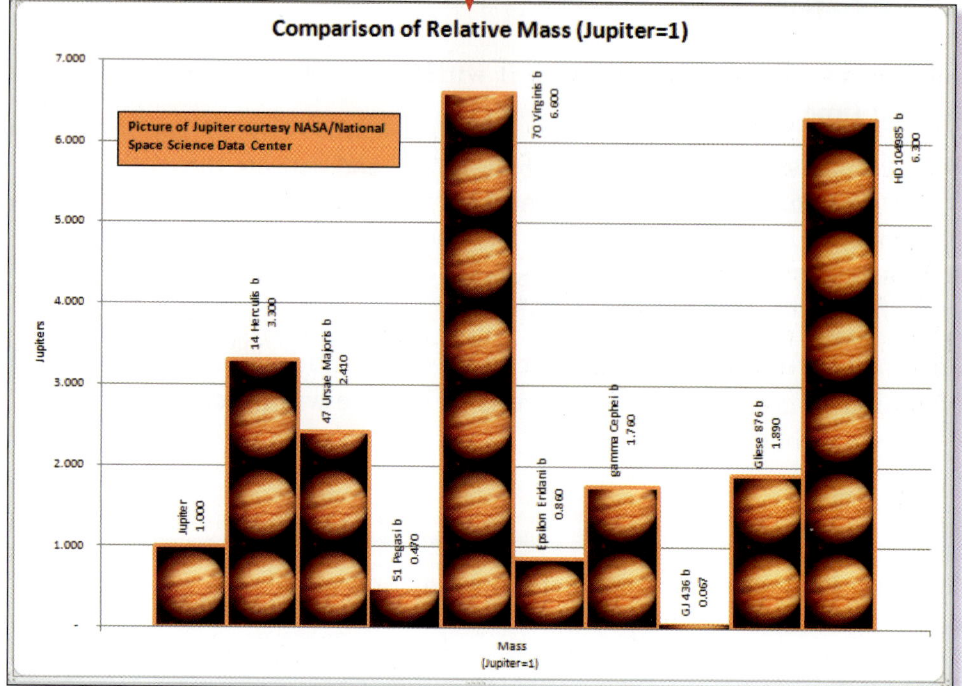


7. Save and close the workbook.

You can preview and print a chart on its own sheet just as you do a worksheet. To preview and print an embedded chart without the accompanying worksheet, first select the embedded chart.

**Let's add a border and a fill color to the range A30:H58.**

Home | Font | Borders or Fill Color

1. Select the range **A30:H58** using the SHIFT + click method.
2. Click the **Home** tab, if necessary, and locate the **Font** group.
3. Click the **Borders** button arrow in the Font group to view a gallery of border options. 
4. Click the **Thick Box Border** option.
5. Click the **Fill Color** button in the Font group. 
6. Click the **White, Background Color 1** color square in the Themes color grid (the first color in the first row).
7. Deselect the range.

**CHECKPOINT**

The top of your formatted range should look like this.

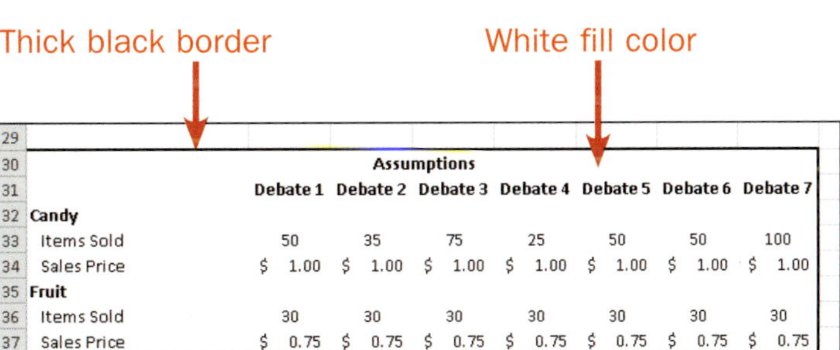


| | A | B | C | D | E | F | G | H |
|---|---|---|---|---|---|---|---|---|
| 29 | | | | | | | | |
| 30 | | | | Assumptions | | | | |
| 31 | | Debate 1 | Debate 2 | Debate 3 | Debate 4 | Debate 5 | Debate 6 | Debate 7 |
| 32 | Candy | | | | | | | |
| 33 | Items Sold | 50 | 35 | 75 | 25 | 50 | 50 | 100 |
| 34 | Sales Price | $ 1.00 | $ 1.00 | $ 1.00 | $ 1.00 | $ 1.00 | $ 1.00 | $ 1.00 |
| 35 | Fruit | | | | | | | |
| 36 | Items Sold | 30 | 30 | 30 | 30 | 30 | 30 | 30 |
| 37 | Sales Price | $ 0.75 | $ 0.75 | $ 0.75 | $ 0.75 | $ 0.75 | $ 0.75 | $ 0.75 |

Look at the row names in the range A6:A25. It would be much easier to read them if the detail items (candy, fruit, popcorn, and so forth) were indented under the main categories (Sales, Expenses).

To indent cell contents, click the Home tab and click the Increase Indent button in the Alignment group. To remove indents, click the Decrease Indent button in the Alignment group.

**Let's indent the row name subcategories and subtotal text.**

Home | Alignment | Increase Indent or Decrease Indent

1. Tap the CTRL + HOME keys, if necessary, to activate the home cell.
2. Click the **Home** tab, if necessary, and locate the **Alignment** group.
3. Select the range **A7:A11** and then use the CTRL key to select the nonadjacent range **A16:A20** and cell **A22**.
4. Click the **Increase Indent** button in the Alignment group once. 
5. Tap the CTRL + HOME keys and save the workbook.

3. Change the mass to **3.600**; then switch back to the *Planets' Relative Mass* chart sheet and view the new position of the data marker for planet *70 Virginis b*. The data marker has changed to reflect the new mass number on the worksheet!
4. Switch back to the *Extrasolar Planets* worksheet and click the **Undo** button on the Quick Access Toolbar to undo your edit and return the *70 Virginis b* mass number to **6.600**.

5. Switch back to the *Planets' Relative Mass* chart sheet. The *70 Virginis b* data marker changes again to reflect the worksheet data.

Now let's use a linking formula to create the chart's title.

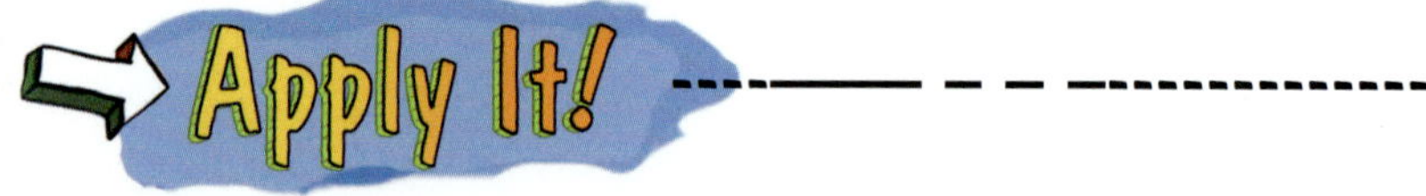


**Let's insert a chart title object and create a linking formula that inserts the contents of cell A2 on the *Extrasolar Planets* worksheet as the column chart's title.**

Chart Tools Layout | Labels | Chart Title

1. Click the **Chart Tools Layout** tab, if necessary, and locate the **Labels** group.
2. Click the **Chart Title** button in the Labels group to view a gallery of chart title options; then click **Above Chart** to insert a chart title object and resize the chart to accommodate it.
3. If you are using *Excel 2010*, observe the ="Chart Title" formula in the formula bar on the *Planet's Relative Mass* chart sheet and the text Chart Title inside the chart title object at the top of the chart. You can select the text inside the chart title object and key new text, or you can edit the formula in the formula bar. Select the "Chart Title" portion of the formula in the formula bar, leaving the equals sign unselected.
4. If you are using *Excel 2007*, key an equals sign (=) in the formula bar to begin your formula.
5. Click the *Extrasolar Planets* sheet tab to activate the worksheet and click cell **A2**. The formula *='Extrasolar Planets'!A2:E2* appears in the formula bar.
6. Tap the ENTER key to insert the formula's results in the chart title object on the chart sheet; then tap the ESC key to deselect the chart title object.

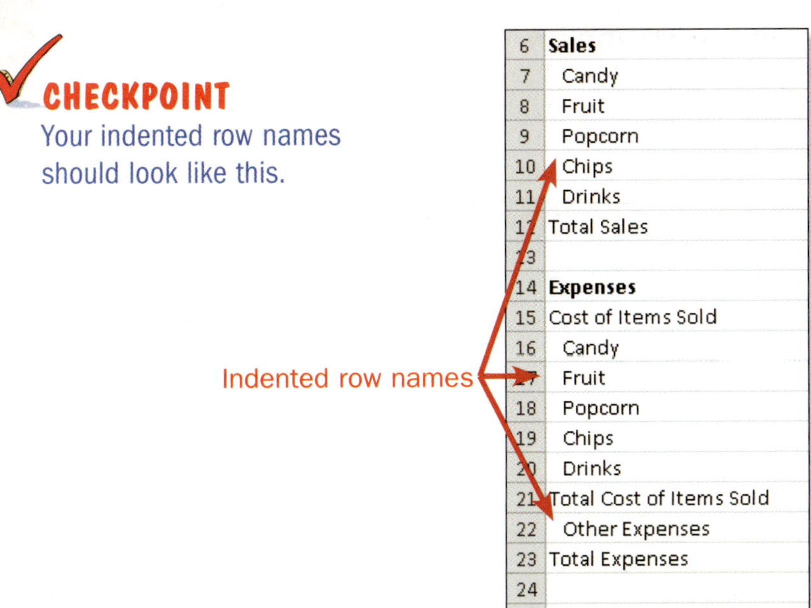


Great! Next, let's enter the formulas to calculate sales, cost of sales, other expenses, subtotals, and totals.

## Entering Budget Formulas

A budget is a plan for receiving and spending money. Perhaps you earn money from a part-time job such as babysitting or mowing the neighbor's lawn. If so, you may plan how much of the money you earn to save for future use and how much to spend now to buy clothes, music or DVDs; eat out; and purchase other items.

**The Snacks and Drinks Budget**

The Explorers Club members are planning a field trip and want to raise money for the trip by selling snacks and drinks during the re-creation of the seven Lincoln-Douglas debates. To determine the amount of money the club can raise for the field trip, a plan, or budget, is necessary.

The budget should include an estimate of the amount of money the club can expect from sales of snacks and drinks and the amount of money necessary to purchase the items for sale in addition to supplies. Any money left over after paying for the snacks, drinks, and supplies, called a surplus, can be used to pay for the field trip.

In addition, if the surplus for all seven debates is more than $500, the historical society will donate 10 percent of the surplus toward the field trip. If the surplus is less than $500, the society will donate $50.

8. Select and bold the text inside the text box and then tap the ESC key twice to deselect the text box and its contents.

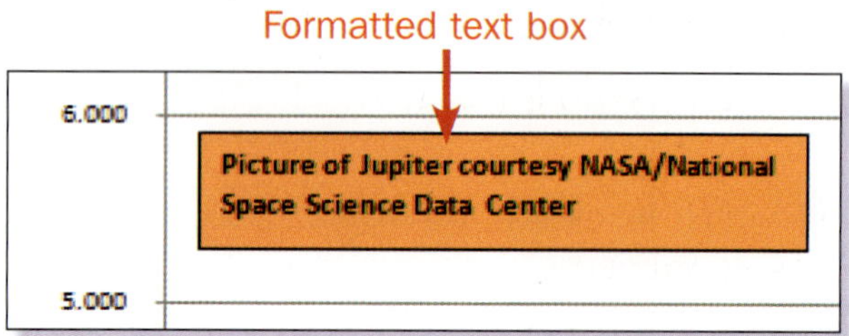


The last step is to add a title to the chart. Ray wants the chart title to contain the same text as cell A2 on the worksheet that contains the chart data, the *Extrasolar Planets* worksheet.

## Creating a Linking Formula

Data on a chart is automatically linked to the underlying worksheet. For example, if you change worksheet numbers or text used to create a chart, the chart automatically updates to reflect those changes. You can also manually link the contents of a worksheet cell to a chart by creating a text box on the chart sheet that contains a special type of formula called a linking formula.

Linking formulas are very powerful and can be used to combine data from multiple worksheets or workbooks into the same formula.

In this Trail Marker, you will create a linking formula to insert the contents of cell A2 on the *Extrasolar Planets* worksheet in a text box on the *Planets' Relative Mass* chart sheet. You build the formula directly in the formula bar on the chart sheet. Then you drag the text box to the top of the chart as the chart's title.

**Let's see how chart data is linked to the worksheet data by changing a planet's mass on the worksheet and viewing the change on the chart. Then you will undo the change. Before you begin, make sure you are viewing the *Planets' Relative Mass* chart sheet.**

1. Look carefully at the chart sheet to see that the extrasolar planet *70 Virginis b* has a mass of 6.600 Jupiters.
2. Click the *Extrasolar Planets* sheet tab to activate the worksheet and find *70 Virginis b* data in row 9.

**Reviewing the Snacks and Drinks Budget Worksheet**

Look carefully at the *Snacks and Drinks Budget* worksheet. It is a complex worksheet that contains the budget layout and estimates for:

- sales—money raised from selling candy, fruit, popcorn, chips, and drinks
- expenses—money that will be spent to purchase the snacks and drinks and other items such as napkins and cleaning supplies

The *Snacks and Drinks Budget* worksheet already contains the estimates, called budget assumptions, for sales and expenses.

You can use these assumptions to build formulas with cell references to calculate the budget's sales, expenses, and surplus numbers.

Using formulas with cell references to calculate the budget numbers takes advantage of a great *Excel* feature—the power of automatic recalculation. After you enter the formulas, you can change the number in an individual assumption cell and *Excel* automatically recalculates all formulas that use that cell!

In Project 8, you learned about entering basic formulas using cell references and functions. To calculate the sales and cost of sales, subtotals, totals, and donation for the *Snacks and Drinks Budget*, you will enter formulas in the cells by keying the equals sign, selecting cell references, and keying the calculation operator (+, -, *, or /) needed to perform the calculation. To calculate the totals in column I, you will use the SUM function.

Look carefully again at the *Snacks and Drinks Budget* worksheet to locate the assumption data for sales, cost of sales, and other expenses. Then review the entire Debate 1 column to locate each of the following cell references:

- Total Sales in cell B12 and the individual item sales in the range B7:B11
- Total Cost of Items Sold in cell B21 and the individual item costs in the range B16:B20
- Other Expenses in cell B22
- Total Expenses in cell B23
- Surplus or (Deficit) in cell B25
- Historical society donation in cell I26
- Total money available for the field trip in cell I27

When you key or edit a formula, *Excel* color-codes the cell reference borders. This gives you a visual cue about where the cells are located in the worksheet. Check it out!

To avoid keying errors, you will use the mouse pointer to select cells as you build the formulas and use the asterisk (*), plus sign (+), and minus sign (-) keys on the numeric keypad. *Don't forget to key the equals sign (=) first to tell Excel you are creating a formula!*

**CHECKPOINT**

What a great job! Your chart should now look like this.

Value (y) axis title

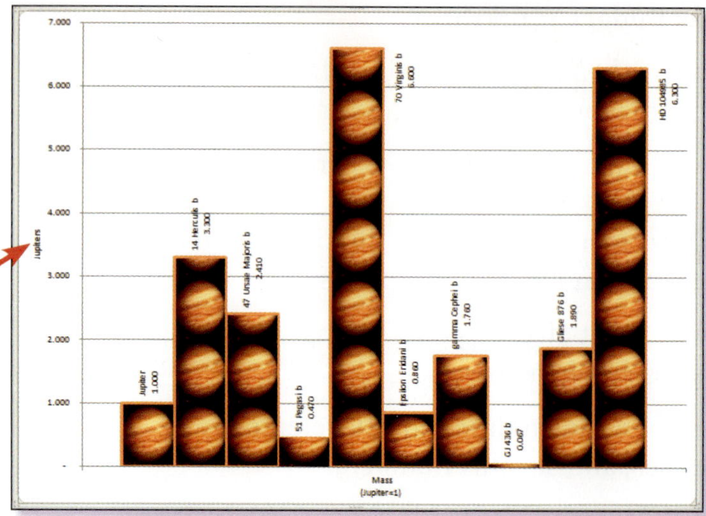


Now let's add a text box to the chart to cite the source of our Jupiter picture.

4 TRAIL MARKER

## Adding a Text Box

You can insert a text box and then key or copy and paste text in the text box just as you did in *Word*. A quick way to create a text box is to draw one with the mouse pointer. When you draw or select a text box, the Drawing Tools Format tab appears on the Ribbon.

**Let's draw a text box on the chart to cite the source of the Jupiter picture and then format the text box.**

Chart Tools Layout | Insert | Text Box

Drawing Tools Format | Shape Styles | Shape Fill or Shape Outline

Home | Font | Bold

1. Click the **Chart Tools Layout** tab, if necessary, and locate the **Insert** group.
2. Click the **Text Box** button in the Insert group to convert the mouse pointer to a drawing pointer.
3. Draw a text box approximately 2 inches wide by 1 inch long in the upper-left area of the plot area.
4. Key **Picture of Jupiter courtesy NASA/National Space Science Data Center** in the text box.
5. Select the text box, if necessary, and drag a sizing handle to resize the text box as necessary to view the text.
6. Click the **Drawing Tools Format** tab and locate the **Shape Styles** group.
7. Fill the text box with the orange fill color and add a black border using the Shape Fill and Shape Outline buttons in the Shapes Styles group.

Text Box

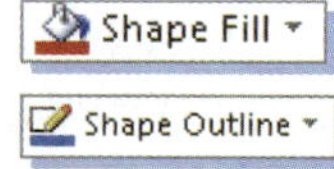

*Excel* follows a specific order when calculating a formula that contains multiple calculation operators. For more information about how *Excel* reads a formula and performs calculations, see the *Calculation Operators and Precedence* topic in *Excel* Help.

**Let's enter Debate 1 formulas.**

**1.** Calculate candy sales:
 **1)** Activate cell **B7** and key an **equals sign** (=) to tell *Excel* you are entering a formula. Scroll to view the assumptions data.
 **2)** Click cell **B33** (the number of candy items sold); tap the **asterisk** key on the numeric keypad (the multiplication symbol).
 **3)** Click cell **B34** (the sales price per candy item) and tap the ENTER key. *Excel* adds the closing parenthesis and enters the formula in the cell.
 **4)** Activate cell **B7** to see the results of the calculation ($50); look at the formula bar to see the actual formula, *=B33*B34*.

B7 | fx =B33*B34

| | A | B | C |
|---|---|---|---|
| 3 | | | F |
| 4 | | | |
| 5 | | **Debate 1** | **Debate** |
| 6 | **Sales** | | |
| 7 | Candy | $ 50 | |

**2.** Calculate fruit sales:
 **1)** Activate cell **B8** and key **=**.
 **2)** Click cell **B36** and key an **asterisk**.
 **3)** Click cell **B37** and tap the ENTER key to calculate fruit sales.

**3.** Using the previous candy sales and fruit sales steps as your guide, calculate popcorn sales in cell **B9** and chips sales in cell **B10**.

The Drinks sales formula will calculate soft drink sales and bottled water sales and then add the two calculations together to get the total Drinks sales.

**4.** Calculate drink sales and total sales:
 **1)** Activate cell **B11** and enter the formula **=B45*B46+B48*B49**.
 **2)** Activate cell **B12**, if necessary, and use the Formula AutoComplete feature to enter the SUM function.
 **3)** Select the range **B7:B11** as the function's argument, if necessary, and tap the ENTER key.

Next, you turn off the legend, which is no longer useful, and add a value (y) axis title.

**Let's turn off the legend and add a value (y) axis title.**

Chart Tools Layout | Labels | Legend

Chart Tools Layout | Labels | Axis Titles

1. Click the **Legend** button in the Labels group to view a gallery of legend options.

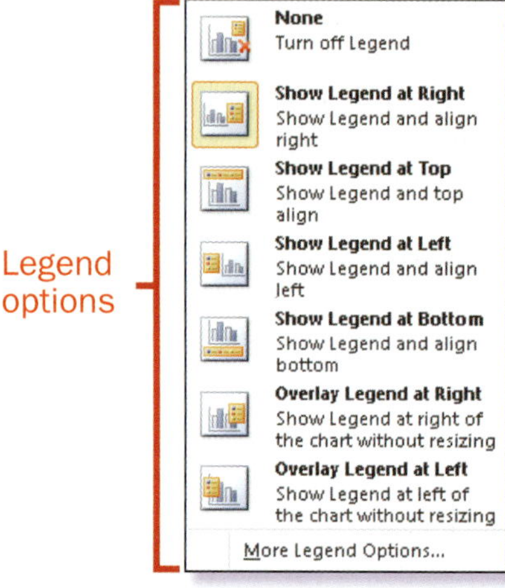


2. Click **None** to turn off the legend.
3. Click the **Axis Titles** button in the Labels group.
4. Point to Primary Vertical Axis to view a gallery of value (y) axis options.

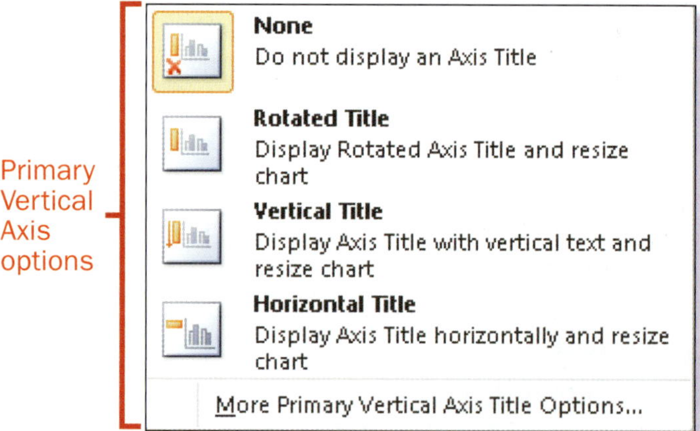


5. Click **Rotated Title** in the gallery to add a value (y) axis title text box and resize the chart.
6. Key **Jupiters** in the formula bar and tap the ENTER key to add the value (y) title text.
7. Tap the ESC key to deselect the value (y) axis title.

Your Debate 1 Sales values should look like this.

| | | |
|---|---|---|
| 6 | **Sales** | |
| 7 | Candy | $ 50 |
| 8 | Fruit | 23 |
| 9 | Popcorn | 113 |
| 10 | Chips | 26 |
| 11 | Drinks | 64 |
| 12 | Total Sales | $ 275 |
| 13 | | |

Would you like to see the actual formulas in the cells instead of the formula results? Just tap the CTRL + ` keys to view formulas in their cells; then tap the CTRL + ` keys again to turn off the view of formulas in the cells. The ` key is located above the TAB key. You can also click the Formulas tab and click the Show Formulas button in the Formula Auditing group. Try it!

Next, let's enter the formula to calculate the cost of the candy to be sold; the cost of each item sold is calculated as a percentage of its sales.

**The cost of the candy is 70% of candy sales. The cost percentages are found in the range B52:B56. You will calculate fruit, popcorn, chips, and drinks costs in a later Trail Marker.**

1. Calculate candy costs:
   **1)** Activate cell **B16** and key =.
   **2)** Click cell **B7** (candy sales) and key an **asterisk**.
   **3)** Click cell **B52** (the percentage of sales) and tap the ENTER key.
   **4)** Activate cell **B16** to see the results of the calculation ($35) and the formula =*B7***B52* in the formula bar.

B16 | fx | =B7*B52

| | A | B | C |
|---|---|---|---|
| 11 | Drinks | 64 | |
| 12 | Total Sales | $ 275 | |
| 13 | | | |
| 14 | **Expenses** | | |
| 15 | Cost of Items Sold | | |
| 16 | Candy | $ 35 | |

9. Click the **Separator** text box arrow and click **(New Line)**.

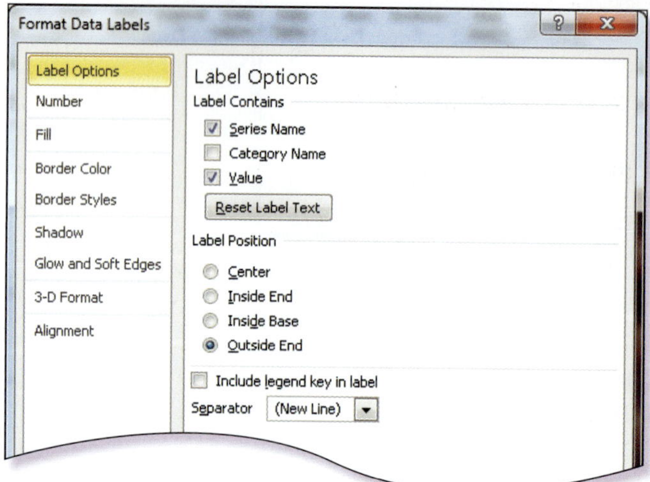


10. Click **Alignment** in the left pane.
11. Click the **Text direction** text box arrow in the right pane and click **Rotate all text 270°**.
12. Click **Close**. The series name *Jupiter* appears on a separate line above the value 1.000 in the rotated data label.
13. Using steps 6–12 as your guide, on a separate line, add the series name to the remaining data labels and rotate them 270°. Deselect the last formatted data label.

If necessary, you can also select a data label and drag it to a new location using the mouse pointer. You need to reposition the data labels for the two tallest data markers.

14. Click the **70 Virginis b** data label to select it; then drag it down and immediately to the right of the data marker.
15. Click the **HD 104985 b** data label to select it; then drag it down and immediately to the right of the data marker.

Your column chart with rotated and repositioned data labels should now look similar to this.

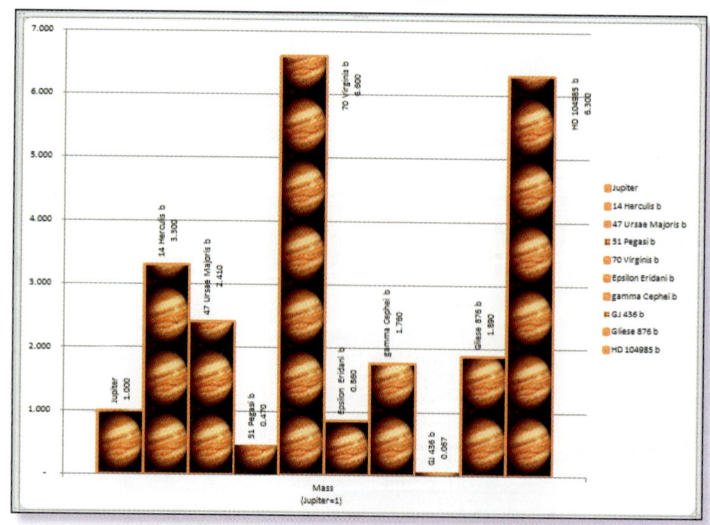

Now let's enter the formulas to calculate the Total Cost of Items Sold, Other Expenses, Total Expenses, and Surplus or (Deficit).

2. Calculate the Total Cost of Items Sold:
   1) Activate cell **B21** and use Formula AutoComplete to insert the SUM function.
   2) Select the range **B16:B20** as the function's argument and tap the ENTER key.
3. Calculate the Other Expenses:
   1) Activate cell **B22**, if necessary, and key =.
   2) Click cell **B12** and key an **asterisk**.
   3) Click cell **D58** and tap the ENTER key.
4. Calculate Total Expenses:
   1) Activate cell **B23**, if necessary, and key =.
   2) Click cell **B21** and key a plus sign (+).
   3) Click cell **B22** and tap the ENTER key.
5. Calculate the Surplus or (Deficit), the difference between Sales and Expenses:
   1) Activate cell **B25** and key =.
   2) Click cell **B12** and key a minus sign (-).
   3) Click cell **B23** and tap the ENTER key.
6. Save the workbook.

**CHECKPOINT**
Your Debate 1 budget column should look like this.

| | | |
|---|---|---|
| 4 | | |
| 5 | | **Debate 1** |
| 6 | **Sales** | |
| 7 | Candy | $ 50 |
| 8 | Fruit | 23 |
| 9 | Popcorn | 113 |
| 10 | Chips | 26 |
| 11 | Drinks | 64 |
| 12 | Total Sales | $ 275 |
| 13 | | |
| 14 | **Expenses** | |
| 15 | Cost of Items Sold | |
| 16 | Candy | $ 35 |
| 17 | Fruit | |
| 18 | Popcorn | |
| 19 | Chips | |
| 20 | Drinks | |
| 21 | Total Cost of Items Sold | $ 35 |
| 22 | Other Expenses | 28 |
| 23 | Total Expenses | $ 63 |
| 24 | | |
| 25 | **Surplus or (Deficit)** | $ 213 |
| 26 | | |

Budget calculations

Wow! What a great job! But before we continue, let's fix a rounding error in the Debate 1 calculations.

Now you are ready to insert data labels, hide the legend, and add a value (y) axis title.

**Let's add value (number of Jupiters) data labels above each data series and then customize each data label to add the data series name on separate line and rotate the data label.**

Chart Tools
Layout | Labels | Data Labels

1. Click the first data series to select it.
2. Click the **Chart Tools Layout** tab and locate the **Labels** group.
3. Click the **Data Labels** button in the Labels group to view a gallery of data label options.

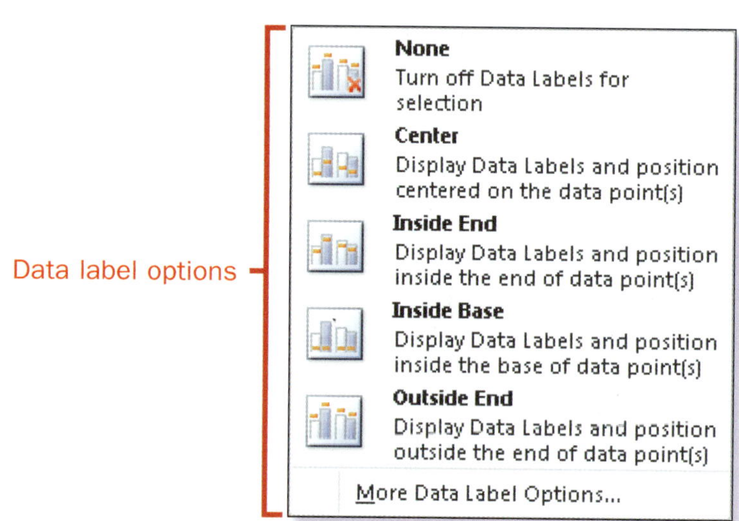


Data label options

4. Click the **Outside End** option in the gallery to add the number of Jupiters value as a data label positioned above the data series.
5. Using steps 3–4 as your guide, add data labels to the remaining data series.
6. Right-click the first data marker's data label and click **Format Data Labels** to open the Format Data Labels dialog box.
7. Click **Label Options** in the left pane, if necessary.
8. Click the **Series Name** checkbox in the right pane to insert a check mark.

## Using the ROUND Function

Budget amounts are usually shown as whole numbers; therefore, Luis formatted cells in his *Snacks and Drinks Budget* worksheet with the Accounting Number Format and Comma styles and no decimal places; the two decimal places for cents in each calculation are not shown.

Let's take a close look at the Debate 1 calculations in column B.

- The formula in cell B8 calculates the cost of fruit (30 fruit x $0.75) and shows the result as $23.
- If you manually multiply 30 times $.075, you will find that the correct answer is $22.50. Because the cell is formatted to show no decimal places, Excel rounded the number up to $23—the nearest whole number.
- However, *Excel* still knows that the actual calculated number is $22.50 and uses this number in other related formulas!

**Let's use the status bar calculations to compare the *Excel* addition of cells B8 and B9 with our manual addition of the cells. Make certain the status bar calculations you learned about in Project 8 are turned on.**

1. Select the range **B8:B9**.
2. Manually add the calculated values formatted with zero decimal places you see in cells B8 (23) and B9 (113). You should get a result of 136.
3. Look at the SUM calculation on the status bar. Excel adds the actual calculated values in cells B8 (22.50) and B9 (112.50) and gets a result of 135.

The $1 difference between your manual calculation and Excel's calculation is called a rounding error.

Rounding errors can happen when you format a cell containing a formula with a different number of decimal places than the 15 places to the right of the decimal point that *Excel* remembers when it calculates the formula's results.

6. Click **Border Color** in the left pane and click the **Solid Line** option button in the right pane to display color options.
7. Click the **Color** button and click **Orange, Accent 6** in the Theme Colors grid.

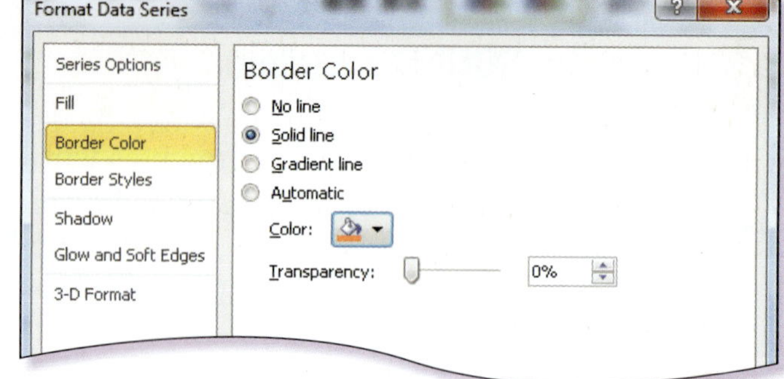


8. Click **Border Styles** in the left pane and key **3 pt** in the Width text box in the right pane to add a thick bright orange border around the data series.
9. Click the **Close** button to apply the formatting to the data series.
10. Using steps 1–9 as your guide, replace the remaining data markers' fill color with the picture of Jupiter and add the 3-point orange border.

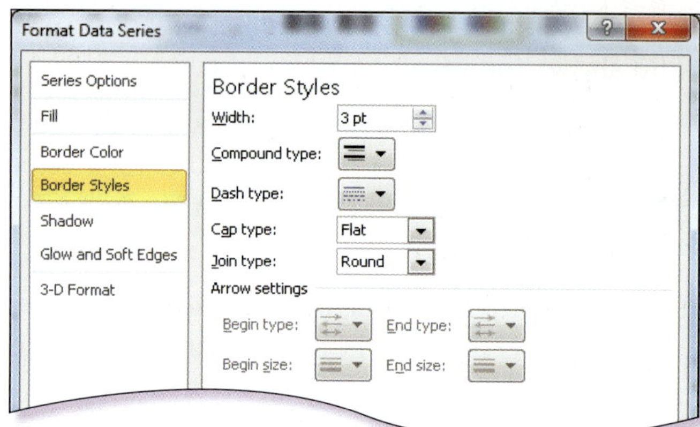


**CHECKPOINT**
Your column chart should look similar to this.

Data plotted with stacked pictures of Jupiter instead of solid color columns

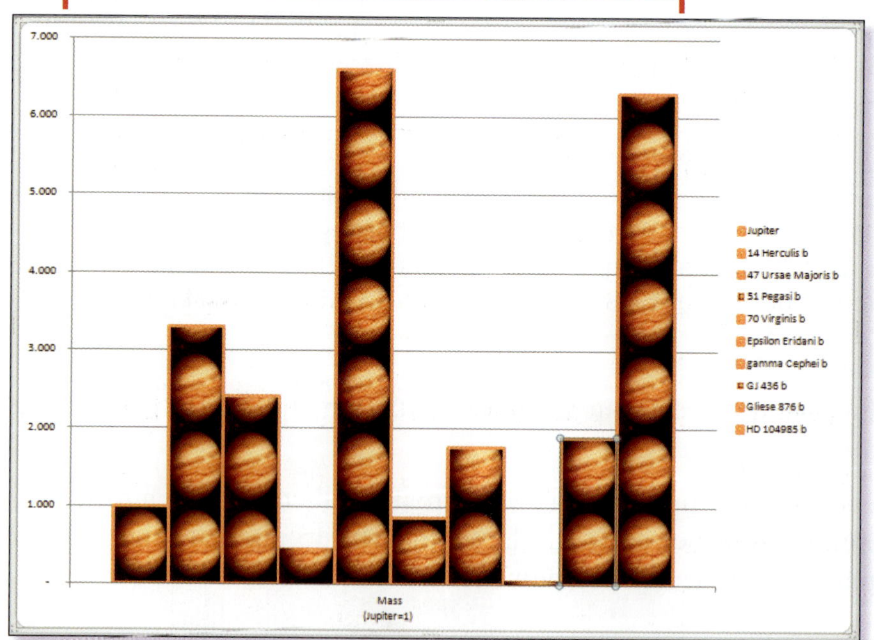

Be careful when creating formulas! It is easy to make a mistake or to create rounding errors when you apply decimal place formatting. *Always* carefully review formula results to make certain the formulas you create are working correctly.

### Avoiding Rounding Errors

You can avoid rounding errors by making sure that *Excel* rounds a formula's calculation to the same number of decimal places as it will be formatted. For example, if you are formatting a cell to show 0 decimal places, you should have *Excel* round the formula's calculation to 0 decimal places. You do this with the ROUND function.

The ROUND function has two arguments separated by commas:

1) the original calculation

2) the number of decimal places to round

Here is an example of a formula containing the ROUND function.

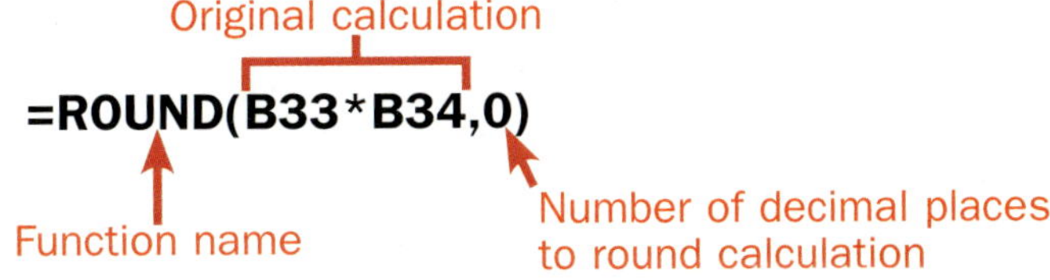


In our *Snacks and Drinks Budget* worksheet, you should edit each of the multiplication formulas to add the ROUND function and specify that the calculated number be rounded to 0 decimal places to make certain the subsequent addition and subtraction formulas produce the correct result.

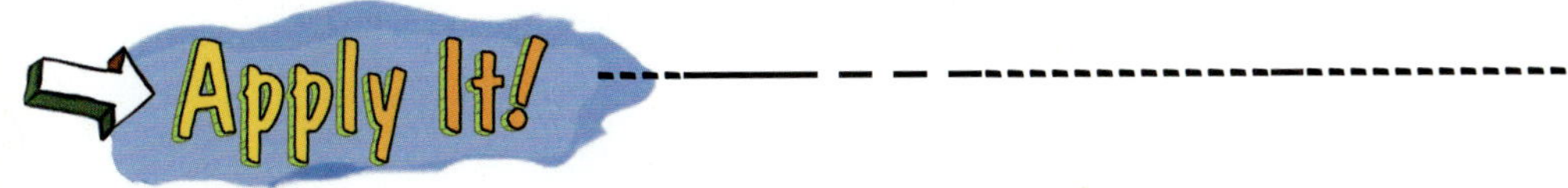


**Let's edit our existing multiplication formulas to add the ROUND function.**

1. Activate cell **B7**.
2. Click the formula bar and position the insertion point between the equals sign and the B33 cell reference.

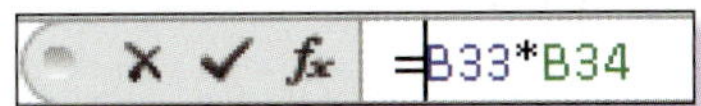

One way to add or remove chart objects such as the legend or data labels is to apply a predefined chart layout to a chart. A gallery of predefined chart layouts is located in the Chart Layouts group on the Chart Tools Design tab. Check it out!

You begin by opening the Format Data Series dialog box and replacing the first data series (the blue Jupiter column) with a picture of the planet Jupiter and adding a thick colored border.

**Let's replace the data markers' fill colors with a picture. Before you begin, make sure the *Planets' Relative Mass* chart sheet is active.**

1. Right-click the **Jupiter** data series column and click **Format Data Series** on the shortcut menu to select the data marker and open the Format Data Series dialog box.
2. Click **Fill** in the left pane and then click the **Picture or texture fill** option in the right pane. You can change the data series or the individual marker's gradient color, fill texture, or pattern, or you can insert a picture with Picture or texture fill options.
3. Click the **Insert From File** button to open the Insert Picture dialog box.
4. Open your data files folder and double-click the **Jupiter** picture filename.
5. Click the **Stack and scale with** option button and key **1** in the units/picture text box, if necessary, to insert one picture of Jupiter for each unit measured and to stack the pictures on top of each other in a column.

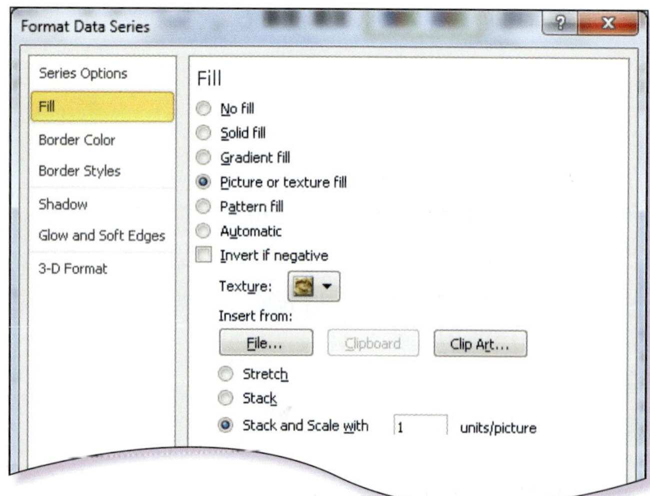

3. Key **ROUND(** to insert the ROUND function and its opening parenthesis in the formula.

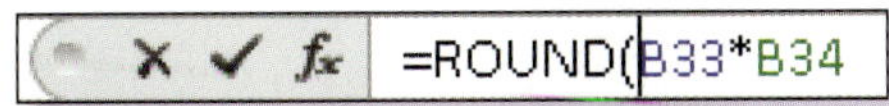


4. Tap the END key to move the insertion point to the end of the formula.
5. Key **,0** to tell *Excel* to round the calculation to the nearest whole number.

=ROUND(B33*B34,0

6. Tap the ENTER key to add the closing parenthesis and enter the formula.
7. Activate cell **B7** to see the results of the calculation and the formula in the formula bar.
8. Using steps 1–3 as your guide, add the ROUND function with 0 decimal places to the formulas in cells **B8**, **B9**, **B10**, **B11**, **B16**, and **B22**. *Do not forget to key the comma and the opening and closing parentheses.*

The Total Sales number is corrected to $276; the Total Expenses number remains the same at $63, and the Surplus or (Deficit) remains the same at $213.

Your Debate 1 Sales values should now look like this.

| 6 | **Sales** | |
|---|---|---|
| 7 | Candy | $ 50 |
| 8 | Fruit | 23 |
| 9 | Popcorn | 113 |
| 10 | Chips | 26 |
| 11 | Drinks | 64 |
| 12 | Total Sales | $ 276 |

Now let's enter the missing formulas for Debate 1 and all of the formulas for Debates 2–7.

## Copying and Pasting Formulas

We still need to create the formulas for the costs of fruit, popcorn, chips, and drinks. You could build formulas to calculate these costs, just as you built the formula for the candy costs. But there is an easier way. You can copy the formula you built in cell B16 to calculate the cost of candy and paste the formula in cells B17:20. *Excel* will do all of the work for you!

### Copying Formulas with Relative References

When you copy a formula in one cell and paste it in the next cell to the right or down, *Excel* automatically changes the column and row references.

**Let's switch the charted data's orientation from column to row.**

**Chart Tools Design | Data | Switch Row/Column**

1. Click the white Chart Area to select the entire chart.
2. Click the **Chart Tools Design** tab and locate the **Data** group.
3. Click the **Switch Row/Column** button in the Data group.

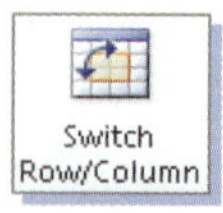


*Excel* reads the data by row, places the data column's name on the category (x) axis, and uses the row names for the legend.

Each data marker is represented by a different-colored column. The legend shows each planet's name and data marker color.

**CHECKPOINT**
Your column chart should now look similar to this.

Chart with data charted in the by rows orientation

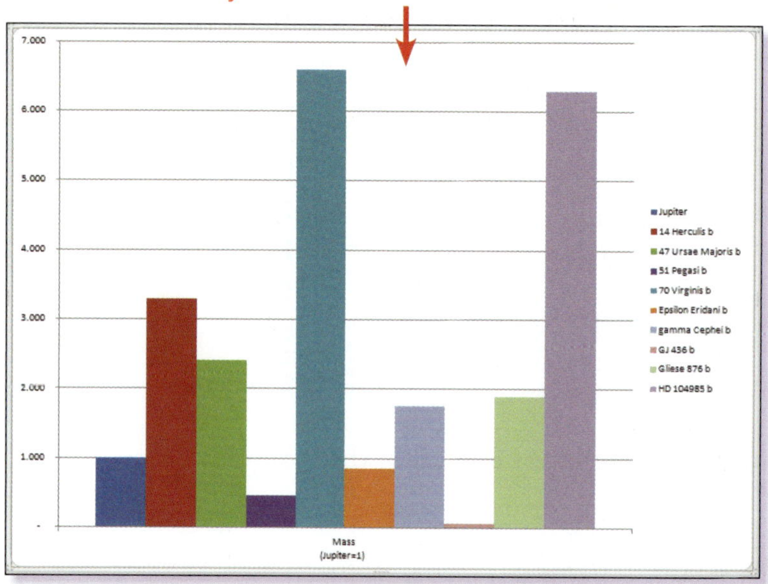


Super! Now let's format the column chart's objects.

## Formatting a Column Chart

In the previous Trail Marker, you learned that a *Jupiter* is a unit of measurement for the mass of an extrasolar planet. Instead of using colors for each column, Ray wants to stack a picture of the planet Jupiter to build the columns, add the number of Jupiters above each column, and hide the legend.

This is called copying formulas with relative references—cell references that automatically change to reflect the formula's new position in the worksheet. By default, *Excel* copies and pastes formulas with relative references.

For example, the formula =ROUND(B33*B34,0) appears as =ROUND(C33*C34,0) when you copy it to the next cell to the right; it appears as =ROUND(B34*B35,0) when you copy it to the next cell down.

Use the Copy and Paste buttons in the Clipboard group on the Home tab to copy and paste formulas anywhere in the worksheet. Use the fill handle to copy and fill formulas into adjacent cells.

**Let's copy the candy cost formula to the range B17:B20 using the fill handle.**

1. Activate cell **B16**.
2. Drag the fill handle down to fill the range B17:B20 with the formula =ROUND(B7*B52,0).
3. Activate cell **B17** and look at the formula in the formula bar. *Excel* copies the formula with relative cell references and changes the formula to =ROUND(B8*B53,0). *Excel* also copies the formatting. The range B17:B20 should be formatted without the dollar sign ($).
4. Select the range **B17:B20** and apply the Comma Style formatting with *no* decimal places; then deselect the range.

Your Debate 1 Expenses values should now look like this.

| 14 | **Expenses** | |
|---|---|---|
| 15 | Cost of Items Sold | |
| 16 | Candy | $ 35 |
| 17 | Fruit | 21 |
| 18 | Popcorn | 40 |
| 19 | Chips | 21 |
| 20 | Drinks | 48 |
| 21 | Total Cost of Items Sold | $ 165 |
| 22 | Other Expenses | 28 |
| 23 | Total Expenses | $ 193 |

Hurrah! The Debate 1 calculations are complete. Now you are ready to enter the formulas for the remaining six debates. But instead of manually entering the formulas, let's copy them!

When a workbook has several worksheets and chart sheets, all of the sheet tabs may not be visible. To see a hidden sheet tab, just click a scrolling button to the left of the sheet tabs or right-click one of the scrolling buttons and click a sheet tab name in the shortcut menu to activate the sheet. Try it!

**Let's create a column chart *on its own chart sheet* that compares the mass of several extrasolar planets to the planet Jupiter and to each other.**

1. Activate the *Extrasolar Planets* worksheet.
2. Select range **A4:B14**.
3. Tap the **F11** key to create the chart on its own sheet.
4. Name the chart sheet ***Planets' Relative Mass***.

Column chart on its own chart sheet

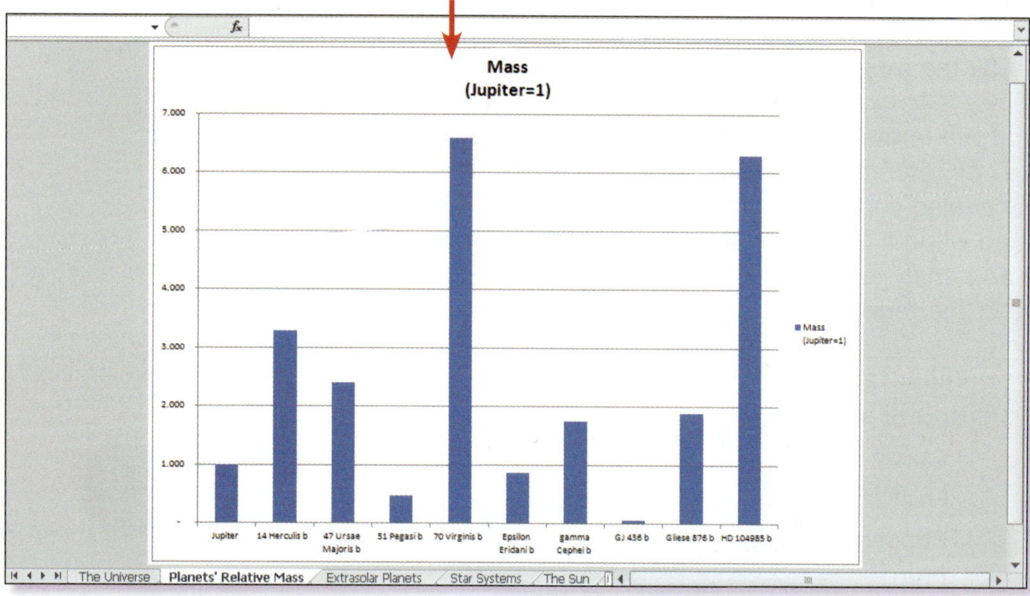


The range you selected on the *Extrasolar Planets* worksheet, A4:B14, is longer than it is wide; *Excel* charted the data using the by column orientation.

The data in A4:A14 (the planet names) is placed along the category (x) axis. You want *Excel* to use the row names as the legend. To do this, you need to change the data orientation from by column to by row. You can change the data orientation by clicking the Chart Tools Design tab and clicking the Switch Row/Column button in the Data group.

### Copying Formulas with Absolute References

Sometimes you do not want *Excel* to change a row or column reference when you copy and paste a formula. Look at the range B52:B56. These cells contain the percentages used to calculate item costs. The percentages are always found in these same cells.

If you copy the Debate 1 candy costs formula *=ROUND(B7*B52,0)* to the next cell to the right, the formula changes to *=ROUND(C7*C52,0)*. Because cell C52 is empty, the formula will calculate a result of zero instead of the correct result. You want the cell reference B52 to stay the same when you copy the formula. Instead of using a relative reference, you must tell *Excel* to use an absolute reference—a cell reference that *does not* change when a formula is copied.

To indicate an absolute reference, insert a dollar sign ($) before the column letter and row number in the cell reference; the cell reference B52 becomes cell reference $B$52. In the formula =ROUND(B7*$B$52,0), the dollar signs ($) tell *Excel* not to change the cell B52 column or row references when the formula is copied to the right.

To add dollar signs to a cell reference, key the dollar signs or tap the F4 key once.

**Let's edit the costs formulas to create absolute cell references.**

1. Activate cell **B16**.
2. Click the **B52** cell reference in the formula bar to position the insertion point inside the cell reference.
3. Tap the **F4** key one time to add the $ to the column and row reference.

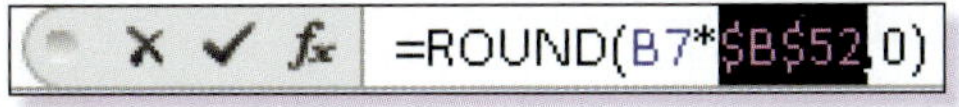


4. Tap the ENTER key.
5. Activate cell **B16** to verify that the formula now includes an absolute reference.
6. Continue to use the formula bar to edit the formulas in cells **B17**, **B18**, **B19**, **B20**, and **B22** to change the cell references for B53, B54, B55, B56, and D58 in each formula, respectively, to an absolute reference.

Nicely done! Now you are ready to copy the formulas from Debate 1 to Debates 2–7.

## Creating a Column Chart

Did you know that there are planets outside our solar system? Astronomers measure the mass, or amount of matter, of these "extrasolar" planets by using a unit of measurement called a *Jupiter*. One *Jupiter* equals the mass of Jupiter, the largest planet in our solar system.

For example, the planet *14 Herculis b* has a mass of 3.3 *Jupiters*—3.3 times the mass of the planet Jupiter. Ray wants you to create a column chart that compares the mass of several extrasolar planets to the mass of the planet Jupiter and each other.

In an *Excel* bar chart, the data markers are represented as horizontal bars instead of vertical columns.

In the column chart you will create, each planet's mass will be represented by a vertical column in the chart's plot area. The plot area has two axes: a vertical axis, called the value (y) axis, and a horizontal axis, called the category (x) axis. The value (y) axis shows the numbers, or values over which the data is to be charted. The category (x) axis shows the names of the categories—each planet—being charted.

Gridlines that help you see each data marker's position appear across the plot area at the value (y) axis.

A quick way to create a column chart on its own chart sheet is to select the data and tap the F11 key. Then you can edit the chart using Ribbon buttons or dialog box options.

When you use the F11 key, *Excel guesses* at how to arrange the data on the chart by looking at the selected data.

- If the selected data on the worksheet is longer than it is wide (more rows than columns), *Excel* creates the chart using the *by column* orientation and places row names on the category (x) axis, all of the data in one column becomes a data series, and the data column name appears in the legend. This arrangement charts the relationship between values in the same row.
- If the selection is wider than it is long (more columns than rows), *Excel* uses the *by row* orientation, places the column names on the category (x) axis, and uses the row names for the legend. This arrangement charts the relationship between values in the same column.

For example, suppose the selected data is arranged in 11 rows and 2 columns. Because there are more rows than columns, *Excel* uses the *by column* orientation to find the data for the category (x) axis, data series, and legend.

**Let's copy all of the formulas at one time using the fill handle.**

1. Select the range **B7:B25**.
2. Drag the fill handle to cell **H25**.
3. Tap the CTRL + HOME keys and save the workbook.

**CHECKPOINT**

The budget area of your worksheet should look like this.

| | A | B | C | D | E | F | G | H | I |
|---|---|---|---|---|---|---|---|---|---|
| 1 | **Historical Society** | | | | | | | | |
| 2 | **Debate Snacks and Drinks Budget** | | | | | | | | |
| 3 | Friday, May 21, 20-- | | | | | | | | |
| 4 | | | | | | | | | |
| 5 | | **Debate 1** | **Debate 2** | **Debate 3** | **Debate 4** | **Debate 5** | **Debate 6** | **Debate 7** | **Total** |
| 6 | **Sales** | | | | | | | | |
| 7 | Candy | $ 50 | $ 35 | $ 75 | $ 25 | $ 50 | $ 50 | $ 100 | |
| 8 | Fruit | 23 | 23 | 23 | 23 | 23 | 23 | 23 | |
| 9 | Popcorn | 113 | 90 | 113 | 83 | 113 | 120 | 105 | |
| 10 | Chips | 26 | 30 | 26 | 38 | 26 | 26 | 53 | |
| 11 | Drinks | 64 | 75 | 71 | 64 | 98 | 64 | 83 | |
| 12 | Total Sales | $ 276 | $ 253 | $ 308 | $ 233 | $ 310 | $ 283 | $ 364 | |
| 13 | | | | | | | | | |
| 14 | **Expenses** | | | | | | | | |
| 15 | Cost of Items Sold | | | | | | | | |
| 16 | Candy | $ 35 | $ 25 | $ 53 | $ 18 | $ 35 | $ 35 | $ 70 | |
| 17 | Fruit | 21 | 21 | 21 | 21 | 21 | 21 | 21 | |
| 18 | Popcorn | 40 | 32 | 40 | 29 | 40 | 42 | 37 | |
| 19 | Chips | 21 | 24 | 21 | 30 | 21 | 21 | 42 | |
| 20 | Drinks | 48 | 56 | 53 | 48 | 74 | 48 | 62 | |
| 21 | Total Cost of Items Sold | $ 165 | $ 158 | $ 188 | $ 146 | $ 191 | $ 167 | $ 232 | |
| 22 | Other Expenses | 28 | 25 | 31 | 23 | 31 | 28 | 36 | |
| 23 | Total Expenses | $ 193 | $ 183 | $ 219 | $ 169 | $ 222 | $ 195 | $ 268 | |
| 24 | | | | | | | | | |
| 25 | **Surplus or (Deficit)** | $ 83 | $ 70 | $ 89 | $ 64 | $ 88 | $ 88 | $ 96 | |

Fantastic! Now let's calculate the row totals.

**Let's use the Sum (AutoSum) button to calculate row totals.**

Formulas | Function Library | Sum (AutoSum)

1. Select the range **B7:I12** and then use the CTRL key to select the following nonadjacent ranges: **B16:I23** and **B25:I25**.
2. View the **Function Library** and click the **Sum** (**AutoSum**) button to insert the SUM function. Each row in the selected ranges is added horizontally, and the results and formulas are entered in the blank cells.
3. Tap the CTRL + HOME keys and save the workbook.

Now you are ready to calculate the historical society's estimated donation.

**Let's use drag and drop to explode the pie by dragging the Dark Energy data marker away from the other two markers.**

1. Select the Dark Energy data marker with two single clicks. *Remember! You click the pie chart in the plot area to select all of the slices; then you click the Dark Energy data marker to select it.*
2. Move the mouse pointer to the selected data marker and drag it slightly to the left, away from the other markers.
3. Deselect the chart and save the workbook.

**CHECKPOINT**

Your chart with the repositioned legend and exploded pie slice should look similar to this.

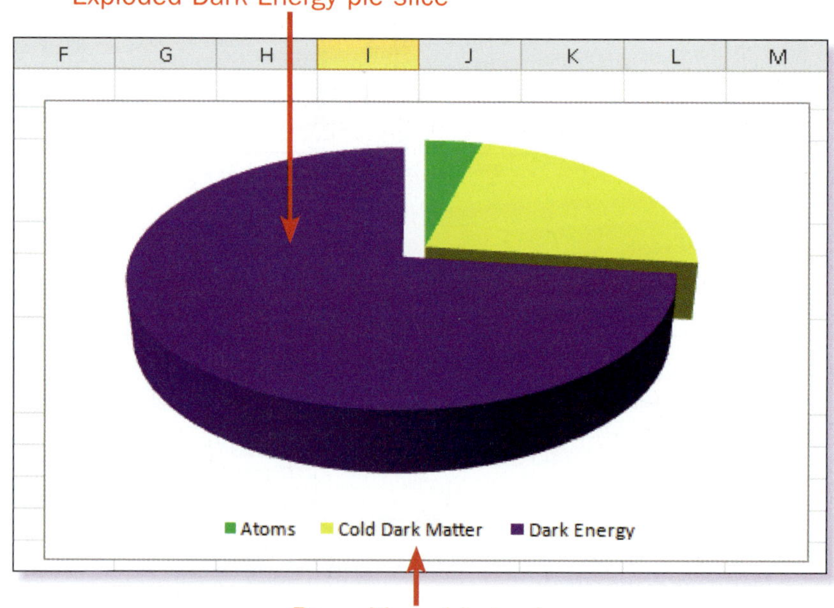


What a super-looking chart! Now let's create a column chart on another worksheet in the *universe10* workbook.

## Using the IF Function

Remember that the historical society is going to donate 10 percent of the surplus *if* the surplus *is greater than* $500. The donation will be $50 *if* the surplus *is equal to or less than* $500.

*Excel* has a logical function, the IF function, that you can use to calculate the donation amount. When you use the IF function, you perform a logical test and then take one of two actions depending on the results of the test.

The IF function has three arguments separated by commas:

1) the logical test

2) the action to take if the test is true

3) the action to take if the test is false

Here is an example of a formula containing the IF function.

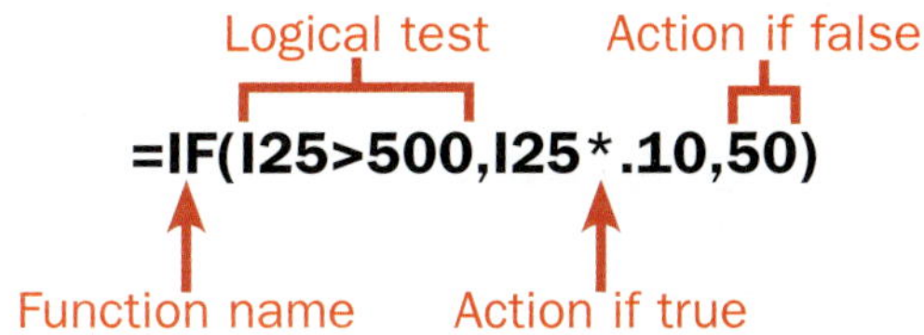

A great way to avoid errors when building a formula containing the IF function is to write down the formula in words and then replace the words with cell references and calculation operators. Try it!

To calculate the donation amount, you create a formula that tests the value of the total Surplus or (Deficit) against $500.

- If the value is greater than $500, then the formula calculates 10 percent of the surplus amount.
- If the value is less than or equal to $500, then the formula enters $50.

7. Repeat the above steps to change the color of the **Cold Dark Matter** to **Yellow** in the Standard Colors and the color of the **Atoms** data marker to **Green** in the Standard Colors; then click outside the chart to deselect it.

You can double-click a chart object to open its Format dialog box. Try it!

### Formatting a Chart Using the Format (Object) Dialog Box

You can also format a chart object using the object's Format dialog box. You can right-click an object to select it, then click Format (Object) to open the Format dialog box.

**Let's reposition the legend to the bottom of the chart using the Format Legend dialog box.**

1. Right-click the legend and click **Format Legend** on the shortcut menu to open the Format Legend dialog box.
2. Click **Legend Options** in the left pane, if necessary, and click the **Bottom** option button in the right pane.

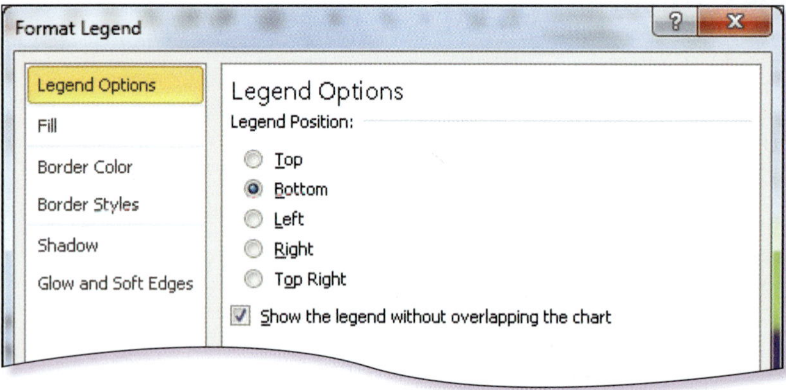
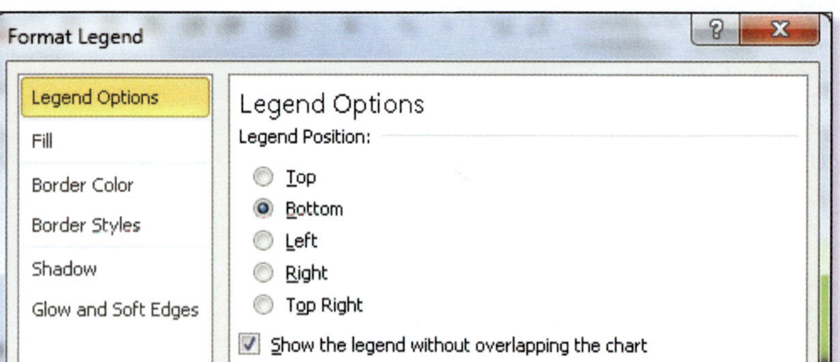


3. Click **Close** and deselect the chart.

The data markers are formatted, and the legend is repositioned.

Some pie charts are created to "explode" the data by separating each slice of the pie. You can make an exploded pie chart two ways—by choosing this type of chart in Excel's chart options or by moving each slice of the pie using drag and drop.

**Let's calculate the estimated donation amount, and then add the total Surplus or (Deficit) and the estimated donation to see how much money may be available for the field trip.**

1. Activate cell **I26**.
2. Key **=IF(**. *Do not forget to key the open parenthesis. Do not key the period.*

| $ 88 | $ 88 | $ 96 | $ 578 | | |
|---|---|---|---|---|---|
| Historical Society Donation | | | =IF( | | |
| Total Available for Field Trip | | | IF(**logical_test**, [value_if_true], [value_if_false]) | | |

3. Key **I25 >500,I25*.10,50)** and tap the ENTER key. *If* the logical test is true (the value in cell I25 is greater than 500), *then* multiply the value in I25 by 10%. *If* the logical test is false (the value in cell I25 is less than or equal to 500), *then* insert 50.

The value in cell I25 is $578; Excel enters 58 in cell I26, which is 10% of $578.

4. Activate cell **I27**, if necessary.
5. Enter the formula **=I25+I26** to calculate the total money available for the field trip.
6. Save the workbook.

Your estimated donation and total available for the field trip should look like this.

| $ 88 | $ 88 | $ 96 | $ 578 |
|---|---|---|---|
| Historical Society Donation | | | 58 |
| Total Available for Field Trip | | | $ 636 |

Well done! Your worksheet looks great! But what will happen if some of Luis's budget assumptions change? Let's see.

3. Click the **Dark Energy** data marker to select just that data marker. *Warning! Steps 2 and 3 involve two single clicks, not a double click!* The selection handles on the boundary of the Dark Energy pie slice indicate that only that slice or data marker is selected.

Selection handles on Dark Energy pie slice indicating only that data marker is selected

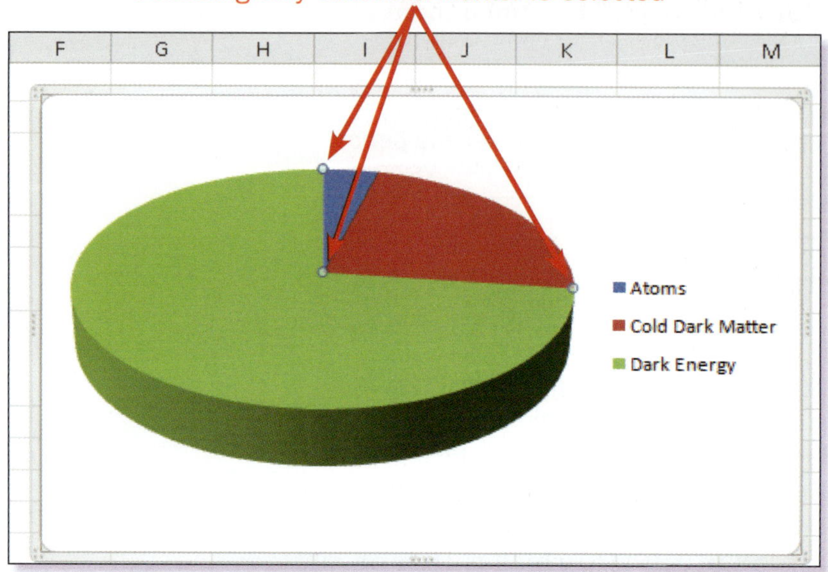


4. Click the **Chart Tools Format** tab and locate the **Shape Styles** group.
5. Click the **Shape Fill** button in the Shape Styles group and point to a color in the color grid to see a live preview of the new formatting.
6. Click the **Purple** color in the Standard Colors grid to apply the purple color to the Dark Energy data marker.

Formatted Dark Energy data marker

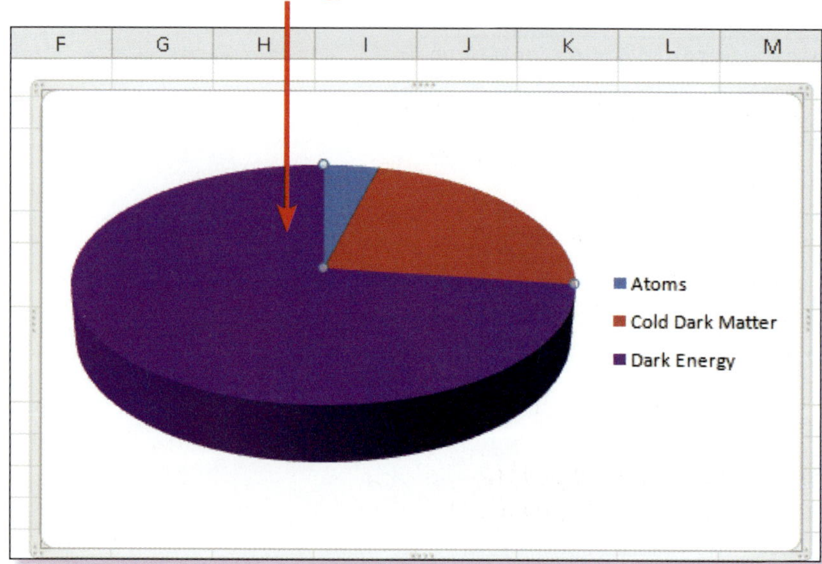

## Performing a What-if Analysis

The estimates in the *Snacks and Drinks Budget* worksheet are based on Luis's current information plus his expectations of future events. If the information or expectations change, the budget should be modified.

For example, the Explorers Club members have now decided to change some information or assumptions about the fund-raising budget:

- Candy should be sold for $0.75 instead of $1.00.
- Only 25 pieces of fruit will be sold at each debate.
- Popcorn cost should be 25 percent of sales.
- Other expenses should be 5 percent of sales.

To understand how making these four changes affects the budget, Luis wants you to perform a what-if analysis—*what* will happen *if* a number is changed.

Good news! Because you used cell references instead of actual values in each of your formulas, performing Luis's what-if analysis is easy.

Each time you change the contents of a cell, *Excel* automatically recalculates the formulas that reference that cell *and* any TODAY or NOW function in the worksheet. Simply enter the new assumption data and let *Excel* do the rest!

**Let's see *what* happens to the budget *if* four budget estimates are changed.**

1. Enter **.75** in cell **B34**.
2. Activate cell **B34** and drag the fill handle to cell **H34**.

All of the formulas that directly or indirectly use the contents of cell B34 recalculate, including candy sales, cost of candy, total sales, surplus, the society's donation, and the total available for the field trip.

3. Enter **25** in cell **B36** and then copy the contents of **B36** to cell **H36** using the fill handle.
4. Enter **.25** in cell **B54**. *Do not forget to key the decimal points.*
5. Enter **.05** in cell **D58**. *Do not forget to key the decimal points.*
6. Activate cell **A1**.

### Formatting a Chart Using Ribbon Buttons

*Excel* allows you to customize a chart by changing its formatting. For example, you can change the colors of the data markers, move the legend, and change the color of the legend's border. You can click the white chart background to select the chart or click an individual chart object, such as a data marker, to select the entire data series.

Selecting a chart or chart object displays the Chart Tools Design, Layout, and Format tabs on the Ribbon. You can click buttons on the Chart Tools tabs to format chart objects, change the chart's layout by adding or removing chart objects, change the chart type, apply a chart style, change the chart's data orientation, and customize your chart in other ways.

Just like formatting text in *Word*, you can live preview formatting when formatting your charts.

Check this out! Move the mouse pointer over a chart to see Chart Tips containing the name of each chart object of the chart.

**Let's format the embedded chart by changing data marker colors, repositioning the legend, changing the legend's border color, and exploding one of the pie slices.**

Chart Tools Format|Shape Styles|Shape Fill

1. Click the white background of the embedded chart to select the entire chart and display the Chart Tools tabs.
2. Click a data marker in the embedded chart to select the entire data series.

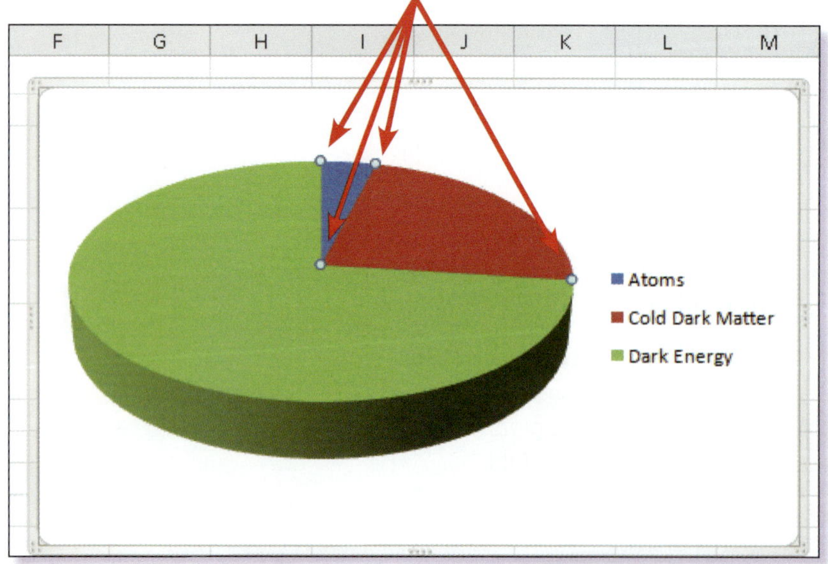

**CHECKPOINT**

Your revised budget should look like this.

| | A | B | C | D | E | F | G | H | I |
|---|---|---|---|---|---|---|---|---|---|
| 1 | **Historical Society** | | | | | | | | |
| 2 | **Debate Snacks and Drinks Budget** | | | | | | | | |
| 3 | Friday, May 21, 20-- | | | | | | | | |
| 4 | | | | | | | | | |
| 5 | | **Debate 1** | **Debate 2** | **Debate 3** | **Debate 4** | **Debate 5** | **Debate 6** | **Debate 7** | **Total** |
| 6 | **Sales** | | | | | | | | |
| 7 | Candy | $ 38 | $ 26 | $ 56 | $ 19 | $ 38 | $ 38 | $ 75 | $ 290 |
| 8 | Fruit | 19 | 19 | 19 | 19 | 19 | 19 | 19 | 133 |
| 9 | Popcorn | 113 | 90 | 113 | 83 | 113 | 120 | 105 | 737 |
| 10 | Chips | 26 | 30 | 26 | 38 | 26 | 26 | 53 | 225 |
| 11 | Drinks | 64 | 75 | 71 | 64 | 98 | 64 | 83 | 519 |
| 12 | Total Sales | $ 260 | $ 240 | $ 285 | $ 223 | $ 294 | $ 267 | $ 335 | $ 1,904 |
| 13 | | | | | | | | | |
| 14 | **Expenses** | | | | | | | | |
| 15 | Cost of Items Sold | | | | | | | | |
| 16 | Candy | $ 27 | $ 18 | $ 39 | $ 13 | $ 27 | $ 27 | $ 53 | $ 204 |
| 17 | Fruit | 17 | 17 | 17 | 17 | 17 | 17 | 17 | 119 |
| 18 | Popcorn | 28 | 23 | 28 | 21 | 28 | 30 | 26 | 184 |
| 19 | Chips | 21 | 24 | 21 | 30 | 21 | 21 | 42 | 180 |
| 20 | Drinks | 48 | 56 | 53 | 48 | 74 | 48 | 62 | 389 |
| 21 | Total Cost of Items Sold | $ 141 | $ 138 | $ 158 | $ 129 | $ 167 | $ 143 | $ 200 | $ 1,076 |
| 22 | Other Expenses | 13 | 12 | 14 | 11 | 15 | 13 | 17 | 95 |
| 23 | Total Expenses | $ 154 | $ 150 | $ 172 | $ 140 | $ 182 | $ 156 | $ 217 | $ 1,171 |
| 24 | | | | | | | | | |
| 25 | **Surplus or (Deficit)** | $ 106 | $ 90 | $ 113 | $ 83 | $ 112 | $ 111 | $ 118 | $ 733 |
| 26 | | | | | | Historical Society Donation | | | 73 |
| 27 | | | | | | Total Available for Field Trip | | | $ 806 |

7. Save and close the workbook.

5. Click the **Pie in 3-D** icon (the first subtype option in the 3-D Pie gallery). A 3-D pie chart is embedded in a window on the worksheet. The window might overlap a portion of the data.

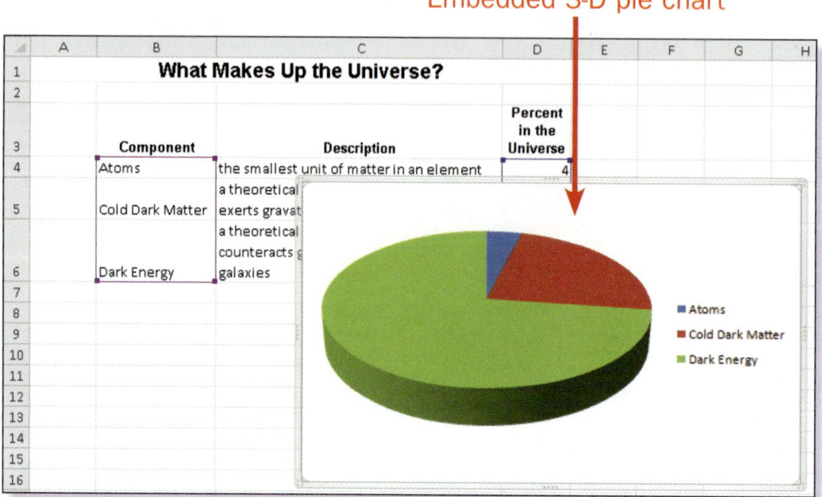


6. Move the mouse pointer to the white chart background area.
7. Drag the chart to position it within the F1:M11 range boundaries; then scroll to view the chart.
8. Click anywhere in the worksheet outside the embedded chart to deselect the chart; then save the workbook.

Each slice in the pie chart is a data marker that represents one of the components of the universe. All three data markers represent the single data series—all of the components in the universe—or the entire pie.

**CHECKPOINT**

Your repositioned and deselected chart should look similar to this.

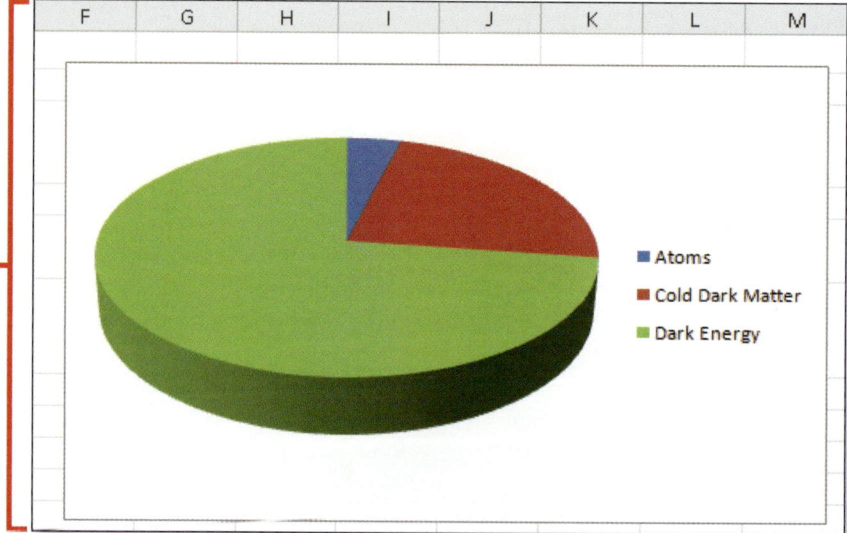

# Project Skills Review

You learned a lot in this project! We are very impressed with your progress. Let's take a few minutes to review the skills that you learned.

| Skill | How to |
|---|---|
| **Add borders and color to cells** | Click the **Borders** or **Fill Color** button arrow in the Font group on the **Home** tab. |
| **Indent cell contents** | Click the **Increase Indent** button in the Alignment group on the **Home** tab.  |
| **Enter formulas** | Key an equals sign (=), use the mouse pointer to select the cell references, key the calculation operator, tap the ENTER or TAB key. |
| **Round formula calculations to agree with number of displayed decimal places** | Build a formula that includes the **ROUND** function. |
| **Copy and paste formulas** | Drag the fill handle. Click the **Copy** and **Paste** buttons in the Clipboard group on the **Home** tab.   |
| **Mark a cell reference as an absolute reference before copying a formula** | Key **$** before the column letter and row number. Tap the **F4** key once. |
| **Perform a logical test; then take one of two actions** | Build a formula using the **IF** function. |
| **Perform a what-if analysis** | Use cell references instead of actual values in a formula. Change cell values, and *Excel* automatically recalculates all related formulas. |

### Creating a Chart

To create a chart, first select both the data and the text that will appear in the chart. Then click the Insert tab and click a button in the Charts group.

A chart can be inserted on its own separate chart sheet or on the same worksheet as the data. When inserted on the same worksheet as the data, it is called an embedded chart.

The type of chart you choose to create depends on the type of data picture you want to show. For example, a pie chart is often used to show percentages.

To create a pie chart from the data on the *The Universe* worksheet, you must first select the cells that contain the data—the cells with the names of the three components and the cells with the percentages. *Remember!* You can select nonadjacent data using the CTRL key.

**Let's use data in *The Universe* worksheet to create an embedded pie chart that shows each component of the universe as a percentage.**

Insert | Charts | Pie

1. Activate *The Universe* worksheet, if necessary.
2. Click the **Insert** tab and locate the **Charts** group.
3. Use the CTRL key to select the nonadjacent ranges **B4:B6** and **D4:D6**. These two ranges include the names of the components in the universe and their percentages.

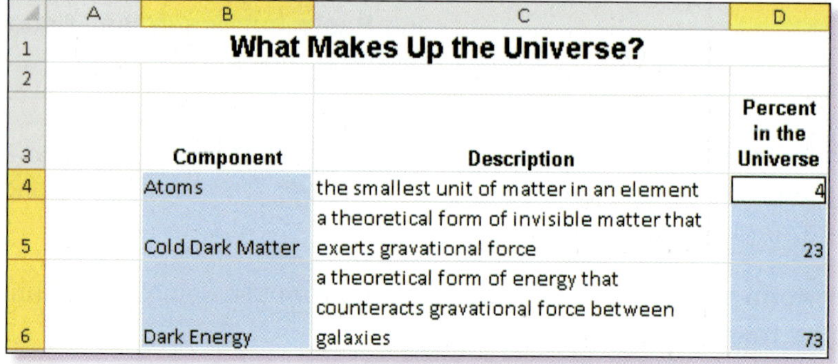

| | A | B | C | D |
|---|---|---|---|---|
| 1 | | What Makes Up the Universe? | | |
| 2 | | | | |
| 3 | | Component | Description | Percent in the Universe |
| 4 | | Atoms | the smallest unit of matter in an element | 4 |
| 5 | | Cold Dark Matter | a theoretical form of invisible matter that exerts gravational force | 23 |
| 6 | | Dark Energy | a theoretical form of energy that counteracts gravitational force between galaxies | 73 |

4. Click the **Pie** button in the Charts group to view a gallery of pie chart subtypes.

Pie chart subtypes

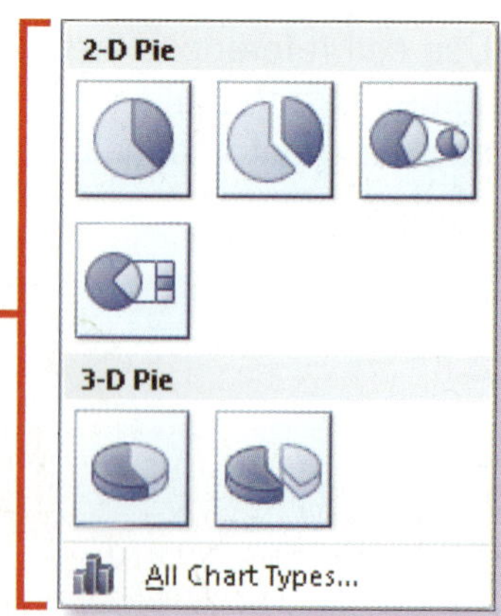

# Exploring *On Your Own*

## Blaze Your Own Trail

You have learned several new skills in this project. Now blaze your own trail by practicing these skills on your own!

1. Open the *budgeting9* workbook and click the *Explorers Club Budget* worksheet.
2. Use the Function Library to insert the NOW function in cell **A3**; format the date as a Long Date and then center the date across the range A3:F3.
3. Add a thick border and the White, Background 1 fill color to the assumptions data in the range H9:I16.
4. Indent the categories below the Revenues and Expenses row names. Do not indent the Total Revenues or Total Expenses lines.
5. Enter formulas to calculate the amounts for Qtr 1, including the calendar costs, using the table below as your guide. Use the IF function to calculate the cost of calendars.
6. Edit the calendar sales and calendar costs formulas to add the ROUND function to round the results of the formulas to 0 decimal places.

| Amounts to Find | How to Calculate the Amount |
|---|---|
| Calendar sales (B7) | Number of calendars (H11) times the sales price per calendar (I11); use absolute references in your formula for the cells that contain assumptions |
| Total Revenues (B10) | Sum of all first-quarter revenues (B7:B9) |
| Cost of calendars (B14) | Based on number of calendars sold (H11) and a percentage (I15, I16) of sales; use absolute references in your formula for the cells that contain assumptions |
| Total Expenses (B17) | Sum of all first-quarter expenses (B13:B16) |
| Surplus or (Deficit) (B19) | Revenues remaining after all expenses are paid (B10, B17) |

7. Use the fill handle to copy the Qtr 1 formulas to Qtrs 2–4.
8. Use the Sum (AutoSum) button to calculate the totals for each row. Then perform a what-if analysis to determine *what* happens to the budget *if*:
   - the number of calendars sold each quarter is 75 and the sales price per calendar is $2.85
   - the calendar cost percentage for 50 or more is 55%
   - field trip expenses are $150 per quarter
9. Save and close the workbook.

**Begin by opening Ray's workbook and saving it with a new name.**

1. Open the *universe* workbook and save it as *universe10*.

Great! Let's start by creating a pie chart to illustrate the components of the universe.

**ERGONOMICS TIP**

Wait! Are your upper arms and elbows close to your body as you work at the keyboard? Fantastic! Now you are ready to go!

## Creating and Formatting a Pie Chart

A chart, or graph, is a picture of worksheet data. Charts help you understand data relationships, such as how data changes over time or how just one portion of the data relates to the data whole. *Excel* has useful charting features, which help you turn selected worksheet data into a pie, column, or line chart.

*Excel* also has special terms for each part of a chart—these are called chart objects.

| Chart Object | Description |
|---|---|
| **Chart area** | The background for the chart |
| **Chart title** | The text title of the chart |
| **Data point** | A number in the worksheet that is converted into a column, point on a line, or pie slice in the chart |
| **Data marker** | A column, point on a line, or pie slice that represents the numbers, or data points, in the worksheet |
| **Data labels** | Text labels that identify the data markers on the chart |
| **Data series** | All of the related data markers |
| **Legend** | Labels and colors that identify each data series |

# Exploring On Your Own

## Reading in Action

### Standardized Test Preparation

When you take a standardized test, you may be asked to use context to determine the meaning of a word. Find the correct answer to this multiple-choice question. Insert each choice into the sentence to determine which one fits best.

Choose the meaning of the word *meet* that BEST fits in this context.

*Because the business had a deficit, the owner could not meet his payments.*

A. to come together for a common purpose

B. to provide for

C. to pay fully

D. to become acquainted with

## Math in Action

### Finding Simple Interest

Banks pay depositors interest—a percentage of the amount in the account. Find the interest earned on $300 deposited for 4 years at a simple interest rate of 5.5% per year.

Formula: Interest = Principal x Rate x Time

Interest = $300 x 0.055 x 4 = $66

Now you try it!

Find the interest earned on $300 deposited for 14 years at a simple interest rate of 3.5% per year. Find the interest earned on $200 deposited for 40 years at a simple interest rate of 3.5%.

# Discovering the Universe

## Explorers' Guide

Data files: universe
Jupiter
Sun

Objectives:
In this project, you will:
- create and format a pie chart
- create a column chart
- format a column chart
- add a text box
- create a linking formula

© ISTOCKPHOTO.COM/PAUL LEFEVRE

## Our Exploration Assignment:

### Using charts to learn more about the universe

Did you know that some scientists believe that the universe is about 15 billion years old? Have you heard about black holes—collapsing stars whose gravitational pull is so strong that light cannot escape? Ray has entered some research data about the universe in a workbook. Can you help him get ready for the next Explorers Club meeting by creating charts from his data? Great! Just follow the Trail Markers to create and format a pie chart, create and format a column chart, add a text box, and create a linking formula.

# Exploring *Across the Curriculum*

## Internet/Web

Work with a classmate to use the Web to help create a budget for the Explorers Club field trip to Lincoln's home in Springfield, Illinois.

- A total of 18 club members and 6 adults will make the two-day trip. Each participant will pay $20; the Explorers Club will pay the remaining trip expenses.
- The club must rent minivans for the trip and pay for rental plus round trip mileage to and from Madison, Wisconsin.
- The budget should include an overnight stay at a motel or hotel in Springfield. Plan for three members and one adult per room.
- The Club will pay for all entrance and parking fees, but members must bring their own spending money and pay for their own meals.

Open your Web browser; use a favorite or bookmark to view the Learning with Computers Web page (www.cengage.com/school/keyboarding/lwcorange). Click the **Links** option and click **Project 9**. Click the links to gather information you will need to create the field trip budget.

1. Create a new workbook and save it as *Lincoln trip9*.
2. Create a budget for the field trip using your online research.
3. Format the budget worksheet attractively. Place all of the assumption data you use to build your formulas in a separate area of the worksheet from the actual budget calculations.
4. Save the workbook.

How does the budget change if 30 members and 10 adults make the trip? If 12 members and 4 adults make the trip?

Explore More

## 9a Build Skill

Key each line twice. Double-space between 2-line groups.

**Alphabet sentences**

1 Jack Vasquez placed my next bid for the two gowns.

2 Jasper amazed Hank by quickly fixing two big vans.

3 Bill Paxton quickly gave away the jazz band forms.

4 Wesley Van Jantz quickly proofed the biology exam.

5 Dr. Kopezy will give Jacques the exam before noon.

gwam 20" | 3 | 6 | 9 | 12 | 15 | 18 | 21 | 24 | 27 | 30 |

## 9b Build Skill

Key each paragraph twice.

For additional practice:
**MicroType 5**
Skill Building, Lesson A

**A** **all letters used** gwam 2'

Atlanta, the capital of Georgia, is a gem of the South. It is 6
the largest city in the state. Atlanta came into existence because of 13
railroads. The original site was selected as the end of the railroad 20
to be built northward. Eight years later the area became known as 27
Atlanta. Because of the railroad, Atlanta was the key supply center 34
for the Confederacy during the Civil War. 38

One of the better known Atlanta citizens was Margaret 44
Mitchell. The book she wrote exquisitely portrays the area during 50
the Civil War. During the war, much of the city was destroyed. 57
However, a few of the older homes in the city have been restored. 64
They are open for the public to view. Today, Atlanta is a modern 70
city that provides visitors and residents of the city with a range of 77
cultural and sporting events for their enjoyment. 82

gwam 2' | 1 | 2 | 3 | 4 | 5 | 6 |

# Exploring Across the Curriculum

## Language Arts: Words to Know

Look up the meaning of the following terms in a classroom dictionary, CD-ROM dictionary or encyclopedia, or online dictionary.

| budget | assumption | what-if | expenditure |
|---|---|---|---|
| revenue | expense | surplus | deficit |

Create a new workbook. Save the workbook as *definitions9*. Rename the Sheet1 sheet tab as **Definitions**. Enter the title **Budget Definitions** in cell **A1**. Enter the system date and time in cell **A2** using the NOW function. Merge and center the title across the range A1:B2. Enter **Term** as the column name in **A4**. Enter **Definition** as the column name in **B4**. Bold the title and column name. Center the column name in the cells.

Enter the terms in the range A5:A12. Enter the term definitions in the range B5:B12. Use the resizing pointer to automatically fit the cell contents for columns A and B. Sort the terms and definitions in ascending alphabetical order by term. Save and close the workbook.

## Math: Creating a Personal Budget

Open the *budgeting9* workbook and click the *My Personal Budget* sheet tab. Use the worksheet to create your own personal budget for an entire year by quarter. Insert or delete budget categories as necessary. Estimate how much money you will earn for the year, how much you will save, and how you will spend the money you do not save.

Add borders and a fill color to the Savings Assumption data. Then enter your estimates for all categories except Savings. Using the IF function, enter a formula to calculate your savings each quarter as a percentage of your total revenues (H9). If your total revenues are greater than or equal to $100 each quarter, save 10% of your revenues. If your total revenues each quarter are less than $100, save $10 per quarter. Enter formulas to calculate Qtr 1 Total Revenues, Total Expenditures, and Surplus or (Deficit). Edit the Savings formula to make the savings percentage cell reference an absolute reference.

Then copy all of the Qtr 1 formulas to Qtrs 2–4. Use the AutoSum button to calculate all of the annual totals. Perform a what-if analysis to determine the effect on your budget if you increase or decrease your quarterly savings percentage or your total revenues. Save and close the workbook.

Explore More

# Exploring *Across the Curriculum*

## Getting Help

Click the Microsoft Excel Help icon below the *Excel* application Close button to open the *Excel* Help window. Key **keyboard shortcuts** in the search box and tap the ENTER key to research ways to insert the current date and time in a cell using keyboard shortcut keys. Then open a workbook and practice what you learned. Close the workbook without saving it.

## Career Day

Financial planning for personal finances, investments, and insurance as well as business financial management often requires the use of complex worksheets. If you enjoy working with complex worksheets, planning, and budgeting, you might like a career in financial planning. Using library, printed, or online resources, identify three interesting careers that involve financial planning. Write a brief summary of each career, print your summary, and save it in your Career Day folder.

## Your Personal Journal

Open your personal journal document. Insert today's date and two blank lines. Write one paragraph about goals you have, such as saving money for a vacation, a college education, or a new computer. Then write a second paragraph explaining how a personal budget can help you attain your goals. Spell-check, save, and close your journal.

## Online Enrichment Games

www.cengage.com/school/keyboarding/lwcorange

# Appendix A Reference

## Three-Level Multilevel List

A three-level multilevel list has main topics, subtopics, and details that support a subtopic. Subtopics are indented under the main topic. Details are indented under subtopics. Each multilevel level is numbered or lettered according to a set system. The most common system is Roman numerals (I, II, III) for main topics, uppercase letters (A, B, C) for subtopics, and Arabic numerals (1, 2, 3) for details.

A multilevel list should have 2-inch top, left, and right margins and a 1-inch bottom margin. Its title should be centered between the left and right margins. Use the default line spacing.

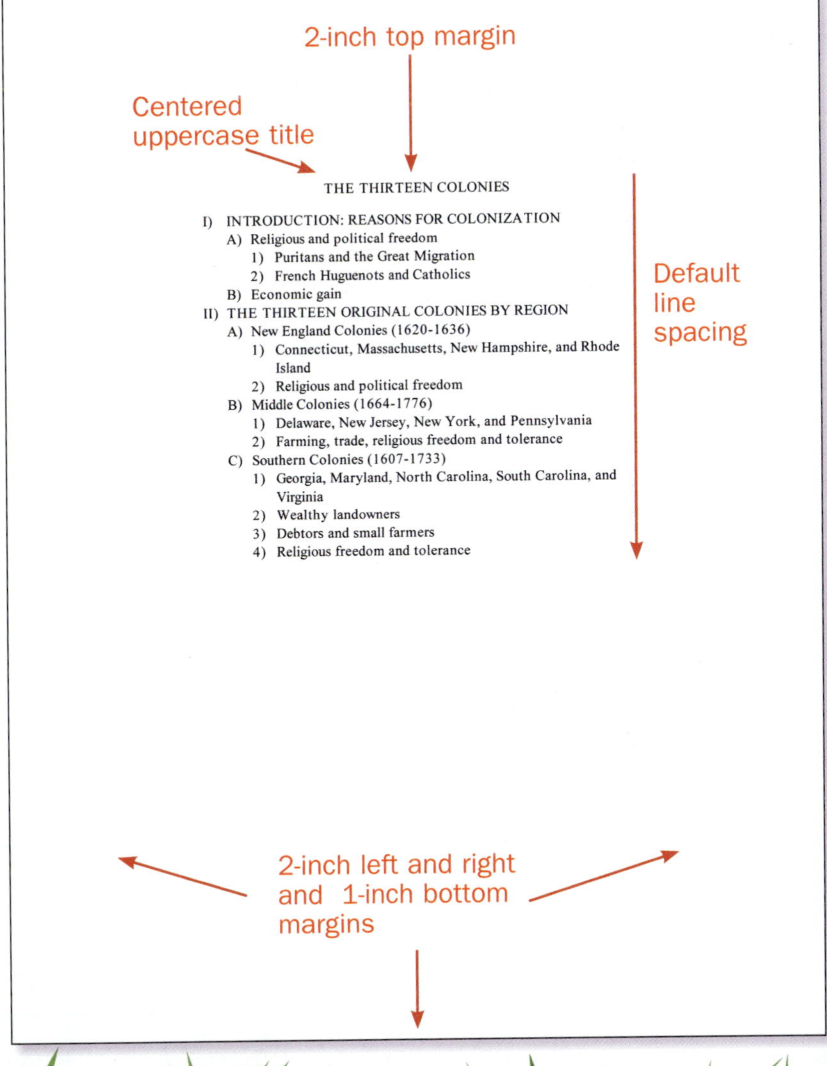



THE THIRTEEN COLONIES

I) INTRODUCTION: REASONS FOR COLONIZATION
   A) Religious and political freedom
      1) Puritans and the Great Migration
      2) French Huguenots and Catholics
   B) Economic gain
II) THE THIRTEEN ORIGINAL COLONIES BY REGION
   A) New England Colonies (1620-1636)
      1) Connecticut, Massachusetts, New Hampshire, and Rhode Island
      2) Religious and political freedom
   B) Middle Colonies (1664-1776)
      1) Delaware, New Jersey, New York, and Pennsylvania
      2) Farming, trade, religious freedom and tolerance
   C) Southern Colonies (1607-1733)
      1) Georgia, Maryland, North Carolina, South Carolina, and Virginia
      2) Wealthy landowners
      3) Debtors and small farmers
      4) Religious freedom and tolerance

# Exploring On Your Own

## Internet/Web

1. There are laws and rules in your community that you must follow to be a good citizen. For example, traffic laws help us get around safely. Laws against stealing protect our personal property; pollution laws protect our health and the environment. In the same way, you also need to follow certain rules to be a good cyber citizen. Develop at least ten cyber citizenship rules that all Internet users should follow. Explain why each rule is important.
2. Don't let spyware sneak onto your computer so that others can peek at information you enter online. To learn more about avoiding spyware, use the Web. Open your Web browser and use a favorite or bookmark to view the Learning with Computers Web page (www.cengage.com/school/keyboarding/lwcorange). Click the **Links** option and click **Appendix B**. Learn how to avoid spyware by taking the Flash quiz from OnGuardOnline, a website maintained by the U.S. Federal Trade Commission that provides tips about how to use the Internet wisely and safely.
3. Your brother needs to step away from the computer to wash the dishes. As you glance up at the monitor, you notice that he's been writing an e-mail to his girlfriend. His e-mail program is still open. You decide to have a look to see what's going on between the two of them. Have you violated anyone's privacy? What problems might your actions cause? Are you being a responsible cyber citizen? Answer these questions in a one-page essay.
4. For each of the following scenarios, tell if plagiarism or piracy has occurred. Briefly explain your answer.
   a. Benjamin finds a really cool animated GIF online and he copies it to his personal Web page.
   b. Mo'nique writes her own opening paragraph for a report on J. K. Rowling; then she copies and pastes text about Rowling that she found online. She changes some of the words in the copied material and adds a paragraph at the end about how much she likes Rowling's books.
   c. Rose finds a beautiful drawing of a medieval castle online. She thinks it would look great on the cover of her report about the Middle Ages. So she downloads it and inserts it on the cover page, along with a credit line.
   d. This morning Will realized that he didn't do his science homework last night. He texts his friend Sara, who offers to send Will her completed science homework in an e-mail attachment.
   e. Abdul takes a direct quote from a website about volcanoes and includes it word for word in his report. He puts quotation marks around the words and includes a footnote telling who wrote the words and where he found them.

## Unbound Single-Page Report

An unbound single-page report has a 2-inch top margin, a 1-inch bottom margin, and 1-inch left and right margins. The main heading is keyed in mixed case and is formatted with the Title style. Line spacing is the default 1.15-inches with 10 points of extra space following each paragraph. The body text font is the default Calibri, 11 point.

Paragraph headings are formatted with the Heading 1 style.

Each paragraph begins at the left margin.

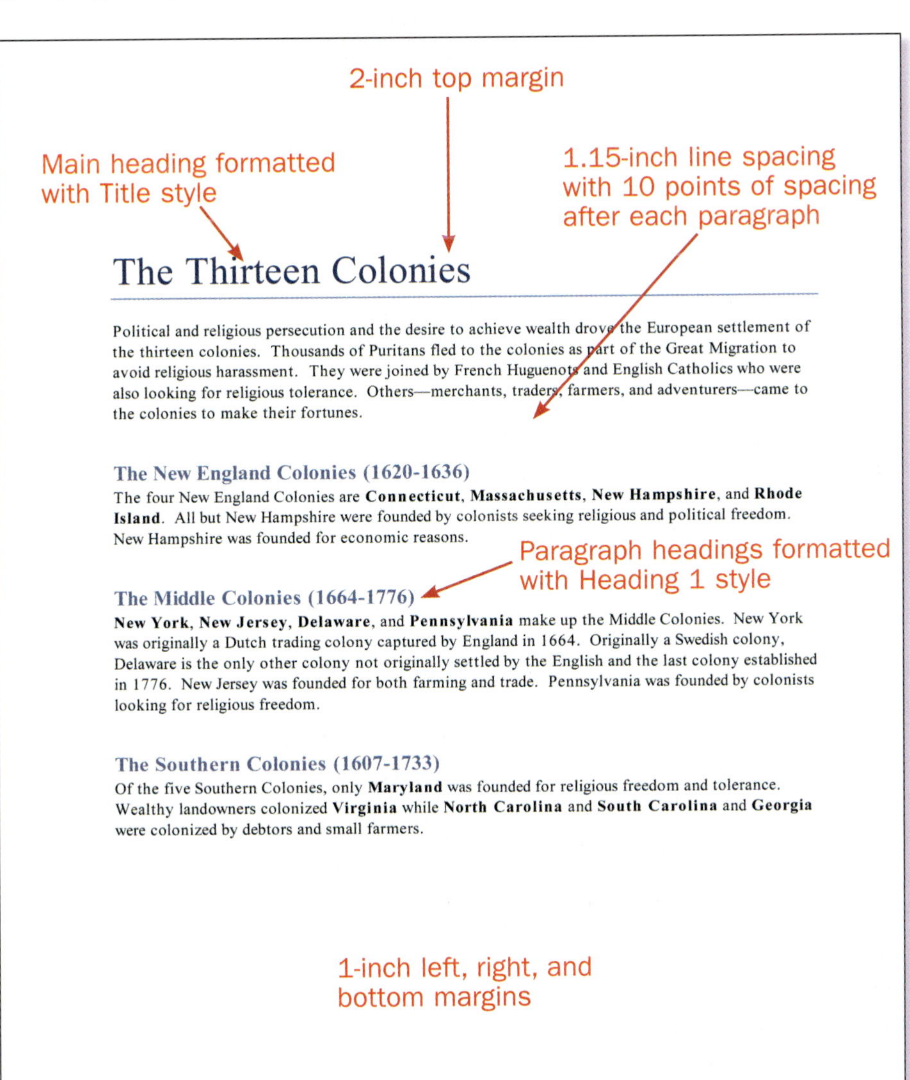

You can learn a lot more about digital piracy at the Peers 2 Peers website (http://www.peers2peers.org/), which offers online guides for intellectual property and piracy. Check it out.

## What Is Appropriate and Inappropriate Cyber Behavior?

You know how to behave at school and in public places such as movie theaters and restaurants. There are certain behaviors you should practice online too.

**Netiquette.** Have you ever heard the word *etiquette*? Etiquette rules govern socially acceptable behavior—for example, covering your mouth when you sneeze or keeping your voice down in the library. Well, there are behavior rules in the virtual world as well. The rules governing appropriate and courteous behavior while you are online are called netiquette. Think of netiquette as online manners—the way you should behave as you surf the Web.

You probably already know plenty of netiquette rules. For example, it's considered impolite to send text messages or e-mails in all caps. (It's like shouting.) Long and wordy postings on discussion groups and forums are another no-no. Sarcasm should be avoided because readers may not pick up on it—they can't hear the tone of your voice. Don't flood your friends' mailboxes with "funny" messages or cute pictures you've found online. And don't start flame wars—hostile and insulting arguments meant mainly to cause trouble rather than actually discuss issues.

It's easy to find netiquette rules online. Just go to your favorite search engine and key *netiquette*. You'll find plenty of guidelines to good online behavior. Following the netiquette rules means you're a good cyber citizen. Your online communication will be more successful if you do.

**File-sharing.** File-sharing technology lets you search for and copy files from someone else's computer. (This is also called "peer-to-peer," or P2P, technology.) File-sharing is most often used to trade MP3s, but movies, games, and software programs can also be shared. BitTorrent, Morpheus, Kazaa, LimeWire, and iMesh are popular file-sharing programs. They give you direct access to other computers without having to go through a central server.

File-sharing programs are a convenient way to share public-domain files (material that isn't owned by anybody). But file-sharing can quickly turn into piracy. Sharing or downloading copyrighted material without paying for it is illegal. Also, shared files may contain viruses and spyware. You may think you're downloading an interesting program, but you could wind up infecting your computer with something nasty. And some P2P programs include access to chat rooms—we've already talked about the dangers involved there. So if you decide to use a file-sharing program, be careful . . . and stay legal.

## Unbound Multipage Report

An unbound multipage report has a 2-inch top margin on the first page, a 1-inch top margin on the remaining pages, and a 1-inch bottom margin and 1-inch left and right margins on all pages. The main heading is formatted with the Title style, and paragraph headings are formatted with the Heading 1 style. The default 1.15-inch line spacing with 10 points of spacing following a paragraph are used.

Each paragraph begins at the left margin.

Page numbers are included in a header in the upper-right corner of the page on all pages except the title (cover) page and the first report page.

2-inch top margin

Main heading formatted with Title style

# Lewis and Clark

In 1801, when Thomas Jefferson took office as President of the United States, American farmers and traders relied on rivers to transport their goods to market. Jefferson was concerned that a secret treaty, in which Spain ceded New Orleans and some of its territories west of the Mississippi River to France, would interfere with access to the Mississippi River and other waterways. To protect the interests of the United States, Jefferson authorized James Monroe and Robert Livingston to negotiate with France for the purchase of New Orleans at the mouth of the Mississippi and portions of western and eastern Florida. Napoleon's representative, Talleyrand, offered to sell not just New Orleans but the entire French territory of Louisiana. Surprised but excited by the chance to gain more territory for the U.S., Monroe and Livingston negotiated a treaty with Talleyrand that authorized the purchase of Louisiana for $15 million dollars.[1]

At more than 800,000 square miles, the Louisiana Purchase almost doubled the size of the United States. After the U.S. Senate ratified the treaty authorizing the Louisiana Purchase, Jefferson assigned his own private secretary, **Meriwether Lewis**, to take charge of an expedition to explore the Louisiana Purchase territories. That expedition was then called the Corps of Discovery. Lewis chose his friend and fellow soldier, **William Clark**, to co-lead the expedition. The expedition, which we now call the **Lewis and Clark Expedition**, became one of the great adventures of all time.

Paragraph heading formatted with Heading 1 style

## Meriwether Lewis

Lewis was born on his parents' Virginia plantation in 1774. As a young boy, Meriwether Lewis lived for a few years on the Georgia frontier developing his frontier survival skills.[2] Returning to Virginia as a teenager, Lewis began his education and assumed the responsibility of managing the family plantation. In 1794, Lewis became a soldier in the state militia and then in the regular army, rising to the rank of captain. He gained a reputation for competence and honesty and, in 1801, President Thomas Jefferson asked him to serve as his private secretary. It is possible that Jefferson already had Lewis in mind to lead a westward expedition because for the next two years, Jefferson had Lewis study with some of the foremost scientists in the country to get ready for the expedition. In the spring of 1803, Lewis was ready for his great adventure.

---

[1] Jon Kukla., *A Wilderness So Immense* (New York: Alfred A. Knopf, 2003), p. 265.

[2] Stephen Ambrose, *Undaunted Courage: Meriwether Lewis, Thomas Jefferson, and the Opening of the American West* (New York: Simon & Schuster, 1996), p. 24.

No page number on first page

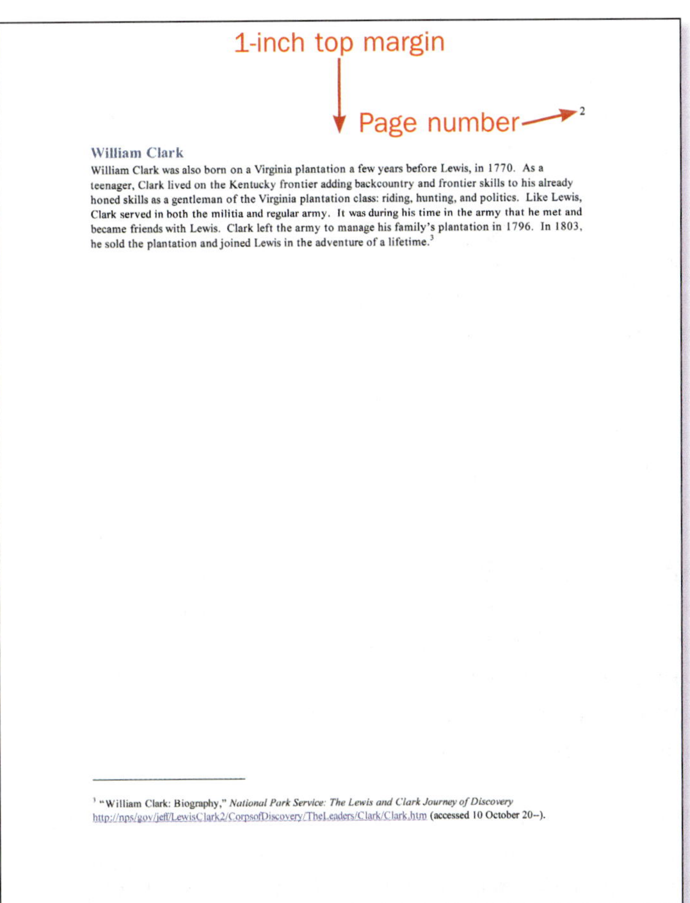

1-inch top margin

Page number

2

## William Clark

William Clark was also born on a Virginia plantation a few years before Lewis, in 1770. As a teenager, Clark lived on the Kentucky frontier adding backcountry and frontier skills to his already honed skills as a gentleman of the Virginia plantation class: riding, hunting, and politics. Like Lewis, Clark served in both the militia and regular army. It was during his time in the army that he met and became friends with Lewis. Clark left the army to manage his family's plantation in 1796. In 1803, he sold the plantation and joined Lewis in the adventure of a lifetime.[3]

---

[3] "William Clark: Biography," *National Park Service: The Lewis and Clark Journey of Discovery* http://nps/gov/jeff/LewisClark2/CorpsofDiscovery/TheLeaders/Clark/Clark.htm (accessed 10 October 20--).

**Plagiarism.** Stealing someone else's work is called plagiarism. Plagiarism happens when you copy another person's ideas, text, or other creative work and present it as your own, without getting permission or crediting the source. All of the following are examples of plagiarism:

- You find an old term paper about the Crusades that your dad wrote in high school and turn it in as your own.
- You lift a paragraph from a Langston Hughes biography word for word and use it in your report, without giving credit to the author.
- You find some artistic photos of flowers online, download the files, and turn them in to your photography class as if you took the photos yourself.
- You do not put quotation marks around words you picked up from another source, and you don't tell who wrote the words and where you found them.
- You copy a Wikipedia article about the water cycle, change a few words here and there, and turn it in as your own work.
- You use so many ideas from an Encyclopedia Britannica article about the Oregon Trail that it makes up the majority of your work, even if you credit the original source.

Sometimes it can be hard figuring out what plagiarism is—and what it isn't. It can also be hard to properly credit your sources. You can find examples of plagiarism as well as guidelines for citations here: http://www.plagiarism.org

All schools take plagiarism very seriously. If you are caught plagiarizing, you will certainly receive a failing grade on your project. You might even be suspended from school. Luckily, you can usually avoid plagiarism by citing your sources. Telling your audience that you're using someone else's work—and providing information about that source—is usually all you need to do to stay above board.

**Piracy.** It's not hard to find music files and software online that you can download for free. And that's OK—as long as you download only from sites where the copyright holder has given permission. But many people download files—or make copies of software programs—without the copyright holder's permission. Piracy is another way people use the Internet to steal what doesn't belong to them. Sometimes pirates burn copies of CDs or DVDs and sell them for a couple of dollars to their friends or at flea markets. But "borrowing" someone's copy of the latest computer game and installing it on your own PC is piracy too. So is swapping MP3 files with your friends.

You may not see the harm in copying "one little song" or sharing "just one software program" with your friends. But piracy is theft, and you can go to jail because of it. Software companies and the music and movie industries lose billions of dollars each year to digital pirates, and they aren't happy about it. They have successfully prosecuted digital pirates—including kids like you. Don't become one of them. Be a good cyber citizen.

## Cover Page for a Multipage Report

A cover or title page is usually added to a multipage report, whether bound or unbound. For these projects, students create a cover page by selecting a preformatted *Word* cover page template and then using the field placeholders to add text, such as name and date, to the page.

When a cover page is created manually, the report title is positioned 2 inches from the top of the page, centered, bolded, keyed in all uppercase, and formatted in the 14-point font. The writer's name appears in 11 point, mixed case, 5 inches from the top of the page. The school name appears two lines below the writer's name. The date is centered 9 inches below the top of the page and is formatted with 11-point font.

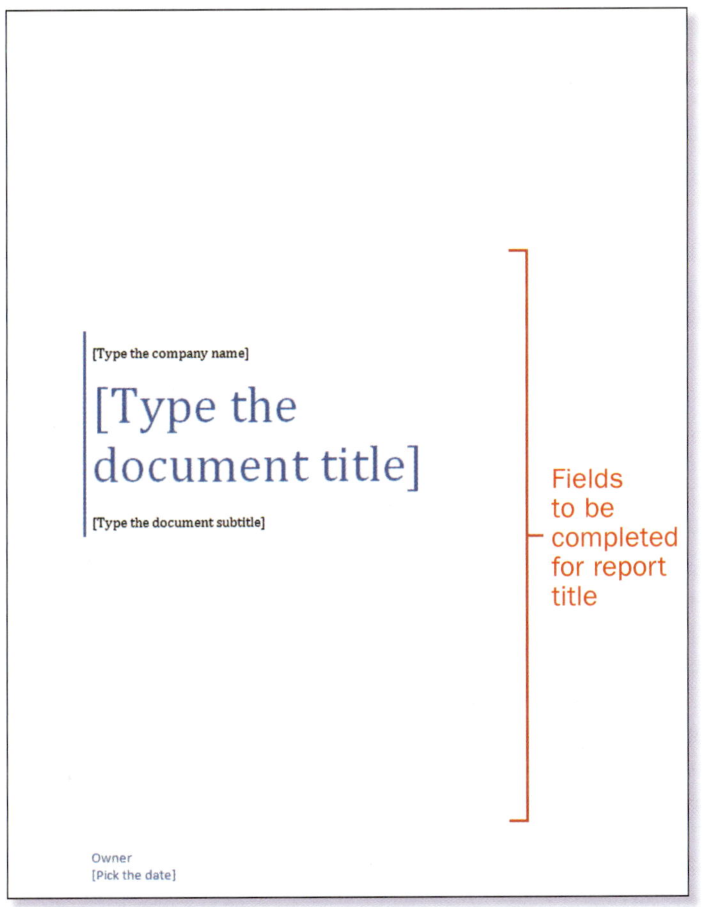


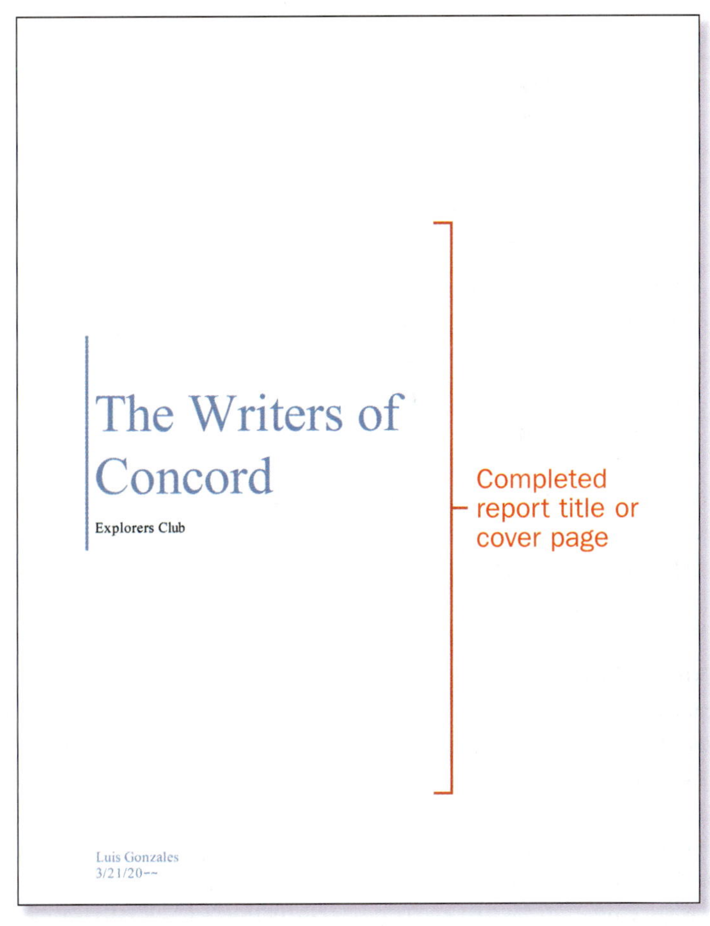

We've already talked about ways to stay safe online, and those rules apply here too. A good way to steer clear of a cyber predator is not to talk to strangers online. Don't arrange a face-to-face meeting with anyone you've met online. Avoid revealing personal information online. And don't respond to messages that are suggestive, obscene, aggressive, or threatening. If something makes you feel uncomfortable, log off right away and tell an adult. Doing so will help keep the Internet safer for everyone.

For more tips for staying safe online, go to the Learning with Computers Web page (www.cengage.com/school/keyboarding/lwcorange), click the **Links** option, and then click **Appendix B**.

It's possible to use location-sharing programs such as Twitter, Foursquare, Loopt, Google Buzz, and even Facebook to "check in" with friends and family and tell people where you are. But this is a very bad idea. Using these kinds of tools makes you vulnerable to unwelcome personal contact.

## When Is It OK to Reuse Web Information?

The Internet makes it easy to copy someone else's work and pass it off as your own. But this is unethical—and sometimes illegal.

Copyright is a form of protection given to the authors or creators of "original works of authorship," including literary, dramatic, musical, artistic, and other intellectual works. That means that only the author has the right to make or distribute copies of the work, perform the work publicly (such as songs or plays), or change it in any way. If you want to use copyrighted material, you have to get the author's permission first. For example, if you wanted to record your own version of a song you heard on iTunes yesterday, you'd have to get permission from the song's copyright holder (probably the person who wrote the song).

Copyright law is only fair. If someone else wrote a great song or did a lot of research about the Underground Railroad, it wouldn't be right for you to take credit for it. Musicians, writers, artists—they all make a living from their hard work. You can't claim it for your own.

There are some limits to copyright law. One of the most important is the doctrine of fair use. The Fair Use doctrine allows limited copying of copyrighted works for educational and research purposes. Suppose, for example, you're doing a report on Antarctica. You want to include a picture of some penguins in your report, and you find a good one online. It would be OK for you to use that picture in your report—as long as you give credit to the copyright holder.

## Sources Cited on the Same Page as Footnotes

Each reference is indicated by a superscript number. The footnote citations are placed at the bottom of the page where the referenced text appears.

# Lewis and Clark

In 1801, when Thomas Jefferson took office as President of the United States, American farmers and traders relied on rivers to transport their goods to market. Jefferson was concerned that a secret treaty, in which Spain ceded New Orleans and some of its territories west of the Mississippi River to France, would interfere with access to the Mississippi River and other waterways. To protect the interests of the United States, Jefferson authorized James Monroe and Robert Livingston to negotiate with France for the purchase of New Orleans at the mouth of the Mississippi and portions of western and eastern Florida. Napoleon's representative, Talleyrand, offered to sell not just New Orleans but the entire French territory of Louisiana. Surprised but excited by the chance to gain more territory for the U.S., Monroe and Livingston negotiated a treaty with Talleyrand that authorized the purchase of Louisiana for $15 million dollars.[1] ← Note reference mark

At more than 800,000 square miles, the Louisiana Purchase almost doubled the size of the United States. After the U.S. Senate ratified the treaty authorizing the Louisiana Purchase, Jefferson assigned his own private secretary, **Meriwether Lewis**, to take charge of an expedition to explore the Louisiana Purchase territories. That expedition was then called the Corps of Discovery. Lewis chose his friend and fellow soldier, **William Clark**, to co-lead the expedition. The expedition, which we now call the **Lewis and Clark Expedition**, became one of the great adventures of all time.

### Meriwether Lewis

Lewis was born on his parents' Virginia plantation in 1774. As a young boy, Meriwether Lewis lived for a few years on the Georgia frontier developing his frontier survival skills.[2] Returning to Virginia as a teenager, Lewis began his education and assumed the responsibility of managing the family plantation. In 1794, Lewis became a soldier in the state militia and then in the regular army, rising to the rank of captain. He gained a reputation for competence and honesty and, in 1801, President Thomas Jefferson asked him to serve as his private secretary. It is possible that Jefferson already had Lewis in mind to lead a westward expedition because for the next two years, Jefferson had Lewis study with some of the foremost scientists in the country to get ready for the expedition. In the spring of 1803, Lewis was ready for his great adventure.

——————— ← Note separator line

[1] Jon Kukla., *A Wilderness So Immense* (New York: Alfred A. Knopf, 2003), p. 265.

[2] Stephen Ambrose, *Undaunted Courage: Meriwether Lewis, Thomas Jefferson, and the Opening of the American West* (New York: Simon & Schuster, 1996), p. 24.

↑ Footnotes

If you've been the victim of a cyberbully, don't fight back. It may be tempting to send your own nasty message in return, but don't. Instead, save the evidence—keep records of offending messages, photos, or online chats. Then tell an adult you trust about the bullying (for example, a parent or guardian or a favorite teacher). You might even want to report the bullying to the service provider (Facebook, YouTube, your ISP).

If cyberbullying is happening in your virtual world, remember that it's affecting a real person. Don't stand back and do nothing. If you see cyberbullying going on, support the victim and report the bullying. How would you feel if no one stood up for you?

## Watch Out for Cyber Predators!

You've probably seen stories like this on the news: a girl exchanges messages with someone online, thinking it's just another kid interested in comics or the latest band. But the "friend" turns out to be an adult, who showed up one day at the girl's after-school job, followed her to the parking lot, forced her into his car, and assaulted her.

It's scary, and it's not something anyone likes to think about, but you have to know: there are bad adults out there waiting to take advantage of vulnerable kids. Every year law enforcement officials estimate that over 5,000 kids become victims as a result of their online activity. It happens.

A cyber predator is someone who uses the Internet to hunt for victims to take advantage of them in many ways—sexually, emotionally, psychologically, or financially. Cyber predators know how to manipulate kids. They create trust and friendship where none should exist.

Cyber predators are the dark side of social networking and other forms of online communication. They frequently log on to chat groups or game sites and pose as other kids. They try to gradually gain your trust and encourage you to talk about your problems. They might ask you to share secrets. Many kids feel safe sharing personal information online because they think the Internet is anonymous . . . and after all, they're sitting in their own house using their own computer, aren't they? But too often, that's just a false sense of security.

Even if you don't chat with strangers, personal information you post on sites such as Xanga, Facebook, and MySpace can make you a target. Along with favorite movies and links to fun websites, kids are putting their phone numbers, class schedules, and other personal information online. This makes it easier for a predator to find them.

## Sources Cited on a Separate References Page

Sources might be cited at the end of the last page of a report, titled References.

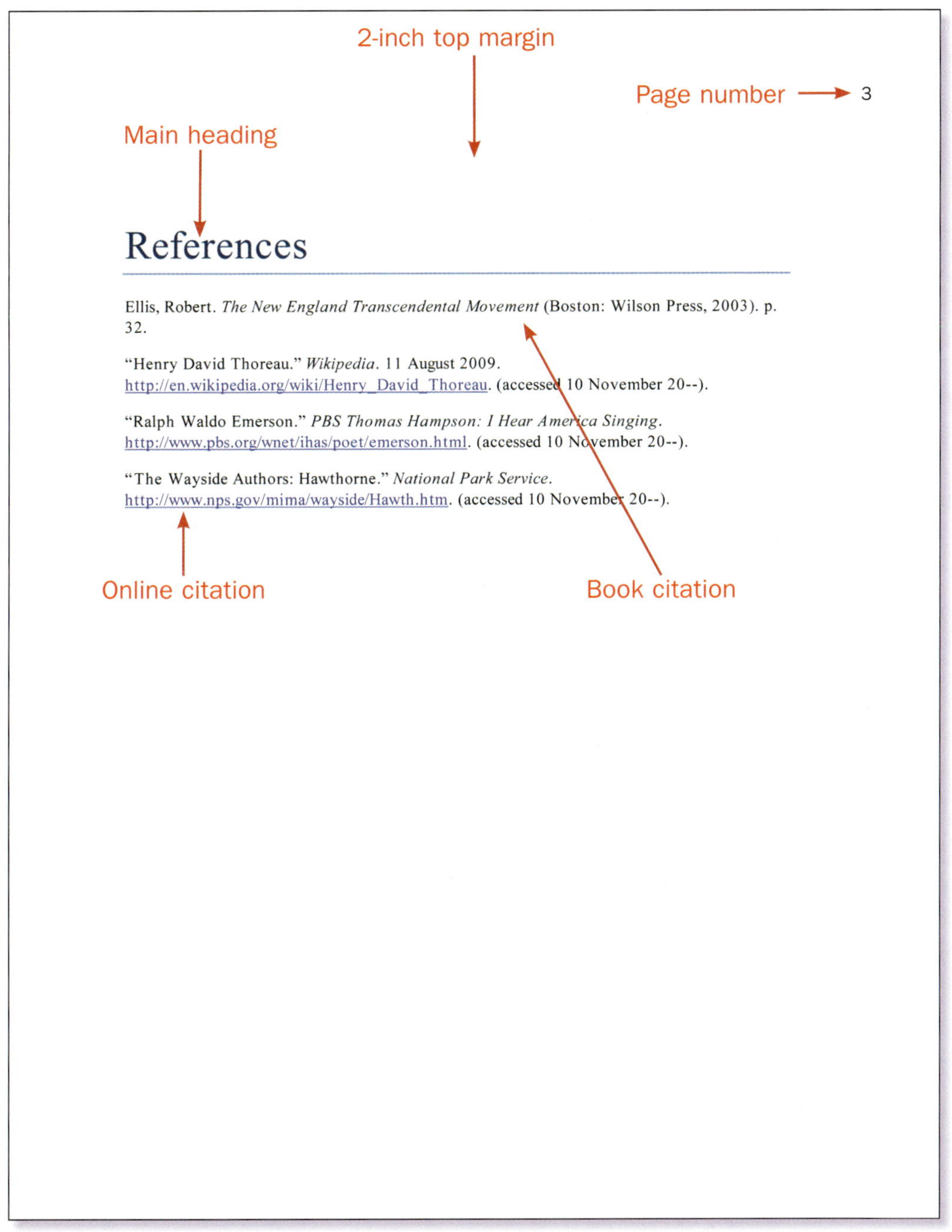


3

# References

Ellis, Robert. *The New England Transcendental Movement* (Boston: Wilson Press, 2003). p. 32.

"Henry David Thoreau." *Wikipedia*. 11 August 2009. http://en.wikipedia.org/wiki/Henry_David_Thoreau. (accessed 10 November 20--).

"Ralph Waldo Emerson." *PBS Thomas Hampson: I Hear America Singing*. http://www.pbs.org/wnet/ihas/poet/emerson.html. (accessed 10 November 20--).

"The Wayside Authors: Hawthorne." *National Park Service*. http://www.nps.gov/mima/wayside/Hawth.htm. (accessed 10 November 20--).

## What Is Cyberbullying?

Unfortunately, bullying has probably been around as long as there have been kids. In the past, bullying involved teasing and name-calling, pushing and hitting, and excluding others from the cool group. But technology has given kids new ways to bully each other. Cyberbullying—using online communications technology to harass or upset someone—has become increasingly common as kids gain access to cell phones and the Internet.

Cyberbullying can happen in many different ways. Cell phones can be used to send hateful calls or text messages or to share humiliating images. Threatening messages can be sent via chat rooms and message boards. Groups of people can decide to pick on or ignore certain people on social networking sites, or someone can create a fake profile using the victim's real name, photo, and contact information. E-mail is used to forward harassing messages or computer viruses to unpopular kids. Name-calling and abusive remarks are thrown at players on gaming sites, or bullies repeatedly "kill" the characters of weaker or less experienced players.

In many ways, cyberbullying is different from the kind of bullying that takes place at school or on the playground. How is it different? Think about this:

- It can happen at any time, day or night. Victims of cyberbullies aren't even safe at home.
- The audience can be very large and reached rapidly. Unkind messages can quickly be sent to large numbers of people and forwarded to even more. Victims always have to worry when and where the messages will resurface.
- Cyberbullies can easily remain anonymous. Victims might not even know who is harassing them.
- Cyberbullying happens between peers and across generations. Sometimes teachers are the targets of cyberbullies. And believe it or not, even parents have become cyberbullies, spreading hateful messages about unpopular kids.

What can you do about cyberbullying? Lots! The first rule is to respect others. Always watch what you say online and be careful about the images you send. You may think only a few people will see, but whatever you send could be made public within minutes. Even little in-jokes among friends can wind up hurting someone if they're forwarded to enough people.

Give your cell phone number or website address only to people you trust. Learn how to block or report people who are bullying others online. Don't share any of your passwords with your friends.

## Sample Footnotes

### Book with one author

[1]Jon Kukla, *A Wilderness So Immense* (New York: Alfred A. Knopf, 2003), p. 265.

### Book with two authors

[1]Robert Morris and Steven Cantrell, *The Transcendentalist Movement* (New York: Weston, 2005), p. 74.

### Book with four or more authors

[1]John Kingston, et al., *Evaluating the Writers of Concord* (New York: Xeon, 2004), p. 96.

### Journal or Magazine Article

[1]Judith Bradley, "Our National Park Service," *RV Travelers*, 15 October 2006, p. 43.

### Encyclopedia or Reference Book

[1]*Compton's Encyclopedia*, Vol. 24 (Chicago: Encyclopædia Britannica, Inc., 2004), p. 325.

### Web Page, Online Journal, Magazine, or Newspaper

[1]"Meriwether Lewis: Biography," *National Park Service: The Lewis and Clark Journey of Discovery*, http://nps.gov/jeff/LewisClark2/CorpsofDiscovery/TheLeaders/Lewis/Lewis.htm (accessed 10 October 20--).

## Sample End-of-Report Citations

### Book with one author

Ellis, Robert. *The New England Transcendental Movement* (Boston: Wilson Press, 2003), p. 32.

### Web Page, Online Journal, Magazine, or Newspaper

"Henry David Thoreau." *Wikipedia*. 11 August 2009. http://en.wikipedia.org/wiki/Henry_David_Thoreau. (accessed 10 November 20--).

You should never respond to e-mails asking for personal information. If your bank needs to contact you about something, an employee will call or send a letter. The bank won't ask for personal data via an e-mail. ALWAYS be suspicious if you get an e-mail or a phone message asking you to verify an account.

For more tips on how to avoid identity theft, go to the Learning with Computers Web page (www.cengage.com/school/keyboarding/lwcorange), click the **Links** option, and then click **Appendix B**.

Pharming or spoofing is a scam where thieves redirect a real website's traffic to a bogus site. The "pharmer" secretly hijacks your computer and takes you to a copycat website that looks just like the real thing. Once there, you'll be asked to provide personal information. Social networking sites such as MySpace and Facebook are frequent targets of this kind of scam.

One way to avoid pharming and spoofing attacks is by checking whether the site you've been directed to includes either a lock icon or a key icon at the bottom of your browser. These icons don't guarantee that the site is legitimate, but they're a good clue. And if the site looks different from the last time you visited, be suspicious. If you have any doubts, don't use the website.

You can also avoid these scams by maintaining up-to-date antivirus software, antispyware, and firewalls (hardware devices or software programs that help protect against unauthorized access) on your computer. These greatly reduce the possibility that you'll be redirected to a bogus website.

And speaking of spyware . . . you guessed it, thieves can use it to steal your identity. Spyware is software that secretly gathers information about you through your Internet connection. Sometimes spyware is attached to freeware or shareware programs that you download. Spyware can also attach itself to a website. Once it's on your computer, it tracks your online activity (for example, the addresses of the websites you visit) and sends that information to someone (often an advertiser). Spyware can also gather information about account numbers and passwords, which can result in identity theft.

Spyware can also slow down your computer's performance and cause your computer to crash. Your Web surfing is usually interrupted with a lot of unwanted pop-up ads if you've picked up spyware, and sometimes your home page is hijacked and defaults to an unwanted page. If those things are happening to you, your computer has probably been infected with spyware.

Firewalls and antivirus/antispyware software can help keep this nasty stuff off your computer. Unfortunately, once you've been infected, spyware can be *really* hard to get rid of. It's probably not something you want to try on your own.

## Personal-Business Letter in Block Format

A personal-business letter is a formal letter written about a personal topic. A personal-business letter contains a return address, a date, a letter address, a salutation, a body, a complimentary close, and the writer's name.

Personal-business letters are usually keyed in block format. In block format, all of the parts of a letter begin at the left margin.

Personal-business letters have a 2-inch top margin, a 1-inch bottom margin, and 1-inch left and right margins. A short letter may be centered vertically on the page.

The default Calibri, 11-point font with 1.15-inch line spacing and 10 points of spacing following each body text paragraph are used.

A colon is keyed after the salutation. A comma is keyed after the complimentary close.

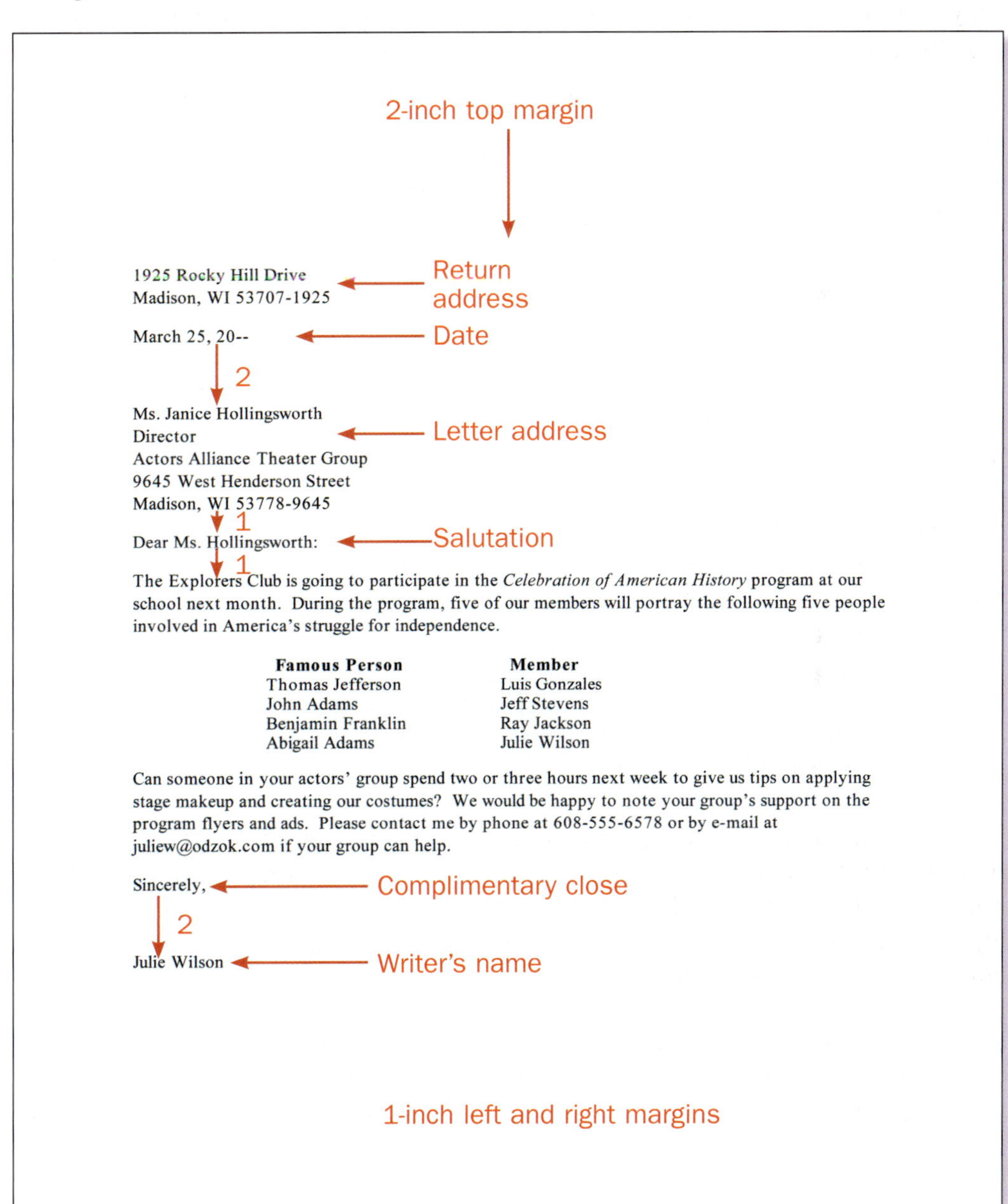


1925 Rocky Hill Drive
Madison, WI 53707-1925

March 25, 20--

Ms. Janice Hollingsworth
Director
Actors Alliance Theater Group
9645 West Henderson Street
Madison, WI 53778-9645

Dear Ms. Hollingsworth:

The Explorers Club is going to participate in the *Celebration of American History* program at our school next month. During the program, five of our members will portray the following five people involved in America's struggle for independence.

| Famous Person | Member |
|---|---|
| Thomas Jefferson | Luis Gonzales |
| John Adams | Jeff Stevens |
| Benjamin Franklin | Ray Jackson |
| Abigail Adams | Julie Wilson |

Can someone in your actors' group spend two or three hours next week to give us tips on applying stage makeup and creating our costumes? We would be happy to note your group's support on the program flyers and ads. Please contact me by phone at 608-555-6578 or by e-mail at juliew@odzok.com if your group can help.

Sincerely,

Julie Wilson

# Appendix B
# Using Technology

## Be a Good Digital Citizen

The Internet may be the world's greatest playground, but you still need to play nice! Sometimes it's hard to remember that the digital community is made up of real people with real feelings. People sometimes take on different personalities online, doing and saying things they would never do face-to-face.

Being a good digital citizen involves more than just staying out of trouble. It involves being web-smart and managing your personal information responsibly. *You* have the power to help build and shape your favorite online communities into places that are creative, fun, and safe.

## Don't Let Someone Steal Your Identity!

Identity theft occurs when someone uses your personally identifying information (for example, your name, Social Security number, or credit card number) without your permission to commit fraud or other crimes. Thieves might use your identity to take money out of your bank account. Or they might establish a credit card in your name, go on a spending spree, and send you the bill. Identity theft is serious.

Thieves don't need a computer to steal your identity. They can go through your garbage looking for bills or other bits of paper that contain account numbers or other personal information. They can steal your purse or wallet or take mail out of your mailbox to get personal information too. But the Internet has given identity thieves plenty of new ways to get what they want.

One common Internet scam is called phishing. In this scam, you get an official-looking e-mail that seems to be from your bank or maybe from eBay or PayPal. The e-mail tells you that there's a problem with your account and asks you to confirm your account number, Social Security number, or some other personal information. But the message is a fake. It's from an identity thief. (Smishing is just like phishing, except it's done with text messaging on your smart phone.)

## Personal-Business Letter in Modified-Block Style

A personal-business letter in modified-block style is similar to a business letter that is written in block style. It also contains a return address, a date, a letter address, a salutation, a body, a complimentary close, and the writer's name.

Personal business letters in modified-block style are usually keyed with the date and the closing lines of the letter beginning near the horizontal center of the page instead of at the left margin. The first line of each paragraph may begin at the left margin or may be indented 0.5 inch.

Personal-business letters in modified-block style have a 2-inch top margin, a 1-inch bottom margin, and 1-inch left and right margins.

The default Calibri, 11-point font with 1.15-inch line spacing and 10 points of spacing following each body text paragraph are used.

A colon is keyed after the salutation. A comma is keyed after the complimentary close.

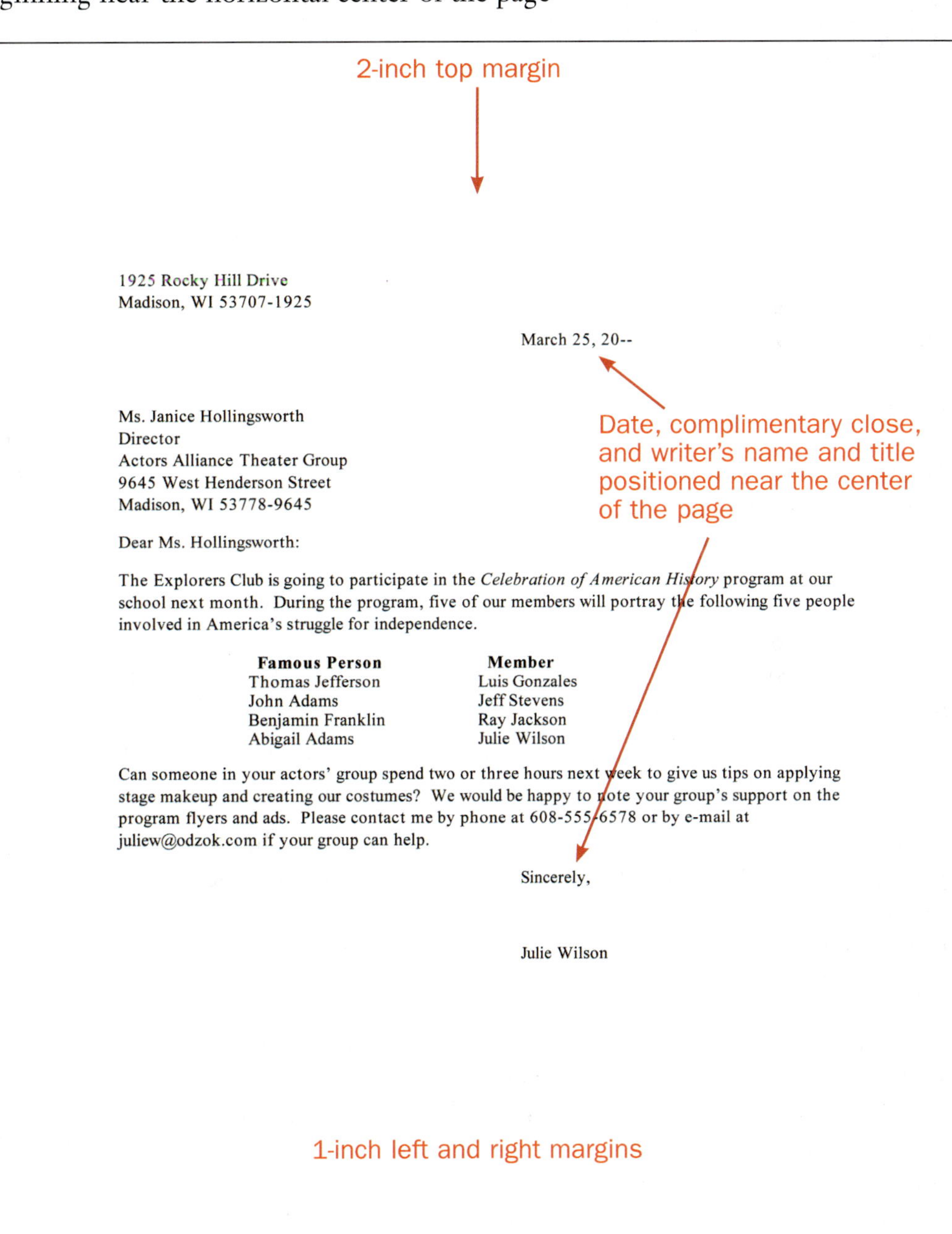


1925 Rocky Hill Drive
Madison, WI 53707-1925

March 25, 20--

Ms. Janice Hollingsworth
Director
Actors Alliance Theater Group
9645 West Henderson Street
Madison, WI 53778-9645

Dear Ms. Hollingsworth:

The Explorers Club is going to participate in the *Celebration of American History* program at our school next month. During the program, five of our members will portray the following five people involved in America's struggle for independence.

| **Famous Person** | **Member** |
|---|---|
| Thomas Jefferson | Luis Gonzales |
| John Adams | Jeff Stevens |
| Benjamin Franklin | Ray Jackson |
| Abigail Adams | Julie Wilson |

Can someone in your actors' group spend two or three hours next week to give us tips on applying stage makeup and creating our costumes? We would be happy to note your group's support on the program flyers and ads. Please contact me by phone at 608-555-6578 or by e-mail at juliew@odzok.com if your group can help.

Sincerely,

Julie Wilson

## Envelope for a Personal-Business Letter

An envelope has a return address and a delivery address. The delivery address has special formatting. It should be keyed in all uppercase without punctuation.

Return address

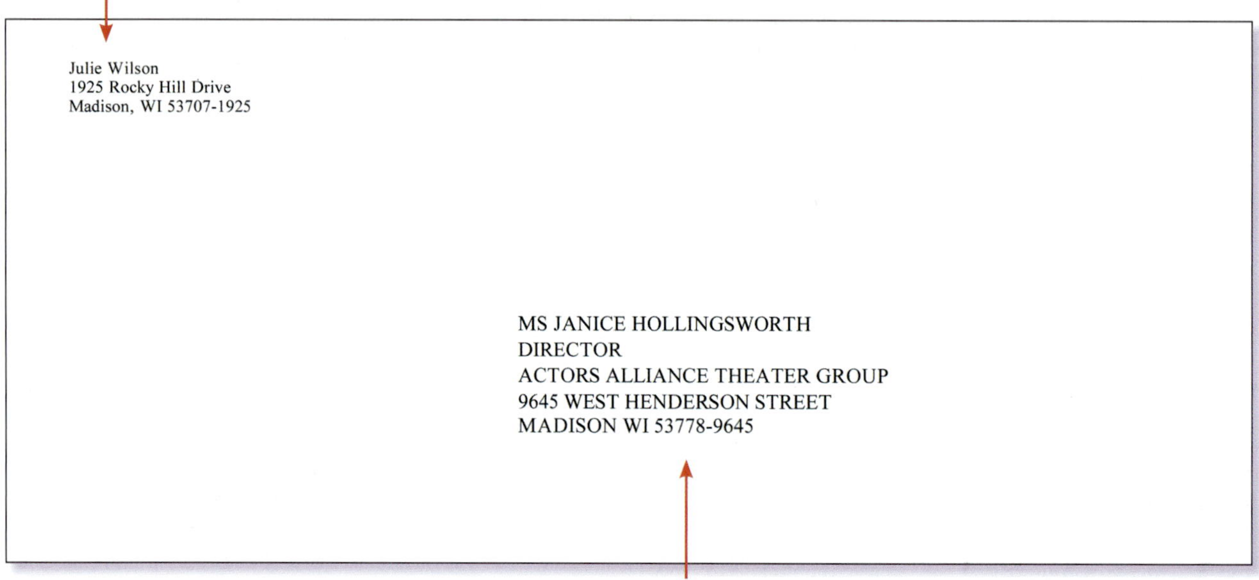


Delivery address in all uppercase characters and no punctuation

## Proofreaders' Marks

Proofreaders' marks are used to mark corrections in keyed or printed text that contains problems and/or errors. As a keyboard user, you should be able to read these marks accurately when revising or editing a rough draft. You also should be able to write these symbols to correct the rough drafts that you and others key. The most-used proofreaders' marks are shown below.

| Mark | Meaning | Mark | Meaning |
|---|---|---|---|
| ‖ | Align copy; also, make these items parallel | #> | Insert space |
| ¶ | Begin a new paragraph | ⋎ | Insert apostrophe |
| Cap ≡ | Capitalize | stet | Let it stand; ignore correction |
| ⁀ | Close up | lc | Lowercase |
| ℓ | Delete | ⊔ | Move down; lower |
| <# | Delete space | ⊏ | Move left |
| No ¶ | Do not begin a new paragraph | ⊐ | Move right |
| ∧ | Insert | ⊓ | Move up; raise |
| ∧, | Insert comma | ○ sp | Spell out |
| ⊙ | Insert period | ∽ tr | Transpose |
| ⋎" | Insert quotation marks | ___ | Underline or italic |

# Glossary

## A

**absolute reference** a cell reference that *Excel* cannot change when it copies a formula

**action button** a predesigned button icon to which you can add hyperlinks

**active cell** the worksheet cell with the dark border that is ready for data entry

**Address bar** toolbar in a *Windows Explorer* or *Internet Explorer* window that has a text box for keying a file location or Web page URL

**align** to position graphics, text boxes, and drawing objects neatly in relation to each other on a slide

**animation effect** motion added to slide objects

**antonym** a word that means the opposite of another word

**application software** software used for a specific purpose, such as word processing

**ascending order** A to Z or 0 to 9

**assumptions** budget criteria that takes for granted an event will occur or that an item has a specific value

**audio** music and other sounds added to a slide

**AutoFill** the *Excel* feature that allows you to place numbers, dates, or text combined with numbers in a range of cells

**AutoFilter** the *Excel* feature used to display rows in a list based on specific criteria

**AutoNumber** a unique identifying number automatically assigned to each record in a database

**AutoPreview feature** a *PowerPoint* feature that automatically plays an animation effect after is it applied to a slide object

**AVERAGE** the *Excel* function that calculates the average value in a range of cells

## B

**bar chart** a chart with horizontal data markers used to compare two or more data series

**Blank** a slide layout that has no placeholders

**Blank document** the default template for a new blank *Word* document

**block format** a letter format in which all of the text starts at the left margin

**body** text in paragraphs that make up a letter's message

**borders** formatting added to the edges of an object or to paragraph boundaries of text

**bound report** a multipage report with the pages bound generally at the left margin

**browser home page** the default Web page that appears when you start your Web browser

**budget** a financial plan based on expectations of future events

**bulleted list** a list of words, phrases, or sentences preceded by a bullet graphic

## C

**cables** insulated wires that connect the computer parts together

**calculation operator** the plus (+), minus (-), multiplication (*), or division (/) symbols in a formula

**Caption property** the field property that specifies the text that appears in a datasheet or form instead of the field name

**case** text in capital letters (uppercase) or noncapital letters (lowercase)

**category (x) axis** shows the names of the categories being charted; categories appear horizontally at the bottom of the chart

**CD** a compact disc; a high-volume external data storage device

**cell** the intersection of a column and a row in an *Excel* worksheet or a *Word* table

**cell reference** a cell's row heading number and column heading letter in an *Excel* worksheet

**Center tab** a tab stop that centers headings over text columns

**character formatting** changing the appearance of individual text characters

**chart** a picture, or graph, of worksheet data

**chart area** the background area of a chart

**chart objects** different parts of a chart, such as its title, legend, or data markers

**chart sheet** a separate sheet in a workbook that contains a chart

**chart title** a chart's title text

**click** to point to a specific area on the screen and tap the left mouse button

**Click and Type** a *Word* Print Layout feature that allows you to double-click anywhere on the page to position the insertion point

**clip art** predesigned pictures or drawings that can be inserted into a document

**Close button** a button in the upper-right corner of a window that you click to close the window

**column chart** a chart with vertical data markers used to compare two or more data series

**column headings** buttons, starting with the letter *A*, that appear across the top of a worksheet

**columns** vertical arrangements of cells in a *Word* table

**columns** vertical arrangements of cells in an *Excel* worksheet

**complimentary closing** the words that come before the signature of a letter, such as *Sincerely yours*

**computer ergonomics** the way people use a computer to avoid injury

**Content pane** a pane in a window that displays the contents of the open folder

**continuous loop** playing a slide show over and over again until it is stopped manually

**copying and pasting** duplicating text and inserting it in a new location

**cover page** the first page of a multipage report that contains the report title, the writer's name, other information (such as a school or organization name), and the date

**CPU** the computer's "brain" that controls the interaction between hardware and software

**cutting and pasting** removing text and placing it in a new location

## D

**dashed-line insertion point** the insertion point's appearance during a drag-and-drop action

**database** a file used to organize data in a structured way

**database objects** tables, queries, forms, or report objects stored in an *Access* database file

**data file** an electronic file you open and change

**data labels** text labels that identify the data markers on a chart

**data marker** a column, point on a line, or pie slice that represents the numbers, called data points, in a worksheet

**data point** a number in a worksheet cell that is converted to a column, point on a line, or pie slice in a chart

**data range** an arrangement of worksheet data in which each row has the same type of data in each column; a header row with column names that defines data in the column so that the list can be sorted and filtered

**data series** all of the related data markers in a chart

**datasheet** a sheet with rows and columns, similar to an *Excel* worksheet, that displays data in an *Access* table or query object

**Datasheet view** the view used to display an *Access* table or query datasheet

**data source document** a *Word* mail merge document that contains the data to be merged

**Data Type property** the field property that specifies the type of data that can be stored in a database table's field

**date** a letter's date with the month spelled out

**Decimal tab** a tab stop that aligns numbers on the decimal point in tabbed columns

**Default Value property** the field property that specifies the text or value that automatically appears in each record

**delivery address** the name and address on an envelope of the person to whom a letter is sent

**demotes** to move multilevel list text down one level in the list

**descending order** Z to A or 9 to 0

**Design view** the view used to create an *Access* database table by specifying fields and field properties

**desktop** the background on the monitor's screen that appears when you start your computer

**Details pane** a window pane that displays information about the open folder or selected file

**dialog box** a small box that presents options you can set while performing a task in an application

**distribute** to arrange slide objects equal distance apart on a slide

**double-click** to point to a specific area on the screen and tap the left mouse button twice very quickly

**Draft view** the *Word* editing view that hides the edges of a page

**drag** to tap and hold down the left mouse button and move the mouse pointer across the screen

**drag and drop** to use the mouse pointer to move or copy selected text in a *Word* document, selected cells in an *Excel* worksheet, or selected slide objects on a *PowerPoint* slide

**drawing canvas** a box or an area that contains a selected SmartArt graphic

**drawing guides** vertical and horizontal lines displayed to help align objects on a slide

**drop cap** an uppercase letter enlarged and positioned at the left margin to create a special effect

**DVD** an external electronic storage device

## E

**editing views** *Word* views such as Draft view and Print Layout view used to add and edit text in a document

**electronic databases** database files stored on electronic media

**electronic mailbox** a folder on a mail server in which a user's e-mail messages are stored

**e-mail address** the address a person uses to receive electronic mail

**e-mail etiquette** rules for good behavior when sending e-mail

**e-mail** electronic messages or mail sent over the Internet

**embedded chart** a chart placed as a floating object on the same worksheet as the data

**embedded workbook object** data from an *Excel* worksheet pasted onto a *PowerPoint* slide ; the data can be edited in *PowerPoint* without changing the original source workbook

**Emphasis** the category of *PowerPoint* animation effects that are used to add emphasis to slide text or objects

**endnotes** source citations that appear on a separate page at the end of a report

**enter data** to key text or numbers in a cell and then tap the ENTER, the TAB, or an arrow key

**Entrance** the category of *PowerPoint* animation effects that are used to add movement to slide text or objects when they appear on a slide

**Exit** the category of *PowerPoint* animation effects that are used to add movement to slide text or objects when they leave a slide

## F

**favorite** a clickable link used to view a Web page or open a file

**field** contains specific data for each record in a table; represented by a column in a datasheet

**Field Name property** the field property that specifies the name of a field

**field properties** multiple criteria that define a field

**Field Properties pane** the *Access* table Design view pane used to set various field properties such as Field Size and Caption

**field selector** the column heading button on a table datasheet used to select a column or show the field name or caption; the row heading button in the Fields pane in Design view used to select a field

**Field Size property** the field property that specifies how many characters can be keyed in a field

**files** documents you open or create and save on your computer

**file server** a computer on a networked computer on which users can store and access electronic files

**File tab** the *Word 2010* tab that displays Backstage view, which contains commands to create, open, save, and print a document

**fill handle** the small black square in the lower-right corner of a worksheet cell used to copy cell contents to adjacent cells

**filter** to display rows in a list that have the same content in a particular column

**filter** to show only those records that have the same content in a specific field

**filtering by selection** specifying the filter criteria by moving the insertion point into the field that contains the value to be filtered

**floating object** a picture or drawing that can be positioned in front of or behind text

**folder** an electronic version of a paper folder in which you can organize and store your computer files

**font** the way letters and numbers look

**font effects** special text effects available in the Font dialog box

**font size** the size of a font, generally measured in points

**font styles** Bold, Italic, and Underline formatting

**footer** text, page numbers, and dates that appear at the bottom of a page

**footnotes** source citations that appear at the bottom of the same page as the information being cited

**form** a database object used to enter or edit data

**Format Painter** an *Office* feature that allows you to copy, or paint, formats from text to text

**formatting marks** nonprinting characters inserted in a *Word* document to control the position and formatting of printed text

**Form tool** an *Access* feature that allows the user to quickly create a database form that lists all of the fields in a record

**Form view** the *Access* view that displays a database form in which table data can be added or edited

**Form Wizard** a step-by-step process used to create a data entry form using fields from an underlying table

**formula** an equation entered in a cell that performs a calculation based on the numerical contents of other cells

**formula bar** the area below the Ribbon that shows the contents of the active worksheet cell

**Full Screen Reading view** a *Word* document view that makes it easier to read the document on a computer screen

**function** a predefined *Excel* formula that performs a common calculation

**function arguments** the cell references and values placed in parentheses and on which a function acts to perform a calculation

**Function AutoComplete** an alphabetical list of functions that appears below a cell when you begin keying a function name in the cell

**Function Library** a group of buttons on the Formulas tab that provides access to functions by category

## G

**Go button** a button in the *Internet Explorer* window you click to load a Web page

**gridlines** dark horizontal lines that help you see each data marker's position in a chart's plot area

**group** to combine multiple selected *PowerPoint* slide objects into a single object

**group** to select multiple *Excel* worksheets to enter common data or perform the same formatting on all of the worksheets

**gutter** an additional 0.5-inch margin added to the left margin for a bound report

## H

**handouts** slide miniatures printed in a variety of formats

**hard drive** a high-volume internal data storage device

**hard page break** a manual page break inserted by the person keying the text

**hardware** computer parts that you can see and touch

**header** text, page numbers, and dates that appear at the top of a page

**home cell** the first cell in the upper-left corner of the worksheet, cell A1

**home page** the primary Web page at a website

**host name** the name of the mail server where the user's electronic mailbox is stored

**hyperlink** text or a picture that is linked to another Web page

## I

**I-beam pointer** the mouse pointer shape used to position the insertion point in a text area

**icons** small graphic symbols

**IF** the *Excel* function that makes one of two possible calculations based on the results of a logical test

**indented** moved inward from the margins

**infographic** a document that combines text, pictures, and drawings to convey a message

**in line** an object positioned in the same line as text

**insertion point** the small black vertical line that indicates the keying position in a document

**Internet** a worldwide network of computers

## K

**keyboard** a set of keys you tap to insert text and numbers or to perform special tasks

**keyboard shortcut** a set of keystrokes used to perform a task

## L

**labels** small pieces of paper, usually with an adhesive backing, used to add information such as mailing addresses and file folder names

**Landscape orientation** a printed page that is wider than it is long

**laptop** a small computer that combines the monitor, keyboard, storage devices, and CPU hardware together in one easy-to-transport case

**Layout view** the view in which a new form or report appears; used to reposition and format elements of the report or form

**Left tab** a tab stop that indents text from the left margin or left-aligns text in tabbed columns

**legend** labels and colors that identify each data series

**letter address** the name and address of the person to whom a letter is addressed

**libraries** *Windows 7* operating system virtual folders used to organize electronic folders

**line spacing** the amount of white space between lines of text

**link** a hyperlink; text or a picture that is linked to another Web page

**linked workbook object** data from an *Excel* worksheet pasted onto a *PowerPoint* slide; the data must be edited in the original workbook

**linking formula** a formula that links data on one worksheet to a calculation on another worksheet or to a text box on a chart

**logical test** a test that compares values to see if they are equal or if one value is less than or greater than the other value

**LOOKUP** the Excel function that looks down a sorted range to find one value and then looks across the data to find a related value in a different range

## M

**mail merge** the process of combining one master document, called the main document, with data from another document, called the data source document, to create multiple letters, envelopes, or labels

**mail server** a computer on a network on which users' e-mail messages are stored

**main document** the primary document in a mail merge that contains the "boilerplate" text for the resulting documents

**main heading** the title of a report

**margin** the white space at the top, bottom, left, and right sides of a page

**MAX** the *Excel* function that calculates the largest value in a range of cells

**Maximize button** a button in the upper-right corner of a window you click to size the window to cover the screen

**menu bar** a bar of expandable menus containing commands in a *Windows Explorer* or *Internet Explorer* window

**merge** to combine multiple cells into one cell

**merge field** a special field in a main document that ties directly to data in a data source

**MIN** the *Excel* function that calculates the smallest value in a range of cells

**Minimize button** a button in the upper-right corner of a window you click to reduce the window to a button on the taskbar

**monitor** a piece of computer equipment with a screen that displays the documents you create

**motion clips** animated clip art

**Motion Path** the category of *PowerPoint* animation effects that are used to add movement to slide text or objects as they travel across a slide

**mouse** a pointing device used to perform a task

**mouse pointer** the white double-headed arrow symbol on the screen that is moved with the mouse

**multilevel list** a list used to organize ideas and topics for an oral presentation or a written report

## N

**Name Box** the area to the left of the formula bar that shows the cell reference of the active cell

**Navigation buttons** Back and Forward buttons you can click to revisit previously viewed window contents

**navigation buttons** buttons in the lower-left corner of a datasheet or form used to navigate between records

**Navigation Pane** a list of tables, queries, forms, and reports in an *Access* database

**Navigation Pane** a *Word* task pane used to find specific body or heading text in a document

**Navigation pane** a window pane that displays shortcuts to frequently used folders, libraries, and computers on your network and to your computer's storage devices

**newsletter columns** a column of text that flows downward to the bottom of the page and then up to the top of the next column like a printed newsletter page

**newspaper-style columns** *See* newsletter columns

**Next page section break** a section break that creates a new document section and a new page at the same time

**Normal view** the default view in which you create and edit slides

**notebook** *See* laptop

**note reference mark** a tiny number or symbol that appears next to cited text

**note separator line** a line that separates footnotes from a report's body text

**Notes Page view** the view that shows a slide miniature and a text box in which presenter notes can be keyed, viewed, and printed

**notes pages** printable pages in which each page contains a slide thumbnail and speaker notes

**notes pane** the area of the *PowerPoint* window in Normal view in which you can key speaker notes

**notification area** the tray on the far right side of the taskbar that displays the current time and icons for system software or applications such as a virus checker

**NOW** the *Excel* function that returns the system date and time

**nudge** to move a selected slide object a small distance by tapping an arrow key

**null screen** a *Word*, *Excel*, or *PowerPoint* application window that is open with a document, workbook, or presentation, respectively

**numbered list** a list of words, phrases, or sentences preceded by a number in sequence

**numeric keypad** the set of keys to the right of the main body of the keypad used to enter numbers

## O

**Office Button** the *Word 2007* button that contains a menu of commands to create, open, save, and print a document

**Office Clipboard** a special place in the computer's memory that stores copied or cut items

**ordered list** a numbered list

**Outline tab** displays slide text in outline form

## P

**page orientation** the way text prints on a page

**pagination** organization of text on pages in a *Word* document based on the amount of text that fits on each page

**paragraph formatting** formatting that changes the layout of text and is applied to complete paragraphs

**paragraph headings** brief text on their own line that introduce paragraphs

**pencil symbol** a symbol in the record selector in a table datasheet indicating that changes to a record have not been saved

**personal-business letter** a formal letter written about a personal topic

**pie chart** a chart used to show each value as a percentage of the total values

**placeholders** areas or boxes on a slide that can contain text, clip art, or other content

**plot area** the area of a chart in which the data markers appear

**point** to place the mouse pointer on a specific area of the screen

**points** font measurements

**Portrait orientation** a printed page that is longer than it is wide

***PowerPoint* table** the default format for *Excel* data pasted on a *PowerPoint* slide

**presentation** a *PowerPoint* file that contains one or more slides

**Preview pane** a pane on the right side of a *Windows Explorer* window that displays a preview of the file selected in the Content pane

**primary key** a special field that contains the unique identifier for each record in a table

**printer** a device that prints a hard copy of electronic documents

**Print Layout view** the *Word* editing view in which the top, bottom, left, and right edges of a page are visible

**Print Place** an area on the File tab in which you can preview a document, set print options, and print a document

**Print Preview** in *Office 2007 applications*, the view that displays a document as it will look when it is printed

**private folder** a folder on a computer network that is not shared with others

**promote** to move multilevel list text up one level in the list

**proofreaders' marks** special symbols noting errors or changes to a proofread document

**proofreading** reading a document to look for errors

## Q

**query** a database object used to answer a question about the data in a table

**query design grid** the query Design view window in which table fields are selected and query criteria are entered

**Quick Access Toolbar** a customizable toolbar that contains, by default, the Save, Undo, and Repeat/Redo buttons

## R

**range** a group of adjacent worksheet cells written with the first and last cell reference separated by a colon, such as A1:B3

**Reading view** a view that makes it easier to read slide text on the screen

**record navigation bar** a bar at the bottom of a datasheet or form that contains navigation buttons and a filter indicator

**record** all of the data for one specific item; represented by a row in a datasheet

**record selector** the row heading button in Datasheet view used to select a record

**relational database** a single file that contains multiple related items called database objects

**relative references** cell references that *Excel* can change when it copies a formula

**repagination** automatic reorganization of text on pages in a *Word* document when text is added, deleted, or formatted or document margins are changed

**report** a database object used to preview and print data

**Report tool** a feature in *Access* that lets a user quickly create a simple report of all of the records and fields in a table

**Report view** the default view for an open report object

**Report Wizard** a step-by-step process used to create a printable report using fields from an underlying table or query

**Required property** the field property that specifies whether data must be entered in a field before the record can be saved

**Restore Down button** a button in the upper-right corner of a window that resizes the window to a smaller size

**return address** a letter sender's name and address

**Reuse Slides pane** a pane in which you can display slides from a saved presentation and add them to the current presentation

**Ribbon** located at the top of the *Office* applications' window, a tabbed arrangement of command buttons used to perform a specific task

**right-click** to point to a specific area on the screen and tap the right mouse button

**right-pointing arrow symbol** the symbol in the record selector in Datasheet view that indicates the current record

**Right tab** a tab stop that aligns dates and other text at the right margin or right-aligns text in tabbed columns

**ROUND** the *Excel* function that rounds a formula's calculated result to the same number of decimal places as shown in the cell

**rounding error** an error that can occur when a formula's calculated result is displayed in the cell with a different number of decimal places than the 15 places retained in the calculation

**row headings** a sequential number starting with 1 that appears down the left side of the worksheet

**rows** horizontal arrangements of cells across a worksheet

**rows** horizontal arrangements of cells in a *Word* table

**rulers** vertical and horizontal tools used to position text on a page

**running a query** opening the query datasheet to view the results of the query

## S

**salutation** a letter's greeting line

**screen** the viewing area on a computer monitor

**ScreenTip** a small flag that contains the name of a window element; it appears when the mouse pointer is placed on a window element

**scroll bars** vertical and horizontal tools you can use to change the view of the open document, workbook, presentation, or database object

**scroll box** a small box on the vertical or horizontal scroll bar you can drag up or down with the mouse pointer

**Search box** a window box used to perform a keyword search for files and folders

**section break** a break that creates areas of a *Word* document that can have margins that are different from the other pages or that can have text in columns

**shading** background color added to text

**sheet tab** the tab at the bottom of a worksheet that shows the worksheet's name

**shortcut menu** a brief menu of commands that appears when you right-click different areas of the screen

**Simple Query Wizard** a step-by-step process used to create a simple query that lists specific fields from a table

**sizing handle** small circles or squares on the boundaries of selected clip art, text boxes, or shapes used to change the object's size using the mouse

**slide** an individual page in a *PowerPoint* file that can contain text, graphics, video, audio, and animation

**slide layout** controls which predefined boxes, called placeholders, appear on a slide

**Slide Master view** the *PowerPoint* view in which you can modify the slide master and its related slide layouts

**slide master** a special hidden slide that contains all of the design elements from the applied template and controls the appearance of all slides except the title slide

**slide pane** the area in the *PowerPoint* window in Normal view in which you add content to slides

**slide show** a series of *PowerPoint* slides projected on a wall or projection screen

**Slide Show view** the view in which *PowerPoint* slides can be projected on a wall or projection screen

**Slide Sorter view** the view in which all of the *PowerPoint* slides in a presentation appear together as thumbnails

**Slides tab** the area of the *PowerPoint* window in Normal view in which you can see slide thumbnails

**slide timings** the preset amount of time between slides as they advance automatically during a slide show

**slide transition effect** a special motion effect that appears as one slide leaves the screen and another one takes its place during a slide show

**SmartArt** predesigned graphic objects

**Smart Guides** a *PowerPoint 2010* alignment tool that appears when slide objects are being aligned using the mouse

**soft page break** an automatic page break created by *Word*

**software** instructions used by a computer to operate its hardware or perform tasks such as word processing

**sources** the origins of facts and ideas used in a report

**speaker notes** notes keyed in a notes page or notes pane for a slide that can be printed and used by a presenter during a slide show

**Start button** a button that opens the Windows operating system's Start menu, which lists the applications on a computer

**status bar** a bar at the bottom of an application window that contains information about the open document

**Step by Step Mail Merge Wizard** the *Word* step-by-step process used to create multiple letters, envelopes, and labels from a main document and a data source

**storage devices** internal hard drives or external devices such as flash drives used to store data

**style** a collection of different formats applied all at one time

**subtotals** temporary column sums, averages, and other calculations created with the *Excel* Subtotal feature

**SUM** the *Excel* function that calculates the total value of a range of cells

**summary slide** a Title and Content slide that lists the title text of other presentation slides

**symbol** a special character inserted in a document that can represent physical things, such as trademarks and copyrights

**synonym** a word that means the same as another word

**system clock** an internal computer clock

**system software** software needed to operate a computer

## T

**tab formatting mark** a formatting mark inserted in a document when you tap the TAB key

**tab indicator** the button to the left of the Horizontal Ruler used to set custom tab stops

**tab stop** an icon on the Horizontal Ruler that indicates a specific keying position

**tabbed columns** columns of text aligned at a tab stop

**table** a grid of vertical columns and horizontal rows

**table** an *Access* database object that contains data

**table design grid** the *Access* table Design view pane used to key the name of the field and set the Data Type property

**taskbar** an area at the bottom of the *Windows 7* and *Windows XP* window that displays buttons for open applications and documents

**templates** model documents

**text box** a container for text or pictures that can be positioned anywhere in a document

**text hyperlinks** text formatted as a hyperlink to another slide, presentation, *Office* document, or Web page

**Text pane** a pane for entering text in a SmartArt object

**theme** a color-coordinated set of fonts, background graphics, and effects

**thesaurus** a tool used to look up synonyms and antonyms for a selected word

**three-level multilevel list** brief text notes organized using a common numbering system such as I. II. III. (first level), A. B. C. (second level), and 1. 2. 3. (third level), with each level representing increasing detail

**thumbnail** a tiny version of a slide

**Title and Content** a slide layout with a title placeholder and a content placeholder

**title bar** the bar along the top of an application or operating system window that contains the window's Minimize, Maximize, Restore Down, Close, and Navigation buttons; the Address Bar; and the Search box

**Title Only** a slide layout with only a title placeholder

**Title Slide** a slide layout with title and subtitle placeholders

**TODAY** a function that returns the system date

**toolbar** a bar in a *Windows Explorer* or application window that contains clickable buttons to manage folder contents; the type of buttons that appear on the toolbar depends on the contents of the window

**triple-click** to point to a specific area on the screen and tap the left mouse button rapidly three times

**typeface** *See* font

## U

**unbound report** a short one- or two-page report that is not bound at a margin

**ungroup** to deselect grouped *Excel* worksheets

**ungroup** to replace a single grouped object with its individual components

**unordered list** a bulleted list

**URL (Uniform Resource Locator)** the address of a Web page

**USB flash drive** a portable external storage device for data

**user name** the name of the person using an electronic mailbox

## V

**value (y) axis** shows the numbers, or values over which the data is to be charted; values appear vertically on the left side of the chart

**video** movies and motion clips added to a slide

**View Shortcuts** buttons on the status bar used to change the editing view

## W

**Web** *See* World Wide Web

**Web browser** the application software used to load and view Web pages

**Web pages** documents containing text, pictures, sound, and animation linked to other Web pages by hyperlinks

**Web servers** computers on a network on which Web pages are stored

**website** a collection of related Web pages

**what-if analysis** a method of analyzing the results of a formula by changing the variables used in the formula's calculations

**window** a rectangular area on the screen in which you can see and work in an application or a document

**wizard** an *Office* application step-by-step process used to complete a task (for example, the Mail Merge Wizard in *Word*, the Chart Wizard in *Excel*, and the Report Wizard in *Access*)

**WordArt** predesigned text formats used to create interesting and colorful text objects

**wordwrap** the process by which text automatically moves to the next line when there is no more room at the right margin

**workbook** a single *Excel* file that contains multiple worksheets

**worksheet** a grid of columns and rows used to enter data and formulas

**workspace** the database window area in which open objects are viewed

**World Wide Web** a special part of the Internet in which computers called servers store documents called Web pages

**writer's name** the name of the person who is writing a letter

# Index

## Q



## R



## S